D0710897

Collins Gem

Dictionary of
Spelling & Word Division

Collins
GEM
Dictionary

Spelling & Word Division

Susie B. Marshall MA CA

Collins
London and Glasgow

General Editor
W. T. McLeod

First Published 1968
Latest Reprint 1987

ISBN 0 00 458749 9

© **William Collins Sons & Co. Ltd. 1968**

Printed in Great Britain by
Collins Clear-Type Press

GUIDE
TO THE USE OF THIS BOOK

The purpose of the written word is to communicate. It is obvious that written matter should be easy to read instantaneously. However, the unavoidable splitting of words which occur at, and overrun, line endings, can impede the flow.

The aim of this book is to illustrate the basis of correct English word splitting, namely, *that the pronunciation of the first part of the word be recognisable before the eye reaches the second part in the succeeding line.* Thus the word *coincidence* must be split *co-incidence* to ensure that it is not confused with *coin-age*. In this way continuity is preserved, and all other considerations are secondary to this.

Method

All possible divisions have been indicated in this book by a hyphen (-). Where a word overruns the column width, it has been correctly divided and the hyphen used. The double hyphen (=) is used for words normally hyphenated.

Warning

A split which gives only two letters at the beginning of the second line is never permissible, and one which gives only two letters at the end of the first line is undesirable except where absolutely necessary.

Once the criteria of pronunciation and style have been satisfied, etymology and familiarity must be taken into account and these may further reduce the possibility of splitting. Etymology applies particularly in compound words where, generally speaking, such elements as prefixes should not be divided. Thus *antedate* should be split *ante-date* and not *an-tedate*. Familiarity applies in related words such as *photograph* and *photographer*: *photo-graph* is correct, but *pho-togra-pher* must be used and not *photo-grapher*.

Stress
The stress mark (′) has been included both in the Word Division and Spelling sections of the book to help in the pronunciation and identification of related words. Where the vowel having the main stress is long, the mark has been placed after the vowel, and where the vowel is short it has been placed after the following consonant, e.g. *ana-bio′sis, ana-biot′ic*. Where two vowels occur together and are pronounced as one, the mark has been placed after the following consonant, whether the vowel is short or long, to indicate that only one is pronounced, and where the sound of either is pronounced the stress mark follows the sounded one.

Word List
In order to reduce the bulk of the word division section only the infinitive of most verbs and the positive of adjectives and adverbs have been included, even though the other parts may be divided according to the normal rules.

A

aard'-vark
aard'-wolf
ab'a-cus
aba-lone'
ab-a'lien-ate
aba mu'rus
aban'-don
aban'-doned
aban'-doner
aban-don-ment
ab-a'pi-cal
aba'se-ment
abash'-ment
aba s-ing
aba't-able
aba'te-ment
aba't-ing
ab'a-tis
ab'at-toir
ab -bacy
ab-ba'tial
ab-ax'ial
ab'-bess
ab'-bey
ab'-bot
ab'-botcy
ab-bre'vi-ate
ab-bre'vi-ated
ab-bre'vi-at-ing
ab-brevi-a'tion
ab'-di-cable
ab'-di-cate
ab-di-ca't-ing
ab-di-ca'tion
ab' di-cator

ab'-di-tory
ab'do-men
ab-dom'i-nal
ab-dom'i-nous
ab'do-men
ab-duct
ab-duc'-tion
ab-duc'-tor
abece-da'rian
at'-el-ite
ab-er'rance
ab-er'rancy
ab-er'rant
ab-er-ra'tion
abet'-ted
abet'-ting
abet'-tor
abev'-ance
abev'-ant
at-hor'
ab-horr'ed
ab-hor'-rence
ab-hor'-rent
ab-hor'-ring
abi'd-ance
abi'd-ing
abi'et-ite
at'i-gail
abil'i-ties
abio-gen'esis
abio-geret'ic
abi-og'en-ist
ab-ject'
ab'-ject
ab ject'-ion

ab-ju'di-cate
ab'-iu-gate
ab juuc'-tion
ab-jur-a'tion
ab/ju'ra-tory
ab-iu re
ab-ju're-ment
at-ju'rer
ab-ju'r-ing
ab-lac'-tate
ab-la te
ab-la'tion
ab -la-tive
ab'-lu-ent
ab-lu'tion
ab-lu'tion-ary
ab'-ne-gate
ab-ne-ga'tion
ab-hor'-mal
ab-nor-mal'i-ties
ab-nor-mal'ity
ab-noi -mally
ab-nor'-mity
aool'-ish
abol-it'ion
abol-it'ion-ism
abol-it'ion-ist
abo-ma-si'tis
abo-ma'sum
abom'-in-able
abom'-in-ably
abom'-in-ate
abom'-in-ated
abom'-in-ation
ab-o'ral

ab-or-ig'i-nal
abor-ig'i-nes
abor'-ti-cide
abor-ti-fa'cient
abor'-tion-ist
abort'-ive
abound'-ing
above-board'
abra-ca-dab'ra
abra'd-ant
abra'd-ing
abran'chi-ate
abra's-ive
ab-re-ac'-tion
ab-rep'-tion
abridg'e-able
abridg'-ing
abridg'e-ment
ab'-ro-gable
ab'-ro-gate
ab'-ro-gated
ab'-ro-gat-ing
ab-ro-ga'tion
ab'-ro-gat- ive
ab'-ro-gator
ab-rupt'
ab-rup'-tion
ab-rupt'ly
ab-rupt'-ness
ab'-scess
ab'-scessed
ab-scind'
ab-scis'sa
ab-scis'sion
ab-scond'
ab-scon'ded
ab-scon'der
ab'-sence

ab'-sent (a.)
ab'-sent (v.)
ab-sen-ta'tion
ab-sen-tee'
ab-sen-tee'-ism
ab'-sinthe
ab-sin'-thian
ab-sin'-thi-ate
ab-sin'-thine
ab-sist'-ence
ab'-sol-ute
ab'-sol-utely
ab-sol-u'tion
ab'-solut-ism
ab'-solut-ist
ab-solu-tis'tic
ab-sol'u-tory
ab-solv'-able
ab-sol'va-tory
ab-solv'e
ab-solv'ed
ab-solv'-ent
ab-solv'-ing
ab-sol'vi-tor
ab-sol'ver
ab'-son-ant
ab-sorb'
ab-sorb-abil'ity
ab-sorb'ed
ab-sorb'-edly
ab-sorb-efa'cient
ab-sorb'-ent
ab-sorb'-ing
ab-sorpti-om'eter
ab-sorp'-tion
ab-sorp'-tive
ab-sorp-tiv'ity
ab-stain'

ab-stain'ed
ab-stain'er
ab-ste'mi-ous
ab-ste'mi-ously
ab-sten'-tion
ab-sten'-tious
ab-sterg'e
ab-ster'-gent
ab-ster'-sion
ab-sters'-ive
ab'-sti-nence
ab'-sti-nency
ab'-sti-nent
ab'-stract (a.n.)
ab-stract' (v.)
ab-strac'-ted
ab-stract'-edly
ab-strac'-tion
ab-strac'-tive
ab-stric'-tion
ab-stru'se
ab-stru'sely
ab-surd'
ab-surd'-ity
ab-surd'ly
abun'-dance
abun'-dant
abun'-dantly
abu's-ing
abu's-ive
abu's-ively
abu's-ive-ness
abu'ti-lon
abut'-ment
abut'-tal
abut'-ted
abut'-ter
abut'-ting

abys'-mal
abys'-mally
ac'a-deme
aca-dem'ic
aca-dem'-ical
aca-dem'i-cally
aca-dem-ic'ian
aca-dem'-i-cism
acad -emy
ac'a-jou
ac'a-leph
acal'y-cene
aca-ly'cen-ous
acan-a'ceous
ac-an-tha'ceous
ac-an-thich'-thy-
    osis
acantho-ceph'a-
    lan
acanth'-oid
acanth-o'sis
acanth'-ous
acap'-su-lar
aca-ri'asis
ac'-ar-oid
acar'i-cide
acar'-perous
acarp'-ous
acata-lec'-tic
acata-lep'sy
acata-lep'-tic
aca-thar'sia
acaul-esc'ent
acaul'-ine
acaul'i-ous
ac-ce'de
ac-ce'd-ence
ac-ce'd-ing

ac-cel-er-an'do
ac-cel'-er-ate
ac-cel-er-a'tion
ac-cel'-er-at-ive
ac-cel'-er-ator
ac-cel'-er-at-ory
ac-celer-om'eter
ac-cen'-sion
ac-cen'-sor
ac'-cent (n.)
ac-cent' (v.)
ac-cen'-tual
ac-cen-tu-al'ity
ac-cen'-tu-ate
ac-cen-tu-a'tion
ac-cept'
ac-cept ability
ac-cept'-able
ac-cept'-ance
ac-cep-ta'-tion
ac-cep'ted
ac-cep'ter
ac-cep-ti-la'tion
ac-cep'-tive
ac-cep'tor
ac'-cess
ac-ces'sar-ily
ac-cess'-ary
ac-cessi-bil'ity
ac-cess'-ible
ac-ces'sion
ac-cess-o'rial
ac-cess-or-ily
ac-cess-o'rius
ac-cess'-ory
ac'-ci-dence
ac'-ci-dent
ac-ci-den'-tal

ac-ci-den'-tally
ac-cip'i-ter
ac-cip'i-tral
ac-cip'i-trine
ac-claim'
ac-cla-ma'tion
ac-clam'a-tory
ac-cli'mat-able
ac-cli'mate
ac-cli'mated
ac-clim-a'tion
ac-climat-is-
    a'tion
ac-cli'mat-ise
ac-cliv'i-tous
ac-cliv'ity
ac-cli'vous
ac-col-a'de
ac-com'-mo-date
ac-com'-mo-dat-
    ing
ac-com-mo-
    da'tion
ac-com'-mo-dat-
    ive
ac-com'panied
ac-com'pani-
    ment
ac-com'pan-ist
ac-com'pany
ac-com'plice
ac-com'plish
ac-com'plished
ac-com'plish-
    ment
ac-compt'
ac-cord'
ac-cord'-able

3

ac-cord'-ance
ac-cord'-ant
ac-cor'de:
ac-cord'-ing
ac-cord'-ingly
ac-cor'-dion
ac-cor'-di-on-ist
ac-cost'
ac-couch'e-ment
ac-cou-cheur'
ac-count'
ac-count-abil'ity
ac-count'-able
ac-c unt'-ancy
ac-count'-ant
ac-count'-ing
ac-coup'le-ment
ac-cou'tre
ac-cou'tre-ments
ac-cred'it
ac-cre-men-
                tit'ion
ac-'resc'ence
ac-cresc'ent
ac-cre'te
ac-cre'tion
ac-cre't-ive
ac-crim'i-nate
ac-cru'al
ac-crue'
ac-cru'-ment
ac-cru'-ing
ac-cu-ba'tion
ac-cumb'-ency
ac-cumb'-ent
ac-cu'mu-late
ac-cu'mu-lat-ing
ac-cumu-la'tion

ac-cu'mu-lat-ive
ac-cu'mu-lator
ac'-cu-racy
ac'-cu-rate
ac'-cu-rately
ac'-cu-rate-ness
ac-curs'ed
ac-cu'sal
ac-cu'sant
ac-cu-sa'tion
ac-cu's-ative
ac-cu's-atory
ac-cu'se
ac-cu'sed
ac-cu'ser
ac-cu'sing
ac-cu'singly
ac-cus'-tom
ac-cus'-tomed
acen-aph'-thy-
                lene
aceph'a-lism
aceph'a-lous
ac'er-ate
acerb'-ity
ac'er-ose
acerv'-ate
acer-va'tion
acer'-vu-late
acer'-vu-line
acer'-vu-lus
acet-ab'u-lar
acet-ab'u-lum
acet-al'de-nyde
acer'a-mide
acet-an'il-ide
acet'-ate
aceti-fi-ca'tion

acet-om'eter
acet'yl-ac'etone
acety-la'tion
acet'y-lene
acet'yl-sali-cyl'ic
acha-la'sia
ache'ni-cal
achiev'-able
achiev'e-ment
achiev'-ing
achl. .-myd'eous
ach-lor-hy'dria
ac ondro-pla'sia
achondro-
                plas'tic
achro-mat'ic
achro-mat'i-cally
achro'ma-tin
achro'ma-tise
achro'ma-tism
achro'ma-tous
acic u-lar
acic'u-larly
acic'u-late
acic'u-lum
aci-dae'mia
aci-dif'er-ous
acidi-fi-ca'tion
acid .-fied
aci-dim'eter
acidi-met'ric
aci-dim'etry
aci-dol'y-sis
acid' -phil
aci-do'sis
acid u-lation
acid'u-lation
acid'u-lent

acid'u-lous
ac'ier-age
ac'ier-ate
ac'i-form
aci-na'ceous
acin-ac'i-form
acin'i-form
ac'i-nous
ac'i-nus
acis'-cu-lis
ac-knowl'-edge
ac-knowl'-edge-
    able
ac-knowl'-edg-
    ing
ac-knowl'edg-
    ment
ac'-mite
ac-no'dal
ac'-ol-yte
acon'-dy-lous
ac'-on-ite
ac-on-it'ic
acon'i-tine
ac-on-i'tum
acoty-le'don
acoty-le'don-ous
acous-tex'tile
acous'-tic
acous'-tics
acous'-ti-cal
acous'-ti-cally
acous-tic'ian
ac-quaint'
ac-quaint'-ance
ac-quaint'-ance-
    ship
ac-quain'ted

acqui-esc'e
acqui-esc'-ence
acqui-esc'-ing
ac-qui're
ac-qui're-ment
ac-qui'rer
ac-qui'r-ing
ac-qui-sit'ion
ac-quis'i-tive
ac-quis'i-tive-
    ness
ac-quit'-tal
ac-quit'-tance
ac-quit'-ted
ac-quit'-ting
a'cre-age
ac'ri-dine
acri-mo'ni-ous
ac'ri-mony
ac'ro-bat
acro-bat'ic
ac'ro-bat'ics
ac'ro-blast
acro-car'-pous
acro-chor'dal
acro-cyan-o'sis
ac'ro-dont
acro-dro'mous
ac'ro-gen
acrog'yn-ous
ac'ro-lith
acro-ma'nia
acro-megal'ic
acro-meg'aly
acron'y-cal
ac'ro-nym
acro-par-aes-
    the'sia

acro-pho'bia
acrop'-olis
acro-po'dium
acro-scop'ic
acro-so'mal
ac'ro-some
ac'ro-spore
acros'-tic
acro-te'rium
ac'rot-ism
ac'ry-late
acry-lon'i-trile
act'-able
ac'-ti-nal
act'-ing
ac-tin'ia
ac-tin'ic
ac-tin'i-form
ac'-tin-ism
ac-tin'-ium
ac-tin'o-graph
ac'-tin-oid
ac-tin'o-lite
ac-tin-ol'ogy
ac'-ti-nom
ac-tin-om'eter
actino-myco'sis
ac-tino-ther'apy
ac'-tion
ac'-tion-able
ac'-ti-vate
ac-ti-va'tion
ac'-ti-vator
ac'-tive
ac'-tively
ac'-ti-vism
ac-tiv'i-ties
ac-tiv'ity

5

ac'-tor
ac'-tress
ac-tu-al'ity
ac'-tu-ally
ac-tu-a'rial
ac'-tu-aries
ac'-tu-ary
ac'-tu-ate
ac'-tu-at-ing
ac-tu-a'tion
ac'-tu-ator
acu'-leate
acu'mi-nate
acumi-na'tion
acu'-mi-nous
acu-na'tion
ac'u-nator
acu-punc'-ture
acu-tan'gu-lar
acu'te-ness
ad'a-mant
ada-man'-tine
ada-mel'-lite
adap-ta-bil'ity
adapt'-able
ad-ap-ta'tion
adapt'-ive
ad-ap-tom'eter
ad-ax'ial
add'-able
ad-den'da
add'-ible
ad'-dict (n.)
ad-dict' (v.)
ad-dic'ted

ad-dic'-tion
ad-dit'a-ment
ad-dit'ion
ad-dit'ional
ad-dit'ion-ally
ad'-di-tive
ad-dors'ed
ad-dress'
ad-dressee'
ad-dress'er
ad-dress'-ing
ad-dress'or
ad-du'ce
ad-du'cent
ad-du'cible
ad-du'cing
ad-duct' (v.)
ad'-duct (n.)
ad-duc'-tion
ad-duc'-tor
adelo-mor'phic
ademp'-tion
aden'i-form
ad'-en-oids
ad-en-oid'al
ad-en-o'ma
ad'-en-ose
ad'-en-ous
adept'-ness
ad'-equacy
ad'-equate
ad'-equately
ad-he're
ad-he'r-ence
ad-her'-ent
ad-her-esc'ent
ad-he'r-ing

ad-he'sion
ad-he'sive
ad-he'sively
ad-hib'it
adia-bat'ic
adi-ac-tin'ic
adi-an'-tum
adi-aph'or-ous
adia-ther'mic
adip'a-mide
ad'-ip-ocere
adi-poc'er-ous
ad'i-pose
adi-pos'ity
ad-ja'c-ency
ad-ja'c-ent
ad-ja'c-ently
ad-jec-ti'val
ad'-jec-tive
ad-join'
ad-join'ed
ad-join'-ing
ad-journ'
ad-journ'ed
ad-journ'-ment
ad-judg'e
ad-judg'-ing
ad-ju'di-cate
ad-ju'di-cat-ing
ad-judi-ca'tion
ad-ju'di-cat-ive
ad-ju'di-cator
ad'-junct
ad-junc'-tive
ad-jur-a'tion
ad-ju'ra-tory
ad-ju're

6

ad-ju′ror
ad-just′
ad-just′-able
ad-just′er
ad-just′-ment
ad-just′or
ad′ju-tage
ad′ju-tancy
ad′ju-tant
ad′ju-vant
ad-lac′ri′mal
ad-lac-tin′ic
ad-lib′i-rum
ad-meas′ure
ad-meas′ure-
    ment
ad-mi-nic′u-lar
ad-min′-is-ter
ad-min′-is-trate
ad-min′-is-trat-
    ing
ad-min′-is-trat-
    ive
ad-min′-is-trator
ad-min′-is-
    tratrix
ad′-mir-able
ad′-mir-ably
ad′-mir-alty
ad-mir-a′tion
ad′-mir-at-ive
ad-mi′red
ad-mi′rer
ad-mi′ring
ad-mi′ringly
ad-missi-bil′ity
ad-miss′-ible
ad-mis′sion

ad-miss′-ive
ad-mit′
ad-mit′-tance
ad-mit′-ted
ad-mit′-tedly
ad-mit′-ting
ad-mix′
ad-mix′-ture
ad-mon′-ish
ad-mon′-ish-
    ment
ad-mon-it′ion
ad-mon′i-tory
ad-na′sal
ad′-nate
ad-na′tion
ad-nex′a
ad-nex′ed
ad-nom′i-nal
ado-lesc′ence
ado-lesc′ent
adopt′-able
adop′-tion
adop′-tive
ado′r-able
ado′r-ably
ado-o′ral
ador-a′tion
ado′r-ing
adorn-ing
adorn′-ment
ad-rec′-tal
adre′na-lin
adroit′-ness
ad-sa-tit′ious
ad-sorb′
ad-sorb′-ate
ad-sorb′-ent

ab-sorp′-tion
ab-sorp′-tive
adu-la′ria
adu-lar-esc′ence
ad′u-late
adu-la′tion
adu-la′t-ory
adul′-ter-ant
adul′-ter-ate
adul-ter-a′tion
adul′-ter-ator
adul′-ter-ess
adul′-ter-ine
adul′-ter-ous
adult′-hood
adul′-ti-cide
ad-um′-bral
ad-um′-brant
ad′-um-brate
ad-um-bra′tion
ad-um-bra′tive
ad-unc′-ate
ad-van′ce
ad-vanc′ed
ad-van′ce-ment
ad-vanc′-ing
ad-van′-tage
ad-van-ta′geous
ad-ve′ne
ad-ve′ni-ence
ad′-vent
ad-ven-tit′ious
ad-ven-tit′iously
ad-ven′-tive
ad-ven′-ture
ad-ven′-turer
ad-ven′-ture-
    some

ad-ven'-tur-ess
ad-ven'-tur-ous
ad'-verb
ad-verb'-ial
ad'-ver-saries
ad'-ver-sary
ad-ver'sa-tive
ad'-verse
ad'-versely
ad'-verse-ness
ad-ver'sity
ad-vert'
ad-vert'-ence
ad-vert'-ent
ad-vert'-ently
ad'-ver-tise
ad-ver'-tise-ment
ad'-ver-tiser
ad'-ver-tis-ing
ad-vi'ce
ad-vis-abil'ity
ad-vi's-able
ad-vi'se
ad-vi'sed
ad-vi'se-ment
ad-vi'ser
ad-vi's-ing
ad-vi'sor
ad-vi's-ory
ad'-vo-cacy
ad'-vo-cate
ad'-vo-cator
ad-voc'a-tory
ad-vow'-son
ady-na'mia
ady-nam'ic
ad'y-tum
aecid'-ium

aeg'ir-ite
aeg'ro-tat
aeo'li-pyle
aeolo-trop'ic
aer'-ate
aer-a'tion
aer'-ator
aeri-al'ity
aer'i-ally
aer-if'er-ous
aeri-fi-ca'tion
aer'i-form
aero-bat'ics
aero-don-et'ics
aero-dro'me
aero-dy-nam'ic
aero-dy-nam'ics
aer'o-foil
aer'o-graph
aer-og'ra-phy
aero-iso-clin'ic
aer'o-lite
aero-lith-ol'ogy
aero-lit'ic
aer-ol'-ogist
aer-ol'ogy
aer'o-mancy
aer-om'eter
aero-met'ric
aer-om'etry
aer'o-motor
aer'o-naut
aero-naut'-ical
aero-naut'-ically
aer'o-naut-ics
aero-pho'bia
aer'o-phyte
aer'o-plane

aer'o-scope
aero-scop'ic
aer-os'copy
aer'-ose
aer'o-sol
aer'o-stat
aero-stat'ics
aero-thera-
  peut'ics
aero-therino-
  ther'apy
aeru'gin-ous
aes-the'sia
aes-thesi-om'eter
aes'-thete
aes-thet'ic
aes-thet'-ically
aes-the-tic'ian
aes-thet'-icism
aes-thet'-ics
aes'-ti-val
aes'-ti-vate
aes-ti-va'tion
aeti-ol'ogy
affa-bil'ity
af'-fable
af'-fably
af-fair'
af-fect'
af-fec-ta'tion
af-fec'-ted
af-fect'-ible
af-fec'-ing
af-fec'-tion
af-fec'-tion-ate
af-fec'-tion-ately
af-fec'-tioned
af-fect'-ive

af'-fer-ent
af-fi'ance
af-fi'anced
af-fi'ant
affi-da'vit
af-fil'i-ate
af-fil'i-ation
af-fin'-ities
af-fin'-ity
af-firm'
af-firm'-ably
af-firm'-ance
af-firm'-ant
af-fir-ma'tion
af-firm'-ative
af-firm'-atively
af-firm'-atory
af-fix' (v.)
af'-fix (n.)
af-fla'tus
af-flict'
af-flict'-ing
af-flic'-tion
af-flic'-tive
af'-flu-ence
af'-flu-ent
af'-flu-ently
af-flux'
af-for'-est
af-for-est-a'tion
af-fran'-chise
af-fray'
af'-fri-cate
af-fric'a-tive
af-fri'ght
af-front'
af-front'-ive
af-fu'sion

afo're-men-
    tioned
afo're-said
afo're-thought
afo're-time '
af'-ter-birth
af'-ter-burner
af'-ter-care
af'-ter-deck
at'-ter-ef-fect'
af'-ter-glow
af'-ter-life
af'-ter-math
af'-ter-most
after-noon'
af'-ter-taste
af'-ter-thought
af'-ter-ward
af'-ter-wards
agamo-gen'-esis
ag'a-mous
aga-pan'-thus
agari-ca'ceous
ag'ate-ware
ag'at-ise
a'ge-less
ager-at'um
ag-glom'-er-ate
ag-glom-er-
    a'tion
ag-glu'tin-ant
ag-glu'tin-ate
ag-gluti-na'tion
ag-glu'ti-nat-ive
ag-gra-da'tion
ag-grand'-ise
ag-gran'dise-
    ment

ag'-gra-vate
ag'-gra-vated
ag'-gra-vat-ing
ag-gra-va'tion
ag'-gra-vator
ag'-gre-gate
ag'-gre-gately
ag'-gre-gat-ing
ag'-gre-gation
ag'-gre-gat-ive
ag'-gre-gat-ory
ag-gress'
ag-gres'sion
ag-gress'-ive
ag-gress'-ive-
    ness
ag-gress'or
ag-griev'-ance
ag-griev'e
ag-griev'ed
ag'ile-ness
ag'io-tage
agist'-ment
ag'i-tate
ag'i-tated
agi-ta't-edly
ag'i-tat-ing
agi-ta'tion
agi'-tat-ive
ag'i-tator
ag'-let
ag'-mi-nated
ag'-nate
ag'-na-thous
ag-nat'ic
ag-na'tion
ag-no'men
ag-nom'i-nal

9

ag-no'sia
ag-nos'-tic
ag-nos'-ti-cal
ag-nos'-ti-cally
ag-nos'-ti-cism
ag'-on-ise
ag'-on-is-ing
ag-on-is'tic
ag-on-is'ti-cal
agora-pho'bia
agra'rian-ism
agree-abil'ity
agree'-able
agree'-aoly
agree'-ing
agree'-ment
agres'-tic
agri-cul'-tural
agri-cul'-tur-al-
　　　　ist
air'-coach
air'-con-dition
air'-con-ditioned
air'-con-dition-
　　　　ing
air'-cooled
air'-craft
air'-drop
air'-field
air'-freight
air'-gun
air'i-ness
air'-ing
air'-less
air'-lift
air'-line
air'-mail
air'-man

air-om'eter
air'-pocket
air'-port
air-press'ure
air'-proof
air'-pump
air'-screw
air'-shaft
air'-ship
air'-sick-ness
air'-space
air'-speed
air'-strip
air'-tight
air'-way
air'-worthy
ala-bam'-ine
ala-bas'-ter
ala-bas'-trine
al'a-nine
al'a-nyl
alarm'-ingly
alarm'-ist
al'-ba-core
al-ba'ta
al'-ba-tross
al-be'it
al'-ber-lite
al-besc'ent
al'-bin-ism
al-bi'no
al-bi-not'ic
al'-bite
al-bu-gin'ea
al-bu-gin'eous
al'-bum
al'bu-men
al-bu'men-ise

al'bu-min
al-bu'min-ise
al-bu'mi-noid
al-bumi-no'sis
al-bu'min-ous
al-bumi-nu'ria
al-bumi-nu'ric
al-bur'-num
al-cal'de
al'-ca-mine
al-caz'ar
al-chem'ic
al-chem'i-cally
al'chem-ist
al'-cohol
al-cohol'ic
al-cohol-ic'ity
al'-cohol-ism
al'co-sol
al'-cove
al'-de-hyde
al'der-man
alder-man'ic
al'-eatory
alem'-bic
alert'-ness
aleth'o-scope
aleur'-one
alex-an'-drite
alexi-phar'mic
al-fal'fa
al-fres'co
al'-gae
alga-ro'ba
al'-gebra
al-gebra'ic
al-gebra'ical
al-gebra'ic-ally

al-gebra'ist
al-gefa'cient
al'-gid
al-gid'ity
al-gin'ic
al'-goid
al-gol'ogy
al-gom'eter
algo-met'ri-cal
al'-gous
algo-pho'bia
al'-gor-ism
al'-gor-ithm
al'ibi-ing
ali-bil'ity
ali-cy'clic
al'i-dade
a'lien-able
a'lien-age
a'lien-ate
a'lien-at-ing
alien-a'tion
a'lien-ist
alif'er-ous
a'li-form
align'-ment
al'i-ment
ali-men'-tally
ali-men'-tary
ali-men-ta'tion
al'i-mony
ali'ne-ment
al'i-ped
ali-phat'ic
al'i-quant
al'i-quot
ali-un'de
aliz'-arin

al-ka-lae'mia
al-kal-esc'ent
al-ka-lim'etry
al'-ka-line
al-ka-lin'ity
al-ka-lis-a'tion
al'-ka-lise
al-ka-loid
al-ka-loid'al
al'-kane
al'-ka-net
al'-kene
al'-kyl
al'-kyl-ate
al-ky-la'tion
al'-kyl-ise
al'-lan-ite
al-lan-to'ic
al-lan-toid'al
al-lay'
al-lay'ing
al-le-ga'tion
al-leg'e
al-leg'e-able
al-leg'ed
al-leg'-edly
al-le'giance
al-leg'-ing
al-le-gor'ic
al-le-gor'i-cal
al'le-gor-ies
al'le-gor-ise
al'le-gor-ist
al'le-gory
al-lel'o-morph
al-lel'o-morphic
al-le-lu'ia
al'ler-gen

al-ler'gic
al'-lergy
al-le'vi-ate
al-le'vi-at-ing
al-levi-a'tion
al-le'vi-at-ive
al'-ley
al'-leyed
al'-ley-way
al-li-a'ceous
al-li'ance
al'-lice
al-lied'
al-lies'
al-li-ga'tion
al'li-gator
all'-im-por'tant
al-lit'-er-ate
al-lit-er-a'tion
al-lit'-er-ative
al'-lo-cable
al'-lo-cate
al'-lo-cat-ing
al-lo-ca'tion
al-lo-cu'tion
al'-lo'dial
al-lo'di-al-ism
al-lo'di-al-ist
al-lo'dium
al-log'a-mous
al-log'amy
al-lom'-er-ism
al-lom'etry
al-lo-mor'phic
al-lo-path'ic
al-lo-path'i-
                    cally
al-lop'a-thy

11

al-lo-pha'ne
al-lo-phyl'-ian
al'-lo-plasm
al'-lo-plast
al'lo-theism
al-lot'-ment
al-lotro-
    mor'phic
allo-trop'ic
al-lot'ro-pism
al-lot'ropy
al-lot'-ted
al-lot'-ter
al-lot'-ting
al-low
al-low'-able
al-low'-ance
al-low'ed
al-low'-edly
al'-loy
all'-spice
al-lu'de
al-lu're
al-lu'red
al-lu're-ment
al-lu'r-ing
al-lu'sion
al-lu's-ive
al-lu's-ively
al-lu's-ive-ness
al-lu'v-ial
al-lu'v-ion
al-lu'v-ium
al-ly'-ing
al'-lyl
al-lyl'a-mine
al'-lyl-ene
al-lyt'ic

al-ma-can'-tar
al'-ma-gest
al'-ma-nac
al-man'-dine
al'-moner
al'-monry
alms'-giving
alms'-house
alms'-man
al'oe-sol
alo-et'ic
al'-ogism
along-si'de
aloof'-ness
alo-pe'cia
al-pac'a
al'pen-stock
al'-pha-bet
al-pha-bet'ic
al'-pha-bet-ise
al-pha-bet'i-cal
al-pha-nu-mer'ic
al-phen'ic
al'-phos
al'-pine
al'-sike
al'tar-piece
al-taz'i-muth
alter-abil'ity
al'ter-able
alter-a'tion
al'ter-at-ive
al'ter-cate
alter-ca'tion
al'ter-nate
al'ter-nately
al'ter-nat-ing
al'ter-nation

alter'na-tive
al'ter-nator
al-the'a
al'ti-meter
al-tis'-onant
al'ti-tude
alti-tu'di-nal
alti-tudi-na'rian
al'-tru-ism
al'-tru-ist
al-tru-is'tic
al-tru-is'ti-cally
al'u-del
alumi-nif'er-ous
alu-min'ium
alu'mi-nise
alu'mi-nous
alu'mi-num
al'u-nite
al-ve'olar
al'veo-late
alveo-la'tion
al-ve'olus
al'-vine
al'ys-sum
am'a-dou
amal'-ga-mate
amal-ga-ma'tion
amal'-ga-mator
am-an-i'-tin
amanu-en'-sis
am'-ar-anth
amar-an'-thine
ama-ryl'lis
amass'-able
amass'-ment
am'a-teur
ama-teur'-ish

12

am'a-teur-ism
am'a-tive
am'a-tol
am'a-tory
amaur-o'sis
ama'z-edly
ama'ze-ment
ama'z-ing
ama'z-ingly
am'a-zon
am'a-zon-ite
am-ba'ges
am-bas'sa-dor
am-bassa-do'rial
am-bas'sa-dress
am'-ber
am'-ber-gris
am'-ber-ite
am-bi-dex'-ter
am-bi-dex-ter'ity
am-bi-dex'-trous
am'-bi-ence
am'-bi-ent
am-bi-gu'ity
am-big'u-ous
ambi-par'-ous
am'-bit
am'-bi-tal
am-bit'ion
am-bit'ious
am'-bi-tus
am-biv'-alence
am-biv'a-lent
am'-bling
am'-blingly
am-bly-o'pia
am-bly-o'pic
am'-broid

am-bro'sia
am-bro'sial
am-bro'sian
am'-bro-type
am'-bry
am-bu-la'crum
am'-bu-lance
am'-bu-lant
am'-bu-late
am-bu-la'tion
am'-bu-lat-ory
am-bus-ca'de
am-bus-ca'der
am'-bush
am'-bushed
am'-busher
am'-bush-ment
amel-ifi-ca'tion
ame'li-or-able
ame'li-or-ate
ameli-or-a'tion
ame'li-or-ator
amel'o-blast
amena-bil'ity
amen'-able
amend'-able
amen'da-tory
amend'-ment
amen'i-ties
amen'-ity
amen'-or-rhea
amen-ta'ceous
amen-tif'er-ous
amen'-ti-form
amer'ce-ment
amer-is'tic
ameta-bol'ic
am'eth-yst

am'eth-ys'-tine
ami-an'thus
ami-ca-bil'ity
am'i-cable
am'i-cably
am'-ide
amid'o-gen
amid'-ships
am'-ine
amino-acet'ic
amino-ben-zo'ic
ami-to'sis
ami-tot'ic
am'-ity
am'-meter
am'mo-dyte
am'-monal
am-mo'nia
am-mo'niac
am-mon-i'acal
am-mo'ni-ate
am'-mon-ite
am-mo'nium
am-mon-ol'y-sis
am-mu-nit'ion
am-ne'sia
am'-nesty
am-ni-ot'ic
amoe'ba-cyte
amoe-bae'an
amoe'-boid
amor-al'ity
am'-or-ist
am'-or-ous
amor'ph-ism
amor'ph-ous
amort-is-a'tion
amort'-ise

13

amort'-is-ing
am'-pèr-age
am'-père
am'-per-sand
am-phi-ar-
    thro'sis
am-phi-as'-ter
am-phi-as'-tral
am-phib'ia
am-phib'-ian
am-phibi-ol'ogy
am-phibi-ot'ic
am-phib'i-ous
am-phib'i-ously
amphi-blas'-tic
am-phi-bol'ic
am-phib'o-lite
am-phibo-log'i-
    cal
am-phi-bol'ogy
am-phib'-olous
am'-phi-brach
amphi-car'pic
amphi-cli'nous
amphi-coel'ous
amphi-con'dy-lar
amphi-con'dy-lous
am-phic'-tyon
amphi-dip'-loid
am'-phi-gam
am'-phi-gen
am-phig'en-ous
amphi-ge'nous
amphi-gor'ic
am'phi-gory
amphi-lep'-sis
am-phi-ox'is
am-phip'-oda

am-phip'o-dous
am-phis-bae'na
am-phis'-tom-ous
amphi-the'atre
amphi-the'rium
am-phor'ic
am-pho-ter'ic
am'ple-ness
am-plex'i-caul
am-pli-a'tion
am-pli-fi-ca'tion
am'pli-fied
am'pli-fier
am'pli-fy-ing
am'-pli-tude
am'-ply
am'-poule
am-pu'la
am-pul-la'ceous
am'-pu-tate
am'-pu-tated
am'-pu-tat-ing
am-pu-ta'tion
am-pu-tee'
am-ri'ta
am'u-let
amu's-able
amu's-edly
amu'se-ment
amu's-ing
amyg'-da-lase
amyg'-da-late
amyg-dal'ic
amyg'-da-lin
amyg'-da-loid
amyg-da-loid'al
amyl-a'ceous
am'yl-ene

amyl-oid'al
amyl-ol'y-sis
amylo-lyt'ic
am'yl-ose
an'a-bas
an-ab'a-sis
ana-bap'tist
ana-bat'ic
ana-bio'sis
ana-biot'ic
anab'-olism
an'a-branch
ana-ca-thar'tic
anach'-ron-ism
anach-ron-is'tic
anach'-ron-ously
ana-clas'-tic
ana-cli'nal
ana-clit'ic
ana-col-u'thon
ana-con'da
ana-cru'sis
an'a-dem
ana-di-plo'sis
anad'ro-mous
an-aer-ob'ic
an-aes-the'sia
an-aes-thet'ic
an-aes'-the-tise
an-aes'-the-tist
an'a-glyph
ana-glyph'ic
anag -lyphy
ana-glyp'-tics
ana-gog'ical
an'a-gogy
an'a-gram
ana-gram-mat'ic

14

ana-kin-et'ic
an'a-lecta
ana-lep'-sis
ana-lep'-tic
an-al-ge'sia
an-al-ge'sic
an-al-lat'ic
ana-log'ic
ana-log'i-cal
ana-log'i-cally
anal'-ogies
anal'-ogise
anal'-ogism
anal'-ogist
anal'-ogous
anal'-ogously
an'a-logue
an'a-lyse
anal'y-ses
anal'y-sis
an'a-lys-ing
an'a-lyst
ana-lyt'ic
ana-lyt'i-cal
ana-lyt'i-cally
an-am-ne'sis
ana-mor'pho-sis
ana-mor'ph-ous
an-an'drous
an'a-paest
ana-paes'-tic
anaph'-oral
an-aphro-dis'iac
ana-phyl-ac'tic
ana-phyl-ax'is
ana-pla'sia
ana-plas-mo'sis
an'a-plasty

an-ap-tot'ic
an'-arch
an-ar'chic
an-ar'chi-cal
an'-arch-ism
an'-arch-ist
an-arch-is'tic
an'-ar-chy
an-ar'throus
ana-sar'ca
ana-stat'ic
an-as'tig-mat
an-as-tig-mat'ic
an-as-to-mo'sis
an-as'tral
anas'-trophe
an'a-tase
anath'-ema
anath'-ema-tise
ana-tom'-ical
anat'-omise
anat'-omist
anat'-omy
an-at'ta
ana-tox'in
anat'ro-pous
an'-ces-tor
an'-ces'-tral
an'-ces-tress
an'-ces-try
an'chor-age
an'chor-ess
an'chor-ite
anchor-it'ic
an'chor-smith
an'chov'-ies
an'-chovy
an'chy-losed

an-cil'-lary
an-cin'o-graph
an-cip'i-tal
an-co'neal
an-co'neus
anda-lu's-ite
an'des-ine
an'des-ite
andes-it'ic
and'-iron
an'-dra-dite
an-dro-cepha'-
    lous
an'-dro-cyte
an-droec'ium
an'-dro-gen
andro-gen'-esis
an-drol'ogy
an-drog'yn-ous
an-ec-do'tage
an'-ec-dotal
an'-ec-dote
an'-ec-dot'ic
an-ec-dot'i-cal
an'-ec-dot-ist
an-emo-log'-i-cal
anem-om'eter
anem-oph'i-lous
an-emo'sis
an-em-ceph'a-
    cous
an'-er-oid
an'-eur-ism
an-frac-tu-os'ity
an-gel'ic
an-gel'ica
an-gel'i-cal
angel-ol'atry

15

ANGELOLOGY

angel-ol'ogy
an-gi'na
an-gi'nous
angio-car'-pic
angio-car'-pous
an'gio-cyst
an-gi-ol'ogy
an-gi-o'ma
angi-om'a-tous
angi-op'a-thy
an'gio-sperm
angio-sper'-mal
angio-sper'-mous
angi-os'tomy
an'gle-site
an'gli-cism
angli-cis-a'tion
an'gli-cise
an'glo-phile
an'glo-phobe
anglo-pho'bia
angos-tu'ra
an'gri-ness
ang'-strom
an'gui-form
anguil'-li-form
an'gu-lar
angu-la're
angu-lar'ity
an'gu-late
angu-la'tion
angu-lom'eter
angu-los'ity
angus-ti-fo'li-ate
angust-ros'-trate
angus'-tate
an-he'dron
an-hi-dro'sis

an-hy-drae'mia
an-hy'-dride
an-hy'-drite
an-hy'-drous
an-idio-mat'i-cal
an'-ile
an'-il-ide
an'i-line
anil'-ity
ani-mad-ver'-sion
ani-mad-vert'
an'i-mal
ani-mal'-cu-lar
ani-mal'-cule
an'i-mal-ism
ani-mal'ity
an'i-mate
an'i-mated
an'i-mat-edly
an'i-mat-ing
ani-ma'tion
an'i-ma'tor
an'i-mism
ani-mos'ity
an'i-mus
an'-ise
an'i-seed
ani-sett'e
anis'i-dine
an-iso-cer'-cal
an-iso-dac'-tyl-ous
an-iso-mer'ic
ani-som'er-ous
aniso-metro'pia
an-iso-ton'ic
an-iso-trop'ic
ani-sot'ropy

an'ker-ite
ank'-let
anky-lo'sis
anky-los'toma
an'-nal
an-nal-is'tic
an'-nals
an'-nal-ist
an-neal'
an-neal'ed
an-nel'-ida
an-nex'
an'-nexe
an-nex'-able
an-nex-a'tion
an-ni'hil-ate
an-nihil-a'tion
an-ni'hil-ator
anni-ver'-sar-ies
anni-ver'-sary
an'-no-tate
an-no-ta'tion
an'-no-tator
an-nounce'e
an-nounce'e-ment
an-noun'cer
an-nounc'-ing
an-noy'
an-noy'-ance
an-noy'ed
an-noy'-ing
an'-nu-ally
an-nu'i-tant
an-nu'ity
an-nul'
an'-nu-lar
an'-nu-lar'ity
an'-nu-lary

16

an'-nu-late
an-nu-la'tion
an'nu-let
an-null'ed
an-nul'-ling
an-nul'-ment
an'-nu-loid
an'-nu-lose
an'-nu-lus
an'-num
an-nun'-ci-ate
an-nun-ci-a'tion
an-nun'-ci-atory
ano-don'tia
an'o-dyne
ano-e'sis
ano-et'ic
an'o-lyte
anom'-al-ism
anom-al-is'tic
anom'-al-ous
anom'-al-ously
anom-er-is'tic
an'o-mite
an'-onym
anon-ym'ity
anon'y-mous
anon'y-mously
anoph'-eles
an-op'-sia
an'-orak
an-or-ex'ia
an-or'-thic
an-or'-thite
an-or-tho'pia
an-or'tho-site
an-os-mat'ic
an-os'-mia

an-ox'ia
an-oxy-bio'sis
an'-ser-ine
an'swer-able
an'swer-ing
ant-ac'id
an-tag'-on-ise
an-tag'-on-ism
an-tag'-on-ist
an-tag-on-is'tic
ant-al'ka-line
ant-aphro-dis'iac
ant-arc'-tic
ant-ar-tic'u-lar
ant-asth-mat'ic
ant'-eater
ante-bra'chium
ante-ce'de
ante-ce'd-ence
an'te-chamber
ante-cu'bi-tal
an'te-date
ante-di-lu'vian
ante-dor'-sal
ante-fix'al
an'te-lope
ante-mer-id'ian
ant-em-et'ic
ante-na'tal
an-ten'-nule
ante-nup'-tial
ante-or'bi-tal
ante-pen'-dium
ante-pen-ult'
ante-pen-ul'ti-
    mate
ante-pran'-dial
an-te'rior

an'te-room
ant-he'lion
an-thel-min'-tic
an'-them
an-the'mion
an'-ther
an'-theral
an-ther-id'-ium
an-the'sis
ant'-hill
an'tho-carp
antho-cy'anin
an-tho'dium
antho-gen'-esis
an'-thoid
an-thog'en-ous
an-tho-log'i-cal
an-thol'-ogise
an-thol'-ogist
an-thol'-ogy
an-thophi'-lous
antho-phyl'-ite
antho-tax'is
an'-thra-cene
an'-thra-cite
an-thra-cit'ic
an-thra-co'sis
an'-thra-flav'-ine
an'-thra-nil
an-thra-nil'ic
an'-thra-nol
an'thra-qui-none
an'-thrax
an-throp'ic
anthro-po-
    cen'tric
anthro-po-gen'-
    esis

ANTHROPOGENY

anthro-pog'eny
anthro-pog'ra-
      phy
an'-thro-poid
an-thro-po-log'i-
      cal
anthro-pol'-ogist
anthro-pol'ogy
anthro-pom'eter
anthro-po-met'ric
anthro-pom'etry
anthro-po-
    mor'phic
anthro-po-
    morph'-ise
anthro-pop'a-thy
anthro-poph'-agi
anthro-poph'-
      agous
anthro-poph'-agy
anthro-pos'-ophy
an'ti-air'-craft
an'-tiar
anti-bil'ious
anti-biot'ic
anti-bodies
anti-body
an'-tic
anti-cat'a-lyst
anti-cath'-ode
an'ti-chlor
anti-chlor-ist'ic
an-tic'i-pant
an-tic'i-pate
an-tic'i-pated
an-tic'i-pat-ing
an-tici-pa'tion
an-tic'i-pat-ive

an-tic'i-pator
an-tic'i-pat-ory
anti-cler'i-cal
anti-cli'max
anti-cli'nal
an'ti-cline
anti-clin-o'rium
anti-co-ag'u-lant
an'ti-cous
anti-cryp'-tic
anti-cy'clone
anti-cyclon'ic
an'ti-dotal
an'ti-dote
anti-drom'ic
an'ti-freeze
an'ti-gen
anti-gen'ic
an-tig'eny
an-tig'or-ite
anti-he'lix
anti-keto-gen'-
      esis
anti-log'-ar-ithm
an-til'o-gism
an-til'ogy
anti-ma-cas'sar
an-tim'er-ism
anti-miss'-ile
anti-mo'ni-ate
an'ti-mon'ic
an'ti-mony
an'ti-node
anti-no'mian
an'-tin'omy
anti-pas'to
anti-pa-thet'ic
anti-pa-thet'i-cal

anti-path'ic
an-tip'a-thy
anti-pep'-sin
anti-peri-stal'-
      sis
anti-peri-stal'-
      tic
anti-phlo-gis'tic
an'ti-phon
an-tiph'-onal
an-tiph'-onary
an-tiph'-ony
an-tiph'ra-sis
an-tip'-odal
an'ti-pode
an-tip-ode'an
an-tip'o-des
an'ti-pole
an'ti-pope
an-ti-pyr-et'ic
anti-qua'rian
an'ti-quary
an'ti-quate
an'ti-quated
an'ti-quat-ing
an-tiq'ue
an-tiq'ui-ties
an-tiq'uity
an-tir-rhi'num
anti-scor-bu'tic
anti-sem-it'ic
anti-sem'i-tism
anti-sep'-sis
anti-sep'-tic
anti-sep'-ti-cise
anti-se'rum
anti-sla'v-ery

18

anti-so'cial
an-tis'-trophe
anti-stroph'ic
an-tith'-esis
anti-thet'ic
anti-thet'i-cal
anti-thet'i-cally
anti-tox'ic
anti-tox'in
anti-tra'des
anti-tra'gus
anti-trop'ic
anti-trust'
anti-tryp'-sin
an'ti-type
anti-typ'ic
anti-typ'i-cal
anti-vene'ne
anti-zymot'ic
ant'-ler
ant'-lered
ant'-lia
an-to-nym
an-ton'-ymous
ant-or'bi-tal
ant'-proof
an-tror'se
an-tros'-tomy
an-trot'omy
an'-vil
an'y-body
an'y-how
an'y-one
an'y-thing
an'y-way
an'y-where
an'y-wise
a'or-ist

a'or-istic
aor-ti'tis
ap'-an-age
apa-go'ge
apart'-heid
apart'-ment
ap-as'-tron
apa-tet'ic
apa-thet'ic
apa-thet'i-cally
ap'a-thy
ap'a-tite
a'pe-like
ape'ri-ent
aperi-od'ic
aper'i-tif
aperi-tif'
aper'i-tive
ap'-er-ture
apet'al-ous
aphaer'-esis
aph-an-ip'ter-ous
aph'-an-ite
apha-nit'ic
apheli-ot'ro-pism
aph'-esis
aphlo-gis'tic
aph'-or-ism
aphor-is'tic
aphoto-met'ric
aphoto-trop'ic
aphro-dis'iac
aphyl'-lous
api-a'rian
a'pi-ar-ist
a'pi-ary
ap'i-cal
ap'i-ces

api-col'y-sis
apic'u-late
api-cul'-tural
a'pi-cul-ture
apic'u-lus
ap'i-ose
apiv'-orous
ap-la-nat'ic
ap'-lite
ap-neus'is
ap-neus'-tic
ap-noe'a
apoc'a-lypse
apoca-lyp'-tic
apo-car'-pous
apo-chro-mat'ic
apoc'ry-pha
apoc'ry-phal
apocy-na'ceous
ap'o-dal
ap'o-deme
apo-dic'-tic
apod'-osis
apo-gam'ic
apog'-amy
apo-ge'al
apo-ge'an
ap'o-gee
ap'o-graph
apo-laus'-tic
apolo-get'ic
apolo-get'-ical
apolo-get'-ically
apolo-get'-ics
apo-lo'gia
apol'o-gies
apol'o-gise
apol'o-gis-ing

apol'o-gist
ap'o-logue
apol'-ogy
apo-me-com'eter
apo-mix'is
apo-morph'-ine
apo-neur-o'sis
apo-pemp'-tic
apo-pet'al-ous
apo-phyl'-lite
apo-plec'=tic
apo-plec'-ti-cal
ap'o-plexy
aposio-pe'sis
apo-sit'ia
apos'-tasy
apos'-tate
apos'-ta-tise
apos'tle-ship
apos'to-late
apos-tol'ic
apos-tol'i-cal
apos-tol'i-cism
apos-tol-ic'ity
apos'-trophe
apos'-troph'ic
apos'-tro-phise
apoth'-ecar-ies
apoth'-ecary
apo-the'cium
ap'o-thegm
apo-theg-mat'ic
apothe-o'sis
apo-the'o-sise
apoth'eo-sise
apo-tro-pa'ic
ap-pal'
ap-pall'ed

ap-pal'-ling
ap-pal'-lingly
ap'pa-nage
ap-par-a'tus
ap-par'el
ap-par'-elled
ap-par'-ent
ap-par'-ently
ap-par-it'ion
ap-par'i-tor
ap-peal'
ap-pcal'-able
ap-peal'ed
ap-peal'er
ap-peal'-ing
ap-peal'-ingly
ap-pear'
ap-pear'-ance
ap-pear'ed
ap-pear'-ing
ap-peas'-able
ap-peas'e
ap-peas'e-ment
ap-peas'er
ap-peas'-ing
ap-peas'-ingly
ap-pel'-late
ap-pel-la'tion
ap-pel'la-tive
ap-pel-lee'
ap-pel'-lant
ap-pel'-lor
ap-pend'
ap-pend'-age
ap-pend'-aged
ap-pend'-ancy
ap-pend'-ant
ap-pen-dec'-tomy

ap-pen'ded
ap-pen'-di-cal
ap-pen-di-ci'tis
ap-pen-di-cos'-
    tomy
ap-pen-dic'u-lar
ap-pen-dic'u-late
ap-pen'-dix
ap-per-ceiv'e
ap-per-cep'-tion
ap-per-cep'-tive
ap-per-tain'
ap'pe-tency
ap'pe-tiser
ap'pe-tis-ing
ap'pe-tite
ap'pe-tit-ive
ap-pet'i-tive
ap'pla'nate
ap-plaud'
ap-plaud'er
ap-plaud'-ing
ap-plaus'e
ap-plaus'eo-
    graph
ap-plaus'-ive
ap'ple-jack
ap'pli'ance
ap-pli-ca-bil'ity
ap'-pli-cable
ap'-pli-cably
ap'-pli-cant
ap'-pli-ca'tion
ap'-pli-cat-ive
ap'-pli-cat-ory
ap-plied'
ap-pli'er
ap-plique'

ap-ply'
ap-ply'-ing
ap-point'
ap-point'-able
ap-pointee'
ap-point'er
ap-point'-ing
ap-point'-ive
ap-point'-ment
ap-point'or
ap-por'tion
ap-por'tion-able
ap-por'tioned
ap-por'tioner
ap-por'tion-ing
ap-por'tion-
     ment
ap-po's-able
ap-po'se
ap'po-site
ap-po-sit'icn
ap-pos'i-tive
ap-prais'-able
ap-prais'al
ap-prais'e
ap-prais'ed
ap-prais'er
ap-prais'-ing
ap-prais'-ingly
ap-prais'-ment
ap-pre'ci-able
ap-pre'ci-ate
ap-pre'ci-ated
ap-pre'ci-at-ing
ap-preci-a'tion
ap-pre'ci-at-ive
ap-pre'ci-at-
     ively

ap-pre'ci-at-ory
ap-pre-hend'
ap-pre-hen'-dcd
ap-pre-hend'-ing
ap-pre-hen-si-
     bil'ity
ap-pre-hen'-sible
ap-pre-hen'-sion
ap-pre-hen'-sive
ap-pre-hen'-
     sively
ap-pren'-tice
ap-pren'-ticed
ap-pren'-tice-
     ship
ap-pri'se
ap-pri'sed
ap-pri's-ing
ap-proach'
ap-proach'-able
ap-proach'-able-
     ness
ap-proach'ed
ap-proach'-ing
ap-pro-ba'tion
ap'-pro-bat-ive
ap'-pro-bat-ive-
     ness
ap'-pro-bat-ory
ap-pro'-pri-able
ap-pro'-pri-ate
ap-pro'-pri-ated
ap-pro'-pri-ately
ap-pro'-pri-ate-
     ness
ap-pro-pri-a'tion

ap-pro'-pri-at-
     ive
ap-prov'-able
ap-prov'al
ap-prov'e
ap-prov'ed
ap-prov'-ing
ap-prov'-ingly
ap-prox'i-mate
ap-prox'i-mat-
     ing
ap-proxi-ma'tion
ap-prox'i-mative
ap-pui'
ap-pul'se
ap-pur'-ten-ance
ap'ri-cot
ap'ro-pos
ap'si-dal
ap'-sis
ap-te'ria
ap'-teral
ap'-teral
ap-ter-yg'ial
ap'-teryx
ap'-ti-tude
apt'-ness
ap-to'te
ap-tot'ic
ap-ty'al-ism
apyr-et'ic
apyr-ex'ia
aq'ua-lung
aq'ua-mar-ine
aq'ua-plane
aqua-rell'e
aquat'i-cally
aq'ua-tint

21

AQUATIVENESS

aquat'-ive-ness
aq'ue-duct
aq'ue-ous
aqui-cul'-ture
aqui-le'gia
aq'ui-line
ara-bes'que
ar-ab'i-nose
ar-ab'i-tol
ar'-able
ar-a'ceous
arach'-nid
arach-ni'tis
arach'-noid
arae'o-style
araeo-sys'-tile
ar-a'neose
ar'-ba-lest
ar'-bi-ter
ar'-bi-trable
ar'-bi-trage
ar'-bi-trager
ar'-bi-tral
ar-bit'ra-ment
ar'-bi-trarily
ar'-bi-trary
ar'-bi-trate
ar'-bi-trated
ar'-bi-trat-ing
ar-bi-tra'tion
ar'-bi-trat-ive
ar'-bi-trator
ar'-bi-tress
ar'-bor
ar-bor-a'ceous
ar-bo'real
ar-bor-esc'ent
ar-bor-e'tum

ar'-bori-cul-ture
ar-bor-is-a'tion
ar'-bor-ise
ar'-bor-ist
ar'-bor-ous
ar'-bour
ar'-bu-tin
ar'-bu-tus
ar-ca'de
ar'ca-num
ar'ca-ture
ar-chae'an
ar-chae-ol'-ogist
ar-chae-ol'ogy
ar-cha'ic
ar-cha'ic-ally
ar'-chaise
ar'-chaism
ar'-chaist
ar-chais'-tic
archan-gel'ic
arch'-bishop
arch-bish'-op-ric
arch'-deacon
arch'-deaconry
arch-di'o-cese
arch-du'cal
arch'-duch-ess
arch'-duchy
arch'-duke
arche-go'nium
arch-en'emy
ar-chen-ceph'a-lon
arch'-ery
arch'che-spore
arche-spo'rium
ar'che-typal

ar'che-type
arch'-fiend
archi-ben'-thal
archi-diac'onal
archi-epis'-co-
     pacy
arch-epis'-co-
     pal
ar'-chil
arch-im'age
archi-man'-drite
archi-neph'-ric
archi-pal'-lium
archi-pel-ag'ic
archi-pel'-ago
archi-pel-agoes
ar'-chi-tect
archi-tec-ton'ic
archi-tec'-tural
archi-tec'-ture
ar'-chi-trave
ar-chi'val
ar'-chive
ar'chi-vist
ar'chi-volt
arch'-ness
ar'-chon
arch'-priest
arch'-way
arc'-ing
arc'-tic
ar'-cu-ate
ar'-dency
ar'-dent
ar'-dently
ar'-dour
ar'-du-ous
ar'-du-ously

22

aren-a'ceous
aren-ic'o-lous
areo-la'tion
areol'-ogy
areo-log'i-cal
areom'-etry
ar'-gent
ar-gen'-tal
ar'-gen-tan
ar'-gen-tate
ar'-gen-teum
ar-gen'-tic
ar-gen-tif'er-ous
ar'-gen-tine
ar'-gen-tite
ar-gen-tom'eter
ar-gen'-tous
ar'-gil
ar'-gil-ite
ar-gil-la'ceous
ar-gil-lic'o-lous
ar-gil-lif'er-ous
ar'-gi-nine
ar'-gol
ar'-gon
ar'-gosy
ar'-got
ar'-gu-able
ar'-gue
ar'-gued
ar'-gu-ing
ar'-gu-ment
argu-men-ta'tion
argu-men'-ta-tive
ar-gu'te
ar-gyr'ia
ar'-gyrol
ar'-id-ness

ar'-il-late
ar'-il-lode
ari's-ing
ar-is-toc'-racy
aris'to-crat
aristo-crat'ic
aristo-crat'i-
        cally
aris'to-gen
aris'to-type
arith'-me-tic (n.)
ar-ith-met'ic (a.)
ar-ith-met'i-cal
arith-me-tic'ian
ar-ith-mom'eter
ark'-ose
ar-mad'a
arma-dil'lo
ar'-ma-ment
ar'-ma-ture
arm'-chair
arm'-ful
arm'-hole
ar'-mies
ar'-miger
ar'-mil-lary
ar-mip'o-tent
ar'-mis-tice
arm'-let
ar-mo'rial
ar'-mour
ar'-mour-bearer
ar'-moured
ar'-mourer
ar'-moury
arm'-pit
ar'-mure
ar'-nica

ar'-oid
aroid'-eous
aro-mat'ic
aro-mat'i-cally
aro'ma-tise
arous'-ing
ar'-que-bus
ar'-rack
ar-raign'
ar-raign'er
ar-raign'-ment
ar-ra'nge
ar-ra'nge-able
ar-ra'nge-ment
ar-ra'ng-ing
ar'-rant
ar'-ras
ar-ray'
ar-ray'al
ar-ray'ed
ar-ray'-ing
ar'-rear
ar-rear'-age
ar-rest'
ar-res'ted
ar-rest'er
ar-rest'-ing
ar-rest'-ive
ar-res'tor
ar-rhyth'm-ia
ar'-ris
ar-ri'val
ar-ri've
ar-ri'v-ing
ar-ro'ba
ar'-ro-gance
ar'-ro-gancy
ar'-ro-gant

23

ar'-ro-gate
ar'-ro-gat-ing
ar-ro-ga'tion
ar'-row
ar'-row-head
ar'-row-root
ar'-rowy
ar-roy'o
ar'-senal
ar'-sen-ate
ar'-senic (n.)
ar-sen'ic (a.)
ar-sen'i-cal
ar'-sen-ide
ar-sen'-ious
ar'-sen-ite
ar'-sine
ar'-sis
ar'-son
ar'-son-ist
ar-te'rial
ar-teri-al-is-
    a'tion
ar-te'ri-al-ise
ar-te'ri-ole
ar-terio-scler-
    o'sis
ar-teri-ot'omy
ar-ter-i'tis
ar'-tery
ar-te'sian
art'-ful
art'-fully
ar-thral'-gia
ar-thrit'ic
ar-thri'tis
ar-throgen'-ous
ar'thro-pod

ar-throp'-odal
ar'-ti-choke
ar-tic'u-lar
ar-tic'u-late
ar-ticu-la'tion
ar-tic'u-lat-ive
ar-tic'u-lator
ar'-ti-fact
ar'-ti-fice
ar-tif'i-cer
ar-ti-fic'ial
ar-ti-fic'i-ally
ar-til'-ler-ist
ar-til'-lery
ar-til'-lery=man
artio-dac'-tyl
ar'-ti-san
art'-ist
ar-ti'ste
ar-tis'-tic
ar-tis'-ti-cal
ar-tis'-ti-cally
art'-istry
art'-less
ar-un-dif'er-ous
ar-un-di-
    na'ceous
ary-lar-sin'ic
ary-te'noid
asa-fet'ida
asa-foet'ida
as-bes'-tos
as-bes-to'sis
as'-bol-ane
as'-bol-ite
as-car'i-dole
as-cend'
as-cend'-able

as-cend'-ancy
as-cend'-ant
as-cend'-ent
as-cend'-ing
as-cen'-sion
as-cent'
ascer-tain'
ascer-tain'-able
ascer-tain'-ment
as-cet'ic
as-cet'i-cally
as-cet'i-cism
as-cid'ian
as-ci'tes
as-co-go'nium
asco-myce'tous
asco-spor'ic
as-cos-por'-ous
as-cri'b-able
as-cri'be
as-cri'b-ing
as-crip'-tion
as'-dic
asep'-alous
asep'-sis
asep'-tate
asep'-tic
asep'-ti-cally
asex'u-ality
asha'm-edly
ash'-lar
ash'-lar-ing
as'-in-ine
asin-in'ity
as-par'a-gine
as-par'a-gus
as'-pect
as'-pen

as'-per-ate
as-per'ge
as-per-gil'-li-
form
as-per-gil'-lum
as-per-gil'-lus
as-per'ity
asperm'-ous
as-per'se
as-pers'er
as-per'sion
as-per-so'rium
as'-phalt
as-phal'tic
as-phal'tum
as'-pho-del
as-phyx'ia
as-phyx'i-ate
as-phyx'i-at-ing
as-phyxi-a'tion
as-phyx'i-ator
as'-pic
as-pi-dis'-tra
as'-pir-ant
as-pi'rant
as-pir-a'tion
as'-pir-ator
as-pir'a-tory
as-pi're
as'-pirin
as-pi'ring
as-pi'ringly
ass'-agai
as-sail'
as-sail'-able
as-sail'-ant
as-sail'-ment
as-sass'in

as-sas'sin-ate
as-sassin-a'tion
as-sault'
as-sault'-able
as-sault'er
as'-say (n.)
as-say' (v.)
as-say'-able
as-say'ed
as-say'er
as-say'-ing
ass'-egai
as-sem'-blage
as-sem'ble
as-semb'-ling
as-sem'bly
as-sent'
as-sen-ta'tion
as-sent'er
as-sen'tient
as-sent'-ingly
as-sent'or
as-sert'
as-sert'er
as-ser'tion
as-sert'-ive
as-ser'tor
as-sert'-ory
as-sess'
as-sess'-able
as-sessee'
as-sess'-ment
as-sess'or
as-sess-o'rial
as-sev'-er-ate
as-sev-er-a'tion
as-sib'i-late

as-sibi-la'tion
as'-si-dent
as-si-du'ity
as-sid'u-ous
as-sid'u-ously
as-sid'u-ous-ness
as-si'gn
as-sign-abil'ity
as-si'gn-able
as'-sig-nat
as-sig-na'tion
as-signee'
as-si'gner
as-si'gn-ment
as-si'gnor
as-simi-la-
bil'ity
as-sim'-i-lable
as-sim'-i-late
as-simi-la't-ing
as-simi-la'tion
as-sim'i-lat-ive
as-sim'i-lator
as-sim'i-lat-ory
as-simu-la'tion
as-sist'
as-sist'-ance
as-sist'-ant
as-sis'ted
as-sist'er
as-sist'-ing
as-sist'or
as-si'ze
as-si'ze-ment
as-si'zer
as-so'ci-able
as-so'ci-ate
as-so'ci-at-ing

25

as-so'ci-ation
as-so'ci-at-ive
as'son-ance
as'son-ant
as-sort'
as-sor'ted
as-sort'-ment
as-sua'ge
as-sua'ge-ment
as-sua'g-ing
as-sua's-ive
as-su'm-able
as-su'm-ably
as-su'me
as-su'm-edly
as-su'mer
as-su'ming
as-sump'-sit
as-sump'-tion
as-sump'-tive
as-su'r-able
as-su'r-ance
as-su're
as-su'r-edly
as-su'red-ness
as-sur'gent
as-su'r-ing
as'-ta-cene
as-ta'sia
as'-ter
as-tereog-no'sis
as-te'ria
as-te'ri-ated
as'-ter-isk
as'-ter-ism
as'-ter-oid
as'-ter-oidal
26

as-ter-oid'-ean
as-ter-os-pon'dy-
   lous
as-the'nia
as-then'ic
as-then-o'pia
asth-mat'ic
asth-mat'i-cal
asth-mat'i-cally
as-tig-mat'ic
astig'-ma-tism
astom'a-tous
as-ton'-ish
as-ton'-ished
as-ton'-ish-ing
as-ton'-ish-ingly
as-ton'-ish-ment
as-tound'
as-toun'ded
as-tound'-ing
as-tound'-ingly
as'-tra-gal
as-trag'a-lus
as'-tra-khan
as'-tral
as-trict'
as-tric'-tion
as-trict'-ive
as-trin'-gency
as-trin'-gent
as'-tro-cyte
as'-tro-dome
as'-tro-graph
as-trog'ra-phy
as'-troid
as'-tro-labe
as-trol'-oger
astrol-og'i-cal

astrol-og'i-cally
as-trol'-ogy
as-trom'-etry
as'tron-aut
as-tron'-omer
astro-nom'ic
astro-nom'i-cally
as-tron'-omy
astro-phys'i-cal
astro-phys'i-cist
astro-phys'ics
as'tro-sphere
as-tu'cious
as-tu'city
as-tu'te
as-tu'tely
as-tu'te-ness
as-tyl'-len
asym'-meter
asym-met'-ric
asym-met'ri-cal
asym-met'ri-cally
asym'-metry
as'ymp-tote
asymp-tot'ic
asymp-tot'i-ca
asyn-ap'sis
asyn -ar-rete
asyn'-chro-nism
asyn'-chro-nous
asyn-det'ic
asyn-det'i-cally
asyn'-de-ton
asyn-er'gia
asyn-gam'ic
asyn-tac-tic
asys'-tole
at'a-bal

atac'a-mite
atac'-to-sol
at'-ar-axy
at'av-ism
at'av-ist
atav-is'-ti-cally
atel-ec'ta-sis
athal'a-mous
atha-na'sia
a'the-ism
a'the-ist
atheis'-tic
atheis'-ti-cal
atheis'-ti-cally
ath'el-ing
ath'-en-aeum
ath'-er-ine
ather'-mancy
ather'-ma-nous
ather-o'ma
ather-o'ma-tous
athero-scler-
                o'sis
ath-eto'sis
ath'-lete
ath-let'ic
ath-let'i-cally
ath-let'i-cism
ath-let'ics
at'-las
at'mo-graph
at-mol'ogy
at-mol'y-sis
at-mom'eter
at'mo-phile
at'-mos-phere
at-mos-pher'ics
at-mos-pher'i-cal

at-mos-pher'i-
              cally
atom'i-cal
atom-ic'ity
atom-is-a'tion
at'om-ise
at'om-iser
at'om-ism
at'om-ist
atom-is'tic
atom-ol'ogy
ato'n-al-ism
aton-al-is'tic
aton-al'ity
ato'ne-ment
ato'n-ing
at'-ony
atra-bil'i-ary
at'ra-tous
at'ri-colour
at'rio-pore
atrio-ven-
          tic'u-lar
at'-rium
atro'pa-mine
at'ro-phied
at'ro-phy
at'ro-pine
at'ro-pism
at'ro-pous
at-tach'
at-tach'-able
at-taché'
at-tach'ed
at-tach'-ment
at-tack'
at-tack'ed

at-tack'er
at-tack'-ing
at-tain'
at-tain-abil'ity
at-tain'-able
at-tain'-able-
              ness
at-tain'-der
at-tain'er
at-tain'-ment
at-taint'
at-tain'-ture
at'-tar
at-tem'-per
at-tem'-per-at-
                ors
at-tempt'
at-tempt'-able
at-tempt'er
at-tend'
at-tend'-ance
at-tend'-ant
at-ten'-tion
at-tent'-ive
at-tent'-ively
at-tent'-ive-ness
at-ten'-u-ate
at-tenu-a'tion
at-ten'u-ator
at-test'
at-test'-ant
at-test-a'tion
at-test'er
at'-tic
at'-ti-cise
at'-ti-cism
at-ti're
at-ti're-ment

27

at-ti'r-ing
at'-ti-tude
atti-tu'di-nise
at-tor'ney
at-tract'
at-tract'a-bility
at-tract'-able
at-tract'-able-
         ness
at-tract'-ant
at-trac'-tion
at-tract'-ive
at-tract'-ively
at-tract'-ive-
         ness
at-trac'-tor
at-trib'u-table
at'tri-bute (n.)
at-trib'ute (v.)
at-trib'u-ting
at-tri-bu'tion
at-trib'u-tive
at-tri'ted
at-trit'ion
at-tri'tus
at-tu'ne
at-tu'ne-ment
at-tu'n-ing
atyp'i-cal
aub'er-gine
auc'-tion
auc-tion-eer'
auc-to'rial
aud-a'cious
aud-ac'ity
audi-bil'ity
aud'-ible
aud'-ibly
28

aud'i-ence
audio-gen'ic
aud'io-gram
audi-om'eter
aud'io-phile
aud'i-phone
aud-it'ion
aud'i-tive
aud'i-tor
audi-to'rial
audi-to'rium
aud'.-tory
aug'i-tite
aug'-ment (n.)
aug-ment' (v.)
augment'-able
aug-men-ta'tion
aug-men-ta'tive
aug-men'-tor
aul'o-phyte
aulo-sto'ma-tous
aur'a-mine
aur-an'tia
aur'-eate
aur'-eole
aureo-my'cin
aur'-icle
aur'-icled
aur-ic'u-lar
aur-ic'u-late
aur-if'er-ous
aur'i-form
aur-ig'ra-phy
aur'i-lave
aur'-ine
aur'i-scope
aur'-ist
auro-ceph'a-lous

aur'-ochs
auro-cy'an-ide
aur'o-phore
aur-o'ra
aur-o'ral
auro-re'an
aur'-ous
aus'-cul-tate
aus-cul-ta'tion
aus'-pi-cate
aus'-pice
aus-pic'ial
aus-pic'ious
aus-pic'iously
aus'-ten-ite
aus-ten-it'ic
aus'-ter
aus-te're
aus-te'rely
aus-ter'ity
aus'-tral
aus'-tra-lite
aut'a-coid
aut-ar'chic
aut'ar-chy
aut-ecol'ogy
auth-en'tic
auth-en'ti-cally
auth-en'ti-cate
auth-enti-ca'tion
auth-en-tic'ity
auth'or-ess
auth-or-is-a'tion
auth'-or-ise
auth'-or-ised
auth'-or-is-ing
auth-ori-ta'rian
auth-or'i-tat-ive

auth-or'ity
auth'or-ship
auto-al-log'amy
aut'o-bahn
auto-bi-og'ra-
 pher
auto-bio-graph'ic
auto-bio-graph'i-
 cal
auto-bi-og'ra-phy
auto-brecci-a'tion
aut'o-cade
aut'o-car
aut'o-carp
auto-cat-al'y-sis
auto-ceph'a-lous
aut'o-chrome
autoch'-thon
autoch-thon'ic
autoch'-thon-ous
aut'o-clave
auto-con-duc'-
 tion
auto-con-den-
 sa'tion
aut'o-crat
auto-crat'ic
auto-crat'i-cally
aut'o-cyst
auto-dy-nam'ic
aut'o-dyne
auto-er-ot'ic
auto-er'-otism
auto-fret'-tage
autog'-amy
auto-gen'-esis
auto-gen-et'ic
auto-gen'ic

autog'en-ous
aut'o-graph
autog'ra-pher
auto-graph'ic
autog'ra-phy
auto-grav'-ure
auto-gy'ro
auto-het'ero-dyne
auto-heter-o'sis
aut'o-infec-tion
auto-in-ocu-
 la'tion
auto-in-toxi-
 ca'tion
auto-kin-et'ic
autol'-atry
autol'y-sis
aut'o-mat
auto-mat'ic
auto-mat'i-cal
auto-mat'i-cally
auto-ma'tion
autom'a-tism
autom'a-ton
auto-mix'is
aut'o-mobile
auto-morph'ic
auto-nom'ic
auton'-omist
auton'-omous
auton'-omy
aut'-onym
auto-pal'a-tine
auto-par'a-site
auto-par-tho-
 gen'esis
autoph'a-gous
autoph'-ony

aut'o-phyte
auto-plas'ma
auto-plas'-tic
auto-po'dium
auto-pot'a-mous
auto-psy-cho'sis
auto-rhyth'-mus
auto-rota'tion
autos'-copy
aut'o-set
aut'o-some
autos'-pasy
aut'o-sphere
auto-sto'per
auto-sug-ges'-
 tion
auto-tox-e'mia
auto-toxi-ca'tion
auto-tox'in
auto-tro'pism
auto-troph'ic
aut'o-type
auto-typ-og'ra-
 phy
auto-zo'oid
autum'-nal
autum'-nally
auxan-om'eter
aux-e'sis
aux-et'ic
auxil'i-ary
aux'-ins
aux'o-chrome
aux'o-cyte
aux-om'eter
auxo-ton'ic
avail-abil'ity
avail'-able

29

av'a-lanche
av'-ar-ice
avar-ic'ious
avar-ic'iously
avas'-cu-lar
ava-tar'
aven-a'ceous
aveng'-ing
av'-ens
av'en-tail
aven'-tur-ine
av'-enue
av'-er-age
aver'-ment
aver'-ring
aver'-sion
avert'-ible
a'vi-ar-ist
a'vi-ary
a'vi-ate
avi-a'tion
a'vi-ator
avicu-la'rium
a'vi-cul-ture
a'vi-cul-tur-ist
avid'-ity
a'vi-fauna
a'vi-form
avita-min-o'sis
avi-zan'-dum
avo-ca'do
avo-ca'dos
avo-ca'tion
avoc'a-tory
av'o-cet
avoid'-able
avoid'-ably
avoid'-ance
30

av'oir-du-pois
avow'-edly
avul'-sion
avun'cu-lar
awa'k'ened
awa'k-en-ing
awa'k-ing
awa're-ness
awe'-some
awe'-stricken
awe'-struck
awk'-ward
awk'-wardly
awk'-ward-ness
awn'-ing
ax'i-ally
axi'i-ate
axi-lem'ma
ax-il'la
ax'il-lary
ax'-in-ite
axio-mat'ic
axio-mat'i-cal
axio-mat'i-cally
ax'le-tree
ax'o-lotl
ax'-on-eme
axo-po'dium
axo-sper'-mous
ax'o-style
az'a-line
azeo-trop'ic
azi-mi'no
az'i-muth
az'i-muthal
azo-meth'-ane
azo-phen'-ine
azo-pro'-teins

azo-tom'eter
a'zu-lene
a'zur-ite
az'y-gous

B

bab'a-coote
ba-bassu'
bab'-bitt
bab'-bittry
ba-bi-ru'ssa
bab'-bler
bab'-bling
ba-boon'
ba-bouch'e
ba-bu'l
ba'by-hood
ba'by-ing
ba'by-ish
ba'by-sit-ter
bacca-laur'-eate
bac'-ca-rat
bac'-cate
bac'-cha-nal
bac-cha-na'lia
bac-cha-na'lian
bac-chant'
bac-chan'te
bac-chan'-tic
bac'-chic
bac-cif'er-ous
bac'-ci-form
bac-civ'or-ous
bach'-elor
bach'-elor-hood
ba-cil-laem'ia

ba-cil'-la-form
ba-cil'-lar
ba-cil'-lary
ba-cil'li
ba-cil-lu'ria
ba-cil'-lus
back'-ache
back'-band
back'-bite
back'-bit-ing
back'-board
back'-boiler
back'-bone
back'-break-ing
back'-drop
back'-fire
back'-gam-mon
back'-ground
back'-hand
back-hand'ed
back'-hander
back'-ing
back'-lash
back'-less
back'-log
back'-rest
back'-saw
back'-set
back-set'-ting
back'-side
back'-sight
back'-slide
back'-slid-ing
back'-stage
back'-stairs
back'-stays
back'-stitch
back'-stop

back'-stroke
back'-sword
back'-talk
back'-track
back'-ward
back-ward-a'tion
back'-wardly
back'-ward-ness
back'-wash
back'-water
back-woods'
back-woods'-man
back'-yard'
bac-te'ria
bac-teri-ae'mia
bac-te'rial
bac-te'ri-cidal
bac-te'ri-cide
bac-te'rio-cyte
bac-terio-log'i-
        cal
bac-teri-ol'-ogist
bac-teri-ol'ogy
bac-teri-ol'y-sin
bac-teri-ol'y-sis
bac-te'rio-lyt'ic
bac-te'rio-phage
bac-te'ri-or-
        rhiza
bac-teri-os'copy
bac-terio-stat'ic
bac-te'rium
bac-teri-u'ria
bac'-ter-oid
bac-ter-oid'al
ba-cu'li-form
bac'u-lite
ba-dig'eon

badl-nog'e
ba'di-ous
bad'-min-ton
bad'-ness
bad'tem-pered
baf'fle-ment
baf'-fler
baf'-fling
baf'-flingly
ba-gass'e
bag'a-telle
bag'-gage
bag'-gage-man
bag'-gage-master
bag'-gage-room
bag'-gily
bag'-ging
bag'-man
bag'-pipe
bag'-piper
ba-guett'e
bail'-able
bail'-ing
bail'-iff
bail'i-wick
bail'-lie
bail'-ment
bails'-man
ba'kel-ite
ba'k-ery
ba'ke-house
ba'k-ing
ba'ke-meat
ba'k-ing powder
bak'-sheesh
bak'-shish
bala-clav'a
bala-laik'a

31

bal'-ance
bal'-ancer
bal'-anc-ing
ba-lat'a
ba-laus'-tine
bal-brig'-gan
bal-conet'
bal'-con-ies
bal'-cony
bal'-da-chin
bal'der-dash
bald'-ness
bald'-pate
bald'-ric
ba-leen'
ba'le-fire
ba'le-ful
bal-is-tra'ria
balk'-ing
bal'-lad
bal-lad'e
bal'-ladry
bal'-last
bal'-last-age
ball-bear'-ing
ball'-cock
bal-ler-i'na
bal'-let
bal-leto-ma'ne
bal-leto-ma'nia
ball'-ing
bal-lis'ta
bal-lis'-tic
bal-lis-tic'ian
bal-lis'-tics
bal-lon-net'
bal-loon'
bal-loon'-ing

bal-loon'-ist
bal'-lot
bal'-lot-age
bal'-lot-box
bal'-lot-ing
ball'-player
ball'-room
balm'i-ness
bal'-neal
bal-ne-a'tion
bal-ne-ol'ogy
bal-neo-ther'apy
balsam'i-cally
balsa-mif'er-ous
bal'sa-mine
bal'-us-ter
bal'-us-trade
bam-bi'no
bam-boo'
bam-booz'le
bam-booz'-ler
ba-nal'ity
ba-nan'a
ban'-dage
ban'-dag-ing
ban-dan'na
ban'-dar
band'-box
band'-elet
ban'-der-ole
ban'-di-coot
band'-ing
ban'-dit
ban'-ditry
ban-dit'ti
band'-let
band'-mas-ter
bando-leer'

bando-lier'
ban'do-line
bands'-man
band'-saw
band'-stand
band'-wagon
ban'dy-ing
ba'ne-ful
ban'-ish
ban'-ish-ment
ban'-is-ter
ban'-jo-ist
ban'-jos
ban-ju-le'le
bank'-able
bank'-ac-count
bank'-book
bank'-draft
bank'-ing
bank'-note
bank'-rupt
bank'-ruptcy
bank's-man
ban'-ner
ban'-neret
ban-ner-ett'e
ban'-ner-ole
ban'-ning
ban'-nis-ter
ban'-nock
ban'-quet
ban-quet'er
ban-quet'-ing
ban-quett'e
ban'-shee
ban'-tam
ban'-tam-weight
ban'-ter

ban'-ter-ing-ly
bant'-ing
bant'-ling
banx'-ring
ban'-yan
ban-zai'
ba'o-bab
bap-ti'se
bap-ti'sed
bap-ti's-ing
bap'-tism
bap-tis'-mal
bap'-tis-tery
bar-ag-no'sis
bara-lip'-ton
bara-the'a
bar-ba'rian
bar-ba'rian-ism
bar-bar'ic
bar-bar'i-cally
bar'-bar-ise
bar-bar-ism
bar-bar'ity
bar'-bar-ous
bar'-bar-ously
bar'-bate
bar'-be-cue
bar'-bel
bar'-bel-late
bar'-belled
bar'-ber
bar'-berry
bar'-ber-shop
bar'-bet
bar-bett'e
bar'-bi-can
bar'-bi-cel
bar'-bier-ite

bar'-bi-tal
bar'-bi-ton
bar-bit'u-rate
bar-bi-tu'ric
barb'-less
bar-bo'la
bar'-bo-tine
bar'-bule
bar'-ca-rolle
bard-ol'-atry
ba're-back
ba're-faced
ba're-foot
ba're-footed
ba're-handed
ba're-headed
ba're-leg-ged
ba're-ness
bar'-gain
bar'-gainer
bar'ge-board
barge-canal'
bar-gee'
bar'ge-man
bar'ge-master
bar-il'la
bar'i-tone
bar'-keeper
bark'-en-tine
bark'-ing
bark-om'eter
bar'-ley
bar'-ley-corn
bar'-ley-mow
bar'-maid
bar'-man
bar-me-ci'dal
bar'-me-cide

bar'-nacle
barn'-dance
barn'-stormer
barn'-storm-ing
barn'-yard
bar'o-graph
bar-ol'ogy
bar-om'eter
baro-met'ric
baro-met'ro-
          graph
bar-om'etry
bar'on-age
bar'on-ess
bar'-onet
bar'on-et-age
bar'on-etcy
bar-o'nial
bar'-ony
baro-phor-e'sis
ba-roq'ue
bar'o-scope
baro-scop'ic
bar'o-stat
baro-therm'o-
          graph
bar'-rack-ing
bar'-racks
bar-ra-coon'
bar-ra-cu'da
bar-rag'e
bar'ra-tor
bar'ra-trous
bar'ra-try
bar'-rel
bar'-relled
bar'-rel-ful
bar'-ren

33

bar'-ren-ness
bar-rett'e
bar-ret'e-ter
bar'-ri-cade
bar-ri-ca'd-ing
bar-ri-ca'do
bar'-rier
bar'-ring
bar'-ris-ter
bar'-room
bar'-row
bar'-ru-lette
bar-tend'er
bar'-ter
bar-ti-zan'
bar'-ton
bary-cen'-tric
bar'y-lite
bary-pho'nia
bar'y-sphere
ba-ry'ta
ba-ry'tes
ba-ryt'ic
ba-ryto-cal'cite
bar'y-tron
ba-sa'lar
basal-metab''-ol-ism
ba-salt'
ba-salt'ic
ba-salt'-ine
ba-salt'i-form
bas'-an-ite
bas'-ci-net
bas'-cule
ba'se-ball
ba'se-board
ba'se-born
34

ba'se-hearted
ba'se-hit
ba'se-less
ba'se-line
ba'se-man
ba'se-ment
ba'se-minded
ba'se-ness
ba-shaw'
bash'-ful
bash'-ful-ness
basi-bran'chial
ba'si-cally
basi-chro'ma-tin
ba-sic'ity
basi-con'ic
basi-cra'nial
ba'si-cyte
ba-sid'ial
ba-sidio-gen-et'ic
ba-sidio-myce'tes
ba-sid'io-phore
ba-sid'io-spore
ba-sid'ium
basi-dor'sal
basi-fu'gal
basi-gam'ic
basi-gam'-ous
basi-hy'al
ba'si-lar
ba-sil'ic
ba-sil'ica
ba-sil'i-cal
ba-sil'i-can
ba-sil'i-con
ba-sil'i-cum
bas'-ilisk
ba'si-nerved

bas'-inet
ba-sip'-etal
ba'si-phil
basi-oc-cip'i-tal
basi-po'dium
basi-scop'ic
basi-sphe'noid
basi-ton'ic
basi-ven'-tral
basi-ver'-tebral
bas'-ket
bas'-ket-ball
bas'-ket-full
bas'-ketry
bas'-ket-work
bask'-ing=shark
baso-phil'ia
bas'-re-lief'
bas'-set
bas'-si-net
bas-soon'
bas-soon'-ist
bass-vi'ol
bass'-wood
bas'-tard
bas'-tard-ise
bas-tard-is-a'tion
bas'-tardy
bas-till'e
bas-ti-na'do
bas'-tion
bas'-tite
ba-ta'ta
batch'-ing
ba-te'a
bat-eleur'
ba'te-ment
bat'-fish

ba-thet'ic
bath'-house
bath'-ing
bath'o-chrome
bath'o-lith
batho-lith'ic
bath-om'eter
batho-phil'i-ous
batho-ton'ic
bath'-robe
bath'-room
bath'y-bic
bathy-lim-net'ic
bathy-met'ric
ba-thys'-mal
bath'y-sphere
ba-tik'
ba-tist'e
ba-tra'chian
bats'-man
bat-ta'lia
bat-tal'ion
bat'-tels
bat'-ten
bat'-ter
bat'-ter-ies
bat'-ter-ing
bat'-tery
bat'-ting
bat'tle-dore
bat'tle-field
bat'tle-flag
bat'tle-front
bat'tle-ground
bat'tle-ment
bat'tle-scarred
bat'tle-ship
bat'-tue

baux'-ite
bawd'i-ness
baya-de're
bay'-berry
bay'er-ite
bay'-onet
bay'-salt
ba-zaar'
ba-zook'a
bdel'-lium
beach'-comber
beach'-head
bea'-con
bead'-ing
bead'le-dom
bead'-work
beag'-ling
beak'-less
beam'i-ness
beam'-ing
beam'-ingly
beam'-less
bean'-feast
bean'-tree
bear'-able
bear'-able-ness
bear'-berry
beard'-less
bear'-ing
bear'-ish
bear'-ish-ness
bear'-skin
beast'-li-ness
be-atif'ic
be-ati-fi-ca'tion
be-at'i-fied
be-at'ify
beat'-ing

be-at'i'tude
beau-mon-tag'o
beaut'-eous
beaut'-ies
beaut'i-fi-ca'tion
beaut'i-fied
beaut'i-fier
beaut'i-ful
beaut'i-fully
beaut'i-fy-ing
beav'-er-teen
be-calm'
be-ca'me
be-caus'e
becca-fi'co
be-chan'ce
be-charm'
beck'-ite
beck'-on-ing
be-cloud'
be-com'e
be-com'-ing
be-dab'ble
be-daub'
be-da'ze
be-daz'zle
be-daz'-zling
bed'-chamber
bed'-clothes
bed'-ded
bed'-ding
be-deck'
be'des-man
be-dev'il
be-dev'illed
be-dev'il-ment
be-dew'
bed'-fast

bed'-fel-low
be-dight'
be-dim'
be-diz'en
bed'-jacket
bed'-lam
bed'-lam-**ite**
bed'-pan
bed'-plate
bed'-post
be-drag'gle
bed'-rid-den
bed'-rock
bed'-room
bed'-sheet
bed'-side
bed'-sore
bed'-spread
bed'-spring
bed'-stead
bed'-straw
bed'-tick
bed'-time
bed'-warmer
beech'-mast
beech'-nut
beef'-eater
beef'i-ness
beef'-wood
bee'-hive
bee'-keeper
beek'-ite
bee'-line
bee'-mas-**ter**
beest'-ings
bees'-wax
beet'-ling
beet'-root

be-fall'
be-fall'en
be-fell'
be-fit'
be-fit'-ting
be-fit'-tingly
be-fog'
be-fogg'ed
be-fog'-ging
be-fool'
be-fo're
be-fo're-hand
be-fo're-time
be-foul'
be-friend'
be-fud'dle
be-gan'
be-gat'
be-get'
be-get'-ter
be-get'-ting
beg'-gar
beg'-gar-li-ness
beg'-garly
beg'-gary
beg'-ging
be-gin'
be-gin'-ner
be-gin'-ning
be-gird'
be-girt'
be-gon'e
be-go'nia
be-got'
be-got'-ten
be-gri'me
be-grudg'e
be-grudg'-ing

be-grudg'-ingly
be-gui'le
be-gui'ler
be-gui'l-ing
be-gui'l-ingly
be'-gum
be-gun'
be-half'
be-ha've
be-ha'v ed
be-ha'v-ing
be-ha'v-iour
be-ha'v-iour-ism
be-hav-iour-is'tic
be-head'
be-head'ed
be-held'
be-he'moth
be-hen'ic
be-hest'
be-hi'nd
be-hi'nd-hand
be-ho'ld
be-ho'lden
be-ho'lder
be-ho'ld-ing
be-hoof'
be-hoov'e
be-ho've
be'-ing
be-jew'el
be-la'bour
be-la'te
be-la'ted
be-la't-edly
be-la't-ed-ness
be-laud'
be-lay'

be-lay'-ing
bel'-dam
be-leag'uer
be-leag'u-ered
be-leag'u-er-ment
bel'-em-nite
bel'-em-noid
hel'-fried
bel'-fry
be-lie'
be-lief'
be-li'er
be-liev'-able
be-liev'e
be-liev'ed
be-liev'er
be-liev'-ing
be-liev'-ingly
be-li'ke
be-lit'tle
be-lit'tle-ment
be-lit'-tling
bel-la-don'na
bell'-bird
bell'-boy
bell'-founder
bell'-flower
bell'-hop
bel'-li-cose
bel-li-cos'-ity
bel-lig'er-ence
bel-lig'er-ency
bel-lig'er-ent
bell'-man
bel'-low
bel'-lows
bell'-shaped
bell'-tower

bell'-wether
bel'ly-band
bel'ly-ful
be-long'
be-long'ed
be-long'-ing
be-long'-ings
be-loved'
be-lov'ed
be-low'
belt'-ing
bel'-vedere
be-ly'-ing
be-ma'zed
be-mi're
be-mi'r-ing
be-moan'
be-moan'ed
be-moan'-ing
be-mu'se
be-mu'sed
be-mu's-ing
be-na'me
bench'-mark
bend'-ing
bend'-wise
be-neath'
ben'-edick
ben'-edict
ben-edic'-tine
ben'-edic'-tion
ben-edic'-tory
ben'-efac-tion
ben'-efac-tor
ben-efac'-tory
ben'-efac-tress
ben-ef'ic
ben'-efice

ben'-eficed
ben-ef'i-cence
ben-ef'i-cent
ben-ef'i-cently
ben-efic'ial
ben-efic'ially
ben-efic'i-aries
ben-efic'i-ary
ben'-efit
ben'-efited
ben'-efit-ing
ben-ev'-olence
ben-ev'-ol-ent
be-night'ed
be-ni'gn
be-nig'-nancy
be-nig'-nant
be-nig'-nantly
be-nig'-nity
be-ni'gnly
ben'i-son
ben-i'to-ite
ben-tho-pot'a-
mous
ben'-thos
ben'-ton-ite
be-numb'
ben'-zal
ben-zal'-dehyde
ben'za-mide
ben'za-mine
ben-zan'-il-ide
ben-zan'-throne
ben'-ze-drene
ben'-zene
ben'-zi-dine
ben'-zil
ben-zil'ic

37

BENZINE

ben'-zine
ben'-zo-ate
ben-zo'ic
ben'-zo-caine
ben'-zol
ben'-zo-line
ben-zon'i-tril
ben'-zoyl
ben'-zoyl-ate
ben'-zyl
ben-zyl'a-mine
ben'-zyl-ate
ben-zyl-chlo'r-
    ide

be-praise'
be-queath'
be-queath'al
be-quest'
be-ra'te
be-ra'ted
be-ra't-ing
ber'-ber-ine
ber'-beris
be-reav'e
be-reav'ed
be-reav'e-ment
be-reav'-ing
be-reft'
ber'-ga-mot
ber-gan'-der
ber'-gylt
ber'i-beri
ber-ke'lium
ber'-ries
ber-serk'
ber-serk'er
berth'-age
berth'-ing

38

ber'yl-line
ber-yl'-lium
ber-yl'-lon-ite
be-seech'
be-seech'ed
be-seech'-ing
be-seem'
be-set'
be-set'-ment
be-set'-ting
be-shrew'
be-si'de
be-si'des
be-sieg'e
be-sieg'er
be-sieg'-ing
be-sla'ver
be-smear'
be-smirch'
be-smirch'er
be-sot'
be-sot'-ted
be-sot'-tedly
be-sought'
be-spang'le
be-spat'-ter
be-speak'
be-spec'-tacled
be-spo'ke
bes'ti-al-ise
besti-al'ity
bes'ti-ally
bes'ti-ary
be-stir'
be-stow'
be-stow'-able
be-stow'al
be-strad'dle

be-strew'
be-strewn'
be-stri'de
be-stro'de
best'-sell'-er
be'ta-caine
be'ta-fite
be'ta-ine
be-ta'ke
be'ta-tron
be-think'
be-thought'
be-ti'de
be-ti'mes
be-to'ken
bet'-ony
be-took'
be-tray'
be-tray'al
be-tray'er
be-tro'th
be-tro'thal
be-tro'thed
be-tro'th-ment
bet'-ter
bet'-ter-ment
bet'-ting
betu-la'ceous
be-tween'
be-twixt'
bev'a-tron
bev'-elled
bev'-el-ling
bev'-er-age
bev'-ies
be-wail'
be-wail'-ing
be-wa're

be-wil'-der
be-wil'-dered
be-wil'-deredly
be-wil'-der-ing
be-wil'-der-ingly
be-wil'-der-ment
be-witch'
be-witch'-ing
be-witch'-ment
be-wray'
bey'-lic
be-yond'
bez'-ant
be-zoar'
bi-an'-nual
bi-an'-nu-ally
bi-ar-tic'u-late
bi'as-ing
bi-aur-ic'u-lar
bi-ax'ial
bi-ba'sic
bib'-li-cal
bib'-lio-graph
bib-li-og'ra-pher
bib-lio-graph'ic
bib-lio-graph'i-cal
bib-li-og'raphy
bib-li-ol'-ater
bib-li-ol'-atry
bib-li-ol'ogy
bib-lio-man'cy
bib-lio-ma'nia
bib-li-op'egy
bib'-lio-phile
bib-li-oph'i-lism
bib-li-ophi-lis'-tic

bib-lio-pol'ic
bib-li-op'oly
bi-brac'-teate
bib'u-lous
bi-cal'-car-ate
bi-cam'-eral
bi-cap'-su-lar
bi-car'-bon-ate
bi-car-pel'-lary
bi-car-pel'-ate
bi-cen-ten'-nial
bi-ceph'a-lous
bi'-ceps
bi-chlo'r-ide
bi-chro'm-ate
bi-cil'i-ate
bi-cip'i-tal
bick'-er-ing
bi-col-lat'eral
bi-col'li-gate
bi-con'ic
bi-con'i-cal
bi-con'-ju-gate
bi-con'-vex
bi'-corn
bi-cor-nu'te
bi-cor'-poral
bi-cren'-ate
bi-cru'ral
bi-cus'-pid
bi-cus'-pi-date
bid'-able
bid'-den
bid'-der
bid'-ding
bi-den'-tate
bi-en'-nial
bi-en'-ni-ally

bi-fa'cial
bi-fa'ri-ous
bi-fa'ri-ously
bif'-fin
bi'-fid
bi-flag'el-late
bi-flo'r-ous
bi-fo'cal
bi'-fold
bi-fo'li-ate
bi'-fur-cate
bi'-fur-cated
bi-fur-ca'tion
big'-am-ist
big'-am-ous
big'-am-ously
big'-ar-oon
bi-gem'-inal
bi-gem'-in-ate
bi-gen-er'ic
big'-ger
big'-gin
big'-headed
big'-hearted
big'-horn
big'-ness
big-noni-a'ceous
big'-otry
bi'-grid
bi-gut'-tu-late
bi-hour'ly
bi-la'bial
bi-la'bi-ate
bil'-an-der
bi-lat'-eral
bi-lat'-er-ally
bil'-berry
bil'-boes

39

BILHARZIA

bil-har'-zia
bil-har-zi'asis
bil'i-ary
bi-lin'-ear
bi-lin'gual
bi-lin'gual-ism
bi-lin'gually
bil'ious-ness
bi-lit'-eral
bill'-able
bill'-board
bil'-let
bill'-fish
bill'-fold
bill'-head
bil'liard-ist
bil'lion-aire
bil'-lon
bil'-low
bil'-lowy
bill'-poster
bill'-sticker
bill'y-boy
bi-lo'bar
bi-lo'bed
bi-loc'u-lar
bi-loc'u-late
bi-loph'o-dont
bil'-tong
bi'-mane
bi'-man-ous
bi-man'u-ally
bi-mas'-tic
bi-men'-sal
bi-mes'-trial
bi-met-al'lic
bi-met'-al-ism
bi-met'-al-list

bi-month'ly
bi'-morph
bi-mo'tored
bi'-nary
bi'-nate
bin-aur'al
bi'nd-ery
bi'nd-ing
bi'nd-weed
bin'-nacle
bin-oc'u-lar
bi'-node
bi'no-graph
bi-no'mial
bi-no'mi-ally
bi-nom'-inal
bi-no'vu-lar
bi-nu'clear
bi-nu'cleo-late
bi'o-blast
bio-cat'a-lyst
bi-oc'el-late
bio-chem'i-cal
bio-chem'-ist
bio-chem'-is-try
bio-coe-no'sis
bio-coe-no'sium
bio-coe-not'ic
bio-dy-nam'-ics
bi'o-gen
bio-gen'-esis
bio-gen-et'ic
bi-og'en-ous
bi-og'eny
bi'o-graph
bi-og'ra-pher
bio-graph'ic
bio-graph'i-cal

bi-og'ra-phy
bio-log'ic
bio-log'i-cal
bi-ol'-ogist
bi-ol'ogy
bio-lumin-
     esc'ence
bio-lyt'ic
bi-om'eter
bio-met'ric
bi-om'etry
bi-on'ics
bio-nom'-ics
bi'-ont
bi'o-phore
bio-phys'-ics
bi'o-plasm
bi'o-plast
bi'-opsy
bi'o-scope
bi-os'copy
bio-se'ries
bi-os'-ophy
bio-stat'-ics
bi-os'-terol
bi-o'ta
bi-ot'ic
bi'o-tite
bio-tit'ic
bi'o-tron
bi'o-type
bi'-pack
bi-pari'etal
bip'-ar-ous
bi-par'-ti-san
bi-par'-tite
bi-par-tit'ion
bi'-ped

40

bi-ped'al
bi-pen'-nate
bi-pen'-ni-form
bi-pin-na'ria
bi-pin'-nate
bi-po'lar
bi'-prism
bi-quad-rat'ic
bi-quar'-terly
bi-ra'dial
bi-ra'mous
birch'-bark
bird'-call
bird'-lime
bird'-lore
bird'-man
bi-refrin'-gence
bi'-reme
bir-et'ta
bi-ros'-trate
birth'-day
birth'-mark
birth'-place
birth'-rate
birth'-right
birth'-stone
bi-sac'-cate
bis'-cuit
bi-sect'
bi-sec'-tion
bi-sec'-tion-ally
bi-sec'-tor
bi-seg'-ment
bi-se'ri-ate
bi-sex'-ual
bi-sexu-al'ity
bish'-op-ric
bis'-muth

bis-muth'in-ite
bis'-mu-tite
bi'-son
bi-sphe'noid
bis-sex'-tile
bis'-tort
bis'-toury
bi-sul'-cate
bi-sul'-phate
bi-sul'-phite
bi-sym-met'ric
bi-syn'-chron-ous
bi-ter'nate
bit'-ten
bit'-ter
bit'-terly
bit'-tern
bit'-ter-ness
bit'-ter-root
bit'-ters
bit'-ter-sweet
bit'-ter-weed
bit'-ter-wort
bit'u-men
bitu'mi-nate
bitu'mi-nise
bitu'mi-noid
bitu'mi-nous
bi-uret'
bi-va'lent
biv'a-lent
bi'-valve
bi-val'vu-lar
bi-va'ri-ant
bi-ven'-tral
bi-vol'-tine
biv'-ouac

biv'ou-acked
biv'ou-ack-ing
bi-week'ly
bizarr'e-ness
blab'-ber
black'a-moor
black'-ball
black'-berry
black'-bird
black'-board
black'-cap
black'-cock
black-damp'
black'-ened
black'-ener
black'-en-ing
black'-eyed
black'-face
black'-friar
black'-head
black'-ing
black'-ish
black'-jack
black'-lead
black'-leg
black'-let-ter
black'-list
black'-mail
black-mail'er
black'-ness
black'-out
black'-poll
black'-ship
black'-shirt
black'-smith
black'-tail
black'-thorn
black'-water

41

blad'-der
bla'de-bone
bla'de-less
bla'de-smith
blae'-berry
bla'm-able
blame-worth'i-
          ness
bla'me-worthy
bla'm-ing
blanch'-ing
bland-il'-oquence
blan'-dish
blan'-dish-ment
bland'-ness
blank'-et-ing
blank'-ness
blar'-ney
blas-phe'me
blas-phe'mer
blas-phe'm-ing
blas'-phem-ous
blas'-phemy
blas-te'ma
blas'-tic
blast'-ing
blas'to-chyle
blas'to-coel
blas'to-cyst
blas'to-derm
blasto-gen'-esis
blasto-gen'ic
blas'-toid
blasto-kin-e'sis
blas'to-mere
blasto-myco'sis
blas-to-phore
blas'to-pore

blasto-zo'oid
blas'-tula
blas-tu-la'tion
bla'z-ing
bla'z-onry
bleach'-ing
blear'-eyed
blear'i-ness
bleat'-ing
bleed'-ing
blem'-ish
blem'-isher
blem-mat'o-gen
blend'-ing
bleph'-ar-ism
bleph-ar-i'tis
bleph-aro-chal'a-
          sis
bleph-aro-ple'gia
bleph-ar-op-
          to'sis
bleph'aro-spasm
bles'-bok
bless'-edly
bless-ed-ness
bless'-ing
bleth'-er-ing
bli'ght-ing
bli'nd-age
bli'nd-fish
bli'nd-fold
bli'nd-ing
bli'nd-ness
bli'nd-worm
blink'-ers
blink'-ing
bliss'-ful
bliss'-fully

blis'-ter
blis'-tery
bli'the-some
blitz'-krieg
bliz'-zard
block-a'de
block-a'ded
block-a'der
block-a'd-ing
block'-buster
block'-head
block'-house
blon'-dine
blond'-ness
blood'-curd-ling
blood'-guilty
blood'-hound
blood'i-ness
blood'-less
blood'-let-ting
blood'-money
blood'-poison-
          ing
blood'-press-ure
blood'-root
blood'-shed
blood'-shed-ding
blood'-shot
blood'-stain
blood'-stained
blood'-stone
blood'-sucker
blood'-test
blood'-thirsty
blood'-vessel
blood'-wort
bloom'-ers
bloom'-ing

bloop'-ing
blot'-less
blot'-ted
blot'-ter
blot-tes'que
blot'-ting
blot'-ting-paper
blow' fish
blow'-fly
blow'-gun
blow'-hole
blow'i-ness
blow'-lamp
blow'-out
blow'-pipe
blow'-torch
blow'-tube
blub'-ber
blub'-berer
blub'-ber-ing
blub'-bery
blu'ch-ers
blue'-beard
blue'-bell
blue'-berry
blue'-bird
blue'-black
blue'-blooded
blue'-bon-net
blue'-bottle
blue'-fish
blue'-grass
blue'-ing
blue'-ish
blue'-jacket
blue'-jay
blue'-ness
blue'-print

blue'-stock-ing
blue'-stone
bluff'-ing
blun'-der
blun'-der-buss
blun'-derer
blun'-der-head
blun'-der-ing
blunt'-ness
blur'-ring
blush'-ing
blus'-ter
blus'-ter-ing
blus'-ter-ous
blus'-tery
bo'a-con-stric'-
    tor
board'-ing
board-ing-house
board'-ing-school
board'-room
board'-walk
boast'-ful
boast'-ingly
boat'-ing
boat'-load
boat'-man
bob'-bin
bob'-bing
bob'-bin-net
bob'-cat
bob'o-link
bob'-sled
bob'-sleigh
bob'-stay
bob'-tail
bob'-white
boc'a-sine

bock'-ing
bo'de-ful
bod'-ice
bod'i-less
bod'-kin
bod'y-guard
bod'y-pol'i-tic
bo'-gey
bog'-gi-ness
bog'-gish
bo'-gie
bog'-gling
bog'-moss
bo'-gus
boil'-ing
bois'-ter-ous
bois'-ter-ously
bo'-las
bo'ld-face
bo'ld-faced
bo'ld-ness
bo-lec'-tion
bol-e'ro
bol-e'tus
bo'-lide
bol'-lard
boll'-worm
bol-om'eter
bolo-met'ric
bo'lt-head
bo'lt-ing
bo'lt-less
bo'-lus
bom-ba-ca'ceous
bom'-bard (n.)
bom-bard' (v.)
bom-bar-dier'
bom-bard'-ment

43

BOMBARDON

bom-bar'-don
bomba-si'ne
bom'-bast
bom-bas'-tic
bom-bas'-ti-cal
bom-bas'-ti-cally
bom'-bic
bomb'-proof
bomb'-shell
bomb'-sight
bon-an'za
bon'-bon
bond'-age
bond-ho'lder
bond'-maid
bond'-man
bond'-servant
bond'-slave
bonds'-man
bond'-woman
bo'ne-black
bo'ne-less
bo'ne-meal
bo'ne-set
bo'ne-set-ter
bo'ne-shaker
bon'-fire
bon-hom'ie
bo'ni-ness
bo-ni'to
bon'-net
bon'-nily
boob'-ies
book'-able
book'-binder
book'-bind-ery
book'-bind-ing
book'-case

book'-dealer
book'-end
book'-ing
book'-ish
book'-keeper
book'-keep-ing
book'-land
book'-let
book'-lore
book'-maker
book'-man
book'-mark
book'-plate
book'-rack
book'-rest
book'-seller
book'-shelf
book'-shop
book'-store
book'-worm
boom'-er-ang
boor'-ish
boost'-ing
boot'-black
boot'-jack
boot'-leg
boot'-leg-ger
boot'-leg-ging
boot'-less
bor-ac'ic
bo'ra-cite
bor'-age
bo'-rate
bo'-rax
bor-bor-yg'mus
bor'-der
bor'-dered
bor'-derer

bor'-der-land
bor'-der-line
bor'-dure
bo're-cole
bo're-dom
bo're-hole
bor'-ley
bor'-neol
born'-ite
bor'-nyl
boro-eth'-ane
bor'-ol-an-ite
bo'-ron
bor'-row
bor'-rower
bor'-zoi
bos'-cage
bos'-ket
boss'-age
bos'-set
boss'-ing
bos'-ton-ite
bos'-tryx
bot-an'-ical
bot-an-ise
bot-an-ist
bot'-any
bot'-fly
both'er-ation
both'er-some
both-rid'ium
both'-rium
bot'-ry-oid
botry-oid'al
botryo-myco'sis
bot'ry-ose
bot'tle-green
bot'tle-neck

44

bot'-tler
bot'-tlɪng
bot'-rom
bot'-rom-ing
bot'-tom-land
bot'-tom-less
bot'-tom-most
bot'-tomry
botu'li-form
bot'u-tism
boud'-oir
bou-gain-vil'-lea
bough-'pot
bou'-gie
boul'der-clay
boul'-evard
bounc'-ing
bound'-aries
bound'-ary
bound'-less
boun'te-ous
boun'ti-ful
bou-quet'
bour'-bon
bour'-don
bour'-geois
bour'-geoise
bour-geoisie'
bour'-non-ite
bou-var'dia
bov'-ate
bov'-ine
bowd-ler-is-
    a'tion
bowd'-ler-ise
bowd'-ler-ism
bow'en-ite
bow'-fin

bow'-knot
bow'-leg
bow'-legged
bow'-line
bowl'-ing
bow'-man
bow'-shot
bow'-sprit
bow'-string
bow-win'-dow
bow'-yer
box-berry
box'-board
box'-calf
box'-car
box'-ful
box'-haul
box'-ing
box'-of'-fice
box'-span-ner
box'-thorn
box'-wood
boy'-cott
boy'-cotter
boy'-cott-ing
boy'-hood
boy'-ish
boy'-ish-ness
brac'-cate
bra'ce-let
bra'chi-ate
brachio-la'ria
brach'io-pod
brach'y-blast
brachy-cephal'ic
brachy-ceph'-aly
brach-yc'er-ous
brachy-cla'dous

brachy-dac-tyl'ic
brach'y-form
bra-chyl'ogy
brachy-mor'-
    phic
brach'yo-dont
bra-chyp'-ter-
    ous
brach'-ysm
bra-chyt'ic
brachy-u'ral
brack'-et-ing
brack'-ish
brac'-te-ate
brac'-teo-late
brac-teo-ma'nia
brac'-te-ose
brad'-awl
brady-ar'-thria
brady-car'dia
brady-kin-e'sis
brady-phre'nia
brad'y-spore
brady-fel'ic
brag'-gart
brag'-gart-ism
brag'-ger
brag'-ging
brain'-less
brain'-sick
brain'-storm
brain'-wash-ing
brain'-wave
brain'-work
brais'-ing
bran'-chial
branch-if'er-ous
branchi-op'oda

45

branchi-os'-te-
        gal
branchi-os'-te-
        gite
bran'ch-ireme
bran'-der-ing
bran'-dish
brand'-ling
brand'-reth
brass'-age
brass'-ard
brass'-erie
brassi-ca'ceous
brass'-ière
brass'i-ness
brass'-ware
brass'-work
brat'-tice
brat'-tic-ing
braun'-ite
bra-va'do
bra've-hearted
bra'v-ery
bra'v-est
brawl'-ing
brawn'i-ness
bra'z-en-faced
bra'z-enly
bra'z-en-ness
braz'i-lin
bra-zil'-wood
bra'z-ing
bread'-fruit
bread'-pan
bread'-root
bread'-stuff
breadth'-ways
breadth'-wise

bread'-win-ner
break'-able
break'-age
break'-away
break'-down
break'-fast
break'-neck
break'-through
break'-up
break'-water
breast'-bone
breast'-pin
breast'-plate
breast'-work
breath'-able
breath'-ing
breath'-less
breath'-lessly
breath'-tak-ing
breech'-cloth
breech'-ing
breech'-loader
breech'-load-ing
breed'-ing
breez'e-way
breez'i-ness
breth'-ren
breun'-ner-ite
brevet'-ted
brev'i-ary
brevi-pen'-nate
brev'-ity
brew'-ery
brew'-ing
bri-a'rean
bri'b-able
bri'b-ery
bri'b-ing

brick'-bat
brick'-dust
brick'-kiln
brick'-layer
brick'-lay-ing
brick'-nog-ging
brick'-work
brick'-yard
bri'de-cake
bri'de-groom
bri'des-maid
bri'de-well
bridg'e-able
bridg'e-board
bridg'e-head
bridg'e-way
bridg'e-work
bridg'-ing
brief'-ing
brief'-less
bri'er-root
bri'er-wood
brig-a'de
briga-dier'
brig'-and
brig'-and-age
brig'-an-dine
brig'-an-tine
bri'ght-ener
bri'ght-en-ing
bri'ght-ness
bril-lian-tine
brim'-ful
brim'-less
brim'-ming
brim'-stone
bring'-ing
bri'ni-ness

46

brink'-man-ship
bris'-ket
brisk'-ness
bris'-ling
bris'tle-tail
brist'-ling
brit'tle-ness
broad'-brim
broad'-cast
broad'-caster
broad'-cast-ing
broad'-cloth
broad'-loom
broad'-minded
broad'-mind-ed-
          ness
broad'-side
broad'-sword
broad'-tail
brob-ding-nag'-
          ian
bro-ca'de
bro-ca'ded
broca-tell'e
broc'-coli
broch'-an-tite
bro-chu're
brock'-ram
bro'-gan
broid'-ery
broil'-ing
bro'k-age
bro'ken-hearted
bro'ker-age
bro'k-ing
bro'-mal
bro'-mate
bro-me'lia

bro'-mel-lite
bro'-mic
bru'-mide
bro-mid'-ic
bro-min-a'tion
bro'-mine
bro'-mo-form
bron'-chial
bronchi-ec'ta-sis
bron'chi-ole
bronchio-lec'ta-
          sis
bronchio-li'tis
bron-chit'ic
bron-chi'tis
bron-chog'ra-phy
bron'cho-scope
bron-chos'copy
bron-chot'omy
bron'-chus
bron'co-cele
bron-coph'ony
bron'-to-saur
bron'-to-saurus
bronz'-ing
bronz'-ite
brood'-ing
brood'-ingly
brood'-mare
brook'-ite
brook'-let
brook'-lime
broom'-ing
broom'-rape
broom'-stick
broth'er-hood
broth'er-li-ness
brow'-beat

brow'-heat-ing
brow'n-ing
brown'-ish
brown'-ness
brown'-stone
brows'-ing
bru'-cine
bru'-cite
bruis'-ing
bru'-mal
bru'-mous
bru-nett'e
brush'-wood
brush'-work
brus'que-ness
bru'-tal-ise
brut-al'ity
bru't-ally
bru't-ish
bru't-ishly
bryo-'log'i-cal
bry-ol'-ogist
bry-ol'ogy
bry'-ony
bryo-zo'a
bryo-zo'on
bu'-ba-line
bub'-bling
bub'-blingly
bub'-bly
bu-bon'ic
bu-bon'o-cele
buc'-cal
buc'-ca-neer
buc'-ci-nal
buc'-ci-nator
buc'-cinat-ory
bu-cen'-taur

47

bu'-chite
buck'a-roo
buck'-board
buck'-et-ful
buck'-eye
buck'-hound
buck'-jumper
buck'-ler
buck'-ling
buck'-ram
buck'-saw
buck'-shot
buck'-skin
buck'-thorn
buck'-tooth
buck'-wheat
bu-col'ic
bu-col'i-cally
bud'-ding
bud'-geri-gar
bud'get-ary
bud'get-ing
bud'-less
buf'-falo
buf'-fa-loes
buf'-fet
buff'-ing
buf-foon'
buf-foon'-ery
bug'a-boo
bug'-bear
bug'-ging
bu'-gloss
bug'-proof
buhr'-stone
build'-ing
bul-ba'ceous
bul-bif'er-ous

bul'-bil
bulb'-let
bulbo-nu'clear
bul'-bous
bul'-bule
bul'-bus
buig'-ing
bu-lim'ia
bulk'-head
bulk'i-ness
bull'-ace
bull'-late
bull'-bait-ing
bull'-dog
bull'-doze
bull'-dozer
bull'-doz-ing
bull'-etin
bull'et-proof
bull'-fight
bull'-fighter
bull'-finch
bull'-frog
bull'-head
bull'-headed
bull'-ied
bull'-ish
bull'-ock
bull'-pen
bull's'-eye
bull'-whip
bull'y-beef
bull'y-ing
bull'y-rag
bum'ble-bee
bum'ble-dom
bumb'-ling
bum'-boat

bum'-malo
bum-ma-ree'
bum'pi-ness
bump'-kin
bump'-tious
bun'-combe
bun'dling
bun'ga-loid
bun'ga-low
bung'-hole
bunk'-house
bu'no-dont
bu'-noid
buno-loph'o-
          dont
bunt'-ing
bunt'-line
bun'-tons
buoy'-age
buoy'-ancy
buoy'-ant
bu-pres'tid
bu-ran'
bur'-bot
bur'-den
bur'-den-some
bur'-dock
bu'-reau
bu-reauc'-racy
bu-reau-crat
bu-reau-crat'ic
bu-rett'e
bur'-gage
bur'-ga-net
bur-gee'
bur'-geon
bur'-gess
bur'-ghal

bur'-gher
bur'-glar
bur'-glar-ies
bur-gla'ri-ous
bur'-glar-ise
bur'-glar-proof
bur'-glary
bur'go-master
bur'-gonet
bur'-goo
bur'-gundy
bu'-rin
bur'-lap
bur-les'que
bur-les'qued
bur-les'quer
bur'li-ness
bur'-ling
bur'-mite
bur'-net
burn'-ing
bur'-nish
bur'-nisher
bur'-nish-ing
bur-noos'e
burn'-sides
bur'-ring
bur'-row
bur'-rower
bur'-sar
bur-sa'rial
bur'-sary
bur-sat'-tee
bur-ser-a'ceous
bur'-si-form
bur-si'tis
burst'-ing

bur'-then
bur'-ton
bur'-weed
bury'-ing
bur'y-ing ground
bush'-buck
bush'-ing
bush'-mas-ter
busn'-ranger
bush'-whacker
bus'i-ness
bus'iness-like
bus'iness-man
bus'-kin
bus'-tard
bust'-ier
bust'-ling
bust'-lingly
bus'y-body
bus'y-ness
buta-di'ene
bu'-tane
bu'-ta-nol
bu'tcher-bird
bu'tch-ery
but'-ler
but'-ter
but'-ter-cup
but'-ter-fat
but'-ter-fingers
but'-ter-fish
but'-ter-fly
but'-ter-milk
but'-ter-nut
but'-ter-scotch
but'-ter-weed
but'-tery
but'-tocks

but'-ton
but'-ton-hole
but'-ton-hook
but'-ton-mould
but'-tons
but'-ton-wood
but'-tress
bu'-tyl
bu'-ty-lene
bu-tyr-a'ceous
bu'tyr-ate
bu-tyr'ic
bu'-tyrin
bux'om-ness
buy'-ing
buz'-zard
buzz'-ing
by'-elec'-tion
by'-gone
by'-law
by'-line
by'-name
by-pass
by'-path
by'-play
by'-pro-duct
byr'-nie
by'-road
bys'-ma-lith
byss-a'ceous
byssi-no'sis
byss'-oid
byss-og'en-ous
by'-stander
by-way
by'-word

49

C

caa'-ing-whale
ca-bal'
cab'-ala
cab'-al-ism
caba-lis'tic
caba-list'i-cal
ca-ball'ed
cab'al-line
ca-ban'a
ca-ba'ne
cab-aret'
cab'-bage
cab'-ezone
cab'-in-boy
cab'i-net
cab'i-net-maker
cab'i-net-work
ca'ble-gram
cab'-man
ca-bob'
ca-boch'ed
ca-boos'e
cab'o-tage
cab'-ri-ole
cab'-ri-olet
cab'-stand
ca-ca'o
cach'a-lot
ca-chec'-tic
ca-chet'
ca-chex'ia
cach''n-nate
cachin-na'tion
cach'o-long
ca-chou'
50

ca-ci'que
cack'-ling
caco-de'mon
cac'o-dyl
caco-dyl'ic
caco-e'thes
caco-gen'-ics
ca-cog'raphy
ca-col'ogy
ca-coon'
ca-coph'-onous
ca-coph'-ony
ca-cos'-mia
cac-ta'ceous
cac'-tus
ca-das'-tral
ca-das'tre
ca-dav'er
ca-dav'-er-ine
ca-dav'-er-ous
cad'-die
cad'-dis
cad'-dish
ca-dell'e
ca-det'
ca-det'cy
ca-det'-ship
cad'-mium
cad'o-phore
cadu-branch'i-ate
ca-du'cary
ca-du'city
ca-du'cous
caec'i-form
caecil'-ian
caecos'-tomy
caeno-gen'-esis
caes'i-ous

caes'-pi-tose
caes-pit'u-tose
cafe-te'ria
caf-fe'ic
caf'-feine
caf'-tan
ca'ge-ling
cai'-man
caino-zo'ic
ca-i'que
cairn'-gorm
cais'-son
cait'-iff
caj'e-put
ca-jo'le
ca-jo'l-ery
ca-jo'l-ing
ca'ke-box
ca'ke-walk
cal'a-bar
cal'a-bash
cal'a-boose
ca-la'dium
cala-man'co
cal'a-man-der
cal'a-mary
cala-mif'er-ous
cal'a-mine
cal'a-mint
cala-mis'-trium
cal'a-mite
ca-lam'i-tous
ca-lam'ity
cal'a-mus
ca-lash'
cal'a-thide
cal'a-thos
cal-ca'neum

cal-ca'neus
cal'-car
cal'-car-ate
cal-ca'reous
cal'-car-ine
cal-ca-vel'lo
ca-ceo-la'ria
cal'-ces
cal'-cic
cal'-ci-cole
cal-cic'o-lous
cal-ci-co'sis
cal-cif'-erol
cal-cif'er-ous
cal-ci-fi-ca'tion
cal'-ci-fuge
cal'-cify
cal-cim'eter
cal'-ci-mine
cal-ci-na'tion
cal-ci'ne
cal-ci'ner
cal'-ci-phile
cal-ciph'i-lous
cal'-ci-phobe
cal'-cite
cal'-cium
calc'-spar
cal'-cu-lable
cal'-cu-late
cal'-cu-lat-ing
cal'-cu-lation
cal'-cu-lat-ive
cal'-cu-lator
cal'-culi
cal'-cu-lus
cal-da'rium
cal-de'ra

ca-lech'e
cal-efa'cient
cal-efac'-tory
cal'-en-dar
cal'-en-der
ca-len'-dula
cal'-en-ture
cal-esc'ence
calf'-skin
cal'i-brate
cali-bra'tion
cali-bra'tor
cal'-ibre
ca'li-ces
cal'-ico
ca-lic'u-lar
cal-id'ity
cal'i-duct
ca-lig'i-nous
ca-li'go
cal'i-pash
cal'i-per
ca'liph-ate
cali-sa'ya
calis-then'-ics
cal'i-ver
calk'-ing
cali'-able
cal-lain'-ite
cal-lig'ra-pher
cal-li-graph'ic
cal-lig'ra-phy
call'-ing
cal-li'ope
cal-li-op'-sis
calli-pyg'ian
cal'-lose
cal-los'ity

cal'-lous
cal'-low
cal'-lus
cal'-luses
calm'-ative
calm'-ness
cal'o-mel
cal-or-esc'ence
ca-lor'ic
cal-or-ic'ity
cal'-orie
cal'-or-ies
cal-or-if'ic
ca-lor'i-fier
calor-im'eter
ca-lor-im'etry
cal'-or-ise
cal-or-i's-ing
calo-so'ma
ca-lott'e
cal'o-type
cal'o-yer
cal'-trop
ca-lum'ba
cal'u-met
ca-lum'-ni-ate
ca-lum-ni-a'tion
ca-lum'-ni-ator
cal'-um-nies
ca-lum'-ni-ous
ca-lum-ni-ous-ly
cal'-umny
cal'u-tron
cal-vit'ies
ca'ly-ces
cal'y-cine
cal'y-ycle
cal'y-coid

51

cal'y-cule
ca-lyc'u-late
ca-lyc'u-lus
ca-lyp'so
ca-lyp'-tra
ca-lyp'-trate
ca-lyp'-tro-gen
cama-rad'-erie
cama-ril'la
cam'-ata
cam'-ber
cam'-bi-form
cam'-hist
cam'-bium
cam-bo'gia
cam'-brel
cam'el-back
cam'el-eer
cam'el-hair
ca-me'llia
ca-mel'o-pard
cam'eo-type
cam'-era
cam'-eral
cam'-era-man
cam'-era-ob-scu-ra
cam'i-sard
cam'i-sole
cam'-let
cam'-mock
cam'o-mile
cam'ou-flage
cam'ou-flet
cam-paign'
cam-paign'er
cam-pan'i-form
cam-pa-nile'
cam-pa-nol'ogy

cam-pan'-ula
cam-pan'u-late
cam-pes'-tral
camp'-fire
cam'-phene
cam-phi'ne
cam'-phor
cam-phor-a'ceous
cam'-phor-ate
cam'-phor-ated
cam-phor'ic
camp'-ing
cam'-pion
camp'-ton-ite
cam'-pus
cam'-shaft
cam'-wood
ca-nal'
canal'-boat
cana-lic'u-lar
cana-lic'u-lated
cana-lic'u-lus
ca-nal-is-a'tion
can'-al-ise
ca-nard'
ca-na'ries
ca-na'ry
ca-nas'ta
can'-can
can'-cel
can'-cel-lated
can-cel-la'tion
can'-celled
can'-cel-ler
can'-cel-ling
can'-cer
can'-cer-ate
can-cero-pho'bia

can'-cer-ous
canc'-roid
can-de-lab'ra
can-de-lab'-rum
cande-lil'la
can'-dent
can-desc'ence
can-desc'ent
can'-did
can'di-dacy
can'di-date
can'di-dature
can'-didly
can'did-ness
can'dle-berry
can'dle-fish
can'dle-grease
can'dle-light
can'dle-nut
can'dle-pin
can'dle-power
can'-dler
can'dle-shade
can'dle-stick
can'dle-wood
cando-lumin-
      esc'ence
can'-dour
can'dy-tuft
ca'ne-brake
can'-ephore
can-esc'ent
can'i-cide
ca-nic'u-lar
can'-ine
can'-is-ter
cank'er-ous
cank'er-worm

can'-na-bin
can'-nel
can'-ner
can'-nery
can'-ni-bal
can'ni-bal-ise
can'ni-bal-ism
can'ni-bal-istic
can'-ni-kin
can'ni-ness
can'-ning
can'-non
can'-non-ade
can'-non-ball
can'-non-bone
can-non-eer'
can'-not
can'-nula
can'-nu-lar
canoe'-ing
canoe'-ist
can'on-ess
ca-non'i-cal
ca-non'i-cals
ca-non'i-cate
can-on-ic'ity
can-on-is-a'tion
can'-on-ise
can'-on-ist
canon-is'tic
can'-onry
can'-opied
can'-opies
can'-opy
ca-no'rous
cano-tier'
can'-ta-loupe
can-tan'ker-ous

can-tat'a
can'ta-trice
can-teen'
can'-ter
can'-ter-bury
can-thar'i-des
can-thar'i-din
can'-thus
can'-ticle
cant'-ing
cant'-ling
can'-ton
can'-tonal
can-ton'ment
can'-tor
can-to'rial
can'-vas
can'-vas-back
can'-vass
can'-vasser
can'-yon
canzo-net'
capa-bil'i-ties
capa-bil'ity
ca-pa'cious
ca-pa'ciously
ca-pac'i-tance
ca-pac'i-tate
ca-pac'i-tive
ca-pac'i-tor
ca-pac'ity
ca-par'i-son
cap'-elin
cap'-el-ine
caper-cail'-zie
cap'-ful
cap'i-bara
capil-la'ceous

ca pil-lar-i'asis
capil-lar'ity
ca-pil'-lary
cap'il-lator
ca-pil'-li-form
ca-pil-lit'ium
cap'-il-lose
cap'i-tal
capi-tal-is-a'tion
cap'i-tal-ise
cap'i-tal-ism
cap'i-tal-ist
capi-tal-is'tic
cap'i-tan
cap'i-tate
capi-ta'tion
capi-tel'-lum
ca-pit'u-lar
ca-pit'u-late
ca-pitu-la'tion
capi-tu'li-form
ca-pit'u-lum
ca'pon-is-ing
ca-po'te
cap'-pa-dine
cap'-ping
cap'reo-late
cap'-ric
ca-pri'ce
ca-pric'ious
cap'ri-corn
capri-fi-ca'tion
capri-fi-ca'tor
cap'ri-fier
cap'ri-fig
cap'ri-form
cap'-rine
cap'ri-ole

53

ca-pro'ic
cap'-ryl
cap'ry-late
ca-pryl'ic
cap'-si-cine
cap'-si-cum
cap'-size
cap'-siz-ing
cap'-stan
cap'-stone
cap'-su-lar
cap'-sule
cap-sul-og'en-ous
cap-tac'-ula
cap'-tain
cap'-taincy
cap-ta'tion
cap'-tion
cap'-tious
cap'-ti-vate
cap'-ti-vating
cap-ti-va'tion
cap'-ti-vator
cap'-tive
cap-tiv'ity
cap'-tor
cap'-ture
cap'-tur-ing
cap'u-chin
cap'u-cine
capy-bar'a
cara-bin-eer'
car'a-cal
cara-car'a
car'a-cole
car'a-cul
car'a-mel
car'a-mote

car'a-pace
cara-pa'cial
car'a-van
cara-van'-sary
cara-van'-serai
car'a-vel
car'a-way
car-bam'ic
car-ba-mide
car-ba-nil'ic
car-ban'i-lide
car'-ba-zole
car'-bide
car'-bi-nal
car'-bine
car-bin-eer'
carbo-cy'clic
car-bo-graph
carbo-hy'drate
car-bol'ic
car'-bol-ise
car-bol-u'ria
car'-bon
car-bon-a'ceous
car-bon-a'do
car'-bon-ate
car'-bon-ator
car-bon'ic
car-bon-if'er-ous
car-bon-is-a'tion
car'-bon-ise
car-bon-om'eter
car'-bon-ous
car'-bon=paper
car'-bonyl
car-bor-un'dum
car-box'yl
car-box'y-lase

car'-boy
car'-buncle
car-bun'cu-lar
car-bu-ret
car'-bu-ret'ted
car'-bu-ret-tor
carbu-ris-a'tion
car'-bu-rise
car-byl-am'ines
car'-ca-jou
car'ca-net
car'-case
car'-cass
car'-cass-ing
car-cer-u'lus
car-cin'o-gen
car-ci-no'ma
car-ci-noma-
to'sis
car-ci-no'ma-
tous
car-ci-no'sis
car'da-mom
card'-board
car'-diac
car'-dia-graph
cardi-al'gia
car'-di-gan
car'-di-nal
car'-di-nal-ate
card'-ing
car'-dio-blast
cardio-cen-te'sis
car'-dio-gram
car'-dio-graph
cardi-og'ra-phy
car'di-oid
car-di-ol'ogy

car-di-ol'-ysis
cardio-ma-la'cia
cardi-om'eter
cardi-om'etry
cardi-or-rhex'is
car'-dio-spasm
car-dio-vas'cu-
        lar
car-di'tis
car-doon'
card'-player
card'-room
card'-sharper
car-du-a'ceous
card-wri'ter
ca-reen'
careen'-age
ca-reer'
career'-ist
ca're-free
ca're-ful
ca're-fully
ca're-ful-ness
ca're-less
ca're-lessly
ca're-less-ness
ca-ress'
ca-ress'-ingly
ca-ress'-ive
ca-ress'-ively
ca're-taker
ca're-worn
car'-fare
car'-fax
car'-goes
car'-i-bou
cari-ca-tu'ral
car'i-ca-ture

car'i-ca-tur-ist
ca-ri'na
car'i-nal
car'i-nate
cari-o'ca
cari-os'ity
ca'ri-ous
cark'-ing
car'-let
car'-line
car'-load
car'-lock
car-magno'le
car'-men
car'-mel-ite
car-min'a-tive
car'-min-at-ive
car'-mine
car'-nage
car'-nal
car'-nal-ise
car'-nal-ism
car-nal'ity
car-nal-lite
car'-nally
car-nass'-ial
car-na'tion
car-naub'a
car-ne'lian
car'-neous
car'-nify
car'-ni-tive
car'-ni-val
car-nlv'-ora
car'-ni-vore
car-niv'or-ous
car'-nose
car'-no-tite

ca-roch'e
car'ol-ler
car'o-tene
ca-rot'id
ca-rous'al
ca-rous'e
carou-sel'
ca-rous'-ing
car'-pal
car-pa'le
car'-pel
car-pel'-lary
car'-pel-loid
car-pen-try
car'-pet
car'-pet-bag
car-pet-bag'-ger
car'-pet-beater
car'-pet-ing
car-pho-lo'gia
car-phol'ogy
carp'-ing
car-poc'er-ite
car-po-go'nium
car-pol'-ogist
car-pol'ogy
carpo-meta-car'-
        pus
car-poph'a-gous
car'po-phore
carpo-trop'ic
car'-pus
car'-ra-geen
car'-rel
car'-riage
car'-rick=bend
car'-ried
car'-rier

55

car'-rier-pig'eon
car'-ri-ole
car'-rion
car'-rol-lite
car'-ron-ade
car'-rot
car'-roty
cart'-age
car-tel'
car-tel-is-a'tion
car-re'sian
car'-ti-lage
carti-lag'i-nous
cart'-load
car-tog'ra-pher
carto-graph'ic
car-tog'ra-pher
car-tog'ra-phy
car'-ton
car-toon'
car-toon'-ist
car-touch'e
car'-tridge
car'tu-lary
cart'-wheel
car'u-cate
car-unc'le
car-un'cu-lar
car-un'-cul-ate
car'va-crol
car'-vel
car'-vel=built
car'-vene
carv'-ing
car'-vone
cary-at'ic
cary-at'id
cary-at'i-dal
56

caryo-phyl-
 la'ceous
cary-op'-sis
cas-ca-bel
cas-ca'de
cas-ca'd-ing
cas-car'a
ca'se=hard'-ened
ca'sein-ate
ca'se-mate
ca'se-ment
ca-sern'
ca-shaw'
cash'-book
ca-shew'
cash-ier'
cash'-mere
cash'=reg'-is-ter
ca-si'no
cas'-ket
cas-sa'tion
ca-sa'va
cas'-ser-ole
cas'si-mere
cas'-sis
cas-sit'er-ite
cass'-ock
casso-lett'e
cas'so-wary
cas-ta'neous
cas'-ta-net
cast'-away
cast'e-less
cas'-tel-lan
cas'-tel-lated
cas-tel-la'tion
cas'-ti-gate
cas-ti-ga'tion

cas'-ti-gator
cas'-ti-gat-ory
cast'-ing
cast'-ing=vote
cas'-tor
cas'-tor-ate
cas'-tor=oil
cas-to'reum
cas-tra-meta'tion
cas'-trate
cas-tra'tion
cas'-ual
cas'-ual-ism
cas'-ual-ness
cas'u-al-ness
cas'u-alty
casua-ri'na
cas'u-ist
casu-is'tic
casu-is'ti-cally
cas'u-istry
cata-bol'ic
cata-bol'i-cally
ca-tab'-olism
cata=chre'sis
cata-chres'-tic
cat'a-clasm
cat'a-clysm
cata-clys'-mal
cata-clys'-mic
cat'a-comb
cata-diop'-tric
cat-ad'-romous
cat'a-falque
cata-lec'-tic
cat'a-lepsy
cata-lep'-tic
cat'a-lise

cat'a-liser
cat'-alo
cat'a-logue
cat'a-loguer
cat'a-logu-ing
ca-tal'pa
ca-tal'y-sis
cat'a-lyst
cata-lyt'ic
cata-maran'
cata-me'nia
cat'a-mite
cat'a-mount
cata-pet'al-ous
cata-phon'ic
cata-phor-e'sis
cata-pla'sia
cata-plasm
cata-plex'y
cat'a-pult
cat'-ar-act
ca-tarrh'
ca-tarrh'al
cat'-arrhine
ca-tarrh'-ous
ca-tas'-ta-sis
ca-tas'-trophe
cata-stroph'ic
cata-stroph'i-
        cally
cata-ton'ic
ca-taw'ba
cat'-bird
cat'-boat
cat'-call
catch'-all
catch'-ing
catch'-ment

catch'-penny
catch'-poll
catch'-word
cat'-eche'sis
cat'-echise
cat'-echism
cat-echis'mal
cat'-echist
cat-echis'tic
cat'-echol
cat'-echu
cat'-echu'men
cat-echumen'i-cal
cat-eg-or'i-cal
cat-eg-or'i-cally
cat'-egor-ise
cat'-egor-ist
ca-te'na
ca-te'nary
cat'-en-ate
cat-en-a'tion
ca'ter-ing
cat'er-pil-lar
cat'er-waul
cat'er-waul-ing
cat'-fish
cat'-gut
cath'-ar-ise
cath-ar'-sis
cath-ar'-tic
cath-ar'-tin
cat'-head
cath-ec'-tic
ca-the'dra
cath'-edra
ca-the'dral
cath'-eter

cath'-eter-ise
cath-et-om'eter
cath'-etron
cath'-ode
cath-og'ra-phy
cath'-olic
cath-ol'i-cise
cath-ol-ic'ity
cathol'-icon
cath'o-lyte
car'-ion
cat'-kin
cat'-like
cat'-ling
cat'-mint
cat'-nip
cat'o-lyte
cat-op'-sis
cat-op'-tric
cato-the'cium
cat'-sup
cat'-ti-ness
cat'-tish
cat'tle-man
cat'-walk
cau'-dal
cau'-dally
cau'-date
cau'-dex
caul'-dron
caul-esc'ent
caul'i-cole
cau-lic'o-lous
cauli-flo'ry
caul'i-flower
caul'-ine
caulo-car'-pic
caul'-ome

caus-al'gia
caus-al'ity
caus-a'tion
caus'a-tive
caus'e-less
caus'-erie
caus'-eway
caus'-ing
caus'-tic
caus'-ti-cally
cau'-ter
cauter-is-a'tion
cau'-ter-ise
cau'-tery
cau'-tion
cau'-tion-ary
cau'-tious
cau'-tiously
cau'-tious-ness
cav'-al-cade
cav'a-lier
ca-val'ly
cav'-alry
cav'-alry-man
cava-ti'na
ca've-man
cav'-ern
cav-er-nic'o-lous
cav-er-no'sis
cav'ern-ous
cav'i-are
cav'i-corn
cav-il-ling
cavi-ta'tion
cav'i-ties
cav'-ity
ca-vort'
ca-vort'-ing
58

cay-enn'e
cay'-enne=pep'-
      per
cay'-man
cay'-use
ceas'e-less
ceas'e-lessly
ceas'-ing
ce-dil'la
ce'-drate
ce'-drine
ced'-ula
ceil'-ing
ceil-om'eter
cel'a-don
cel'-an-dine
cel'-ebrant
cel'-ebrate
cel'-ebrated
cel-ebra'tion
cel'-ebrator
cel-eb'rity
cel-er'iac
cel-er'ity
cel'-ery
cel-es'ta
cel-es'tial
cel'-es-tine
cel'-es-tite
cel'i-bacy
celi-ba-ta'rian
cel'i-bate
ce'-lite
cel'-lar
cel'-lar-age
cel'-larer
cel'-lar-ette
cel'-lar-man

cel-lif'er-ous
cel'-li-form
cel-loid'in
cel'lo-phane
cel'lu-lar
cellu-la'tion
cell'-ule
cel'lu-lith
cellu-li'tis
cel'lu-loid
cel'lu-lose
cellu-lo'sic
cellu-los'ity
cel'-si-tude
cemen-ta'tion
cement'-ite
cemen-tit'ious
cem'-eteries
cem'-etery
cen'-acle
ce-no'bian
ce'no-bite
ceno-bit'ic
ceno-gen-et'ic
cen'o-taph
cen'-sor
cen-so'rial
cen-so'ri-ous
cen'-sor-ship
cen'-sur-able
cen'-sure
cen'-sured
cen'-sur-ing
cen'-sus
cen'-tal
cen'-tare
cen'-taur
cen'-taury

cen-tav'o
cen-ten-a'rian
cen-ten'-ary
cen-ten'-nial
cen'-ter-ing
cen-tes'i-mal
cen'tl-grade
cen'ti-gramme
cen'ti-litre
cen-til'lion
cen'ti-metre
cen'ti-pede
cent'-ner
cen'-tral
cen-tral-is-a'tion
cen'-tral-ise
cen'-tral-ism
cen'-tral-ist
cen'tre-bit
cen'tre-board
cen'tre-piece
cen'-tric
cen'-tri-cally
cen'tric'ity
cen-trif'u-gal
cen'-tri-fuge
cen'-tri-ole
cen-trip'-etal
cen'-trist
centro-bar'ic
centro-cli'nal
centro-des'mose
cen-troid'al
centro-lec'i-thal
cen'-tro-plasm
cen'-tro-some
cen'-trum
cen'-tuple

cen-tu'pli-cate
cen-tu'r-ial
cen-tu'r-ion
cen'-tury
ceph'a-lad
cephal-al'gia
ceph'a-late
ceph'a-lin
ceph-al-is-a'tion
cepha-li'tis
ceph'a-lo-cele
cepha-lo-chord'-
ate
ceph-al-om'eter
ceph'a-lo-pod
ce-ra'ceous
cer-am'ic
cer-am'ics
cer'a-mist
cer'a-noid
cer-ar'gyr-ite
cer'a-sin
cer-as'tes
ce'-rate
ce'-rated
cer'a-toid
cer'-cal
cer-ca'ria
cer'-cus
cer-ebel'-lar
cer-ebel'-lum
cer'-ebral
cer-eb'ri-form
cer'-cbro=spi'nal
cer'-ebrum
ce're-cloth
ce're-ments
cer-emo'nial

cer'-emon-ies
cer-emo'ni-ous
cer'-emony
ce'-reous
ce-rif'er-ous
ce'-rite
ce'-rium
cer'-met
cer'-nu-ous
ce'ro-graph
ce-rog'ra-phy
cero-plas'-tic
ce-rot'ic
ce'-rous
cer'-tain
cer'-tainly
cer'-tain-ties
cer'-tainty
cer-ta'tion
cer'-ti-fi-able
cer-tif'i-cate
cer-ti-fi-ca'tion
cer'-ti-fied
cer'-ti-fies
cer'-tify
cer'-ti-fy-ing
cer'-ti-tude
cer-u'lean
ce-ru'men
ce-ru'mi-nous
ce'-ruse
ce'ru-site
cer'-van-tite
cer'-velat
cer'-vi-cal
cer'-vices
cer-vi-ci'tis
cer'-vi-cum

cer'-vine
cer'-vix
cess-a'tion
cess'ion-ary
cess'-pit
cess'-pool
ces'-toid
cet-a'cean
cet-a'ceous
ce'-tane
ceteo-saur'us
chab'a-zite
chae-tif'er-ous
chae-toph'-or-ous
chaeto-plank'-ton
chae'-to-pod
chaet'o-taxy
chaf'-finch
chain'o-matic
chain-re-ac'-tion
chair'-man
chair'-man-ship
chal-a'za
chal-can'-thite
chal-ced'-ony
chal'-cid
chal'-co-cite
chal-cog'ra-phy
chalco-py'rite
chal'-dron
chal'-ice
chalk'i-ness
chalk'-stone
chal'-lenge
chal'-lenge-able
chal'-lenger
chal'-leng-ing

chal'-lis
chal-yb'-eate
chal'y-bite
cha'mber-lain
cha'mber-maid
cham'-bray
cha-me'leon
cham'-fer
cham'o-site
cham-pa'gne
cham'-per-tous
cham'-perty
cham'-pion
cham'-pion-ship
chan'ce-ful
chan'-cel
chan'-cel-lery
chan'-cel-lor
chan'-cel-lor-
　　　　　ship
chan'-cery
chand-elier'
chand'-ler
chand'-lery
change-abil'ity
cha'nge-able
cha'nge-ful
cha'nge-less
cha'nge-ling
chan'g-ing
chan'-nel
chan'-nelled
chan'-nel-lise
chan'-nel-ling
chan'ti-cleer
chant'-late
chan'-try

chap-ar-ral'
chap'-book
chap'-fallen
chap'i-ter
chap'-lain
chap'-laincy
chap'-let
chap'-man
chap'-ter
chap'-ter-house
char'a-banc
char'ac-ter
charac-ter-is-
　　　　a'tion
char'ac-ter-ise
charac-ter-ist'ic
charac-ter-is'ti-
　　　　cally
char'ac-tery
char'-coal
charg'e-able
charg'-ing
cha'ri-ness
char'-iot
chario-teer'
char-is'ma
char-is'mata
char-is-mat'ic
char'i-table
char'i-ties
char'-ity
chari-var'i
char'-la-tan
char'-la-tan-ism
char'-la-tanry
char'-lock
charm'-ing
charm'-ingly

char'-nel
char'-nel-house
char'-pie
char'-poy
char'-qui
char-ta'ceous
char'-ter
char'-tist
chart'-let
chart'-room
char'-woman
chas'-mal
chasmo-gam'ic
chasmog'-am-ous
chas'mo-phyte
chas-ti'si
chas-tise-ment
chas-ti'ser
chas'-tity
chas'-uble
chat'el-ain
chat'el-aine
chatoy'-ance
chatoy'-ant
chat'-tel
chat'-ter
chat'-ter-box
chat'-terer
chat'-ti-ness
chat'-ting
chauf'-fer
chauf'-feur
chaul-moog'ra
chauv'in-ism
chauv'in-ist
chauvin-is'ti-
      cally
cheap'-ened

cheap'-ness
check'er-berry
check'er-board
check'-ered
check'-ers
check'-mate
check'-out
check'-rein
check'-room
ched'-dar
chedd'-ite
cheek'-bone
cheer'-ful
cheer'-fully
cheer'-ful-ness
cheer'-ily
cheer'-ing
cheer'-less
chees'e-cake
chees'e-monger
chees'e-par-ing
chees'i-ness
chee'-tah
chei-li'tis
cheir-op'-tera
cheir-op'-teran
cheir-op'-ter-ous
che'-late
che-lic'era
che'li-form
che-lo'nian
chemi-at'ric
chem'i-cal
chemi-lumi-
      nesc'ence
chemi-sorp'-tion
chem'-ist
chem'-is-try

chem'i-type
chemo-recep' tor
chem-o'sis
chemo-syn'-
      thesis
chemo-tax'is
chemo-ther'apy
chem'-urgy
cheno-po'dium
cheq'ue-book
cheq'uer-board
cher'-ish
cher'-no-zem
cher'-ries
cher'-son-ese
cher-u'bic
cher-u'bi-cally
cher'u-bim
cher'-vil
cher-vo'nets
chess'-board
chess'-man
ches'-ter-field
chest'-nut
cheva-lier'
chev'-eril
chev'-ron
chev'ro-tain
chev'ro-tin
chi-as'ma
chi-as'mal
chi-as'mus
chi-buk'
chica'n-ery
chick'a-dee
chick'a-ree
chick'-en-pox
chick'-ling

CHICKPEA

chick'-pea
chick'-weed
chic'-ory
chid'-den
chief'-tain
chief'-taincy
chief'-tain-ship
chiff'-chaff
chif-fon'
chif-fon-ier'
chif'-fo-robe
chig'-ger
chi'ld-hood
chi'ld-ish
chi'ld-ishly
chi'ld-ish-ness
chi'ld-less
chi'ld-like
chil'-dren
chil'-iad
chil'i-asm
chil'i-ast
chil'li-ness
chilli'-ing
chill'-ingly
chi'lo-plasty
chi-lop'oda
chim-aer'-oid
chim-e'ra
chim-er'i-cal
chim-er'i-cally
chim'-ney
chim'-ney-piece
chim'-ney-pot
chim'-ney-sweep
chim'-pan-zee
chi'na-berry
chi'na-ware
62

chin-chil'la
chin'io-fon
chin'-ning
chin-ook'
chin'-qua-pin
chip'-munk
chip'-per
chip'-ping
chi-rag'ra
chi'ro-graph
chi-rog'ra-pher
chi-rog'ra-phy
chi'ro-mancy
chi-rop'-odist
chi-rop'-ody
chiro-prac'-tic
chiro-prac'-tor
chir'-rup
chir'-ruped
chir'-rup-ing
chir-rur'-geon
chis'-elled
chis'-el-ler
chis'-el-ling
chit'-chat
chi'-tin
chi'-tin-ase
chi'-tin-ous
chi'-ton
chit'-ter-lings
chit'-ting
chiv'-al-ric
chiv'-al-rous
chiv'-alry
chla-myd'-eous
chlo-an'thite
chlo-as'ma
chlor-am'-ide

chlo'ra-mine
chlo'r-ate
chlo'ra-zide
chlor'-dane
chlo'r-ide
chlo'ri-dise
chlor-im'eter
chlo'ri-nate
chlori-na'tion
chlo'r-ine
chlo'r-ite
chlori-tis-a'tion
chlor'o-form
chloro-hy'drin
chlor-o'ma
chloro-my'cetin
chlo'ro-phyll
chloro-phyl'-lous
chlor-o'sis
chlor-ot'ic
chlo'r-ous
cho'-ana
cho-an'o-cyte
chock'-stone
chock'-taw
choc'-olate
cho'ke-berry
cho'ke-bore
cho'ke-cherry
cho'ke-damp
cho'k-ing
chol-aem'ia
chol'a-gogue
chol-an-gi'tis
chol-an'-threne
chol'-era
chol'-eric
chol'-er-ine

chol-es'-terol
cho'li-amb
choli-am'bic
chol'-ine
chol-in-es'ter-ase
chol-u'ria
cho'mo-phyte
chon'-dral
chon-dri-fi-
    ca'tion
chon'-drin
chon-dro-
    cranium
chon-drol'ogy
chon-dro'ma
chon-dro'sa-mine
chon -drule
choos'-ing
chop-i'ne
chop'-per
chop'-ping
chop'-stick
chor-a'gus
chor-al'e
chor-da-cen'-tra
chor-da-cen'-
    trous
chor'-dal
chor'-date
chor-dot'omy
chor-eog'ra-pher
chor-eog'ra-phy
cho'ri-amb
chori-am'-bus
chor'-ion
chori-on'ic
chorio-reti-ni'tis
chor'-is-ter

cho-rog'ra-pher
choro-graph'i-cal
cho-rog'ra-phy
cho'-roid
cho-roid-i'tis
cho-rol'ogy
chort'-ling
chow'-chow
chow'-der
chre-ma-tis'tic
chres-tom'a-thy
chris'-mal
chris'ma-tory
chris'ten-dom
chris-ti-an'a
chris'-tian-ise
chro'-mate
chro-mat'ic
chro-mat'i-cally
chroma-tic'ity
chro'ma-tin
chro'ma-tism
chro-mat'o-scope
chro'ma-tron
chro'ma-trope
chro'-mic
chromi-dro'sis
chro'mi-nance
chro'-mite
chro'-mium
chro'mo-gen
chro'mo-graph
chromo-lith'o-
    graph
chromo-lith-
    og'ra-phy
chro-mom'eter
chro'mo-scope

chro'-mous
chro'-mule
chron'-icle
chron'-icler
chron'-icling
chron'o-gram
chron'o-graph
chron-og'ra-phy
chrono-log'ic
chrono-log'i-cal
chron-ol'-ogist
chron-ol'ogy
chron-om'eter
chron-om'etry
chrono-met'ric
chron'o-scope
chron'o-tron
chrys'a-lid
chrys'a-lis
chrys-an'-
    themum
chrys-el-ephan'-
    tine
chrys'-ene
chrys'o-beryl
chryso-col'la
chrys'o-lite
chrys'o-prase
chrys'o-tile
chtho'-nian
chuck'le-head
chuck'-ling
chug'-ging
chuk'-ker
chunk'i-ness
church'-man
church'-warden
church'-yard

churl'-ish
churl'-ish-ness
chut'-ney
chy-la'ceous
chyli-fac'-tion
chyli-fi-ca'tion
chylo-caul'-ous
chylo-peri-
        to'neum
chylo-phyl'-lous
chylo-tho'rax
chy-lu'ria
chymi-fi-ca'tion
chy'-mous
cib-o'rium
cic-a'da
cic-a'la
cic'a-trice
cic'a-trices
cica-tric'ial
cic'a-tricle
cica-tris'-ant
cica-tris-a'tion
cica-tri'se
cic-a'trix
cichor-a'ceous
cid'-aris
ciga-rett'e
cil'i-ate
cim'i-coid
cim'o-lite
cin-cho'na
cin-chon'i-dine
cin'-cho-nine
cin'-chon-ism
cin'-cho-phen
cinc'-ture
cin'-der

cin'e-cam'-era
cine-fac'-tion
cin'-ema
cin'e-ma-scope
cine-mat'ic
cine-mat'o-graph
cine-ma-tog'ra-
        pher
cine-ma-tog'ra-
        phy
cin-er-am'a
cin-er-a'ria
cin-er-a'rium
cin'-er-ary
cin-er-a'tion
cin-e'reous
cin'-er-ous
cin'gu-late
cin'gu-lum
cin'-na-bar
cin'na-baric
cin'na-bar-ine
cin'-na-mate
cin-nam'ic
cin'-na-mon
cin-na-mon'ic
cin'-no-line
cinq'ue-foil
cinq'ue-pace
cip'o-lin
cip'-pus
cir'-ci-nate
circ'-let
circ'-ling
cir'-cuit
cir-cu'-itous
cir'-cu-lar

circu-lar-is-
        a'tion
cir'cu-lar-ise
cir-cu-lar'ity
cir'-cu-late
cir'-cu-lation
cir'-cu-lator
cir'-cu-lat-ory
cir'-cu-lus
cir-cum-am'bi-
        ent
cir-cum-am'bu-
        late
cir-cum-ambu-
        la'tion
cir-cum-am'bu-
        lat-ory
cir'-cum-cise
cir'-cum-cision
cir-cum-duc'-tion
cir-cum'-fer-
        ence
cir-cum-fer-
        en'tial
cir-cum'-fer-
        entor
cir'-cum-flex
cir-cum-flex'ion
cir-cum'flu-ent
cir-cum'flu-ous
cir-cum-fu'se
cir-cum-fu'sion
cir-cum-ja'cent
cir-cum-lit'-toral
cir-cum-lo-
        cu'tion
cir-cum-loc'u-
        tory

cir-cum-nav'i-gate

cir-cum-navi-ga'tion

cir-cum-nav'i-gator

circum-nu'tate

cir-cum-nu-ta'tion

cir-cum-po'lar

cir-cum-sciss'ile

cir'-cum-scribe

cir'-cum-scrip-tion

cir-cum-scrip'-tive

cir'-cum-so'lar

cir'-cum-spect

cir'-cum-stance

cir'-cum-stanced

cir'-cum-stances

cir-cum-stan'-tial

cir-cum-stan'-tially

cir-cum-stan'-tiate

cir-cum-val'-late

cir-cum-val-la'tion

cir'-cum-vent

cir'-cum-venter

cir-cum-ven'-tion

cir-cum-vo-lu'tion

cir-cum-volv'e

cir'-cus

cir'-rate

cir-rho'sis

cir-rhot'ic

cir-rif'er-ous

cir'-ri-pede

cir'-ro-cu'mu-lus

cir'-rose

cir'-ro-stra'tus

cir'-rous

cir'-rus

cir'-soid

cis-al'pine

cis-at-lan'tic

cis-mon'-tane

cispa-da'ne

ciss'-oid

cis-ta'ceous

cis'-tern

cit'a-del

cit-ta'tion

ci'ta-tory

cith'-ara

cith'-ern

cit'-ies

cit'i-zen

cit'i-zen-ess

cit'i-zenry

cit'i-zen-ship

cit'-rate

cit'-reous

cit'-ric

cit'-ri-form

cit'-rine

cit'-ron

cit-ron-el'la

cit'-rous

cit'-rus

civ'-ery

civ'-ics

civ-il'ian

civi-lis-a'tion

civ'i-lise

civ'i-lised

civ'i-lis-ing

civ'-ility

civ'-illy

civ'-ism

clab'-ber

clad'-ding

clad'-ode

clag'-ging

claim'-ant

clair-voy'-ance

clair-voy'-ant

clam'-ant

clama-to'rial

clam'-bake

clam'-ber

clam'mi-ness

clam'-or-ous

clam'-our

clam'-shell

clan-des'tine

clang'or-ous

clan'-nish

clans'-man

clap'-board

clap'-per

clap'-ping

clap'-trap

clar'-en-don

clari-fi-ca'tion

clar'i-fied

clar'i-fy-ing

clar'i-net

clar'-ion

clar'-ity

65

CLASSICAL

clas'si-cal
clas'si-cally
clas'si-cism
clas'si-cist
clas'si-fi-a-ble
classi-fi-ca'tion
clas'si-fi-cat-ory
clas'si-fied
clas'si-fy-ing
class'-mate
class'-room
clas'-tic
clath'-rate
clat'-ter
clat'-tered
claudi-ca'tion
claus'-tral
claus-tro-pho'bia
claus'-trum
clav'-ate
clav'i-chord
clav'-icle
clav'i-corn
clav-ic'u-lar
cla-vier'
clav'i-form
clav'u-late
claw'-like
clay'-more
clead'-ing
clean'li-ness
clean'-ness
cleans'-ing
clear'-age
clear'-ance
clear'-ing
clear'-ing-house

clear'-ness
clear'-starch
cleav'-able
cleav'-age
cleav'-ing
cleisto-gam'ic
cleis-tog'a-mous
cleis-tog'amy
clem'a-tis
clem'-ency
clem'-ent
clep'-sy-dra
cle-re-story
cler'gy-man
cler'i-cal
cler'i-cal-ism
cler'i-hew
cler'-isy
clerk'-ship
clev'-erly
clev'-er-ness
cli-an'thus
cli'-ent
cli'ent-age
cli-en'tal
cli-en-tel'e
cli-mac'-teric
cli-mac'-tic
cli'-mate
cli-mat'ic
cli-ma-tise
clima-tol'ogy
cli'-max
climb'-able
climb'-ing
clin-nan'-drium
cling'-ing
cling'-stone

clin'i-cal
clin-ic'ian
cli'no-graph
cli-nom'eter
clino-met'ric
clin-to'nia
clip'-per
clip'-ping
clit'-oris
clo-a'ca
clo-a'cal
cloak'-room
clob'-ber
clob'-ber-ing
clock'-maker
clock'-tower
clock'-wise
clock'-work
clod'-dish
clod'-hopper
clod'-pate
clog'-ging
clois'-ter
clois'-tral
clois'-tered
clo'-nus
clo'se-fit-ting
clo'se-ness
clo's-ure
clo'th-ier
clo'th-ing
cloth'-yard
clo'-ture
clot'-ted
clot'-tine
cloud'-berry
cloud'-burst
cloud'i-ness

cloud'-less
cloud'-let
clo'-ver
clown'-ish
cloy'-ing
cloy'-ingly
club'-bable
club'-bing
club'-foot
club'-haul
club'-house
club'-man
club'-room
club'-woman
clum'si-ness
clus'-ter
clut'-ter
clyp'-eate
clys'-ter
co-ac'er-vate
co-acer-va'tion
coach'-box
coach'-man
coach'-man-ship
co-ac'-tion
co-ac'-tive
co-ad'ju-tant
co-ad'ju-tor
co-ad'u-nate
co-a'gent
co-ag'u-lable
co-ag'u-lant
co-ag'u-late
co-agu-la'tion
co-ag'u-lator
co-ag'u-lum
coal-cel'-lar
coal-deal'er

co-alesc'e
co-alesc'-ence
co-alesc'-ent
co-alesc'-ing
coal'-field
coal'-heaver
coal'-hole
coal'-ite
co-alit'ion
coam'-ing
co-ap-ta'tion
co-arc'-tate
co-arc-ta'tion
coars'e-ness
coast'-guard
coast'-line
coast'-wise
co-a'ti
coat'-ing
coat'-room
co-auth'or
co-ax'ial
coax'-ing
coax'-ingly
co-azer-va'tion
co'-balt
co-balt'ic
co-balt-'ous
cob'-bler
cob'ble-stone
co-bel-lig'er-ent
co'-bra
cob'-ric
cob'-web
co-cain'e
co-cain-is-a'tion
co-cain'-ise
co-cain'-ism

coc-cidi-o'sis
coc-cif'er-ous
coc-cin'-eous
coc-ci-dyn'ia
coc'-cus
coc-cyg'eal
coc'-cyx
coch'i-neal
coch'-lea
cock-a'de
cocka-tiel'
cock'a-too
cock'a-trice
cock'-boat
cock'-chafer
cock'-crow
cock'-erel
cock'-eyed
cock'-fight
cock'-horse
cock'le-bur
cock'le-shell
cock'-ling
cock'-loft
cock'-ney
cock'-pit
cock'-roach
cocks'-comb
cocks'-foot
cock'-shy
cock'-spur
cock'-sure
cock'-tail
co'-coa
co-co-bo'-lo
co'co-nut
coc-sig'eal
coc'-tile

coc'-tion
co'-cus
co-defend'-ant
co'-deine
co'-dex
cod'-fish
co'di-ces
cod'i-cil
codi-fi-ca'tion
co'di-fied
co'di-fier
cod'-lin
cod'-ling
co-edu-ca'tion
co-edu-ca'tional
co-ef-fic'ient
coel'a-canth
coelen'-ter-ate
coel'-iac
coel'o-mate
coelo-sperm'-ous
coel'o-stat
coelo-zo'ic
co-emp'-tion
coe-nes-the'sia
coe-nu'rus
co-e'qual
co-erc'e
co-erc'-ible
co-erc'-ing
co-er'cion
co-erc'-ive
co-es-sen'-tial
co-eter'nal
co-exist'
co-exist'-ence
co-exist'-ent
co-ex-tend'

co-ex-ten'-sion
co-ex-ten'-sive
co-e'val
cof'-fee
cof'-fee-house
cof'-fee-pot
cof'-fee-room
cof'-fer
cof'-fer-dam
cof'-fin
co'-gency
co'-gent
cog'-ging
cog'i-table
cog'i-tate
cogi-ta'tion
cog'i-tat-ing
cog'i-tat-ive
cog'-nate
cog-na'tion
cog'ni-sable
cog'ni-sance
cog'ni-sant
cog-ni'se
cog-nit'ion
cog'-ni-tive
cog-nom'i-nal
cog-nosc'ible
cog-no'vit
cog'-wheel
co-hab'it
co-hab'i-tant
co-habi-ta'tion
co'-heir
co-heir'-ess
co-he're
co-he'r-ence

co-he'r-ency
co-he'r-ent
co-he'rer
co-he'sion
co-he's-ive
co-he's-ive-ness
co-ho-ba'tion
co'-hort
coif'-feur
coif'-fure
coin'-age
co-inci'de
co-in'ci-dence
co-in'ci-dent
co-inci-den'-tal
co-inci'd-ing
co-inher'it-ance
co-insu're
cois'-trel
co-it'ion
co'-itus
co-ju'ror
co'k-ing
col'-an-der
col'-chi-cine
col'-chi-cum
col'-co-thar
co'ld-ness
co'ld-proof
co'le-man-ite
coleop'-tera
coleop'-ter-oid
coleop'-ter-ous
coleop'-tile
co'le-slaw
co'-leus
co'le-wort
col'-ic-root

col'-ic-weed
coli-se'um
col-i'tis
col-lab'-or-ate
col-lab-or-a'tion
col-lab'-or-ator
col'-lage
col-laps'e
col-laps'ed
col-laps'-ible
col-laps'-ing
col'-lar
col'-lar-band
col'-lar-bone
col-la-ret'
col'-lar-ing
col-lat'eral
col-la't-ing
col-la'tion
col-la'tor
col'-league
col-lect' (v.)
col'-lect (n.)
col-lec-ta'nea
col-lec'ted
col-lect'-ible
col-lec'-tion
col-lec'-tive
col-lec'-tively
col-lec'-tiv-ism
col-lec'-tiv-ist
col-lec'-tor
col'-leen
col'-lege
col'-leger
col-le'gial
col-le'gian
col-le'gi-ate

col-len'-chyma
col-lic'u-lose
col-lic'u-lus
col-li'de
col-li'd-ing
col'-lie
col'-li-gate
col'li-ga'tion
col'li-gat-ive
col'-li-mate
col lo-cu'tion
col-loc'u-tor
col-lo'dion
col-lo'gue
col'-loid
col-loid'al
col'-lop
col-lo'quial
col-lo'qui-al-ism
col-lo'qui-ally
col'-lo-quist
col'-loquy
col'lo-type
col-lu'de
col-lu'd-ing
col-lu'sion
col-lu's-ive
col-lu's-ively
col-lu'vies
col-lyr'ium
col'o-cynth
co'-lon
co-lon'el
col-o'nial
col-o'nial-ise
co-lon'ic
col'-on-ies
col-on-is-a'tion

col'-on-ise
col'-on-ist
col-on-na'de
col-on-na'ded
col'-ony
col'o-phon
col'o-phony
co-lop-to'sis
col'or-ation
color-if'ic
color-im'eter
color-im'etry
col'or-ine
col-os'sal
col-os'sus
co-los'-tomy
col-os'trum
col'ot'omy
col'our-ful
col'our-ing
col'our-ist
col'our-less
col'our-man
col'our-pro'-cess
col-por'-tage
col-por-teur'
co'lt-ish
co'lts-foot
col'u-brine
col-u'go
col-um-ba'rium
col'um-bary
col'um-bine
col-um'-bium
colu-mel'la
col-um'-nar
col'-um-nated
col-umni-a'tion

69

col'um-nist
col-lu're
co'-mate
com'a-tose
com'a-tosely
com'-bat (n. v.)
com-bat' (v.)
com'-ba-tant
com'-bat-ing
com-ba'tive
com-ba'tively
com-ba'tive-ness
com'-bi-na'tion
com'-bi-nat-ive
com-bi-na-to'rial
com-bi'ne (v.)
com'-bine (n.)
comb'-ing
com-bi'n-ing
com-bre'tum
com-busti-bil'ity
com-bust'-ible
com-bus'-tion
com-e'-back
com'-edo
com-e'dian
com-edienn'e
com'-edies
com'-edy
come'-li-ness
com-est'ible
com'-fit
com'fort-able
com'fort-ably
com'fort-less
com'i-cal
comi-cal'ity
com-it'ia

com-it'ial
com'-ity
com-mand'
com'-man-dant
com-man-deer'
com-mand'er
com-mand'-ing
com-mand'-ment
com-man'do
com-meas'-ure
com-mem'-or-ate
com-mem'-or-at-
    ing
com-mem-or-
    a'tion
com-mem'-or-at-
    ive
com-menc'e
com-menc'e-ment
com-menc'-ing
com-mend'
com-mend'-able
com-men'-dam
com-men-da'tion
com-men-da'tory
com-men'-sal
com-men'-sal-
    ism
com-men-sura-
    bil'ity
com-men'-sur-
    able
com-men'-sur-
    ate
com-men'-sur-
    ately
com-men-sur-
    a'tion

com'-ment (n).
com-ment' (v.)
com'-men-tary
com'-men-tate
com'-men-tator
com'-merce
com-mer'-cial
com-mer'-cial-
    ise
com-mer'-cial-
    ised
com-mer'-cial-
    ism
com-mer'-cially
com-mi-na'tion
com-min'a-tory
com-min'gle
com-min'gling
com'-min-ute
com-mi-nu'tion
com-mis'er-able
com-mis'er-ate
com-miser-a'tion
com'-mis-sar
com-mis-sa'riat
com'-mis-sary
com-mis'sion
com-mission-
    air'e
com-mis'sioned
com-mis'sioner
com-miss'u-ral
com'-missure
com-mit'
com-mit'-ment
com-mit'-tal
com-mit'-ted
com-mit'tee

com-mit'tee-man
com-mit'-ting
com-mix'
com-mix'-ture
com-mo'de
com-mo'di-ous
com-mod'i-ties
com-mod'ity
com'mo-dore
com'-mon
com'-mon-able
com'-mon-age
com'-mon-alty
com'-moner
com'-monly
com'-mon-place
com'-mons
com'-mon-sense
com'-mon-weal
com'-mon-wealth
com-mo'tion
com'-mu-nal
com-mu'ne (v.)
com'-mune (n.)
com-mu'ni-cable
com-mu'ni-cant
com-mu'ni-cate
com-mu'ni-cat-
                 ing
com-muni-ca'tion
com-mu'ni-cat-
                 ive
com-mu'ni-cator
com-mu'nion
com-muniqué'
com-mu-nis-
           a'tion
com'-mu-nise

com'-mu-nism
com'-mu-nist
com'-mu-nistic
com-mu'ni-ties
com-mu'nity
com-mu't-able
com'-mu-tate
com-mu-ta'tion
com-mu'ta-tive
com'-mu-tator
com-mu'te
com-mu'ter
com-mu't-ing
co'-mose
com'-pact (n.)
com-pact' (a. v.)
com-pa'ges
com-pag'i-nate
com-pagi-na'tion
com-pan'-dor
com-pan'ion
com-pan'ion-able
com-pan'ion-ate
com-pan'ion-less
com-pan'ion-ship
com-pan'ion-way
com'-par-able
com-par'a-tive
com-par'a-tively
com-par'a-tor
com-pa're
com-par'i-son
com-part'
com-part'-ment
com-pas'sion
com-pas'sion-ate
com-pati-bil'ity
com-pat'-ible

com-pa'triot
com-pat'-riot
com'-peer
com-peer'
com-pel'
com-pel-la'tion
com-pell'ed
com-pel'-ling
com-pen'di-ous
com-pen'di-
              ously
com-pen'-dium
com-pens'-able
com'-pen-sate
com'-pen-sat-ing
com-pen-sa'tion
com-pen'sa-tive
com'-pen-sator
com-pen'sa-tory
com'-pere
com-pe'te
com'-petence
com'-petent
com-pe't-ing
com-pe-tit'ion
com-pet'i-tive
com-pet'i-tively
com-pet'i-tor
com-pi-la'tion
com-pi'le
com-pi'ler
com-pi'l-ing
com-pla'cence
com-pla'cency
com-pla'cent
com-plain'
com-plain'-ant
com-plaint'

71

com-plais'-ance
com-plais'-ant
com'-pla-nate
comp'-lement
comp-lemen'-tal
comp-lemen'-tary
com-ple'te
com-ple'tely
com-ple'te-ness
com-ple'tion
com'-plex
com-plex'ion
com-plex'ioned
com-plex'ity
com-pli'able
com-pli'ance
com-pli'ant
com'-pli-cant
com'-pli-cate
com'-pli-cated
com-pli-ca'tion
com-plic'ity
com-plied'
com'-pli-ment
com-pli-men'-
      tary
com'-pline
com-ply'
com'-posite
com'-positely
com-po-sit'ion
com-pos'i-tor
com-posi-to'rial
com'-post
com-po'sure
com-po-ta'tion
com'-po-ta'tor
com'-pound (n.a.)

com-pound' (v.a.)
com-pra-dor'
com-pre-hend'
com-pre-hend'-
      ible
com-pre-hen'-
      sible
com-pre-hen'-
      sion
com-pre-hen'-
      sive
com'-press (n.)
com-press' (v.)
com-press'ed
com-press-
      ibil'ity
com-press'-ible
com-press'-ing
com-pres'sion
com-press'-ive
com-press'or
com-pri'sal
com-pri'se
com-pri's-ing
com'pro-mise
comp-tom'-eter
comptro'l-ler
com-pul'-sion
com-pul'-sive
com-pul'-sorily
com-pul'-sory
com-punc'-tion
com'-pur-ga'tion
com'-pur-gator
com-put'-able
com-pu-ta'tion
com-pu'te
com-pu'ter

com-pu't-ing
com'-pu-tist
com'-rade
com'-rade-ship
co-na'tion
con'a-tive
con-cat'-enate
con-cat-ena'tion
con-ca-va'tion
con'-cave
con-cav'ity
con-ceal'
con-ceal'-ment
con-ce'de
con-ce'ded
con-ce'der
con-ce'd-ing
con-ceit'
con-ceit'ed
con-ceit'-edly
con-ceiv-abil'ity
con-ceiv'-able
con-ceiv'-ably
con-ceiv'e
con-ceiv'-ing
con'-cen-trate
con-cen-trat-ing
con-cen-tra'tion
con-cen-tra'tion-
      camp
con'-cen-trator
con-cen'tre
con-cen'-tric
con-cen'-tri-cal
con-cen-tric'ity
con'-cept
con-cept'-acle
con-cep'-tion

con-cep'-tive
con-cep'-tual
con-cep'-tu-al-ise
con-cep'-tu-al-ism
con-cep'-tu-al-ist
con-cern'
con-cern'ed
con-cern'-ing
con-cern'-ment
con'-cert (n.)
con-cert' (v.)
con-cer'ted
con-cer-ti'na
con-cer'to
con-ces'sion
con-cession-air'e
con-ces'sion-ary
con-ces'sive
con'chi-fer
con-chif'er-ous
con'chi-form
con-chi'tis
con'-choid
con-choid'al
con-cho-log'i-cal
con-chol'-ogist
con-chol'ogy
con-cil'i-able
con-cil'iar
con-cil'i-ate
con-cil'i-at-ing
con-cili-a'tion
con-cil'i-ator
con-cil'i-atory
con-cin'-nity

con-ci'se
con-ci'sely
con-ci'se-ness
con-cis'ion
con'-clave
con'-clav-ist
con-clu'de
con-clu'd-ing
con-clu'sion
con-clu's-ive
con-clu's-ively
con-coct'
con-coct'er
con-coc'-tion
con-col'or-ous
con-col'or-ate
con-com'i-tance
con-com'i-tant
con'-cord (n.)
con-cord' (v.)
con-cord'-ance
con-cord'-ant
con-cor'dat
con'-course
con-cresc'ence
con-cresc'ent
con'-crete
con-cre'te
con-cre'tely
con-cre'tion
con-cre'tion-ary
con-cu'bi-nage
con-cu'bi-nary
con'-cu-bine
con-cu'pis-cence
con-cu'pis-cent
con-cur'
con-curr'ed

con-cur'-rence
con-cur'-rent
con-cur'-ring
con-cuss'
con-cus'sion
con-cy'c-lic
con-demn'
con-dem-na'tion
con-dem'na-tory
con-demn'ed
con-demn'er
con-demn'-ing
con-dens'-able
con'-den-sate
con-den-sa'tion
con-dens'e
con-dens'er
con-dens'-ing
con-de-scend'
con-de-scend'-ence
con-de-scend'-ing
con-de-scend'-ingly
con-de-scen'-sion
con-di'gn
con'-di-ment
con-dit'ion
con-dit'ional
con-dit'ioned
con-dit'ion-ing
con-do'la-tory
con-do'le
con-do'l-ence
con-do'l-ing
con-do-min'ium

73

con-do-na'tion
con-do'ne
con'-dor
con-du'ce
con-du'cive
con-duct' (v.)
con'-duct (n.)
con-duc'-tance
con-duc'-ted
con-duc'-tible
con-duc-ti-bil'ity
con-duc-ti-met'ric
con-duc'-tion
con-duc'-tive
con-duc-tiv'ity
con-duc'-tor
con-duc'-tress
con'-duit
con-du'pli-cate
con'dy-lar
con'-dyle
condy-lo'ma-tous
co'-ney
con-fab'u-late
con-fabu-la'tion
con-far-re-a'tion
con-fec'-tion
con-fec'-tion-ary
con-fec'-tion-er
con-fec'-tion-ery
con-fed'-er-acy
con-fed'-er-ate
con-fed-er-a'tion
con-fer'
con-feree'
con'-fer-ence
con-fer'-ment

con-fer'-rable
con-ferr'ed
con-fer'-ring
con-fer'va
con-fer'-void
con-fess'
con-fess'ed
con-fess'-edly
con-fes'sion
con-fes'sional
con-fes'sor
con-fet'ti
con'-fi-dant
con-fi'de
con-fi'ded
con'-fi-dence
con'-fi-dent
con-fi-den'-tial
con-fi-den'-tially
con'-fi-dently
con-fi'd-ing
con-figur-a'tion
con-fig'ure
con-fi'n-able
con-fi'ne (v.)
con-fi'ne-ment
con-fi'ner
con'-fines (n.)
con-fi'n-ing
con-firm'
con-firm'-able
con-fir-ma'tion
con-fir'ma-tory
con-firm'ed
con-fis'cable
con'-fis-cate
con'-fis-cat-ing

con-fis-ca'tion
con'-fis-cator
con-fis'ca-tory
con-fit'eor
con-fla-gra'tion
con-fla'te
con-fla'tion
con'-flict (n.)
con-flict' (v.)
con-flict'-ing
con-flic'-tion
con-flic'-tive
con'-flu-ence
con'-flu-ent
con'-flux
con-fo'cal
con-form'
con-form'-able
con-form'-ance
con-for-ma'tion
con-form'-ist
con-form'-ity
con-found'
con-foun'ded
con-found'-edly
con-fra-ter'nity
con-front'
con-fron-ta'tion
con-fu'se
con-fu'sed
con-fu's-edly
con-fu's-ing
con-fu'sion
con-fu't-able
con-fu't-ant
con-fu-ta'tion
con-fu'ta-tive
con-fu'te

con-geal'
con-geal'-ment
con-gel-a'tion
con'-gener
con-gen-er'ic
con-gen'er-ous
con-ge'nial
con-genial'ity
con-gen'i-tal
con-ger'ies
con-gest'
con-ges'ted
con-ges'-tion
con-ges'-tive
con-gla'ci-ate
con'-glo-bate
con-glo-ba'tion
con-glom'-er-ate
con-glom-er-
a'tion
con-glu'ti-nant
con-glu'ti-nate
con-gluti-na'tion
con-grat'u-lant
con-grat'u-late
con-grat'u-lat-ing
con-gratu-la'tion
con-grat'u-lator
con-grat'u-lat-
ory
con'-gre-gate
con-gre-ga'tion
con-gre-ga'tional
con'-gress
con-gres'sional
con'-gress-woman
con'gru-ence
con'gru-ency

con'gru-ent
con'gru-ity
con'gru-ous
con'i-cal
con'i-cally
con'-ics
co-nid'ial
co'ni-fer
co-nif'er-ous
co'ni-form
co'ni-ine
co'-nium
con-jec'-tural
con-jec'-tur-ally
con-jec'-ture
con-join'
con-joint'
con'ju-gal
con'ju-gally
con'-ju-gate
con-ju-ga'tion
con'-ju-gator
con-junct'
con-junc'-tion
con-junc-ti'va
con-junc-ti'val
con-junc'-tive
con-junc-ti-vi'tis
con-junc'-ture
con-jur-a'tion
con'-jure (v.i.)
con-ju're (v.t.)
con-ju're-ment
con'-jurer
con'-jur-ing
con'-juror
con'-nate
con-nect'

con-nec'-ted
con-nect'-edly
con nect'er
con-nec'-tion
con-nec'-tive
con-nec-tiv'ity
con-nec'-tor
con-nex'ion
con-nex'ion-al-
ism

conn'-ing
con-ni'v-ance
con-ni've
con-ni'v-ent
con-ni'v-ently
con-noisseur'
con-no-ta'tion
con'-no-tat-ive
con-no'te
con-no't-ing
con-nu'bial
co'-noid
co-noid'al
co'no-scope
con'quer-ing
con-quis'ta-dor
con-san'guine
con-sanguin'-
eous
con-sanguin'-ity
con'-science
con'-science-less
con'-science-
strick'en
con-scien'-tious
con-scion-able
con'-scious
con'-sciously

75

CONSCIOUSNESS

con'-scious-ness
con'-script (n.)
con-script' (v.)
con-scrip'-tion
con'-se-crate
con'-se-crat-ing
con-se-cra'tion
con-sec'-tary
con-se-cu'tion
con-sec'u-tive
con-sec'u-tively
con-sen-esc'ence
con-sen'-sual
con-sen'-sus
con-sent'
con-senta-ne'ity
con-sen-ta'neous
con-sent'er
con-sen'tient
con'se-quence
con'se-quent
con-se-quen'-tial
con-se-quen'-
    tially
con'se-quently
con-serv'-ancy
con-serv'-ant
con-ser-va'tion
con-ser'va-tism
con-ser'va-tive
con-serva-toire'
con'-ser-vator
con-ser'va-tory
con-serv'e
con-serv'-ing
con-sid'er
con-sid'er-able
con-sid'er-ably

con-sid'er-ate
con-sid'er-ately
con-sider-a'tion
con-sid'ered
con-sid'er-ing
con-si'gn
con-si'gn-able
con-sig-na'tion
con-signee'
con-sig'nify
con-si'gn-ment
con-si'gn-or
con-sil'i-ence
con-sil'i-ent
con-sist'
con-sist'-ence
con-sist'-ency
con-sist'-ent
con-sist'-ently
con-sis-tom'eter
con-sis'-tory
con-so-la'tion
con-sol'a-tory
con-so'le (v.)
con-sol'e (n.)
con-sol'ı-dant
con-sol'i-date
con-sol'i-dat-ing
con-soli-da'tion
con-sol'i-dat-ive
con-so'l-ing
con-so'l-ingly
con'-sols
con-sommé'
con'-son-ance
con'-son-ancy
con'-son-ant
con-son-an'tal

con'-son-antly
con'-sort' (v.)
con'-sort (n.)
con-sor'-tium
con-spec'-tus
con-spi-cu'ity
con-spic'u-ous
con-spic'u-ously
con-spir'acy
con-spi'r-ant
con-spir'a-tor
con-spira-to'rial
con-spi're
con-spi'r-ing
con'-stable
con-stab'u-lary
con'-stancy
con'-stant
con'-stantly
con'-stel-late
con-stel-la'tion
con'-ster-nate
con-ster-na'tion
con'-sti-pate
con'-sti-pated
con'-sti-pat-ing
con-sti-pa'tion
con-stit'u-ency
con-stit'u-ent
con'-sti-tute
con-sti-tu'tion
con-sti-tu'tional
con-sti-tu'tion-
    al-ise
con-sti-tu'tion-
    al-ism
con-sti-tu'tion-
    al-ist

con-sti tu'tion-
    ally
con'sti-tut-ive
con'-sti-tutor
con-strain'
con-strain'ed
con-strain'-ing
con-straint'
con-strict'
con-stric'-tion
con-stric'-tive
con-stric'-tor
con-strin'ge
con-strin'-gent
con-struct' (v.)
con'-struct (n.)
con-struc'-tion
con-struc'-tional
con-struc'-tive
con-struc'-tiv-
    ism
con-struc'-tor
con-strue'
con-strued'
con-stru'-ing
con-sub-stan'-tial
con-sub-stan'-
    tiate
con-sub-stan-
    tia'tion
con'-suetude
con-suetu'd-
    inary
con'-sul
con'su-lar
con'-sul-ate
con'-sul-ship
con-sult'

con-sul'-ant
con-sul-ta'tion
con-sul'ta-tive
con-su'm-able
con-su'me
con-su'med
con-su'm-edly
con-su'mer
con-su'm-ing
con-sum'-mate
    (a.)
con'-sum-mate
    (v.a.)
con-sum-ma'tion
con-sumpt'
con-sump'-tion
con-sump'-tive
con-ta-besc'ence
con-ta-besc'ent
con'-tact
con'-tact-breaker
con'-tac-tor
con-tact'-ual
con-ta'gion
con-ta'gious
con-ta'gium
con-tain'
con-tain'er
con-tain'-ing
con-tain'-ment
con-tam'i-nant
con-tam'i-nate
con-tam'i-nated
con-tam'i-nat-ing
con-tami-na'tion
con-tam'i-nat-ive
con-tang'o
con-temn'

con-temn'er
con-tem'-per
con'-tem-plate
con'-tem-plated
con-tem-plat-ing
con-tem-pla'tion
con-tem'pla-tive
con-tem-por-
    a'neous
con-tem'-por-ary
con-tem' por-isc
con-tempt'
con-tempt'-ible
con-tempt'-ibly
con-temp'tu-ous
con-tend'
con-ten'dent
con-tend'er
con-tent' (a.v.n.)
con'-tent (n.)
con-ten'ted
con-tent'-edly
con-ten'-tion
con-ten'-tious
con-ten'-tiously
con-tent'-ment
con'-tents
con-ter'mi-nal
con-term'i-nate
con-ter'mi-nous
con'-test (n.)
con-test' (v.)
con-test'-able
con-test'-ant
con-tes-ta'tion
con'-text
con-tex'-tual
con-tex'-ture

77

con-ti-gu'ity
con-tig'u-ous
con-tig'u-ously
con'-ti-nence
con'-ti-nent
con-ti-nen'-tal
con-tin'-gency
con-tin'-gent
con-tin'-ual
con-tin'u-ally
con-tin'u-ance
con-tin'u-ant
con-tinu-a'tion
con-tin'u-at-ive
con-tin'u-ator
con-tin'ue
con-tin'u-ing
con-ti-nu'ity
con-tin'uo
con-tin'u-ous
con-tin'u-ously
con-tin'uum
con-tor'-ni-ate
con-tort'
con-tor'-tion
con-tor'-tion-ist
con-tort-ive
con'-tour
con'-tra-band
con'tra-band-ist
con'tra-bass
con'tra-cep'-tion
con-tra-cep'-tive
con'-tract (n.v.)
con-tract' (v.)
con-tract-abil'ity
con-tract'-able
con-trac'-ted

con-tract'-ible
con-trac'-tile
con-trac-til'ity
con-trac'-tion
con-tract'-ive
con-trac'-tor
con-trac'-tual
con-trac'-ture
con-tra-dict'
con-tra-dic'-tion
con-tra-dic'-
       torily
con-tra-dic'-tory
contra-dis-tinc'-
       tion
contra-dis-
       ting'uish
con'-trail
contra-in'di-cate
contra-indi-
       ca'tion
con-tral'to
con-trap'-tion
contra-pun'-tal
contra-pun'-tist
contra-ri'ety
con'-trar-ily
con'-tra'ri-ness
con'-trari-ness
con'-trari-wise
con'-trary
con-trast' (v.)
con'-trast (n.)
con'-trate
contra-val-la'tion
con-tra-ve'ne
con-tra-ve'n-ing
con-tra-ven'tion

con-trib'u-table
con-trib'u-tary
con-trib'-ute
con-trib'u-ting
con-tri-bu'tion
con-trib'u-tive
con-trib'u-tor
con-trib'u-tory
con-tri'te
con-tri'tely
con-trit'ion
con-tri'v-ance
con-tri've
con-tri'ver
con-tri'v-ing
con-tro'l
con-tro'l-lable
con-troll'ed
con-tro'l-ler
con-tro'l-ling
con-tro-ver'sial
con-tro-ver'sion
con'tro-versy
con'-tro-vert
contro-vert'-ible
con-tu-ma'cious
con'tu-macy
con-tu-me'li-ous
con'tu-mely
con-tu'se
con-tu'sion
con-un'drum
con-ur-ba'tion
con-va-lesc'e
con-va-lesc'-ence
con-va-lesc'-ent
con-va-lesc'-ing
con-vect'

con-vec'-tion
con-vec'-tor
con-vec'-tive
con-ve'ne
con-ve'ner
con-ve'nience
con-ve'nient
con-ve'niently
con-ve'ning
con'-vent
con-vent'-icle
con-ven'-tion
con-ven'-tional
con-ven'-tion-
        al-ise
con-ven'-tion-
        al'ity
con-ven'-tion-ary
con-ven'-tual
con-verg'e
con-ver'-gence
con-ver'-gent
con-verg'-ing
con-vers'-able
con-vers'-ance
con-vers'-ant
con-ver-sa'tion
con-ver-sa'tional
con-ver-sa'tion-
        al-ist
con'-verse (n.a.)
con-vers'e (v.)
con-vers'ely
con-vers'-ing
con-ver'-sion
con-vers'-ive
con'-vert (n.)
con-vert' (v.)

con-vert'er
con-vert'-ible
con-ver'tor
con'-vex
con-vex'ity
con-vey'
con-vey'-ance
con-vey'-ancer
con-vey'-anc-ing
con-vey'er
con-vey'-ing
con-vey'or
con'-vict (n.)
con-vict' (v.)
con-vic'-tion
con-vinc'e
con-vinc'-ible
con-vinc'-ing
con-vinc'-ingly
con-vi've
con-viv'-ial
con-vivi-al'ity
con-vo-ca'tion
con-vo'ke
con-vo'king
con'-vol-ute
con'-vol-u'tion
con-volv'e
con-vol-vu-
        la'ceous
con-vol'-vu-lus
con'-voy
con'-voyed
con-voy'-ing
con-vuls'e
con-vul'sion
con-vul'-sion-ary
con-vul'-sive

con-vul'-sively
coo'-ing
cook'-book
cook'-ery
cook'-stone
cool'-ant
cool'-ness
coon-skin
coop'-er-age
co-op'-er-ate
co-op'-er-a'tion
co-op'-er-at-ive
co-op'-er-ator
coop'-ery
co-opt'
co-or'-di-nate
co-or'-di-na'tion
co-or'-di-nator
co-paib'a
co'-pal
co-par'-cen-ary
co-par'-cener
co-part'-ner
co-part'-nery
co-part'-ner-ship
co'-peck
co'pe-stone
cop'-ies
co'-pilot
co'pi-ous
co'pi-ously
co'pi-ous-ness
cop'-per
cop'-peras
cop'-per-head
cop'-per-ing
cop'-per-ise
cop'-per-plate

cop'-per-smith	cor'-di-ally	corn'-field
cop'-per-ware	cor'di-er-ite	corn'-flour
cop'-pery	cor'di-form	corn'-flower
cop'-pice	cor'-dite	corn'-husk-ing
cop'-ping	cor'-don	cor'-nice
cop-roph'a-gous	cor'-do-van	cor-nic'u-late
cop'-ula	cor'-duroy	cor-nifi-ca'tion
cop'u-late	cord'-wainer	cor'-ni-form
cop'u-lation	cord'-wood	corn'-loft
cop'u-lat-ive	co-re'gent	corn'-stalk
cop'y-book	co-re-la'tion	corn'-starch
cop'y-hold	co're-less	corn'-stone
cop'y-holder	coreop'-sis	cor'-nua
cop'y-ing-ink	co-re-spon'-dent	cor'-nual
cop'y-ist	cori-a'ceous	cor-nu-co'pia
cop'y-right	cori-an'-der	cor'-nus
cop'y-writer	cork'-age	cor'-nute
coq'ueli-cot	cork'-screw	cor-ol'la
coquett'-ing	cork'-wood	cor-ol'lary
coquett'-ish	cor'-mo-phyte	cor'-ol-late
cor'-acle	cor'-mor-ant	cor-o'na
cor'a-coid	cor'-mus	cor-on-ach
coral-lif'er-ous	cor-na'ceous	cor-o'na-graph
cor'a-line	corn'-brash	cor-o'nal (a.)
cor'-al-line	corn'-chand-ler	cor'o-nal (n.)
cor'-al-lite	corn'-cob	cor'-on-ary
cor'-al-loid	corn'-cockle	cor'-on-ate
cor-al'-lum	corn'-crake	cor-on-a'tion
cor-an'to	cor'-nea	cor'-oner
cor'-ban	cor'-neal	cor'-onet
cor'-bel	cor'-nel	cor'-poral
cor'-bel-ling	cor-ne'lian	cor'-por-ally
cor-bic'-ula	cor'-neous	cor-por-al'ity
cor'-bie	cor'-ner	cor'-por-ate
cord'-age	cor'-ner-stone	cor-por-a'tion
cor'-date	cor'-ner-wise	cor-po'real
cor'-dial	cor'-net	cor-poreal'-ity
cordi-al'ity	cor'-net-ist	cor-por-e'ity

cor'po-sant	cor-rob'-or-ator	cor-ti'na
cor'-pu-lence	cor-rob'or-at-ory	cor'-ti-nate
cor'-pu-lent	cor-rob'-oree	cor'-tisol
cor'-pus	cor-ro'de	cor'-ti-sone
cor'-puscle	cor-ro'd-ent	cor-un'dum
cor-pus'cu-lar	cor-ro'd-ible	cor-us'cant
cor-ral'	cor-ro'd-ing	cor'-us-cate
cor-ra'sion	cor-ro's-ible	cor-us-ca'tion
cor-rect'	cor-ro'sion	cor-vée'
cor-rec'-tant	cor-ro's-ive	cor-vett'e
cor-rec'-tion	cor'-ru-gate	cor'-vine
cor-rec'-tional	cor'-ru-gated	cory-ban'-tic
cor-rec'ti-tude	cor'-ru-gated= i'ron	cor-yd'a-line
cor-rec'-tive	cor-ru-ga'tion	cor'-ymb
cor-rect'ly	cor'-ru-gator	cor-ym'-bose
cor-rec'-tor	cor'rug-meter	cory-phae'us
cor-reg'i-dor	cor'-rupt	cory-phée'
cor'-re-late	cor-rupt'er	cor-y'za
cor-re-la'tion	cor-rupti-bil'ity	co-se'cant
cor-rel'a-tive	cor-rupt'-ible	co-seis'mal
cor-re-spond'	cor-rup'-tion	co-seis'mic
cor-re-spon'-dence	cor-rup'-tive	co-sig'na-tory
cor-re-spon'-dent	cor'-sac	co'-sine
cor-re-spond'-ing	cor'-sair	cos-met'ic
cor-re-spon'-sive	cors'e-let	cos'-mic
cor'-ri-dor	cor'-set	cos'-mi-cally
cor'-rie	cor'-setry	cos'-min
corri-gen'-dum	cor'-site	cos'-mism
cor'ri-gible	cors'-let	cos'-mist
cor-rob'-or-ant	cor'-tège	cosmo-gon'ic
cor-rob'-or-ate	cor'-tex	cos-mog'-on-ist
cor-rob-or-a'tion	cor'-ti-cal	cos-mog'ony
cor-rob'-or-at- ive	cor'-ti-cate	cos-mog'ra-pher
	cor'-ti-cated	cos-mog'ra-phy
	cor-ti-ca'tion	cos'-moid
	cor-tic'o-lous	cos-mo-log'i-cal
	cor'-tin	cos-mol'ogy
		cosmo-pol'i-tan

cos-mop'-olite
cosmo-ra'ma
cos'-mos
cos'-mo-tron
cos'-set
cos'-tal
cos-tal'gia
cos'-tard
cos'-tate
cos-tean'
cos-tean'-ing
cos'-ter
cos'-ter-monger
cost'-ing
cos'-tive
cost'-li-ness
cost'-mary
cos'-trel
cos'-tume
cos'-tumer
cos-tu'mier
co-tan'-gent
co-tan-gen'-tial
co-ten'-ancy
co-ter'mi-nous
co-thur'-nus
co-ti'dal
co-til'lion
co-toneas'-ter
cot'-tage
cot'-tager
cot'-tar
cot'-ter
cot'-tier
cot'-ton
cot'-ton-seed
cot'-ton-tail
cot'-ton-wool

coty-le'don
coty-le'don-ary
coty-le'don-ous
cot'y-loid
cou'-cal
couch'-ant
couch'-grass
couch'-ing
cou'-gar
coug'-nar
cou-liss'e
cou-lomb'
coul'-ter
cou'-marin
cou'-mar-one
coun'-cil
coun'-cil-lor
coun'-cil-man
coun'-sel
coun'-sel-lor
coun'-ter
coun'ter-act
coun'ter-at-tack'
coun'ter-bal-ance
coun'ter-blast
coun'ter-charge
coun'ter-charm
coun'ter-check
coun'ter-claim
coun'ter-clock'-
    wise
coun'ter-es'pion-
    age
coun'ter-feit
coun'ter-feiter
coun'ter-foil
coun'ter-fort

coun'ter-ir'-ri-
    tant
coun'ter-mand
coun'ter-march
coun'ter-mark
coun'ter-mine
coun'ter-mure
coun'ter-pane
coun'ter-part
coun'ter-plea
coun'ter-plot
coun'ter-point
coun'ter-poise
coun'ter-rev-ol-
    u'tion
coun'ter-shaft
coun'ter-sign
coun'ter-sink
coun'ter-stroke
coun'ter-vail
coun'ter-weight
count'-ess
count'-ing-house
count'-less
coun-tri-fied
coun'try-man
coun'try-side
coun'try-wide
coun'try-woman
count'-ship
coup'-ler
coup'-let
coup'-ling
cou'-pon
cour'-age
cour-a'geous
cour-ant'
cour'-ier

cours'-ing
cour'-teous
court'-esan
cour'-tesy
court'-house
court'-ier
court'-li-ness
court'-mar'-tial
court'-room
court'-ship
court'-yard
co-va'lency
co-va'ri-ance
co-va'ri-ant
cov'-en-anter
cov'-en-antor
cov'er-age
cov'er-ing
cov'er-let
cov'-ert
cov'er-ture
cov'et-ous
cov'et-ous-ness
cow'-ard
cow'-ard-ice
cow'-ardly
cow'-bane
cow'-bell
cow'-bird
cow'-boy
cow'-catcher
cow'-grass
cow'-herd
cow'-hide
cow'-lick
cow'-ling
cow'-path
cow'-pox
cow'-shed
cow'-slip
cox-al'gia
cox'-comb
cox-comb'i-cal
cox'-combry
coy'-ness
coz'en-age
crab-ap'ple
crab'-bed
crab'-bing
crab'-grass
crack'-brained
crack'-ing
crack'-ling
crack'-nel
cracks'-man
craft'-ily
craf'ti-ness
crafts'-man
crafts'-man-ship
crag'gi-ness
crags'-man
cram'-mer
cram'-ming
cram'-pon
cran'-berry
crani-ol'ogy
crani-om'eter
crani-om'etry
crani-os'copy
crani-ot'omy
crank'-case
crank'i-ness
cran'-nied
crap'u-lent
crap'u-lous
crass'i-tude
crassu-la'ceous
crater'i-form
cra-vat'
crav'-ing
craw'-fish
crawl'-ing
cray'-fish
cra'z-ily
cra'zi-ness
cra'z-ing
cream'-ery
creas'-ing
cre-a'te
cre'-atine
cre-a'ting
cre-a'tion
cre-a'tion-ism
cre-a'tion-ist
cre-a'tive
cre-a'tively
cre-a'tor
crea'-tural
crea'-ture
cre'-dal
cre'-dence
cre-den'-tial
credi-bil'ity
cred'-ible
cred'-ibly
cred'i-table
cred'i-tor
cred-u'lity
cred'u-lous
creep-ing
crem-a'te
crem-a'tion
crema-to'rium
crem'a-tory

cre'mo-carp
cren'-ate
cren-a'tion
cren'a-tive
cren'-el-late
cren'-el-lated
cren-ell'e
cren'u-lated
crenu-la'tion
cre'o-sote
crep'i-tant
crep'i-tate
crepi-ta'tion
crep'i-tus
crep-us'cu-lar
crep-us'cle
cres'-cent
cres'-cive
cre'-sol
crest'-fallen
cre-syl'ic
cre-ta'ceous
cre'-tify
cre-ti-fi-ca'tion
cret'-in-ism
cret'-in-ous
cret'-onne
crev-ass'e
crev'-ice
crib'-bage
crib'-bing
crib'ri-form
crib'-rose
crick'-eter
cri'-coid
crim'i-nal
crimi-nal'ity
crim'i-nate

crimi-na'tion
crim'i-nat-ive
crim'i-nat-ory
crimi-no-log'i-cal
crimi-nol'-ogist
crimi-nol'ogy
crim'-son
crin'-an-ite
cring'-ing
cri'-nite
crin'-oid
crin'-ol-ine
crip'-pling
cris'-pate
cris-pa'tion
crisp'-ing
crisp'-ness
cris'-tate
cris-to'ba-lite
cri-te'ria
cri-te'rion
crit'i-cal
crit'i-cally
crit'i-cas-ter
crit'i-cise
crit'i-cis-ing
crit'i-cism
criz'-zling
cro'-ceate
cro'chet-ing
cro-cid'o-lite
crock'-ery
croc'o-dile
croco-dil'ian
croc'o-dil-ing
cro'-co-ite
cro'-cus
crom'-lech

crook'-edly
crook'-ed-ness
crop'-per
crop'-ping
cross'-bar
cross-bear'-ings
cross'-bell
cross'-bill
cross'-bones
cross'-bow
cross'-bow-man
cross'-bred
cross'-breed
cross'-cut
cross-exam-in-a-'tion
cross-exam'-ine
cross'-hair
cross'-head-ing
cross'-ing
cross'-let
cross'-piece
cross-pol'-li-nate
cross-pol-li-na'tion
cross-pur'-poses
cross-ques'-tion
cross-ref'-er-ence
cross'-road
cross-sec'-tion
cross'-tree
cross'-walk
cross'-ways
cross'-wise
cross'-word
crotch'-ety
cro'-ton

84

cro-ton-al'de-
        hyde
cro-ton'ic
croup'-ier
croup'-ous
crow'-bar
crow'-berry
crow'-foot
crow'-ing
crow'n-post
crow'-quill
cru'-cial
cru'-cian
cru'-ciate
cru'-cible
cru'-ci-fer
cru-cif'er-ous
cru'-ci-fied
cru'-ci-fix
cru-ci-fix'ion
cru'-ci-form
cru'-cify
cru'd-ity
cruis'-ing
crul'-ler
crum'-bling
crum'-bly
crum'-pet
crump'-ling
crunch'-ing
crup'-per
cru-sa'de
cru-sa'der
cru-sa'd-ing
crus-ta'cean
crus-ta'ceous
crus'ti-ness
crus'-tose

crutch'-ing
cry'-ing
cry'o-gen
cryo-gen'-ics
cry-og'eny
cry'o-lite
cry-om'eter
cry-oph'-orus
cryo-plank'-ton
cry'o-scope
cry'o-scop'ic
cry'o-stat
cry'o-tron
cryp'-tic
cryp'-to-gam
cryp'to-crys-tal-
        line
cryp-tog'-amous
cryp-tog'amy
cryp'-to-gram
cr0p'-to-graph
cryp-tog'ra-pher
crypto-graph'ic
cryp-tog'ra-phy
cryp-tol'ogy
cryp'-to-mere
crypto-mer'-ism
cryp-tom'eter
cryp'-tonym
cryp'to-phyte
crypto-zo'ic
crys'-tal
crys'-tal-line
crys-tal-lin'ity
crys-tal-lis-
      a'tion
crys'-tal-lise
crys'-tal-lite

cryst'-allo-gram
crys-tal-log'ra-
        pher
crys-tal-log'ra-
        phy
crys'-tal-loid
crys'-tal-lose
crys'-to-dyne
crys-to'leum
cten-id'ium
cten'-oid
cu'-bage
cu'ba-ture
cub'-bing
cub'by-hole
cu'-beb
cu'-bic
cu'bi-cal
cu'bi-cally
cu'-bicle
cu-bic'u-lum
cu'bi-form
cu'-bism
cu'-bist
cu'-bit
cu'bi-tal
cu'bi-tus
cu'-boid
cu-boid'al
cuck'-old
cu'-cul-late
cu'-cum-ber
cu-cur'-bit
cu-curbi-ta'ceous
cud'-bear
cud'-dling
cud'gel-ler
cud'-weed

85

CUIRASS

cuir-ass'
cuir-ass-ier'
cu'-let
cu'-lex
cul'i-nary
cul'-let
cull'-ing
cul'-men
cul'-mi-cole
cul-mif'er-ous
cul'-mi-nant
cul'-mi-nate
cul-mi-na'tion
cul-pa-bil'ity
culp'-able
cul'-prit
cul'-ti-vable
cul'-ti-vate
cul'-ti-vated
cul-ti-va'tion
cul'-ti-vator
cul'-trate
cul'-tri-form
cul'-tural
cul'-tured
cul'-ver
cul'-verin
cul'-vert
cum'-ber
cum'-ber-some
cum'-brous
cum'-mer-bund
cum'-quat
cu'mu-late
cumu-la'tion
cu'mu-lat-ive
cu'mu-lus
86

cunc-ta'tion
cu'-neal
cu'-neate
cune'i-form
cun'-ning
cup'-bearer
cup'-cake
cu'-pel
cu-pel-la'tion
cup'-ful
cup'-like
cu'-pola
cup'-ping
cu'-preous
cu'-pric
cu-prif'er-ous
cu'-prite
cupro-cy'an-ide
cu'-prous
cu'-pu-lar
cu'-pu-late
cu'-pule
cura-bil'ity
cu'ra-coa
cu'ra-çao
cu-ra're
cu'ra-rine
cu'ra-rise
cu'ra-tive
cu-ra'tor
curb'-ing
curb'-stone
cur-cu'lio
cur-cu'ma
curd'-ling

cu're-less
cu-rett'e
cur'-few
curi-o'sa
curi-os'ity
cu'ri-ous
cu'-rium
cur'-lew
cur'li-cue
curl'i-ness
curl'-ing
cur-mud'geon
cur'-rant
cur'-rency
cur'-rent
cur'-rently
cur'-ricle
cur-ric'u-lar
cur-ric'u-lum
cur'-ried
cur'-rier
cur'-ri-ery
cur'-rish
cur'ry-comb
cur'ry-ing
curs'-ing
cur'-sitor
cur'-sive
cur'-sively
cur'-sor
cur-so'rial
cur'-sori-ness
cur'-sory
cur'-sus
cur-tail'
cur-tail'-ment
cur'-tain
cur'-tal

cur-ta′na
curt′i-lage
cu′-rule
cur-va′ceous
cur′-va-ture
cur-vet′
cur-vet′-ted
cur-vet′-ting
curvi-cos′-tate
curvi-fo′li-ate
curvi-lin′ear
curv′-ing
cus′-pate
cus′-pid
cus′-pi-dal
cus′-pi-date
cus′-pi-dor
cuss′-ed-ness
cus′-tard
cus′tard-apple
cus-to′d-ial
cus-to′d-ian
cus′-tody
cus′-tom
cus′-tom-able
cus′-tom-arily
cus′-tom-ary
cus′-tomer
cus′-tom-house
cus′-tom=made
cus′-toms
cus′-tu-mal
cu-ta′neous
cut′-away
cu-tic′u-lar
cu-ticu-lar-is-
       a′tion
cu′-tin

cu-tin-is-a′tion
cu′-tis
cut′-lass
cut′-ler
cut′-lery
cut′-let
cut′-off
cut′-out
cut′-purse
cut′-ter
cut′-ting
cut′-tingly
cut′tle-fish
cut′-tling
cut′-water
cut′-worm
cy-an′a-mide
cy-an′ic
cy-ani-da′tion
cy′-an-ide
cy′-an-id-ing
cy′-an-ine
cy-an′o-gen
cy-an-om′eter
cy-an-om′etry
cy-an-o′sis
cy-an-ot′ic
cy-an-u′ric
cy-ath′i-form
cy-ber-net′-ics
cy-ca-da′ceous
cyc′la-men
cy′c-lic
cy′c-li-cal
cy′c-ling
cy′c-list
cy-cli′tis
cy′clo-gram

cy′clo-graph
cy′c-loid
cyc-loid′al
cyc-lom′eter
cy′c-lone
cyc-lon′ic
cyclo-pe′an
cyclo-pe′dia
cyclo-ple′gia
cyclo-ra′ma
cy-clo′sis
cy-clos′to-mous
cy′clo-style
cyclo-thy′mia
cy′clo-tron
cyg′-net
cyl′-in-der
cyl-in′-dri-cal
cyl′-in-droid
cyl-in′do-scope
cy′-mar-ose
cy-ma′tium
cym′-bal
cym′-balo
cym′-bi-form
cymbo-cephal′ic
cym′o-graph
cy′-mose
cy-mot′ri-chous
cyn′i-cal
cyn′i-cism
cyno-ceph′a-lus
cy-nop′o-dous
cy′no-sure
cyper-a′ceous
cy′-pher
cy′-press
cyp′ri-noid

87

CYPRIPEDIUM

cypri-pe'dium
cys'-tic
cys'-tine
cys-ti'tis
cys'-toid
cys-to'ma
cys-tot'omy
cy'-tase
cy-tas'-ter
cyt'i-sine
cy'-tode
cyto-gen'-esis
cyto-gen-et'ics
cy-tog'en-ous
cyto-kin-e'sis
cy-tol'ogy
cy-tol'y-sis
cyto-mor-pho'sis
cy'to-plasm
cyto-plas'-mic
cyto-tax-on'omy
cyto-zo'ic
czar'-evitch
czar-ev'na
czar-i'na
czar'-ism

D

dab'-ber
dab'-bing
dab'-bling
dab'-chick
dab'-ster
dachs'-hund
da-coit'
da-coit'y
88

dac'-tyl
dac'-ty-lar
dac-tyl'ic
dac'-ty-line
dac-tyli-og'ly-
      phy
dac-tyli-og'ra-
      phy
dac-tyl-i'tis
dac-tyl'o-gram
dac-tyl-og'ra-phy
dac'-ty-loid
dac-tyl-ol'ogy
dad'-ding
dae'-dal
dae-da'leous
dae-da'lian
dae'-mon
dae-mon'ic
daf'-fodil
dag'-ger
dag'-ging
da-guer'reo-type
dail'-ies
dain'-ties
dain'-tily
dain'ti-ness
dair'-ies
dair'y-ing
dair'y-maid
dair'y-man
dais'-ies
dais'-ite
da'les-man
dal'-li-ance
dal'-lied
dal'ly-ing
dal-mat'ic

dal'ton-ism
dam'-age
dam'-ag-ing
dam'-as-cene
dam'-ask
dam'-mar
dam'-nable
dam-na'tion
dam'-na-tory
dam-ni-fi-ca'tion
dam'-nify
dam'-ning (a.)
damn'-ing (n.)
dam'-ningly
dam'o-sel
damp'-ener
damp'-ing
damp'-ish
damp-proof'-ing
dam'-sel
dam'-son
danc'-ing
dan'-delion
dan'-der
dan'-di-fied
dan'-dify
dan'-druff
dan'-dy-ism
da'ne-wort
da'nger-ous
da'nger-ously
dank'-ness
dap'-per
da're-devil
dark'-en-ing
dark'-ling
dark'-ness
dark'-room

dark'-some
dar'-ling
dar'-nel
dash'-board
dash'-ing
das'-tard
das'-tard-li-ness
das'-tardly
dasy-phil'-lous
das'y-ure
da'te-less
dat'o-lite
daub'-ery
daub'-ing
daub'-ster
daugh'-ter
daugh'-ter-in-law
daunt'-less
daunt'-lessly
dav'-en-port
dawd'-ler
dawd'-ling
dawn'-ing
day'-book
day'-break
day'-dream
day'-light
day'-mark
day'-spring
day'-star
day'-time
daz'-zling
daz'-zlingly
dea'-con
dea'-con-ate
dea'-con-ess
dea'-conry
de-acti-va'tion

dead'-en-ing
dead'-eye
dead'-fall
dead'-head
dead'-light
dead'-line
dead'-li-ness
dead'-lock
dead'-ness
dead'-nettle
dead-reck'-on-ing
dead'-wood
deaf'-en-ing
deaf'-en-ingly
deaf'-ness
de-alb'-ate
deal'-ing
dean'-ery
dear'-ness
death'-bed
death'-blow
death'-deal-ing
death'-less
death'-like
deaths'-head
death-war'-rant
death'-watch
de-bac'le
de-bar'
de-bark-a'tion
de-bar'-ment
de-bar'-ring
de-ba'se
de-ba'sed
de-ba'se-ment
de-ba's-ing
de-ba's-table
de-ba'te

de-ba'ter
de-ba't-ing
de-bauch'
de-bauch'ee
de-bauch'er
de-bauch'-ery
de-ben'-ture
de-bil'i-tate
de-bil'i-tated
de-bili-ta'tion
de-bil'ity
deb-onair'
de-bouch'
de-bouch'-ment
de-bouch'ure
de-bunk'
deb'u-tant
dec'-ade
dec'a-dence
dec'a-dent
dec'a-gon
dec'a-gram
deca-he'dron
deca-la'ge
de-cal-ci-fi-
　ca'tion
de-cal'-ci-fied
de-cal'-cify
de-calco-ma'nia
de-cal-esc'ence
dec'a-litre
dec'a-logue
dec-am'er-ous
dec'a-metre
de-camp'
de-camp'-ment
de-ca'nal
dec'a-nal

89

de-ca'ni
de-cant'
de-can-ta'tion
de-can'ter
de-cap'i-tate
de-capi-ta'tion
dec'a-pod
de-cap-su-la'tion
de-car-bon-is-
    a'tion
de-car'-bon-ise
de-car-bu-ris-
    a'tion
de-car'-bu-rise
dec'-are
dec'a-stere
dec'a-style
deca-syl-lab'ic
dec'a-syl-lable
de-cay'
de-cay'ed
de-cay'-ing
de-ceas'e
de-ceas'ed
de-ce'd-ent
de-ceit'
de-ceit'-ful
de-ceit'-ful-ness
de-ceiv'e
de-ceiv'er
de-ceiv'-ingly
de-cel'er-ate
de-cel-er-a'tion
decem'-vir
decem'-vir-ate
de-cen'-nary
decen'-niad
decen'-nial

decen'-ni-ally
decen'-nium
de'-cent
de'-cently
de-cen-tra-lis-
    a'tion
de-cen'-tra-lise
de-cen'tre
de-cep'-tion
de-cep'-tive
dech'-en-ite
dec'i-bel
de-ci'de
de-ci'ded
de-ci'd-edly
de-cid'ua
de-cid'u-ous
de-cid'u-ously
deci'-gramme
de'-cile
dec'i-litre
dec'i-mal
deci-mal-is-
    a'tion
dec'i-mal-ise
dec'i-mate
deci-ma'tion
dec'i-mator
dec'i-metre
de-ci'pher
de-ci'pher-able
de-cis'ion
de-ci's-ive
de-ci's-ively
dec'i-stere
de-claim'
de-claim'-ant
dec-la-ma'tion

de-clam'a-tory
de-cla'r-able
dec-lar-a'tion
de-clar'a-tive
de-clar'-ator
de-clar'a-tory
de-cla're
de-class'ed
de-class'-ify
de-clen'-sion
de-cli'n-able
dec-li-na'tion
de-cli'na-tory
de-cli'ne
de-cli'n-ing
dec-li-nom'eter
de-cliv'i-tous
de-cliv'-ity
de-cliv'-ous
de-coct'
de-coc'-tion
de-co'de
de-co'd-ing
de-col'-late
de-col-la'tion
de-col'or-ant
de-col'or-ate
de-col'or-iser
de-col'our-ise
de-com-po's-able
de-com'-posite
de-compo-sit'ion
de-com-pound'
de-com-press'
de-com-pres'sion
de-con'-secrate
de-con-tam'i-
    nate

de-con-tami-
    na'tion
de-con-trol'
dec'-or-ate
dec-or-a'tion
dec'-or-at-ive
dec'-or-ator
de-cor'ti-cate
de-corti-ca'tion
dec'-or-ous
de-co'rum
de-coup'-ling
de-coy'
de-coy'ed
de-coy'-ing
de'-crease (n.)
de-creas'e (v.)
de-cree'
de-cree'-ing
dec'-rement
de-crem'-eter
de-crep'it
de-crep'i-tate
de-crepi-ta'tion
de-crep'i-tude
de-cresc'ence
de-cresc'ent
de-cre'tal
de-cre'tist
de-cre't-ively
de-cre't-ory
de-cri'al
de-cried'
de-cri'er
de-cry'
dec'u-man
de-cum'-bent
de-cum'-bi-ture

dec'-uple
dec-u'rion
de-cur'-rent
dec'-ury
de-cuss'-ate
de-cuss-a'tion
de-den'-dum
ded'i-catee'
dedi-catee'
ded'i-cat-ive
ded'i-cator
ded'i-cat-ory
de-du'ce
de-du'ced
de-du'c-ing
de-duct'
de-duct'-ible
de-duc'-tion
de-duct'-ive
deem'-ster
deer'-hound
deer'-meat
deer'-skin
deer-stalk'er
de-fa'ce
de-fa'ced
de-fa'ce-ment
de-fa'c-ing
de'-fal-cate
de-fal-ca'tion
def'-al-cator
defa-ma'tion
de-fam'a-tory
de-fa'me
de-fat'i-gable
de-fault'

de-fault'er
de-feas'-ance
de-feas'-ible
de-feat'
de-feat'ed
de-feat'-ism
de-feat'-ist
de-feat'ure
def'-ecate
def-eca'tion
de'-fect (n.)
de-fect' (v.)
de-fec'ted
de-fec'-tion
de-fec'-tive
de-fen'ce
de-fenc'e-less
de-fend'
de-fend'-ant
de-fend'er
de-fen-es-
    tra'tion
de-fens'-ible
de-fensi-bil'ity
de-fens'-ive
de-fer'
def'-er-ence
def'-er-ent
def-er-en'-tial
de-fer'-ment
de-fer'-rable
de-ferr'ed
de-fer'-ring
de-fer-vesc'ence
de-fi'ance
de-fi'ant
de-fi'antly
de-fibri-na'tion

DEFICIENCY

de-fic'iency
de-fic'ient
def'i-cit
defi-la'de
de-fi'le
de-fi'le-ment
de-fi'l-ing
de-fi'n-able
de-fi'ne
de-fi'ned
de-fi'n-ing
def'i-nite
def'i-nitely
defi-nit'ion
de-fin'i-tive
de-fin'i-tude
def'-la-grate
def'-la-grat-ing
def-la-gra'tion
def'-la-grator
de-fla'te
de-fla'tion
de-fla'tion-ary
de-flect'
de-flec'-tion
de-flec'-tive
de-flec-tom'eter
de-flec'-tor
de-flex'ed
de-flex'-ure
de-flor-a'tion
de-flow'er
de-flu'ent
de-fo'li-ate
de-foli-a'tion
de-fo'rci-ant
de-for'-est
de-for-es-ta'tion
92

de-form'
de-form'-able
de-for-ma'tion
de-form'ed
de-form'-ity
de-fraud'
de-fraud-a'tion
de-fraud'ed
de-fray'
de-fray'al
de-fray'ed
de-fray'-ing
de-fray'-ment
de-frost'
de-frost'er
deft'-ness
de-funct'
de'fy'-ing
de-gas'-sing
de-gauss'e
de-gauss'-ing
de-gen'er-acy
de-gen'er-ate
de-gener-a'tion
de-gen'er-at-ive
de-ger'min-ator
de-glu'tin-ate
de-glu-tit'ion
degra-da'tion
de-gra'de
de-gra'ded
de-gra'd-ing
de-gree'
de-gres'sion
de-gress'-ive
de-gus-ta'tion
de-hisc'e
de-hisc'ence

de-hisc'ent
de-hor-ta'tion
de-hor'ta-tive
de-hu'man-ise
de-humid'i-fier
de-hy'dra'te
de-hy-dra'tion
de-hy'dro-gen-
        ase
de-hyp'-no-tise
de'-icide
deic'-tic
de-if'ic
de-ifi-ca'tion
de'-ified
de'-iform
de'-ify
de'-ism
de'-ist
de'-ities
de'-ity
de-jec'ted
de-ject'-edly
de-jec'-tion
de-lac-ta'tion
de-lain'e
de-lami-na'tion
de-la'tion
de-lay'
de-lay'-ing
de-lec'-table
de-lec-ta'tion
del'-egacy
del'-egate
del-ega'tion
de'-leing
de-le'te
de-le'ted

del-cte'ri-ous
de-le'tion
delft'-ware
de-lib'-er-ate
de-lib-er-a'tion
de-lib'-er-at-ive
del'-i-cacies
del'i-cacy
del'i-cate
del'i-cately
deli-ca tess'en
de-lic'ious
de-lict'
de-li'ght
de-li'ghted
de-li'ght-ful
de-lim'it
de-limi-ta'tion
de-lin'-eate
de-lin-ea'tion
de-lin'-quency
de-lin'-quent
deli-quesc'e
deli-quesc'ence
deli-quesc'ent
de-lir'i-ous
de-lir'ium
deli-tesc'ent
de-liv'er
de-liv'-er-able
de-liv'-er-ance
de-liv'-erer
de-liv'-er-ies
de-liv'-ery
de-local-is-a'tion
de-lo'cal-ise
del'-phi-nine
del-phin'-ium

del-ta'ic
del'-toid
de-lu'de
dc-lu'ded
de-lu'ding
del'-uge
del'-uged
de-lu'sion
de-lu's-ive
de-lu's-ory
delv'-ing
de-mag-net-is-
    a'tion
de-mag'-net-ise
dem'a-gogic
dema-gog'i-cal
dem'a-gogue
dem'a-goguery
dem'a-gogy
de-mand'
de-mand'-able
de-mand'-ant
de-man'ded
de'-mar-cate
de-mar-ca'tion
de-mate'ri-al-ise
de-mean'
de-mean'-our
de-ment'
de-men'ted
de-men'ti
de-men'tia
de-mer'it
de-meri-to'ri-ous
de-mer'-sal
de-me'sne
dem'i-bas-tion
dem'i-god

dem'i-john
de-mili-tar-is-
    a'tion
dc-mil'i-tar-ise
dem'i-lune
dem'i-monde
demi-rep
de-mi's-able
de-mi'se
de-mis'sion
dc-mit'
dem'i-tasse
demi-ur'gic
de-mob-il-is-
    a'tion
de-mob'-il-ise
democ'-racy
dem'o-crat
demo-crat'ic
democ'-ra-tise
de-modu-la'tion
de-mod'u-lator
de-mog'ra-pher
demo-graph'ic
de-mog'ra-phy
de-mol'-ish
demo-lit'ion
de'-mon
de-monet-is-
    a'tion
de-mon'et-ise
de-mo'niac
de-mo'ni-acal
de-mon'ic
de'-mon-ise
de'-mon-ism
de-mon-ol'a-try
de-mon-ol'-ogist

93

de-mon-ol'ogy
de-mon'-strable
de-mon'-strably
dem'-on-strate
dem'-on-strat-ing
dem-on-stra'tion
de-mon'-stra-tive
dem'-on-strator
de-moral-is-
     a'tion
de-mor'al-ise
de-mor'al-is-ing
de'-mos
de-mo'te
de-mo'ted
de-mot'ic
de-mo'tion
de-mul'-cent
de-mul-si-fi-
     ca'tion
de-mur'
de-mu're
de-mu'rely
de-mur'-rage
de-mur'-ral
de-mur'-rant
de-murr'ed
de-mur'-rer
de-mur'-ring
de-na'rius
de'-nary
de-nat'ion-al-ise
de-nat'u-ral-ise
de-na'tur-ant
de-na'ture
de-na'tured
den'-dri-form
den'-drite

den-drit'ic
den'-dro-graph
den'-droid
den'-dro-lite
den-drol'-ogist
den-drol'-ogy
den-ega'tion
de-ni'able
de-ni'al
de-nied'
de-ni'er
den'-ier
de-nies'
den'i-grate
deni-gra'tion
den'i-grator
den'i-zen
de-nom'i-nate
de-nomi-na'tion
de-nomi-na'tional
de-nomi-na'tion-
     al-ism
de-nom'i-nat-ive
de-nom'i-nator
de-no-ta'tion
de-no't-ative
de-no'te
de-no'te-ment
de-no't-ing
de-nounc'e
de-nounc'ed
de-nounc'e-ment
de-nounc'-ing
den-sim'eter
den-si-tom'eter
den'-sity
den'-tal
den'-tary

den'-tate
den-ta'tion
den-tell'e
den'-ticle
den-tic'u-lar
den-tic'u-late
den-ticu-la'tion
den'-ti-form
den'-ti-frice
den-tig'er-ous
den'-til
den'-ti-lated
den'-tine
den'-tist
den'-tis-try
den-tit'ion
den'-toid
den'-ture
de-nu'd-ate
de-nu-da'tion
de-nu'de
de-nu'mer-ant
de-nu'mer-ator
de-nun'ci-ate
de-nunci-a'tion
de-nun'ci-at-ive
de-nun'ci-at-ory
deny'-ing
de-ob'stru-ent
de-o'dand
deo-dar'
de-o'dor-ant
de-odor-is-a'tion
de-o'dor-ise
de-o'dor-iser
de-on-tol'ogy
de-oxi-da'tion
de-ox'i-dise

94

de-ox'y-gen-ate
de-part'
de-par'ted
de-part'-ment
de-part-men'-tal
de-part-men'-
    tal-ism
de-par'-ture
de-pas'-ture
de-paup'er-ise
de-pend'
de-pend-abil'ity
de-pend'-able
de-pend'-ant
de-pen'-dence
de-pen'-dency
de-pen'-dent
de-per-son-al-is-
    a'tion
de-per'-son-al-ise
de-phleg'ma-tor
de-pict'
de-pic'-tion
dep'i-late
de-pil'a-tory
de-plen'-ish
de-ple'te
de-ple'ted
de-ple'tion
de-ple'tive
de-plo'r-able
de-plor-a'tion
de-plo're
de-plo'red
de-plo'r-ing
de-ploy'
de-ploy'-ment
de-plu'me

de-polar-is-a'tion
de-po'lar-ise
de-po'lar-iscr
de-po'ne
de-po'nent
de-pop'u-late
de-popu-la'tion
de-port'
de-port-a'tion
de-port'ed
de-portee'
de-port'-ment
de-po'sal
de-po'se
de-po'sed
de-po's-ing
de-pos'it
de-pos'i-tary
de-pos'ited
de-po-sit'ion
de-pos'i-tor
de-pos'i-tory
dep-ra-va'tion
de-pra've
de-pra'ved
de-prav'ity
dep'-recate
dep'-recat-ing
dep-reca'tion
dep'-recat-ory
de-pre'ciable
de-pre'ciate
de-precia'tion
dep'-redate
dep-reda'tion
dep'-redator
dep'-redat-ory
de-press'

de-press'-ant
de-press'ed
de-press'-ible
de-press'-ing
de-pres'sion
de-press'-ive
de-press'or
de-pri'val
depri-va'tion
de-pri've
de-pri'ved
de-pri'v-ing
dep'u-rant
dep'u-rate
depu-ra'tion
de-pu'ra-tive
depu-ta'tion
de-pu'te
dep'u-ties
dep'u-tise
dep'u-ty
de-rac'i-nate
de-rail'
de-rail'-ment
de-ra'nge
de-ra'nge-ment
de-ra'ng-ing
de-ra'te
de-ra'tion
der'-el-ict
der-el-ic'tion
de-requi-sit'ion
de-ri'de
de-ri'd-ing
de-ris'-ible
de-ris'ion
de-ri's-ive
de-ri's-ively

de-ri'sory
deri-va'tion
de-riv'a-tive
de-ri've
de-ri'ved
de-riv'ing
der'-mal
der-ma-ti'tis
der-mat'o-gen
der-ma-to-
        graph'ia
der'-ma-toid
der-ma-tol'-ogist
der-ma-tol'ogy
der-mat'o-phyte
der-ma-top'sy
der-ma-to'sis
der'-mic
der'-mis
der'o-gate
dero-ga'tion
de-rog'a-torily
de-rog'a-tory
der'-rick
der'-rin-ger
der'-ris
der'-trum
der'-vish
de-satu-ra'tion
des'-cant
de-scend'
de-scend'-ant
de-scend'ed
de-scend'-ent
de-scend'er
de-scend'-ible
de-scent'
de-scri'b-able

de-scri'be
de-scri'bed
des-cried'
de-scrip'-tion
de-scrip'-tive
des-cry'
des-cry'-ing
des'-ecrate
des-ecra'tion
des'-ecrator
de-seg'-re-gate
de-seg-re-ga'tion
de-sensi-tis-
        a'tion
de-sen'-si-tise
des'-ert (n.)
de-sert' (v.)
de-sert'er
de-ser'-tion
de-serv'e
de-serv'ed
de-serv'-edly
de-serv'-ing
de-sex'-ual-ise
des'-ic-cate
des-ic-ca'tion
des'-ic-cat-ive
des'-ic-cator
de-sider-a'ta
de-sid'er-ate
de-sid'er-at-ive
de-sider-a'tum
de-si'gn
de-si'gn-able
des'-ig-nate
des-ig-na'tion
des'-ig-nat-ive
des'-ig-nator

de-si'gn-edly
des'-ig-nee
de-si'gn-er
de-si'gn-ing
de-si'gn-less
de-sil'-ver-ise
de-sip'i-ence
de-sir-abil'ity
de-sir'-able
de-si're
de-si'r-ous
de-sist'
de-sist'-ance
des-mog'ra-phy
des-mol'ogy
des'o-late
deso-la'tion
de-sorp'-tion
de-spair'
de-spair'ed
de-spair'-ing
de-spatch'
des-per-a'do
des-per-a'does
des'-per-ate
des'-per-ately
des-per-a'tion
de-spic'able
de-spi's-able
de-spi'se
de-spi'sed
de-spi'ser
de-spi's-ing
de-spi'te
de-spi'te-ful
des-pit'eously
de-spoil'
de-spoil'er

de-spoil'-ing
de-spoli-a'tion
de-spond'
de-spon'-dence
de-spon'-dency
de-spon'-dent
de-spond'-ing
des'-pot
des-pot'ic
des-pot'i-cal
des'-pot-ism
des'-pu-mate
des-pu-ma'tion
des'-qua-mate
des-qua-ma'tion
des-sert'
des-ti-na'tion
des'-tine
des'-ti-nies
des'-tiny
des'-ti-tute
des-ti-tu'tion
de-stroy'
de-stroy'ed
de-stroy'er
de-struc-ti-
    bil'ity
de-struc'-tible
de-struc'-tion
de-struc'-tive
de-struc'-tive-
        ness
de-struc'-tor
de-sul'-phur-ise
des'-ul-tory
de-syn-ap'sis
de-tach'
de-tach'-able

de-tach'ed
de-tach'-ment
de-tail'
de-tail'er
de-tain'
de-tainee'
de-tain'er
de-tect'
de-tect'-able
de-tec'-ta-phone
de-tec'-tion
de-tec'-tive
de-tec'-tor
de-ten'-tion
de-ten'-tive
de-ter'
de-ter'ge
de-ter'-gent
de-te'rio-gate
de-te'rio-rate
de-terio-ra'tion
de-te'rio-rat-ive
de-ter'-ment
de-ter'-min-able
de-ter'-mi-nant
de-ter'-mi-nate
de-ter-mi-na'tion
de-ter'-mi-nat-ive
de-ter'-mine
de-ter'-mined
de-ter'-min-edly
de-ter'-min-ism
de-ter'-min-ist
de-terr'ed
de-ter'-rence
de-ter'-rent
de-ter'-ring
de-ter'-sive

de-test'
de-test'-able
de-tes-ta'tion
de-thro'ne
de-thro'ne-ment
det'i-nue
det'-on-ate
det'-on-at-ing
det-on-a'tion
det'-on-ator
de-tor'-sion
de-tor'-tion
de'-tour
de-tract'
de-trac'-tion
de-trac'-tor
de-trac'-tory
de-train'
det'-ri-ment
det-ri-men'-tal
de-tri'ted
de-trit'ion
de-tri'tus
de-tru'de
de-trun'-cate
de-tu-mesc'ence
deu-tera-no'pic
deu'-ter-ide
deu-te'rium
deu-ter-og'amy
deu'-teron
deu-ter-op'a-thy
de-val'u-ate
de-valu-a'tion
de-vap-or-a'tion
dev'-as-tate
dev'-as-tated
dev'-as-tat-ing

dev-as-ta'tion
dev'-as-tator
de-vel'op
de-vel'-oped
de-vel'-oper
de-vel'-op-ment
de-vel-op-men-
       tal
de-vest'
de'-vi-ate
de-vi-a'tion
de-vi-a'tion-ist
de-vi'ce
dev'il-fish
dev'il-ish
dev'il-ling
dev'il-ment
dev'-ilry
dev'-il-try
de'-vi-ous
de'-vi-ously
de-vi's-able
de-vi'se
de-vi'ser
de-visee'
de-vi'sor
de-vital-is-
     a'tion
de-vi'tal-ise
de-vitri-fi-
     ca'tion
de-vit'-rify
de-vo'cal-ise
de-void'
de-volu'te
de-vol-u'tion
de-vol've
de-vol've-ment
98

de-volv'-ing
de-vo'te
de-vo'ted
de-vo't-edly
dev'o-tee
de-vo'tion
de-vo'tional
de-vour'
de-vout'
de-vout'ly
dew'-berry
dew'-claw
dew'-drop
dew'i-ness
dew'-lap
dew'-point
dex'-ter
dex-ter'ity
dex'-ter-ous
dex'-ter-ously
dex'-tral
dex'-trin
dex-tro-car'-dia
dex-tror'se
dex'-trose
dex'-trous
di'a-base
dia-be'tes
dia-bet'ic
dia-beto-gen'ic
dia-bol'ic
dia-bol'i-cal
di-ab'o-lism
di-ab'o-list
di-ab'-olo
dia-caus'-tic
dia-cet'ic
di-ac'etyl

dia-chron'ic
di-ach'-ron-ism
di-ach'y-lon
di-ac'id
di'a-coele
di-ac'-onal
di-ac'-on-ate
dia-crit'ic
dia-crit'i-cal
di-ac-tin'ic
dia-del'-phous
di'a-dem
di-aer'-esis
di'a-glyph
di'-ag-nose
di-ag-no'sis
di-ag-nos'-tic
di-ag-nos-tic'ian
dia-gom'eter
di-ag'-onal
di-ag'-on-ally
di'a-gram
dia-gram-mat'ic
dia-gram-mat'i-
     cal
dia-gram'-ma-
     tise
di'a-graph
dia-kin-e'sis
di'a-lect
dia-lec'-tal
dia-lec'-tally
dia-lec'-tic
dia-lec'-ti-cal
dia-lec-tic'ian
dia-lec'-ti-cism
di'-al-lage
di'-alled

di'-al-ling
di-al'o-gism
di'a-logue
di-al'y-sis
dia-lyt'ic
dia-lyt'i-cally
di'a-lyse
din-mag-net'ic
dia-man-tif'er-
    ous
di-am'-eter
dia-met'ric
dia-met'ri-cal
di'a-mond
di-an'-drous
dia-no-et'ic
di-an'-thus
dia-pa'son
di-a-per
di-aph'a-nous
di'a-phone
dia-phor-e'sis
dia-phor-et'ic
di'a-phragm
dia-phrag-mat'ic
di-aphy-se'al
di-aph'y-sis
dia-phy-si'tis
di-ap'-sid
di-ar'-chal
di'-ar-chy
di'ar-ies
di'-ar-ise
di'-ar-ist
di-ar-rhoe'a
di-ar-rhoet'ic
di-ar-thro'sis
di-as'chi-sis

di'a-spore
di'-as-tase
dia-stas'ic
di-as'ta-sis
dia-stat'ic
di-as'ter
di-as'tole
di-as-tol'ic
dia-stroph'ic
di-as'tro-phism
di'a-style
dia-tess'-aron
dia-ther'-mal
dia-ther'-mancy
dia-ther'-ma-
    nous
dia-ther'-mic
dia-ther'my
di-ath'-esis
dia-thet'ic
di'a-tom
di-ato-ma'ceous
dia-tom'ic
di-at'om-ite
dia-ton'ic
di'a-tribe
di-at'ro-pism
di-az'o
di'a-zole
di-az'o-tise
di-ba'sic
dib'-ber
di-bran'chi-ate
di'-cast
di-cas'-tery
di-cas'-tic
di-cen'-trene
di-ceph'a-lous

di-cha'sium
di-chlor'-ide
di-chot'-omous
di-chot'-omy
di-chro'ic
di-chro-mat'ic
di-chro'ma-tism
di'-chro-mism
di-cli'n-ous
di-coty-le'don
di-coty-le'don-
    ous
di-cou'-marin
di-crot'ic
dic'-ta-phone
dic'-tate (n.)
dic-ta'te (v.)
dic-ta't-ing
dic-ta'tion
dic-ta'tor
dic-ta-to'rial
dic-ta'tor-ship
dic-ta'tor-y
dic'-tion
dic'-tion-ar-ies
dic'-tion-ary
dic'-tum
didac'-tic
didac'-ti-cism
di-dac'-tyl
di-dac'-tyl-ous
did'y-mate
didym'-ium
die'-cast
die'-cast-ing
die-cut'-ter
di-elec'-tric
die'-maker
di-en-ceph'a-lon

di'-esis
di'et-ary
diet-et'ic
diet-ic'ian
dif'-fer
dif'-fered
dif'-fer-ence
dif'-fer-ent
dif-fer-en'-tia
dif-fer-en'-tial
dif-fer-en'-tiate
dif-fer-en-
    tia'tion
dif'-fi-cult
dif'-fi-cult-ies
dif'-fi-culty
dif'-fi-dence
dif'-fi-dent
dif'-flu-ence
dif'-flu-ent
dif-fract'
dif-frac'-tion
dif-frac'-tive
dif-frangi-bil'ity
dif-fran'-gible
dif-fu'se
dif-fu'ser
dif-fusi-bil'ity
dif-fu's-ible
dif-fu'sion
dif-fu's-ive
dig'-amy
di-gas'-tric
di-gen'-esis
di-gen-et'ic
di'-gest' (n.)
di-gest' (v.)
di-gesti-bil'ity

di-gest'-ible
di-ges'-tion
di-ges'-tive
dig'-ger
dig'-ging
dig'i-tal
digi-tal'i-form
digi-ta'lin
digi-ta'lis
dig'i-tal-ise
dig'i-tate
digi-ta'tion
dig'i-ti-form
dig'i-ti-grade
di'-glot
dig'-ni-fied
dig'-ni-fiedly
dig'-nify
dig'-ni-fy-ing
dig'-ni-tar-ies
dig'-ni-tary
dig'-ni-ties
dig'-nity
di'-graph
di-gress'
di-gres'sion
di-gress'-ive
di-he'dral
di-lac'er-ate
dil-ap'i-date
dil-ap'i-dated
dil-api-da'tion
dil-at-abil'ity
di-la't-able
di-la't-ancy
di-la't-ant
di-la-ta'tion
di-la't-ative

di-la'te
di-la't-ing
di-la'tion
di-la't-ive
di-la-tom'eter
di-la-tom'etry
di-la'tor
dil'a-tori-ness
dil'a-tory
di-lem'ma
dilettant'-ism
dil'i-gence
dil'i-gent
dil'u-ent
di-lu'te
di-lu't-ing
di-lu'tion
di-lu'v-ial
di-men'-sion
dim'-er-ous
dim'-eter
di-mid'i-ate
dimin'-ish
dim-in'-ish-able
dim-in-u'tion
dim-in'u-tive
dim'-iss-ory
dim'-ity
dim'-mer
dim'-ming
dim'-ness
di-mor'-phic
di-mor'-phism
di-mor'-phous
dim'-pling
di-ner'ic
din'gi-ness
din'-ner

din'-ner-time
din'-ner-ware
di'-no-saur
dino-saur'-lan
di'-no-there
di-oc'esan
di'o-cese
di-oec'ious
di-op'-side
di-op'-sis
di-op'-rase
di-op'-ter
di-op-tom'eter
di-op'-tral
di-op'tre
di-op'-tric
dio-ram'a
di'-or-ite
di-ox'-ide
di-par'-tite
di'-phase
di-phe'nyl
diph-the'ria
diph-the'rial
diph-ther'ic
diph-ther-it'ic
diph'-ther-oid
diph'-thong
diph-thong'al
diph-thong-ise
di-ple'gia
diplo-coc'-cus
dip-lod'-ocus
dip'-lo-gen
dip'-loid
dip-lo'ma
dip-lo'-macy
dip'lo-mat

diplo-mat'ic
dip-lo'ma-tist
dip-lo'pia
dip-lo'p'ic
dip-lo'sis
dip'-noan
dip'-ody
di-po'lar
di-po'lar-ise
di'-pole
dip'-per
dip-so-ma'nia
dip-so-ma'niac
dip'-tera
dip'-teral
dip'-ter-ous
dip'-tych
di-rect'
di-rec'-tion
di-rec'-tional
di-rec'-tive
di-rec-tiv'ity
di-rect'ly
di-rect'-ness
di-rec'-tor
di-rec-to'rial
di-rec'-tor-ate
di-rec'-tory
di-rec'-trix
di're-ful
dir'i-gible
dir'i-ment
dir'ti-ness
dis-abil'ity
dis-a'ble
dis-a'bled
dis-a'bling
dis'-abuse

di-sac'-char-ide
dis-ac-cord'
dis-ac-cred'it
dis-ac-cus'tom
dis-ad-van'-tage
dis-ad-van-ta'geous
dis-af-fect'
dis-af-fect'ed
dis-af-fec'-tion
dis-af-firm'-ance
dis-af-fir-ma'tion
dis-agree'
dis-agree'-able
dis-agree'-ment
dis-al-low'
dis-al-low'-able
dis-al-low'-ance
dis-ap-pear'
dis-ap-pear'-ance
dis-ap-pear'ed
dis-ap-point'
dis-ap-point'ed
dis-ap-point'-ment
dis-ap-pro-ba'tion
dis-ap-prov'al
dis'-ap-prove
dis-ap-prov'-ing
dis-ap-prov'-ingly
dis-arm'
dis-ar'ma-ment
dis-ar-ra'nge
dis-ar-ra'nge-ment

dis-array'
dis-ar-tic'u-late
dis-ar-ticu-
     la'tion
dis-as-sem'ble
dis-as-sim'i-late
dis-as-simi-
     la'tion
dis-as-so'ciate
dis-as'-ter
dis-as'-trous
dis-as'-trously
dis-avow'
dis-avow'al
dis-band'
dis-bar'
dis-bar'-ment
dis-bar'-ring
dis-be-lief'
dis-be-liev'e
dis-be-liev'er
dis-bur'-den
dis-bur'se
dis-bur'se-ment
dis-burs'-ing
dis-cal'-ceate
dis-calc'ed
dis'-card (n.)
dis-card' (v.)
dis-car'-nate
dis-cern'
dis-cern'-ible
dis-cern'-ibly
dis-cern'-ing
dis-cern'-ment
dis-cerp'-tible
dis-cerp'-tion
dis'-charge (n.)
102

dis-char'ge (n. v.)
dis-ci'ple
dis'ci-plin-able
disci-pli'nal
dis'ci-plin-ant
disci-pli-na'rian
dis'ci-plin-ary
dis'ci-pline
dis'ci-pliner
dis-cis'sion
dis-claim'
dis-claim'er
dis-cla-ma'tion
dis-clo'se
dis-clo's-ure
dis-cob'-olus
dis-co-dac'-tyl-
     ous
dis-cog'ra-phy
dis'-coid
dis-coid'al
dis-col'our
dis-colour-a'tion
dis-col'our-ment
dis-com'fit
dis-com'fi-ture
dis-com'fort
dis-com'fort-able
dis-com-mo'de
dis-com-mod'ity
dis-com-po'se
dis-com-po'sure
dis-con-cert'
dis-con-cert'-
     ment
dis-con-form'-ity
dis-con-nect'
dis-con-nect'ed

dis-con-nec'-tion
dis-con'-so-late
dis-con'-so-
     lately
dis-con-tent'
dis-con-ten'ted
dis-con-tent'-
     ment
dis-con-tig'u-ous
dis-con-tin'u-
     ance
dis-con-tinu-
     a'tion
dis-con-tin'ue
dis-conti-nu'ity
dis-con-tin'u-ous
dis'-cord
dis-cor'-dance
dis-cor'-dant
dis'-count
dis-coun'-ten-
     ance
dis-cour'-age
dis-cour'-age-
     ment
dis-cour'-ager
dis-cour'-ag-ing
dis'-course (n.)
dis-cour'se (v.)
dis-cour'-teous
dis-cour'-tesy
dis-cov'er
dis-cov'erer
dis-cov'er-ies
dis-cov'ert
dis-cov'ery
dis-cred'it
dis-cred'i-table

dis-creet'
dis-creet'ly
dis-crep'-ancy
dis-crep'-ant
dis-cre'te
dis-cre'tion
dis-cre'tion-ary
dis-crim'i-nate
dis-crim'i-nat-ing
dis-crimi-na'tion
dis-crim'i-nat-ory
dis-crown'
dis-cul'-pate
dis-cur'-sion
dis-cur'-sive
dis-cur'-sively
dis'-cus
dis-cuss'
dis-cuss'ed
dis-cuss'-ible
dis-cus'sion
dis-dain'
dis-dain'-ful
dis-dain'-fully
dis-eas'e
dis-eas'ed
dis-eas'es
dis-em-bark'
dis-em-bar-ka'tion
dis-em-bar'rass
dis-em-bod'i-ment
dis-em-bod'y
dis-em-bo'gue
dis-em-bow'el
dis-em-broil'
dis-en-a'ble

dis-en-chant'
dis-en-chant'-ment
dis-en-cum'-ber
dis-en-dow'
dis-en-ga'ge
dis-en-ga'ge-ment
dis-en-no'ble
dis-en-ro'l
dis-en-tail'
dis-en-tang'le
dis-en-thral'
dis-en-ti'tle
dis-en-tomb'
dis-es-tab'-lish
dis-es-tab'-lish-ment
dis-es-teem'
dis-fa'vour
dis-figur-a'tion
dis-fig'ure
dis-fig'ure-ment
dis-fig'ur-ing
dis-fran'-chise
dis-fran'-chise-ment
dis-gor'ge
dis-gor'ger
dis-gra'ce
dis-gra'ce-ful
dis-grun'tled
dis-guis'e
dis-guis'-edly
dis-gust'
dis-gust'ed
dis-gust'-edly
dis-gust'-ing
dis-gust'-ingly

dis-har-mo'ni-ous
dis-har'-mony
dish'-cloth
dis-heart'en
dis-her'i-son
dish'-mop
dis-hon'est
dis-hon'esty
dis-hon'our
dis-hon'our-able
dish'-pan
dish'-towel
dish'-washer
dish'-water
dis-il-lu'sion
dis-il-lu'sion-ment
dis-in-cli-na'tion
dis-in-cli'ne
dis-in-cli'ned
dis-in-clo'se
dis-in-fect'
dis-in-fec'-tant
dis-in-fec'-tion
dis-in-fec'-tor
dis-in-fes-ta'tion
dis-in-gen'uous
dis-in-her'it
dis-in-her'i-tance
dis-in'-te-grate
dis-in-te-gra'tion
dis-in'-te-grator
dis-inter'
dis-in'-terest
dis-in'-terested

103

dis-in'-terested-
ness
dis-in-ter'-ment
dis-in-ter'red
dis-in-ter'-ring
dis-join'
dis-joint'
dis-join'ted
dis-junc'-tion
dis-junc'-tive
dis-junc'-tor
dis-li'ke
dis-limn'
dis'-lo-cate
dis-lo-ca'tion
dis-lodg'e
dis-lodg'e-ment
dis-loy'al
dis-loy'alty
dis'-mal
dis'-mally
dis-man'tle
dis-man'-tling
dis-mast'
dis-may'
dis-mem'-ber
dis-mem'-ber-
ment
dis-miss'
dis-miss'al
dis-mis'sion
dis-miss'-ive
dis-miss'-ory
dis-mount'
dis-obe'dience
dis-obe'dient
dis-obey'
104

dis-obey'ed
dis-obli'ge
dis-obli'g-ing
dis-obli'g-ingly
di-so'mic
dis-or'der
dis-or'dered
dis-or'der-li-ness
dis-or'derly
dis-or-gan-is-
a'tion
dis-or'-gan-ise
dis-o'rien-tate
dis-orien-ta'tion
dis-own'
dis-own'-ment
dis-par'-age
dis-par'-age-ment
dis-par'-ag-ingly
dis'-par-ate
dis-par'-ity
dis-part'
dis-pas'sion-ate
dis-patch'
dis-patch'er
dis-pel'
dis-pell'ed
dis-pel'-ling
dis-pens-abil'ity
dis-pens'-able
dis-pens'-ary
dis-pen-sa'tion
dis-pen'sa-tory
dis-pens'er
dis-per'-sal
dis-per'-sant
dis-pers'e
dis-pers'-ible

dis-per'-sion
dis-per'-sive
dis-pir'it
dis-pir'i-ted
dis-pla'ce
dis-pla'ced
dis-pla'ce-**ment**
dis-plant'
dis-play'
dis-pleas'e
dis-pleas'-ing
dis-pleas'ure
dis-port'
dis-po's-able
dis-po'sal
dis-po'se
dis-po'ser
dis-po-sit'ion
dis-pos-sess'
dis-prais'e
dis-proof'
dis-pro-po'rtion
dis-pro-
po'rtional
dis-pro-
po'rtion-ate
dis-prov'al
dis-prov'e
dis-puta-bil'ity
dis-pu't-able
dis'-pu-tant
dis-pu-ta'tion
dis-pu-ta'tious
dis-pu'ta-tive
dis-pu'te
dis-quali-fi-
ca'tion
dis-qual'i-fied

dis-qual'-ify
dis-qui'et
dis-qui'et-ude
dis-qui-sit'ion
dis-ra'te
dis-re-gard'
dis-rel'-ish
dis-re-pair'
dis-rep'u-table
dis-rep'u-tably
dis-re-pu'te
dis-re-spect'
dis-re-spect'-able
dis-re-spect'-ful
dis-ro'be
dis-rupt'
dis-rup'-tion
dis-rup'-tive
dis-sat-is-
     fac'tion
dis-sat'-is-fied
dis-sat'-isfy
dis-sect'
dis-sec'ted
dis-sec'-tion
dis-sec'-tor
dis-seis'e
dis-seisee'
dis-seis'in
dis-semb'-lance
dis-sem'ble
dis-semb'-ler
dis-sem'i-nate
dis-semi-na'tion
dis-sem'i-nator
dis-sen'-sion
dis-sent'
dis-sent'er

dis-sen'-tient
dis-sen'-tious
dis'-ser-tate
dis-ser-ta'tion
dis'-ser-tat-ive
dis-serv'-ice
dis-sev'er
dis-sev'er-ance
dis'-si-dence
dis'-si-dent
dis-sil'i-ency
dis-sil'i-ent
dis-sim'i-lar
dis-simi-lar'ity
dis-sim'i-late
dis-simi-la'tion
dis-sim'i-lat-ive
dis-sim-il'i-tude
dis-sim'u-late
dis-simu-la'tion
dis-sim'u-lator
dis'-si-pate
dis'-si-pated
dis-si-pa'tion
dis'-si-pat-ive
dis'-si-pator
dis-so'ciate
dis-socia'tion
dis-solu-bil'ity
dis-sol'-uble
dis'-sol-ute
dis-sol-u'tion
dis-solv'-able
dis-solv'e
dis-solv'-ent
dis-solv'-ing
dis'-son-ance
dis'-son-ancy

dis'-son-ant
dis-sua'de
dis-sua'sion
dis-sua's-ive
dis-sua's-ively
dis-sym-met'ri-
     cal
dis-sym'-metry
dis'-taff
dis-tain'
dis'-tal
dis'-tance
dis'-tant
dis'-tantly
dis-ta'ste
dis-ta'ste-ful
dis-tem'-per
dis-tend'
dis-ten'-sible
dis-ten'-sion
dis-ten'-tion
dis'-tich
dis'-ti-chous
dis-til'
dis-til'-lable
dis'-til-late
dis-til-la'tion
dis-til'-ler
dis'-til-lery
dis-til'-ling
dis-tinct'
dis-tinc'-tion
dis-tinc'-tive
dis-tinct'ly
dis-tinct'-ness
dis-tin'guish
dis-tin'guish-able
dis-tin'guish-ably

dis-tin'guished
di'-tone
dis-tort'
dis-tor'ted
dis-tor'-tion
dis-tor'-tive
dis-tract'
dis-tract'-ible
dis-trac'-tion
dis-trac'-tive
dis-train'
dis-train'er
dis-traint'
dis-traught'
dis-tress'
dis-tress'ed
dis-tress'-ful
dis-tress'-ing
dis-trib'u-tary
dis-trib'-ute
dis-tri-bu'tion
dis-trib'u-tism
dis-trib'u-tist
dis-trib'u-tive
dis-trib'u-tor
dis'-trict
dis-trust'
dis-trust'-ful
dis-turb'
dis-turb'ance
dis-turb'er
di-sul'-phide
dis-u'nion
dis-u-ni'te
dis-u'se
di'-theism
dis-thi-on'ic
dith'y-ramb

dithy-ram'-bic
dit-tan'-der
dit'-tany
dit-tog'ra-phy
di-ure'sis
di-uret'ic
di-ur'-nal
di'-va-gate
di-va-ga'tion
di-va'lent
di-van'
di-var'i-cate
di-vari-ca'tion
di-verg'e
di-ver'-gence
di-ver'-gency
di-ver'-gent
di-ver'-gently
di'-vers
div'-ers
di-vers'e
di-vers'ely
di-ver-si-fi-
    ca'tion
di-ver'-si-fied
di-ver'si-form
di-ver'-sify
di-ver'-sion
di-ver'-sity
di-vert'
di-vert'-ible
di-ver-tic'u-lar
di-ver-ticu-li'tis
di-ver-ticu-lo'sis
di-ver-tic'u-lum
di-vert'-ing
di-ver'-tive
di-vest'

di-ves'ti-ture
div-i'de
div-i'ded
div'i-dend
div-i'der
divi-na'tion
div-in'a-tory
div-i'ne
div-i'ncly
div-i'ner
div-in'ity
div-isi-bil'ity
divis'-ible
div-is'ion
div-is'ional
div-i'sive
div-i'sor
div-o'rce
div-orcee'
div-o'rce-ment
di-vul'-gate
di-vul'ge
di-vul'ge-ment
di-vulg'-ing
diz'-zily
diz'-zi-ness
dob'-bin
do'-cile
do'-cilely
do-cil'-ity
dock'-age
dock'-et-ing
dock'-hand
dock'-man
dock-mas-ter
dock'-side
dock'-yard

doc'-tor
doc'-toral
doc'-tor-ate
doc'-tri-naire
doc-tri'nal
doc-tri-na'rian
doc'-trine
doc'-trin-ism
doc'-trin-ist
doc'u-ment
docu-men'-tal
docu-men'-tary
docu-men-ta'tion
do-deca-he'dral
do-deca-he'dron
dod'-der
do-dec'a-gon
do-dec-ag'o-nal
dodg'-ing
doe'-skin
dog'-berry
dog'-bite
dog'-cart
dog'-catcher
dog-col'-lar
dog'-fight
dog'-fish
dog'-ged
dog'-gedly
dog'-ger
dog'-gerel
dog'-gery
dog'-ging
dog'-house
dog-mat'ic
dog-mat'i-cal
dog-mat'i-cally
dog'-ma-tise

dog'-ma-tism
dog'-ma-tist
dog'-trot
dog'-watch
dog'-wood
doil'-ies
do'-ing
do-lab'ri-form
dol'-drum
do'le-ful
do'le-fully
dol'-er-ite
do'l-ing
dol'-lar
dol'-man
dol'-men
dol'o-mite
dol'-or-ous
dol'-our
dol'-phin
dolt'-ish
do-main'
dom-es'tic
dom-es'ti-cate
dom-es-ti-ca'tion
dom-es-tic'ity
do'mi-cal
dom'i-cile
domi-cil'iar
domi-cil'i-ary
dom'i-nance
dom'i-nant
dom'i-nate
domi-na'tion
dom'i-nat-ive
dom'i-nator
dom'i-neer
domi-neer'-ing

dom-in'i-cal
dom'-inie
do-min'ion
do-min'ium
dom'-ino
dom'i-noes
do'-nate
do-na't-ing
do-na'tion
don'a-tive
do-na't-ory
do-nee'
don'-jon
don'-key
do'-nor
dood'-ling
dooms'-day
door'-bell
door'-keeper
door'-knob
door'-man
door'-nail
door'-plate
door'-post
door'-sill
door'-step
door'-stone
door'-way
do'p-ing
dor-ad'o
dor'-mancy
dor'-mant
dor'-mer
dor'-mi-tive
dor'-mi-tor-ies
dor'-mi-tory
dor'-mouse
dor'-sal

dor-sal'-gia
dor-sa'lis
dor-sif'er-ous
dor-si-flex'ion
dor'si-grade
dor-so-dyn'ia
dor'-sum
do's-age
do-sim'-etry
do's-ing
dos'-sier
dos'-sil
do't-age
do'-tard
do't-ing
dot'-ted
dot'-terel
doub'le=bar'-relled
doub'le=deal'-ing
doub'-let
doub'-ling
doub-loon'
doubt'-able
doubt'-ful
doubt'-fully
doubt'-less
douch'-ing
dough'-boy
dough'-nut
dous'-ing
dov'e-cote
dov'e-tail
dow'-able
dow'a-ger
dowd'i-ness
dow'-el-ing
dow'-las
108

down'-cast
down'-fall
down'-hearted
down'-hill
down'i-ness
down'-pour
down'-right
down'-stairs
down'-stream
down'-throw
down'-town
down'-trod-den
down'-ward
dows'-ing
doxo-log'i-cal
dox-ol'ogy
do'zi-ness
do'z-ing
drab'-bet
drab'-ness
drag'-ging
drag'-net
drag'o-man
drag'-onet
drag'on-fly
dra-goon'
drag'-rope
drain'-age
drain'-pipe
dra-mat'ic
dra-mat'i-cally
drama-tis-a'tion
dram'a-tise
dram'a-tis-ing
dram'a-tist
drama-tur'-gic
drama-tur'-gist
dram'a-turgy

dra'p-ery
dra'p-ing
dras'-tic
dras'-ti-cally
draughts'-man
draw'-back
draw'-bridge
draw'-ing
drawl'-ing
dray'-age
dray'-man
dread'-ful
dread'-fully
dread'-nought
dream'i-ly
dream'i-ness
dream'-ing
dream'-land
dream'-less
drear'-ily
drear'i-ness
dredg'-ing
drench'-ing
drep-a'nium
dress'-age
dress'-ing
dress'-ing-room
dress'-maker
dress'-making
drib'-bler
drib'-let
drift'-age
drift'-ing
drift'-wood
drill'-ing
drill'-mas-ter
drill'-stock
drink'-able

drip'-ping
driv'el-ler
driv'el-ling
dri've-way
dri'v-ing
droll'-ery
drom'-edary
drom'-ond
dro'n-ing
droop'-ing
drop'-let
drop'-per
drop'-ping
drop'-si-cal
drop'-sied
drows'-ily
drows'i-ness
drub'-bing
drudg'-ery
drudg'-ing
drug'-get
drug'-ging
drug'-gist
drug'-store
drum'-lin
drum'-mer
drum'-ming
drum'-stick
drunk'-ard
drunk'-en-ness
dru-pa'ceous
dry'-goods
dry'-ing
dry'-ness
dry-salt'er
dry-salt'-ery
du'a-lin
du'-al-ise

du'-al-ism
du'-al-ist
du-al-ist'ic
du-al'ity
du'-ally
dub'-bin
dub'-bing
du-bi'ety
dubi-os'ity
du'bl-ous
du'bi-ously
du'bi-table
dubi-ta'tion
du'bi-tat-ive
du'-cal
duch'-ess
duck'-bill
duck'-ling
duck'-weed
duc'-tile
duc-til'ity
duct'-less
dud'-geon
du'el-ler
du'el-ling
du'el-list
du'el'lo
du-en'na
du-et'-tist
duf'-fel
duf'-fer
du'-gong
dug'-out
du'ke-dom
dul'-cet
dul-ci-an'a
dul'-cify
dul'-ci-mer

dull'-ard
dull'-ness
dumb'-bell
dumb'-found
dumb'-show
dum'-dum
dum'-my-ing
dump'i-nees
dump'-ling
dun'-der-head
dun'ga-rees
dun'-geon
dung'-hill
dun'-lin
dun'-ite
dun'-nage
dun'-ning
dun'-nock
duo-dec'i-mal
duo-dec'imo
duo-de'nal
duo-den'-ary
duo-de'num
du'o-logue
du'p-able
du'p-ery
du'p-ing
du'-plex
du'pli-cate
dupli-ca'tion
du'pli-cat-ive
du'pli-cator
du-plex'-ity
du-plic'i-dent
du-plic'ity
dura-bil'ity
du'r-able

du-ra'men
du'-rance
dur-a'tion
dur'-bar
dur-ess'
du'-rian
du'r-ing
dur'-mast
dusk'i-ness
dust'-bin
dust'-cloth
dust'-heap
dust'-ily
dust'i-ness
dust'-less
dust'-man
dust'-pan
dust'-proof
du'-teous
du'-teously
du'ti-able
du'-ties
du'ti-ful
du-um'-vir-ate
dwarf'-ish
dwell'-ing
dwin'-dling
dy-ad'ic
dye'-ing
dy'-ing
dy'na-graph
dy-nam'ic
dy-nam'i-cal
dy-nam'-ics
dy-na-mism
dyna-mis'tic
dy'na-mite
dy'na-mited

dy'na-miter
dy'-namo
dyna-mom'eter
dy'na-mos
dy'na-motor
dyn'-ast
dyn-as'tic
dyn'-asty
dy'-na-tron
dy'-node
dys-ar'-thria
dys-ba'sia
dys-cra'sia
dys-en-ter'ic
dys'-en-tery
dys-func'-tion
dys-gen'ic
dys-lo-gis'tic
dys-pep'-sia
dys-pep'-tic
dys-pha'gia
dys-pho'nia
dysp'-nea
dys-pro'sium
dys'-trophy

E

eag'er-ness
eag'-let
ear'-ache
ear'-drop
ear'-drum
earl'-dom
ear'-mark
ear'-muff
earn'-est

earn'-estly
earn'-est-ness
earn'-ing
ear'-phone
ear'-ring
ear'-shot
ear'-split-ting
earth'-born
earth'-bound
earth'-en-ware
earth'i-ness
earth'-ing
earth'-li-ness
earth'-nut
earth'-quake
earth'-ward
earth'-wax
earth'-work
earth'-worm
ear'-wax
ear'-wig
eas'e-ful
eas'e-ment
eas'-ily
eas'i-ness
eas'-ing
east'-erly
east'-ern
east'-erner
east'-ing
east'-ward
eas'y-go-ing
eat'-able
eat'-ing
cav'es-drop
cav'es-drop-per
cav'es-drop-ping
ebb'-ing

eb'-on-ise
eb'-on-ist
eb'-on-ite
eb'-ony
ebrac'-teate
ebul'-lience
ebul-li-om'eter
ebul-li-os'copy
ebul-li-scop'ic
ebul-lit'ion
ebur-na'tion
ebur'-nean
ebur'-neum
ecal'-car-ate
ecau'-date
ec-bol'ic
ec-cen'-tric
ec-cen'-tri-cal
ec-cen'-tri-cally
ec-cen-tric'ity
ec-chon-dro'ma
ec-chon-dro'sis
ec-chy-mo'ma
ec-chy-mo'sis
ec-cle'sia
ec-cle'si-ast
ec-clesi-as'tic
ec-clesi-as'-ti-
        cal
ec-clesi-as'-ti-
        cism
ec-clesi-ol'a-try
ec-clesi-ol'ogy
ec'-crine
ec-crin-ol'ogy
ec-dem'ic
ec-dys'-ial
ec-dys'i-ast

ec'-dy-sis
ec'-go-nine
echi'n-ate
echi'n-ite
echi'no-derm
ech'-oed
ech'-oes
ech'o-ing
ech'o-ism
echo-la'lia
echo-prax'ia
ec-lamp'-sia
ec-lec'-tic
ec-lec'-ti-cal
eclips'-ing
eclip'-tic
eco-log'i-cal
ecol'-ogist
ec'-lo-gite
ec'-logue
ecol'-ogy
econo-met'ric
econ-om'ic
econ-om'i-cal
econ-om'i-cally
econ'-om-ies
econ'-om-ise
econ-om'-is-er
econ-om'-is-ing
econ'-om-ist
econ'-omy
ec'o-sphere
ec'-sta-sies
ec'-sta-sise
ec'-stasy

ec-stat'ic
ec-stat'i-cally
ec'-to-blast
ec'-to-derm
ec-to-der'-mal
ec-to-der-moi'dal
ec-tog'en-ous
ecto-par'a-site
ecto-para-sit'ic
ec'-to-phyte
ec-top'ic
ec'-to-plasm
ec-to-plas'-mic
ec-tos-to'sis
ec-tro-me'lia
ec'-type
ec-ty-pog'ra-phy
ecu-men'i-cal
ecu-men-ic'ity
ec'-zema
ec-ze'ma-tous
ed'-died
ed'-dies
ed'-dish
ed'dy-ing
e'del-weiss
edent'-ate
edg'e-ways
edg'e-wise
edg'-ing
edi-bil'ity
ed'-ible
edic'-tal
edi-fi-ca'tion
edi-fi-ca't-ory
ed'i-fice
edi-fic'ial
ed'i-fied

111

ed'i-fies
ed'-ify
ed'i-fy-ing
ed'i-tor
edi-to'rial
edi-to'ri-al-ise
edi-to'ri-ally
ed'i-tor-ship
edri-op-thal'-mic
edu-ca-bil'ity
ed'u-cable
ed'u-cate
ed'u-cat-ing
edu-ca'tion
edu-ca'tional
edu-ca'tion-al-ist
edu-ca'tion-ally
ed'u-cat-ive
ed'u-cator
ed'u-cat-ory
edu'c-ible
educ'-tion
educ'-tive
educ'-tor
edul'-cor-ate
edul-cor-a'tion
eel'-buck
eel'-grass
eer'-ily
eer'i-ness
ef-fa'ce
ef-fa'ce-able
ef-fa'ce-ment
ef-fa'c-ing
ef-fect'
ef-fect'-ible
ef-fec'-tive
ef-fec'-tive-ness

ef-fec'-tor
ef-fects'
ef-fec'-tual
ef-fec-tu-al'ity
ef-fec'-tu-ally
ef-fec'-tu-ate
ef-fec-tu-a'tion
ef-fem'i-nacy
ef-fem'i-nate
ef'fer-ent
ef-fer-vesc'e
ef-fer-vesc'ence
ef-fer-vesc'ent
ef-fer-vesc'ible
ef-fer-vesc'ing
ef-fe'te
ef-fi-ca'cious
ef'-fi-cacy
ef-fic'iency
ef-fic'ient
ef-fic'iently
ef-fig'ial
ef-fig'ur-ate
ef'-figy
ef-flor-esc'e
ef-flor-esc'ence
ef-flor-esc'ent
ef-flu-ent
ef'-flu'v-ial
ef-flu'v-ium
ef'-flux
ef-fo'di-ent
ef'-fort
ef'-fort-less
ef-front'-ery
ef-ful'-gence
ef-ful'-gent
ef-fu'se

ef-fusi-om'eter
ef-fu'sion
ef-fu's-ive
ef-fu's-ively
eft-soon'
egali-ta'rian
egali-ta'rian-ism
egest'-ive
eges'-tion
egg'-head
egg'-nog
egg'-plant
egg'-shaped
egg'-shell
eg'-lan-tine
ego-cen'-tric
ego-cen-tric'ity
ego-cen'-trism
e'go-ism
e'go-ist
ego-is'tic
ego-is'ti-cal
ego-ma'nia
ego-ma'niac
e'go-tism
e'go-tist
ego-tis'-tic
ego-tis'-ti-cal
ego-tis'-ti-cally
egre'gi-ous
ei'der-dówn
eid'o-graph
eidour-a'nion
eig'en-period
eig'en-ton
eight'-een
eight'-eenth
eight'-fold

eight'i-eth
ein'-stein-ium
eire'ni-con
ejac'u-late
ejac'u-lat-ing
ejacu-la'tion
ejac'u-lat-ive
ejac'u-lat-ory
ejec'-tion
ejec'-tive
eject'-ment
ejec'-tor
elab'-or-ate
elab'-or-ately
elab'-or-ate-ness
elab'-or-at-ing
elab-or-a'tion
elab'-or-at-ive
elae'o-lite
elae-op'-tene
elai'o-plast
elai'o-some
elaps'-ing
elas'-mo-branch
elas'-tance
elas'-tic
elas'-ti-cally
elas-tic'ity
elas'-tin
elas'-to-mer
elas-tom'eter
elas-to'sis
elat'-erid
elat'-erin
elat'-er-ite
ela-te'rium
el-aul'ic
el'-bow

el'-bow-room
el'der-berry
eld'-erly
eld'-est
el'-dritch
el-ecam-pa'ne
elec'-tion
elec-tion-eer'
elec'-tive
elec'-tor
elec'-toral
elec'-tor-ate
elec'-tric
elec'-tri-cal
elec'-tri-cally
elec-tric'ian
elec-tric'ity
elec-tri-fi-
     ca'tion
elec'-tri-fied
elec'-trify
elec-tro-anal'y-
     sis
elec-tro-car'-
     dio-gram
elec-tro-car'-
     dio-graph
elec-tro-chem'i-
     cal
elec-tro-chem'-
     is-try
elec-tro-crat'ic
elec-tro-cute
elec-tro-cu'tion
elec'-trode
elec-tro-dy-
     nam'-ics
elec-tro-fa'c-ing

elec-tro-form'-
     ing
elec'-tro-gram
elec-tro-graph'ic
elec-trog'ra-phy
elec'-tro-lise
elec'-trol'y-sis
elec'-tro-lyte
elec-tro-lyt'ic
elec-tro-lyt'i-cal
elec-tro-mag'-net
elec-tro-mag-
     net'ic
elec-tro-mag'-
     net-ism
elec-tro-mech-
     an'i-cal
elec-trom'eter
elec-tro-met'ric
elec-tro-mo'tive
electro-mo'tor
elec'-tron
elec-tro-neg'a-
     tive
elec-tron'ic
elec'-tro-os-
     mo'sis
elec-troph'-orus
elec'-tro-plate
elec'-tro-pos'i-
     tive
elec'-tro-scope
elec-tro-scop'ic
elec'-tro-sol
elec-tro-son'ic
elec-tro-stat'ic
elec-tro-syn-
     ton'ic

elec-tro-tel-
  lu'ra-graph
elec-tro-thera-
    peut'ics
elec-tro-ther'-
      apy
elec-tro-ther'-
      mics
elec'-tro-tint
elec-tro-ton'ic
elec'-tro-type
elec'-tro-typer
elec'-trum
elec'-tu-ary
eleemos'y-nary
el'-egance
el'-egancy
el'-egant
el'-egantly
el-egi'ac
el'-egise
el'-egist
el'-egy
el'-ement
el-emen'-tal
el-emen'-tarily
el-emen'-tary
el'-emi
elenc'-tic
el'-eph-ant
el-ephan-ti'asis
el-ephan'-tine
el-ephan'-toid
el'-ev-ate
el'-ev-ated
el-ev-a'tion
el'-ev-ator
el'-ev-at-ory
114

elf'-ish
elici-ta'tion
elic'i-tor
eli'd-ible
eli'd-ing
el-igi-bil'ity
el'i-gible
elim'-in-able
elim'-in-ant
elim'-in-ate
elim-in-a'tion
elim-in-ator
eli-qua'tion
el-lips'e
el-lips'es
el-lip'-ses
el-lip'-sis
el-lip'-soid
el-lip-soid'al
el-lip'-tic
el-lip'-ti-cal
el-lip-tic'ity
el-lit'-toral
elo-cu'tion
elo-cu'tion-ary
elo-cu'tion-ist
elo'-gium
elo'pe-ment
elo'p-ing
el'o-quence
el'o-quent
el'o-quently
el'se-where
elu'ci-date
eluci-da'tion
elu'ci-dat-ive
elu'ci-dator
eluci-da't-ory

elu'd-ible
elu'd-ing
elu's-ive
elu's-ory
elu'tri-ate
elu'v-ial
elu'v-ium
el'-van
el'-ver
el'y-tron
em-a'ciate
em-a'ciated
emaci-a'tion
em'a-nate
ema-na'tion
em'a-nat-ive
eman'-ci-pate
eman-ci-pa'tion
eman'-ci-pator
eman'-ci-pat-ory
emar'-gin-ate
emas'-cu-late
emas-cu-la'tion
emas'-cu-lat-ory
em-balm'
em-balm'-ment
em-bank'
em-bank'-ment
em-bar'
em-bar-ca-de'ro
em-bar'go
em-bar'-goed
em-bar'-goes
em-bark'
em-bar-ka'tion
em-bar'-rass
em-bar'-rassed
em-bar'-rasses

em-bar'-rass-ing
em-bar'-rass-
          ingly
em-bar'-rass-
          ment
em'-bass-age
em'-bass-ies
em'-bassy
em-bat'tle
em-bat'tle-ment
em-bay'
em-bay'-ment
em-bed'
em-bed'-ded
em-bel'-lish
em-bel'-lish-ment
em'-ber
em'-ber-days
em-bez'zle
em-bez'zled
em-bez'zle-ment
em-bez'-zler
em-bit'-ter
em-bla'zon
em-bla'z-on-ment
em-bla'z-onry
em'-blem
em-blem-at'ic
em-blem-at'i-cal
em-blem-at'i-
          cally
em-blem'a-tise
em'-blement
m'-blem-ise
m-bod'i-ment
m-bod'y
m-bo'lden
m-bol-ec'tomy

em-bol'ic
em'-bol-ism
em-bol-is'mic
em'-bolus
em'-boly
em-bos'om
em-boss'
em-boss'ed
em-boss'er
em-boss'-ing
em-boss'-ment
em-bouchu're
em-bow'el
em-bow'er
em-bra'ce
em-bra'ce-able
em-bra'ceor
em-bra'cer
em-bra'c-ery
em-bra'c-ing
em-brang'le-ment
em-bra'sure
em'-bro-cate
em-bro-ca'tion
em-broid'er
em-broid'-erer
em-broid'-ery
em-broil'
em-broil'-ment
em-bron'ze
em-brown'
em-bry-ec'tomy
em'-bryo
em-bryo-gen-et'ic
em-bry-og'eny
em-bryo-log'i-cal
em-bry-ol'ogy
em'-bry-onal

em-bry-on'ic
em'-bryos
em-bry-ot'omy
emen-da'tion
em'en-dator
emen'-da-tory
em'-er-ald
em'-er-al-dine
emerg'-ence
emerg'-encies
emerg'-ency
emerg'-ent
emerg'-ing
emer'i-tus
emer'-sion
em'-ery
em'-esis
em'-etine
emic'-tion
emic'-tory
em'i-grant
em'i-grate
em'i-grat-ing
emi-gra'tion
emi-gra't-ory
em'i-nence
em'i-nency
em'i-nent
em'i-nently
em'-iss-ar-ies
emiss-a'rium
em'-iss-ary
emiss'-ive
emiss-iv'ity
emit'-ted
emit'-ter
emit'-ting
em'-met

115

em-me-tro'pia
em'o-drin
emol'-li-ent
emol'u-ment
emo'tion-al
emo'tion-al-ise
emo'tion-al-ism
emo'tion-ally
emo't-ive
emo-tiv'ity
em-pais'-tic
em-pa'le
em-pan'el
em-pan'-el-ling
em-path'ic
em'pa-thy
em-pen'-nage
em'-peror
em'-pery
em'-pha-ses
em'-pha-sis
em'-pha-sise
em'-pha-sis-ing
em-phat'ic
em-phat'i-cally
em-phy-se'ma
em'-pire
em-pir'ic
em-pir'i-cal
em-pir'i-cism
em-pir'i-cis t
em-pir-is'tic
em-pla'ce-ment
em-plec'-tite
em-plec'-tum
em-ploy'
em-ploy'-able
em-ploy'ee

em-ploy'er
em-ploy' ment
em-po'rium
em-pow'er
em'-press
em-pri'se
emp'-tied
emp'-ti-ness
emp'tion
emp'-ty-ing
em-pur'pled
em-pye'ma
em-pyre'al
em-pyre'an
em-pyr-eum'a
em'u-late
emu-la'tion
em'u-lat-ive
em'u-lator
em'u-lat-ory
emul'-gent
em'u-lous
em'u-lously
emul-si-fi-
              ca'tion
emul'-si-fied
emul'-si-fier
emul'-sify
emul'-sin
emul'-sion
emul'-sive
emul'-soid
emunc'-tory
en-a'ble
en-a'bling
en-act'
en-ac'-tive

en-act'-ment
en-ac'-tory
en-am'el
en-am'-elied
en-am'-eller
en-am'our
en-am'oured
enan-thal'de-
              hyde
en-an'-them
en-an-the'ma
enan'-thic
en-an'tio-morph-
              ous
en-an-ti-o'sis
en-ar'-gite
en-ar-thro'sis
en-caen'ia
en-cal'-low
en-camp'
en-camp'-ment
en-cap'-su-late
en-car'-nal-ise
en-ca'se
en-ca's-ing
en-cas'-tered
en-caus'-tic
en-cephal-al'gia
en-cephal'ic
en-cepha-lit'ic
en-cepha-li'tis
en-ceph'a-lo-cele
en-ceph'a-lo-
              coele
en-ceph'a-lo-
              gram
en-cepha-lo-
              graph'ic

en-cepha-log'ra-phy
en-ceph'a-loid
en-cepha-lo-ma-la'cia
en-ceph'a-lon
en-cepha-lop'a-thy
en-chain'
en-chant'
en-chant'er
en-chant'-ing
en-chant'-ment
en-chan'-tress
en-cha'se
en-chir-id'ion
en-chon-dro'ma
en-chon-drom'a-tous
en-cho'rial
en-cir'cle
en-cir'cle-ment
en-circ'-ling
en-clasp'
en'-clave
en-chit'ic
en-clo'se
en-clo'ser
en-clo's-ing
en-clo's-ure
en-co'mi-ast
en-comi-as'tic
en-co'mium
en-com'pass
en-coun'-ter
en-cour'-age
en-cour'-age-ment

en-cour'-ag-ing
en-cri'nal
en-crin'ic
en'-cri-nite
en'-croach'
en-croach'-ment
en-crust'
en-crus-ta'tion
en-cum'-ber
en-cum'-brance
en-cy'c-lic
en-cy'c-li-cal
en-cyc-lo-pe'dia
en-cyc-lo-pe'dic
en-cyc-lo-pe'dism
en-cyc-lo-pe'dist
en-cyst'
en-cys-ta'tion
en-cyst'-ment
en-dam'-age
en-da'nger
en-dar-ter-i'tis
en-dear'
en-dear'-ing
en-dear'-ment
en-deav'-our
en-deav'-oured
en-dec-an'-drous
en-de'mial
en-dem'ic
en-dem'i-cally
en-dem-ic'ity
en-demi-ol'ogy
en'-dem-ism
en-der'-mic
end'-ing
en'-dive

end'-less
end'-lessly
end'-long
end'-most
en-do-blas'-tic
en-do-car'-diac
en-do-car-di'tis
en-do-car'-dium
en'-do-carp
en-do-cell'u-lar
en-do-chon'-dral
endo-cri'nal
en'-do-cr ne
endo-crino-log'ic
endo-crin-ol'ogy
endo-crino-path'ic
endo-crin-op'a-thy
en-doc'ri-nous
en'-do-derm
en-do-der'-mal
en-do-der'-mis
en-do-gam'ic
en-dog'a-mous
en-dog'amy
en'-do-gen
endo-gen-et'ic
endo-gen-ic'ity
en-dog'en-ous
en-dog'en-ously
en-do-lith'ic
en'-do-lymph
endo-lym-phan'-gial
endo-lym-phat'ic
endo-metri'tis
endo-me'trium

117

en'-do-morph
en-do-mor'-phic
en-do-mys'-ium
endo-par'a-site
endo-phrag'-mal
en-doph-thal-
    mi'tis
en-do-phyl'-lous
en'-do-phyte
en'-do-plasm
en-do-plas'ma
en-do-plas'-mic
endo-rha'cis
en-dors'-able
en-dorse'
en-dor-see'
en-dors'e-ment
en-dors'er
en-dors'-ing
en'-do-scope
en-dos'-copy
en-dos-mo'sis
en'-do-sperm
endo-spo'rium
en-dos'-porous
en-dos'-teum
en-dos-to'sis
en-do-the'cium
en-do-the'lial
en-do-theli-o'ma
en-do-the'lium
en-do-the'loid
en-do-ther'mic
en-do-tox'in
en-dow'
en-dow'-ment
en-do-zo'ic
en-due'
118

en-du'r-able
en-du'r-ance
en-du're
en-du'r-ing
end'-ways
end'-wise
en-dy'sis
en'-ema
en'-em-ies
en'-emy
en-er-get'ic
en-er-get'i-cal
en-er-get'i-cally
en'-er-gies
en'-er-gise
en'-er-giser
en'-er-gism
en-er-gu'men
en'-ergy
en-er-va'tion
en'-er-vate
en'-er-vator
en-fa'ce
en-feeb'le
en-feeb'-ling
en-feoff'
en-feoff'-ment
en-fet'-ter
en-fi-la'de
en-fleur-ag'e
en-fo'ld
en-fo'rce
en-fo'rce-able
en-fo'rc-edly
en-fo'rce-ment
en-fo'rcer
en-fo'rc-ing
en-fran'-chise

en-fran'-chise-
        ment

en-ga'ge
en-ga'ged
en-ga'ge-ment
en-ga'g-ing
en-gen'-der
en'-gine
en-gin-eer'
en-gin-eer'-ing
en'-gine-room
en-gir'dle
en-graft'
en-grain'
en-gra've
en-gra'ver
en-gra'v-ing
en-gross'
en-gross'-ing
en-gross'-ment
en-gulf'
en-han'ce
en-han'ce-ment
en-hanc'-ing
en-har-mon'ic
enig-mat'ic
enig-mat'i-cal
enig-mat'i-cally
enig'-ma-tise
en-jamb'-ment
en-join'
en-join'er
en-joy'
en-joy'-able
en-joy'-ably
en-joy'-ment
en-kin'dle
en-kin'-dling

en-la'ce
en-larg'e
en-larg'e-ment
en-larg'-ing
en-li'ghten
en-li'ght-en-ment
en-list'
en-list'-ment
en-li'ven
en-mesh'
en'-mi-ties
en'-mity
en'-nead
en-no'ble
en-no'bler
en-no'bling
enor'-mity
enor'-mous
enor'-mously
en-phy-tot'ic
en-qui're
en-qui'ry
en-ra'ge
en-rapt'
en-rap'-ture
en-rav'-ish
en-rich'
en-rich'-ment
en-ro'be
en-ro'l
en-ro'll
en-ro'lled
en-ro'l-ling
en-ro'l-ment
en-sam'ple
en-san'guine
en-scon'ce
en-sconc'-ing

en-shri'ne
en-shroud'
en'-si-form
en'-sign (n.)
en-si'gn (v.)
en'-signcy
en'si-lage
en-si'le
en-sla've
en-sla've-ment
en-sla'ver
en-sla'ving
en-sna're
en'-sor
en-sue'
en-su'-ing
en-su'-ingly
en-su're
en-su'r-ing
en-tab'-la-ture
en-ta'ble-ment
en-tail'
en-tail'-ment
en-tan'gle
en-tan'gle-ment
en-tan'gler
en-tan'gling
en'-ta-sis
en-tel'-echy
en'-ter
en-ter-al'gia
en-ter-ec'-tomy
en-ter'ic
en-ter-i'tis
en-tero-col-i'tis
en-tero-col-
        os'tomy
en'-teron

en-ter-op-to'sis
en-ter-os'tomy
en-ter-ot'omy
en'-ter-pris-ing
en'-ter-pris-
        ingly
en-ter-tain'
en-ter-tain'er
en-ter-tain'-ing
en-ter-tain'-ment
en-thal'py
en-thet'ic
en-thral'
en-thral'-ling
en-thral'-lingly
en-thral'-ment
en-thro'ne
en-thron-is-
        a'tion
en-thu'se
en-thu'si-asm
en-thu'si-ast
en-thusi-as'tic
en-thusi-as'ti-
        cally
en'-thy-meme
en-ti'ce
en-ti'ce-ment
en-ti'c-ing
en-ti're
en-ti'rely
en-ti'rety
en-ti'ta-tive
en'-ti-ties
en-ti'tle
en'-tity
en-to-gas'-tric
en-tomb'

119

ENTOMBMENT

en-tomb'-ment
en-tom'ic
ento-mo-log'i-cal
en-to-mog'en-ous
en-to-mog'ra-phy
en-to-mol'-ogist
en-to-mol'ogy
en-to-moph'a-
    gous
en-to-moph'i-lous
ento-mos'tra-can
en'-to-phyte
en-to-zo'ic
en-to-zo'on
en'-trails
en'-train'
en-tram'-mel
en'-trance (n.)
en-tran'ce (v.)
en'-trance-way
en-tranc'-ing
en-tranc'-ingly
en'-trant
en'-trap'
en-trap'-ment
en-trap'-ping
en-treat'
en-treat'-ies
en-treat'-ing
en-treat'-ingly
en-treat'y
en-trench'
en-trench'-ment
en'tre-sol
en'-tries
en'-tropy
en-trust'
en'-try
120

en-twi'ne
en-twist'
enu'-cleate
enu'-mer-ate
enu-mer-a'tion
enu'-mer-at-ive
enu'-mer-ator
enun'-ci-able
enun'-ci-ate
enun-ci-a'tion
enun'-ci-at-ive
enun'-ci-ator
en-u're
en-vel'op
en-vel'ope
en-vel'-oped
en-vel'-op-ing
en-vel'-op-ment
en-ven'-om
en'-vi-able
en'-vi-ably
en'-vied
en'-vies
en'-vi-ous
en'-vi-ously
en-vi'ron
en-vi'ron-ment
en-viron-men'-
    tal
en-vi'rons
en-vis'-age
en-vis'ion
en'-voy
en'-vy-ing
en'-vy-ingly
en-wrap'
en-wrap'-ping
en-zo-ot'ic

en-zy-mat'ic
en'-zyme
en-zy-mol'ogy
e'o-lith
eo-lith'ic
eosin'o-phil
epa-go'ge
ep'-arch
ep-arch'-ial
ep-ar-tc'rial
ep-aul-ett'e
é'pée-ist
epeiro-gen'ic
epeir-og'eny
ep-en-ceph'a-lon
ep-en'-dyma
epen-dy-mi'tis
epen-dy-mo'ma
ep-en'-thesis
ep-ex-ege'sis
eph'-edrine
ephem'-era
ephem'-eral
ephem'-eris
ephem'-eron
epi-ben'-thos
epi-bol'ic
epib'-oly
ep'i-cal
ep'i-cally
epi-ca'lyx
epi-can'-thic
epi-can'-thus
epi-car'-dium
ep'i-carp
ep'i-cede
epi-ce'dium
ep'i-cene

ep'i-cen-ism
epi-cen'tre
epi-cen'-trum
epi-cot'yl
ep'i-crit'ic
epi-cure'an
ep'i-cur-ism
ep'i-cycle
epi-cy'c-loid
epi-cyc-loid'al
epi-deic'-tic
epi-dem'ic
epi-dem'i-cal
epi-demi-ol'ogy
epi-der'-mal
epi-der'-mic
epi-der'-mis
epi-der'-moid
epi-der-moid'al
epi-di'ascope
epi-did'y-mis
epi-di'or-ite
ep'i-dote
epi-du'ral
epi-fo'cal
epi-gam'ic
epi-gas'-tric
epi-gas'-trium
epi-ge'al
epi-ge'an
epi-ge'ic
epi-gen'-esis
epi-gen-et'ic
epig'en-ous
epi-glot'-tis
ep'i-gram
epi-gram-mat'ic

epi-gram-mat'i-
    cal
epi-gram'-ma-
    tist
ep'i-graph
epig'ra-phist
epi-graph'ic
epig'ra-phy
epig'yn-ous
epi-la'tion
ep'i-lator
ep'i-lepsy
epi-lep'-tic
epi-lith'ic
epi-lit'-oral
ep'i-logue
ep'i-mere
epi-mer-isa'tion
ep'i-mer-ise
epi-my'sium
ep'i-nasty
epi-neph'-rine
epi-neur'ium
ep'i-nine
epi-phen-om'-
    enon
epiphy-se'al
epiph'y-sis
ep'i-phyte
epi-pter'ic
epis'-co-pacy
epis'-co-pal
epis'-co-pal-ism
epis'-co-pate
ep'i-sode
epi-sod'ic
epi-sod'i-cal
epi-sod'i-cally

epi-spas'-tic
ep'i-sperm
epis'-ta-sis
epi-stat'ic
epi-stax'is
epis-temo-log'i-
    cal
epis-tem-ol'ogy
epi-ster'-num
epis'-tol-ary
ep'i-stome
epis'-trophe
ep'i-style
epit'a-sis
epitha-la'mion
epitha-la'mium
epi-the'lial
epi-theli-o'ma
epi-theli-om'a-
    tous
epi-the'lium
ep'i-them
ep'i-thet
epit'-ome
ep'i-tomi-cal
epit'-om-ise
epit'ro-phy
epi-zo'on
epi-zo-ot'ic
epi-zo'oty
ep'-ode
ep'-onym
epo-nym'ic
epon'y-mous
epon'-ymy
ep-ox'y
ep'-si-lon
equa-bil'ity

121

EQUALISATION

equal-is-a'tion
e'qual-ise
e'qual-iser
equali-ta'rian
e'qual-ling
equa-nim'ity
equa-to'rial
eques'-trian
eques'-tri-enne
equi-an'gu-lar
equi-angu-lar'ity
equi-dis'-tant
equi-la-bra'tion
equi-lat'eral
equil'i-brant
equi-lib'-rate
equi-li-bra'tion
equi-lib'-rist
equi-lib'-rium
equi-mul'-tiple
equi-noc'-tial
eq'ui-nox
eq'ui-page
equip'-ment
eq'ui-poise
equi-pol'-lence
equi-pol'-lent
equi-pon'-der-ance
equi-pon'-der-ant
equi-pon'-der-ate
equi-po-ten'-tial
equip'-ping
equi-se'tum
eq'ui-table
eq'ui-tant
equi-ta'tion
eq'ui-tes
122

eq'ui-ties
equiv'-al-ence
equiv'-al-ency
equiv'o-cal
equiv'o-cate
equivo-ca'tion
equiv'o-cator
eq'ui-voque
eradi-a'tion
erad'i-cable
erad'i-cate
eradi-ca'tion
erad'i-cat-ive
erad'i-cator
era's-able
era's-ing
era's-ure
er'-bium
erec'-tile
erec-til'ity
erec'-tion
erec'-tive
erec'-tor
erect'-ness
er-ema-caus'is
er-ep'-sin
er'-eth-ism
er-gas'-tic
er'ga-tive
er-ga-toc'racy
erg-om'eter
er'-gon
er-go-nom'i-cal
er-go-nom'-ics
er-gos'-terol
er'-got
er-got'ic
er'-go-tism

er'-got-ism
cr'-go-tisc
er'-got-ise
er-go-tox'-ine
eri-ca'ceous
er'i-coid
erin'-eum
eri-om'eter
cris'-tic
er'-ken-sator
er'-mine
ero'd-ent
ero'd-ible
erog'en-ous
ero's-ive
erot'i-cism
er'ot-ism
ero-to-ma'nia
err-abil'ity
err'-ancy
err'-rand
er'-rant
er'-rantry
er-rat'a
er-rat'ic
er-rat'i-cally
er-rat'um
er'-rhine
err'-ing
err'-ingly
er-ro'neous
er-ro'neously
er-ro'neous-ness
er'-ror
er'-satz
erst'-while
eru-besc'ence
eru-besc'ent

eru'ci-form
eruc'-tate
eruc-ta'tion
er'u-dite
eru-dit'ion
erum'-pent
erup'-tion
erup'-tive
erup-tiv'ity
ery-sip'-elas
ery-si-pel'a-tous
ery-the'ma
ery-the'ma-tous
ery-thras'ma
ery-thre'mia
er'y-thrine
er'yth-rism
eryth'-rite
eryth'-ri-tol
eryth'-ro-blast
eryth'-ro-cyte
eryth-ro-cytom'-
    eter
eryth-ro-mel-
    al'gia
eryth-ro-pe'nia
eryth'-ro-phore
ery-throp'-sia
ery-throp'-sin
eryth'-ro-scope
er'y-throse
es'-ca-lade
es'-ca-late
es'-ca-lator
es-cal-lo'nia
es-cal'-loped
es-cam'-bio
es-ca'p-able

es'-ca-pade
es-ca'pe
es-capee'
es-ca'pe-ment
es-ca'p-ing
es-ca'p-ism
es-ca'p-ist
es-carp'-ment
escha-lot'
es'-char
es-char-ot'ic
es-cha-tol'-ogist
es-cha-tol'ogy
es-cheat'
es-chew'
es-chew'al
es'-chy-nite
es'-cort (n.)
es-cort' (v.)
es'-cri-toire
es-crow'
es'-cu-age
es-cu'do
es-cu'dos
es'-cu-lent
es'-cu-line
es-cutch'eon
es'-kar
eso-pho'ria
eso-ter'ic
eso-ter'i-cally
eso-ter'i-cism
es-pal'ier
es-par'to
es-pec'ial
es-pec'ially
es-pi'al

es'pion-age
es'-pla-nade
es-plees'
es-pous'al
es-pous'e
es-pous'er
es-pous'-ing
es-pun'dia
es-qui're
es'-say (n.)
es-say' (v.)
es'-say-ist
es'-sence
es-sen'-tial
es-sen'-tiality
es-sen'-tially
es'-son-ite
es-tab'-lish
es-tab'-lished
es-tab'-lish-ment
es-ta'te
es-teem'
es'-ter
es-teri-fi-ca'tion
es'-ter-ase
es-ter'i-fy
es'-ter-ise
es-tif'er-ous
es'-ti-mable
es'-ti-mate
es'-ti-mat-ing
es-ti-ma'tion
es'-ti-mator
es'-ti-vator
es-top'
es-topp'ed
es-top'-pel
es-top'-ping

123

es-to'vers
es-tra'nge
es-tra'nge-ment
es-tra'ng-ing
es-tray'
es-treat'
es'-tro-gen
es-tro-gen'ic
es'-trone
es'-tu-ar-ine
es'-tu-ary
esu'ri-ence
esu'ri-ent
esu'-rine
et'a-lon
et-cet'-era
etch'-ing
eter'-nal
eter'-nally
eter'-nity
eth'-ane
eth'a-nol
etha-nol'a-mine
eth'-ene
eth'-en-oid
eth-e'real-ise
eth-e'real-ity
eth-e'really
eth-e'reous
etheri-fi-ca'tion
e'ther-ify
ether-is-a'tion
e'ther-ise
eth'i-cal
eth'-ics
ethi-on'ic
eth'-moid

eth-moid'al
eth-moid-i'tis
eth'-nic
eth'-ni-cal
eth'-ni-cally
eth-nic'ity
eth-no-cen'tric
eth-no-cen'trism
eth-nog'ra-pher
eth-no-graph'ic
eth-no-graph'i-
                cal
eth-nog'ra-phy
eth-no-log'i-cal
eth-nol'-ogist
eth-nol'ogy
etho-log'i-cal
eth-ol'ogy
eth-ox'yl
eth-ox'y-line
ethyl'-amine
eth'-yl-ate
eth'-yl-ene
ethy-len'ic
eth-yl-ephed'-
                rine
e'tio-late
etio-la'tion
et'i-quette
ety-mo-log'i-cal
ety-mol'-ogise
ety-mol'-ogist
ety-mol'ogy
et'y-mon
eu'ca-lypt
euca-lyp'tic
euca-lyp'-tole
euca-lyp'-tus

eu-car'-pic
eu'char-ist
eu'chro-ite
eu'-clase
eu'-crite
eu-cy'c-lic
eu-dae'-mon
eu-dae-mon'ic
eu-dae'-mon-ism
eudi-om'eter
eudio-met'ric
eu-di-om'etry
eu-gam'ic
eu-gen'ic
eu-gen'i-cal
eu-gen'i-cist
eu-gen'-ics
eu'gen-ist
eu'-genol
eu-he'mer-ism
eu'-logies
eu'-logise
eu'-logist
eu-logis'tic
eu-logis'ti-cal
eu-lo'gium
eu'-logy
eu'mer-ism
eu'-nuch
eu-on'y-mous
eu-on'ymy
eu-pa'tor-ine
eu-pa-to'rium
eu-pat'-rid
eu-pat'ri-dae
eu-pep'-sia
eu-pep'-tic
eu'-phem-ise

124

eu'-phem-ism
eu-phem-is'tic
eu-phon'ic
eu-pho'ni-ous
eu'-phon-ism
eu-pho'nium
eu'-phony
eu-phor'-bia
eu-phor-bi-
    a'ceous
eu-pho'ria
eu-phor'ic
eu'-phrasy
eu'-phroe
eu'-phu-ism
eu-phu-is'tic
eu'p-nea
eu-pot'a-mous
eu-re'ka
eu-ri'pus
eu-ro'pium
eury-bath'ic
eury-ha'line
eury-ther'-mous
eu-ryth'-mics
eu-ryth'my
eu-stat'ic
eu'-taxy
eu-tec'-tic
eu-tec'-toid
eu-tha-na'sia
eu-tnen'-ics
eux'-en-ite
evac'u-ant
evac'u-ate
evac'u-at-ive
evacu-a'tion
eva'd-ing

evag'i-nate
evagi-na'tion
eval'u-ate
evalu-a'tion
evan-esc'e
evan-esc'ence
evan-esc'ent
evan'-gel
evan-gel'ic
evan-gel'i-cal
evan'-gel-ise
evan'-gel-ism
evan'-gel-ist
evan-gel-is'tic
evap'or-able
evap'or-ate
evap'-or-at-ing
evap-or-a'tion
evap'-or-at-ive
evap'-or-ator
evap-or-im'eter
eva's-ible
eva's-ive
evec'-tion
e'ven-fall
e'ven-handed
e'ven-ing
e've-ning
e'ven-ness
e'ven-song
event'-ful
e'ven-tide
even-tra'tion
event'-ual
eventu-al'ity
even'tu-ally
even'tu-ate
ev'er-green

ever-last'-ing
ever-last'-ingly
ever-mo're
evers'-ible
ev'ery-body
every-day'
ev'ery-one
ev'ery-thing
ev'ery-where
evic'-tion
evic'-tor
ev'i-dence
ev'i-denc-ing
ev'i-dent
evi-den'-tial
ev'i-dently
e'vil-doer
e'vil-ness
evinc'-ible
evinc'-ing
evin'-cive
evis'-cer-ate
evis-cer-a'tion
evis'-cer-ator
ev'i-table
ev'o-cable
evo-ca'tion
evoc'a-tive
ev'o-cator
evoc'-atory
evo'k-ing
ev'ol-ute
evol'-ution
evol-u'tion-ary
evol-u'tion-ist
evol'-vable
evol'-vate
evol've-ment

evolv'-ing
evul'-sion
ex-ac'er-bate
ex-ac'er-bat-ing
ex-acer-ba'tion
exact'-able
exact'-ing
exac'-tion
exac'-ti-tude
exact'-ment
exact'-ness
exag'-ger-ate
exag'-ger-ated
exag-ger-a'tion
exag'-ger-ative
exag'-ger-ator
exal-ta'tion
exam'-in-able
exam-in-a'tion
exam'-ine
exam-inee'
exam'-iner
ex-an'i-mate
ex-an-the'ma
ex-an-them-at'ic
ex-an-the'ma-tous
ex'-arch
ex'-ar-chate
exas'-per-ate
exas'-per-at-ing
exas'-per-at-
    ingly
exas-per-a'tion
ex-car-din-a'tion
ex'-ca-vate
ex-ca-va'tion
ex'-ca-vator
ex-ceed'

ex-ceed'-ingly
ex-cel'
ex-cell'ed
ex'-cel-lence
ex'-cel-lency
ex'-cel-lent
ex'-cel-lently
ex-cel'-ling
ex-cel'-sior
ex-cept'
ex-cept'-able
ex-cept'-ing
ex-cep'-tion
ex-cep'-tion-able
ex-cep'-tional
ex-cep'-tion-ally
ex-cep'-tive
ex'-cerpt (n.)
ex-cerpt' (v.)
ex-cerp'-ter
ex-cerp'-tible
ex-cess' (n.)
ex'-cess (a.)
ex-cess'-ive
ex-cess'-ively
ex-cha'nge-able
ex-cha'ng-ing
ex-cheq'-uer
ex-cip'i-ent
ex-ci-pu'li-pene
ex-ci's-able
ex'-cise (n.)
ex-ci'se (v.)
ex-ci'se-man
ex-cis'ion
ex-cit-abil'ity
ex-ci't-able
ex-ci't-ant

ex-ci-ta'tion
ex-ci't-ative
ex-ci't-atory
ex-ci'te
ex-ci'te-ment
ex-ci'ter
ex-ci't-ing
ex-ci'tor
ex-claim'
ex-cla-ma'tion
ex-clam'a-tory
ex-clu'd-able
ex-clu'de
ex-clu'd-ing
ex-clu'sion
ex-clu's-ive
ex-clu's-ively
ex-clu's-ive-ness
ex-clu's-ory
ex-cog'i-tate
ex-cogi-ta'tion
ex-com-mu'ni-
        cate
ex-com-muni-
       ca'tion
ex-con'-vict
ex-co'ri-ate
ex-cori-a'tion
ex-cor'ti-cate
ex'-cre-ment
ex-cresc'ence
ex-cresc'ency
ex-cresc'ent
ex-cre'ta
ex-cre'te
ex-cre'tion
ex-cre't-ory
ex-cru'-ciate

ex-cru'-ciat-ing
ex-cru-cia'tion
ex'-cul-pate
ex-cul-pa'tion
ex-cul'pa-tory
ex-cur'-rent
ex-cur'-sion
ex-cur'-sion-ist
ex-cur'-sive
ex-cur'-sus
ex-cu's-able
ex-cu'sa-tory
ex-cu'se
ex-cu's-ing
ex'-eat
ex'-ecrable
ex'-ecrate
ex-ecra'tion
ex'-ecrat-ive
ex'-ecrat-ory
ex'-ecut-able
exec'u-tant
ex'-ecute
ex-ecu'tion
ex-ecu'tioner
exec'u-tive
exec'u-tor
execu-to'rial
exec'u-tory
exec'u-trix
ex-ege'sis
ex'-egete
ex-eget'ic
ex-eget'i-cal
exemp'-lar
exemp'-lary
exemp-li-fi-
        ca'tion

exemp'-lify
exempt'-ible
exemp'-tion
exemp'-tive
ex-en-ter-a'tion
ex-equa'tur
ex-er-ci's-able
ex'-er-cise
ex'-er-ciser
ex-er'-esis
ex'-ergue
exer'-tion
exert'-ive
ex'-eunt
ex-fo'li-ate
ex-foli-a'tion
ex-ha'lant
ex-ha-la'tion
ex-ha'le
exhaus'-ted
exhaus'-ter
exhaust'-ible
exhaus'-tion
exhaus'-tive
exhaus'-tively
exhaust'-less
exhi-bi'tion
exhi-bit'ioner
exhi-bit'ion-ism
exhi-bit'ion-ist
exhib'i-tive
exhib'i-tor
exhib'i-tory
exhil'-ar-ant
exhil'-ar-ate
exhil'-ar-at-ing
exhil-ar-a'tion
exhil'-ar-at-ive

exhor-ta'tion
exi-gu'ity
ex-ig'u-ous
ex-in-an-it'ion
exist'-ence
exist'-ent
ex-is-ten'-tial
ex-is-ten'-tial-
        ism
ex-is-ten'-tial-
        ist
exo-car'-diac
ex'o-crine
ex'o-derm
exo-der'-mis
exo-don'-tia
exo-don'-tist
ex'-odus
ex'o-gamic
ex-og'amy
ex'o-gen
ex-og'en-ous
ex-o'mis
exon'-er-ate
exon-er-a'tion
exo-pho'ria
ex-oph-thal'-mia
ex-oph-thal'-mic
exor'-bi-tance
exor'-bi-tant
ex'-or-cise
ex'-or-ciser
ex'-or-cism
ex'-or-cist
exor'-dial
exor'-dium
exo-skel'etal
exo-skel'eton

127

ex-os-to'sis
exo ter'ic
exo-ther'-mic
exo-therm-ic'ity
exot'i-cally
exot'i-cism
ex'o-type
ex-pand'
ex pand'-able
ex-pan'der
ex-pan'dor
ex-pans'e
ex-pan-si-bil'ity
ex-pans'-ible
ex-pan'-sile
ex-pan'-sion
ex-pans'-ive
ex-pa'tiate
ex-patia'tion
ex-pat'ri-ate
ex-patri-a'tion
ex-pect'
ex-pect'-able
ex-pect'-ancy
ex-pect'-antly
ex-pec-ta'tion
ex-pec'ta-tive
ex-pect'-ant
ex-pec'-tor-ant
ex-pec'-tor-ate
ex-pec-tor-a'tion
ex-pec'-tor-ator
ex-pe'di-ency
ex-pe'di-ent
ex-pe'di-ently
ex'-pedite
ex'-pediter
ex'-pedit-ing

ex-pedit'ion
ex-pedit'ion-ary
ex-pedit'ious
ex-pedit'iously
ex-pel'
ex-pel'-lable
ex-pel'-lant
ex-pell'ed
ex-pel-lee'
ex-pel'-ling
ex-pend'
ex-pend'-able
ex-pen'-di-ture
ex-pens'e
ex-pens'-ive
ex-pens'-ively
ex-pe'ri-ence
ex-pe'ri-enced
ex-pe'ri-enc-ing
ex-per-imen-
    ta'tion
ex-per'-imenter
ex-peri-en'-tial
ex-per'-iment
ex-per-imen'-tal
ex-per-imen'-tally
ex-pert' (a.)
ex'-pert (n. a.)
ex-per-ti'se
ex'-pert-ise
ex'-pertly
ex'-pert-ness
ex'-pi-ate
ex'-pi-ate
ex-pi-a'tion
ex'-pi-ator
ex'-pi-at-ory
ex-pir-a'tion

ex-pir'a-tory
ex-pi're
ex-pi'red
ex-pi'r-ing
ex-pi'ry
ex-pis'-cate
ex-plain'
ex-plain'-able
ex'-pla-nate
ex-pla-na'tion
ex-plan'a-tive
ex-plan'a-tory
ex-plan-ta'tion
ex'-ple-tive
ex-ple'-tive (n.)
ex-plic'-able
ex'-pli-cate
ex-pli-ca'tion
ex-plic'a-tive
ex-plic'a-tor
ex-plic'a-tory
ex-plic'it
ex-plic'itly
ex-plo'de
ex-plo'der
ex-plo'd-ing
ex-ploit' (v.)
ex'-ploit (n.)
ex-ploit'-able
ex-ploi-ta'tion
ex-ploit'er
ex-plo-ra'tion
ex-plo'ra-tive
ex-plo'ra-tory
ex-plo're
ex-plo'rer
ex-plo'r-ing
ex-plo's-ible

ex-plo'sion
ex-plo's-ive
ex-plo's-ively
ex-po'nent
ex'-po-nen'-tially
ex'-port (n. v.)
ex-po'rt (v.)
ex-po'rt-able
ex-por-ta'tion
ex-po'rter
ex-po'sal
ex-po'se
ex-po'sed
ex-po'ser
ex-po's-ing
ex-po-sit'ion
ex-pos'i-tive
ex-pos'i-tor
ex-pos'i-tory
ex-pos'tu-late
ex-postu-la'tion
ex-pos'tu-lat-ory
ex-po'sure
ex-pound'
ex-pound'er
ex-press'
ex-press'-age
ex-press'er
ex-press'-ible
ex-press'-ing
ex-pres'sion
ex-pres'sion-ism
ex-pres'sion-ist
ex-pres'sion-less
ex-press'-ive
ex-press'-ively
ex-press'ly
ex-press'-man

ex-press'or
ex'-pro-brate
ex-pro-bra'tion
ex-pro'bra-tory
ex-pro'-pri-ate
ex-pro-pri-a'tion
ex-pro'-pri-ator
ex-pul'-sion
ex-pul'-sive
ex-pun'ge
ex-pung'-ing
ex'-pur-gate
ex-pur-ga'tion
ex'-pur-gator
ex-pur-ga-to'rial
ex-pur'-ga-tory
ex-quis'-ite
ex-quis'-itely
ex-san'gui-nate
ex-scind'
ex-sert'
ex-sert'ed
ex-ser'-tile
ex-ser'-tion
ex'-sic-cate
ex-sic'-cant
ex-sic-ca'tion
ex-stip'u-late
ex'-tant
ex-tant'
ex-tem'-poral
ex-tem-pora-
      ne'ity
ex-tem-por-
      a'neous
ex-tem'-pore
ex-tem-por-is-
      a'tion

ex-tem'-por-ise
ex-tem'-por-iser
ex-tend'
ex-ten'd-able
ex-ten'ded
ex-ten'der
ex-ten'd-ible
ex-ten-si-bil'ity
ex-ten'-sible
ex-ten'-sile
ex-ten'-sion
ex-ten'-sity
ex-ten'-sive
ex-ten'-sively
ex-ten-som'eter
ex-ten'-sor
ex-tent'
ex-ten'u-ate
ex-ten'u-at-ing
ex-tenu-a'tion
ex-ten'u-ator
ex-ten'u-atory
ex-te'rior
ex-te'ri-or-ise
ex-ter'-mi-nate
ex-ter-mi-na'tion
ex-ter'-mi-nat-
      ive
ex-ter'-mi-nator
ex-ter'-mi-nat-
      ory
ex-ter'-nal
ex-ter'-nal-ise
ex-ter'-nal-ism
ex-ter-nal'ity
ex-ter-nal'ly
ex-tero-cep'-tive
ex-tero-cep'-tor

129

ex-ter-ri-to'rial
ex-tinct'
ex-tinc'-tion
ex-tinc'-tive
ex-tin'guish
ex-tin'guish-able
ex-tin'guisher
ex'-tir-pate
ex-tir-pa'tion
ex'-tir-pator
ex-to'l
ex-to'lled
ex-to'l-ling
ex-tor'-sion
ex-tort'
ex-tor'ted
ex-tor'-tion
ex-tor'-tion-ary
ex-tor'-tion-ate
ex-tor'-tioner
ex-tor'-tion-ist
ex-tor'-tive
ex'-tra
extra-canon'i-cal
ex'-tract (n.)
ex-tract' (v.)
ex-tract'-able
ex-tract'-ant
ex-trac'-tion
ex-trac'-tive
ex-trac'-tor
extra-cur-ric'u-
      lar
ex-tra-di't-able
ex'-tra-dite
ex'-tra-dit-ing
ex-tra-dit'ion
ex-tra'dos

extra-ju-dic'ial
extra-mar'i-tal
extra-mun'-dane
extra-mu'ral
extra'neous
extra-or'di-
      narily
extra-or'di-nary
ex-trap'o-late
ex-trap'o-lated
extra-pol-a'tion
extra-pol-a'tory
extra-sen'-sory
extra-terri-
      to'rial
extra-terri-tori-
      al'ity
ex-trav'a-gance
ex-trav'a-gant
ex-trava-gan'za
ex-trav'a-sate
ex-trava-sa'tion
extra-vas'cu-lar
ex-tre'me
ex-tre'mely
ex-tre'm-ism
ex-tre'm-ist
ex-trem'ity
ex'-tri-cable
ex'-tri-cate
ex-tri-ca'tion
ex-trin'-sic
ex-trin'-si-cally
ex-tror'se
ex-tro-ver'-sion
ex'-tro-vert
ex-tro-ver'-tive
ex-tru'de

ex-tru'der
ex-tru'd-ing
ex-tru's-ible
ex-tru'sion
ex-tru'sive
ex-tu'ber-ance
exu'ber-ance
exu'ber-ant
ex'u-date
exu-da'tion
ex-u'de
exult'-ancy
exult'-ant
exul-ta'tion
exult'-ingly
exu'-vial
exu'vi-ate
exuvi-a'tion
eye'-ball
eye'-bright
eye'-brow
eye'-cup
eye'-glass
eye'-hole
eye'-ing
eye'-lash
eye'-less
eye'-let
eye'-let-eer
eye'-lid
eye'-piece
eye'-shade
eye'-sight
eye'-sore
eye'-spot
eye'-strain
eye'-strings
eye'-tooth

eye'-wash
eye'-water
eye'-wink
eye'-wit-ness

F

fab-a'ceous
fa-bel'la
fab'-liau
fab'-ric
fab'-ri-cant
fab'-ri-cate
fab-ri-ca'tion
fab'-ri-cator
fab'u-list
fab'u-lous
fab'u-lously
fa-ça'de
fa'ce-able
fa-ce'tious
fac'ile-ness
fa-cil'i-tate
fa-cili-ta'tion
fa-cil'i-ties
fa-cil'ity
fa-cin'-or-ous
facio-plas'ty
fac-sim'i-le
fac'-tice
fac'-tion
fac'-tional
fac'-tion-al-ism
fac'-tion-ary
fac'-tious
fac'-tiously

fac'-tious-ness
fac-tit'ious
fac-tit'iously
fac'-ti-tive
fac'-tor
fac'-tor-age
fac-to'rial
fac'-tor-ies
fac-tor-is-a'tion
fac'-tor-ise
fac'-tory
fac-to'tum
fac'-tual
fac-tu-al'ity
fac'-tu-ally
fac'-tum
fac'-ture
fac'-ula
fac'-ul-tat-ive
fac'-ul-ties
fac'-ulty
fa-cun'-dity
fad'-di-ness
fad'-dist
fa'de-less
fae'-cal
fae'-ces
fa-ga'ceous
fag'-got
fag'-got-ing
fa-got'to
fail'-ing
fail'-ingly
fail'-ure
faint'-hearted
faint'-ish
faint'-ness
fair'-ies

fair'-ing
fair'-lead
fair'-ness
fair'-sized
fair'-way
fair'y-hood
fair'y-land
fair'y-like
fair'y-tale
faith'-ful
faith'-fully
faith'-ful-ness
faith'-heal-ing
faith'-less
fal'-bala
fal'-cate
fal'-chion
fal'-ci-form
fal'-con
fal'-coner
fal-conet
fal'-conry
fal-cu'la
fal'-cu-late
fal'-deral
fald'-stool
fal'-la-cies
fal-la'cious
fal-la'ciously
fal'-lacy
fal-li-bil'ity
fal'-lible
fall-'ing
fall'-out
fal'-low
fals'e-hearted
fals'e-hood
fals'e-ness

131

fal-set'to
fals'e-work
falsi-fi-ca'tion
fals'i-fied
fals'i-fier
fals'i-fy-ing
fals'-ity
fal'ter-ing
fam-il'ial
fam-il'iar
fam-iliar-is-
    a'tion
fam-il'iar-ise
fam-ili-ar'ity
fam-il'iarly
fam'-il-ies
fam'-il-ism
fam'-ily
fam'-ine
fam'-ish
fam'u-lus
fa-nat'ic
fa-nat'i-cal
fa-nat'i-cism
fan'-cied
fan'-cier
fan'-cies
fan'-ci-ful
fan'-ci-fully
fan'cy-ing
fan'cy-work
fan-dan'gle
fan-dan'go
fan'-fare
fan-faro-na'de
fan'-ning
fan'-tail

fan-ta'sia
fan'-ta-sise
fan'-tast
fan-tas'-tic
fan-tas'ti-cal
fan-tas'ti-cally
fan'-tasy
fan'-tod
fan'-wise
far-ad'ic
fara-dis-a'tion
far'a-dise
far'a-dism
far'-an-dole
far'-away
far'-ci-cal
far-ci-cal'ity
far'-del
fare-well'
far'-fetched
far'-flung
fari'-na
fari-na'ceous
fari'-nose
farm'-house
farm'-ing
farm'-stead
farm'-yard
far-ra'gi-nous
far-ra'go
far-reach'-ing
far'-rier
far'-row
far'-see-ing
far'-sighted
far'-ther
far'-ther-most
far'-thest

far'-thing
far'-thingale
fas'-cicle
fas-cic'u-lar
fas-cic'u-late
fas'-ci-cule
fas'-ci-nate
fas'-ci-nated
fas'-ci-nat-ing
fas'-ci-nat-ingly
fas-ci-na'tion
fas'-ci-nator
fas-ci'ne
fascio'la
fas-cio-li'asis
fas'-cism
fash'ion-able
fash'ion-ably
fa'sten-ing
fas-tid'i-ous
fas-tid'i-ous-
    ness
fas-tig'i-ate
fas-tig'i-ated
fas-tig'ium
fa'st-ing
fa'st-ness
fa'tal-ism
fa'tal-ist
fatal-is'tic
fatal-is'ti-cally
fatal'-ity
fa'te-ful
fa'ther-land
fa'ther-less
fa'ther-like
fa'ther-li-ness
fath'-om-able

fath'om-less
fa-tid'ic
fa-tid'i-cal
fat'i-gable
fa-ti'gued
fa-ti'guing
fa-ti'guingly
fat'-ling
fat'-ness
fat'-ten
fat'-tener
fat'-ter
fat'-tish
fa-tu'itous
fa-tu'ity
fat'u-oid
fat'u-ous
fat'u-ously
fau'-cal
fau'-cal-ise
fau'-ces
fau'-cet
fault'-find-ing
fault'-ily
fault'i-ness
fault'-less
fau'-nal
fau'-ton
fav-e-llid'ium
fav-e'olate
fav-e'olus
fav-o'nian
fa'vour-able
fa'vour-ably
fa'vour-ite
fa'vour-it-ism
fawn'-ing
fay'-al-ite

fear'-ful
fear'-fully
fear'-ful-ness
fear'-less
fear'-lessly
fear'-less-ness
fear'-nought
fear'-some
feas'-ance
feasi-bil'ity
feas'-ible
feath'-er-bed-ding
feath'-er-brain
feath'-ered
feath'-er-edge
feath'-er-head
feath'-er-ing
feath'-er-less
feath'-er-veined
feath'-er-weight
feath'-ery
fea'-ture
fea'-tured
fea'-ture-less
feb'-ri-cide
feb-ric'ity
feb-ric'-ula
feb-ri-fa'cient
feb-rif'er-ous
feb-rif'ic
feb-rif'u-gal
feb'-ri-fuge
feb'-rile
feb-ril'ity
feck'-less
fec'-ula
fec'u-lence

fec'u-lent
fec'-und
fec'-und-ate
fec-und-a'tion
fec-un'da-tive
fec-un'dity
fed'-er-al
fed-er-al-is-
            a'tion
fed'-er-al-ise
fed'-er-al-ism
fed'-er-al-ist
fed-er-al-is'tic
fed'-er-ate
fed-er-a'tion
fed'-er-at-ive
feeb'le-hearted
feeb'le-minded
feeb'le-ness
feed'-bin
feed'-ing
feed'-stuff
feel'-ing
feel'-ingly
feld'-spar
feld-spath'ic
feld'-spa-thoid
feld-spa-thoid'al
fe-li-cide
feli-cif'ic
fel-ic'i-tate
fel-ici-ta'tion
fel-ic'i-tous
fel-ic'ity
fe'-lid
fe'-line
fe-lin'ity
fell'-monger

FELLNESS

fell-ness
fel'-loe
fel'-low
fel'-low-ship
fel-o'ni-ous
fel-o'ni-ously
fel'-ony
fel'-site
fel-sit'ic
fel'-spar
fel'-stone
fel'-teric
felt'-ing
fel-ucc'a
fe'-male
fe-mal'ity
fem'-er-ell
fem'i-nacy
fem-in-al'ity
femi-ne'ity
fem'i-ninc
femi-nin'-ity
fem'-in-ise
fem'-in-ism
fem'-in-ist
fem-in'ity
fem'-mer
fem'-oral
fe'-mur
fen'ce-less
fen'-chene
fen'-chone
fenc'-ible
fenc'-ing
fen'-der
fen-es-tel'la
fen-es'tra
fen-es'tral

fen'-estrated
fen-estra'tion
fen'-nec
fen'-nel
fen'u-greek
feoff'-ment
fer-a'cious
fer-ac'ity
fer'-etory
fe'-rine
fer'-ity
fer-ment' (v.)
fer'-ment (n.)
fer-ment-abil'ity
fer-ment'-able
fer-men-ta'tion
fer-men'ta-tive
fer-ment'er
fer-ment'-ive
fer'-mious
fer'mium
fern'-ery
fer-o'cious
fer-o'cious-ness
fer-oc'ity
fer'-rate
fer'-reous
fer'-ret
fer'-retter
fer'-riage
fer'-ric
fer-ri-cyan'ic
fer-ri-cy'an-ide
fer'-ried
fer'-ries
fer-rif'er-ous
fer'-rite
fer-rit'ic

fer'-ri-tin
fer-ro-cal'-cite
fer'-ro-cene
fer-ro-con'-crete
fer-ro-cy'an-ide
fer-ro-mag-
        net'ic
fer-ro-mag'-net-
        ise
fer-ro-man'gan-
        ism
fer'-ro-type
fer'-rous
fer-rox'yl
fer-ru'gi-nous
fer'-rule
fer'-ry-boat
fer'-ry-ing
fer'-ry-man
fer'-tile
fer-ti-lis-able
fer-ti-lis-a'tion
fer'-ti-lise
fer'-ti-liser
fer'-ti-lism
fer-til'ity
fer'-ula
feru-la'ceous
fer'-ule
fer'-vency
fer'-vent
fer'-vently
fer'-vid
fer'-vour
fes'-cue
fes'-tal
fes'-tally
fes'-ter

fes-ti-na'tion
fes'-ti-val
fes'-tive
fes-tiv'-ity
fes-toon'
fetch-'ing
fe-tip'ar-ous
fet'-ish
fe'-tish
fet'-ish-ism
fe'-tish-ism
fet'-ish-ist
fe'-tish-ist
fet-ish-is'tic
fe-tish-is'tic
fet'-lock
fet'-ter
fet'-ter-lock
feu'-dal
feu-dal-is-a'tion
feu'-dal-ise
feu'-dal-ism
feu'-dal-ist
feu-dal-is'tic
feu-dal'ity
feud'a-tory
feu'-dist
fe'-ver
fe'-vered
fe'-ver-few
fe'-ver-ish
fe'-ver-ishly
fe'-ver-ous
fe'ver-weed
few'-ness
fib'-ber
fib'-bing
fi'bre-board

fi'bri-form
fi'-bril
fi-bril'la
fi-bril'lary
fi-bril-late
fib-ril-la'tion
fi'-bril'li-form
fi'-bril-lose
fi'-bril-lous
fi'-brin
fi-brin'o-gen
fi-bri-nog'en-ous
fi'-bri-nous
fi'-bro-blast
fi-bro-cys'-tic
fi'-broid
fi'-broin
fi'-bro-lite
fi-bro'ma
fi-brom'a-tous
fi-bro-myo'ma
fi-bro-myo-si'tis
fi'-brose
fi-bro'sis
fi-bro-si'tis
fi-brot'ic
fi'-bro-tile
fi'-brous
fib'-ula
fib'u-iar
fick'ie-ness
fic'-tile
fic'-tion
fic'-tional
fic'-tion-ist
fic'-ti'tious
fic-tit'iously
fic'-tive

fid'-dler
fid'-dle-sticks
fid'-dling
fid-el'ity
fid'i-bus
fidu'-cial
fidu'-cially
fidu'-ciary
field'-fare
field'-piece
fields'-man
field'-stone
field-worker
fiend'-ish
fierc'e-ness
fier'-ily
fi'eri-ness
fif-teen'
fif-teen'th
fif'-ti-eth
fi'ght-ing
fig'-ment
fig'u-line
fig'u-rable
fig'u-rant
fig'ur-ate
fig'ur-ately
figu-ra'tion
fig'u-rat-ive
fig'u-rat-ively
fig'-ure
fig'-ured
fig'-ure-head
fig'ur-ine
fig'-wort
fil'a-ment
fila-men'-tory
fila-men'-tous

135

fi'-lar
fil-a'ria
fil-a'rial
fil-ari-a'sis
fil'a-ture
fil'-bert
fil'-emot
fil'-ial
fil'i-ate
fili-a'tion
fil'i-beg
fil'i-bus-ter
fili-ci'dal
fil'i-cide
fili-cin'-ean
fil'i-form
fil'i-gree
fili-pen'-du-lous
fill'-ing
fil'-lis-ter
fil-mo-gen'ic
fil'o-plumes
filo-po'dia
fi'-lose
fil'o-selle
fil'-ter
fil-ter-abil'ity
fil'-ter-able
fil'-terer
filth'-ily
filth'i-ness
fil-tra-bil'ity
fil'-trable
fil'-trate
fil-tra'tion
fim'-bria
fim'-bri-ate
fim'-bri-ated

fim-bri-a'tion
fim'-bril-late
fim-et'ic
fim-ic'o-lous
fi'-nal
fi'-nality
fi'ne-ness
fi'ne-spun
fin-ess'e
fin'-gent
fin'ger-board
fin'ger-ing
fin'ger-plate
fin'ger-post
fin'ger-print
fin'ger-stall
fin'ger-tip
fin'-ial
fin'i-cal
fini-cal'ity
fin'-ick-ing
fin'-icky
fin'-ish
fin'-ished
fin'-isher
fi'-nite
fin'i-tude
fin'-let
fin'-ner
fi're-arm
fi're-back
fi're-ball
fi're-bird
fi're-board
fi're-box
fi're-brand
fi're-brick
fi're-bug

fi're-clay
fi're-cracker
fi're-damp
fi're-dog
fi're-es-ca'pe
fi're-fly
fi're-less
fi're-light
fi're-man
fi're-place
fi're-plug
fi're-power
fire-re-sist'-
       ant
fi're-ship
fi're-side
fi're-stone
fi're-tower
fi're-trap
fi're-watcher
fi're-water
fi're-wood
fi're-works
fir'-kin
fir'-ma-ment
fir-ma-men'-tal
fir'-man
fir-mi-ster'-nous
firm'-ness
fir'-ring
first'-born
first'-hand
first'-ling
fis'-cal
fis'-cally
fish'er-man
fish'-ery
fish'-garth

fish'-hook
fish'-ily
fish'-i-ness
fish'-ing
fish'-line
fish'-monger
fish'-plate
fish'-tail
fish'-wife
fish -worm
fis'-sile
fissi-lin'gual
fis'-sil'ity
fis'sion-able
fis-sip'ar-ous
fiss'i-ped
fissi-ros'-tral
fis'-sure
fis'-sur-ing
fist'i-cuffs
fis-tu'ca
fis'-tula
fis'-tu-lar
fis'-tu-lose
fis'-tu-lous
fitch'-er-ing
fit'-ful
fit'-fully
fit'-ment
fit'-ness
fit'-ted
fit'-ter
fit'-ting
fit'-tingly
fi've-fold
fix'-able
fix-a'te
fix-a'tion

fix'a-tive
fix'a-ture
fix'-edly
fix'-ed-ness
fix'-ing
fix'-ity
fix'-ture
fiz'-zling
flab'-ber-gast
fla'bel'-late
fla-bel'-li-form
fla-bel'-lum
flab'-bi-ness
flac -cid
flac-cid'ity
flac'-cidly
flag'el-lant
flag'el-late
flagel-la'tion
flag'el-lator
fla-gel'-li-form
fla-gel'-lum
flag'eo-let
flag'-ging
fla-git'ious
fla-git'iously
flag'-man
fla'-gon
flag -pole
flag'-ship
flag'-staff
flag'-stone
flail -ing
flam'-beau
flam-boy'-ance
flam-boy'-ancy
flam-boy'-ant
fla-men'co

fla'me-proof
flam'e-thrower
fla-min'go
fla-min'goes
flam'-mable
flam'-mule
flam'-per
flan'-ger
flan'-ging
flan'-nel
flan-nel-ett'e
flan'-ning
flap'-per
flap'-ping
fla're-back
flash -back
flash'-board
flash'-ily
flash'i-ness
flash'-ing
flash'-light
flash-point
flat'-boat
flat-bot'-tomed
flat'-fish
flat'-foot
flar'-head
flat'-let
flat'-ness
flat'-ten
flar-tener
flat'ter-ing
flat'-ting
flat'-tish
flat'-top
flat'u-lence
flat'u-lent
flat'-ware

137

flat'-wise
flat'-worm
flaun'ch-ing
flaun't-ing
flaut'-ist
fla-van'-threne
fla-vesc'ence
fla-vesc'ent
flav'-one
fla-vo-pur'-purin
fla'vour-ing
flaw'-less
flax'-seed
flea'-bane
flea'-bite
flea'-bit-ten
fleak'-ing
flea'-wort
flec'-tion
flec'-tional
fledg'-ling
fleec'i-ness
flee'-ing
fleet'-ing
fleet'-ness
flem'-ish
flesh'i-ness
flesh'-ing
flesh'-less
flesh'-li-ness
flesh'-pot
fletch'-er-ise
fiet'-ton
flexi-bil'ity
flex'-ible
flex'-ile
flex-om'eter
flex'u-ose

flexu-os'ity
flex-u-ous
flex'-ural
flex'-ure
flib-ber-ti-gib-' bet
flick'-er-ing
flick'-er-ingly
flick'-ery
fli'ghti-ness
fli'ght-less
flim's-ily
flim'-si-ness
flin'ch-ing
flin'-ders
fling'-ing
flint'-lock
flip'-pancy
flip'-pant
flip'-per
flip'-ping
flir-ta'tion
flir-ta'tious
flir't-ing
flir't-ingly
flitch'-ing
flit'-ter
flit'-ter-mouse
flit'-ting
float'-able
float'-age
float'-ing
floc-cil-la'tion
floc-ci-ta'tion
floc'-cose
floc'-cu-lant
floc-cu-la'tion
floc'-cu-lator

floc'-cule
floc'-cu-lence
floc'-cu-lent
floc'-cu-lose
floc'-cu-lous
floc'-cu-lus
floc'-cus
flog'-ging
flood'-gate
flood'-ing
flood'-light
flood-om'eter
flood'-proof
flood'-tide
floor'-ing
floor'-walker
flop'-ping
flor-esc'ence
flor-esc'ent
flor'i-ate
flor'i-ated
flori-cul'-tural
flori-cul'-tur-al-ist
flor'i-cul-ture
flor-id'ity
flor'-idly
flor'-id-ness
flor-if'er-ous
flor'-ist
flor-is'tic
flor'u-lent
flos'-cu-lar
flos'-cu-lous
flo-ta'tion
flo-til'la
flot'-sam
floun'c-ing

floun'-der
floun'-dered
floun'-der-ing
flou'rish-ing
flour-om'eter
flout'-ing
flow'er-ily
flow'er-ing
flow'er-pot
fluc'-tu-ant
fluc'-tu-ate
fluc'-tu-ated
fluc-tu-a't-ing
fluc-tu-a'tion
flu'-ency
flu'-ent
fluff'i-ness
flu-id'ic
flu-id'-ify
flu'-id-ise
flu-id'ity
flu'-ing
flum'-mery
flun'-key
fluo-bo'rate
fluo-bor'ic
fluo-bo'rite
flu'-or-ene
flu-or-esc'e
flu-or-es'cein
flu-or-esc'ence
flu-or-esc'ent
flu-or-esc'ing
flu-or'ic
flu'-ori-date
flu-ori-da'tion
flu'-or-ide
flu'-ori-dise

flu'-ori-nate
flu'-or-ine
flu'-or-ite
flu'-oro-phore
flu'-oro-scope
flu-or-os'copy
flu-or-o'sis
flu'or-spar
fluo-sil'i-cate
fluo-si-lic'ic
flur'-ried
flur'-ries
flur'-ry-ing
flush'-ing
flus'-ter
flus'-tra
flus-tra'tion
flu-ti'na
flut'-ter
flut'-tered
flut'-ter-ing
flut'-tery
flu'-vial
flu'-vial-ist
flu'-via-tile
flu-vi-ol'ogy
flux'-ible
flux'ion-ary
flux'-meter
fly'-away
fly'-blow
fly'-blown
fly'-boat
fly'-catcher
fly'-ing
fly'-ing-fish
fly'-ing-jib

fly'-leaf
fly'-paper
fly'-speck
fly'-trap
fly'-weight
fly'-wheel
foam'-ing
fo'-cal
fo-cal-is-a'tion
fo'-cal-ise
fo-cim'eter
fo-com'eter
fo'-cus
fo'-cused
fo'-cuser
fo'-cus-ing
fod'-der
foe'-man
foeti-ci'dal
foet'i-cide
foe'-tus
fog'-horn
fog'-ram
foil'-ing
fol'-de-rol
fo'ld-ing
foli-a'ceous
fo'-li-age
fo'-li-ate
fo'-li-ated
fo-li-a'tion
fo'-lic
fo'-li-cole
fo'-lio
fo-lio-bran'chi-ate
fo'-lio-late
fo'-li-ole

fo'-lio-lose
fo'-li-ose
fo'-lium
fo'lk-lore
fo'lk-ways
fo'lk-weave
fol'-licle
fol-lic'u-lar
fol-licu-li'tis
fol-licu-lo'ma
fol'-low
fol'-lowed
fol'-lower
fol'-low-ing
fol'-low-through
fol'-low-up
fo-ment'
fo-men-ta'tion
fo-ment'er
fon'-dant
fond'-ler
fond'-ling
fond'-ness
fon'-tal
fon-ta-nel'
food'-stuff
fool'-ery
fool'-hardi-ness
fool'-hardy
fool'-ing
fool'-ish
fool'-ishly
fool'-ish-ness
fool'-proof
fools'-cap
foot'-age
foot'-ball

foot'-bath
foot'-board
foot'-bridge
foot'-boy
foot'-candle
foot'-fall
foot'-hill
foot'-hold
foot'-ing
foot'-less
foot'-light
foot'-ling
foot'-loose
foot'-man
foot'-mark
foot'-note
foot'-pad
foot'-path
foot'-plate
foot'-print
foot'-room
foot'-rule
foot -sore
foot'-step
foot'-stool
foot'-walk
foot'-wear
foot'-work
foot'-worn
fop'-pery
fop'-pish
for'-age
for'-aged
for'-ager
for'-ag-ing
for-a'men
for-am'-ina
fora-min'i-fer

for-amin-if'eral
for-amin-if'er-
    ous
for-am'i-nous
for-as-much'
for-bear'
for-bid'
fo'rce-ful
fo'rce-meat
for'-ceps
fo'rc-ible
fo'rc-ibly
fo'rc-ing
for'-ci-pate
for-cip'i-form
for'-cyte
fo'rd-able
fo're-arm
fo're-bear
fore-bo'de
fore-bo'd-ing
fo're-cast
fo're-caster
fore-clo'se
fore-clo's-ure
fo're-court
fore-doom'
fo're-father
fo're-finger
fo're-foot
fo're-front
fore-go'er
fo're-go-ing
fo're-gone
fo're-ground
fo're-hand
fo're-handed
fo're-head

fo're-hook
for'eign-ness
fore-judg'e
fore-judg'e-ment
fore-know'
fore-know'l-edge
fo're-land
fo're-leg
fo're-look
fo're-man
fo're-mast
fore-men'-tioned
fo're-most
fo're-name
fo're-noon
for-en'-sic
for-en'-si-cal
for-en'-si-cal-ly
fore-or-dain'
fore=or'di-nate
fore-or-di-
    na'tion
fo're-part
fo're-paw
fo're-peak
fo're-quarter
fore-run' (v.)
fo're-run (n.)
fo're-run-ner
fo're-sail
fore-saw'
fore-see'
fore-see'-able
fore-see'-ing
fore-seen'
fore-shad'ow
fo're-sheet
fo're-shore

fore-short'en
fo're-side
fo're-sight
fo're-skin
for'-est
for'-estal
fore-stall'
for-est-a'tion
fo're-stay
for'-ested
for'-ester
for'-estry
fo're-taste (n.)
fore-ta'ste (v.)
fore-tell'
fore-tell'er
fore-tell'-ing
fo're-thought
fo're-token (n.)
fore-to'ken (v.)
fore-to'ld
fore-top'
for-ev'er
fore-warn'
fo're-woman
fo're-word
fo're-yard
for'-fars
for'-feit
for'-feit-able
for'-feiter
for'-feit-ure
for'-fend'
for'-fi-cate
for-fic'i-form
for-fic'u-late
for-gath'er
for-ga've

forg'e-able
forg'-ery
for-get'
for-get'-ful
for-get'-ful-ness
forg'-etive
for-get'-me-not
for-get'-table
for-get'-ting
forg'-ing
for-giv'-able
for-giv'e
for-giv'en
for-giv'e-ness
for-giv'-ing
for-go'-ing
for-gon'e
for-got'
for-got'-ten
for'-int
fork'-edly
for-lorn'
for-lorn'ly
for'-mal
for-mal'-dehyde
for'-mal-ise
for'-mal-iser
for'-mal-is-ing
for'-mal-ism
for'-mal-ist
for-mal-is'tic
for-mal'ity
for'-mally
form'-ant
for'-mat
for-ma'te
for'-mates
for'-matin

141

for-ma´-tion
for´-ma-tive
for´-mene
for´-mer
for´-merly
for´-mic
for´-mi-cary
for´-mi-cate
for-mi-ca´tion
for´-mi-cide
for-mida-bil´ity
for´-mi-dable
form´-less
for´-moxy
for´-mula
formu-lar-is-
    a´tion
for´-mu-lar-ise
for´-mu-lary
for´-mu-late
for-mu-la´tion
for´-mu-lator
for´-mu-lise
for´-mu-lism
for-mu-list
for-mu-lis´tic
for´-myl
for´-my-late
for-nent´
for´-ni-cate
for-ni-ca´tion
for´-ni-cator
for´-nix
for-sa´ke
for-sa´ken
for-sook´
for-sooth´
for´-ster-ite

for-swear´
for-sworn´
for-sy´thia
for´ta-lice
forth´-coming
forth-go´ing
forth´-right
forth-with´
for´ti-eth
for-ti-fi-ca´tion
for´-ti-fied
for´-ti-fier
for´-tify
for´-ti-tude
for-ti-tu´di-nous
fort´-night
fort´-nightly
for´-tress
for-tu´-itism
for-tu´-itist
for-tu´-itous
for-tu´-ity
for´-tu-nate
for´-tu-nately
for´-tune
for´-tune-tell-er
fo´-rum
for´-ward
for´-warder
for´-wardly
for´-ward-ness
for-went´
foss-ett´e
fos´-sick
fos´-sil
fos-si-late
fos-si-la´tion
fossi-lif´er-ous

fos-sil-is-a´tion
fos´-sil-ise
fos-so´ri-al
fos´-ter
fos´-ter-age
fos´-ter-ling
fou-droy´-ant
fou-gass´e
fou´-lard
foul´-ing
foul´-ness
fou´-mart
foun-da´tion
foun´-der
foun´-der-ous
found´-ling
foun´-dries
foun´-tain
foun´-tain-head
foun´-tain-pen
four´-fold
four´-score
four´-some
four´-square
four´-teen
four´-teenth
fo´-vea
fo-ve´ola
fo-ve´o-lar
fo-ve´o-late
fo-vil´la
fowl´-ing
fox´-glove
fox´-hole
fox´-hound
fox´i-ness
fox´-tail

frac'-tion
frac'-tional
frac'-tion-ary
frac'-tion-ate
frac'-tion-at-ing
frac-tion-a'tion
frac'-tion-ise
frac'-tious
frac-tog'ra-phy
frac'-tural
frac'-ture
fra-ga'ria
fra-gil'ity
frag'-ment
frag-men'tal
frag'-men-tary
frag-men-ta'tion
frag'-mented
frag'-men-tise
frail'-ties
fram-be'sia
fra'me-work
fran'-chise
fran'ci-um
franc'o-lin
fran-gi-bil'ity
fran'-gible
frangi-pan'i
frank'-furter
frank'-in-cense
frank'-ing
frank'-lin
frank'-lin-ite
frank'-ness
fran'-tic
fran'-ti-cally
fra-ter'-nal
fra-ter'-nal-ism

frat-er-nis-
    a'tion
frat'-er-nise
fra-ter'-nity
frat-ri-ci'dal
frat'-ri-cide
fraud'u-lence
fraud'u-lent
fraud'u-lently
fraxi-nel'la
fraz'-zling
freak'-ish
free'-board
free'-booter
free'-born
freed'-man
free'-dom
free'-hand
free'-handed
free'-hold
free'-lance
free-lan'cing
free'-man
free'-mar-tin
free-ma'sonry
free'-sia
free'-stone
free'-thinker
free-think'-ing
free'-way
free'-wheel
free-wheel'-ing
free'-will
freez'-ing
freight'-age
frem'i-tus
fren-et'ic
fren-et'i-cal

fren-et'i-cally
fren'u-lum
fre'-num
fren'-zied
fre'-quency
fre'-quent (a.)
fre-quent' (v.)
fre-quen-ta'tion
fre-quen'ta-tive
fre-quen'-ter
fre'-quently
fres'-coer
fres'-coes
fresh'-ener
fresh'-en-ing
fresh'-man
fresh'-ness
fresh'-water
fret'-ful
fret'-fully
fret'-saw
fret'-ted
fret'-ting
fret'-work
fri-abil'ity
fri'-able
fri'-ary
fric'a-tive
fric'-tion
fric'-tional
friend'-less
friend'-lily
friend'-li-ness
friend'-ship
frig'-ate
fri'ght-ened
fri'ght-en-ing
fri'ght-ful

FRIGHTFULLY

fri'ght-fully
fri'ght-ful-ness
frig-id'ity
frigor-if'ic
frill'-ing
frin'-gil-line
frin'-ging
frip'-pery
fris'-ket
frisk'-ily
frisk'i-ness
frisk'-ing
frit-il'-lary
frit'-ter
frit'-ting
friv-ol'ity
friv'-olled
friv'-ol-ling
friv'-ol-ous
frizz'-ing
friz'-zling
frog'-bit
frog'-ging
frog'-man
frol'-icked
frol'-ick-ing
frol'-ic-some
fron-desc'ence
fron'-dose
front'-age
fron-tier'
fron-tiers'-man
front'-is-piece
front'-less
front'-let
fronto-gen'-esis
fron-tol'y-sis
fron-to-par-i'etal

frost'-bite
frost'-bitten
frost'i-ness
frost'-ing
frost'-proof
froth'-ily
fro'-ward
frown'-ing
frow'zi-ness
fruc-tesc'ence
fruc-tif'er-ous
fruc-ti-fi-
    ca'tion
fruc'-ti-fied
fruc'-tify
fruc-tiv'or-ous
fruc-tol'y-sis
fruc'-tose
fruc'-to-side
fruc'-tu-ous
fru'-gal
fru-gal'ity
fru'-gally
fru'-gal-ness
fru-giv'or-ous
fruit'-age
fruit-a'rian
fruit'-erer
fruit'-ful
fruit'-ful-ness
fruit'i-ness
fru-it'ion
fruit'-less
fru-men-ta'ceous
fru'-menty
frump'-ish
frus-tr_'te
frus-tra'ted

frus-tra'ter
frus-tra't-ing
frus-tra'tion
frus'-tule
frus'-tum
fru-tesc'ence
fru-tesc'ent
fru'-tex
fru'ti-cose
fuch'-sine
fuch'-site
fu-civ'or-ous
fu'-coid
fu-coid'al
fu-cos'-terol
fuco-xan'-then
fu'-cus
fud'-dling
fu'el-ler
fu'el-ling
fu-ga'cious
fu-ga'ciously
fu-gac'ity
fu'-gal
fu'gi-tive
fu'gle-man
ful'-crum
fulfil'-ling
fulfil'-ment
ful'gur-at-ing
fulgur-a'tion
ful'gur-ite
ful'gur-ous
fu-lig'i-nous
full'-back
full'-ness
fu'l-mar

144

fu'lmi-nate
fu'lmi-nat-ing
fulmi-na'tion
fu'lmi-nator
fu'lmi-nat-ory
fu'lmi-nous
fu'l-some
fu'l-some-ness
fu-made'
fu-mar'ic
fu'-ma-role
fu'-mar-ose
fu-ma-to'rium
fu'-ma-tory
fum'-bler
fum'-bling
fu'-mi-gate
fu'-mi-gat-ing
fu-mi-ga'tion
fu-mi-gator
fu'-mi-tory
fu'-mous
fu'-mu-lus
fu-nam'bu-list
func'-tion
func'-tional
func'-tion-ary
func'-tion-ate
fun'-da-ment
fun-da-men'-tal
fun-da-men'-tal-
      ism
fun-da-men'-tal-
      ist
fun-da-men'-tally
fun'-dus
fu'-neral
fu'-ner-ary

fu-ne'real
fun-gi-bil'ity
fun'-gible
fun'gi-cidal
fun'gi-cide
fun-giv'or-ous
fungos'-ity
fu'-nicle
fu-nic'u-lar
fu-nic'u-lose
fu-nic'u-lus
fu'-ni-form
fu'-nnel
fun'-nelled
fun'-nel-ling
fun'-nily
fu'-ran
fu'-rane
fur'-be-low
fur'-bish
fur'-bisher
fur'-cate
fur-ca'tion
fur'-cu-lum
fur-fur-a'ceous
fur -fural
fu'ri-bund
fu'ri-ous
fu'ri-ously
fur'-long
fur'-lough
fur'-nace
fur'-nish
fur'-nisher
fur'-nish-ings
fur'-ni-ture
fu-ro'ic
fu'-ror

fu-ro're
fur'-rier
fur'-ri-ness
fur'-row
fur'-ther-ance
fur'-ther-more
fur'-ther-most
fur'-tive
fur'-tively
fu'-runcle
fu-run'cu-lar
fu-runcu-lo'sis
fu-sain'
fu'sa-role
fus'-cous
fu'-sel
fu'-sel-age
fu-si-bil'ity
fu's-ible
fu'si-form
fu'sil-ier
fu'sil-lade
fuso-spi'ro-chete
fuss'-ily
fus'-tian
fus'-tic
fus'-ti-gate
fus'-tily
fus'-ti-ness
fu'-thorc
fu'-tile
fu'-tilely
fu-tili-ta'rian
fu-til'ity
fut'-tock
fu'-tural
fu-tur-am'ic
fu'-ture

FUTURISM

fu'-tur-ism
fu'-tur-ist
fu-tur-is'tic
fu-tu'rity
fuzz'i-ness
fyl'-fot

G

gab'-ar-dine
gab'-bart
gab'-bing
gab'-bro
gab'-er-dine
gad'-about
gad'-ding
gad'-fly
gad'o-lin-ite
gado-lin'-ium
gad-droon'
gad'-wall
gaf'-fer
gag'-ger
gag'-ging
gahn'-ite
gai'-ety
gail-lar'-dia
gain'-ful
gain'-said
gain'-say
gai'-ter
ga-lac'-ta-gogue
ga-lac'-tan
ga-lac'-tic
ga-lac'-tin
ga-lac'-tite
ga-lac-tom'eter

ga-lac-tom'etry
ga-lacto-phor-
    i'tis
ga-lacto-poi-
    e'sis
ga-lac-tor-rhe'a
ga-lac'-tose
ga-lac-to'sis
ga-la'go
gal-an'-thus
gal'-an-tine
gal-an'ty
gal-ate'a
gal'-axy
gal'ba-num
gal'-bu-lus
gal'-eate
gal-een'y
gal'-eiform
gal-e'na
gal-en'ic
gal-en'i-cal
gal-er-ic'u-late
gal-er'i-form
gal'-ets
gali-ma'tias
gal'-ingale
gal'-lantly
gal'-lan-tries
gal'-lan-try
gal'-leass
gal'-leon
gal'-lery
gal'-let
gal'-ley
gal'-leys
gal-li-am'bic
gal'-liard

gal'-li-cism
gal-li-gas'-kins
gal-li-na'ceous
gal-li-na'zo
gall'-ing
gal'-li-nule
gal'-liot
gal'-li-pot
gal'-lium
gal'-li-vant
gal'-lon
gall'i-wasp
gal-loon'
gal'-lop
gal-lop-ade'
gal'-loped
gal'-loper
gal'-lop-ing
gal'-lo-way
gal'-lows
gall'-stone
ga-lo're
ga-losh'
ga-losh'es
gal-van'ic
gal-van-is-a'tion
gal'-van-ise
gal'-van-iser
gal'-van-is-ing
gal'-van-ism
gal-vano-caut'-
    ery
gal-vano-mag-
    net'ic
gal-va-nom'eter
gal-va-nom'etry
gal-van'o-scope
gal'-va-no-scope

gal-van-os'copy
gal-van-os'tegy
gal-vano-trop'ic
gal-va-not'ro-
   pism
gal'-yak
ga-mash'es
gam-ba'do
gam'-be-son
gam'-bier
gam'-bit
gam'-bler
gam'-bling
gam-bo'ge
gam'-bol
gam'-boled
gam'-bol-ling
gam'-brel
gam-broom'
ga'me-cock
ga'me-keeper
ga'me-ness
ga'me-some
ga'me-ster
ga-met-an'-gium
ga-me'te
ga-me'tic
ga-me'ti-cally
ga-me'to-cyst
ga-me'to-cyte
ga-meto-gen'-esis
ga-meto-nu'clear
ga-me'to-phore
ga-me'to-phyte
ga-meto-phyt'ic
gam-ma'dion
gamma-glob'u-lin
gam'-ma-graph

gam'-mer
gam'-mon
gamo-gen'-esis
gamo-gen-et'ic
gamo-gen'ic
gam-og'ony
gamo-pet'a-lous
gamo-pet'-aly
gam'o-phase
gamo-phyl'-lous
gamo-sep'a-lous
gan'-der
gan'gli-ate
gan'gli-ated
gangli-ec'-tomy
gan'gli-form
gangli-i'tis
gan'gli-oid
gan'gli-on-ated
gangli-on'ic
gan-gli-on-i'tis
gang'-plank
gan'gren-ous
gang'-ster
gang'-way
gan'-is-ter
gan'-net
gan'-oid
gan'-trees
gan'-try
gar'-bling
gar'-board
gard'-ant
gar'-dener
gar-de'nia
ga're-fowl
gar'-fish
gar-gan'-tuan

gar'-get
gar'-gling
gar'-goyle
gar'-land
gar'-lic
gar'-licky
gar'-ment
gar'-ner
gar'-net
gar-ni-er-ite
gar'-nish
gar-nishee'
gar-nishee'-ing
gar'-nisher
gar'-nish-ing
gar'-nish-ment
gar'-ni-ture
gar'-ret
gar'-ret-ing
gar-ri-son
gar'-ron
gar'-rot
gar-rott'e
gar-rott'ed
gar-rott'-ing
gar-ru'lity
gar'-ru-lous
gar'-ru-lously
gar'-ter
gas-con-a'de
gas-elier'
gas'i-fi-able
gasi-fi-ca'tion
gas'-ify
gas'-ket
gas'-light
gas'o-line
gas-om'eter

gaso-met'ric
gas-om'etry
gas'-ser
gas'-sing
gas-ter-ec'-tomy
gas-ter-op'oda
gas-ter-op'o-dous
gas-tero-zo'id
gas-tral'-gia
gas-tra'lia
gas-trec'-tomy
gas'-tric
gas-tri'tis
gas'-tro-cele
gas-tro-cen'-
    trous
gastro-cne'mius
gas-tro-col'ic
gas-tro-duo-
    de'nal
gas-tro-duo-den-
    i'tis
gas-tro-duo-den-
    os'tomy
gas-tro-en-ter-
    i'tis
gas-tro-en-ter-
    os'tomy
gas-tro-in-tes'-
    ti-nal
gas'-tro-lith
gas'-trol'-oger
gas-trol'-ogist
gas-trol'ogy
gas-tro-my-
    ot'omy
gas-tron'-omer
gas-tron-om'ic

gas'-tro-nom'i-cal
gas-tron'-omist
gas-tron'-omy
gas-tro-pex'y
gas'-tro-pod
gas-trop'o-dous
gas'-tro-pore
gas-trop-to'sis
gas'-tro scope
gas-tros'copy
gas-tros'tomy
gas-tro-tax'is
gas-tro-vas'cu-
    lar
gas'-trula
gas-tru-la'tion
gas'-works
ga'te-post
ga'te-way
gath'-ered
gath'-erer
gath'-er-ing
gat'-ling
gauch'-erie
gaud'-ery
gaud'-ily
gaud'-ness
gaud'-ness
gaug'-ing
gaul-the'ria
gaunt'-let
gauz'i-ness
ga-vag'e
gav'-eler
gav'-el-kind
ga-vott'e
gawk'i-ness
gay'-ness
ga-ze'bo

ga'ze-hound
ga-zell'e
ga-zett'e
gaz'et-teer
gaz'o-gene
ge-ant-cli'nal
ge-an'ti-cline
gear'-ing
gear'-shift
gear'-wheel
geito-nog'amy
gel'a-tin-ase
gel-at'i-nate
gel'a-tine
gela-tin'i-form
gel-a'tino-chlor'-
    de
gel-ati-nis-
    a'tion
gel-at'i-nise
gel-at'i-niser
gel-at'i-noid
gel-at'i-nous
gel-a'tion
geld'-ing
gel-id'ity
gel'-ig-nite
gel-om'eter
gel-se'mic
gel-se'mium
gem'i-nate
gemi-na'tion
gem'i-nat-ive
gem'-ini
gem-ma'ceous
gem-ma'te (v.)
gem'-mate (a.)
gem-ma'tion

gem'-ma-tive
gem-mic'er-ous
gem'-mi-form
gem-mip'ar-ous
gem-mo-log'i-cal
gem-mol'ogy
gem'-mule
gems'-bok
gen'-der
genea-log'i-cal
genea-log'i-cally
gen-eal'ogist
gen-eal'ogy
gen-ecol'ogy
gen'-era
gen'-eral
gen-er-al-is-
     a'tion
gen'-er-al-ise
gen-er-al-is'simo
gen-er-al'ity
gen'-er-ally
gen'-er-al-ship
gen'-er-ate
gen'-er-at-ing
gen-er-a'tion
gen'-er-at-ive
gen'-er-ator
gen'-era-trix
gen-er'ic
gen-er'i-cal
gen-er'i-cally
gen-er-os-'ity
gen'-erous
gen'-er-ously
gen'-esis
gen-eth'-liac
gen-eth-li'acal

gen-et'ic
gen-et'i-cal
gen-et'i-cist
gen-et'ics
ge'-nial
ge-nial'-ity
ge-'nially
gen-ic'u-lar
gen-ic'u-late
ge'-nie
ge'nio-plasty
gen-is'ta
gen'i-tal
geni-ti'val
gen'i-tive
gen'ito-u'ri-nary
gen'i-ture
ge'-nius
geno-ci'dal
gen'o-cide
gen'o-mere
gen'o-type
geno-typ'ic
gen-teel'
gen-teel'ly
gen'-tian
gen-tian-a'ceous
gen-tian-el'la
gen'-tianin
gen-til'ity
gen'tle-folk
gen'tle-man
gen'tle-ness
gen'tle-woman
gen'-trice
gen'-try
gen'-ual
gen'u-flect

genu-flec'-tion
genu-flec'-tor
genu-flec'-tory
genu-flex'ion
gen'u-ine
gen'u-inely
gen'u-ine-ness
ge'-nus
geo-bio'tic
geo-car'-pic
geo-car'py
geo-cen'-tric
geo-cen'-tri-cal
geo-cen'-tri-cism
geo-chem'i-cal
geo-chem'-is-try
ge-och'-rony
ge-oc'ro-nite
ge'-ode
geo-des'ic
ge-od'-esist
ge-od'-esy
geo-det'ic
geo-det'i-cal
ge-od'ic
ge'o-duck
geo-g-nos'tic
geo-g'-nosy
geo-gon'ic
ge-og'ony
ge-og'ra-pher
geo-graph'ic
geo-graph'i-cal
geo-graph'i-cally
ge-og'ra-phy
ge'-oid
ge-oid'al
ge-ol'-atry

149

geo-log'ic
geo-log'i·cal
ge-ol'o-gise
ge-ol'-ogist
ge-ol'ogy
geo-mag-net'ic
geo-mag'-net-ism
ge'o-mancy
gc-om'a trisc
ge-om'eter
geo-met'ric
geo-met'ri-cal
ge-om-etric'ian
gc-om'-etrid
ge-om'-etriser
ge-om'etry
geo-nas'ty
ge-oph'a-gist
ge-oph'a-gous
ge-oph'-agy
geo-phil'ic
geo-phys'i-cal
geo-phys'i-cist
geo-phys'-ics
ge'o-phyte
geo-phyt'ic
geo-pol-it'i-cal
geo-poli-tic'ian
geo-pol'i-tics
geo-pon'-ics
ge-os'copy
geo-syn'-cline
geo-tac'-tic
geo-tax'is
geo-tech-no-
    log'i-cal
geo-tech-nol'ogy
geo-tec-ton'ic
150

geo-ther'-mal
ge'o-tome
geo-trop'ic
ge-ot'ro-pism
ger-ani-a'ceous
ger-a'nial
ger-a'nium
ger'-bil
ger'-fal-con
geria-tric'ian
geri-at'rics
ger-man'-der
ger-ma'ne
ger'-ma-nite
ger-ma'nium
ger-ma'rium
ger'-men
ger'-mi-cidal
ger'-mi-cide
ger'-min-able
ger'-mi-nal
ger'-mi-nant
ger'-mi-nate
ger-mi-na'tion
ger'-mi-nat-ive
ger'-mi-nator
ger-mi-par'ity
ger'-mon
germ'-proof
gero-don'-tics
ger-on'-tic
ger-on-toc'racy
ger-on-to-log'i-
    cal
ger-on-tol'-ogist
ger-on-tol'ogy
ger'-ry-man-der
ger'-und

ger-un'-dial
ger-un-di'val
ger-un'-dive
ges'-tate
ges-ta't-ing
ges-ta'tion
ges-ta-to'rial
ges'-ta-tory
ges'-tic
ges-tic'u-late
ges-ticu-la'tion
ges-tic'u-lat-ive
ges-tic'u-lat-ory
ges'-ture
ges'-tur-ing
get'-away
get'-ter
get'-ting
gew'-gaw
gey'ser-ite
gha'st-li-ness
gho'st-like
gho'st-li-ness
gho'st-writer
gho'st-writ-ten
ghoul'-ish
gi'ant-ess
gi'ant-ism
giar-di'asis
gib'-ber
gib-ber-el'lic
gib-ber-el'lin
gib'-ber-ish
gib'-bet
gib'-bon
gib-bos'ity
gib'-bous
gibbs'-ite

gib'-lets
gi'-bus
gid'-dily
gid'-di-ness
gigan-te'an
gigan-tesq'ue
gigan'-tic
gigan'-tism
gigan-tom'achy
gig'-ger-ing
gig'-gling
gil'-bert
gild'-ing
gil'-lie
gil'-ly-flower
gil'-son-ite
gil'-vous
gim'-bal
gim'-balled
gim'-crack
gim'-let
gim'-mal
gim'-mick
gin'-gal
gin'-ger
gin'-ger-bread
gin'-ger-li-ness
gin'-gerly
gin'-gery
gin'-gili
gin-gi'val
gin-gi-vi'tis
ging'ly-moid
ging'ly-mus
gin'-ney
gin'-seng
gir-aff'e

gir'an-dole
gir'a-sol
gir'-der
gird'-ing
gird'-ler
gird'-ling
girl'-hood
girl'-ish
girl'-ishly
gi-sarm'e
git'-tern
giv'e-away
giv'-ing
giz'-zard
gla-bel'la
gla-bresc'ent
gla'cial-ist
gla'ci-ate
glaci-a'tion
gla'-cier
glaci-ol'ogy
glaci-om'eter
gla'-cis
glad'-den
glad'i-ate
glad'i-ator
gladia-to'rial
gladi-o'lus
glad'-ness
glad'-some
glad'-stone
glair'-eous
glam'-or-ise
glam'-or-ous
glam'-our
glanc'-ing
glan'-der-ous
glan'-ders

glan-dif'er-ous
glan'-di-form
glan'du-lar
glan'-dule
glan-du-lif'er-
ous
glan'-du-lous
glass'-blower
glass'-cloth
glass'-cut'ter
glass'-ful
glass'-ily
glass'-ine
glass'i-ness
glass'-ware
glass'-wort
glau'ber-ite
glau-co'ma
glau-co'ma-tous
glau'-con-ite
glau-con-it'ic
glau'-co-phane
glau'-cous
gla'z-ier
gla'z-ing
gleam'-ing
glean'-ing
gleb'u-lose
glen-do-veer'
glee'-ful
gle'-noid
gli'a-din
gli'd-ing
glim'-mer
glim'-mer-ing
glim'-mer-ingly
glimps'-ing
glint'-ing

151

GLIOMA

gli-o'ma
gli-oma-to'sis
gli-om'a-tous
glis-sad'e
glis-san'do
glis'ten-ing
glis'-ter
glit'-ter
glit'-ter-ing
glit'-tery
gloam'-ing
gloat'-ing
glo'-bal
glo'-bal-ism
glo-bal'ity
glo'-bally
glo'-bate
glo'be-trot'-ter
glo-biger-i'na
glo'-bin
glo'-boid
glo'-bose
glo-bos'ity
glob'u-lar
globu-lar'ity
glob'-ule
globu-lif'er-ous
glob'u-lin
glob'u-lite
glob'u-lose
glo'-bus
glo-chid'i-ate
glock'-en-spiel
gloco-cys-tid'ium
glom'-er-ate
glom-er-a'tion
glom-er'u-lar
glom-er'u-late

glom'-er-ule
glom-eru-li'tis
glom-er'u-lus
glo'-mus
glon'o-ine
gloom'-ily
gloom'i-ness
gloom'-ing
glori-fi-ca'tion
glo'-ri-fied
glo'-ri-fier
glo'-rify
glo'-ri-fy-ing
glo'-ri-ole
glo'-ri-ous
glo'-ri-ously
glos'-sal
gloss-a'rial
gloss'-ar-ist
gloss-a'rium
gloss'-ary
gloss'-ate
gloss-a'tor
gloss-ec'tomy
gloss'-ily
gloss'i-ness
gloss-i'tis
gloss'-meter
glosso-dyn'ia
gloss-og'ra-pher
gloss-ol'ogy
glos-soph'a-gine
glosso-ple'gia
gloss'o-spasm
glot'-tal
glot'-tis
glot-tol'ogy
glow'er-ing

glow'er-ingly
glow'-ing
glow'-worm
glox-in'ia
glu-cin'-ium
glu'-ci-num
glu-con'ic
glu'-co-phore
gluco-pro'tein
glu-co'sa-mine
glu'-co-san
glu'-cose
glu'-co-sidase
glu'-co-side
glu-cu-ron'ic
glu'ey-ness
glu'-ing
glu-ma'ceous
glu-mif'er-ous
glum'-ness
glu-mo'se
glu-tam'ic
glu'-ta-mine
glu-te'al
glu'-telin
glu'-ten
glu'-tenin
glu-te'us
glu'-ti-nate
glu'-tin-ise
glu-tin-os'ity
glu'-ti-nous
glu'-ti-nously
glut'-ted
glut'-ting
glut'-ton
glut'-ton-ous
glut'-tony

152

glyc'er-ate
glyc'er-ide
glyc'er-ine
glycero-phos-
      phor'ic
gly'-ceryl
gly-cid'ic
gly'-cine
gly-clon'ic
gly'-co-coll
gly'-co-gen
gly-co-gen'-esis
gly-co-gen'ic
gly'-col
gly-col'ic
gly-col'y-sis
gly-co-lyt'ic
gly-co-pro'tein
gly-co-su'ria
gly-cu-ron'ic
gly-ox'al
gly-ox-al'ic
gly-ox-yl'ic
glyph'o-graph
glyph-og'ra-pher
glypho-graph'ic
glyph-og'ra-phy
glyp'-tal
glyp'-tic
glyp'-to-don
glyp'-to-dont
glyp-tog'ra-phy
gmel'-in-ite
gnath'-ism
gnath'-ite
gnath'o-base
gnath-on'ic
gnath'o-pod

gnath-op'o-dite
gnatho-the'ca
gnat'-like
gnaw'-ing
gneiss'-oid
gno'm-ish
gno-mol'ogy
gno'-mon
gno-mon'ic
gno'-sis
gnos'-tic
gnos'-ti-cism
gnoto-biot'ics
goal'-keeper
goat'-herd
goat'-ling
goat'-skin
goat'-sucker
go-bang'
gob'-ber
gob'-bet
gob'-bler
gob'-bling
go'-be-tween'
gob'-let
gob'-lin
god'-child
god'-daugh-ter
god'-dess
god'-father
god'-fear-ing
god'-for-saken
god'-head
god'-less
god'-less-ness
god'-like
god'-li-ness
god'-mother

go-down'
god'-parent
go-droon'
god'-send
god'-ship
god'-son
god'-wit
goeth'-ite
go-et'ic
go'-fer
gof'-fer
gof'-fer-ing
gog'-gling
gog'-let
go'-ing
goi-tro-gen'ic
goi-tro-gen-
      ic'ity
goi-trog'en-ous
goi'-trous
gold'-beater
gold'-brick
gold'-crest
gold'-dig-ger
gold'en-eye
gold'-en-haired
gold'-en-rod
gold'-fields
gold'-finch
gold'-fish
gold'i-locks
gold'-smith
gol'i-ard
goli-ar'dic
gol'-li-wog
gom-been'
gom-broon'
gom'-eral

153

GOMPHOSIS

gom-pho'sis
go-mu'ti
gona-dec'tomy
gon-a'dial
gon-ad'ic
gon-ado-tro'phin
gon'-dola
gon-do-lier'
gon-do-li'no
gon'-fa-lon
gon-fa-lon-ier'
gon'-fa-non
go-nid'-ial
go-nid'-ium
gon'i-mo-blast
go-ni-om'eter
go-nio-met'ric
go-ni-om'etry
go'-nion
go'-nites
go'-no-blast
gono-chor'-ism
gono-chor-is'tic
gono-coc'ci
gono-coc'-cus
go'-no-coel
go'-no-phore
gon-or-rhe'a
gon-or-rhe'al
go'-no-some
go-no-the'ca
go-nyd'-ial
goo'-ber
good=for=noth'-
　　　　ing
good'-ies
good'-ish
good'-li-ness
154

good=look'-ing
good'-man
good=na'tured
good'-ness
good=tem'-pered
good'-wife
good=will'
goo'-gly
goo'-gol
goo'-gol-plex
goos-an'-der
goos'e-berry
goos'e-flesh
goos'e-foot
goos'e-herd
goos'e-neck
go'-pher
go'-ral
gor'-gerin
gor'-get
gor'g-ing
gor'-gon-ise
gor-gon-zo'la
gor'-hen
gor-il'la
gor'-man-dise
gos'-hawk
gos'-lar-ite
gos'-ling
gos'-pel
gos'-pel-ler
gos'sa-mer
gos'-san
gos'-sip
gos'-sip-ing
gos'-sip-red
gos'-sipy
gos-soon'

gos'-sy-pine
gos-syp'i-trin
goth'i-cise
gou'-ache
gouf'-ing
goug'-ing
gou'-lash
gour-ami
gour'-mand
gour'-man-dise
gour'-man-diser
gour'-mand-ism
gour'-met
gout'-ily
gov'ern-able
gov'ern-ance
gov'ern-ess
gov'ern-ment
govern-men'tal
gov'ernor=
　　　gen'eral
gov'ernor-ship
grab'-ber
grab'-bing
gra'ce-ful
gra'ce-fully
gra'ce-ful-ness
gra'ce-less
gra'-cile
gra'-cilis
gra-cil'ity
gra-da'te
gra-da'tion
gra-da'tional
grad'a-tory
gra'di-ent
gra'di-ne
gra'dio-graph

gradi-om'eter
grad'-ual
grad'u-al-ism
grad'u-al-ist
grad'u-ally
grad'u-ate
grad'u-ating
gradu-a'tion
grad'u-ator
graf-fi'to
gra'ft-age
graft'-ing
grain'-ing (a.)
gral-la-to'rial
gral'-loch
gram'-ary
gra-mer'cy
gra-mic'i-din
gra-mi-na'ceous
gra-min'-eous
gra-mi-niv'or-ous
grami-niv'or-ous
gram'-ma-logue
gram'-mar
gram-ma'rian
gram-mat'ic
gram-mat'i-cal
gram-mat'i-cally
gram-mat'i-cise
gram'o-phone
gram'-pus
grana-dil'la
gran'-ary
gran'-dam
grand'-aunt
grand'-child
grand'-children
grand'-daugh-ter

gran'-dce
gran'-deur
grand'-father
gran-di-fo'li-ate
gran-dil'o-quence
gran-dil'o-quent
gran'-di-ose
gran-di-os'ity
grand'-ma
grand'-mother
grand'-nephew
grand'-ness
grand'-niece
grand'-pa
grand'-parent
gran'-drelle
grand'-sire
grand'-son
grand'-stand
grand'-uncle
granger-is-a'tion
gra'nger-ise
gra'nger-iser
gra'nger-ism
gra'nger-ite
gran-if'er-ous
gran'i-form
gran'-ite
gran'-ite-ware
gran-it'ic
gran'i-tite
gran'i-toid
gran'i-vore
gran-iv'or-ous
gran'-nom
grano-blas'-tic
grano-di'or-ite
grano-lith'ic

gran'o-phyre
grant'-able
gran'u-lar
granu-lar'ity
gran'u-late
gran'u-lated
gran'u-later
gran'u-lat-ing
granu-la'tion
gran'u-lous
gran'-ule
gran'u-lite
granu-lit'ic
granu-lit-is-
     a'tion
gra-nu'lo-cyte
granu-lo'ma
granu-lo-ma-
     to'sis
granu-lom'a-tous
gran'u-lous
gra'pe-fruit
gra'pe-shot
gra'pe-skin
gra'pe-vine
graph'i-cal
graph'i-cally
graph'-ite
gra-phit'-ic
graph'i-tise
graph'i-tised
graph'i-toid
graph'i-ure
graph-ol'ogy
grapho-ma'nia
grapho-met'ric
graph'o-type
grap'-nel

grap'-pel
grap'-pler
grap'-pling
gra'sp-ing
gra'sp-ingly
gra'ss-hopper
gra'ssi-ness
gra'ss-ing
gra'ss-land
gra'te-ful
gra'te-fully
grat'i-cule
grati-fi-ca'tion
grat'i-fied
grat'i-fier
grat'-ify
grat'i-fy-ing
grat'i-nate
gra'-tis
grat'i-tude
gra-tu'-ities
gra-tu'-itous
gra-tu'ity
grat'u-lant
grat'u-late
gratu-la'tion
grat'u-lat-ory
grau'-pel
gra-va'men
gra've-clothes
gra've-digger
grav'-elled
grav'-elly
grav'e-ness
grav'eo-lent
gra've-stone
gra've-yard
gra'-vid
156

grav'-ida
gra-vid'ity
gra-vim'eter
gravi-met'ric
gra-vim'etry
gravi-per-cep'-
      tion
grav'i-tate
grav'i-tator
grav'i-tat-ing
gravi-ta'tion
gravi-ta'tional
grav'i-tat-ive
gravi-tom'eter
grav'i-ton
grav'-ity
gra-vu're
gray'-beard
gray'-ish
gray'-ling
gray'-ness
gra'z-ier
gra'z-ing
greas'e-proof
greas'e-wood
greas'-ily
greas'i-ness
great'-coat
great'-hearted
great'-ness
greed'-ily
greed'i-ness
green'-back
green'-brier
green'-ery
green'-finch
green'-fly
green'-gage

green'-grocer
green'-heart
green'-horn
green'-house
green'-ing
green'-ish
green'-ling
green'-ness
gree'-nock-ite
green'-room
green'-sand
green'-stick
green'-sward
green'-wood
greet'-ing
gref'-fier
greg'-ar-ine
greg-ar-in'-iform
greg-a'ri-ous
greg-a'ri-ous-
      ness
grei'-sen
grei-sen-is-
      a'tion
gre'-mial
grem'-lin
gren-a'de
gren'a-dier
gren'a-dine
gres-so'rial
grey'-beard
grey'-ish
grey'-lag
grey'-ness
grey-wack'e
grey'-wethers
grid'-iron
grief'-stricken

griev'-ance
griev'-ing
griev'-ingly
griev'-ous
griev'-ously
grif'-fin
grif'-fon
gril'-lage
grill-room
grim-a'ce
grim-a'cing
gri-mal'-kin
gri'mi-ness
grim'-mer
grim'-ness
grin-de'lia
gri'nd-ery
gri'nd-ing
gri'nd-stone
grin'-ning
grip'-pers
grip'-ping
gris'-eous
gris'-kin
gris'li-ness
grist'-mill
grit'-stone
grit'-ting
griz'-zling
griz'-zly
groan'-ingly
gro'cer-ies
grog'-gi-ness
grog'-ram
grog'-shop
grom'-met
groom'-ing
grooms'-man

groov'-ing
gro'-per
gros'-beak
gross'-ness
gros'-su-lar-ite
gro-tes'que
gro-tes'quely
gro-tes'querie
grouch'i-ness
ground'-age
ground'-bait
ground'-hog
ground'-ing
ground'-less
ground'-ling
ground'-mass
ground'-nut
ground'-sel
ground'-sill
grounds'-man
ground'-work
group'-age
group'-ing
grous'-ing
grout'-ing
grout'-nick
grov'el-ler
grov'el-ling
grow'-able
grow'-ing
growl'-ing
grub'-ber
grub'-bing
grub'-stake
grudg'-ing
grudg'-ingly
gru'el-ling
grue'-some

grum'-bler
grum'-bling
grum'-met
gru'-mose
gru'-mous
grump'i-ness
grunt'-ing
gry's-bok
guai-acol
guai'-acum
gua'ni-dine
guan'-ine
guaran-tee'
guaran-tee'-ing
guar'an-ties
guar'an-tor
guard'-edly
guard'-ed-ness
guard'-house
guard'-ian
guard'-ian-ship
guard'-room
guards'-man
guber-nac'u-lum
guber-na-to'rial
guel'-der rose
guer'-don
guer-ril'la
guess'-ing
guess'-work
guest'-room
guf-faw'
guid'-able
guid'-ance
guid'e-book
guid'e-post
guid'-ing
guild'-hall

157

guild'-master
gui'le-ful
gui'le-less
guil'le-mot
guil'lo-tine
guilt'-ily
guilt'i-ness
guilt'-less
guitar'-ist
gu'-lar
gulch'-ing
gul'-let
gul'-let-ing
gulli-bil'ity
gull'-ible
gul'-lies
gu'-lose
gu-los'ity
gulp'-ing
gum'-boil
gum'-drop
gum-mat'a
gum'-ma-tous
gum'-mer
gum'-mi-ness
gum'-ming
gum-mo'sis
gum'-mous
gump'-tion
gun'-boat
gun'-cot-ton
gun'-fire
gun'-flint
gun'-ite
gun'-lock
gun'-man
gun'-nage
gun'-nel

gun'-ner
gun'-nera
gun'-nery
gun'-ning
gun'-powder
gun'-run-ner
gun'-run-ning
gun'-shot
gun'-smith
gun'-stock
gun'-ter
gur-gi-ta'tion
gurg'-let
gurg'-ling
gur'-jun
gur'-let
gur'-nard
gur'-net
gush'-ing
gus'-set
gus-ta'tion
gus'-ta-tive
gus'-ta-tory
gust'-ily
gus'-ti-ness
gut'-ta-per'-cha
gut'-tate
gut'-ted
gut'-ter
gut'-ter-ing
gut'-ter-snipe
gut-tif'er-ous
gut'-ti-form
gut'-ting
gut'-tu-late
gut'-tural
gut-tur-al'ity
guy'-ing

guz'-zling
gym-khan'a
gym-na'si-arch
gym-na'si-ast
gym-na'sium
gym'-nast
gym-nas'-tic
gym-nas'-tics
gym'-no-cyte
gym-nog'en-ous
gym'-no-plasm
gym-no-rhi'nal
gym-no-som'a-
    tons
gym-nos'o-phist
gym-nos'o-phy
gym'-no-sperm
gymno-sperm'-
    ous
gym'no-spore
gynae-ce'um
gynae-coc'racy
gynae-co-log'i-
    cal
gynae-col'o-gist
gynae-col'ogy
gynae-ol'-atry
gy-nan'-dro-
    morph
gy-nan-dro-
    morph'ism
gyn-an'-drous
gyn-an'-dry
gyn'-archy
gy'-nase
gyn-eco-mor'-
    phous
gyni-at'rics

gyno-ba'sic
gyno-dioe'cious
gyno-gen'-esis
gyno-mon-
   oe'cious
gyn'o-phore
gyp'-ping
gyp'-seous
gyp-sif'er-ous
gyp-sog'ra-phy
gyp-soph'-ila
gyp'-sum
gy'-ral
gy-ra'te
gy-ra'tion
gy-ra't-ing
gy-ra'tor
gy'ra-tory
gyr'-fal-con
gy'ro-compass
gy-roi'dal
gy-rom'eter
gy'ro-plane
gy'ro-scope
gyro-scop'ic
gy'-rose
gyro=sta'bil-iser
gy'ro-stat
gyro-stat'-ics
gy'-rus

H

ha-ben'-dum
ha-ben'-ula
ha-ben'u-lar
hab'-er-dasher

hab-er-dash'-ery
hab'er-geon
hab'-ile
ha-bil'i-ment
ha-bil'i-tate
ha-bili-ta'tion
hab-it-abil'ity
hab'-it-able
hab'i-tant
hab'i-tat
habi-ta'tion
ha-bit'-ual
ha-bit'u-ally
ha-bit'u-ate
ha-bitu-a'tion
hab'i-tude
ha-bit'ué
ha-chu're
hack'a-more
hack'-berry
hack'-ery
hack'-ing
hack'-ler
hack'-let
hack'-ling
hack'-ma-tack
hack'-ney
hack'-ney-coach
hack'-neyed
hack'-saw
had'-dock
had'-romal
had'-rom-ase
had'-rome
haem'a-chrome
hae'-mad
hae'-mal
hae-man-gi-o'ma

hae-ma-poi-e'sis
hae-ma-poph'y-
   sis
hae-mar-thro'sis
haem'a-tal
hae-ma-tem'-esis
hae-mat'ic
hae'-ma-tin
hae-ma-tin'ic
hae'-ma-tite
hae-ma-tit'ic
hae-ma-to'bium
hae'-ma-to-blast
hae'-ma-to-cele
hae'-ma-to-
   chrome
hae-ma-to'gen-
   ous
hae'-ma-toid
hae-ma-tol'-ogist
hae-ma-tol'ogy
hae-ma-to'ma
hae-ma-toph'a-
   gous
haema-tox'y-lin
hae-mato-zo'on
hae-ma-tu'ria
haemo-chroma-
   to'sis
hae-mo-chrom'-
   ogen
hae'-mo-coele
hae-mo-cy'anin
hae'-mo-cytes
hae-mo-ge'nia
hae-mo-glo'bin
hae-mo-globi-
   nae'mia

159

hae-mo-globi-
    nom'eter
hae-mo-globi-
    nu'ria
hae'-mo-lymph
hae-mol'y-sins
hae-mol'y-sis
hae-mo-lyt'ic
hae-mo-phil'ia
hae-mo-phil'iac
hae-mop'-ty-sis
haem'-or-rhage
haem-or-rha'gic
haem'-or-rhoid
haem-or-rhoid'al
haem'-or-rhoids
hae-mo-sider-
    o'sis
hae-mo-sta'sis
hae-mo-stat'ic
hae-mot'ro-phy
hae-mo-trop'ic
haf'-nium
hag'-berry
hag'-gard
hag'-ging
hag'-gis
hag'-gler
hag'-gling
hag'i-archy
hagi-oc'racy
hagi-og'ra-pher
hagi-og'ra-phy
hagi-ol'-ater
hagi-ol'-atrous
hagi-ol'-atry
hagio-log'ic
hagi-ol'ogy

hag'io-scope
hag'-rid-den
hail'-stone
hail'-storm
hair'-breadth
hair'-brush
hair'-cloth
hair'-cord
hair'-cut
hair'-dresser
hair'-dress-ing
hair'i-ness
hair'-like
hair'-line
hair'-pin
hair'-rais-ing
hair'-split-ter
hair'-split-ting
hair'-spring
hair'-streak
hair'-stroke
hair-trig'-ger
ha'-kim
ha-kim'
hal-a'tion
hal'-berd
hal-ber-dier'
hal'-cyon
half'-back
half'-hearted
half'-mast
half-ti'tle
half-'tone
half'-way
half-wit'-ted
hal'i-but
ha-lic'-ore
hal'-ide

hal'i-dom
hali-eu'tics
hali-plank'-ton
hali-ster-e'sis
hal'-ite
hali-to'sis
hal'i-tus
hal'-lan
hal-lel'
hal'-ling
hall'-mark
hal-loo'
hal'-low
hal'-lowed
hal'-lowed-ness
hal-loy'-site
hal-lu'ci-nate
hal-luci-na'tion
hal-lu'ci-nat-ory
hal-luci-no'sis
hal'-lux
hall'-way
halo-bion'tic
halo-biot'ic
hal'-ogens
hal-ogen-a'tion
hal-og'en-ous
hal'-oid
halo-lim'-nic
hal'o-phile
hal'o-phobe
ha'lo-phyte
halo-phyt'ic
ha-lot'ri-chite
hal'-teres
halt'-ing
halt'-ingly
hal'-vans

halv'-ing
hal'-yard
hama-dry'ad
hama-meli-
da'ceous
ham-ar-ti-ol'ogy
hami-ros'-trate
ham'-let
ham'-mer
ham'-mer-head
ham'-mer-less
ham'-mer-toe
ham'-mock
ham'-per
ham'-shackle
ham'-ster
ham'-string
ham'-strung
ham'-ula
ham'u-lar
ham'u-lose
ham'u-lus
han'a-per
hand'-bag
hand'-ball
hand'-bell
hand'-bill
hand'-book
hand'-cart
hand'-cuff
hand'-fast
hand'-ful
hand'-hold
hand'i-cap
hand'i-capped
hand'i-cap-per
hand'i-cap-ping
hand'i-craft

hand'i-crafts-man
hand'-ily
hand'i-ness
hand'i-work
hand'ker-chief
han'dle-able
han'dle-bar
hand'-ler
hand'-less
hand'-ling
hand'-made
hand'-maid
hand'-maiden
hand'-out
hand'-rail
hand'-saw
hand'-screw
hand'-sel
hand'-shake
hand'-some
hand'-somely
hand'-spike
hand'-spring
hand'-work
hand'-worked
hand'-writing
hand'-writ-ten
hand'y-man
hang'-dog
hang'-ing
hang'-man
hang'-nail
hang'-out
hang'-over
han'ker-ing
han'-sel
han'-som
ha-pan'-thous

hap-haz'-ard
hap'-less
hap'-lo-dont
hap'-loid
hap-log'ra-phy
hap'-lont
hap-lo'sis
hap-lo-stem'-on-
ous
hap'-pen
hap'-pily
hap'-pi-ness
hap'-py-go-
lucky
hap'-tene
hap'-teron
har-ang'ue
ha-rang'ued
har-ang'uer
har-ang'uing
har'-ass
har'-assed
har'-ass-ing
har'-ass-ment
har'-bin-ger
har'-bour
har'-bour-age
hard-bit'-ten
hard'-board
hard'-ener
hard'-en-ing
har'di-hood
hard'-ily
har'di-ness
hard'-pan
hard'-ship
hard'-tack
hard'-top

161

hard'-ware
hard'-wood
ha're-bell
ha're-lip
har'i-cot
har'-le-quin
har-le-quin-a'de
har'-lot
har'-lotry
har'-ma-line
har-mat-tan'
harm'-ful
harm'-fully
harm'-less
harm'-lessly
harm'-less-ness
har-mo'nial
har-mon'ic
har-mon'-ica
har-mon'-ics
har-mo'ni-ous
har-mon-is-
         a'tion
har'-mon-ise
har'-mon-is-ing
har'-mon-ist
har-mon-is'tic
har-mo'nium
har-mon-om'eter
har'-mony
har'-ness
har-pae-toph'a-
        gous
harp'-ing
harp'-ist
har-poon'
harp'-si-chord
har'-ri-dan
162

har'-rier
har'-row
harsh'-ness
har'-tal
har'te-beest
harts'-horn
harus'-pex
harus'-pi-cal
har'-vest
har'-vester
hash'-ish
has'-lets
hass'-ock
has'-tate
ha'sti-ness
hat'-band
hat'-box
hat'-brush
hatch'-ery
hatch'-ing
hatch'-ment
hatch'-way
ha'te-ful
ha'te-fully
hat'-rack
hat'-stand
hat'-ter
hau'-berk
hau'er-ite
haugh'-tily
haugh'-ti-ness
haul'-age
haunch'-ing
haunt'-ing
haus'-man-ite
hav'e-lock
hav'-er-sack
hav'-er-sine

hav'-il-dar
hav'-ocked
hav'-ock-ing
haw'-finch
hawk'-ing
hawk'-moth
haws'e-hole
haw'-ser
haw'-thorn
hay'-cock
hay'-field
hay'-loft
hay'-maker
hay'-mow
hay'-rack
hay'-rick
hay'-seed
hay'-stack
hay'-ward
hay'-wire
haz'-ard
haz'-ard-ous
ha'zel-nut
ha'z-ily
ha'zi-ness
ha'z-ing
head'-ache
head'-band
head'-dress
head'-first
head-fo're-most
head'-frame
head'-gear
head'-ily
head'i-ness
head'-ing
head'-land
head'-less

head'-light
head'-line
head'-long
head'-man
head'-master
head'-piece
head'-quarters
head'-room
head'-ship
heads'-man
head'-spring
head'-stall
head'-stock
head'-stone
head'-strong
head'-waiter
head'-waters
head'-way
head'-work
heal'-ing
health'-ful
health'-ful-ness
health'-ily
health'i-ness
heap-stead
hear'-ing
hear'-say
heart'-ache
heart'-beat
heart'-break
heart'-break-ing
heart'-broken
heart'-burn
hearth'-stone
heart'-ily
heart'i-ness
heart'-ing

heart'-land
heart'-less
heart'-rend-ing
heart's'-ease
heart'-sick
heat'-edly
hea'-then
hea'-then-dom
hea'-then-ish
hea'-then-ism
heav'en-ward
heav'i-ness
heav'-ing
heav'y-set
heav'y-weight
heb'-domad
heb-dom'a-dal
hebe-phre'nia
heb'-etate
he-bet'ic
he'-etude
hec'a-tomb
heck'-ler
heck'-ling
hec'-tare
hec'-tic
hec'-ti-cally
hecto-cot'y-lus
hec'-to-gramme
hec'-to-graph
hec-to-graph'ic
hec'-to-litre
hec'-to-metre
hec'-tor
hed'-en-ber-gite
hed'-er-ine
hed-er-a'ceous
hedg'e-hog

hedg'e-row
hedg'-ing
he-don'ic
he-don'-ics
he'-don-ism
he-don-is'tic
he-don-is'ti-cal
heed'-ful
heed'-less
heed'-less-ness
heel'-ball
heel'-ing
heel'-tap
he-gem-on'ic
he-gem'ony
he-gu'men
heir'-dom
heir'-ess
heir'-loom
heir'-ship
hel'-enin
heleo-plank'-ton
he-li'acal
heli-an'-the-mum
heli-an'-thine
he-li-an'-thus
hel'i-cal
hel'i-ces
hel'i-coid
heli-coid'al
hel'i-con
hel-i-cop-ter
he-lio-cen'-tric
he-li-och'romy
he'-lio-dor
he'-lio-gram
he'-lio-graph
he-li-og'ra-phy

163

HELIOGRAVURE

he-lio-gravu're
he-li-om'eter
he-lio-met'ric
he-li-om'etry
he'-lion
he-lio-pho'bic
he'-lio-phyte
he'-lio-scope
he-li-o'sis
he'lio-stat
he'-lio-therapy
he'-lio-trope
he-li-ot'ro-pism
he'lio-type
he'lio-typ-ogra-phy
hel'i-port
he'-lium
he'-lix
hell'-bent
hell'-cat
hell'e-bore
hell'e-bor-ine
hell'-fire
hell'-gram-mite
hell'-ish
hel'-met
hel'-meted
hel'-minth
hel-min-thi'asis
hel-min'-thic
hel-min'-thoid
hel-min-thol'ogy
helms'-man
hel'o-phyte
hel'-ot-ism
hel'-otrise
hel'-otry
164

help'-ful
help'-ing
help'-less
help'-lessly
help'-less-ness
help'-mate
help'-meet
hel'-ter-skel-ter
hel'-vite
hem-era-lo'pia
hemia-no'pia
hemia-tax'ia
hemi-col'-loid
hemi-cra'nia
hemi-cryp'-to-phyte
hemi-crys'-tal-line
hem'i-cycle
hemi-he'dral
hemi-kary-ot'ic
hemi-kar'yon
hemi-mor'-phism
hemi-mor'-phite
hemi-ple'gia
hemi-sec'-tion
hem'i-sphere
hemi-spher'ic
hemi-spher'i-cal
hem-spher'i-cally
hemi-sphe'roid
hem'i-stich
hem-is'ti-chal
hem'i-trope
hem'-lock
hem'-ming

hemp'-seed
hem'-stitch
hen'-bane
henc'e-forth
hence-for'-ward
hench'-man
hen'-coop
hen-dec'a-gon
hen-dec-ag'onal
hen-deca-syl-lab'ie
hen-di'adys
hen'-equen
hen'-house
hen'-naed
hen'-na-ing
hen'-nery
hen'o-theism
hen'-peck
he'-par
hep'-arin
hepa-tec'tomy
hep-at'ic
hep-at'ica
hepa-tis-a'tion
hep'a-tise
hep'a-tite
hepa-ti'tis
hepa-tog'en-ous
hep'a-tol-ith
hepa-tol'ogy
hepa-tol'-ogist
hepa-to'ma
hepa-top-to'sis
hepa-tor-rhex'is
hepa-tos'copy
hepa-tot'omy
hep-ta-chord

hep'-tad
hep'-ta-glot
hep'-ta-gon
hep-tag'-onal
hep-ta-he'dral
hep-ta-he'dron
hep-tam'-er-ous
hep-tam'eter
hep'-tane
hep-tan'gu-lar
hep'-tarch
hep-tar'-chi-cal
hep'-tarchy
hep-ta-syl-lab'ic
hep'-ta-teuch
hep'-tode
hep'-tose
her'-ald
her-al'-dic
her-al-dry
her-ba'ceous
herb'-age
herb'-al-ist
her-ba'rium
herbi-ci'dal
her'bi-cide
her-bif'er-ous
her-biv'or-ous
her-bor-is-a'tion
her'-bor-ist
her'-dic
herds'-man
he're-abouts
here-af'ter
her-edi-ta-bil'ity
her-ed'i-table
her-edit'a-ment
her-ed'i-tarily

her-ed'i-tary
her-ed'ity
here-in-af'ter
here-in-befo're
her-e'si-arch
her'-esy
her'-etic
her-et'i-cal
here-to-fo're
here-un'to
here-upon'
here-with'
her'-iot
her'-iot-able
heri-ta-bil'ity
her'i-table
her'i-tage
her'i-tance
her'i-tor
her-maph'ro-dite
her-maphro-dit'ic
her-maph'ro-dit-
          ism
her-men-eu'tics
her-met'ic
her-met'i-cal
her-met'i-cally
her'-mit
her'-mi-tage
her'-nia
her'-nial
her'-niary
her-ni-ot'omy
her-o'ic
her'-oin
her'-oine
her'-oism
her'-onry

her'-pes
her-pet'ic
her-peto-log'i-
          cal
her-pet-ol'-ogist
her-pet-ol'ogy
her'-ring
her'-ring-bone
her-self'
hes'i-tance
hes'i-tancy
hes'i-tant
hes'i-tantly
hes'i-tate
hes'i-tater
hes'i-tat-ing
hes'i-tat-ingly
hesi-ta'tion
hes'i-tat-ive
hes-per'i-din
hes-per-id'ium
hes'-peris
hess'-ian
hess'-ite
hess'-on-ite
het'-aero-lite
het-er-an'-drous
het-ero-aux'in
het-ero-car'-pous
het-ero-chro-
          mat'ic
het-ero-chro'-
          mous
het-er-och'ron-
          ism
het-ero-chro'-sis
het'-ero-clite
het-ero-cy'clic

het-ero-dac′-tyl-
ous

het′-er-odont
het′-ero-dox
het′-ero-doxy
het′-ero-dyne
het′-ero-dyn-ing
het-er-oe′cious
het-cro-game′te
het-er-og′a-mous
het-er-og′amy
het-er-og-en-e′ity
het-er-og′neous
het-er-og-gen′-esis
het-er-og′eny
het-er-og′ony
het-er-og′ra-phy
het-er-og-kin-e′sis
het-er-ol′ogy
het-er-ol′y-sis
het-er-om′er-ous
het-ero-mor′-phic
het-er-on′om-ous
het-er-on′-omy
het′-er-onym
het-er-on′y-mous
het-ero=ous′ia
het-ero-phyl′-
lous

het-ero-plas′ma
het-ero-plas′-tic
het-cro-plas′ty
het-ero-sex′-ual
het-ero-sexu-
al′ity

het-er-o′sis
het-ero-stat′ic
het-ero-tax′is
166

het-ero-to′pes
het-cro-to′pia
hct-ero-top′ic
het-ero-troph′ic
het-ero-zygo′sis
het-ero-zy′gote
het-ero-zy′gous
het′-man
hcu′-lan-dite
heu-ris′-tic
hew′-ing
hex′a-chord
hexa-em′eron
hex′a-gon
hex-ag′-onal
hex′a-gram
hexa-he′dral
hexa-he′dron
hex-am′-er-ous
hex-am′eter
hexa-met′ric
hex′-ane
hex-ang′u-lar
hexa-no′ic
hex′a-phase
hex′a-pla
hex′a-pod
hex-ap′ody
hex-ap′-ter-ous
hex′-arch
hex′a-style
hex′a-teuch
hexo-es′-trol
hex-o′sa-mine
hex′y-lene
hey′-day
hi-a′tus
hi-ber-nac′u-lum

hi-ber′-nal
hi′-ber-nant
hi′-ber-nate
hi-ber-na′tion
hi′-ber-nator
hib-is′-cus
hic′-cough
hic′-cup
hick′-ory
hid′-den
hi′de-bound
hid′-eous
hid′-eously
hid′-eous-ness
hi′-de-out
hi-dro′sis
hi-drot′ic
hi-e′mal
hi′-er-arch
hi-er-ar′chal
hi-er-ar′chic
hi-er-ar′chi-cal
hi-er-ar′chism
hi′-er-archy
hi-er-at′ic
hi-ero-crat′i-cal
hi′ero-dule
hi′ero-glyph
hiero-glyph′ic
hiero-glyph′i-cal
hiero-glyph′i-
cally

hi′-ero-phant
hi-ero-phan′-tic
high′-ball
high′-born
high′-boy

high'-bred
high'-brow
high'-fre'-
    quency (a.)
high'-land
high'-light
high'-ness
high'-road
high'-way
high'-way-man
hi'-jacker
hil-a'ri-ous
hil-ar'ity
hild'-ing
hill'-billy
hill'i-ness
hill'-ock
hill'-ocked
hill'-side
hill'-top
hi'-lum
hi-mat'-ion
him-self'
hin'-der
hi'nd-most
hi'nd-quarter
hin'-drance
hi'nd-sight
hin'-ter-land
hip'-bone
hip-pa'rion
hip-po-cam'-pus
hip'-po-cras
hip-po-crep'i-
    form
hip'-po-drome
hip'-po-griff
hip-poph'agy

hip-po-pot'a-mus
hip-po'ric
hip'-pus
hir'-cine
hi're-ling
hi're-pur'-chase
hir'-su-tal
hir'-sute
hiru-din'-ean
hir-un'-dine
his'-pid
hiss'-ing
his-tam'i-nase
his'-ta-mine
his'-ti-dine
his-ti-o'ma
his'-to-cyte
his-to-gen'-esis
his-to-gen-et'ic
his-tog'eny
his'-to-gram
his-to-hae'ma-tin
his-to-log'i-cal
his-tol'o-gist
his-tol'ogy
his-tol'y-sis
his'-tones
his-to'rian
his-tor'i-ated
his-tor'ic
his-tor'i-cal
his-tor'i-cally
his-tor-ic'ity
his'-tor-ies
his-tori-og'ra-
    pher
his-torio-
    graph'i-cal

his-tori-og'ra-
    phy
his'-tory
his-to-zo'ic
his'-trion
his-tri-on'ic
his-tri-on'i-cal
his-tri-on'i-cism
his-tri-on'ics
his'-tri-on-ism
hith'-er-most
hith'-erto
hit'-ter
hit'-ting
hoard'-ing
hoar'-frost
hoar'i-ness
hoar'se-ness
hoar'-stone
ho'-at-zin
hob'-bies
hob'-bing
hob'ble-de-hoy
hob'-bler
hob'-bling
hob'-by-horse
hob'-gob-lin
hob'-nail
hob'-nob
hob'-nob-bing
ho'-boes
ho'-bo-ism
ho'-cus
ho'-cus-po'-cus
ho-di-er'nal
hod'-man
hod'o-graph
hod-om'eter

hog'-back
hog'-get
hog'-gin
hog'-ging
hog'-gish
hogs'-head
hog'-skin
hog'-tie
hog'-wash
hol'-ard
hol'-co-dont
ho'ld-all
ho'ld-back
ho'ld-er-bat
ho'ld-fast
ho'ld-ing
ho'ld-over
ho'le-proof
hol'-iday
ho'li-ness
hol'-ism
hol'-land
hol-lan-dais'e
hol'-lan-der
hol'-low
hol'-low-ness
hol'-ly-hock
hol'-mium
holo-ben'-thic
hol'o-caust
hol-og'na-thous
hol'o-graph
holo-graph'ic
holo-he'dral
holo-neph'-ros
holo-pho'tal
hol'o-phote
hol-oph'ra-sis
168

holo-phyt'ic
holo-plank'-ton
hol-op'tic
hol'o-type
holo-zo'ic
ho'l-ster
ho'ly-stone
hom'-age
hom'-ager
ho'me-bred
ho'me-land
ho'me-less
ho'me-like
ho'me-li-ness
ho'me-maker
ho'me-own-ing
ho'me-sick
ho'me-sick-ness
ho'me-spun
ho'me-stead
ho'me-steader
ho'me-ward
ho'me-work
hom'i-cidal
hom'i-cide
homi-let'-ics
hom'i-lies
hom'il-ist
hom'-ily
hom'i-nid
hom'-iny
homo-cen'-tric
hom-och'romy
homo-cys'-teine
homoe-om'er-ism
homoeo-mor'-
       phous
hom'oeo-path

homoeo-path'ic
homoe-op'a-thy
homoeo-ther'-
       apy
homo-er'o-tism
hom-og'amy
hom-ogen-e'ity
homo-ge'neous
hom-ogen'-esis
hom-ogen-is-
       a'tion
hom-og'en-ise
hom-og'en-iser
hom-og'en-is-ing
hom-og'en-ous
hom-og'eny
hom-og'ony
hom'o-graph
homo-graph'ic
hom-og'ra-phy
hom-ol'-ogate
hom-ol-oga'tion
homo-log'i-cal
hom-ol'o-gise
hom-ol'o-gous
hom'-ol-ogue
hom-ol'-ogy
hom-ol'y-sis
homo-mor'-phic
homo-mor'-
       phism
hom'-onym
homo-nym'ic
hom-on'y-mous
hom'o-phone
homo-phon'ic
hom-oph'on-ous
hom-oph'ony

homo-phyl'-lous
homo-plas'ma
homo-plas'-tic
homo-po'lar
hom-op'ter-ous
homo-sex'-ual
homo-sexu-al'ity
hom-os'per-ous
homo-tax'is
homo-thet'ic
homo-typ'ic
homo'zygo'sis
homo-zy'gous
hom-un'cu-lus
hon'ey-comb
hon'ey-dew
hon'ey-moon
hon'ey-suckle
honor-a'rium
honor-if'ic
hon'our-able
hon'our-ably
hood'-lum
hoo'-doo
hood'-wink
hoof'-beat
hoof'-print
hoo'-kah
hook'-worm
hool'i-gan
hoop'-ing
hoo'-poe
hoo-ray'
ho'pe-ful
ho'pe-fully
ho'pe-ful-ness
ho'pe-ite

ho'pe-less
ho'pe-lessly
hop'-per
hop'-sack
hop'-scotch
ho'-ral
ho'-rary
hor'-dein
ho're-hound
hor-i'zon
hori-zon'-tal
hori-zon'-tally
hor'-monal
hor-mone
hor-mon'ic
horn'-beam
horn'-bill
horn'-blende
horn'-book
hor'-net
hor-ni'to
horn'-less
horn'-pipe
horn'-stone
hor'-ologe
hor-ol'-oger
hor-ol-og'ic
hor-ol'-ogist
hor-ol'ogy
hor-op'ter
hor'-oscope
hor-os'copy
hor-ren'-dous
hor'-rible
hor'-ribly
hor'-rid
hor-rif'ic
hor'-ri-fied

hor'-rify
hor-rip'-ilate
hor-rip-ila'tion
hor'-ror
hor'-ror-
　　　　　strick'en
hor'se-back
horse-car
horse-chest'-nut
hor'se-flesh
hor'se-fly
hor'se-hair
hor'se-hide
hor'se-laugh
hor'se-leech
hor'se-less
hor'se-man
hor'se-man-ship
hor'se-play
hor'se-power
hor'se-shoe
hor'se-shoer
hor'se-tail
hor'se-whip
hor'se-woman
hor'-ta-tive
hor'-ta-tory
hor-ti-cul'-tural
hor-ti-cul-ture
hor-ti-cul'-tur-
　　　　　　ist
ho-san'na
ho'-sier
ho'-siery
hos'-pice
hos-pit'-able
hos-pit'-ably
hos'-pi-tal

hos-pi-tal-is-
      a'tion
hos'-pi-tal-ise
hos-pi-tal'ity
hos'-pi-tal-ler
hos-pit'ium
hos-po-dar'
hos'-tage
hos'-tel
hos'-tel-ler
hos'-telry
ho'st-ess
hos'-tile
hos-til'ity
hot'-bed
hot'-box
hotch-'potch
ho-tel'
ho-tel'-ier
hot'-foot
hot'-head
hot-head'ed
hot'-house
hot'-ness
hot'-pot
hot'-press
hot'-spur
hot=tem'-pered
hour'-glass
house'-boat
house'-bound
house'-breaker
house'-break-ing
house'-broken
house'-coat
house'-fly
house'-ful
house'-hold
170

house'-holder
house'-keeper
hous'e-keep-ing
hous'e-less
hous'e-line
hous'e-maid
hous'e-room
hous'e-top
hous'e-warm-ing
hous'e-wife
hous'e-wifery
hous'e-work
hous'-ing
houst-o'nia
hov'-er-ing
how-be'it
how'-dah
how-ev'er
how'-it-zer
how-so-ev'er
hoy'-den
hub'-bub
hub'-ner-ite
hu-bris'-tic
huck'a-back
huck'le-berry
huck'-ster
hud'-dling
huff'-ily
huff-i'ness
huff'-ish
hu-ge'ous
hug'-ger=mug'-ger
hug'-gery
hug'-ging
hu'-la=hu'la
hulk'-ing
hul'-la-bal-oo

hu'-man
hu-ma'ne
hu-ma'nely
hu-man-is-a'tion
hu'-man-ise
hu'-man-iser
hu'-man-ism
hu'-man-ist
hu-man-is'tic
hu-mani-ta'rian
hu-mani-ta'ri-
     an-ism
hu-man'i-ties
hu-man'ity
hu'-man-kind
hu'-manly
hum'ble-ness
hum'-bling
hum'-bug
hum-bug'-gery
hum'-bug-ging
hum'-drum
hu-mec'-tant
hu-mec-ta'tion
hu'-mer-al
hu'-mer-us
hu'-mic
hu'-mi-cole
hu-mic'o-lous
hu'-mid
hu-midi-fi-
     ca'tion
hu-mid'i-fied
hu-mid'i-fier
hu-mid'i-ify
hu-mid'ity
hu'-mi-dor
hu-mi-fi-ca'tion

hu'-mify
hu-mil'i-ate
hu-mil'i-at-ing
hu-mili-a'tion
hu-mil'ity
hu'-min
hu'-mite
hum'-ming
hum'-ming-bird
hum'-mock
hu'mor-al-ism
hu'mor-al-ist
humor-al-is'tic
humor-esq'ue
hu'mor-ist
humor-is'tic
hu'mor-ous
hu'mor-ously
hu'mor-some
hu'-mous (a.)
hump'-back
hump'-backed
hu'-mu-lene
hu'-mus
hunch'-back
hunch'-backed
hun'-dred
hun'-dred-fold
hun'-dredth
hun'-dred-weight
hun'ger-ing
hun'gri-ness
hunt'-ing
hunt'-ress
hunts'-man
hurd'-ler
hurd'-ling
hur'-dy-gur'-dy

hur'-ler
hur'-ly-bur'ly
hur-rah'
hur'-ri-cane
hur'-ried
hur'-riedly
hur'-ry-scur'ry
hurt'-ful
hurt'-ing
hurt'-ling
hus'-band
hus'-band-man
hus'-bandry
hush'-ing
husk'-ily
hus'ki-ness
husk'-ing
hus-sar'
hust'-ings
hus'-tler
hus'-tling
hut'-ment
hut'-ting
hy'a-cinth
hya-cin'-thian
hya-cin'-thine
hy-aen'a
hy'a-line
hya-lin-is-a'tion
hy'-al-ite
hy-al'-ogen
hy-al-og'ra-phy
hy'a-loid
hy'-al-ophane
hy-al-op'-ter-ous
hya-lu-ron'i-dase
hy'-brid
hy-brid-i's-able

hy-brid-is-a'tion
hy'-brid-ise
hy'-brid-ism
hy-brid'ity
hy'-da-tid
hy'-da-toid
hyd-no-car'-pic
hy'-dra
hy-drac'id
hydra-cryl'ic
hy'-dra-gogue
hy-dral'a-zine
hy-dra'ngea
hy'-drant
hy-drar'-gyr-ism
hy-drar-thro'sis
hy-dras'-ti-nine
hy'-drate
hy-dra'tion
hy'-drator
hy-draul'ic
hy-draul'i-cally
hy'-dra-zide
hy'-dra-zine
hy-dra-zo'ate
hy-dra-zo'ic
hy'-dra-zone
hy-dre'mia
hy'-dric
hy'-dride
hy-dri-od'ic
hy-dro'a
hy-dro-bro'mic
hy-dro-car'bon
hy-dro-car'-pous
hy'-dro-cele
hy-dro-cephal'ic

hy-dro-ceph'a-
lous
hy-dro-ceph'a-lus
hy-dro-cer-am'ic
hy-dro-chlor'ic
hy-dro-chlo'-ride
hy-dro-chor'ic
hy-dro-cin-nam'ic
hy-dro-cor'-ti-
sone
hy-dro-cyan'ic
hy-dro-dyn-am'ics
hy-dro-elec'-tric
hy-dro-elec-
tric'ity
hy-dro-flu-or'ic
hy'-dro-foil
hy'-dro-gel
hy'-dro-gen
hy'-dro-gen-ate
hydro-gen-a'tion
hy-drog'en-ise
hy-drog'en-ous
hy-drog'-nosy
hy'-dro-graph
hy-drog'ra-pher
hy-dro-graph'ic
hy-drog'ra-phy
hy-dro-hae'ma-
tite
hy'-droid
hy'-dro-kin-et'ics
hy'-drol
hy'-dro-lase
hy-drol'ogy
hy'-dro-lyse
hy-drol'y-sis
hy-dro-lyt'ic

hy-dro-ma'nia
hy-dro-mechan'i-
cal
hy'-dro-mel
hy-dro-me'lia
hy-dro-me'teor
hy-drom'-eter
hy-dro-met'ric
hy-drom'-etry
hy-dro-path'ic
hy-drop'a-thist
hy-drop'a-thy
hy'-dro-phane
hy-dro-phil'-lic
hy-droph'i-lous
hy'-dro-phobe
hy-dro-pho'bia
hydro-pho'bic
hy'-dro-phone
hy'-dro-phyte
hy-drop'ic
hy'-dro-plane
hy-dro-pneu-
mat'ic
hy-dro-pon'-ics
hydro-quino'ne
hy'-dro-scope
hy-dro-scop'ic
hy'-dro-skis
hy'-dro-sol
hy'-dro-some
hy'-dro-sphere
hy'-dro-stat
hy-dro-stat'-ics
hy-dro-sul'-phide
hy-dro-sul-
phu'ric
hy-dro-tax'is

hy-dro-thera-
peu'tics
hy-dro-ther'apy
hy-dro-ther'-mal
hy-drot'ro-pism
hy'-drous
hy'-dro-vane
hy-drox'-ide
hy-drox'yl
hy-drox-yl-a'tion
hy-drox'y-zine
hy-dro-zo'an
hy'-dryl
hy-e'na
hy'-eto-graph
hy-etog'ra-phy
hy-etol'-ogy
hy-etom'eter
hy'-geist
hy'-giene
hygi-en'ic
hy-gien'ic
hygi-en'i-cally
hy-gien'i-cally
hy'-gien-ist
hy'-gro-deik
hy'-gro-graph
hy-grol'ogy
hy-grom'eter
hy-gro-met'ric
hy-grom'etry
hy-gro-pet'ri-cal
hy'-gro-phile
hy'-gro-phyte
hy'-gro-scope
hy-gro-scop'ic
hy'-gro-stat
hy'-lic

hy-lo-mor'-phism
hy-loph'a-gous
hy'-lo-phyte
hy-lo-the'ism
hy-lo-the'ist
hy-lo-theis'tic
hy-lot'o-mous
hy-lo-zo'ic
hy-lo-zo'ism
hy-lo-zo'ist
hy'-men
hy-men-e'al
hy-men-op'-ter-
    ous
hym'-nal
hym'-nary
hym'-nist
hym'-nod-ist
hym'-nody
hym-nog'ra-pher
hym-nol-og'ic
hym-nol'-ogist
hym-nol'ogy
hy'-oid
hy-oid'eus
hypa-cu'sic
hyp-ae'thral
hyp-al-ge'sia
hy-pal'-lage
hy-par-te'rial
hy-pax'-ial
hy-per-ac'id
hy-per-acid'ity
hy-per-acu'sis
hy-per-aes-
    the'sia
hy-per-aes-
    thet'ic

hy-per'ba-ton
hy-per'-bola
hy-per'-bole
hy-per-bol'ic
hy-per-bol'i-cal
hy-per-bol'i-
    cally
hy-per'-bol-ise
hy-per'-bol-ist
hy-per'-bol-oid
hy-per-bol-oid'al
hy-per-bor'-ean
hy-per-cal-
    cae'mia
hy-per-cap'-nia
hy-per-cata-
    lec'-tic
hy-per-crit'i-cal
hy-per-crit'i-
    cism
hy-per-du'lia
hy-per-e'mia
hy-per-fo'cal
hy-per-gly-
    cae'mia
hy'-per-gol
hy-per-go'nar
hy-per'i-cin
hy-peri-dro'sis
hy-per-kera-
    to'sis
hy-per-kin-e'sia
hy-per-met'ric
hy-per-met'ri-cal
hy-per-me-tro'pia
hy-per-me-trop'ic
hy-per-mne'sia
hy'-peron

hy-per-o'pia
hy-per-os-to'sis
hy-per-phys'i-cal
hy-per-pie'sia
hy-per-pla'sia
hy-perp-ne'a
hy-per-pne'a
hy-per-ploid
hy-per-sen-si-
    tis-a'tion
hy-per-sen'-si-
    tive
hy-per-son'ic
hy'-per-sthene
hy-per-sthen'ic
hy-per-sthe'nite
hy-per-ten'-sion
hy-per-ten'-sive
hy-per-ton'ic
hy-per-thy'roid
hy-per-thy'rum
hy-per-tri-
    cho'sis
hy-per-troph'ic
hy-per'tro-phied
hy-per'tro-phy
hyp-esthe'sia
hy'-pha
hy'-phen
hy'-phen-ate
hy'-phen-ated
hy-phen-a'tion
hyp-na-gog'ic
hyp'-nody
hyp'-noid
hyp-noid'al
hyp-nol'ogy
hyp-no-pae'tia

HYPNOSIS

hyp-no'sis
hyp-not'ic
hyp-not'i-cally
hyp'-not-ise
hyp'-not-is-ing
hyp'-not-ism
hyp'-not-ist
hypo-cal-cae'mia
hy'-po-caust
hypo-chlo'rite
hypo-chlo'rous
hyp-ochon'-dria
hyp-ochon'-driac
hyp-ochon-
   dri'acal
hyp-ochon-
   dri'asis
hypoc'-risy
hyp'-ocrite
hyp-ocrit'i-cal
hyp-ocrit'i-cally
hy'-po-derm
hy-po-der'-mal
hy-po-der'-mic
hy-po-der'mi-
   cally
hy-po-der'mis
hy'-po=en-tec'-
   tic
hy-po-gae'ous
hy-po-gas'-tric
hy-po-gas'-trium
hy-po-ge'al
hy-po-ge'an
hy'-po-gene
hy-po-gen'-esis
hy-po-gen'ic
hy-pog'en-ous

hypo-ge'um
hy-po-gloss'al
hy-po-glot'-tis
hy-pog'na-thous
hy-pog'y-nous
hy'-poid
hy-po-ma'nia
hypo-phos'-phite
hy-po-phos-
      phor'ic
hy-po-phos'-
      phor-ous
hypo-phyl'-lous
hy-poph'y-sis
hy-po-pla'sia
hy'-po-ploid
hy-pos'-ta-sis
hy-pos'-ta-sise
hy-po-stat'ic
hy-po-stat'i-
      cally
hy-pos-then'ic
hy-po-sto'ma-tous
hy'-po-style
hy-po-sul'-phate
hy-po-sul'-phite
hy-po-sul-phu'ric
hy-po-sul'-phur-
      ous
hy-po-ten'-sion
hy-pot'-en-use
hypo-thal'a-mus
hy-poth'ec
hy-poth'-ecary
hy-poth'-ecate
hy-poth-eca'tion
hy-poth'-ecator
hy-poth'-eses

hy-poth'-esis
hy-poth'-esise
hy-po-thet'ic
hy-po-thet'i-cal
hy-po-thet'i-
      cally
hy-po-tra-
    che'lium
hy-pox-e'mia
hyp'-so-chrome
hyp'-so-dont
hyp'-so-graph
hyp-sog'ra-phy
hyp-som'eter
hyp-so-met'ri-cal
hyp-som'etry
hy'-rax
hy'-son
hys-ter-an'-thous
hys-ter-ec'tomy
hys-ter-e'sis
hys-ter-et'ic
hys-te'ria
hys-ter'ic
hys-ter'i-cal
hys-ter'i-cally
hys-ter'-ics
hys-ter'i-form
hys-ter-og'eny
hys-ter-ol'ogy
hys-ter-ot'omy
hy'-ther-graph

I

iam'-bic
iam'-bus

iat ri-cal
i'ce-blink
iatro-chem'is-try
iat ro-genic
iatro-gen-ic'ity
ib'i-dem
i ce-berg
i'ce-blink
i'ce-bound
i'ce-box
i'ce=man
ich-neu'-mon
ich'-no-graph
ich-no-graph'i-
     cal
ich-nog'ra-phy
ich'-no-lite
ich-nol'ogy
i'chor-ous
ich'-thus
ich'-thyic
ich-thy-og'ra-
     pher
ich-thy-og'ra-phy
ich'-thy-oid
ich'-thy-ol'-atry
ich'-thy-olite
ich-thyo-log'i-
     cal
ich-thy-ol'-ogist
ich-thy-ol'ogy
ich-thy-oph'a-
     gist
ich-thy-oph'a-
     gous
ich-thy-oph'agy
ich'-thyo-saur
ich-thyo-sau'rus
ich-thy-o'sis

ich-thy-ot'ic
ich'-thys
i'ci-ness
icon'o-clasm
icon'o-clast
icono-clas'-tic
icon-og'ra-pher
icon-og'ra-phy
icon-ol'ater
icon-ol'-atry
icon-ol'ogy
icon-om'eter
icon'o-scope
icon-os'ta-sis
icosa-he'dron
ic-ter'ic
ic'-terus
ic'-tus
ideal-is-a'tion
ide'al-ise
ide al-ism
ide al-ist
ideal-is'tic
ident'-ical
ident'-ifi-able
identi-fi-ca'tion
ident'-ified
ident'-ifies
ident'-ify
ident'-ity
i'deo-gram
i'deo-graph
ideo-graph'ic
ideog'ra-phy
ideo-log'i-cal
ideol'-ogist
i'deo-logue
ideol'-ogy

idio-chro'ma-tin
idi-oc'racy
id'i-ocy
idio-gloss'ia
id'io-gram
id'-iom
idi-om-at'ic
idio-path'ic
idio-op'a-thy
id'io-some
idio-stat'ic
idio-syn'-crasy
idio-syn-crat'ic
id'-iot
idi-ot'ic
idi-ot'i-cal
idi-ot'i-cally
id'iot-ism
i'dle-ness
idol'-ater
idol'-atrise
idol'-atrous
idol'-atry
idol-is-a'tion
i'dol-ise
i'dol-ism
idyl'-lic
i'dyl-list
ig'-loo
ig'-neous
ig-nesc'ent
ig-nif'er-ous
ig-ni'ti-able
ig-ni'te
ig-ni'ter
ig-ni't-ing
ig-ni'tion
ig-ni'tron

175

ig-no-bil'i-ty
ig-no'ble
ig-nom-in'i-ous
ig-nom-in'i-ously
ig'-nom-iny
ig-nor-a'mus
ig'-nor-ance
ig'-nor-ant
ig'-nor-antly
ig-no're
iguan'-odon
il'-eal
il-ei'tis
il-eos'-tomy
il'-eum
il'-iac
il'-ium
ill=ad-vi'sed
il'-lam
il-lap'se
il-la'tion
il-la't-ive
ill=dis-po'sed
il-le'gal
il-le'gal-ise
il-legal'ity
il-le'gally
il-legi-bil'ity
il-leg'ible
il-legit'-imacy
il-legit'-imate
ill=fit'-ting
ill=got'-ten
il-lib'-eral
il-lib-er-al'ity
il-lic'it
il-limi-ta-
     bil'ity

il-lim'i-table
il-lin'-ium
il-lit'-er-acy
il-lit'-er-ate
ill=man'-nered
ill'-ness
il-log'i-cal
il-logi-cal'ity
ill=tem'-pered
ill=treat'-ment
il-lu'de
il-lu'me
il-lu'mi-nant
il-lu'mi-nate
il-lu'mi-nat-ing
il-lumi-na'tion
il-lu'mi-nat-ive
il-lu'mi-nator
il-lu'mine
il-lu'miner
il-lu'min-ing
il-lumi-nom'eter
il-lu'sion
il-lu'sion-ism
il-lu'sion-ist
il-lu'sive
il-lu'sory
il'-lus-trate
il'-lus-trat-ing
il-lus-tra'tion
il-lus'tra-tive
il'-lus-trator
il-lus'-tri-ous
il'-men-ite
im'-age
im'a-gery
im-ag'in-able
im-ag'inal

im-ag'in-ary
im-agin-a'tion
im-ag'in-at-ive
im-ag'ine
im-ag'in-ing
im'a-gism
im'a-gist
ima-gis'tic
im-bal'-ance
im'-be-cile
im-be-cil'ic
im-be-cil'ity
im-bed'
im-bi'be
im-bi'ber
im-bi-bit'ion
im'-brex
im'-bri-cate
im'-bri-cated
im-bri-ca'tion
im-bri-cat-ive
im-brog'lio
im-brue'
im-bru'-ing
im-bue'
im-bu'-ing
im-bur'se
imi-daz'-ole
imi-daz'-ol-ide
im'-ide
im'-ido
imid'-ogen
im-in-az'ole
im'-ine
im'-ino
imi-ta-bil'ity
im'i-table
im'i-tate

im-i-ta'tion
im'i-tat-ive
im'i-tator
im-mac'u-lacy
im-mac'u-late
im-mal'-eable
im'-ma-nence
im'-ma-nent
im-mar'-gin-ate
im-ma-te'rial
im-ma-te'ri-al-ism
im-ma-te'ri-al-ist
im-ma-teri-al'ity
im-ma-tu're
im-ma-tu'rity
im-meas'ur-able
im-meas'ur-ably
im-me'di-acy
im-me'di-ate
im-me'di-ately
im-med'ic-able
im-mem'-or-able
im-mem-o'rial
im-mens'e
im-mens'ely
im-men'-sity
im-men'-sur-able
im-merg'e
im-mers'e
im-mers'ed
im-mers'-ible
im-mers'-ing
im-mer'-sion
im'-mi-grant
im'-mi-grate

im-mi-gra'tion
im'-mi-nence
im'-mi-nent
im-mis-ci-bil'ity
im-mis'-cible
im-mit'i-gable
im-mo'-bile
im-mo-bil-is-a'tion
im-mo'bi-lise
im-mo-bil'ity
im-mod'-er-acy
im-mod'-er-ate
im-mod-er-a'tion
im-mod'-est
im-mod'-esty
im'-mo-late
im-mo-la'tion
im'-mo-lator
im-mor'al
im-mor-al'ity
im-mor'-ally
im-mor'-tal
im-mor-tal-is-a'tion
im-mor'-tal-ise
im-mor-tal'ity
im-mor-tell'e
im-mo'-tile
im-mov-abil'ity
im-mov'-able
im-mov'-ably
im-mu'ne
im-mu-nis-a'tion
im'-mu-nise
im-mu'n-ity
im-mu-nol'ogy
im-mu're

im-mu'r-ing
im-muta-bil'ity
im-mu't-able
im'-pact
im-pac'-ted
im-pac'-tion
im-pac'-tive
im-pair'
im-pair'-ment
im-pa'le
im-pa'le-ment
im-pa'ling
im-pal-pa-bil'ity
im-pal'-pable
im-pal'u-dism
im-pa-na'tion
im-pan'el
im-pan'elled
im-pari-syl-lab'ic
im-par'ity
im-park'
im-par'-lance
im-part'
im-par-ta'tion
im-par'-tial
im-par-tial'ity
im-par'-tially
im-part'-ible
im-passa-bil'ity
im-pass'-able
im'-passe
im-passi-bil'ity
im-pass'-ible
im-pas'sion
im-pas'sion-ate
im-pas'sioned
im-pass'-ive

im-pass'-ively
im-pass-iv'ity
im-pa'ste
im-pa'tience
im-pa'tiens
im-pa'tient
im-pa'tiently
im-pav'id
im-peach'
im-peach-abil'ity
im-peach'-able
im-peach'er
im-peach'-ment
im-pearl'
im-pec-ca-bil'ity
im-pec'-cable
im-pec'-cant
im-pecuni-os'ity
im-pecu'ni-ous
im-pe'dance
im-pe'de
im-pe'dible
im-pe'dient
im-ped'i-ment
im-ped'i-menta
im-pedi-men'-tal
im-pedi-men'-tary
im-pe'ding
im-ped'i-tive
im-pel'
im-pell'ed
im-pel'-lent
im-pel'-ler
im-pel'-ling
im-pen'
im-pend'

im-pend'-ence
im-pend'-ent
im-pend'-ing
im-pen-etra-bil'ity
im-pen'-etrable
im-pen'-etrate
im-pen'i-tence
im pen'i-tent
im-pen'-nate
im-per'a-tive
im-per'a-tively
im-per-a'tor
im-pera-to'rial
im-per-cep'-tible
im-per-cep'-tibly
im-per-cep'-tive
im-per-cip'i-ent
im-per'-fect
im-per-fec'-tion
im-per-fec-ti-bil'ity
im-per-fec'-tible
im-per'-fectly
im-per'-fect-ness
im-per'-for-ate
im-per'-for-ated
im-per-for-a'tion
im-pe'rial
im-pe'ri-al-ise
im-pe'ri-al-ism
im-pe'ri-al-ist
im-peri-al-is'tic
im-pe'ri-ally
im-per'il
im-per'illed
im-per'il-ling
im-pe'ri-ous

im-per-ish-
abil'ity
im-per'-ish-able
im-pe'rium
im-per'-ma-
nence
im-per'-ma-nent
im-per-mea-
bil'ity
im-per'-meable
im-per-miss'-ible
im-per-scrip'-
tible
im-per'-sonal
im-per-son-al'ity
im-per'-son-ate
im-per-son-
a'tion
im-per-son-at-
ive
im-per'-son-ator
im-per-spi-cuity
im-per-sua'sible
im-per'-ti-nence
im-per'-ti-nency
im-per'-ti-nent
im-per-turb-
abil'ity
imper-turb'-able
im-per-tur-
ba'tion
im-per'-vi-ous
im-peti'go
im'-petrate
im-petu-os'ity
im-pet'u-ous
im-pet'u-ously
im'-petus

im-pi'ety
im-pig'-nor-ate
im-pig-nor-a'tion
im-pin'ge
im-pin'ge-ment
im-pin'gent
im-pin'ger
im-pin'ging
im'-pi-ous
imp'-ish
im-placa-bil'ity
im-plac'-able
im-plac'-ably
im-placen'-tal
im-plant'
im-plan-ta'tion
im-plas-tic'ity
im-plaus'-ible
im'-plement
im-plemen'-tal
im-plemen-
        ta'tion
im-ple'tion
im'-pli-cate
im-pli-ca'tion
im'-pli-cat-ive
im-plic'it
im-plic'itly
im-pli'ed
im-pli'edly
im-plo'de
im-plo're
im-plo'r-ing
im-plo'r-ingly
im-plo'sion
im-plo'sive
im-ply'
im'-pol-ite

im-pol'i-tic
im-pon-der-
        abil'ity
im-pon'-der-able
im-por-os'ity
im-po'rt (v.)
im'-port (n. v.)
im-po'rt-able
im-po'rt-ance
im-po'rt-ant
im-po'rt-antly
im-port-a'tion
im-po'rter
im-por'-tu-nacy
im-por'-tu-nate
impor-tu'ne
im-por-tu'n-ing
im-por-tu'n-ity
im-po'se
im-po'sing
im-po-sit'ion
im-possi-bil'ity
im-poss'-ible
im-poss'-ibly
im'-post
im-pos'-tor
im-pos'-tume
im-pos'-ture
im'-po-tence
im'-po-tency
im'-po-tent
im-pound'
im-pound'-able
im-pov'-er-ish
im-pov'-er-ish-
        ment
im-pow'er

im-prac-ti-ca-
        bil'ity
im-prac'-ti-cable
im-prac'-ti-cal
im-prac'-ti-cally
im'-pre-cate
im-pre-ca'tion
im'-pre-cator
im'-pre-cat-ory
im-pre-cis'ion
im-preg-na-
        bil'ity
im-preg'-nable
im-preg'-nate
im-preg-na'tion
im'-preg-nator
im-pre-sar'io
im-pre-scrip'-
        tible
im-pressi-bil'ity
im-press'-ible
im-pres'sion
im-pression-
        abil'ity
im-pres'sion-able
im-pres'sion-ary
im-pres'sion-ism
im-pres'sion-ist
im-pression-
        is'tic
im-press'-ive
im-press'-ive-
        ness
im-press'-ment
im-press' (v.)
im'-press (n.)
im-press'-able
im'-prest

im'-print (n.)
im-print' (v.)
im-pris'on
im-pris'-on-ment
im-proba-bil'ity
im-prob'-able
im-prob'-ably
im-pro'-bity
im-promp'tu
im-prop'er
im-prop'erly
im-pro'-pri-ate
im-pro-pri-a'tion
im-pro-pri'ety
im-prov'-able
im-prov'e
im-prov'e-ment
im-prov'er
im-prov'i-dence
im-prov'i-dent
im-prov'-ing
im-pro-vis-a'tion
im-pro-vis-a'tor
im'-pro-vise
im'-pro-vis-ing
im-pru'd-ence
im-pru'd-ent
im-pru'd-ently
im'-pu-dence
im'-pu-dent
in-pu-dic'ity
im-pu'gn
im-pugn'-able
im-pug-na'tion
im-pu'gner
im-pu'gn-ment
im-puis'sance
im-puis'sant

im'-pulse
im-pul'-sion
im-pul'-sive
im-pul'-sively
im-pu'nity
im-pu're
im-pu'rity
im-pu't-able
im-pu-ta'tion
im-pu'ta-tive
im-pu'te
im-pu't-ing
in-abil'ity
in-ab-sen'-tia
in-ac-cessi-
     bil'ity
in-ac-cess'-ible
in-ac'-cur-acy
in-ac'-cur-ate
in-ac'-tion
in-ac'-ti-vate
in-ac-ti-va'tion
in-ac'-tive
in-ac-tiv'ity
in-ad-ap-ti-
     bil'ity
in-ad-ap'-tible
in-ad'-equacy
in-ad'-equate
in-ad-he'sion
in-ad-mis-si-
     bil'ity
in-ad-mis'-sible
in-ad-ver'-tence
in-ad-ver'-tent
in-ad-ver'-tently
in-ad-vi's-able
in-a'lien-able

in-al'ter-able
in-am-or-at'a
in-a'ne
in-an'i-mate
in-anit'ion
in-an'ity
in-ap-peas'-able
in-ap'-petence
in-ap-pli-ca-
     bil'ity
in-ap'-pli-cable
in-ap-pli-ca'tion
in-ap'-pos-ite
in-ap-pre'ci-able
in-ap-pre-
     cia'tion
in-ap-pre'ci-at-
     ive
in-ap-pre-hen'-
     sible
in-ap-pre-hen'-
     sion
in-ap-proach'-
     able
in-ap-pro'-pri-
     ate
in-apt'
in-ap'-ti-tude
in-apt'-ness
in-arch'
in-ar-tic'u-late
in-ar-ti-fic'ial
in-ar-tis'-tic
in-as-much'
in-at-ten'-tion
in-at-ten'-tive
in-audi-bil'ity
in-aud'-ible

180

in-aug'-ural
in-aug'-ur-ate
in-aug'-ur-at-ing
in-aug-ur-a'tion
in-aug'-ur-ator
in-aug'-ur-at-ory
in-aus-pic'ious
in-aus-pic'iously
in'-board
in'-born
in'-bred
in'-breed
in'-breed-ing
in'-built
in-cal-cu-la-
         bil'ity
in-cal'-cu-lable
in-cal'-cu-lably
in-cal-esc'ent
in-can-desc'e
in-can-desc'ence
in-can-desc'ent
in-can-ta'tion
in-capa-bil'i-ty
in-ca'pable
in-ca-pa'cious
in-ca-pac'i-tate
in-ca-paci-ta'tion
in-ca-pac'ity
in-car'-cer-ate
in-car-cer-a'tion
in-car'-cer-ator
in-car'-di-nate
in-car'-na-dine
in-car'-nate (a.)
in'-car-nate (v.)
in-car-na'tion
in-ca'se

in-caut'ious
in-cen'-di-ar-ism
in-cen'-di-ary
in'-cense (n.)
in-cens'e (v.)
in-cen'-sing
in-cen'-sory
in-cen'-tive
in-cept' (v.)
in'-cept (n.)
in-cep'-tion
in-cep'-tive
in-cep'-tor
in-cer'-ti-tude
in-cess'-ancy
in-cess'-ant
in-cess'-antly
in-cess'-ive
in'-cest
in-ces'-tuous
in'-cho-ate
in'-cho-ately
in-cho-a'tion
in-cho'a-tive
inch'-worm
in'-ci-dence
in'-ci-dent
in-ci-den'-tal
in-ci-den'-tally
in-cin'-er-ate
in-cin-er-a'tion
in-cin'-er-ator
in-cip'i-ence
in-cip'i-ency
in-cip'i-ent
in-ci'se
in-cis'ion
in-ci's-ive

in-ci't-ant
in-ci-ta'tion
in-ci'te
in-ci'te-ment
in-ci'ter
in-ci't-ing
in-civ-il'ity
in'-civ-ism
in-clem'-ency
in-clem'-ent
in-cli'n-able
in-cli-na'tion
in-cli'n-atory
in-cli'ne (v. n.)
in'-cline (n.)
in-cli'ned
in-cli'n-ing
in-cli-nom'eter
in-clo'se
in-clo's-ure
in-clu'd-able
in-clu'de
in-clu'ded
in-clu'd-ing
in-clu'sion
in-clu's-ive
in-co-erc'-ible
in-cog-ni'to
in-co-he'r-ence
in-co-he'r-ency
in-co-he'r-ent
in-co-he's-ive
in-cog'-ni-sable
in-cog'-ni-sance
in-cog'-ni-sant
in-com-bus'-tible
in'-come
in'-coming

in-com-men'-sur-
able
in-com-men'-
sur-ate
in-com-mo'de
in-com-mo'di-ous
in-com-mu'ni-
cable
in-com-muni-
ca'do
in-com-mu'ni-
cat-ive
in-com-mu't-able
in-com-pact'
in-com'-par-able
in-com'-par-ably
in-com-pass'ion-
ate
in-com-pati-
bil'ity
in-com-pat'-ible
in-com'-petence
in-com'-petency
in-com'-petent
in-com-ple'te
in-com-ple'tely
in-com-pli'ant
in-com-pre-hen-
si-bil'ity
in-com-pre-hen'-
sible
in-com-pre-hen'-
sion
in-com-pre-hen'-
sive
in-com-press'-
ible
in-com-pu't-able
182

in-con-ceiv-
abil'ity
in-con-ceiv'-able
in-con-ceiv'-ably
in-con-clu's-ive
in-con-cuss'-ible
in-con-dens'-able
in-con'-dite
in-con-for'-mity
in-con-ge'nial
in-con'-gru-ent
in-con-gru'ity
in-con'-gru-ous
in-con-sec'u-tive
in-con'-sequence
in-con'-sequent
in-con-sequen'-
tial
in-con-sid'-er-
able
in-con-sid'-er-
ate
in-con-sider-
a'tion
in-con-sist'-ency
in-con-sist'-ent
in-con-so'l-able
in-con'-son-ance
in-con'-son-ant
in-con-spic'u-ous
in-con'-stancy
in-con'-stant
in-con-su'm-able
in-con-sum'-mate
in-con-test-
abil'ity
in-con-test'-able
in-con'-ti-nence

in-con'-ti-nent
in-con-tro'l-
lable
in-con-tro-vert'-
ible
in-con-ve'nience
in-con-ve'niency
in-con-ve'nient
in-con'-ver-sant
in-con-ver-ti-
bil'ity
in-con-vert'-ible
in-con-vin'-cible
in-co-or'-di-nate
in-co-or-di-
na'tion
in-cor'-por-able
in-cor'-por-ate
in-cor'-por-ated
in-cor-por-a'tion
in-cor'-por-at-
ive
in-cor'-por-ator
in-cor-por'-eal
in-cor-por-e'ity
in-cor-rect'
in-cor-rigi-
bil'ity
in-cor'-ri-gible
in-cor-ro'd-ible
in'-cor-rupt
in-cor-rupti-
bil'ity
in-cor-rupt'-ible
in-crass'-ate
in-creas'-able
in-creas'e (v.)
in'-crease (n.)

in-creas'er
in-creas'-ing
in-credi-bil'ity
in-cred'-ible
in-cred'-ibly
in-cred-u'lity
in-cred'u-lous
in-cred'u-lously
in'-crement
in-cremen'-tal
in-cresc'ent
in-cre't-ory
in-crim'i-nate
in-crimi-na'tion
in-crim'i-nat-ory
in-crust'
in-crus-ta'tion
in'-cu-bate
in'-cu-ba'tion
in'-cu-bator
in'-cu-bous (a.)
in'-cu-bus (n.)
in'-cul-cate
in-cul-ca'tion
in-cul'-cator
in'-cul-pate
in-cul-pa'tion
in-cul-pa'tory
in-cum'-bency
in-cum'-bent
in-cu-nab'-ula
in-cu-nab'-ulum
in-cur'
in-cura-bil'ity
in-cu'rable
in-cu'ri-ous
in-cur'-rable
in-curr'ed

in-cur'-rence
in-cur'-ring
in-cur'-sion
in-cur'-sive
in-cur-va'tion
in-cur've
in-cu'se
in'-da-gator
in'-da-mine
in-debt'ed
in-debt'-ed-ness
in-de'cency
in-de'cent
in-de-cid'u-ous
in-de-ci'pher-
    able
in-de-cis'ion
in-de-ci'sive
in-de-cli'n-able
in-de-com-po's-
    able
in-dec'-or-ous
in-de-co'rum
in-deed'
in-de-fati-ga-
    bil'ity
in-de-fat'i-gable
in-de-feas'-ible
in-de-fect'-ible
in-de-fen'-sible
in-de-fi'n-able
in-def'i-nite
in-def'i-nitely
in-de-hisc'ent
in-de-lib'er-ate
in-deli-bil'ity
in-del'-ible

in-del'i-cacy
in-del'i-cate
in-dem-ni-fi-
    ca'tion
in-dem'-ni-fied
in-dem'-ni-fies
in-dem'-nity
in-dem'-ni-tor
in-dem'-nity
in-de-mons'-
    trable
in'-dene
in-dent'
in-den-ta'tion
in-den'ted
in-den'ter
in-den'-tion
in-den'-ture
in-de-pen'-dence
in-de-pen'-dency
in-de-pen'-dent
in-de-pen'-dently
in-de-scri'b-
    able
in-de-struc-ti-
    bil'ity
in-de-struc'-
    tible
in-de-ter'-min-
    able
in-de-ter'-mi-
    nate
in-de-ter-mi-
    na'tion
in-de-ter'-mi-
    nism
in'-dex
in'-dexer

183

in-du'bi-table
in-du'ce
in-du'ce-ment
in-du'cer
in-du'cible
in-du'cing
in-duct'
in-duct'-ance
in-ductee'
in-duct'-ile
in-duc-til'ity
in-duc'-tion
in-duc'-tive
in-duc-tiv'ity
in-duc-tom'eter
in-duc'-tor
in-duc-to'rium
in-due'
in-dulg'e
in-dul'-gence
in-dul'-gent
in-dul'-gently
in-dulg'er
in-dulg'-ing
in'-du-line
in-dult'
in-du-men'-tum
in-du'na
in-du'pli-cate
in'-du-rate
in-du-ra'tion
in'-du-rat-ive
in-du'-siate
in-du'-sium
in-dus'-trial
in-dus-tri-al-is-
          a'tion
in-dus'-tri-al-ise

in-dus'-tri-al-
          ism
in-dus'-tri-al-ist
in'-dus-tries
in-dus'-tri-ous
in'-dus-try
in'-dwell-ing
in-e'bri-ant
in-e'bri-ate
in-ebri-a'tion
in-ebri'ety
in-edi-bil'ity
in-ed'-ible
in-ed'-ited
in-ef-fa-bil'ity
in-ef'-fable
in-ef-fa'ce-able
in-ef-fec'-tive
in-ef-fec'-tively
in-ef-fec'-tual
in-ef-fec-tu-
          al'ity
in-ef-fi-ca'cious
in-ef'-fi-cacy
in-ef-fic'iency
in-ef-fic'ient
in-elas'-tic
in-elas-tic'ity
in-el'-egance
in-el'-egant
in-eli-gi-bil'ity
in-el'i-gible
in-el'-oquent
in-eluc'-table
in-elu'd-ible
in-ept'
in-ep'-ti-tude
in-equal'ity

in-eq'ui-table
in-eq'uity
in-erad'i-cable
in-era's-able
in-err'-able
in-err'-ant
in-ert'
in-ert'-ance
in-er'-tia
in-er'-tial
in-ert'-ness
in-es-ca'p-able
in-es-sen'-tial
in-es'-ti-mable
in-evi-ta-bil'ity
in-evi'ta-ble
in-ev'i-table-
          ness
in-ev'i-tably
in-exact'
in-exac'-ti-tude
in-ex-cu's-able
in-exhaust-
          ibil'ity
in-exhaust'-ible
in-exhaust'-ive
in-exis'-tence
in-exis'-tent
in-exor-abil'ity
in-ex'or-able
in-ex'or-ably
in-ex-pe'di-ence
in-ex-pe'di-ency
in-ex-pe'di-ent
in-ex-pen'-sive
in-ex-pe'ri-ence
in-ex-pe'ri enced
in-ex'-pert

in-ex'-pi-able
in-ex-plain'-able
in-ex-plic-a-
      bil'ity
in-ex-plic'-able
in-ex-plic'it
in-ex-plo'r-able
in-ex-plo'sive
in-ex-press'-ible
in-ex-press'-ive
in-ex-pug'-nable
in-ex-pun'-gible
in-ex-ten'-sible
in-ex-tin'guish-
      able
in-ex'-tir-pable
in-ex-trica-
      bil'ity
in-ex'-tri-cable
in-ex'-tri-cably
in-fal-li-bil'ity
in-fal'-lible
in'-fa-mous
in'-famy
in'-fancy
in'-fant
in-fan'ta
in-fan-ti-ci'dal
in-fan'-ti-cide
in'-fan-tile
in'-fan'-ti-lism
in'-fan-tine
in'-fan-try
in'-fan-try-man
in'-farct
in-farc'-tion
in-fat'u-ate
in-fat'u-ated
186

in-fatu-a'tion
in-feas'-ible
in-fect'
in-fect'-ant
in-fec'-tion
in-fec'-tious
in-fec'-tive
in-fec-tiv'ity
in-fec'-tor
in-fec'-und
in-fec-un'dity
in-fel-ic'i-tous
in-fel-ic'ity
in-fer'
in-fer'-able
in'-fer-ence
in-fer-en'-tial
in-fe'rior
in-feri-or'ity
in-fer'-nal
in-fer'no
in-ferr'ed
in-fer'-ring
in-fer'-tile
in-fer-til'ity
in-fest'
in-fes-ta'tion
in-fest'er (n. v.)
in-feu-da'tion
in'-fi-del
in-fi-del'ity
in'-field
in'-fil'-trate
in'-fil-tra'tion
in'-fil-trat-ive
in'-fil'-trator
in'-fi-nite
in'-fi-nitely

in-fini-tes'i-mal
in-fini-ti'val
in-fin'i-tive
in-fin'i-tude
in-fi-ni'tum
in-fin'-ity
in-firm'
in-firm'-ary
in-firm'-ity
in-fla'me
in-fla'ming
in-flam-ma-
      bil'ity
in-flam'-mable
in-flam-ma'tion
in-flam'-ma-tory
in-fla't-able
in-fla'te
in-fla'ted
in-fla'ter
in-fla't-ing
in-fla'tion
in-fla'tion-ary
in-fla'tion-ism
in-fla'tion-ist
in-fla'tor
in-flect'
in-flec'-tion
in-flec'-tive
in-flec'-tor
in-flex'ed
in-flexi-bil'ity
in-flex'-ible
in-flex'ion
in-flict'
in-flic'-table
in-flict'er
in-flic'-tion

in-flic'-tor
in-flor-esc'ence
in-flor-esc'ent
in'-flow
in'-flu-ence
in'-flu-encer
in'-fluent
in-flu-en'-tial
in-flu-en'za
in'-flux
in-fold'
in-form'
in-for'-mal
in-for-mal'ity
in-for'-mally
in-form'-ant
in-for-ma'tion
in-form'a-tive
in-for'-ma-tory
in-form'er
in-fract'-ible
in-frac'-tion
in'-fra-dyne
infra-hu'man
in-fran'-gible
in-fra▪red'
in-fra-son'ics
in'-fra-sound
in'-fra-struc'-
      ture
in-fre'quency
in-fre'quent
in-fre'quently
in-fring'e
in-fring'e-ment
in-frin'ger
in-frin'-ging
in-truc'-tu-ous

in-fun-dib'u-lar
in-fun-di-bu'li-
      form
in-fun-dib'u-lum
in-fu'ri-ate
in-fu'ri-at-ing
in-furi-a'tion
in-fusc'-ate
in-fu'se
in-fu'ser
in-fusi-bil'ity
in-fu's-ible
in-fu'sion
in-fu-so'ria
in-fu-so'rial
in-fu-so'rian
in'-gate
in-gath'-er-ing
in-gem'i-nate
in-gen'-er-ate
in-ge'ni-ous
in-ge'ni-ously
in-gen-u'ity
in-gen'u-ous
in-gest'
in-gest'-ant
in-ges'-tion
in-gest'-ive
ing'le-nook
in-glo'ri-ous
in'-got
in-graft'
in-grain'
in-grain'ed
in'-grate
in-gra'tiate
in-gra'tiat-ing
in-gratia'tion

in-grat'i-tude
in-gra-vesc'ence
in-gra-vesc'ent
in-grav'i-date
in-gre'di-ent
in'-gress
in-gres'sion
in'-grow-ing
in'-grown
in'-growth
ing'ui-nal
in-gulf'
in-gur'-gi-tate
in-gur-gi-ta'tion
in-hab'it
in-habi-ta-bil'ity
in-hab'-it-able
in-hab'i-tancy
in-hab'i-tant
in-habi-ta'tion
in-hab'i-ter
in-ha'l-ant
in-ha-la'tion
in'-ha-lator
in-hala-to'rium
in-ha'le
in-ha'ler
in -ha'ling
in-har-mon'ic
in-har-mo'ni-ous
in-he're
in-he'rence
in-he'rent
in-her'it
in-her'it-able
in-her'it-ance
in-her'itor
in-her'itress

187

in-her'i-trix
in-he'sion
in-hib'it
in-hib'i-ter
in-hi-bit'ion
in-hib'i-tor
in-hib'i-tory
in-hos'-pi-table
in-hos-pi-tal'ity
in-hu'man
in-hu-ma'ne
in-hu-man'ity
in-hu'man-ism
in-im'i-cal
in-im'i-cally
in-imi-ta-bil'ity
in-im'i-table
in'-ion
in-iq'ui-tous
in-iq'uity
in-it'ial
in-it'ial-ling
in-it'ially
in-it'iate
in-itia'tion
in-it'iat-ive
in-it'iator
in-it'iat-ory
in-ject'
in-jec'-tion
in-jec'-tor
in-ju-dic'ial
in-ju-dic'ious
in-junct'
in-junc'-tion
in-junc'-tive
in'-jure
in'-jur-ies
188

in'-jur-ing
in-ju'ri-ous
in'-jury
in-jus'-tice
ink-horn
ink'-ling
ink'-stain
ink'-stand
ink'-well
in'-laid
in'-land
in'-lay
in'-let
in'-lier
in'-ly-ing
in'-mate
in-'most
in-na'te
in-na'tely
in-nav'i-gable
in'-ner
in'-ner-most
in-nerv'-ate
in-ner-va'tion
in'-nings
inn'-keeper
in'no-cence
in'no-cent
in'no-cently
in-noc'u-ous
in-nom'i-nate
in'no-vate
inno-va'tion
in'no-vator
in'no-vat-ory
in-nox'ious
in-nu-en'do
in-nu-en'-does

in-nu'mer-able
in-nu-trit'ion
in-nu-trit'ious
in-ob-serv'-ance
in-oc'u-lable
in-oc'u-lar
in-oc'u-late
in-oc'u-lat-ing
in-ocu-la'tion
in-oc'u-lat-ive
in-oc'u-lator
in-oc'u-lum
in-o'dor-ous
in-of-fen'-sive
in-of-fic'ious
in-op'-er-able
in-op'-er-at-ive
in-op'-por-tune
in-op-por-tu'ne-
    ness
in-or'-di-nacy
in-or'-di-nate
in-or'-di-nately
in-or-gan'ic
in-or-gan'i-cally
in-or-gan-is-
    a'tion
in-os'-cu-late
in-os-cu-la'tion
in-os'-i-tol
in-ox'i-dis-able
in'-put
in'-quest
in-qui'etude
in'-qui-line
in-qui're
in-qui'rer
in-qui'r-ies

in-qui'r-ing
in-qui'r-ingly
in-qui'ry
in-qui-sit'ion
in-quis'i-tive
in-quis'i-tively
in-quis'i-tive-
        ness
in-quis'i-tor
in-quisi-to'rial
in'-road
in'-rush
in-sal'i-vate
in-sali-va'tion
in-sa-lu'bri-ous
in-sa-lu'brity
in-sal'u-tary
in-sa'ne
in-san'i-tary
in-san'ity
in-satia-bil'ity
in-sa'tiable
in-sa'tiate
in-sa-ti'ety
in-sat'-ur-able
in'-scape
in'-science
in'-scient
in-scri'b-able
in-scri'be
in-scri'ber
in-scri'b-ing
in-scrip'-tion
in-scrip'-tional
in-scrip'-tive
in-scro'le
in-scro'll
in-scru'-table

in-scru-ta-
        bil'ity
in-scru'-tably
in-sculpt'
in-sculp'-tate
in-sculp'-ture
in'-sect
in-sec'ta
in-sec-ta'rium
in-sec'-tary
in-sec-ti-ci'dal
in-sec'-ti-cide
in-sec'-ti-form
in-sec'-ti-fuge
in-sec'-tile
in-sec'-tion
in-sec-ti'val
in-sec'-ti-vore
in-sec-tiv'or-
        ous
in-sec-tol'ogy
in-secu're
in-secu'r-ity
in-sel-ec'-tive
in-sem'i-nate
in-semi-na'tion
in-sen'-sate
in-sen-si-bil'ity
in-sen'-sible
in-sen'-sibly
in-sen'-si-tive
in-sen'-su-ous
in-sen'-tient
in-sep-ar-
        abil'ity
in-sep'-ar-able
in-sert' (v.)
in'-sert (n.)

in-ser'-tion
in-ses-so'rial
in'-set (n.)
in-set' (v.)
in'-shore
in-si'de
in-si'der
in-sid'i-ous
in-sid'i-ously
in-'sight
in-sig'-nia
in-sig-nif'i-
        cance
in-sig-nif'i-cant
in-sin-ce're
in-sin-ce'rely
in-sin-cer'ity
in-sin'u-ate
in-sin-ua'tion
in-sin'u-at-ive
in-sin'u-ator
in-sip'id
in-si-pid'ity
in-sip'i-ence
in-sist'
in-sist'-ence
in-sist'-ent
in-sist'-ently
in-sist'er
in-so-bri'ety
in'-so-late
in-so-la'tion
in-'sole
in'-sol-ence
in'-sol-ent
in-sol-id'ity
in-solu-bil'ity
in-sol'-vable

189

in-sol'-vency
in-sol'-vent
in-som'-nia
in-som'-niac
in-so-much'
in-souc'i-ance
in-souc'i-ant
in-span'
in-span'ned
in-span'-ning
in-spect'
in-spec'-tion
in-spec'-tor
in-spec'-tor-ate
in-spec-to'rial
in-spect'-oscope
in-spec'-tress
in-spi'r-able
in-spi-ra'tion
in-spi-ra'tional
in-spi-ra'tion-
    ism
in-spi-ra'tion-ist
in-spir'a-tive
in'-spir-ator
in-spir'a-tory
in-spi're
in-spi'rer
in-spi'r-ing
in-spir'it
in-spiss'-ate
in-spiss-a'tion
in-spiss'-ator
in-sta-bil'ity
in-sta'ble
in-stall'
in-stal-la'tion
in-stall'ed

in-stal'-ling
in-stal'-ment
in'-stance
in'-stancy
in'-stant
in-stan-ta'neous
in-stan-
    ta'neously
in-stan'-ter
in'-stantly
in'-star
in-sta'te
in-staur-a'tion
in-stead'
in'-step
in'-sti-gate
in'-sti-gat-ing
in-sti-ga'tion
in'-sti-gator
in-stil'
in-stil-la'tion
in-still'ed
in-stil'-ling
in-stil'-ment
in'-stinct (n.)
in-stinct' (a.)
in-stinc'-tive
in-stinc'-tively
in'-sti-tute
in-sti-tu'tion
in-sti-tu'tional
in-sti-tu'tion-
    al-ise
in-sti-tu'tion-
    al-ism
in'-sti-tutor
in-struct'
in-struc'-tion

in-struc'-tional
in-struc'-tive
in-struc'-tor
in-struc'-tress
in'-stru-ment
in-stru-men'-tal
in-stru-men'-tal-
    ist
in-stru-men-
    tal'ity
in-stru-men-
    ta'tion
in-sub-or'-di-
    nate
in-sub-or-di-
    na'tion
in-sub-stan'-tial
in-sub-stan-
    tial'ity
in-suf'-fer-able
in-suf-fic'iency
in-suf-fic'ient
in'-suf-flate
in-suf-fla'tion
in'-suf-flator
in'-su-lar
in-su-lar'ity
in'-su-late
in-su-la'tion
in'-su-lator
in'-su-lin
in'-sult (n.)
in-sult' (v.)
in-sul-ta'tion
in-super-abil'ity
in-su'per-able
in-sup-port'-able
in-su'rable

in-su'rance
in-su'rant
in-su're
in-su'red
in-su'rer
in-sur'-gence
in-sur'-gency
in-sur'-gent
in-su'ring
in-sur-rec'-tion
in-sur-mount'-
            able
in-sur-rec'-tion-
            ary
in-sur-rec'-tion-
            ist
in-sus-cep-ti-
            bil'ity
in-sus-cep'-tible
in-tact'
in-ta'gli-ated
in-ta'glio
in'-take
in-tan-gi-bil'ity
in-tan'-gible
in-tar'-sia
in'-teger
in'-te-grable
in'-te-gral
in-te-gral'ity
in'-te-grant
in'-te-grate
in-te-gra'tion
in-te-gra'tion-
            ist
in'-te-grat-ive
in'-te-grator
in-teg'-rity

in-teg'u-ment
in-tegu-men'-tal
in-tegu-men'-tary
in'-tel-lect
in-tel-lec'-tion
in-tel-lec'-tive
in-tel-lec'-tual
        is-a'tion
in-tel-lec'-tu-al-
            ise
in-tel-lec'-tu-
            al-ism
in-tel-lec'-tu-
            al-ist
in-tel-lec-tu-
            al'ity
in-tel-lec'-tu-
            ally
in-tel'-li-gence
in-tel'-li-gencer
in-tel'-li-gent
in-tel-li-gen'-
            tial
in-tel'-li-gently
in-tel-li-gent'-
            sia
in-tel-li-gi-
            bil'ity
in-tel'-li-gible
in-tem'-per-ance
in-tem'-per-ant
in-tem'-per-ate
in-ten'-able
in-tend'
in-tend'-ance
in-tend'-ancy
in-tend'-ant

in-tend'-ment
in-ten'-er-ate
in-tens'e
in-tens'ely
in-ten-si-fi-
            ca'tion
in-ten'-si-fied
in-ten'-si-fier
in-ten'-si-fies
in-ten'-sify
in-ten'-sion
in-ten-si-
            tom'eter
in-ten'-sity
in-ten'-sive
in-ten'-sively
in-tent'
in-ten'-tion
in-ten'-tional
in-ten'-tion-ally
in-ten'-tioned
in-tent'ly
in-tent'-ness
in-ter'
in-ter-act'
in-ter-ac'-tion
in-ter-blend'
in-ter-breed'
in-ter'ca-lary
in-ter'ca-late
in-ter-cal-a'tion
in-ter-ce'de
in-ter-ce'd-ing
in-ter-cel'lu-lar
in'-ter-cept (n.)
in-ter-cept' (v.)
in-ter-cep'-tion
in-ter-cep'-tive

in-ter-cep'-tor
in-ter-ces'sion
in-ter-cess'or
in-ter-cess'-ory
in'-ter-change (n.)
in-ter-cha'nge (v.)
in-ter-change-
    abil'ity
in-ter-cha'nge-
    able
in-ter-clav'-icle
in-ter-col-le'gi-
    ate
in-ter-col-o'nial
in'-ter-com
in-ter-com-
    mu'ni-cate
in-ter-com-muni-
    ca'tion
in-ter-com-
    mu'nion
in-ter-com-
    mu'nity
in-ter-con-nect'
in-ter-con-ti-
    nen'-tal
in-ter-cos'-tal
in'-ter-course
in-ter-crop'
in-ter-cur'-rence
in-ter-cur'-rent
in-ter-de-nomi-
    na'tional
in-ter-de-pend'
in-ter-de-pen'-
    dence
in-ter-de-pen'-
    dent

in-ter-dict'
in-ter-dic'-tion
in-ter-dic'-tor
in-ter-dig'i-tal
in-ter-fe'ro
in-ter-fe'rence
in-ter-fer-en'-
    tial
in-ter-fe'ring
in-ter-fer-
    om'eter
in-ter-fer-
    om'etry
in-ter-fer'on
in-ter-flu'-ent
in-ter-fu'se
in-ter-fu'sion
in-ter-gla'cial
in-ter-gra'de
in'-terim
in-te'rior
in-ter-ja'cent
in-ter-ject'
in-ter-jec'-tion
in-ter-jec'-tor
in-ter-jec'-tory
in-ter-jec'-tural
in-ter-knit'
in-ter-la'ce
in-ter-lam'i-nate
in-ter-lard'
in-ter-lay'
in'-ter-leaf
in-ter-leav'e
in-ter-li'ne
in-ter-lin'eal
in-ter-lin'ear

in-ter-li'ning
in-ter-link'
in-ter-lock'
in-ter-locu'tion
in-ter-loc'u-tor
in-ter-loc'u-tory
n-ter-loc'u-
    tress
in-ter-loc'u-trix
in-ter-lo'po
in-ter-lo'per
in'-ter-lude
in-ter-lu'nar
in-ter-mar'-riage
in-ter-mar'ry
in-ter-med'dle
in-ter-med'-dler
in-ter-me'di-ary
in-ter-me'di-ate
in-ter-me'dium
in-ter'-ment
in-ter-mez'zo
in-ter'mi-nable
in-ter'mi-nably
in-ter-ming'le
in-ter-ming'ling
in-ter-mis'sion
in-ter-mit'
in-ter-mit'-tence
in-ter-mit'-tent
    tently
in-ter-mix'
in-ter-mix'-ture
in-ter-mu'ral
in-tern' (v.)
in'-tern (n.)
in-tern'-ally

in-ter-nat′ional
in-ter-national-
is-a′tion
in-ter-nat′ional-
ise
in-ter-nat′ional-
ism
in-ter-nat′ional-
ist
in-ter-nat′ionally
in-ter-ne′cine
in-tern′ed′
in-ter-nee′
in-tern′-ist
in-tern′-ment
in′-tern-ship
in-ter-nun′-cial
in-ter-nun′-cio
in-tero-cep′-tive
in-ter-os′-cu-
late
in-ter-os-cu-
la′tion
in-ter-pa′ge
in-ter-pel′-late
in-ter-pel-
la′tion
in-ter-pel-la′tor
in-ter-pen′-
etrate
in-ter-pen-
etra′tion
in-ter-plan′-
etary
in-ter-plan-
ta′tion
in′-ter-play
in-ter-plead′

in-terp′-olate
in-terp′-olater
in-terp-ola′tion
in-terp′-olator
in-ter-po′sal
in-ter-po′se
in-ter-po′s-ing
in-ter-po-si′tion
in-ter′-pret
in-ter′-pret-able
in-terpret-a′tion
in-ter′pret-ative
in-ter′preter
in-ter-ra′cial
in-ter-ra′dial
in-terr′ed′
in-ter-reg′-num
inter-rela′te
inter-rela′ted
inter-rela′tion
inter-rela′tion-
ship
in-ter′-ring
in′-ter′rog-ate
in-ter-rog-a′tion
in-ter′rog′a-tive
in-ter′rog-ator
in-ter′rog′a-tory
in-ter-rupt′
in-ter-rup′-ted
in-ter-rup′-ter
in-ter-rup′-tible
in-ter-rupt′-ing
in-ter-rup′-tor
in-ter-sect′
in-ter-sec′-tion
in-ter-sec′-
tional

in-ter-sep′-tal
in-ter-sex′-ual
in-ter-spa′ce
in-ter-spers′e
in-ter-sper′-sion
in-ter-sta′te
in-ter-stel′-lar
in-ters′-tice
in-ters′-tices
in-ter-stit′ial
in-ter-ti′dal
in-ter-twi′ne
in-ter-twist′
in-ter-ty′pe
in-ter-ur′-ban
in′-ter-val
in-ter-ve′ne
in-ter-ve′ner
in-ter-ve′nor
in-ter-ven′tion
in-ter-ven′tion-
ist
in′-ter-view
in′-ter-viewer
in-ter-volv′e
in-ter-weav′e
in-ter-wo′ven
in-tes′-tacy
in-tes′-tate
in-tes′-ti-nal
in-tes′-tine
in′-tima
in′-ti-macy
in′-ti-mate
in′-ti-mately
in′-ti-mater
in-ti-ma′tion
in-tim′i-date

INTIMIDATION

in-timi-da'tion
in-tim'i-dator
in-tim'i-dat-ory
in-tinc'-tion
in-tit'-ule
in'-toed
in-tol'-er-able
in-tol'-er-ably
in-tol'-er-ance
in-tol'-er-ant
in'-ton-ate
in-ton-a'tion
in-to'ne
in-to'ning
in-tox'i-cant
in-tox'i-cate
in-tox'i-cat-ing
in-toxi-ca'tion
in-tra-cel'lu-lar
in-tra-cer'-ebral
in-tra-cra'nial
in-trac-ta-
    bil'ity
in-trac'-table
in-tra-der'-mal
in-tra'dos
in-tra-mol-ec'u-
    lar
in-tra-mu'ral
in-tran'-si-gence
in-tran'-si-gent
in-tran'-si-tive
in'-trant
intra-sta'te
in-tra-tel-lu'ric
in-trava-sa'tion
in-tra-ve'nous
in-treat'
194

in-trep'id
in-trep-id'ity
in'-tri-cacy
in'-tri-cate
in'-trigant
in-tri'gue
in-tri'gued
in-tri'guer
in-tri'guing
in-tri'guingly
in-trin'-sic
in-trin'-si-cal
in-trin'-si-cally
in-tro-du'ce
in-tro-duc'-tion
in-tro-duc'tory
in'-troit
intro-jec'-tion
in-tro-mis'sion
in-tro-mit'
in-tro-mit'-tent
in-tro-spect'
in-tro-spec'-tion
in-tro-spec'-tive
in-tro-ver'-sion
in'-tro-vert
in-tro-ver'-tive
in-tru'de
in-tru'der
in-tru'sion
in-tru's-ive
in-trust'
in'-tu-bate
in-tu-ba'tion
in-tuit'ion
in-tuit'ion-al
in-tuit'ion-al-
    ism

in-tui'tion-al-
    ist
in-tu'it-ive
in-tu'it-ively
in-tu'it-iv-ism
in-tu'it-iv-ist
in-tu-mesc'e
in-tu-mesc'ence
in-tu-mesc'ent
in-tus-sus-cep'-
    tion
in'u-lase
in'u-lin
in-unc'-tion
in-un'-dant
in'-un-date
in'-un-da'tion
in'-un-dator
in-un'da-tory
in-ur-ba'ne
in-ur-ban'ity
in-u're
in-u're-ment
in-u'r-ing
in-u'tile
in-util'ity
in-va'de
in-va'der
in-va'd-ing
in-varia-bil'ity
in-va'riable
in-va'riably
in-va'riant
in-va'sion
in-va's-ive
in-vec'-tive
in-veigh'
in-vei'gle

in-veig'-ling
in-vent'
in-vent'-able
in-ven'-tion
in-ven'-tive
in-ven'-tor
in-ven-to'rial
in'-ven-tories
in'-ven-tory
in-ver-ac'ity
in-ver'-sion
in-ver'-sive
in-vert'
in'-ver-tase
in-vert'-ebrate
in-vert'er
in-vert'-ible
in-ver'tor
in-vest'
in-ves'-ti-gate
in-ves-ti-ga'tion
in-ves'-ti-gator
in-ves'-ti-gat-
    ory
in-ves'-ti-ture
in-vest'-ment
in-ves'-tor
in-vet'-er-acy
in-vet'-er-ate
in-vid'i-ous
in-vig'i-late
in-vigi-la'tion
in-vig'i-lator
in-vig'-or-ate
in-vig'-or-at-ing
in-vig-or-a'tion
in-vig'-or-at-ive

in-vig'-or-ator
in-vin-ci-bil'ity
in-vin'-cible
in-viol-abil'ity
in-vi'ol-able
in-vi'ol-ate
in-visi-bil'ity
in-vis'-ible
in-vi-ta'tion
in-vi'tatory
in-vi'te
in-vi'ter
in-vi't-ing
in-vi't-ingly
in'-vo-cate
in-vo-ca'tion
in-voc'a-tive
in'-vo-cator
in-voc'a-tory
in'-voice
in'-voic-ing
in-vo'ke
in-vo'k-ing
in-vol'u-cel
in-vo-lu'cral
in'-vo-lucre
in-vo-lu'crum
in-vol'-un-tar-
    ily
in-vol'-un-tary
in'-vol-ute
in'-vol-uted
in-vol-u'tion
in-volv'e
in-volv'e-ment
in-volv'-ing
in-vul'-ner-
    abil'ity

in-vul'-ner-able
in-vul-tu-a'tion
in'-ward
in'-wardly
in-weav'e
in-wo'ven
in-wrought'
i'od-ide
i'od-ine
io'do-form
iod-om'etry
i'ol-ite
ion-is-a'tion
i'on-ise
ion'o-sphere
iono-spher'ic
io'ta-cism
ip'-ecac
ip-ecacu-an'ha
ipo-me'a
ira-cun'-dity
iras-ci-bil'ity
iras'-cible
i're-ful
i're-fully
i're-stone
iri-da'ceous
iri-dal'gia
iri-dec'-tomy
iri-desc'ence
iri-desc'ent
ir-id'ic
iri-dis-a'tion
ir'i-dise
irid'-ium
iris-a'tion
i'ri-scope
irk'-some

i'ron-bound
i'ron-clad
i'ron-gray
iron'i-cal
iron'i-cally
i'ron-ing
i'ron-master
i'ron-monger
i'ron-mould
i'ron-stone
i'ron-ware
i'ron-wood
i'ron-work
i'ron-worker
ir-ra'diance
ir-ra'diant
ir-ra'diate
ir-radia'tion
ir-rad'i-cable
ir-rat'ional
ir-rat'ion-al-ise
ir-ration-al'ity
ir-re'al-is-able
ir-re-claim'-able
ir-rec-og-ni's-
      able
ir-rec-on-ci'l-
      able
ir-re-cov'er-able
ir-re-deem'-able
ir-re-den'ta
ir-re-den'-tism
ir-re-den'-tist
ir-re-duc-
     ibil'ity
ir-re-du'ci-ble
ir-ref'ra-gable
ir-re-fran'-gible
196

ir-re-fut-
      abil'ity
ir-re-fu't-able
ir-reg'u-lar
ir-regu-lar'ity
ir-reg'u-larly
ir-rel'-ative
ir-rel'-evance
ir-rel'-evant
ir-re-lig'ion
ir-re-lig'ious
ir-re'meable
ir-re-me'di-able
ir-re-mov'-able
ir-rep'-ar-able
ir-re-pla'ce-able
ir-re-press'-ible
ir-re-proach'-
      able
ir-re-sis-ti-
     bil'ity
ir-re-sist'-ible
ir-re-sist'-ibly
ir-re-sol'-uble
ir-res'-ol-ute
ir-res'-ol-utely
ir-res-ol-u'tion
ir-re-solv'-able
ir-res-pec'-tive
ir-re-spon-si-
     bil'ity
ir-res-pon'-sible
ir-res-pon'-sive
ir-re-ten'-tion
ir-re-ten'-tive
ir-re-triev-
     abil'ity
ir-re-triev'-able

ir-rev'-er-ence
ir-rev'-er-ent
ir-re-versi-
     bil'ity
ir-re-vers'-ible
ir-revo-ca-
     bil'ity
ir-rev'o-cable
ir-rev'o-cably
ir'-ri-gable
ir'-ri-gate
ir-ri-ga'tion
ir'-ri-gator
ir-rig'u-ous
ir-ris'ion
ir-ri-ta-bil'ity
ir'-ri-table
ir'-ri-tably
ir'-ri-tancy
ir'-ri-tant
ir'-ri-tate
ir'-ri-tat-ing
ir-ri-ta'tion
ir'-ri-tat-ive
ir'-ro-rate
ir-ro-ra'tional
ir-rup'-tion
ir-rup'-tive
isa-cous'-tic
i'sa-goge
isa-gog'ics
i'sa-gon
isal'-lo-bar
i'sa-tin
i'sa-tinic
is-che'mia
is'-chial
is-chi-at'ic

is'-chium

isen-trop'ic

iso-an'yl

i'so-bar

iso-bar'ic

i'so-bath

iso-bath'y-therm

i'so-chore

iso-chro-mat'ic

isoch'-ronal

i'so-chrone

isoch'-ron-ism

isoch'-ron-ous

iso-cli'nal

iso-crat'ic

iso-dis-per'se

i'so-dont

iso-dyn-am'ic

isog'a-mous

isog-en-et'ic

isog'en-ous

iso-ge'o-therm

iso-gloss'al

isog'-onal

iso-gon'ic

i'so-lable

i'so-lat-able

i'so-late

iso-la'tion

iso-la'tion-ism

iso-la'tion-ist

i'so-lator

iso-leuc'ine

isol'o-gous

i'so-logue

iso-mag-net'ic

i'so-mer

iso-mer'ic

isom'-er-ise

isom'-er-ism

iso-met'ric

iso-met'ri-cally

iso-metro'pia

iso-mor'-phic

iso-mor'-phism

iso-oc'-tane

i'so-phase

isoph-thal'ic

iso-pies'tic

i'so-pleth

i'so-pod

iso-pol'ity

i'so-preno

iso-pro'-panol

iso-pro'-pyl

isos'-celes

iso-seis'-mal

isos'-tasy

iso-stat'ic

iso-ster'ic

iso-ten'i-scope

isoth'-eral

i'so-there

i'so-therm

iso-ther'mal

iso-ton'ic

iso-ton-ic'ity

i'so-tope

iso-top'ic

i'so-tron

iso-trop'ic

isot'ro-pous

is'su-able

is'su-ance

is'su-ing

isth'-mian

isth'-mus

ita-col'u-mite

ital'i-cise

ital'i-cis-ing

ital'-ics

itch'i-ness

item-is-a'tion

i'tem-ise

it'er-ance

it'er-ate

iter-a'tion

it'er-at-ive

ithy-phal'-lic

itin'-er-acy

itin'-er-ancy

itin'-er-ant

itin'-er-ary

itin'-er-ate

it-self'

J

jab'-ber

jab'-bing

jab'-iru

jab-or-an'di

jac'a-mar

jac'-ana

jac-ar-an'da

ja'-cinth

jack'-a-napes

jack'-ass

jack'-boot

jack'-daw

jack'-ham-mer

jack'-knife

jack-o-lan'-tern

jack'-pot
jack'-stays
jack'-straw
jack'-yard
jac'-obin
ja-co'bus
jac'-onet
jac'-quard
jac-ta'tion
jac-ti-ta'tion
jac'u-late
ja-de'ite
jag'-ged
jag'-gery
jag'-uar
jail'-bird
jail'-break
jam-ba-lay'a
jam-boree'
jam'-ming
jan'is-sary
jan'i-tor
jan'i-tress
ja-pann'ed
ja-pon'-ica
jar'-gon
jar-gon-ell'e
jar'-gon-ise
jar'-gon-ist
jar-goon'
jar'-osite
jar-ovis-a'tion
jar'-ovise
jar'-rah
jar'-ring
jas'-mine
jas'-pel-line
198

jas'-per
jas-pid'-ean
jaun'-dice
jaunt'-ily
jaunt'i-ness
jav'-elin
jaw'-bone
jay'-walker
jeal'-ous
jeal'-ously
jeal'-ousy
jeer'-ingly
je-ju'nal
je-ju'ne
je-jun-i'tis
je-jun-os'to-my
je-ju'num
jel'-lied
jel'-lify
jel'-ly-fish
jem'a-dar
jen'-net
jen'-net-ting
jeop'-ard
jeop'-ard-ise
jeop'-ard-is-ing
jeop'-ardy
jequir'-ity
jer-bo'a
jer-emi'ad
jerk'-ily
jer'-kin
jerk'i-ness
jero-bo'am
jer'-ry-built
jer'-ry-can
jer'-sey
jer'-vine

jess'a-mine
jest'-ingly
jesu-it'i-cal
jet'-liner
jet-pro-pell'ed
jet-pro-pul'-sion
jet'-sam
jet'-ties
jet'-ting
jet'-ti-son
jet'-ton
jew'-elled
jew'el-ler
jew'el-weed
jew'-ing
jib'-bing
jig'-ger
jig'-gling
jig'-saw
jim'-son-weed
jin'go-ism
jin'go-ist
jingo-is'tic
jin-nee'
jin-rik'-sha
jit'-ters
jit'-tery
jo-ba'tion
job'-ber
job'-bery
job'-bing
job'-holder
job'-less
jo-co'se
jo-cos'ity
joc'u-lar
jocu-lar'ity

joc'-und
joc-un'dity
jodh'-purs
jog'-ging
jog'-ging
john'-ny-cake
join'-der
join'-ery
join'-ture
jo'ke-ster
jo'k-ing
jo'k-ingly
jol'-ley
jol-li-fi-ca'tion
jol'-lify
jol'-lily
jol'-lity
jol'-ly-boat
jon'-quil
jo'-rum
jos'-tling
jot'-ted
jot'-ting
jounc'-ing
journal-e'se
jour'nal-ist
journal-is'tic
journal-is'ti-
cally
jour'nal-ise
jour'ney-ing
jour'ney-man
jo'v-ial
jovi-al'ity
jo'vi-ally
joy'-ance
joy'-ful
joy'-fully

joy'-ous
joy'-ously
joy'-ous-ness
joy'-ride
ju'-bate
ju'-bi-lance
ju'-bi-lant
ju'-bi-late
ju-bi-la'tion
ju'-bi-lee
judg'e-ship
judg'-ing
judg'e-ment
ju'-di-cat-ive
ju'-di-cat-ory
ju'-di-ca-ture
ju-dic'ial
ju-dic'iary
ju-dic'ious
ju-dic'iously
ju'-gal
jug'-ger-naut
jug'-gler
jug'-glery
jug'-gling
jug'u-lar
jug'u-late
juic'-ily
juic'i-ness
ju-lit'su
ju'-jube
ju'ke-box
ju'-lep
jum'-bling
jump'-ing
junc-a'ceous
junc'-tion
junc'-tural

junc'-ture
ju'n-ior
juni-or'ity
ju'-ni-per
junk'-et-ing
junk'-ing
junk'-man
ju'-ral
jur-ass'ic
ju'-rat
ju-rid'i-cal
jur-is-con-sult'
jur-is-dic'-tion
jur-is-pru'-dence
jur-is-pru'-dent
jur-is-pru-den'-
tial
ju'r-ist
jur-is'tic
jur-is'-ti-cally
ju'ry-man
ju'ry-mast
juss'-ive
jus'-tice
jus-tic'iable
jus-tic'iar
jus-tic'iary
jus-ti-fi-
abil'ity
jus-ti-fi'-able
jus-ti-fi-ca'tion
jus'-ti-fi-cat-
ive
jus'-ti-fi-cat-
ory
jus'-ti-fied
jus'-ti-fier
jus'-tify

199

jus'-tl-fy-ing
just'-ness
jut'-ting
juv-en-esc'ence
juv-en-esc'ent
juv'-en-ile
ju-ven-il'ia
juv-en-il'ity
jux'-ta-pose
jux-ta-po-sit'ion

K

kain'-ite
kak-emo'no
kal-eid'o-scope
kal-eido-scop'ic
ka'le-yard
kal-ig'en-ous
kal'-in-ite
kali-oph'i-lite
kal'-li-type
ka'-long
kam'a-cite
ka-ma'la
kamp-tu'li-con
kan'-da-har
kang'a-roo
ka-noon'
kan-tar'
kaoli-ang'
ka'o-lin
kao-lin'ic
kao-lin-is-a'tion
ka'o-lin-ise
ka'o-lin-ite
ka'-pok

kar'a-gan
kar'a-kul
kar'-ite
ka-ross'
kar-roo'
kar'-tel
kary-as'-ter
karyo-gam'ic
kary-og'amy
karyo-kin-e'sis
kary-ol'ogy
kar'yo-lymph
kary-ol'y-sis
karyo-mi'cro-
some
kary-om'i-tome
kar'yo-plasm
kar'yo-some
kash'-gar
kas'-pine
ka-tab'a-sis
ka-tab'at-ic
ka-tab'-ol-ism
kata-gen'-esis
kata-kin-et'ic
kata-klas'-tic
kata-mor'-phism
kat'a-plexy
kata-ther-
mom'eter
kata-to'nia
kata-voth'-ron
kat'-ion
ka'ty-did
keck'-ling
ked'-dah
ked'-geree
keel'-age

keel'-haul
keel'-son
keen'-ness
keep'-ing
keep'-sake
keit-lo'a
ke'-loid
kel'-pie
ken'-nel
ken-o'sis
ken'o-tron
ken-tal'-len-ite
kent'-ledge
kent'-rogon
ken'-yte
ker-ar'-gyr-ite
ker'a-sine
kera-tal'-gia
ker'a-tin
kera-tin-is-
a'tion
ker'a-tin-ise
ker-at'i-nous
kera-ti'tis
kera-tog'en-ous
ker'a-toid
kera-to'ma
ker'a-tose
kera-to'sis
kera-tot'omy
ker-aun'o-graph
kerb'-stone
ker'-chief
ker'-chiefed
ker'-ite
ker'-mes
ker'-mes-ite
ker'-mis

ker'-nel
ker'-nelled
ker'-nite
ker'o-gen
ker'o-sene
ker'o-type
ker'-san-tite
ker'-sey
ker'-sey-mere
ker-sey-nett'e
kes'-trel
ke'-tene
ke'-ti-mine
keto-gen'-esis
keto-gen'ic
keto-hex'-ose
ke-tol'y-sis
ke-to-lyt'ic
ke'-tone
ke-ton'ic
keto-nu'ria
ke-to'sis
ket'tle-drum
key'-board
key'-hole
key'-note
key'-stone
khad'-dar
kham'-sin
khan'-ate
kib'-bler
kib'-itzer
kick'-back
kick'-off
kick'-shaw
kid'-ded
kid'-ding
kid'-nap

kid'-napped
kid'-nap-per
kid'-nap-ping
kid'-ney
kies'el-guhr
kies'er-ite
kil'-der-kin
kil'-erg
kil'-la-dar
kill'-dee
kill'-deer
kil'-lick
kil'-li-fish
kill'-ing
kill'-joy
kil'o-cycle
kil'o-gramme
kil'o-litre
kil'o-metre
kilo-met'ric
kil'o-ton
kil'o-var
kil'o-watt
kil'o-watt-hour
kim'-ber-lite
kim-o'no
kin-aes-the'sia
kin-aes-the'sis
kin-aes-thet'ic
kin'-der-gar-ten
ki'nd-hearted
kin'-dler
ki'nd-less
ki'nd-li-ness
kin'-dling
ki'nd-ness
kin'-dred
kin-emat'-ics

kin-esi-at'rics
kin-e'sics
kin-esio-log'ic
kin-esi-ol'ogy
kin-et'ic
kin-eto-gen'-esis
kin-e'to-graph
kin-eto-graph'ic
kin-eto-scop'ic
kin-eto'sis
kin'-folk
king'-bird
king'-bolt
king'-craft
king'-dom
king'-fish
king'-fisher
king'-less
king'-let
king'-li-ness
king'-ling
king'-pin
king'-post
king'-ship
king'-wood
kink'a-jou
kin-ni-kin-nick'
kins'-folk
kin'-ship
kins'-man
kins'-woman
kip'-per
kir'-ki-fier
kis'-met
kiss'-able
kist'-vaen
kit'-cat
kitch'-ener

kitch-en-ett'e
kitch'-en-maid
kitch'-en-ware
kit'-mut-gar
kit'-ten
kit'-ten-ish
kit-ter-een'
kit'-tl-wake
klep-to-ma'nia
klep-to-ma'niac
kli'no-stat
klip'-springer
kly'-dono-gram
kly'-dono-graph
klys'-tron
knack'-ery
knap'-per
knap'-ping
knap'-sack
knap'-weed
kna'v-er-y
kna'v-ish
knead'-ing
knee'-cap
knee'-hole
knee'-joint
kneel'-ing
knee'-pan
knick'-er-bock-
          ers
knick'-ers
knick'-knack
knick'-knack-ery
kni'fe-board
kni'fe-grinder
kni'ght-age
knight-err'-ant
knight-err'-antry

kni'ght-hood
kni'ght-li-ness
knit'-ter
knit'-ting
knob'-bing
knob'-ker-rie
knock'-about
knock'-down
knock'-out
knot'-grass
knot'-hole
knot'-ted
knot'-ter
knot'-ting
know'-able
know'-ing
know'-ingly
knowl'-edge
knowl'-edge-able
knuck'le-bone
knuck'le-duster
knuck'le-ling
knur'-ling
ko-al'a
ko'-bold
kohl-rab'i
ko'-jic
kol-in'sky
kol-khoz'
ko'ni-meter
ko-ni-ol'ogy
kon'i-scope
kon-om'eter
koo'-doo
koo'ka-burra
koo'-lah
koo'-miss
ko'-peck

ko'-sher
kour'-bash
kow-tow'
kra'-ken
kra-toc'-racy
krem'-no-phyte
krim'-mer
kro-mes'ky
kro'-mo-gram
kro'-mo-scope
kry-om'eter
kryp'-tol
kryp'-ton
ku-lak'
kum'-quat
kur'-bash
kur-to'sis
kwashi-or'kor
ky'-an-ise
ky'-an-is-ing
ky'-an-ite
ky'-ass
kyl-lo'sis
ky'-loe
ky'-mo-graph
ky-mo-graph'ic
ky-mog'ra-phy
ky-pho'sis
ky-phot'ic
kyrio-log'ie

L

laa'-ger
lab'-arum
lab'-da-num
lab-efac'-tion

la'bel-ler
la'bel-ling
la-bel'lum
labial-is-a'tion
la'bial-ise
la-bil'ity
la'bio-den-tal
lab-or'a-tory
la-bo'ri-ous
la-bo'ri-ously
lab'-ra-dor
lab-ra-dor-
 esc'ence
lab'-ra-dor-ite
lab'-ret
lab'-roid
lab'-rys
la-bur'-nin
la-bur'-num
lab'-yr-inth
lab-yr-inth'-ian
lab-yr-inth'i-
 form
lab-yr-in'-thine
lab-yr-in-thi'tis
lab-yr-inth'-
 odont
lac'-cate
lac'-cic
lac'-cine
lac'-co-lite
lac'-co-lith
lac-co-lith'-ic
lac-co-lit'ic
lac'er-able
lac'er-ate
lac'er-at-ing
lacer-a'tion

lac'er-at-ive
la-cer'-tian
lacer-til'-ian
la-cer'-tine
la'ce-work
lach'ry-mal
lach'ry-mat-ory
lach'ry-mose
la-cin'i-ate
lacka-dais'i-cal
lack'-ing
lack'-lustre
la-con'ic
la-con'i-cally
la-con'i-cism
lac'-on-ism
lac'-quer
la-cross'e
lac-tal-bu'min
lac'-tar-ene
lac'-tary
lac'-tase
lac'-tate
lac-ta'tion
lac'-teal
lac'-teous
lac-tesc'ence
lac-tesc'ent
lac'-tic
lac-tif'er-ous
lac-tif'ic
lac'-tine
lacto-bacil'-lus
lacto-flav'in
lac'-toid
lac-tom'eter
lacto-pro'-tein
lac'-to-scope

lac'-tose
lac-to'sis
la-cu'na
la-cu'nal
la-cu'nar
la-cu'nary
la-cu'nose
la-cus'-tral
la-cus'-trine
lad'-der
lad'-die
la'dle-ful
la'dy-bird
la'dy-bug
la'dy-finger
la'dy-like
la'dy-love
la'dy-ship
laevo-gy'rate
laevo-ro-ta'tion
laevo-ro-ta't-ory
laevu-lin'ic
lae'vu-lose
lag'-gard
la-gen'i-form
lag'-ger
lag'-ging
la-goon'
la-goon'al
la-gop'o-dous
lag-oph-thal'-
 mia
lait'-ance
la'ke-side
lal-la'tion
la-lop'a-rhy
la-man'-tin
lam'a-sery

203

lam-ba'ste
lam'-ba-tive
lamb'-da-cism
lamb'-doid
lam'-bency
lam'-bent
lam'-bert
lamb'-kin
lamb'-like
lam'-brequin
lamb'-skin
la-mel'la
la-mel'-lar
lam'-el-late
la-mel'-li-corn
la-melli-
    bran'chi-ate
lam-el-lif'er-ous
la-mel'-li-form
lam-el-li-ros'-
       tral
lam'-el-lose
la'me-ness
la-ment'
lam'-en-table
lam'-en-tably
lam-en-ta'tion
la-men'ted
lami-a'ceous
lam'-ina
lam'-in-able
lam'i-nal
lam'i-nar
lami-nari-a'ceous
lam'-in-ary
lam'i-nate
lami-na'tion

lam'i-nator
lam-in-if'er-ous
lam-in-i'tis
lam'-in-ose
lam'-mer-geier
lam'-pad
lam'pa-dary
lam'-pas
lamp'-black
lam'-pion
lamp'-light
lam-poon'
lam-poon'er
lam-poon'-ist
lamp'-post
lam'-prey
lamp'-stand
lan'-ark-ite
lan'ce-let
lan'-ceo-lar
lan'-ceo-late
lan'-cet
lan'-cet-wood
lan-cif'er-ous
lan'-ci-form
lan'-ci-nate
lan'-ci-nat-ing
lan-ci-na'tion
lanc'-ing
lan'-dau
lan'-dau-let
land'-fall
land'-grave
land'-holder
land'-ing
land'-ing-craft
land'-ing-field
land'-ing-gear

land'-ing-strip
land'-lady
land'-less
land'-locked
land'-loper
land'-lord
land'-lord-ism
land'-lub-ber
land'-mark
land'-owner
land'-rail
land'-scape
land'-slide
land'-slip
lands'-man
land'-ward
lan'guish-ing
lan'guor-ous
lan-gu'ria
lan'i-ary
lan'i-ate
lan-if'er-ous
lan-ig'er-ous
lan'-ner
lan'-neret
lan'o-lin
lans'-quenet
lan-ta'na
lan'-tern
lan'-tern-jawed
lan'-tha-nide
lan'-tha-num
lan'-tharin
la-nu'gin-ous
la-nu'go
lan'-yard
lap-ar-ot'omy
lap'-dog

204

la-pel'
lap'i-cide
lapi-da'rian
lap'i-dary
lap'i-date
lapi-da'tion
la-pid'-eous
lapi-desc'ent
lapi-dic'o-lous
lapi-dif'ic
la-pid'-ify
lap'i-dose
la-pil'li
la-pil'-li-form
la-pil'-lus
lap-is∗la-zu'li
lap'-per
lap'-pet
lap'-ping
laps'-able
laps'-ing
lap'-wing
lar'-board
lar'-cen-ist
lar'-cen-ous
lar'-ceny
lar-da'ceous
lar'-der
lar'-don
larg'e-ness
lar-gess'
larg'-ish
lar'-iat
lar'-ine
lar-ith'-mics
lark'-spur
lar'-mier
lar'-ri-gan

lar'-ri-kin
lar'-ry-ing
lar'-vae
lar'-val
lar'-vi-cidal
lar'-vi-cide
lar'-vi-form
lar-vip'ar-ous
lar-viv'or-ous
lar-yn'gal
lar-yn'geal
lar-yn-gec'tomy
lar-yn'ges
lar-yn-git'ic
lar-yn-gi'tis
la-ryn'go-logi-
        cal
laryn-gol'o-gist
lar-yn-gol'ogy
lar-yn'go-phone
lar-yn'go-scope
laryn-gos'copy
lar-yn-got'omy
lar'-ynx
las'-car
lasciv'-ious
lash'-ing
lash'-kar
las'-ket
las'-pring
las'si-tude
last'-ing
lata-ki'a
latch'-ing
latch'-key
latch'-string
lat-ebric'-olous
la-teen'

la'te-ness
lat'-eral
lat'-erally
lat-eri'ceous
lat'-eri-grade
lat-eris-a'tion
lat'-erite
lat-erit'ious
lath'er-ing
lath'-ing
lath'-work
lati-cif'er-ous
lat'i-clave
lati-cos'-tate
lati-den'-tate
lati-fo'li-ate
lati-fun'-dia
lati-fun'-dium
lati-pen'-nate
lati-ros'-tral
lati-ros'-trate
lati-ros'-trous
lat'i-tude
lati-tu'di-nal
lati-tudi-na'rian
lati-tu'di-nous
la-tri'ne
lat'-ten
lat'-ter
lat'-ter-kin
lat'-terly
lat'-tice
lat'-tice-work
lat'-tic-ing
lauda-bil'ity
laud'-able
laud'a-num
laud-a'tion

LAUDATIVE

laud'a-tive
laud'a-tory
laugh'-able
laugh'-ing
laugh'-ing-stock
laugh'-ter
laun'-der
laun-derett'e
laun'-dress
laun'-dries
laun'-dry
laun'-dry-man
laur-a'ceous
laur'-ate
laur'-da-lite
laur'-eate
laur'-eate-ship
laur'-elled
laur'-ion-ite
laur'-ite
laur-us'-tine
laur-us-ti'nus
la-va'bo
lav'a-form
lav'-age
lav-a'tion
lav'a-tory
la've-ment
lav'-en-der
la'ver-ock
lav'-ish
lav'-ishly
law-abi'd-ing
law'-breaker
law'-ful
law'-giver
law'-less
law'-less-ness

law'-maker
law'-mak-ing
lawn'-mower
lawn=ten'-nis
law'-ren-cite
law'-suit
law'-yer
lax a'tion
lax'a-tive
lax'a-tor
lax'-ity
lay'-er-ing
lay-ett'e
lay'-man
lay'-out
laz'a-ret
lazar-et'to
la'zi-ness
laz'u-lite
laz'u-rite
leach'-ing
lead-er-ett'e
lead'-er-ship
lead'-ing
leads'-man
leaf'-age
leaf'i-ness
leaf'-less
leaf'-let
leak'-age
leak'-ance
leak'-proof
lean'-ing
lean'-ness
leap'-frog
leap'-ing
learn'-edly
learn'-ing

leas'-able
leas'e-hold
leas'-ing
least'-ways
least'-wise
leath'er-ine
leath'er-work
leav'en-ing
leav'-ing
lech'-er-ous
lech'-ery
lech'os-os
lec'i-thin
lec'i-thin-ase
lec'-tern
lec'-tion
lec'-tion-ary
lec'-tor
lec'-tual
lec'-ture
lec'-tured
lec'-turer
lec'-tur-ing
lec'y-thus
ledg'e-ment
lee'-board
lee'-fang
leer'-ing
leer'-ingly
lee'-ward
lee'-way
left'-ist
left'-over
leg'a-cies
leg'-acy
legal-is-a'tion
le'gal-ise
le'gal-ism

le'gal-ist
legal-is'tic
leg'a-tee
leg-a'tion
leg'end-ary
leg'-ged
leg'-gings
legi-bil'ity
le'gion-ary
le'gion-naire
leg'is-late
legis-la'tion
leg'is-lat-ive
leg'is-lator
legis-la-to'rial
leg'is-lature
leg'i-tim
legit'-imacy
legit'-imate
legit'-ima-tise
legit'-imise
legit'-imis-ing
legit'-imist
leg'-man
leg'-ume
leg-u'min
leg-u'min-ous
lei-os'-por-ous
lei-ot'ri-chous
leish-man-i'asis
leis'-ter
leis'-terer
leit-motiv'
lem'-ming
lem'-nis-cate
lem-nis'-cus
lem-on-a'de
lem'n-res

lend'-ing
length'-en-ing
length'-ily
length'i-ness
length'-ways
length'-wise
len-it'ic
len'i-tive
len'-ity
lenta-men'te
len'-tic
len'-ti-cel
len'-ticle
len-ti-co'nus
len-tic'u-lar
len-ticu-la'tion
len'-ti-form
len-tig'i-nous
len-ti'go
len'-til
len'-tisk
len'-ti-tude
len'-toid
le'o-nine
le'o-nite
le'o-tard
lepido-cro'cite
lepi-do-den'-dron
lepid'o-lite
lepi-dop'-ter-ist
lepi-dop'-ter-ous
lepi-do'sis
lep'i-dote
lep'-orid
lep'-or-ine
lep'-rechaun
lep-rol'ogy
lepro-sa'rium

lep'-rosy
lep'-rous
lep-to-ceph'a-
              lous
lep-to-ceph'a-lus
lep-to-ceph'aly
lep-to-cer'-cal
lep-to-cer'-cous
lep-to-dac'-tyl-
              ous
lep-to-der'-ma-
              tous
lep-to-kur'-tic
lep-to-kur-to'sis
lep-tol'ogy
lep-to-men-in'ges
lep-to-men-in-
              gi'tis
lep'-ton
lep'-tor-rhine
lep'-to-some
lep'-tus
les-pe-de'za
let'-down
leth-ar'gic
leth-ar'gi-cally
leth'-ar-gise
leth'-argy
let'-ter
let'-ter-box
let'-tered
let'-ter-head
let'-ter-ing
let'-ter-per'-
              fect
let'-ter-press
let'-ting
let'-tuce

LEUCINE

leu'-cine
leu'-cite
leu-cit'ic
leu-co-crat'ic
leu'-co-cyte
leu-co-cythe'mia
leu-co-cyt'ic
leu-co-der'-mia
leu'-col
leu'-col-ine
leu-co'ma
leu'-co-maine
leu'-con
leu'-con-oid
leu-cop'a-thy
leu-co-pe'nia
leu-cop'-terin
leu-cor-rhe'a
leu-co'sis
leu-cot'omy
leu-kae'mia
leu-kae'mic
lev'-ant
lev-a'tor
lev'-elled
lev'-el-ler
lev'-el-ling
lev'-elly
le'ver-age
lev'-eret
lev'-i-able
lev-i'athan
lev'-ied
lev'-i-gable
lev'-i-gate
lev-ga'tion
lev'i-gator
208

lev'i-rate
levi-rat'ic
lev'i-tate
lev'i-tat-ing
levi-ta'tion
lev'-ity
levo-glu'co-san
lcvo-gy'r-ate
levo-gyr-a'tion
lev'y-ing
lewd'-ness
lew'-is-ite
lew'-is-son
lex'i-cal
lexi-cog'ra-pher
lexi-co-graph'i-cal
lexi-cog'ra-phist
lexi-cog'ra-phy
lexi-col'-ogist
lexi-col'ogy
lex'i-con
lexi-graph'ic
lex-ig'ra-phy
liab-il'ity
li'-able
li-as'sic
li'-bant
li-ba'tion
li'ba-tory
li'bel-lant
libel-lee'
li'bel-ler
li'bel-ling
li'bel-lous
lib'-eral
lib-er-al-is-a'tion

lib'-er-al-ise
lib'-er-al-ism
lib'-er-al-ist
lib-er-al-is'tic
lib-er-al'ity
lib'-er-ally
lib'-er-ate
lib-er-a'tion
lib'-er-ator
lib-er-ta'rian
lib-er-ta'rian-ism
lib'-er-tine
lib'-er-tin-ism
lib'-erty
lib-id'-inal
lib-id'-in-ous
li-bra'rian
li'-brary
li'-brate
li-bra'tion
li'bra-tory
li'-bri-form
li'-cence
li'cens-able
li'-cense
li'-censed
li-censee'
li'-censer
li'cens-ing
li'-censor
li-cen'tiate
li-cen'tious
li-cen'tious-ness
li'-chen
li-chen'i-cole
li-cheni-fi-ca'tion

li-chen'i-form
li'-chenin
li-chen-og'ra-
    pher
li-chen-og'ra-phy
li'-chen-oid
li-chen-ol'o-gy
li'-chen-ous
lic'-tor
lid'-ded
li-enter'ic
li'-entery
li-er'ne
lieuten'-ancy
lieuten'-ant
li'fe-belt
li'fe-blood
li'fe-boat
li'fe-buoy
li'fe-guard
li'fe-less
li'fe-like
li'fe-line
li'fe-long
li'fe-saver
li'fe-saving
li'fe-time
lig'a-ment
liga-men'tal
liga-men'-tary
liga-men'-tous
li'-gan
lig'-ate
lig-a'tion
lig'a-ture
lig'-ger
li'ght-ened
li'ght-en-ing

li'ght-er-age
li'ght-er-man
light=fing'ered
light=foot'ed
light=hand'ed
light=head'ed
light=heart'ed
li'ght-house
li'ght-ing
light=mi'nded
li'ght-ness
li'ght-ning
li'ght-proof
li'ght-ship
li'ght-some
li'ght-weight
li'ght-wood
lig'-neous
lig-nesc'ent
lig-nic'o-lous
lig-nif'er-ous
lig-ni-fi-ca'tion
lig'-ni-fied
lig'-ni-form
lig'-nify
lig'-nin
lig-ni-per'-dous
lig-nip'er-ous
lig'-nite
lig-nit'ic
lig-niv'or-ous
lig'-num
lig'-roin
lig'-ula
lig'u-late
lig'-ule
lig'u-rite

li'ke-able
li'ke-li-hood
li'ke-ness
li'ke-wise
li'-lac
lil'a-cine
lili-a'ceous
lil'-ies
li-ma'ceous
lim-ac'i-form
li-ma'cine
li-ma'tion
lim'-bate
lim'-ber
lim'-bric
lim'-bus
li'me-ade
li'me-kiln
li'-men
lim'-er-ick
li'me-stone
li'me-water
li'me-wort
li-mic'o-line
li-mic'o-lous
lim'i-nal
lim'-it-able
lim'i-tary
lim'i-tate
limi-ta'tion
lim'i-tat-ive
lim'-ited
lim'-it-less
lim'i-trophe
lim-iv'or-ous
lim'-ner
lim-net'ic
lim-no-biot'ic

lim-nol'ogy
lim-noph'i-lous
lim-no-plank'-ton
lim'-on-ene
lim-on'i-form
li'-mon-ite
li-mon-it'ic
li-mo'sis
lim'ou-sine
lim'-pet
lim'-pid
lim'-pid'ity
lim'-pidly
limp'-kin
lim'u-lus
lin-al'ool
lin'a-ment
li'-nar-ite
linch'-pin
linc'-tus
lin'-dane
lin'-den
lin'-eage
lin'-eal
lin'-eally
lin'-eament
lin'-ear
lin-ear'ity
lin'-eate
lin-ea'tion
li'ne-man
lin'eo-late
lingua-den'-tal
ling'ui-form
linguis'-tic
linguis'-ti-cally
linguis-tic'ian
linguis'-tics
210

lin'guis-try
lin'gu-lar
lin'gu-late
lini'-ment
li'-nin
lin-i'tis
link'-age
link'-ing
lin'-net
li'no-cut
lino-le'ic
lino-le'nic
lin-o'leum
li'no-type
lin-ox'yn
lin'-sang
lin'-seed
lin'-sey
lin'-stock
lin'-tel
lint'-ers
lint'-white
li'on-cel
li'on-esque
li'on-ess
lion-is-a'tion
li'on-ise
li'on-ism
li'on-like
lip'-ar-ite
li'-pase
li-phae'mia
lip'o-chrome
li-pog'en-ous
lip-og'ra-phy
lip'-oid
lip-ol'y-sis
lipo-lyt'ic

lip-o'ma
lipo-ma-to'sis
lip'o-plast
lipo-pro'-tein
lip'o-some
lipo-trop'ic
lip-ot'ro-pism
lip'-per
lip'-stick
liquefac'-tion
liquefac'-tive
liq'uefi-able
liq'uefy-ing
liquesc'-ence
liquesc'-ent
liquid-am'-bar
liq'ui-date
liqui-da'tion
liq'ui-dator
liq'ui-dise
liquid'-ity
liq'ui-dus
liq'uor-ice
lir-el'li-form
lirio-den'-dron
lir'i-pipe
lir-oc'o-nite
lisp'-ing
lisp'-ingly
lis-son-ceph'a-lous
lis-ter-el-lo'sis
lis'-ter-ine
lis'-ter-ise
list'-less
list'-less-ness
lit'-any
lit'-er-acy

lit'-eral
lit'-er-al-ise
lit'-er-al-ism
lit'-er-al-ist
lit'-er-al-ly
lit'-er-ate
lit-er-a'ti
lit-er-a'tim
lit'-er-ator
lit'era-ture
lith-e'mia
li'the-some
lith-i'asis
lithi-fi-ca'tion
lith'-ium
litho-chro-
    mat'ics
lith'o-clast
lith-od'om-ous
lith-og'en-ous
lith'o-glyph
litho-glyph'-ics
lith'o-graph
litho-graph'ic
lith-og'ra-pher
lith-og'ra-phy
lith'-oid
lith-ol'-atry
lith-ol'-atrous
lith'o-logic
lith-ol'-ogist
lith-ol'ogy
lith-ol'y-sis
lith'o-mancy
lith-on-trip'-tic
lith oph'a-gous

lith'o-phane
lith-oph'i-lous
lith'o-phyte
lith'o-pone
lith'o-scope
lith'o-sere
lith'o-sphere
lith'o-tome
lith-ot'o-mous
lith-ot'omy
lith'o-trite
lith-ot'rity
lith'o-type
lith-ox'yl
lith-u'ria
lit'i-gable
lit'i-gant
lit'i-gate
liti-ga'tion
lit'i-gator
litigi-os'ity
lit-ig'ious
lit-ig'iously
lit'-mus
li'-totes
lit'-ter
lit'tle-ness
lit'-toral
lit'u-ate
lit'u-rate
lit-ur'ge
lit-ur'gic
lit-ur'gi-cal
lit-ur'gi-cally
lit-ur'gics
lit-urgi-ol'-ogist
lit-urgi-ol'ogy
lit'-ur-gist

lit'-urgy
liv'-able
li'veli-hood
li'veli-ness
liv'e-long
liv'-er-ied
liv'-er-ish
liv'-er-leaf
liv'-er-wort
liv'-ery
liv'ery-man
li've-stock
liv-id'ity
liv'-ing
lix-iv'i-ate
lix-ivi-a'tion
lix-iv'ium
liz'-ard
load'-line
loath'-ing
loath'-some
lo'-bar
lo'-bate
lo-ba'tion
lob'-bied
lob'-bing
lob'-by-ing
lob'-by-ist
lo-bec'-tomy
lob-e'lia
lo'bel-ine
lo-bot'omy
lob'-ster
lob'u-lar
lob'u-late
lob'-ule
lob'u-lose
lob'-worm

LOCAL

lo'-cal
lo-cal'e
lo'cal-is-able
local-is-a'tion
lo'cal-ise
lo'cal-iser
lo'cal-ism
lo-cal'ity
lo-ca'te
lo-ca'ter
lo-ca't-ing
lo-ca'tion
loc'a-tive
lo-ca'tor
lock'-age
lock'-fast
lock'-jaw
lock'-out
lock'-ram
lock'-rand
locks'-man
lock'-smith
lock'-step
lock'-stitch
lo'co-mote
loco-mo'tion
loco-mo'tive
loco-mo'tor
lo'co-mot-ory
lo'co-weed
loc'u-lar
loc'u-late
loc'u-lose
loc'u-lous
loc'u-lus
lo'-cus
lo'-cust
loc'u-tary
212

loc-u'tion
lo'de-star
lo'de-stone
lodg'-ing
lodg'-ment
lod'i-cule
lo'-ess
loft' ily
loft'ti-ness
loga-graph'ia
lo'gan-berry
lo-gani-a'ceous
loga-oed'ic
log'-ar-ithm
log-ar-ith'-mic
log-ar-ith'-mi-
cal
log-ar-ith'-mi-
cally
log'a-tom
log'-book
log'-ger
log'-ger-head
log'-ging
log'i-cal
log'i-cally
logis'-tic
logis-tic'ian
logis'-tics
log'o-gram
logo-gram-mat'ic
log-og'ra-pher
log-og'ra-phy
log'o-griph
log-om'-achy
lo-gom'eter
log-or-rhe'a
log'o-thete

log'o-type
log'-roll-ing
log'-wood
loin'-cloth
loi'-ter
loi'-terer
loll'-ing
lol'-li-pop
lo'-ment
lo-men-ta'ceous
lo-men'-tose
lo-men'-tum
lo'ne-li-ness
lo'ne-some
longa-nim'ity
long-an'im-ous
long'-boat
long'-bow
long-dis'tance
lon-gev'ity
lon-ge'vous
long'-hand
long'-headed
long'-horn
lon'-gi-corn
long'-ing
lon-gi-pen'-nate
lon-gi-ros'-tral
lon'gi-tude
longi-tu'di-nal
long'-shore
long'-shore-man
long'-sighted
long-stand'-ing
long-suf'-fer-ing
look'-ing
look'-out
loop'-hole

loos'e-ness
loos'e-strife
loph'o-dont
loph'o-phore
lop'-ol-ith
lop'-per
lop'-ping
lop'-sided
lo-qua'cious
lo-quac'ity
lo'-quat
loq'ui-tur
lo'-ran
lo'-rate
lor'-cha
lord'-li-ness
lord'-ling
lor-do'sis
lord'-ship
lor-i'ca
lor'i-cate
lori-ca'tion
lor'i-keet
lor'i-ner
lo'-ris
lor'-ries
lo'-rum
lo'-tic
lo'-tion
lot'-tery
lo'-tus
loud'-ness
loud'-speaker
loung'-ing
lous'i-ness
lout'-ish
lov'-able
lov'-age

lov'e-bird
lov'e-less
lov'e-li-ness
lov'e-lorn
lov'e-sick
lov'-ing
lov'-ing=kind'-
        ness
lov'-ingly
low'-born
low'-boy
low'-bred
low'-brow
low'-er=case
low'-er-ing
low'-er-most
low'-est
low'-ing
low'-land
low'-li-ness
low'-ness
low=press'-ure
low=spir'-ited
lox'o-drome
loxo-drom'ic
loy'-al-ism
loy'-al-ist
loy'-ally
loy'-alty
loz'-enge
lub'-ber
lub'-berly
lu'-bri-cal
lu'-bri-cant
lu'-bri-cate
lu-bri-ca'tion
lu'-bri-cat-ivo
lu'-bri-cator

lu-bric'ious
lu-bric'ity
lu-bri-cous
lu-bri-fac'-tion
lu-car'ne
lu'-cency
lu'-cent
lu-cer'nal
lu-cer'ne
lu'-cid
lu-cid'ity
lu'-cidly
lu'-cid-ness
lu'-ci-fer
lu-cif'er-ase
lu-cif'-erin
lu-cif'er-ous
lu-cif'u-gal
lu-cif'u-gous
lu'-ci-gen
lu-ciph'i-lous
luck'-ily
luck'-less
lu'-cra-tive
luc-ta'tion
lu'-cu-brate
lu-cu-bra'tion
lu'-cu-brator
lu'-cu-brat-ory
lu'-cu-lent
lu'-di-crous
lu'-di-crous-ness
lu-di-fi-ca'tion
lu'-gar-ite
lug'-gage
lug'-ger
lug'-ging
lu-gu'bri-ous

lug'-worm
lu'ke-warm
lull'-aby
lum-ba'gin-ous
lum-ba'go
lum'-bar
lum'-ber
lum'-berer
lum'-ber-jack
lum'-ber-man
lum'-ber-some
lum'-ber-yard
lum'-bri-cal
lum'-bri-coid
lu'-men
lu'mi-nant
lu'-min-ary
lu-mi-nesc'e
lu-mi-nesc'ence
lumi-nesc'ent
lu-mi-nif'er-ous
lu-min'o-phore
lu-min-os'ity
lu'-mi-nous
lu-mis'-terol
lum'-mox
lump'-ily
lump'-ish
lu'-nacy
lu'-nar
lu-na'rian
lu'-nate
lu'-na-tic
lu-na'tion
lunch'-eon
lunch-eon-ett'e
lunch'-room

lu-nett'e
lung'-fish
lung'-wort
lu'-ni-form
lu'-nik
luni-so'lar
lu'-ni-tidal
lu'-nula
lu'-nu-late
lu'-nule
lu'-pin
lu'-pine
lu'-pin-ine
lupi-no'sis
lu'pu-lin
lu'pu-lone
lu'-pus
lurch'-ing
lu'-rid
lu'-ridly
lurk'-ing
lust'-ful
lust'ily
lust'i-ness
lus'-tral
lus'-trate
lus-tra'tion
lus'-trine
lus'-tring
lus'-trous
lus'-trum
lust'-wort
lu'-tan-ist
lu'-tein
lu'-tein-ise
lu'teo-lin
lu'-teous
lu'te-string

lu-te-tium
lu'-thern
lu'-ti-dine
lu'-tist
lux'-ate
lux-a'tion
luxu'r-iance
luxu'r-iant
luxu'r iate
luxu'r-iat-ing
lux'ur-ies
luxu'r-ious
luxu'r-ious-ness
ly'-can-thrope
ly-can-throp'ic
ly-can'-thropy
ly-ce'um
lych-nid'i-ate
ly'-co-pene
ly-co-per'-don
ly'-copin
ly'-co-pod
ly-co-po'dium
lydd'-ite
ly'-ing
ly'-ing-in'
lymph-aden-i'tis
lymph-ad'en-oid
lym-phan'-gial
lym-phat'ic
lym'-pho-cyte
lym-phog'en-ous
lymph'-oid
lympho-sar-
     co'ma
lyn-ce'an
lynch'-ing
ly-om'er-ous

lyo-phil´ic
ly-oph´i-lise
ly´-rate
lyr´i-cal
lyr´i-cally
lyr´i-cism
ly´ri-form
lyr´-ist
ly-sim´eter
ly´-sin
ly´-sine
ly´-sis
ly-so-gen´ic
ly´-so-zime

M

ma-cab´re
ma-ca´co
ma-cad´am
ma-cadam-is-
a´tion
ma-cad´am-ise
ma-caq´ue
maca-ro´ni
maca-ron´ic
maca-roon´
ma-cass´ar
ma-caw´
mac´-ca-boy
mac´er-ate
macer-a´tion
mac´er-ator
machia-vel´-lian
ma-chic´o-late
ma-chico-la´tion
ma-chi´nal

mach´i-nate
machi-na´tion
mach´i-nator
ma-chi´ne
ma-chi´ne-gun
ma-chi´n-ery
ma-chi´ne-shop
ma-chi´ne-tool
ma-chi´n-ist
mach´-meter
mack´-erel
mack´i-naw
mack´-in-tosh
ma-cro´bian
macro-bio´sis
macro-bi´otic
macro-ceph´a-
lous
macro-chem´-is-
try
mac´-ro-cosm
mac-ro-cos´-mic
macro-cy´c-lic
mac´-ro-cyte
macro-dac´-tyl-
ous
ma-crog´ra-phy
ma-crom´eter
macro-mol´-ecule
mac´-ron
macro-phys´-ics
mac´ro-pod
macro-p´sia
ma-crop´-ter-ous
macro-scop´ic
macros-mat´ic
ma-cru´al
ma-cru´rous

mac-ta´tion
mac´-ula
mac´u-lar
mac´u-late
macu-la´tion
mac´u-lature
mac´-ule
macu-lif´er-ous
ma-cu´li-form
mac´u-lose
mada-ro´sis
mad´-cap
mad´-den
mad´-den-ing
mad´-der
mad´-dest
mad´-house
mad´-man
mad´-ness
ma-dras´
mad´-re-pore
mad´-ri-gal
ma-du´ra
mael´-strom
mae´-nad
mae-nad´ic
maf´-fick
maf´-fick-ing
mag´a-zine
maga-zin´-ist
ma-gen´ta
mag´-got
mag´-goty
mag´i-cal
mag´i-cally
ma-gic´ian
ma-gilp´
ma-gis´-ter

magis-te'rial
mag'is-tery
mag'is-tracy
mag'is-tral
mag'is-trate
mag'is-tra-ture
mag-na'lium
mag-na-nim'ity
mag-nan'i-mous
mag'-na-scope
mag'-nate
mag-ne'sia
mag-nesio-chro'mite
mag-nesio-fer'-rite
mag'-nes-ite
mag-ne'sium
mag'-neson
mag-net'ic
mag-net'i-cally
mag'-net-is-able
mag-net-is-a'tion
mag'-net-ise
mag'-net-iser
mag'-net-ism
mag'-net-ite
mag-ne'to
mag-ne'to-graph
mag-neto-hydro-dyn-am'ics
mag-net-om'eter
mag-neto-met'ric
mag-net-om'etry
mag-neto-mo'tive
mag'-neton
mag-ne'tos
216

mag-neto-stric'-tion
mag'-netron
mag-ni-fi-ca'tion
mag-nif'i-cence
mag-nif'i-cent
mag-nif'-ico
mag'-ni-fied
mag'-ni-fier
mag'-nify
mag'-ni-fy-ing
mag-nil'-oquence
mag-nil'-oquent
mag'-ni-tude
mag-no'lia
mag-noli-a'ceous
mag'-num
mag'-pie
mahl'-stick
main'-ten-ance
main'-yard
ma-hog'-any
ma-hout'
maid'-en-hair
maid'-en-head
maid'-en-hood
maid'-enly
maid'-ser-vant
mai-eut'ic
mail'-able
mail'-bag
mail'-box
mail'-man
main'-boom
main'-deck
main'-land
main'-mast
main-per'-nor

main'-prise
main'-sail
main'-sheet
main'-spring
main'-stay
main'-stream
main'-tain
main-tain'-able
main'-ten-ance
main'-yard
ma-jes'-tic
ma-jes'-ti-cal
ma-jes'-ti-cally
maj'-esty
ma-jol'-ica
major-do'mo
ma-jor'i-ties
ma-jor'ity
ma'jor-ship
ma-jus'cu-lar
ma-jus'-cule
ma'ke-be-lieve
ma'ke-shift
ma'ke-weight
ma'k-ing
ma-lac'ca
mal'a-chite
ma-la'cia
mal'a-coid
mala-col'-ogist
mala-col'ogy
mala-coph'i-lous
mala-co-phyl'-lous
mala-cos'-tra-can
mala-cos'-tra-cous

mal-address'
mal-adjust'ed
mal-adjust'-
      ment
mal-ad-min'-is-
      ter
mal-ad-min-is-
      tra'tion
mal-adroit'
mal-adroit'ly
mal'-ady
mal-ais'e
mal'a-mute
mal'an-ders
mal'a-pert
mal'a-prop-ism
ma-la'ria
ma-la'rial
ma-lari-om'etry
mal-as-simi-
      la'tion
mal'-ate
mal-ax'-ate
mal-ax-a'tion
mal'-chite
mal'-con-tent
mal-edic'-tion
mal-efac'-tion
mal-efac'-tor
mal-ef'ic
mal-ef'i-cence
mal-ef'i-cent
ma-le'ic
mal-ev'ol-ence
mal-ev'ol-ent
mal-feas'-ance
mal-feas'-ant
mal-for-ma'tion

mal-form'ed
mal'-ice
ma-lic'ious
ma-lic'iously
ma-lif'er-ous
ma-li'gn
ma-lig'-nancy
ma-lig'-nant
ma-lig'-nity
ma-ling'er
ma-ling'erer
mal'-ism
mal'i-son
mal'-lard
mallea-bil'ity
mal'-leable
mal'-leate
mal'-leo-lar
mal-le'olus
mal'-let
mal'-leus
mal'-low
malm'-sey
mal-nu-trit'ion
ma-lo'dor-ous
ma-lo'dor-ously
mal-o dour
ma-lo'nic
mal'-onyl
mal-pighi-a'ceous
mal-po-sit'ion
mal-prac'-tice
malt'-ase
mal'-tha
malt'-ose
mal-treat'
mal-treat'-ment
malt'-ster

mal-va'ceous
mal-va'sia
mal-ver-sa'tion
mam'-elon
mam-elu'ca
mam-il'la
mam'-il-late
mam'-mal
mam-ma'lian
mam-ma-lif'er-
      ous
mam-ma-log'i-
      cal
mam-mal'-ogist
mam-mal'ogy
mam'-mary
mam'-mate
mam'-mee
mam-mif'er-ous
mam'-mi-form
mam-mil'-lary
mam'-mil-late
mam'-mon
mam'-mon-ism
mam'-mon-ist
mam'-mon-ite
mam'-moth
man'-acle
man'-acling
man'-age
man-age-abil'ity
man'-age-able
man'-age-ment
man'-ager
man'ager-ess
mana-ge'rial
man'-ag-ing
man'a-kin

MANATEE

man'a-tee
man'-chet
man-chi-neel'
man'-ci-pate
man-ci-pa'tion
man'-ciple
man-do'mus
man'-da-rin
man-da't-ary
man'-date
man-da'tor
man'da-tory
man'-del-ate
man-del'ic
man'-dible
man-dib'u-lar
man-dib'u-late
man-do'la
man-do-lin
man-do-lin'-ist
man-do'ria
man-drag'-ora
man'-drake
man'-drel
man'-drill
man'-du-cate
man-du-ca'tion
man'-du-cat-ory
man'-eton
man'-ful
man'-fully
man'ga-bey
man'ga-nate
man'ga-nese
manga-ne'sian
man-gan'ic
manga-nif'er-ous

man'ga-nin
man'ga-nite
man-gan'o-site
man'ga-nous
mang'-corn
ma'ngi-ness
man'go-steen
man-'grove
man'-handle
man'-hole
man'-hood
ma-ni'acal
man'i-cate
man'i-cure
man'i-curist
man'i-fest
mani-fes'-tant
mani-fes-ta'tion
mani-fes'ta-tive
man'i-festly
mani-fes'to
mani-fes'-tos
man'i-fold
man'i-folder
man'i-form
ma-nil'la
man'-ioc
man'-iple
ma-nip'u-late
ma-nipu-la'tion
ma-nip'u-lat-ive
ma-nip'u-lator
ma-nip'u-lat-ory
man'i-tose
man'i-tou
man-ki'nd
man'-like
man'-li-ness

man'-nequin
man'-ner
man'-ner-ism
man'-ner-ist
man-ner-is'tic
man'-ner-less
man'-nerly
man'-ni-kin
man'-nish
man'-nite
man'-ni-tol
man'-nose
ma-noeuvr'-able
ma-noeuv're
ma-noeuvr-
          ability
ma-noeuv'rer
man-om'eter
mano-met'ric
man-om'etry
man-o'rial
man'-power
man'-rope
man'-sard
man'-serv-ant
man'-sion
man'-slaughter
man'-slayer
man'-suetude
man'-tel
man'-telet
man'-tel-piece
man'-tel-shelf
man'-tic
man'-tid
man-til'la
man'-tis
man-tiss'a

218

man'-tling
man'-tra
man'-ual
ma-nu'ally
ma-nu'brium
manu-duc'-tive
manu-fac'-tory
manu-fac'-ture
manu-fac'-turer
manu-fac'-tur-ing
manu-mis'sion
manu-mit'
manu-mit'-ted
manu-mit'-ting
manu-mo'tive
ma-nu're
ma-nu'rial
man'u-script
man-za-ni'ta
map'-ping
ma-quett'e
mar'a-bou
mar'a-bout
ma-ra'ca
mar-as-chi'no
ma-ras'-mic
ma-ras'-mus
mar'a-thon
ma-raud'
ma-raud'er
ma-raud'-ing
mara-ve'di
mar'ble-ise
mar'-bling
mar'-ca-site
mar-ca-sit'i-cal
mar-cel'
mar-cel'la

mar-cell'ed
mar-cesc'ence
mar-cesc'ent
mar-che'sa
mar-che'se
mar'-chion-ess
march'-pane
mar'-cus
mar-em'ma
mar'-gar-ate
mar'gar'ic
mar'-garin
mar'-gar-ine
mar'-gar-ite
mar'-gay
mar'-gin
mar'-ginal
mar'-gin-a'lia
mar'-gin-ate
mar'-grave
mar'-gra-vine
mar'-guer-ite
mar'ial-ite
mar'i-gold
mar'i-got
mar'i-graph
mari-huan'a
mari-juan'a
mar-im'ba
ma-ri'na
mari-na'de
mar'i-nate
mar'i-nat-ing
mari-na'tion
mar-i'ne
mar'i-ner
mari on-ctt'e
mar'i-tage

mar'i-tal
mar'i-tally
mar'i-time
mar'-joram
mark'-edly
mar'-ket
mar-ket-abil'ity
mar'-ket-able
mar'-keter
mar'-ket-ing
mar'-ket-place
mar'-khor
marks'-man
marks'-man-ship
mar-la'ceous
mar'-lin
mar'-line
mar'-line-spike
mar'-lite
mar-lit'ic
mar'-ma-lade
mar'-mar-ise
mar-mar-o'sis
mar'-ma-tite
mar'-mol-ite
mar-mor-a'ceous
mar'-mor-ate
mar-mor-a'tion
mar-mo'real
mar'-moset
mar'-mot
ma-roon'
mar'-plot
mar-quee'
mar'-quess
mar'-quess-ate
mar'-quetry
mar'-quis

mar'-quis-ate
mar-qui-sett'e
mar'-ram
mar'-riage
mar'-riage-able
mar'-ried
mar'-ring
mar'-row
mar'-row-bone
mar'-rowy
mar'-shal
mar'-shalcy
mar'-shalled
mar'-shal-ler
marsh'i-ness
marsh'-mal-low
mar-soon'
mar-su'pial
mar-su'pi-al-ise
mar-su'pium
mar-tel'lo
mar'-ten
mar'-ten-site
mar'-tial
mar'-tial-ise
mar'-tially
mar'-tin
mar'-ti-net
mar-ti'ni
mar'-tite
mart'-let
mar'-tyr
mar'-tyr-dom
mar'-tyr-ise
mar-tyr-ol'-atry
mar-tyro-log'i-cal

mar-tyr-ol'-ogist
mar-tyr-ol'ogy
mar'-vel
mar'-velled
mar'-vel-ling
mar'-vel-lous
mar'-vel-lously
mar'-ver
mar'-zi-pan
mas-car'a
mas'-cot
mas'-cu-line
mas-cu-lin'ity
mas'o-chism
mas'o-chist
maso-chis'-tic
ma-son'ic
mas'-quer-ade
mass'-acre
mass'-acred
mass'-acrer
mass'-acring
mass-ag'e
mass-ag'ing
mas-se'ter
mass-eur'
mass-eus'e
mass'i-cot
mass'i-ness
mass'-ive
mass'-ive-ness
masso-ther'apy
mas'-taba
mas-tec'-tomy
mas'-ter
mas'-ter-at-arms
mas'-ter-dom
mas'-ter-ful

mas'-ter-li-ness
mas'-terly
mas'-ter-piece
mas'-ter-ship
mas'-ter-stroke
mas'-ter-work
mas'-tery
mast'-head
mas'-tic
mas'-ti-cate
mas-ti-ca'tion
mas'-ti-cator
mas'-ti-cat-ory
mas'-tiff
mas-tit'ic
mas-ti'tis
mas'-to-don
mas-to-don'-tic
mas-to-don'-toid
mas'-toid
mas-toid'al
mas-toid-ec'tomy
mas-toid-i'tis
mas-toid-ot'omy
mas-tur-ba'tion
ma-su'rium
mat'a-dor
match'-able
match'-board
match'-less
match'-lock
match'-maker
match'-making
match'-wood
ma-te'rial
ma-teri-al-is-a'tion

MECHANISM

ma-te'ri-al-ise
ma-te'ri-al-ism
ma-te'ri-al-ist
ma-teri-al-is'tic
ma-teri-al-is'ti-
       cally
ma-teri-al'ity
ma-te'ri-ally
ma-ter'nal
ma-tern'ally
ma-ter'nity
math-emat'-ical
math-emat'-
       ically
math-ema-tic'ian
math-emat'-ics
mat'-inal
mat'-ins
mat'-lock-ite
mat'-rass
ma'tri-arch
matri-ar'-chal
ma'tri-arch-ate
ma'tri-archy
matri-ci'dal
mat'ri-cide
ma-tric'u-lant
ma-tric'u-late
ma-tricu-la'tion
matri-lin'-eal
matri-mo'nial
mat'ri-mony
matro-cli'nous
matro-mor'-phic
ma'tron-age
ma'tron-ise
ma'tron-li-ness
matro-nym'ic

mat'-ta-more
mat'-ted
mat'-ter
mat'-ting
mat'-tock
mat'-toid
mat'-tress
mat'u-rate
matu-ra'tion
ma-tu'ra-tive
ma-tu're
ma-tu'rely
ma-tu're-ness
matu-resc'ent
ma-tu'rity
ma-tu'ti-nal
mat'u-tine
mat'-zoth
maud'-lin
maul'-stick
maun'-der
mauso-le'um
mauv'-ine
mav'-er-ick
mawk'-ish
max-il'la
maxil'-lary
maxil'-li-form
maxil'-li-ped
max'i-mal
max'i-mal-ise
max'-im-ite
max'i-mise
max'i-miser
max'i-mum
may'-fish
may'-fly
may'-hap

may'-hem
may'-on-naise
may'-or-alty
may'-or-ess
may'-pole
maz'-ar-ine
ma-zur'ka
ma-zout'
maz'-zard
mead'ow-sweet
meal'-ies
meal'i-ness
meal'-time
meal'-worm
meal'y-mouthed
me-an'der
me-an'der-ing
me-an'drine
me-an'drous
mean'-ing
mean'-ing-ful
mean'-ing-less
mean'-ness
mean'-time
mean'-while
measur-abil'ity
meas'ur-able
meas'ure-less
meas'ure-ment
me-a'tus
mech-an'ic
mech-an'-ical
mech-an-ic'ian
mech-an'ics
mech-an-is-
       a'tion
mech'-an-ise
mech'-an-ism

221

MECHANIST

mech'-an-ist
mech-an-is'tic
mech-ano-mor'-
        phic
mechano-ther'apy
mec-on'ic
mec'-onin
mec-o'nium
med'-alled
med-al'lic
med-al'lion
med'-al-list
med'-dler
med'dle-some
med'dling
me'-dia
medi-aev'al
medi-aev'al-ism
medi-aev'al-ist
me'-dial
me'-dian
me'-diant
medias-ti'nal
medias-ti-ni'tis
medias-ti'num
me'-diate
me'-diately
me-dia'tion
me-dia-tis-a'tion
me'dia-tive
me'dia-tise
me'-diator
media-to'rial
me'dia-tory
me'dia-tress
med'i-cable
med'i-cal
med'i-cally

medic'-ament
med'i-cate
medi-ca'tion
med'i-cat-ive
med'i-cator
med-ic'in-able
med-ic'inal
med'i-cine
med'-ico
medi-co-le'gal
me-dio'cre
me-dioc'-rity
med'i-tate
medi-ta'tion
med'i-tat-ive
med'i-tator
me'-dium
me-dium-is'tic
med'-lar
med'-ley
med-u'lla
med-ul'-late
med-ul'-lary
meek'-ness
meer'-schaum
meet'-ing
meet'-ing-house
mega-cephal'ic
mega-ceph'a-lous
meg'a-cycle
meg'-a-death
meg'a-gamete
meg'a-line
meg'a-lith
megalo-cephal'ic
megalo-ceph'-aly
mega-lo-ma'nia

mega-lo-ma'niac
mega-lop'-olis
meg'a-lo-pol-itan
meg'a-lo-saur
mega-par'-sec
meg'a-phone
meg'a-pode
mega-scop'ic
mega-spor-an'-
        gium
meg'a-spore
meg'-aton
meg'a-volt
meg'a-watt
meg'-ohm
meg'-ohm-meter
mei'o-cyte
mei-om'er-ous
mei'-onite
mei-o'sis
mci-ot'ic
mei-zo-seis'-mal
mel-ac'-on-ite
mel'a-mine
mel-an-ae'mia
mel-an-cho'lia
mel-an-cho'liac
mel-an-chol'ic
mel'-an-choly
mel-an'ic
mel'-anin
mel'-an-ism
mel'-an-ite
mel'-ano
mel'-ano-cyte
mel'a-noid
mela-no'ma
mela-no'sis

mel-an-os'-por-
    ous
mela-not'ic
mel-an'-ter-ite
mel-an-tha'ceous
mela-nu'ria
mel'a-phyre
mel-ez'i-tose
me-lia'ceous
mel'i-lite
mel'i-lot
mel'-in-ite
me'-lior-ate
me-lior-a'tion
me'-lior-at-ive
me'-lior-ism
me'-lior-ist
me-lior'-ity
mel-is'ma
mel-is-mat'ic
mel-iss'ic
mel-lif'er-ous
mel-lif'-lu-ence
mel-lif'-lu-ent
mel-lif'-lu-ous
mel-liph'a-gous
mel-li-su'gent
mel'-li-tate
mel-lit'ic
mel-liv'or-ous
mel'-low
mel'-low-ness
mel-o'deon
mel-o'dia
mel-od'ic
mel-od'i-cal-ly
mel-o'dious
mel-o'diously

mel'-odise
mel'-odist
mel'o-drama
melo-dram-at'ic
melo-dram'a-tise
melo-dram'a-tist
mel'-ody
mel'-oid
melo-ma'nia
melt-abil'ity
melt'-able
mel'-ton
mem'-ber
mem'-ber-ship
mem-bra-na'ceous
mem'-brane
mem-bra-nif'er-
    ous
mem'-bra-nous
mem-en'to
mem-or-abil'ia
mem-or-abil'ity
mem'-or-able
mem-or-an'da
mem-or-an'dum
mem-o'rial
mem-o'rial-ise
mem-o'rial-is-ing
mem-o'rial-ist
mem'-or-ies
mem-or-is-a'tion
mem'-or-ise
mem'-or-iser
mem'-or-is-ing
mem'-ory
men-ac'ca-nite
men'-ace
men'-ac-ing

men-ag'erie
men-ar'che
mend'-able
men-da'cious
men-da'ciously
men-dac'ity
men'-di-cancy
men'-di-cant
men-dic'ity
men'-di-pite
men'-folk
men-ha'den
me'-nial
men'-il-ite
men-in-geal
men-in'ges
men-ingi-o'ma
men-in-git'ic
men-in-gi'tis
men-in'go-cele
men-ingo-coc'-
    cus
men-ingo-myel-
    i'tis
men-is'-cal
men-is'ci-form
men-is'-cus
me-nol'ogy
meno-paus'al
men'o-pause
men-or-rha'gia
men-or-rhe'a
meno-tax'is
men'-ses
men'-strual
men'-stru-ate
men-stru-a'tion
men'-stru-ous

223

men'-struum
men-sur-abil'ity
men'-sur-able
men'-sural
men-sur-a'tion
men-sur-a't-ive
men'-tal
men-tal'ity
men'-tally
men-ta'tion
men-tha'ceous
men'-thene
men'-thol
men'-thol-ated
men'-ti-cide
men'-tion
men'-tion-able
men'-tioner
men'-tor
men'-tum
mep'a-crine
meper'i-dine
meph-it'ic
meph-i'tis
mepro'-ba-mate
mer'-can-tile
mer'-can-til-ism
mer-cap'-tal
mer-cap'-tan
mer-cap'-tides
mer-cap'-tol
mer-cap'-tu-rine
mer'-cen-ary
mer'-cer
mer-cer-is-a'tion
mer'-cer-ise
mer'-cer-is-ing
mer'-cery

mer'-chan-dise
mer'-chan-diser
mer'-chan-dis-ing
mer'-chant
mer'-chant-able
mer'-chant-man
mer'-cies
mer'-ci-ful
mer'-ci-fully
mer'-ci-ful-ness
mer'-ci-less
mer-cu-rate
mer-cu'rial
mer-cu'ri-al-ise
mer-cu'ri-al-ism
mer-curi-al'ity
mer-cu'ric
mer'-cu-rous
mer'-cury
mer-etric'ious
mer-gan'-ser
mer'-gence
mer'i-carp
mer-id'-ian
mer-id'i-onal
mer-i'no
mer-i'nos
mer'-ion
mer'-ism
mer'i-spore
mer'-is-tem
mer-is-temat'ic
mer-is'tic
mer'-ited
meri-to'ri-ous
mer'-kin
mer'-lin
mer'-ling

mer'-lon
mer'-maid
mer'-man
mer'o-blast
mero-blas'-tic
mer-og'amy
mero-gen'-esis
mero-gen'ic
mer-og-nos'tic
mer-ogon'ic
mer-og'ony
mer-o'pia
mer'o-some
mer-os-then'ic
mer-ox'ene
mer'-rily
mer'-ri-ment
mer'-ri-ness
mer'-ry-an'-drew
mer'-ry-maker
mer'-ry-mak-ing
mer'-sa-line
mer'y-cism
mes-cal'
mes-ca-line
mes-en-cephal'ic
mes-en-ceph'a-
    lon
mes-en'chyma
mes-en-chy-mal
mes-en-chym'a-
    tous
mes'-en-chyme
mes-en-te'rial
mes-en-ter'ic
mes-en-ter-i'tis
mes-en'-teron
mes'-en-tery

mes-eth'-moid
mesh'-work
me'-siad
me'-sial
me'-sian
mes'i-tite
mes'-ityl
mes-it'yl-ene
mes-mer'ic
mes-mer-is-a'tion
mes'-mer-ise
mes'-mer-is-ing
mes'-mer-ism
me'sn-alty
meso-ben'-thos
mes'o-blast
meso-blas'-tic
mes'o-carp
meso-cephal'ic
meso-ceph'a-lous
meso-crat'ic
mes'o-coele
mes'o-derm
meso-der'-mal
meso-gas'-tric
meso-gas'-trium
mes-og'na-thous
mes'o-lite
meso-lith'ic
meso-mer'ic
mes-om'er-ism
me'-son
meso-neph'-ric
meso-neph'-ros
mes'o-phyll
mes'o-phyte
meso-phyt'ic
meso-po'dium

meso-po'dial
mes'o-sphere
meso-ster'-num
meso-tar'-sal
meso-the'lium
meso-tho'rium
mes'o-tron
mes-ox-al'ic
meso-zo'ic
mes'o-zole
mes-quit'e
mess'-age
messa-li'ne
mess'-en-ger
mess'i-ness
mess'-mate
mes'-suage
mes-ti'zo
metab'-asis
meta-bio'sis
meta-biot'ic
met'a-bolic
metab-oli's-able
metab'-olise
metab'-olism
metab'-olite
meta-car'-pal
meta-car'-pus
met'a-centre
meta-cen'-tric
meta-chem'-is-try
meta-chro-mat'ic
meta-chro'ma-tin
meta-chro'sis
met'a-coele
meta-gen'-esis
meta-gen-et'ic
metag'-na-thous

met-al'-dehyde
met-al'lic
met-al-lif'er-ous
met'-al-line
met'-al-ling
met-al-lis-a'tion
met'-al-lise
met'-al-list
met-al'lo-chrome
met-allo-graph'ic
met-al-log'ra-phy
met'-al-loid
met-al-lur'-gic
met-al-lur'-gi-cal
metal'-lur-gist
met'-al-work
met'a-mere
meta-mer'ic
metam'-er-ised
metam'-er-ism
meta-mor'-phic
meta-mor'-phism
meta-mor'-phose
meta-mor'-phosis
met-a-neph'-ric
met-a-neph'-ros
met-an-il'-lic
met'a-phase
met'a-phor
meta-phor'ic
meta-phor'-ical
met'a-phrase
met'a-phrast
meta-phras'-tic

225

meta-phys'-ical
meta-phys-ic'ian
meta-phys'i-cise
meta-phys'-ics
meta-phy'sis
meta-pla'sia
meta-pla'sis
met'a-plasm
meta-plas'-mic
meta-plas'-tic
meta-po'dium
meta-pol-it'i-cal
meta-poli-tic'ian
meta-pol'i-tics
meta-pro'-tein
meta-so'ma-tism
meta-soma-to'sis
met'a-stable
met-as'ta-sis
meta-stat'ic
meta-tar'-sal
meta-tar-sal'-gia
meta-tar'-sus
met-ath'-esis
meta-thet'ic
meta-tho'rax
meta-xe'nia
met-em-pir'ic
met-em-pir'i-cal
met-em-pir'i-cist
met-empsy-cho'-
        sis
met-empsych-o's-
        ist
met-en-ceph'alon
met-en'-teron
me-teor'ic
me'teor-ism

me'teor-ite
meteor-it'ics
meteor'-ograph
meteor-og'ra-phy
me'teor-oid
meteor-oid'al
meteoro-log'i-cal
meteor-ol'ogist
meteor-ol'ogy
me'teoro-scope
meteor-os'copy
meth-ac'ry-late
meth-acryl'ic
meth'a-done
meth'-ane
meth'-an-ide
meth'-anol
metha-nom'eter
meth-an'the-line
meth-eg'-lin
meth-e'na-mine
meth'-ene
meth'-ine
meth-ion'ic
meth-i'on-ine
meth-od'i-cal
meth-od'i-cally
meth'-od-ise
meth-od-ol'ogy
meth-ox'yl
meth'-yl-amine
meth'-yl-ate
meth'-yl-ated
meth'-yl-ene
meth'yl'ic
meth-yl'i-dyne
meth-yl-naph'-
        tha-lene

met-icu-los'ity
metic'u-lous
me'-tis
me'-tol
met-on'ic
meton'-ymy
met'-ope
met-op'ic
meto-pos'copy
met'-ric
met'ri-cal
met'ri-cise
met'ri-cist
met'-rify
metro-log'i-cal
metrol'-ogist
metrol'-ogy
metro-mor'-phic
met'ro-nome
metro-nom'ic
metro-nym'ic
met'ro-pole
metrop'-olis
met'ro-poli-tan
met'tle-some
mez'za-nine
mez'zo-tint
mi-ar'-gyr-ite
mi-ca'ceous
mica-fo'lium
mi'-can-ite
mi-cel'-lar
mi-cell'e
micra-cous'-tic
micro-aer'o-phile
micro-anal'-ysis
micro-ana-lyt'ic
mi'cro-bar

mi'-crobe
mi-cro'bial
mi-cro'bic
mi-cro'bi-cide
micro-biol'ogy
micro-cephal'ic
micro-ceph'-aly
mi'cro-copy
mi'cro-cosm
mi'cro-cos-mic
mi'cro-dot
micro-far'ad
mi'cro-film
mi'cro-graph
micro-graph'ic
mi-crog'ra-phy
mi'cro-groove
micro-gyr'ia
mi'-crohm
mi'cro-lite
mi-crol'-ogy
mi'cro-lux
micro-lyth'ic
mi'cro-mesh
mi-crom'eter
micro-met'ri-cal
mi-crom'-etry
mi'-cron
mi'-cron-ise
micro-or'-gan-ism
mi-croph'a-gous
mi'cro-phone
micro-phon'ic
micro-pho'to-graph
micro-pho-tog'ra-phy

micro-phyl'-line
micro-phyl'-lous
mi'cro-phyte
micro-po'dous
mi-crop'sia
mi-crop'-ter-ous
micro-pyr'-om'eter
mi'cro-scope
micro-scop'ic
micro-scop'i-cally
mi-cros'-copist
mi-cros'copy
mi-cro-seism
micro-seis'-mic
micro-seis'-mo-graph
micro-seis-mol'ogy
mi-cros-mat'ic
mi'cro-some
micro-spe'cies
mi'cro-spore
micro-stom'a-tous
micro-struc'-tural
micro-struc'-ture
mi'cro-tome
mi-crot'-omy
mi'cro-wave
mi'cro-zyme
mic'-tur-ate
mic-tur-it'ion
mid'-brain
mid'-day
mid'-den

mid'dle-man
mid'dle-weight
mid'-dling
mid'-iron
mid'-land
mid'-most
mid'-night
mid'-rib
mid'-riff
mid'-ship-man
mid'-ships
mid'-stream
mid'-sum-mer
mid'-way
mid-week'ly
mid'-west
mid-west'-ern
mid'-wife
mid'-wifery
mid'-win-ter
mid'-year
mi'ght-ily
mi'ghti-ness
mignon-ett'e
migrain'-oid
mi'-grant
mi-gra'te
mi-gra't-ing
mi-gra'tion
mi-gra'tor
mi'-gratory
mil'-dew
mil'-dew-proof
mil'-dewy
mi'ld-ness
mi'le-age
mi'le-post
mi'le-stone

mil'-foil
mili-a'ria
mil'i-ary
mil'i-tancy
mil'i-tant
mil'i-tantly
mil'i-tarily
mili-tar-is-
       a'tion
mil'i-tar-ise
mil'i-tar-is-ing
mil'i-tar-ism
mil'i-tar-ist
mili-tar-is'tic
mil'i-tary
mil'i-tate
mil'i-tat-ing
mil-it'ia
mil'-ium
milk'i-ness
milk'-leg
milk'-liv-ered
milk'-man
milk'-sop
milk'-weed
milk'-wood
mill'-board
mill'-dam
mil-len-a'rian
mil'-len-ary
mil-len'-nial
mil-len'-nium
mil'-leped
mil'-ler-ite
mil-les'i-mal
mil'-let
mil-li-am'meter
mil-li-am'-pere

mil'-liard
mil'-li-ary
mil'-li-bar
mil'-li-curie
mil'-li-gramme
mil'-li-lam-bert
mil'-li-litre
mil'-li-lux
mil'-li-metre
mil'-li-micron
mil'-li-ner
mil'-linery
mill'-ing
million-air'e
mill'ion-ary
mil'lion-fold
mil'-li-pede
mill'-pond
mill'-race
mill'-stone
mill'-stream
mill'-wright
mil-reis'
mil'-vine
mim'-bar
mim'eo-graph
mi-me'sis
mi-met'ic
mim'-etite
mim'-icked
mim'-icker
mim'-ick-ing
mim'-icry
mim-og'ra-phy
mim-o'sa
mimo-sa'ceous
mim'o-type
mim'u-lus

min-a'cious
min'-aret
min'a-torily
min'a-tory
minc'e-meat
minc'-ing
minc'-ingly
mi'nd-ful
mi'nd-less
mi'ne-field
mi'ne-layer
min'-eral
min-er-al-is-
       a'tion
min'-er-al-ise
min'-er-al-is-er
min-er-al-og'i-
       cal
min-er-al'-ogist
min-er-al'ogy
min'-eral-oid
mi'ne-sweeper
min-ett'e
min'i-ate
min'ia-ture
min'ia-tur-ist
mini-fi-ca'tion
min'-ify
min'i-kin
min'i-mal
mini-mis-a'tion
min'i-mise
mini'-miser
min'i-mum
min'-is-ter
min-is-te'rial
min-is-te'rium
min'-is-trant

min-is-tra'tion
min'-is-tries
min'-is-try
min'i-track
min'-ium
min'i-ver
min'i-vet
min'-now
min-or'ity
min'-ster
min'-strel
min'-strelsy
mint'-age
min'u-end
min-uet'
min-us'cu-lar
min'-us-cule
min'-ute
mi-nu'te
min'-utely
mi-nu'tely
mi-nu'te-ness
min-u'tia
mir'a-belle
mir-ab'i-lite
mir'-acle
mir-ac'u-lous
mir-ac'u-lously
mir'a-dor
mir-ag'e
mir'-bane
mi'ri-ness
mir'-ror
mirth'-ful
mirth'-less
mis-ad-ven'-ture
mis-al-li'ance
mis'-an-thrope

mis-an-throp'ic
mis-an-throp'i-
cally
mis-an'throp-ist
mis-an'-thropy
mis-ap-pli-ca'-
tion
mis-ap-pli'ed
mis-ap-ply'
mis-ap-pre-hend'
mis-ap-pre-hen'-
sion
mis-ap-pro'-pri-
ate
mis-ap-pro-pri-
a'tion
mis-ar-ra'nge-
ment
mis-be-com'-ing
mis-be-got'-ten
mis-be-ha've
mis-be-ha'v-ing
mis-be-ha'v-iour
mis-be-lief'
mis-be-liev'e
mis-be-liev'er
mis-cal'cu-late
mis-cal-cu-
la'tion
mis-call'
mis-car'-riage
mis-car'-ried
mis-car'ry
mis-car'-ry-ing
mis'-cegen-ate
mis-cegen-a'tion
mis-cel-la-ne'ity
mis-cel-la'neous

mis'-cel-lany
mis-chan'ce
mis'-chief
mis'-chief-maker
mis-chiev-ous
mis-ci-bil'ity
mis'-cible
mis-con-ceiv'e
mis-con-cep'-
tion
mis-con'-duct
mis-con-struc'-
tion
mis-con-strue'
mis-count'
mis'-cre-ance
mis'-cre-ancy
mis'-cre-ant
mis-cre-a'te
mis-cre-a'tion
mis-deal'
mis-deed'
mis-de-mean'-
ant
mis-de-mean'-
our
mis-di-rect'
mis-di-rec'-tion
mis-do'er
mis-do'ing
mis-doubt'
mis'-er-able
mi'ser-li-ness
mis'-ery
mis-feas'-ance
mis-feas'or
mis-fi're
mis'-fit

229

mis-form'
mis-for'-tune
mis-ga've
mis-giv'e
mis-giv'-ing
mis-got'-ten
mis-gov'ern
mis-gov'ern-ment
mis-guid'-ance
mis-guid'e
mis-guid'ed
mis-han'dle
mis-hand'-ling
mis'-hap
mis-hear'
mis-in-form'
mis-in-for-
    ma'tion
mis-in-struct'
mis-in-ter'-pret
mis-in-ter-pret-
    a'tion
mis-join'
mis-join'-der
mis-judg'e
mis-judg'-ment
mis-laid'
mis-lay'
mis-lay'-ing
mis-lead'
mis-lead'-ing
mis-led'
mis-li'ke
mis-man'-age
mis-man'-age-
    ment
mis-match'
mis-ma'te

mis-ma'ting
mis-na'me
mis-no'mer
miso-cap'-nic
mis-og'-amist
mis-og'-amy
mis-og'yn-ist
mis-og'yny
mis-ol'ogy
miso-ne'ism
mis-pla'ce
mis-pla'ce-ment
mis'-print
mis-pris'ion
mis-pro-noun'ce
mis-pro-nounc'-
    ing
mis-pro-nun-ci-
    a'tion
mis-pro-por'tion
mis-quo-ta'tion
mis-quo'te
mis-quo't-ing
mis-read'
mis-reck'on
mis-rep-resent'
mis-rep-resen-
    ta'tion
mis-re-po'rt
mis-ru'le
mis-ru'ling
mis-sha'pe
mis-sha'pen
miss'-ile
miss'-ing
mis'sion-ary
miss'-ive
mis-speak'

mis-spell'
mis-spell'ed
mis-spell'-ing
mis-spelt'
mis-spend'
mis-spent'
mis-sta'te
mis-sta'te-ment
mis-step'
mis-ta'k-able
mis-ta'ke
mis-ta'ken
mis-ta'kenly
mis-ta'k-ing
mist'-ily
mist'i-ness
mis-ti'me
mis'tle-toe
mis-took'
mis-treat'
mis-treat'-ment
mis'-tress
mis-trust'
mis-trust'-ful
mis-un-der-
    stand
mis-un-der-
    stand'-ing
mis-un-der-
    stood
mis-u'sage
mis-u'se
mith'-ri-date
mith'ri-dat-ism
mit'i-gable
mit'i-gant
mit'i-gate
mit'i-gat-ing

miti-ga'tion
mit'i-gat-ive
mit'i-gator
mit'i-gat-ory
mito-chon'-dria
mi-to'sis
mi-tot'ic
mi'-tral
mi'-trate
mit'ri-form
mit'-ten
mit'-ti-mus
mix'-ti-form
mix-ti-lin'-eal
mix'-ture
miz'zen-mast
mnemo-tax'is
moan'-ing
mob'-bing
mob'-cap
mo'-bile
mo-bil-is-a'tion
mo'-bil-ise
mo-bil'ity
mob-oc'racy
moc'-ca-sin
mo'-cha
mock'-ery
mock'-ing
mock'-ing-bird
mock'-ingly
mo'-dal
mo'-dal-ism
mo-dal'ity
mod'-elled
mod'-el-ler
mod'-el-ling
mod'-er-ate

mod'-er-ately
mod'-er-at-ing
mod-er-a'tion
mod'-er-ator
mod-er-ator-ship
mod'-ern
mod-ern-is-a'tion
mod'-ern-ise
mod'-ern-is-ing
mod'-ern-ism
mod'-ern-ist
mod-ern-is'tic
mod-er'nity
mod'-ernly
mod'-ern-ness
mod'-est
mod'-estly
mod'-esty
mod'i-cum
modi-fi'-able
mod'i-fi-cand
modi-fi-ca'tion
mod'i-fi-cat-ory
mod'i-fied
mod'i-fier
mod'-ify
mod-il'lion
mo-di'olus
mo-di'ste
modu-la-bil'ity
mod'u-lar
mod'u-late
modu-la'tion
mod'u-lator
mod'-ule
mod'u-lus
mo-fett'e
mo'-hair

mo'-hole
mo-hur'
moi'-dore
moi'-ety
moil'-ing
moist'-ener
moist'-ness
moist'-ure
mois'-ture-proof
mo-lal'ity
mo'-lar
mo-lar'ity
mo'-lary
mol-as'ses
mol-ec'u-lar
mol-ecu-lar'ity
mol'-ecule
mo'le-hill
mo'le-skin
mol-es-ta'tion
mo'-line
mol-lesc'ent
mol'-leton
mol-li-fi-ca'tion
mol'-li-fied
mol'-lify
mol'-li-fy-ing
mol-lusc
mol-lus'ca
mol-lus'-coid
mol-lus'-cous
mol-yb'-date
mol-yb'-den-ite
mol-yb'-denum
mol-yb'-dic
mol-yb'-dite
mol-yb'-dous
mo'-ment

mo'-men-tarily
mo'-men-tary
mo'-mently
mo-men'-tous
mo-men'-tum
mon'a-chal
mon'a-chism
mon-ac'-ti-nal
mona-del'-phous
mon-ad'ic
mon-ad'i-form
mon'a-dism
mon-ad'-nock
mona-dol'ogy
mon-an'-drous
mon-an'-dry
mon-an'-thous
mon'-arch
mon-ar'chal
mon-ar'chi-an-ism
mon-ar'chic
mon-ar'chi-cal
mon'-ar-chism
mon'-ar-chist
mon-as-te'rial
mon'-as-tery
mon-as'tic
mon-ast'i-cally
mon-as'ti-cism
mon-as'ti-con
mon-atom'ic
mon-aur'al
mon-ax'-ial
mon'-az-ite
mon'-er-gism
mon-e'sia
mon'-et-arily
mon'-et-ary
232

mon-et-is-a'tion
mon'-et-ise
mon'ey-less
mon'ey-maker
mon'ey-mak-ing
mon'ey-order
mon'ey-wort
mon'gol-ism
mon-il'i-corn
mon-il'i-form
mon'-ism
mon'-ist
mon-is'tic
mon-it'ion
mon'i-tor
moni-to'rial
mon'i-tor-ing
mon'i-tor-ship
mon'i-tory
mon'i-tress
monk'-ery
mon'key-pot
mon'key-rail
monk'-hood
monks'-hood
mono-ac'etin
mono-ac'id
mono-acid'ic
mono-ba'sic
mono-blep'-sis
mon'o-bloc
mono-car'-dian
mono-car'-pic
mono-car'-pous
mon'o-chord
mono-chro-mat'ic
mono-chro'ma-
tism

mono-chro'ma-
tor
mon'o-chrome
mon-och'rony
mon-och'ry-nous
mon'-ocle
mono-coty-
ledon
mon-oc'racy
mono-crat'ic
mon-oc'u-lar
mon'o-cule
mono-dac'-tyl-
ism
mono-dac'-tyl-
ous
mon-od'ic
mon'o-drama
mon'-ody
mono-oe'cious
mono-gam'ic
mon-og'-amist
mon-og'-amous
mon-og'amy
mono-gen'-esis
mono-gen-et'ic
mon-og'en-ism
mon-og'eny
mon-og'ony
mon'o-gram
mono-gram-
mat'ic
mon'o-grammed
mon'o-graph
mon-og'ra-pher
mono-graph'ic
mon-og'yny
mon'o-lith

mono-lith'ic
mon-ol'-ogist
mon'o-logue
mon-ol'ogy
mon-om'-achy
mono-ma'nia
mono-ma'niac
mono-man-i'acal
mon'o-mer
mon-om'er-ous
mono-met-al'lic
mono-met'-al-
lism
mon-om'eter
mon-o'mial
mono-mor'-phic
mon'o-plane
mono-pet'-alus
mon-oph'a-gous
mono-ple'gia
mono-po'dium
mon-op-ol-is-
a'tion
mon-op'-ol-ise
mon-op'-ol-ist
mon-op-ol-is'tic
mon-op'oly
mon-op'-sony
mon-op'-teral
mono-sep'-al-ous
mono-spo'rous
mon'o-stich
mon'o-stone
mono-stroph'ic
mono-syl-lab'ic
mono-syl'-lable
mon'o-theism
mon'o-theist

mono-theis'-tic
mono-thet'ic
mon'o-tint
mon-ot'-onous
mon-ot'-ony
mon'o-treme
mon-ot'ri-chous
mono-trop'ic
mon-ot'ropy
mono-typ'ic
mono-va'lent
mon-ox'-ide
mon-soon'
mon'-ster
mon'-strance
mon-stros'ity
mon'-strous
mon-tag'e
mon'-tane
mon'-tant
mon-tic'o-lous
mon-tic'u-late
mon'-ti-cule
mont-mor-il'-lon-
ite
mon'u-ment
monu-men'-tal
mon'-zon-ite
mood'-ily
mood'i-ness
moo'-ing
moon'-beam
moon'-blind
moon'-calf
moon'-eye
moon'-fish
moon'-less
moon'-light

moon'-lit
moon-ra'ker
moon'-rise
moon'-shine
moon'-shiner
moon'-stone
moon'-struck
moor'-age
moor'-cock
moor'-game
moor'-hen
moor'-ing
moor'-land
mop'-pet
mop'-ping
mo-quett'e
mo-ra'ceous
mor-ain'ic
mor-al'e
mor-al-is-a'tion
mor'-al-ise
mor'-al-ism
mor'-al-ist
mor-al-is'tic
mor'-ally
mor'-als
mora-to'rium
mor'a-tory
mor'-bid
mor-bid'ity
mor'-bidly
mor-bif'ic
mor-bo'se
mor-da'cious
mor-dac'ity
mor'-dancy
mor'-dant
mor'-dent

233

mor-el'lo
more-o'ver
mor-gan-at'ic
mor'-gan-ite
mor'i-bund
mori-bun'-dity
mo'-rion
morio-plas'ty
mor'-kin
mor'-lap
mor'-ling
morn'-ing
mor-on'ic
mo-ro'se
mo-ro'se-ness
mo-ros'ity
mor-ox'-ite
mor'-pheme
mor'-phe'mics
mor'-phic
mor'-phine
mor'-phin-ism
mor-phino-ma'nia
mor-phino-
        ma'niac
mor-phio-ma'nia
mor-phio-ma'niac
mor-pho-gen'-esis
mor-pho-gen-et'ic
mor-phog'eny
mor-phog'ra-pher
mor-phog'ra-phy
morph'-oline
mor-pho-log'ic
mor-pho-log'i-cal
mor-phol'-ogist
mor-phol'ogy
mor-phon'omy
234

mor-pho'sis
mor'-ris
mor'-row
mor'-sel
mor'-tal
mor'-tal-ise
mor-tal'ity
mor'-tally
mor'-tar
mor'-tar-board
mort'-gage
mort-gagee'
mort'-gag-ing
mort'-gagor
mor-tic'ian
mor-tif'er-ous
mor-ti-fi-ca'tion
mor'-ti-fied
mor'-tify
mor'-ti-fy-ing
mor'-tise
mor'-tiser
mort'-tis-ing
mort'-main
mor-to'rio
mor'-tu-ary
mor'-ula
mo-sa'ic
mosa-saur'us
mos'cha-tel
mos-chif'er-ous
mos'-lings
mos-qui'to
mos-qui'toes
moss'i-ness
moss-troop'er
mot'a-cil
mo-tel'

mo-tet'
moth'er-hood
moth'er-land
moth'er-less
moth'er-li-ness
moth'-proof
mo-tif'
mo'-tile
mo-til'ity
mo'-tion
mo'-tion-less
mo'-tiv-ate
mo'-tiv-at-ing
mo-tiv-a'tion
mo'-tive
mo'-tive-less
mo-tiv'ity
mot'-ley
mot'-mot
mo'tor-boat
mo'tor-bus
mo'tor-cade
mo'tor-car
mo'tor-cycle
mo'tor-cyc-list
motor-is-a'tion
mo'tor-ise
mo'tor-ist
mo'tor-man
motor-path'ic
mo-tor'pa-thy
mot'-tling
mot'-toes
mouf'-flon
mou-jik'
mou-lag'e
mould'i-ness
mould'-ing

mou'-lin-age
mou'-line
mount'-able
moun'-tain
moun-tain-eer'
moun-tain-eer'-
    ing
moun'-tain-ous
moun'-te-bank
mount'-ing
mourn'-ful
mourn'-fully
mourn'-ing
mous'e-hole
mous'e-tail
mous'e-trap
mouth'-ful
mouth'-piece
mov-abil'ity
mov'-able
mov'e-ment
mov'-ing
mow'-burn
mow'-burnt
mow'-ing
mu-ced'-inous
mu'-cic
mu'-cid
mu'-ci-dine
mu'-ci-dous
mu-cif'er-ous
mu-cif'ic
mu'-ci-gen
mu'-ci-lage
mu-ci-la'gin-ous
mu'-cin
mu'-cin-oid
mu'-cin-ous

mu-cip'ar-ous
mu-civ'or-ous
muck'-rake
mu'-co-cele
mu'-coid
mu-coid'al
mu-con'ic
mu'-cor
mu-co'sa
mu-cos'ity
mu'-cous
mu'-cron-ate
mu-cron'u-late
mu'-cus
mu'-da-rin
mud'-dily
mud'-di-ness
mud'-fish
mud'-flat
mud'-guard
mud'-lark
mud'-skip-per
muf'-fin
muf-fin-eer'
muf'-fler
muf'-fling
mug'-ger
mug'-gi-ness
mug'-wort
mug'-wump
mu-lat'to
mu-lat'-toes
mul'-berry
mulc'-tu-ary
mu-leteer'
mu-li-eb'rity
mu'li-erose
muli-eros'ity

mul'-lein
mul'-let
mul-li-ga-taw'ny
mull'-ite
mult-an'gu-lar
multi-cap'i-tate
mul'ti-coloured
multi-den'-tate
multi-dig i-tate
multi-fa'rious
mul'ti-fid
mul-tif'i-dous
mul'ti-form
multi-form'-ity
multi-lat'-eral
multi-lin'-eal
multi-lin'-ear
multi-loc'u-lar
mul-til'-oquent
mul-tim'eter
multi-million'-
    aire
multi-no'mial
multi-nom'-inal
multi-nom'-in-
    ate
multi-nu'clear
multi-nu'cleate
mul-tip'-ara
mul-tip'-arous
multi-par'-tite
mul'ti-ped
mul'ti-phase
mul'-tiple
multi-plic'-able
multi-pli-cand'
mul-ti-pli-
    ca'tion

235

MULTIPLICATIVE

mul'-ti-pli-cat-
      ive
mul-ti-plic'ity
mul'-ti-plied
mul'-ti-plier
mul'-ti-ply
mul'-ti-ply-ing
mul-tis'on-ous
multi-syl'-lable
mul'-ti-tude
mul-ti-tu'd-in-
      ous
multi-va'lent
mul'-ti-valve
multi-val'-vu-lar
multi-ver'-sant
mul-toc'u-lar
mul'-ture
mum'-bling
mum'-mer
mum'-mery
mum'-mi-fi-
      ca'tion
mum'-mify
mun-da'ne
mun-dan'ity
mun'-da-tory
mun-dif'i-cant
mun-div'a-gant
mu'-ner-ary
mu-nic'i-pal
mu-nic'i-pal-ise
mu-nici-pal'ity
mu-nif'i-cence
mu-nif'i-cent
mu'-ni-ment
mu-nit'ion
mu'-rage
236

mu'-ral
mur'-der
mur'-derer
mur'-der-ess
mur'-der-ous
mu'-ri-ate
mu-ri-at'ic
mu'-ri-cate
mu'-rine
murk'-ily
mur'-mur
mur'-murer
mur'-mur-ing
mur'-mur-ous
mur'-rhine
mu-sa'ceous
mus'-ca-del
mus'-ca-dine
mus'-car-ine
mus'-cat
mus-ca-tel'
mus'-coid
mus-col'-ogist
mus-co-va'do
mus'-cu-lar
mus-cu-lar'ity
mus'cu-lature
mus'-cu-lite
mu-seog'-raphy
mu-seol'-ogy
mu-sett'e
mu-se'um
mush'-room
mu'-sic
mu'-si-cal
mu-si-cal'e
mu'-si-cally
mu-sic'ian

mu-si-col'-ogy
mus'-kel-unge
mus'-ket
mus-keteer'
mus'-ketry
musk'-melon
musk-rat
mus'-lin
mus'-quash
mus'-rol
muss'i-tate
muss-ta'tion
mus'-tang
mus'-tard
mus'-tel-ine
mus'-tel-oid
mus'-ter
must'i-ness
mu-ta-bil'ity
mu'-table
mu-ta-gen'ic
mu-tan'-dum
mu'-tant
muta-ro-ta'tion
mu'-tage
mu'-tase
mu'-tate
mu'-tat-ing
mu-ta'tion
mu'ta-tive
mu'ta-tory
mu'te-ness
mu'-ti-late
mu-ti-la'tion
mu'-ti-lator
mu'-ti-lous
mu-tin-eer'
mu't-ing

mu'-tin-ied
mu'-tin-ous
mu'-tiny
mu'ti-nying
mu'to-scope
mut'-ter
mut'-ter-ing
mut'-ton
mur'-ton-head
mutu-al-is-a'tion
mu'tu-al-ism
mutu-al'ity
mu-tu-ally
mu'-tule
mu'-tuum
mu-zhik'
muz'-zling
my-al'-gia
my-al'gic
my'-al-ism
my-as-the'nia
my-as-then'ic
my-ce'li-oid
my-ce'lium
my-ce'tes
my-cet-ol'ogy
my-ceto'ma
my-co-log'i-cal
my-col'-ogist
my-col'ogy
my-coph'a-gist
my-coph'-agy
my'-cose
my-co'sis
my-cot'ic
my-co-troph'ic
myc-ter'ic
myd-ri'asis

myd-ri-at'ic
my-el-as-the'nia
my-ela-rroph'ia
my'-elin
my-el-it'ic
my-el-i'tis
my'-elo-cyte
my'eloid
my-elo-ma-to'sis
my-el-om'-atous
mv-lo-hy'oid
my'o-blast
myo-blas'-tic
myo-car'-dial
myo-car-di'tis
myo-car'-dium
my'o-cyte
myo-dyn-am'ics
my'o-graph
my-og'ra-phy
my'-oid
my-o'ma
my'o-mancy
my-on-ic'ity
my-op'-athy
my-o'pia
my-op'ic
my-o'sin
my-o'sis
myo-sit'ic
myo-si'tis
my-o'ta-sis
my-ot'ic
my'o-tome
my-ot'omy
myr'-iad

myr'ia-metre
myr'ia-pod
myr'i-cyl
myr-in-gi'tis
myr-in'go-scope
myr-in-got'omy
myrio-phyl'-lous
myrio-ram'a
myr-is'tic
myr-mecol'-ogy
my-rob'-alan
my'-ro-sin
myr-ta'ceous
myr'-ti-form
my-self'
my-so-pho'bia
mys-ta-gog'ic
mys'-ta-gogue
mys'-ter-ies
mys-te'ri-ous
mys-te'ri-ously
mys'-tery
mys'-tic
mys'-ti-cal
mvs'-ti-cally
mys'-ti-cism
mys-ti-fi-ca'tion
mys'-ti-fied
mys'-tify
mys'-ti-fy-ing
mys'-ti-fy-ingly
mys-tiq'ue
myth'i-cal
myth'i-cally
myth'i-cise
myth'i-cist
myth-og'ra-pher
mytho-log'i-cal

237

MYTHOLOGICALLY

mytho-log'i-cally
myth-ol'-ogist
myth-ol'ogy
mytho-ma'nia
mytho-poe'ic
mytho-po-e'sis
myt-il'i-form
myt'-il-ite
myt'-il-oid
myt-og'ra-phy
myx'-ine
myx-oede'ma
myx-o'ma
myxo-ma-to'sis
myx-o'ma-tous

N

nab'-bing
nac'-arat
na-cell'e
nac'-void
nae'-vus
na-gan'a
nag'-ging
nai'-ant
nail'-ery
nail'-wort
nain'-sook
naiss'-ant
na'ked-ness
na'me-able
na'me-less
na'me-sake
na'm-ing
nan'-dine
nanis-a'tion

nan-keen'
naph'-tha
naph'-tha-lene
naph-tha-len'ic
naph'-thal'ic
naph'-thal-ise
naph'-thene
naph-then'ic
naph-thi-on'ic
naph-tho'ic
naph'-thol
naph-tho-qui-
   no'ne
naph'-thyl-ene
nap'i-form
nap'-kin
nap'-less
nap'-per
nap'-ping
nap'-ra-path
na-prap'-athy
nar'-ceine
nar-ciss'-ism
nar-ciss'-ist
nar-ciss'us
nar'-co-lepsy
nar-co-lep'-tic
nar-co'ma
nar-co-ma'nia
nar-co'sis
nar-co-syn'-
   thesis
nar-co-ther'apy
nar'-cot'ic
nar'-cot-ine
nar'-cot-ise
nar'-cot-ism
nar-doo'

nar'-dus
nar'-gileh
nar'i-corn
nar'i-form
nar'-ras
nar-ra't-able
nar-ra'te
nar-ra'tion
nar'-ra'tive
nar-ra'tor
nar'-row
nar'-row=gauge
nar'-rowly
nar'-row-ness
nar'-thex
nar'-whal
nasal-is-a'tion
na'sal-ise
nasal'-ity
nas'-ard
na'sc-berry
na'si-corn
na'si-form
na'so-scope
nas'-tic
nas'-tily
nas'-ti-ness
nas-tur'-tium
na-ta'tion
nata-to'rial
nata-to'rium
na'ta-tory
national-is-
   a'tion
nat'ional-ise
nat'ional-ism
nat'ional-ist
national-is'tic

national'-ity
na'tion-wide
na'tive-ness
na'tiv-ism
nativ-is'tic
nativ'-ity
na'trol-ite
nat'-ter-jack
nat'-tily
nat'u-ral
natu-ral-is-
      a'tion
nat'u-ral-ise
nat'u-ral-ism
nat'u-ral-ist
natu-ral-is'tic
nat'-urally
nat'u-ral-ness
na'tur-ism
na'tur-ist
natur-is'tic
na'turo-path
natur-op'a-thy
naught'-ily
naugh'ti-ness
nau'-machy
naup'li-form
naup'-lius
nauro-pom'eter
naus'-eant
naus'-eate
naus'-eated
naus'-eat-ive
naus'-eous
naut'i-cal
naut'i-cally
naut'i-lus
naut'o-phone

nav-ic'ula
nav-ic'u-lar
navi-ga-bil'ity
nav'i-gable
nav'i-gate
navi-ga'tion
nav'i-gator
na-wab'
na'ya-gite
near'-est
near'-ness
near'-sighted
neat'-herd
neat'-ness
neb'-ris
neb'-ula
neb'u-lae
neb'u-lar
neb'u-ule
neb'u-lise
neb'u-liser
neb-u'lium
nebu-los'ity
neb'u-lous
necess-ar'ily
nec'ess-ary
necessi-ta'rian
necessi-ta'rian-
         ism
necess'i-tate
necess'i-ties
necess'i-tous
necess'i-tously
necess'-ity
neck'-band
neck'-cloth
neck'-er-chief
neck'-ing

neck'-lace
neck'-let
neck'-line
neck'-piece
neck'-tie
neck'-wear
necro-bio'sis
necrog'en-ous
necrog'-ra-pher
necrol'-ater
necrol'-atry
necro-log'ic
necro-log'i-cal
necrol'-ogist
necrol'-ogy
nec'ro-man-cer
nec'ro-mancy
necro-man'-tic
necroph'-agous
necroph'-il-ism
necroph'-il-ous
necro-pho'bia
necroph'-ori
necroph'-or-ous
necrop'-olis
nec'-ropsy
necro-scop'ic
necros'-copy
nec'ro-sin
nec'ro-tise
necrot'-om-ise
necrot'-omy
nec'-tar
nec-ta'real
nec-ta'rean
nec'-tared
nec-ta'reous
nec-tar-if'er-ous

239

nec'-tar-ine
nec'-tar-iv'or-ous
ncc'-tar-ous
nec'-tary
nec'-to-calyx
nec-ton'ic
nec'-to-pod
nec'-to-some
need'-ful
need'i-ness
need'le-bush
need'le-craft
need'le-fish
need'le-ful
need'le-like
need'le-point
need'-ler
need'-less
need'-lessly
need'-less-ness
need'le-woman
need'le-work
need'-ling
nef-a'rious
nef-a'riously
ne-ga'te
ne-ga'tion
ne-ga'tion-ist
neg'a-tive
neg'a-tively
neg'a-tiv-ism
nega-tiv-is'tic
nega-tiv'ity
neg'a-tory
neg'a-tron
neglect'-ful
neg'-li-gence
neg'-li-gent

neg'-li-gently
neg-li-gi-bil'ity
neg'-li-gible
nego'-ciant
nego-tiabil'-ity
nego'-tiable
nego'-tiate
nego'-tiat-ing
nego-tia'tion
nego'-tiator
negun'-dium
neigh'-bour
neigh'-bour-hood
neigh'-bour-ing
neigh'-bour-li-
          ness
neigh'-bourly
nek'-ton
nem'a-lite
ne-mat'ic
nem'a-tode
nema-to-di'asis
nem'a-toid
nema-tol'ogy
nemer'-tine
nem'-esis
nem-oph'-il-ous
nem-oph'-ily
nem'-oral
nem'-or-ose
nem'-or-ous
nen'u-phar
neo-ba-lae'na
ne'o-blast
ne'o-cene
neo-class'i-cal
neoc'-racy
neo-dym'-ium

neog'-amy
ne'o-gen
ne'o-lite
neo-lith'ic
neo-log'ic
neo-lo'gian
neo-log'ical
neol'-ogise
neol'-ogism
neol'-ogist
neol'-ogy
neo-man'o-scope
neo-my'cin
neo-na'tal
neon'-omous
neon-to-log'i-cal
neon-tol'-ogist
neon-tol'-ogy
neo-pho'bia
ne'o-phyte
neo-pla'sia
ne'o-plasm
neo-plas'-tic
neo-plas'ty
ne'o-prene
neo-sal'-var-san
neo-stig'-mine
neo-ter'ic
neot'-er-ism
neot'-er-ist
neo-vi'tal-ism
nepen'-the
nepen'-thean
neph'a-lism
neph'a-list
neph'-el-ine
neph'-elin-ite
neph'-elite

240

neph'-el-oid
neph-el-om'eter
neph'o-graph
nepho-log'ic
neph-ol'-ogist
neph-ol'ogy
neph'o-scope
neph-ral'-gia
neph-rec'-tomy
neph'-ric
neph-rid'-ial
neph-rid'-ium
neph'-rite
neph-rit'ic
neph-ri'tis
neph'-ro-cyte
neph-ro'dium
neph'-roid
neph-rol'-ogy
neph'-ron
nephro-pto'sis
neph-ro'sis
neph-rot'ic
neph-rot'omy
nepi-on'ic
nep-ot'ic
nep'-ot-ism
nep-tu'nium
ner-it'ic
ner'-oli
ner'-olin
ner'-vate
ner-va'tion
ner'-va-ture
ner've-less
ner'-vine
nerv'-ing
ner-vos'-ity

ner'-vous
ner'-vously
ner'-vous-ness
ner'-vure
ner-vu-ra'tion
ner'-vure
ne'si-ote
nes'-tling
nesto-ca'lyx
neth'-er-most
net'-ting
net'-tling
net'-work
neur-al'-gia
neur-al'-gic
neur-as-the'nia
neur-as-then'ic
neur-a'tion
neur-ax'is
neur-ec'-tomy
neur-il'ity
neur'-ine
neur-it'ic
neur-i'tis
neu'ro-blast
neuro-blas-to'ma
neu'ro-coele
neuro-gen'-esis
neuro-gen'ic
neur-og'-lia
neur-og'ra-phy
neuro-log'i-cal
neur-ol'-ogist
neur-ol'-ogy
neur-ol'-ysis
neur-o'ma
neuro-mus'cu-lar
neur-on'ic

neur-on-i'tis
neu'ro-path
neuro-path'ic
neuro-path'i-
            cally
neuro-path-
        ol'ogy
neur-op'-athy
neur-op'-teral
neur-op'-ter-ous
neur-o'ses
neur-o'sis
neur'o-sur-gery
neur-ot'ic
neur-ot'i-cism
neur-ot'omy
neuro-trop'ic
neur-ot'ro-pism
neus'-ton
neu'-ter
neu'-tral
neu-tral-is-
        a'tion
neu'-tral-ise
neu'-tral-iser
neu'-tral-ism
neu-tral'ity
neu'-trally
neu-tri'no
neu'-tron
nev'er-more
nev'er-the-less
new'-born
new'-comer
new-fang'led
new'-ish
new'-ness
news'-agent

news'-cast
news'-caster
news'-dealer
news'-let-ter
news'-man
news'-monger
news'-paper
news'-paper-man
news'-print
news'-reel
news'-room
news'-stand
news'-ven-dor
ni'a-cin
nia-cin'a-mide
nib'-bling
nib'-lick
nic'-col-ite
ni'ce-ness
nick-el-if'er-ous
nick'-el-ine
nick-el-o'deon
nick'el-plate
nick'-el-type
nick'-nacks
nick'-name
nic-otin'a-mide
nic'-otine
nic-otin'ic
nic'-otin-ism
nic-ta'tion
nic'-ti-tate
nic'-ti-tat-ing
nic-ti-ta'tion
nida-men'-tal
nid-ic'-olous
nid'i-fi-cate
nidi-fi-ca'tion
242

nid-if'u-gous
nid'-ify
ni'-dor
ni'dor-ous
nidu-la'tion
ni'-dus
nig'-gard
nig'-gard-li-ness
nig'-gardly
nig'-gling
ni'ght-cap
ni'ght-club
ni'ght-fall
ni'ght-gown
ni'ght-hawk
ni'ght-ingale
ni'ght-long
ni'ght-mare
ni'ght-shade
ni'ght-shirt
ni'ght-time
ni-gresc'ence
ni-gresc'ent
nig'-ri-cant
nig'-rify
nig'-grine
nig'-ri-tude
nig'ro-sine
ni'-hil-ism
ni'-hil-ist
ni-hil-is'tic
ni-hil'-ity
nim-bif'er-ous
nim'ble-ness
nim'-bly
nimbo-stra'tus
nim'-bus
nim'i-ous

nin'-com-poop
ni'ne-fold
ni'ne-pins
ni'ne-teen
ni'ne-teenth
ni'ne-ti-eth
ni-o'bic
ni-o'bium
nip'-per
nip'-per-kin
nip'-ping
nip'-ter
ni'-sus
nitid'-ity
nit'i-dous
nitra-mi'ne
ni'-trate
ni'tra-tine
ni-tra'tion
ni'-tric
ni'-tride
ni'-tri-dise
ni-tri-fi-ca'tion
ni'tri-fied
ni'-trify
ni'-trile
ni'-trite
ni'tri-toid
ni-tro-an'il-ine
nitro-ben'-zene
nitro-cel-lu-lose
ni'-tro-gen
ni'tro-gen-ate
ni-trog'en-ise
ni-trog'en-ous
ni-tro-glyc'er-
    ine
ni-trol'ic

ni-trom'eter
ni'-tron
ni'-tro-sate
nitro-sa'tion
ni-tro'so
ni-tro-tol'u-ene
ni'-trous
ni-trox'yl
ni'-tryl
nit'-wit
ni'-val
ni-va'tion
niv'-eous
ni-zam'
no-bel'-ium
no-bil'i-ary
no-bil'i-tate
no-bili-ta'tion
no-bil'ity
no'ble-man
no'ble-ness
no'ble-woman
no'-body
no-car-di'asis
no'-cent
no-cicep'-tive
no-cicep'-tor
noc-tam-bu-
    la'tion
noc-tam'-bu-lism
noc-tam'-bu-list
noc-tif'lor-ous
nocti-lu'ca
nocti-lu'cent
nocti-lu'cine
nocti-lu'cous
noc-tiv'a-gant
nocti-vaga'tion

noc-tiv'a-gous
noc'-to-graph
noc'-to-vision
noc'-tu-ary
noc'-tuid
noc'-tule
noc'-turn
noc-tur'-nal
noc'-turne
noc'u-ous
no'-dal
no-dal'-ity
no'-dated
nod'-ding
no'di-cal
no-do'se
no-dos'ity
nod'u-lar
nod'u-lated
nodu-la'tion
nod'-ule
nod'u-lose
nod'u-lous
no-egen'-esis
no-egen-et'ic
no-emat'-ical
no-e'sis
no-et'ic
nog'-gin
nog'-ging
nois'e-less
nois'e-lessly
nois'-ily
nois'i-ness
nois'-ing
noi'-some
no'-mad
no-mad'ic

no-mad'i-cal
no'-mad-ism
nom'-arch
nom'-archy
nom'-bril
no'-men-clator
no-men'cla-ture
nom'-in-able
nom'-inal
nom'-in-al-ise
nom'-in-al-ism
nom'-in-al-ist
nom'i-nate
nom'i-nated
nomi-na'tion
nom'i-na-tive
nom'i-nator
nomi-nee'
no'-mism
nom-is'tic
nom-oc'-racy
nom-og'en-ist
nom-og'eny
nom'o-gram
nom-og'ra-pher
nomo-graph'ic
nom-og'ra-phy
nomo-log'i-cal
nom-ol'-ogist
nom-ol'ogy
nom'o-thete
nomo-thet'ic
non-ac-cept'-
    ance
non'-age
nona-gen-a'rian
nona-ges'i-mal
non-ag-gres'sion

non'a-gon
no'-nane
nona-no'ic
non-ap-pear'-ance
non'-chalance
non'-chalant
non'-chalantly
non-com'-ba tant
non-com-
    mis'sioned
non-com-mit'-tal
non-con-duc'-tor
non-con-form'-ist
non-con-form'-ity
non'-de-script
non-en'-tity
non-essen'-tial
non'e-such
non-exist'-ence
non-exist'-ent
non-feas'-ance
non-ful-fil'-ment
non-in-ter-ven'-
      tion
non-join'-der
non-ju'ror
non-met-al'lic
non-pareil'
non'-par-ous
non-par-tic'i-
     pat-ing
non-par'-ti-san
non'-plus'
non-pluss'ed
non-plus'-sing
non-pro-duc'-tive
non-prof'it
non-res'i-dence

non-res'i-dent
non-sec-ta'rian
non'-sense
non-sen'-si-cal
non-sen-si-
      cal'ity
non'-skid
non'-stop
non'-suit
non'-sup-port
non-u'nion
non'u-plet
no-ol'ogy
noon'-day
noon'-tide
noon'-time
no'-pal
no'-ria
nor'-mal
nor'-malcy
nor-mal-is-a'tion
nor'-mal-ise
nor'-mal-is-er
nor-mal'ity
nor'-mally
nor'-ma-tive
north'-cock
north-east'-erly
north-east'-ern
north-east'-ward
north'-erly
north'-ern
north'-erner
north'-ern-most
north'-ing
north'-land
north'-ward
north'-wardly

north-west'-erly
north-west'-ern
no'se-band
no'se-bleed
no'se-gay
no'-sel-ite
no-se-piece
noso-co'mial
nos og'ra-pher
noso-graph'ic
nos-og'ra-phy
noso-log'i-cal
nos-ol'-ogist
nos-ol'ogy
nos-on'omy
noso-pho'bia
nos'o-taxy
nos-tal'-gia
nos-tal'-gie
nos-tol'ogy
nos'-tril
nos'-trum
nota-bil'ity
no'-table
no'-table-ness
no'-tably
no-tan'da
no-tan'-dum
no-ta'rial
no'-tar-ies
no'-tar-ise
no'-tary
no-ta'tion
no'te-book
no'te-less
no'te-let
no'te-paper
no-te-worth-ily

no'te-worthi-ness
no'te-worthy
noth'ing-ness
no'-tice
no'-tice-able
no'-tice-ably
no'-tic-ing
no'-ti-fiable
no-ti-fi-ca'tion
no'-ti-fied
no'-ti-fier
no'tify
no'-ti-fy-ing
no'-tion
no'-tional
no'-tion-ist
no-tit'ia
no'-to-chord
noto-chor'dal
noto-nec'-tal
no-tor-i'ety
no-to'ri-ous
no-to'ri-ously
noto-ung'u-late
not-with-stand'-
ing
nou'-gat
nou'-menal
nou'-men-al-ism
nou'-menon
nour'ish-able
nour'ish-ing
nour'ish-ment
nour'i-ture
no-vac'u-lite
no-va'lia
no-va'tion
novel-ett'e

nov'el-ise
nov'el-ist
novel-is'tic
nov'el-ties
no-ve'na
nov'-en-ary
nov-en'dial
nov-en'-nial
no-ver'-cal
nov'-ice
no-vit'iate
now'-adays
no'-ways
no'-where
no'-wise
nu'-ance
nu-bec'-ula
nu'-becule
nu'-bia
nu-bif'er-ous
nu'-bi-form
nu'-bile
nu-bil'ity
nu'-bi-lous
nu'ca-ment
nu'-chal
nu-cif'er-ous
nu'-ci-form
nu-civ'or-ous
nu'-clear
nu'-cleate
nu-clea'tion
nu'-cleator
nu'-clei
nu-cle'ic
nu'-clein
nu-clein-a'tion
nu-cle'olar

nu'-cleo-late
nu'-cleole
nu-cle'olus
nu-cleol'-ysis
nu'-cleon
nu-cleon'-ics
nu'-cleo-plasm
nucleo-ti'dase
nu'-cleus
nu'-clide
nu-clid'ic
nu'-cule
nu-da'tion
nu'de-ness
nudg'-ing
nu'-disma
nu'-dist
nu'-dity
nu'ga-tory
nug'-get
nuis'-ance
nul-li-fi-ca'tion
nul-li-fid'-ian
nul'-li-fied
nul'-li-fier
nul'-lify
nul'-li-fy-ing
nul'-li-pore
nul'-lity
num'-ber
num'-bered
num'-berer
num'-ber-less
numb'-fish
numb'-ing
numb'-ingly
numb'-ness

245

nu'-men
nu'-mer-able
nu'-meral
nu'-mer-ary
nu'-mer-ate
nu-mer-a'tion
nu'-mera-tive
nu'-mer-ator
nu-mer'ic
nu-mer'i-cal
nu-mer'i-cally
nu-mer-ol'ogy
nu-mer-os'ity
nu'-mer-ous
nu'-mi-nous
nu-mis-mat'-ics
nu-mis'ma-tist
nu-mis-ma-
    tog'ra-phy
nu-mis-ma-tol'-
    ogist
nu-mis-ma-
    tol'ogy
num'-mery
num'-mi-form
num'-mu-lar
num'-mu-lated
num-mu-la'tion
num'-mu-line
num'-mu-lite
num-mu-lit'ic
num'-skull
nun'-ciature
nun'-cio
nun'cu-pate
nuncu-pa'tion
nun'cu-pat-ive
nun'cu-pator

nun'cu-pat-ory
nun'-di-nal
nun'-di-nary
nun'-dine
nun'-like
nun'-nery
nup'-tial
nup-tial'ity
nur'se-maid
nur'-sery
nurs'-ery-man
nurs'-ing
nurs'-ling
nur'-tural
nur'-ture
nur'-tur-ing
nu'-tant
nu'-tate
nu-ta'tion
nut'-cracker
nut'-hatch
nut'-meg
nu'-tria
nu'-tri-cism
nu'-tri-ent
nu'-tri-lite
nu'-tri-ment
nu'-tri-men-tal
nu-trit'ion
nu-trit'ional
nu-trit'ion-ist
nu-trit'ious
nu'-tri-tive
nut'-shell
nut'-ter
nut'-ti-ness
nut'-ting
nych-the'meral

nych-the'meron
nyc-ta-gin-
    a'ceous
nyc-ta-lo'pia
nyc-ta-lop'ic
nyc'-ta-lops
nyc-tan'-thous
nyc-ti-nas'-tic
nyc'-ti-nasty
nycti-pel-ag'ic
nyc-ti-trop'ic
nyc-tit'ro-pism
ny'-lon
nymphae-a'ceous
nymph'a-lid
nympho-lep'sy
nympho-ma'nia
nympho-ma'niac
nys-tag'-mic
nys-tag'-moid
nys-tag'-mus
nys'-ta-tin
ny'-tril

O

oak'-moss
oar'-fish
oar'-lock
oars'-man
oars'-man-ship
oat'-cake
oat'-meal
ob-com-press'ed
ob-con'ic
ob-cord'-ate
ob'-du-racy

ob'-du-rate
obe'di-ence
obe'di-ent
obe'di-ently
obeis'-ance
obeis'-ant
ob-el-is'cal
ob-el-is'coid
ob'-el-ise
ob'-elisk
ob'-elus
obe's-ity
obey'-ing
ob-fus'-cate
ob-fus-ca'tion
ob-fus'-cator
ob-fus'ca-tory
ob'i-tal
obit'u-ar-ies
obit'u-ary
ob'-ject (n.)
ob-ject' (v.)
ob-jec-tee'
ob-jec-ti-fi-
    ca'tion
ob-jec'-tify
ob-ject'-ing
ob-jec'-tion
ob-jec'-tion-able
ob-jec'-tive
ob-jec'-tively
ob-jec'-tive-ness
ob-jec'-tiv-ism
ob-jec'-tiv-ist
ob-jec-tiv'ity
ob'-ject-less
ob-jec'-tor
ob-jur-a'tion

ob-ju're
ob'-jur-gate
ob-jur-ga'tion
ob-jur'ga-tive
ob'-jur-gator
ob-jur'ga-tory
ob'-last
ob-la'tion
ob-la'tory
ob'-li-gant
ob'-li-gate
ob'-li-gat-ing
ob-li-ga'tion
ob'-li-gator
oblig'a-tory
ob-li-gee'
obli'ge-ment
obli'g-ing
obli'g-ingly
ob'-li-gor
obli'que-ness
ob-liq'ui-tous
ob-liq'ui-ty
ob-lit'-er-ate
ob-lit-er-a'tion
ob-lit'-er-at-ive
ob-lit'-er-ator
ob-liv'-ion
ob-liv'i-ous
ob-li-visc'ence
ob'-long
ob'-longated
ob'-loquy
ob-mu-tesc'ence
ob-mu-tesc'ent
ob-nox'ious
ob-nu'bi-late

ob-nubi-la'tion
o'bo-ist
ob'-olus
ob-o'vate
ob-o'void
ob-rep'-tion
ob-rep-tit'ious
ob-sce'ne
ob-sce'nely
ob-scen'ity
ob'-sequent
ob-scu'r-ence
ob-scu'r-an-tism
ob-scur-a'tion
ob-scu're
ob-scu'rely
ob-scu're-ness
ob-scu'r-ing
ob-scu'r-ity
ob'-secrate
ob-secra'tion
ob'-sequies
ob-se'qui-ous
ob-se'qui-ous-
    ness,
ob-serv'-able
ob-serv'-ance
ob-serv'-ant
ob-ser-va'tion
ob-serv'-ative
ob-serv'-atory
ob-serv'e
ob-serv'er
ob-serv'-ing
ob-sess'
ob-ses'sion
ob-ses'sion-ist
ob-sess'-ive

247

ob-sess'or
ob-sid'-ian
ob-sid'i-onal
ob-si'gn
ob-sig'-nate
ob-sig-na'tion
ob-sig'-na-tory
ob-sol-esc'e
ob-sol-esc'ence
ob-sol-esc'ent
ob'-sol-ete
ob'-sol-ete-ness
ob'-stacle
ob-stet'-ri-cal
ob-ste-tric'ian
ob-stet'-rics
ob'-sti-nacy
ob'-sti-nate
ob'-sti-nately
ob-strep'er-ous
ob-stric'-tion
ob-struct'
ob-struc'-ter
ob-struc'-tion
ob-struc'-tion-
ism
ob-struc'-tion-
ist
ob-struc'-tive
ob-struc'-tor
ob'-stru-ent
ob-tain'
ob-tain'-able
ob-tain'-ment
ob-tect'
ob-tend'
ob-ten'-tion
ob-test'

ob-tes-ta'tion
ob-tru'de
ob-tru'der
ob-tru'd-ing
ob-trunc'-ate
ob-tru'sion
ob-tru'sive
ob-tru's-ively
ob-tund'
ob-tund'-ent
ob'-tu-rate
ob-tu-ra'tion
ob'-tu-rator
ob-tu'se
ob-tu'se-ness
ob-vers'e (a.)
ob'-verse (n.)
ob-vers'ely
ob-ver'-sion
ob-vert'
ob'-vi-ate
ob'-vi-at-ing
ob-vi-a'tion
ob'-vi-ator
ob'-vi-ous
ob'-vi-ously
ob'-vi-ous-ness
ob'-vol-ute
oca-ri'na
oc-ca'sion
oc-ca'sional
oc-ca'sion-al-ism
oc-ca'sion-al-ist
oc-ca'sion-ally
oc'-ci-dent
oc-ci-den'-tal
oc-ci-den'-tal-
ise

oc-cip'i-tal
oc-cipi-ta'lia
oc'-ci-put
oc-clu'de
oc-clu'd-ent
oc-clu'd-ing
oc-clu'sal
oc-clu'sion
oc-clu's-ive
oc-clu'sor
oc-cult'
oc-cul-ta'tion
oc-cult'-ism
oc-cult'-ist
oc'-cu-pancy
oc'-cu-pant
oc-cu-pa'tion
oc-cu-pa'tional
oc'-cu-pat-ive
oc'-cu-pied
oc'-cu-pier
oc'-cupy
oc'-cu-py-ing
oc-cur'
oc-curr'ed
oc-cur'-rence
oc-cur'-rent
oc-cur'-ring
ocean-a'rium
ocean-og'ra-pher
oceano-graph'ic
ocean-og'ra-phy
o'cean-ite
oc'el-late
ocel'-lus
och-le'sis
och-let'ic
och-loc'-racy

och'-lo-crat
och-lo-crat'ic
och-lo-pho'bia
ochro-no'sis
oc'-ta-chord
oc'-tad
octa-deca-no'ic
oc-tad'ic
oc'-ta-gon
oc-tag'-onal
oc-ta-he'dral
oc-ta-he'dron
oc'-tal
oc'-ta-mer
oc-tam'er-ous
oc-tam'eter
oc'-tane
oc-tan'gu-lar
oc'-tant
oc-tan'-tal
oc'ta-ploid
oc-ta-pod'ic
oc-tap'-ody
oc'ta-stich
oc-tas'ti-chon
oc'ta-style
oc'ta-teuch
oc-ta'val
octa-va'lent
oc'-tave
oc-ta'vo
oc-ten'-nial
oc-tet'
oc-til'lion
oc'-to-fid
oc-to-gen-a'rian
oc-tog'en-ary
oc-to-na'rian

oc'-to-nary
oc'-to-pod
oc'-to-pus
oc-to-roon'
oc'-tose
octo-syl-lab'ic
oc-to-syl'-lable
oc'-troi
oc'-tuple
oc'tu-plet
oc'-tyl-ene
oc'u-lar
oc'u-lar-ist
oc'u-late
oc'u-list
o'da-lisque
odd'-ity
odd'-ment
odd'-ness
o'di-ous
o'do-graph
odom'-eter
odon-tal'-gia
odon'-tic
odon-ti'tis
odon-to-gen'ic
odon-tog'eny
odon'-to-graph
odon-tog'ra-phy
odon'-toid
odon'to-lite
odon-tol'-ogist
odon-tol'ogy
o'dor-ant
odor-if'er-ous
odor-im'etry
o'dor-ise
o'dor-ous

o'dour-less
oede'ma-tous
oed'i-pal
oenan'-thic
oenol'-ogist
oenol'-ogy
oe'no-mancy
oenom'-eter
oenoph'-il-ist
oeso-phag'eal
oesoph'-agus
off'-beat
off'-cast
of-fen'ce
of-fend'
of-fend'er
of-fend'-ing
of-fens'-ive
of-fens'-ive-ness
of'-fer
of'-fer-ing
of-fer-to'rial
of'-fer-tory
off-hand'ed
of'-fice
of'-fice-holder
of'-fi-cer
of-fic'ial
of-fic'ial-dom
of-ficial-e'se
of-fic'ially
of-fic'iant
of-fic'iary
of-fic'iate
of-ficia'tion
of-fic'iator
of-fic'inal
of-fic'ious

249

of-fic'iously
off'-ing
off'-print
off'-scour-ings
off'-set (n. a.)
off-set' (v.)
off-set'-ting
off'-shoot
off-sho're
off'-side
off'-spring
o'gre-ish
ohm'-age
ohm'-meter
oil'-cloth
oil'i-ness
oil'-man
oil'-skin
oil'-stone
oint'-ment
oiti-ci'ca
old'-ish
old'-ness
old'-ster
oleag'i-nous
olean'-der
olec'-ra-nal
olec'-ra-non
oleif'-er-ous
o'leo-graph
oleog'-ra-phy
oleo-mar'-gar-ine
oleom'-eter
oleo-res'in
ol-er-a'ceous
ol-fac'-tion
ol-fac'-tive
ol-fac-tom'eter

ol-fac'-tory
ol-ib'a-num
ol'i-fant
ol'i-garch
oli-gar'-chal
oli-gar' chic
ol'i-garchy
oli-ge'mia
ol'i-go-chaete
ol'i-go-clase
oli-gom'er-ous
oli-gop'-oly
oli-gop'-sony
ol'i-tory
oliv-a'ceous
ol'iv-ary
ol'-ive
oliv'-en-ite
ol'i-ver
ol'i-vet
ol'i-vil
ol'i-vine
om-brol'ogy
om-brom'eter
om'-bro-phile
om-broph'i-lous
om'-bro-phobe
om-broph'o-bous
om'-bro-phyte
omen-ol'ogy
omen'-tum
om'-in-ous
om'-in-ously
omiss'-ible
omis'-sion
omiss'-ive
omit'-ted
omit'-ting

om-ma-te'um
om-ma-tid'ium
om-ne'ity
om'-ni-bus
om'ni-com-
        petent
om-ni-fa'rious
om-nif'ic
om-nif'i-cence
om-nif'i-cent
om'-ni-form
om-ni-for'mity
om-nig'en-ous
om'-ni-graph
om-nim'eter
om-ni-par'ity
om-nip'ar-ous
om-nip'-otence
om-nip'-otent
omni-pres'-ence
omni-pres'-ent
om'-ni-range
om-nisc'ience
om-nisc'ient
om'-nium
om-niv'or-ous
omo-hy'oid
omo-pha'gia
omoph'-agous
om'-pha-cite
om-phal'ic
om-pha-li'tis
om'-pha-los
on'a-ger
ona-gra'ceous
o'nan-ism
o'nan-ist
onan-is'tic

on-col'ogy
on-com'eter
on'-coming
on'-cost
on-cot'omy
on'-do-graph
on-dom'-eter
oneiro-crit'i-cal
oneiro-crit'i-
    cism
oneir-ol'ogy
oneir'o-mancy
on'-er-ous
one-self'
on'e-time
on'ion-skin
on'-looker
ono-mas'-tic
ono-mas'-ti-con
ono-mato-poe'ia
ono-mato-poe'ic
ono-mato-poet'ic
on'-rush
on'-set
on'-shore
on'-slaught
on-to-gen'-esis
on-to-gen-et'ic
on-tog'eny
on-to-log'i-cal
on-tol'-ogist
on-tol'ogy
on'-ward
ony-chi'tis
onycho-myco'sis
ony-choph'a-gist
ony-choph'-agy
ooz'-ing

opac'i-fier
opa-cim'eter
opal-esc'e
opal-esc'ence
opal-esc'ent
o'p-al-ine
opeid'o-scope
o'pen-cast
o'pen-ing
o'pen-ness
o'pen-work
op'-era
op'-er-able
op'-era-glass
op-er-am'eter
op'-er-ant
op'-er-at-able
op-er-at'ic
op-er-at'i-cally
op-er-a'tion
op-er-a'tional
op'-er-at-ive
op'-er-ator
oper'cu-lar
oper'cu-late
oper'cu-lum
op-er-et'ta
op'-er-ose
ophi-cal'-cite
ophi-ceph'a-lous
oph'i-cleide
ophid'-ian
ophi-di'asis
ophi-ol'-ater
ophi-ol'-atrous
ophi-ol'-atry
ophio-log'i-cal

ophi-ol'ogy
oph'io-mancy
ophi-oph'a-gous
ophi-ophil'-ist
oph'-ite
oph-thal'-mia
oph-thal'-mic
oph-thal-mi'tis
oph-thal-mo-
    log'ic
oph-thal-mo-
    log'i-cal
oph-thal-mol'-
    ogist
oph-thal-
    mol'ogy
oph-thal-
    mom'eter
oph-thal-mom'-
    etry
oph-thal'-mo-
    scope
oph-thal-
    moscopy
opi-an'ic
o'pi-ate
opi-at'ic
opin'ion-ated
opin'ion-at-ive
opin'ion-ator
opi-som'eter
op-is-thog'-na-
    thous
op-is'-tho-graph
o'pi-um-ism
opop'a-nax
opo-ther'apy
op'-pi-dan

OPPILATE

op'-pi·late
op-pi·la'tion
op'-pi-lat-ive
op-po'nency
op-po'nent
op-por-tune'
op-por-tu'nely
op-por-tu'ne-ness
op-por-tu'n-ism
op-por-tun-ist
op-por-tun-is'tic
op-por-tu'nity
op-pos-abil'ity
op-po's-able
op-po'se
op-po'ser
op-po's-ing
op'-posite
op-po-sit'ion
op-press'
op-press'-ible
op-pres'sion
op-press'-ive
op-press'or
op-pro'-bri-ous
op-pro'-brium
op-pugn'
op-pug'-nancy
op-pug'-nant
op-pug-na'tion
op-pugn'er
op'-si-math
op-sim'-athy
op-so-ma'nia
op-so-ma'niac
op-son'ic
op'-sonin
op-so'nium
252

op-tat'-ive
op'-tic
op'-tical
op-tic'ian
op'-tics
op'-ti-macy
op'-ti-mal
op-tim'eter
op'-ti-mism
op'-ti-mist
op-ti-mis'-tic
op-ti-mis'-ti-
     cally
op'-ti-mum
op'-tion
op'-tional
op'-to-gram
op-tom'eter
op-to-met'ric
op-tom'-etrist
op-tom'-etry
op'-to-phone
op'u-lence
op'u-lency
op'u-lent
or'-ache
or'-acle
orac'u-lar
oracu-lar'ity
orac'u-lous
or'-ange
or-ange-a'de
or'-angery
or'-ange-wood
or'a-tor
ora-to'rial
ora-tor'ian
ora-tor'i-cal

ora-tor'i-cally
ora-to'rio
or'a-tory
or-bic'u-lar
or-bicu-lar'ity
or-bic'u-late
or'-bit
or'-bital
or'-bited
or'-biter
or'-bit-ing
or'-chard
or'-chard-ist
or-che'sis
or-chesog'   raphy
or'-ches-tra
or-ches'-tral
or-ches-trate
or-ches-tra'tion
or'-chid
or-chi-da'ceous
or-chid-ol'-ogist
or-chid-ol'ogy
or'-chil
or-chit'ic
or-chi'tis
or'-cin
or'-cine
or'-cinol
or-dain'
or-dain'-ment
or'-deal
or'-der
or'-der-li-ness
or'-derly
or'-di-nal
or'-di-nance

or-di-nand'
or-di-nar'ily
or'-di-nary
or'-di-nate
or-di-na'tion
or-di-nee'
ord'-nance
or'-don-nance
or'-dure
or'-dur-ous
or-ec'tic
or-ex'is
or'-gan
or'-gan-die
or-gan'ic
or-gan'i-cally
or-gan'i-cism
or-gan'i-cist
or-gan-i's-able
or-gan-is-a'tion
or'-gan-ise
or'-gan-iser
or'-gan-is-ing
or'-gan-ism
or'-gan-ist
or-gano-gen'-esis
or-gano-gen'ic
or-ga-nog'eny
or-ga-nog'ra-phy
or-gano-lep'-tic
or'-ga-non
or-ga-nos'copy
or-gan'o-sol
or-gano-ther'apy
or'-ga-num
or'-gan-zine
or'-gasm
or-gas'-tic

or'-geat
or'-gi-ast
or-gi-as'-tic
or'-gies
or'-gone
or'-gu-lous
orien'-tal
o'rien-tate
orien-ta'tion
o'rien-tator
or'i-fice
ori-fic'ial
or'i-flamme
or'i-gan
orig'-anum
or'i-gin
orig'-inal
orig-inal'ity
orig'-inally
orig'-inate
orig-inat-ing
orig-ina'tion
orig'-in-at-ive
orig'-in-ator
ori-na'sal
or-is-mol'ogy
or'i-son
or'-lop
or'-mer
or'-molu
or'-na-ment
or-na-men'-tal
or-na-men-ta'tion
or-na'te
or-na'te-ness
or-nith'ic
or-ni-thich'-nite
or'-ni-thine

or'-ni-choid
or-nith'o-lite
or-nitho-log'ical
or-ni-thol'-ogist
or-ni-thol'-ogy
or-nith'o-mancy
or-nitho-man'tic
or-nith'o-morph
or'-ni-thop-ter
or-nitho-
    rhyn'chus
or-ni-thos'copy
oro-gen'-esis
oro-gen-et'ic
oro-gen'ic
or-og'eny
oro-graph'ic
or-og'ra-phy
o'ro-ide
or-ol'-ogist
or-ol'ogy
orom'-eter
oro-met'ric
oro-pe'sa
orotun'-dity
or'-phan
or'-phan-age
or'-phan-hood
or'-phan-ism
or-pha'rian
or'-phic
or'-phism
or'-phite
or'-phrey
or'-pi-ment
or'-pine
or'-rery
or'-ris

or'ris-root
or'-ta-nique
orth'-ian
or'-thi-con
or'-tho-centre
ortho-cephal'ic
ortho-ceph'-aly
ortho-chrom-at'ic
or'-tho-clase
ortho-di'agraph
or-tho-don'tia
or-tho-don'-tic
or-tho-don'-tist
or'-tho-dox
or-tho-doxy
or-tho-drom'ic
or-thod'-romy
ortho-ep'ic
ortho-ep'i-cally
or-tho'epist
or-tho'epy
or-tho-for'-mic
ortho-gen'-esis
or-thog'na-thous
or'-tho-gon
or-thog'-onal
or'-tho-graph
or-thog'ra-pher
ortho-graph'ic
or-thog'ra-phy
or-thom'-etry
or-tho-paed'ic
or-tho-paed'ist
ortho-paed'y
or-tho-pho'ria
or-thop-ne'a
or-thop'-ter-al
or-thop'-ter-ous
254

or-thop'-tics
or-tho-scop'ic
or-thos'-tichy
ortho-trop'ic
or-thot'ro-pism
or-thot'ro-pous
or'-tolan
oryc-tog'-nosy
oryc-tol'ogy
o'sa-zone
os'-cil-late
os-cil-la'tion
os'-cil-lator
os'-cil-lat-ory
os-cil'la-tron
os-cil'lo-gram
os-cil'lo-graph
os-cil'lom'eter
os-cil'lo-scope
os'-ci-tancy
os'-ci-tant
os'-ci-tate
os-ci-ta'tion
os'-cu-lant
os'-cu-lar
os'-cu-late
os-cu-la'tion
os'-cu-lat-ory
os'-cule
os'-cu-lum
os'-mate
os'-mi-ate
os'-mic
os-mi-dro'sis
os'-mious
os-mir-id'ium
os'-mium
os-mom'eter

os'-mo-metric
os-mom'-etry
os'-mose
os-mo'sis
os-mot'ic
os'-mous
os'-prey
oss'-eous
os-set'er
oss'-icle
oss-ic'u-lar
oss-if'er-ous
ossi-fi-ca'tion
oss'i-fied
oss-if'-raga
oss'i-frage
oss'-ify
oss'-ify-ing
oss-iv'or-ous
os'su-ary
os'-teal
oste-ec'tomy
oste-it'ic
oste-i'tis
os-tend'
os-ten'-sible
os-ten'-sibly
os-ten'-sive
os-ten'-sively
os-ten-ta'tion
os-ten-ta'tious
os-ten-ta'tiously
os'-teo-ar-
thri'tis
os'-teo-blast
os-teo-chon-
dri'tis
os-te-oc'-la-sis

os'-teo-clast
os-teo-der'-mal
osteo-gen'-esis
osteo-gen-et'ic
os-te-og'en-ous
os'-te-og'eny
os-te-og'ra-phy
os-te-ol'o-gist
os-te-ol'ogy
os-te-o'ma
os-teo-ma-la'cia
os-te-o'ma-tous
os-te-om'-etry
osteo-myel-i'tis
os'-teo-path
os-teo-path'ic
os-te-op'a-thy
os'-teo-phyte
os-teo-phyt'ic
os-teo-plas'-tic
os'-teo-plasty
os-te-ot'omy
os'-ti-ary
os'-ti-ate
os'-tio-late
os'-ti-ole
os'-tium
os-to'sis
os-tra'cean
os-tra'ceous
os'-tra-cise
os'-tra-cis-ing
os'-tra-cism
os'-tra-cod
os'-treicul-ture
os'-trich
otal'-gia
o'theo-scope

oth'er-wise
oto-laryn-go-
  log'i-cal
oto-lar-yn-
  gol'ogy
ot'o-lith
oto-log'ic
otol'-ogist
otol'-ogy
o'to-scope
oto-scop'ic
otos'-copy
ot'-to-man
ot'-trel-ite
our-self'
our-sel'ves
out-bal'-ance
out-bid'
out'-board
out'-bound
out'-break
out'-build
out'-build-ing
out'-burst
out'-cast
out-class'
out-class'ed
out'-come
out'-crop
out'-crop-ping
out'-cry
out-da'ted
out'-did
out-dis'-tance
out-do'
out-don'e
out'-door
out-doors'

out'-er-most
out-fa'ce
out'-fall
out'-field
out'-fielder
out'-fit
out'-fit-ter
out-flank'
out'-flow
out-gen'-eral
out'-go
out'-go-ing
out-grew'
out-grow'
out'-growth
out'-house
out'-ing
out'-land
out'-lander
out-land'-ish
out-last'
out'-law
out'-lawry
out'-lay
out'-let
out'-lier
out-liv'e
out'-look
out-ly-ing
out-man-oeuv're
out'-moded
out-num'-ber
out'-patient
out-play'
out'-point
out'-port
out'-post
out'-pour

255

OUTPOURING

out'-pour-ing
out'-put
out'-rage
out-ra'ge-ous
out-ra'ge-ously
out'-rager
out-ran'
out-ra'nge
out-rank'
out'-reach
out'-rider
out'-rigged
out'-rig-ger
out'-right
out-root'
out-run'
out'-run-ner
out-sail'
out-sell'
out'-set
out-shi'ne
out-shon'e
out-si'de
out-si'der
out-sit'
out'-size
out'-skirts
out-smart'
out-soar'
out'-span
out-speak'
out-spo'ken
out'-spread
out-stand'
out-stand'-ing
out-stay'
out-stretch'
out-stretch'ed
256

out-strip'
out-stripp'ed
out'-ward
out'-wardly
out-wear'
out-weigh'
out-wit'
out'-with
out-wit'-ted
out'-work
out-wo'rn
oval'i-form
oval'-ity
ovari-ec'tomy
ova'ri-ole
ovari-ot'omy
ova'ri-ous
ovar-i'tis
ov'en-ware
over-act'
over-ac-tiv'ity
o'ver-all
o'ver-arm
over-aw'e
over-bal'-ance
over-bear'
over-bear'-ing
over-bid'
over-blown'
o'ver-board
over-bo'ld
over-bo're
over-bo'rne
over-build'
over-bur'-den
over-ca'me
over-cap'i-tal-
                ise

o'ver-cast
over-char'ge
over-cloud'
o'ver-coat
over-com'e
over-crowd'
over-did'
over-do'
over-don'e
o'ver-dose
o'ver-draft
over-draw'
over-drawn'
over-dress'
o'ver-drive
over-due'
over-eat'
over-es'ti-mate
over-fed'
over-feed'
o'ver-flow
over-grow'
over-grown'
o'ver-growth
o'ver-hand
over-hang'
over-haul'
o'ver-head
over-hear'
over-hung'
over-joy'
over-joy'ed
o'ver-laid
o'ver-land
o'ver-lander
o'ver-lap
over-lap'-ping
o'ver-lay

over-leaf'
over-load'
over-look'
o'ver-lord
o'ver-mantle
over-match'
o'ver-much
over-ni'ght
over-pass'
over-pay'
over-play'
o'ver-plus
over-popu-la'tion
over-pow'er
over-pro-duc'tion
over-proof'
over-ran'
over-ra'te
over-reach'
over-ri'de
over-ru'le
over-run'
over-seas'
over-see'
o'ver-seer
over-set'
over-shad'ow
o'ver-shoe
over-shoot'
over-shot'
o'ver-sight
over-si'ze
over-sleep'
over-slept'
over-spread'
over-sta'te
over-stay'
over-step'

over-stock'
o'ver-stuffed
over-sup-ply'
over-ta'ke
over-ta'ken
over-task'
over-tax'
over-threw'
over-throw'
over-thrown'
o'ver-time
over-ti'red
o'ver-tone
o'ver-took'
over-top'
over-tra'de
o'ver-ture
over-turn'
o'ver-wear
over-wear'y
over-ween'-ing
o'ver-weight
over-whelm'
over-whelm'-ing
over-whelm'-ingly
over-work'
over-work'ed
over-wrought'
ovi-ci'dal
o'vi-cide
o'vi-duct
ovif'-er-ous
ovig'er-ous
ovi-na'tion
ovip'-ara
ovi-par'-ity
ovip'ar-ous

ovi-pos'it
ovi-pos'i-tor
o'vi-sac
ovo-vi-vip'ar-ous
o'vu-lar
o'vu-late
ovu-la'tion
ovu-lif'er-ous
ow'-ing
owl'-et
owl'-ish
own'-er-ship
ox'a-late
ox-al'ic
ox'a-lis
oxa-lu'ric
ox'a-lyl
ox-am'ic
ox-am'ide
ox-am'i-dine
ox'a-zine
ox'-bow
ox'-cart
ox'-heart
ox'i-dant
ox'i-dase
ox'i-date
oxi-da'tion
ox'i-dat-ive
ox'-ide
oxi-dim'-etry
ox'i-dis-able
oxi-dis-a'tion
ox'i-dise
ox'i-diser
ox-id'u-lated
oxim'-eter
oxi-met'ric

ox-in-'dole
ox'-lip
ox-o'nium
ox'-tail
ox'-tongue
oxya-can'-thine
oxya-can'-thous
oxy-acet'y-lene
oxy-dac'-tyl-ous
oxy'-gen
ox'y-gen-ate
oxy-gen-a'tion
oxy-gen'ic
ox'y-gen-ise
oxy-haemo-glo'bin
ox'y-mel
oxy-mo'ron
ox-yn'tic
oxy-rhinc'us
oxy-sul'-phide
oxy-tetra-
    cy'cline
oxy-to'cic
oxy-to'cin
ox'y-tone
oys'-ter
oys'-ter-man
oys'-ter-rake
oys'-ter-shell
ozo-ke'rite
o'zon-ate
o'zon-ide
ozon-if'er-ous
ozon-is-a'tion
o'zon-is-er
ozon-ol'y-sis
ozon-om'eter
ozo'no-sphere
258

o'zon-ous
o'zo-type

P

pab'u-lar
pab'u-lous
pab'u-lum
pa'ce-maker
pachy-dac'-tyl
pach'y-derm
pachy-der'-mal
pachy-der'-ma-
    tous
pachy-der'-mia
pachy-der'-mic
pachy-der'-mous
pach'y-tene
pac'i-fi-able
pa-cif'ic
pa-cif'i-cal
pa-cif'i-cally
pa-cif'i-cate
paci-fi-ca'tion
pa-cif'i-cator
pa-cif'i-cat-ory
pac'i-fied
pac'i-fier
pac'i-fism
pac'i-fist
paci-fis'tic
pac'i-fy-ing
pack'-age
pack'-ager
pack'-ag-ing
pack'-horse
pack'-ing

pack'-ing-house
pack'-man
pack'-sack
pack'-saddle
pack'-thread
pac'-tion
pad'-ding
pad'dle-box
pad'dle-fish
pad'-dler
pad'-dling
pad'-dock
pad'-lock
pad'ua-soy
paed'-er-asty
paedo-gen'-esis
pa'gan-ish
pa'gan-ism
pa'gan-ise
pa'gi-nal
pa'gi-nate
pagi-na'tion
pa-go'da
pag'o-dite
pag-u-u'rian
pail'-ful
pain'-ful
pain'-fully
pain'-less
pain'-lessly
pains'-tak-ing
paint'-brush
paint'-ing
paint'-work
pal'-ace
pal'a-din
palae-eth-
    nol'ogy

palae-og'ra-pher
palaeo-graph'ic
palae-og'ra-phist
palae-og'ra-phy
pal'aeo-lith
palaeo-lith'ic
palae-og'-ologist
palae-og'ology
palae-on-tol'-
      ogist
palae-on-tol'ogy
pal'aeo-type
palaeo-typ'ic
palaeo-zo'ic
pal-ag'o-nite
pal'-ama
palan-quin'
pal-at-abil'ity
pal'-at-able
pal'a-tal
pala-tal-is-
      a'tion
pal'a-tal-ise
pal'-ate
pa-la'tial
pa-lat'-in-ate
pal'a-tine
pala-to-ple'gia
pal-av'er
pa'le-face
pa'le-ness
pal-es'tra
pal'-ette
pal'-frey
pal-il'-logy
pal'-imp-sest
pal'-in-drome
pal-in-drom'ic

pal-in-gen'-esis
pal-in-gen'-es-
        ist
pal-in-gen-et'ic
pal-in-gen-et'i-
        cal
pal'i-node
pali-sa'de
pali-san'-der
pal-la'dian
pal-la'din-ised
pal-la'dium
pal'-la-site
pall'-bearer
pal-lesc'ence
pal-lesc'ent
pal'-let
pal-lett'e
pal'-lial
pal'-li-asse
pal'-li-ate
pal'-li-at-ing
pal'-li-ation
pal'-li-ative
pal'-li-ator
pal'-li-atory
pal'-lid
pal'-lium
pal'-lor
pal-ma'ceous
pal'-mar
pal-ma'rian
pal'-mary
pal'-mate
pal-mat'i-fid
pal'-ma-tine
pal-ma'tion
pal'-melt

palm'-ery
pal-met'to
pal-mi-fi-ca'tion
pal'-mi-grade
pal'-mi-ped
palm'-ist
palm'-is-try
pal'-mi-tate
pal-mit'ic
pal'-mi-tin
pal-mu'la
pal-my'ra
palo-mi'no
pal-pa-bil'ity
pal'-pable
pal'-pably
pal'-pate
pal-pa'tion
pal'-pebral
pal-pif'er-ous
pal-pig'er-ous
pal'-pi-tant
pal'-pi-tate
pal'-pi-tat-ing
pal-pi-ta'tion
pal'-pu-lus
pal'-pus
pal'tri-ness
pal'u-dal
palu-dic'o-lous
pal'u-dine
pal-u'di-nous
pal'u-dism
pal'u-dose
pal'u-dous
pal'u-drine
pal-us'-tral
pal-us'-trian

259

pal-us'-trine
paly-nol'ogy
pam'a-quine
pam'-pas
pam-pe'an
pam-pe'ro
pam'-phlet
pam-phlet-eer'
pamph'-let-ise
pana-ce'a
pa-na'da
pan'-ary
pana-tel'a
pan'a-trope
pan'-cake
pan-car-di'tis
pan'-cheon
pan-chro-mat'ic
pan-crat'ic
pan-cra'tium
pan'-creas
pan-crea-tec'-
       tomy
pan-cre-at'ic
pan'-crea-tin
pan-crea-ti'tis
pan-crea-tot'omy
pan-da'tion
pan'-dect
pan-de'mia
pan-dem'ic
pan-de-mo'niac
pan-de-mo'nium
pan'-der
pan-der'-mite
pan-dicu-la'tion
pan-do-mon'ic
260

pan'-dore
pan-do're
pan'-dow'dy
pan'-du-rate
pan-du'ri-form
pan-eg'o-ism
pan-egyr'ic
pan-egyr'i-cal
pan'-egyr-ise
pan-egyr'-ist
pan'-elled
pan'-el-ling
pan'-el-ist
pan-gam'ic
pan-gen-et'ic
pang'o-lin
pan'-handle
pan'-hand-ling
pan'-icked
pan'-ick-ing
pan'-icle
pan-ic'u-late
pani-fi-ca'tion
pan-jan'-drum
pan'-lo-gism
pan-mix'ia
pan-na'de
pan'-nage
pan-nicu-li'tis
pan'-nier
pan'-ni-form
pan'-ni-kin
pan'-ning
pan'-nose
pano-is'tic
pan'-oply
pan-op'-ti-con
pan-or-am'a

pan-or-am'ic
pan'o-trope
pan-phar'-ma-
          con
pan'-sies
pan-soph'ic
pan'-soph-ism
pan'-sophy
pan-sper-mat'ic
pan-sper'ma-
          tism
pan-tag'-amy
pan-ta-lets'
pan-ta-loon'
pan-tech'-ni-con
pan'-the-ism
pan'-the-ist
pan-the-is'tic
pan-the-ol'-ogist
pan-the-ol'ogy
pan'-ther
pan'-ther-ine
pan'-tile
panti-soc'-racy
pan'-to-graph
pan-to-graph'er
pan'-to-graph'ic
pan-tog'ra-phy
pan-to-log'ic
pan-tol'ogy
pan-tom'eter
pan'-to-mime
pan-to-mim'ic
pan-to-mor'-phic
pan'-ton
pan-toph'a-gist
pan-toph'a-gous
pan-toph'agy

pan'-to-scope
pan-to-scop'ic
pan-to-then'ic
pan'-tries
pan'-try
pan-ur'gic
pan'-zer
pa-paver-a'ceous
pa-pav'er-ine
pa-pav'er-ous
pa'per-back
pa'per-board
pa'per-boy
pa'per-chase
pa'per-cut-ter
pa'per-hanger
pa'per-knife
pa'per-like
pa'per-weight
pa'per-work
pa-pili-on-
 a'ceous
pa-pil'la
pap'-il-lary
pap'-il-late
pap-il-lif'er-ous
pap-il-li'tis
pap-il-lo'ma
pap-il-lo-ma-
 to'sis
pap-il-lom'a-tous
pap'-il-lose
papil-os'ity
pa-poos'e
pap'-pose
pap'-rika
pap'u-lar
papu-la'tion

pap'-ule
pap'u-lose
pap'u-lous
papyr-a'ceous
pa-py'rine
papyr-og'ra-phy
papyr-ol'-ogist
papyr-ol'ogy
pa-py'ro-type
pa-py'rus
para-ba'sic
par-ab'a-sis
para-be'ma
para-bio'sis
para-biot'ic
par'-able
para-blep'-sis
para-blep'-tic
par-ab'-ola
para-bol'ic
para-bol'i-cal
par-ab'-olise
par-ab'-olist
par-ab'-oloid
par-ab-oloid'al
para-cen-te'sis
par'a-chor
par'a-chor-dal
par-ach'-ron-ism
par'a-chute
par'a-chut-ist
par'a-clete
par-ac'me
par'a-coele
para-cros'-tic
para-cu'sis
par-a'de
par-a'der

par'a-digm
para-dig-mat'ic
par-a'd-ing
para-dis-a'ic
par'a-dise
para-dis'-ean
para-dis'-iac
para-dis'ia-cal
para-dis'-ial
para-dis'-ian
par'a-dos
par'a-dox
para-dox'i-cal
para-dox'ure
par'a-doxy
par-aes-the'sia
par'af-fin
paraf-fin'ic
para-gen'-esis
par-ag'-na-thous
par-ag-no'sis
para-go'ge
para-gog'ic
par'a-gon
par-ag'-on-ite
par'a-gram
para-gram'-ma-
 tist
par'a-graph
par'a-grapher
para-graph'ia
para-graph'ic
para-graph'i-
 cally
par'a-graph-ist
para-helio-
 trop'ic
par'a-keet

261

PARALDEHYDE

par-al'-dehyde
para-leip'-sis
para-lex'ia
par-al-lac'-tic
par'-al-lax
par'-al-lel
par'-al-leled
par-al-lel-
      epi'ped
par-al-lel-epip'-
      edal
par'-al-lel-ing
par'-al-lel-ism
par-al-lel'o-gram
par-al-lel-
      om'eter
par-al'-ogise
par-al'-ogism
par-al'-ogy
para-lys-a'tion
par'a-lyse
par'a-lysed
par'a-lyser
par'a-lys-ing
par-al'-ysis
para-lyt'ic
para-mag-net'ic
para-mag'-net-
      ism
para-mat'ta
para-me'cium
para-am'eter
para-met'ric
par-am-ne'sia
par'a-morph
para-mor'-phic
para-morph'-ism
par'a-mount

par'a-mour
para-myo-sin'-
      ogen
para-neph'-ric
para-neph'-ros
par'-ang
para-nitro-an'il-
      ine
para-noi'a
para-noi'ac
par'a-noid
par-a-noid'al
par-an-the'lion
par'a-pet
par'a-peted
par'-aph
par'a-phase
para-pha'sia
para-pha'sic
para-pher-na'lia
para-pho'nia
par'a-phrase
par'a-phraser
par'a-phras-ing
par-aph'ra-sis
par'a-phrast
para-phras'-tic
para-phrax'ia
para-phre'nia
par-aph'y-sis
para-ple'gia
para-ple'gic
para-ros-an'il-
      ine
par-ar'-thria
par'a-sang
par'a-sceve
para-sel-e'ne

par'a-site
para-sit'ic
para-sit'i-cal
para-siti-ci'dal
para-sit'i-cide
par'a-sit-ise
par'a-sit-ism
par'a-sit-oid
para-sito-log'ic
para-sit-ol'-
      ogist
para-sit-ol'ogy
para-sit-o'sis
par'a-sol
para-syn'-thesis
para-syn-thet'ic
para-syn'-theton
para-tac'-tic
para-tax'is
par-ath'-esis
para-thi'on
para-thy'roid
para-ton'ic
par'a-trooper
par'a-troops
para-ty'phoid
par'a-vane
par-ax'ial
par'-boil
par'-buckle
par'-cel
par'-celled
par'-cel-ling
par'-cel-post
par'-cen-age
par'-cen-ary
par'-cener
parch'-ment

parch'-men-tis-
      ing
par'-close
par'-don
par'-don-able
par'-doner
par-egor'ic
par-egor'i-cal
par-en-ceph'a-
      lon
pa'rent-age
par-en'tal
par-en'teral
par-enth'-eses
par-enth'-esis
par-enth'-esise
par-en-thet'ic
par-en-thet'i-cal
par-en-thet'i-
      cally
pa'rent-hood
par-en'ti-cide
par-er'ga
par-er'gon
par'-esis
par-esthe'sia
par-et'ic
par'-ga-site
par'-get
par'-geter
par'-get-ing
par-he'lion
par-i'etal
pari-mu'tuel
par'-ish
par-ish'ioner

par'i-son
pari-syl-lab'ic
par'-ity
park'-way
par'-lance
par'-lay
par'-ley
par'-lia-ment
par-lia-men-
      ta'rian
par-lia-men'-tary
par-lour
par'-lous
par-oc-cip'i-tal
par-o'chial
par-o'chial-ism
par-ochial'-ity
par'-odied
par'-odist
par-odis'tic
par'-ody
par'-ody-ing
par-oem'ia
par-oemi-og'ra-
      pher
par-oemi-og'ra-
      phy
par-oemi-ol'ogy
par-o'le
par-o'led
par-olee'
par-o'l-ing
par-ono-ma'sia
par-ono-mas'tic
par'-onym
par-on'y-mous
par-os'mia

par-ot'ic
par-ot'id
par-otid-ec'-
      tomy
par-otit'ic
par-oti'tis
par'-ox-ysm
par-ox-ys'mal
par-ox'y-tone
par'-pen
par-quet'
par'-quetry
par'-ra-keet
par'-ral
par-ri-ci'dal
par'-ri-cide
par'-ried
par'-rot
par'-ry-ing
par'-sec
par-si-mo'ni-ous
par'-si-mony
pars'-ing
par'-snip
par'-son
par-son-age
par-ta'ke
par-ta'ken
par-terr'e
par-theno-gen'-
      esis
par-theno-gen-
      et'ic
par'-tial
par-tial'-ity
par'-tially
parti-bil'ity
part'-ible

263

PARTICIPANT

par-tic'i-pant
par-tic'i-pate
par-tici-pa'tion
par-tic'i-pator
parti-cip'ial
par'ti-ciple
par'-ticle
par-tic'u-lar
par-tic'u-lar-ism
par-ticu-lar'ity
par-tic'u-lar-ise
par-tic'u-larly
par-tic'u-late
par'-ties
part'-ing
par'-ti-san
par'-ti-san-ship
par'-tite
par-tit'ion
par-tit'ioner
par-tit'ion-ing
par-tit'ion-ist
par'-ti-tive
par-ti-tu'ra
part'-ner
part'-ner-ship
par-took'
par'-tridge
par-tu'ri-ent
par-tur-it'ion
par-va-nim'ity
par'-venu
par-vi-fo'li-ate
par'-vis
pas'-chal
pas'-cual
pash'a-lik
pasi-graph'ic
264

pa-sig'ra-phy
pas-quin-a'de
pass'-able
pass'-ably
pass'-age
pass'-age-way
pass'-book
pass'-en-ger
pass'-er-ine
pass'-ible
pas'si-meter
pass'-ing
pas'sion-ate
pas'sion-ately
pas'sion-less
pass'i-vate
pass'-ive
pass'-ively
pass'-ive-ness
pass'-iv-ism
pass'-iv-ist
pass-iv'ity
pass'-key
pass'-port
pass'-word
pa'ste-board
pas'-tel
pas'-tern
pas-teur-is-
         a'tion
pas'-teur-ise
pas'-teur-isor
pas-ti'che
pas'-tille
pas'-time
pa'sti-ness
pas'-tor
pas'-tor-age

pas'-toral
pas-toral'e
pas'-tor-al-ise
pas'-tor-al-ism
pas'-tor-al-ist
pas'-tor-ate
pas'-tor-ship
pas-tra'mi
pa'stry-cook
pas'-tur-able
pas'-tur-age
pas'-ture
pata-gi'um
pat'a-mar
pat'-and
patch'-able
patch'-ery
patch'-ily
patch'i-ness
patch'-work
pa-tel'la
pa-tel'-late
pa-tel'-li-form
patent-abil'ity
pa'tent-able
pat'-era
pa-ter'nal
pa-ter'nal-ism
pa-ternal-is'tic
pa-tern'-ally
pa-ter'nity
pa-thet'ic
pa-thet'i-cally
path'-finder
path'-less
path'o-gen
patho-gen'-esis
patho-gen-et'ic

patho-gen'ic	pa-tro'l-man	peac'e-able
patho-gen-ic'ity	patro-mor'-phic	peac'e-ably
path-og'eny	pat'ron-age	peac'e-ful
path-og-no-mon'ic	pa'tron-ess	peac'e-fully
path-og'-nomy	pat'-ron-iser	peac'e-ful-ness
patho-log'ic	pat'-ron-is-ing	peac'e-maker
patho-log'i-cal	patro-nym'ic	peac'e-time
path-ol'-ogist	patro-nym'i-cally	pea'-cock
path-ol'-ogy	pa-troon'	pea'-hen
patho-pho'bia	pat'-ten	pea'-nut
pa-tho'sis	pat'-ter	pearl-esc'ent
path'-way	pat'-tern	pearl'i-ness
pat'-ible	pat'-terned	pearl'-ite
pa-tib'u-lary	pat'-tern-maker	pear'-main
pat'-ina	pat'-ting	pea'-vey
pat'i-nate	pat'u-lin	peat'-crete
pati-na'tion	pat'u-lous	peb'-bling
pa'tri-arch	paul'-dron	peb'-bly
patri-ar'-chal	paunch'i-ness	pecca-bil'ity
pa'tri-arch-ate	pauper-is-a'tion	pec'-cable
pa'tri-archy	paup'er-ise	pecca-dil'lo
pa-tric'ian	paup'er-ism	pecca-dil'-loes
pa-tric'iate	pauro-meta-bol'ic	pec'-cancy
patri-ci'dal	paus'-ing	pec'-cant
pat'ri-cide	pa-van'	pec'-cary
patri-lin'-eal	pa've-ment	peck'-ing
patri-lo'cal	pav-il'ion	pec'-tase
patri-mo'nial	pav'-on-ine	pec'-tate
pat'ri-mony	pawn'-broker	pec'-ten
patri-ot'ic	pawn'-brok-ing	pec'-tic
patri-ot'i-cally	pawn'-shop	pec'-tin
pa'tri-ot-ism	pay'-able	pec-tin-a'ceous
pa-tris'-tic	pay'-day	pec'-ti-nal
patro-clin'ic	pay'-ing	pec'-ti-nate
pa-tro'l	pay'-master	pec-tin-a'tion
pa-tro'lled	pay'-ment	pec-tin'-eal
pa-tro'l-ler	pay-o'la	pec-tis-a'tion
pa-tro'l-ling	pay'-roll	pec'-tise

pec'-tol-ite
pec-to-lyt'ic
pec'-toral
pec-tor-il'-oquy
pec'-tose
pec'-tous
pec'-tus
pec'u-late
pec'u-lat-ing
pecu-la'tion
pec'u-lator
pecu'-lium
pecu'ni-arily
pecu'ni-ary
peda-gog'ic
peda-gog'i-cal
ped'a-gogue
ped'a-goguery
ped'a-gogy
ped'-alled
ped'-al-ler
ped'-al-ling
ped'-ant
ped-an'tic
ped-an'ti-cally
ped-an'ti-cism
ped-an-toc'-racy
ped'-an-try
ped'-ate
ped'-dler
ped'-dlery
ped'-dling
ped'er-ast
ped'er-asty
ped'-estal
ped-es'trian
ped-es'tri-an-ism
pedi-at'ric
266

pedia-tric'ian
pedi-at'rics
ped'i-cel
ped'i-cel-late
ped'-icle
ped-ic'u-lar
ped-ic'u-late
ped-icu-lo'sis
ped-ic'u-lous
ped'i-cure
ped'i-form
ped'i-gree
ped'i-greed
ped'i-ment
ped'i-men-tal
pedi-men-ta'tion
ped'i-palp
ped'-lar
ped'-lary
ped-ol'-ocal
ped-ol'-ogist
ped-ol'ogy
ped-om'eter
pedo-met'ri-cal
ped'-rail
ped-unc'le
ped-unc'u-late
peel'-ing
peep'-hole
peer'-age
peer'-ess
peer'-less
peev'-ish
peev'-ish-ness
pee'-wit
peg'a-moid
peg'-ging
peg'-ma-tite

peg-ma-tit'ic
pei-ram'eter
pe'jor-ate
pejor-a'tion
pe'jor-at-ive
pel'-age
pel-ag'ic
pel ar-gon'ic
pel-ar-go'nium
pel-ar-gop'-sis
pel'-er-ine
pel'i-can
pel-la'gra
pel-la'grous
pel'-let
pel'-licle
pel-lic'u-lar
pel'-li-tory
pel-lu'cid
pel-lu-cid'ity
pel-mat'ic
pel'-met
pel'o-phile
pel-o'ria
pel-or'ic
pel'-or-ised
pel'-or-ism
pel-o'rus
pel'-ory
pel-o'ta
pel'-tast
pel'-tate
pelo-ther'apy
pel'-vic
pel-vi-form
pel-vim'-eter
pel-vim'-etry
pel'-vis

pem'-mi-can
pem'-phi-gus
penal-is-a'tion
pe'nal-ise
pe'nal-is-ing
pen'-al-ties
pen'-alty
pen'-ance
pen-an'nu-lar
pen-cat'-ite
pen'-cil
pen'-cilled
pen'-cil-ling
pen'-cil-ler
pen'-dant
pen'-dency
pen'-dent
pen-den'-tive
pen'-dicle
pend'-ing
pen-drag'on
pen'-du-lar
pen'-du-late
pen'-du-line
pen-du-los'ity
pen'-du-lous
pen'-du-lum
pen'-eplain
pen-eplan-a'tion
pen-etra-bil'ity
pen'-etrable
pen-etra'lia
pen-etram'-eter
pen'-etrance
pen'-etrate
pcn'-etrat-ing
pen-etra'tion
pen'-etrat-ive

pen'-etrator
pen'-etrom'-eter
pen'-guin
pen'-holder
peni-cil'-late
peni-cil'-li-form
peni-cil'-lin
peni-cil'-lium
pen-in'-sula
pen-in'-su-lar
pen-in'-su-late
pen'i-stone
pen'i-tence
pen'i-tent
peni-ten'-tial
peni-ten'-tiary
pen'i-tently
pen'-knife
pen'-man
pen'-man-ship
pen-na'ceous
pen'-nant
pen'-nate
pen'-nies
pen'-ni-form
pen'-ni-less
pen'-ning
pen'-nin-ite
pen'-non
pen'ny-weight
pen'ny-wort
pen'ny-worth
peno-log'i-cal
penol'-ogist
penol'-ogy
pen'-sile
pen-sil'ity
pen'-sion

pen'-sion-able
pen'-sion-ary
pen'-sioner
pen'-sive
pen'-sively
pen'-stock
pen'-ta-chord
pen'-tacle
pent'-act
pent-ac'-tinal
pen'-tad
penta-dac'-tyl-
　　　　ous
pen'-ta-glot
pen-tag'-noid
pen'-ta-gon
pen-tag'-onal
pen-tag'-on-ally
pen'-ta-gram
pen-ta-he'dral
pen-ta-he'dron
pen-ta-hy'drite
pen'-ta-mer
pen-tam'er-ous
pen-tam'-eter
pen'-tane
pent-an'gu-lar
penta-pet'al-ous
pen'-ta-ploid
pen-tap'-ody
pen'-tar-chy
pen'-ta-style
penta-syl-lab'ic
pen-tath'-lon
penta-tom'ic
penta-ton'ic
penta-va'lent
pen'-tene

PENTETERIC

pent-eter'ic
pent'-house
pent'-land-ite
pen'to-bar-bi-tal
pen'-tode
pen-tom'ic
pen'-to-san
pen'-tose
pent-ox'-ide
pent'-roof
pen'-tryl
pen'tu-lose
pen'-tyl
pen'-tyl-ene
pen-ult'
pen-ul'-ti-mate
pen-um'-bra
pen-um'-brae
pen-u'ri-ous
pen'-ury
pen'-written
pe'on-age
pep-er-i'no
pep-i'no
pep'-los
pep'-lum
pep'-per
pep'-per-box
pep'-per-corn
pep'-per-mint
pep'-pery
pep'-sin
pep-sin'-ogen
pep'-tic
pep'-ti-dase
pep'-tide
pep-tis-a'tion
pep'-tise
268

pep'to-nate
pep'-tone
pep-ton-is-a'tion
pep'-ton-ise
per-acu'te
per-ad-ven'-ture
per-am'-bu-late
per-am'-bu-lat-ing
per-am-bu-la'tion
per-am'-bu-lator
per-am'-bu-lat-ory
per-bo'rate
per-cal'e
per'-ca-line
per-ceiv'-able
per-ceiv'-ably
per-ceiv'e
per-cent'-age
per-cen'-tal
per-cen'-tile
per'-cept
per-cep-ti-bil'ity
per-cep'-tible
per-cep'-tibly
per-cep'-tion
per-cep'-tive
per-cep-tiv'ity
per-cep'-tual
per-chan'ce
per'-cheron
per-chlo'r-ate
per-chlo'ric
per-chro'm-ate
per'-ci-form
per'-cine

per-cip'i-ence
per-cip'i-ency
per-cip'i-ent
per'-coid
per-coid'ean
per'-co-late
per-co-la'tion
per'-co-lator
per-cur'-rent
per-cur'-sory
per-cuss'
per-cuss'-ant
per-cus'sion
per-cuss'-ive
per-cu-ta'neous
per-cu'tient
per-den'do
per-dit'ion
per-dura-bil'ity
per-du'r-able
per-du'r-ance
per-dur-a'tion
per'-egrin-ate
per-egrin-a'tion
per'-egrin-ator
per'-egrine
per-egrin'-ity
per-eir'a
per-eir'ine
per-emp'-tive
per-emp'-torily
per-emp'-tori-ness
per-emp'-tory
per-en'nate
per-en-na'tion
per-en'-nial
per'-fect (a.)

per-fect' (v.)
per-fect'er
per-fec-ti-bil'ity
per-fec'-tible
per-fec'-tion
per-fec'-tion-ism
per-fec'-tive
per'-fectly
per-fec'to
per-fec'-tor
per-fer'vid
per-fer-vid'ity
per-fic'ient
per-fid'i-ous
per-fid'i-ously
per-fid'i-ous-
ness
per'-fidy
per-fo'li-ate
per'-for-ate
per'-for-ated
per'-for-a'tion
per'-for-at-ive
per'-for-ator
per-fo'rce
per-form'
per-form'-able
per-form'-ance
per-form'er
per'-fume
per-fu'mer
per-fu'mery
per-func'-torily
per-func'-tori-
ness
per-func'-tory
per-fu'se
per-fu'sion

per-fu's-ive
per-ga-me'neous
per-ga-men-
ta'ceous
per'-gola
per-haps'
per'i-anth
peri-ar-thri'tis
peri-as'-tron
peri-car'-diac
peri-car'-dial
peri-car-di'tis
peri-car'-dium
per'i-carp
peri-car'-pial
peri-cen'-tral
peri-cen'-tric
peri-chon'-drium
per'i-clase
peri-cli'nal
per'i-cline
per-ic'opal
per-ic'ope
per-ic'opic
peri-cra'nial
peri-cra'nium
per'i-cycle
per'i-derm
peri-des'mium
per-id'-ium
per'i-dot
peri-do'tite
per'i-drome
peri-ege'sis
peri-ge'an
per'i-gee
peri-gen'-esis
per-ig'yn-ous

peri-he'lion
per'il-ling
per'il-ous
per'il-ously
per-im'eter
peri-met'ric
peri-met'ri-cal
per-im'etry
per'i-morph
peri-ne'al
peri-ne-or'rha-
phy
peri-neph'-rium
peri-ne'um
peri-neur'ium
per-in'-ium
per-i'odate
per-iod'ic
period'-ical
period'-ically
period-ic'ity
peri-os'-teal
peri-os'-teum
peri-os-ti'tis
peri-ot'ic
peri-pa-tet'ic
peri-petei'a
per-ip'ety
per-iph'-eral
per-iph'-er-ally
per-iph'-ery
per'i-phrase
per-iph'-ra-sis
peri-phras'-tic
per'i-plus
per-ip'-teral
per-ip'-tery
per-i'que

269

per-is′cian
per-is′cii
per′i-scope
per′i-scop′ic
per′-ish
per′-ish-able
peri-so′mal
per′i-sperm
per-iss′ad
per-iss-ol′ogy
per-is′-ta-lith
peri-stal′-sis
peri-stal′-tic
per-is′-ter-ite
per-is-ter-on′ic
per′i-stome
peri-sto′mial
peri-streph′ic
peri-sty′lar
per′i-style
peri-the′cium
peri-theli-o′ma
per-ito-ne′al
per-ito-ne′um
per-ito-nit′ic
per-ito-ni′tis
per-vis′-ceral
per′i-wig
per′i-winkle
per′-jure
per′-jurer
per′-jur-ing
per-ju′ri-ous
per′-jur-ous
per′-jury
perk′i-ness
per′-lite
per-lit′ic
270

per-lus′-trate
per-lus-tra′tion
per′-ma-frost
per′-ma-nence
per′-ma-nency
per′-ma-nent
per′-ma-nently
per-man′ga-nate
per-meabil′ity
per′-meable
per′-meameter
per′-meance
per′-meant
per′-meate
per′-mea′tion
per′-meat′ive
per-missi-bil′ity
per-miss′-ible
per-mis′sion
per-miss′-ive
per-mit′ (v. n.)
per′-mit (n.)
per-mit′-ted
per-mit-tee′
per-mit′-ting
per-mit-tiv′ity
per′-mu-table
per′-mu-tate
per′-mu-ta′tion
per′-mu-tator
per-mu′te
per′-mu-toid
per′-nancy
per-neur′al
per-nick′-ety
per-ni-o′sis
per-noc-ta′tion
pero-ne′al

per′-or-ate
per-or-a′tion
per-o′sis
per-os-to′sis
per-ox′i-dase
per-oxi-da′tion
per-ox′ide
per-ox′i-dise
per-pend′
per-pen-dic′u-lar
per′-petrate
per-petra′tion
per′-petrator
per-pet′ual
per-pet′u-ally
per-pet′u-ate
per-petu-a′tion
per-pet′u-ator
per-petu′ity
per-plex′
per-plex′ed
per-plex′-edness
per-plex′-ing
per-plex′-ity
per′-qui-site
per-qui-sit′ion
per-quis′i-tor
per′-ron
per-scru-ta′tion
per′-secute
per-secu′tion
per′-secutor
per′-secut-ory
per-se′ity
per-seve′r-ance
per-sev′-erant
per-sev′-erate
per-sev-era′tion

per-sev'-erator
per-seve're
per-seve'r-ing
per-si-ca'ria
per'-si-cot
per'-si-enne
per'-si-flage
per-sim'-mon
per-sist'
per-sist'-ence
per-sist'-ency
per-sist'-ent
per-sist'-ently
per-sist'er
per-son
per-so'na
per-son-able
per'-son-age
per'-sonal
per-son-al'ity
per'-son-al-ise
per'-son-ally
per'-son-alty
per'-son-ate
per-son-a'tion
per'-son-ator
per-soni-fi-
　　　　ca'tion
per-son'i-fier
per-son'ify
per-son'i-fy-ing
per-son-nel'
per-sorp'-tion
per-spec'-tive
per-spec'-to-
　　　　graph
per-spec-tog'ra-
　　　　phy

per-spi-ca'cious
per-spi-cac'ity
per-spi-cu'ity
per-spic'u-ous
per-spi'r-able
per'-spir-ate
per-spir-a'tion
per-spi'ra-tive
per-spir'-acy
per-spi're
per-spi'r-ing
per-sua'd-able
per-sua'de
per-sua'der
per-sua'd-ing
per-sua's-ible
per-sua'sion
per-sua's-ive
per-sua's-ively
per-sul'-phate
per-tain'
per'-thite
per-ti-na'cious
per-ti-na'ciously
per-ti-nac'ity
per'-ti-nence
per'-ti-nency
per'-ti-nent
per-turb'
per-turb'-able
per-tur-ba'tion
per-tuss'al
per-tuss'is
per-u'ke
per-u's-able
per-u'sal
per-u'se
per-u'ser

per-u's-ing
per-va'de
per-va'd-ing
per-va'sion
per-va's-ive
per-va's-ively
per'-veance
per-vers'e
per-vers'ely
per-vers'e-ness
per-ver'-sion
per-ver'-sity
per-ver'-sive
per-vert' (v.)
per'-vert (n.)
per-vert'ed
per-vert'er
per-vert'-ible
per'-vi-ate
per-vi-ca'cious
per-vi-cac'ity
per'-vi-ous
per-yg'in-ous
pes-an'te
pess'-ary
pes-si-mism
pes'si-mist
pessi-mis'tic
pessi-mis'ti-
　　　　cally
pest'-ered
pest'-house
pesti-ci'dal
pes-tif'er-ous
pes'ti-lence
pes'ti-lent
pesti-len'-tial
pest-ol'-ogist

271

pest-ol'o-gy
pet'-aled
pet-al-if'er-ous
pet'-al-ine
pet'-al-ism
pet'-al-ite
pet'a-lody
pet'-al-oid
pet'-alon
pet'-al-ous
pet-ard'
pet'a-sus
petaur'-ist
pet'-cock
pet-e'chia
pe'ter-sham
peth'i-dine
pet'io-lar
pet'io-late
pet'i-ole
pet-it'ion
pet-it'ion-ary
pet-it'ioner
pet'-rail
pet'-rel
pet-resc'ent
petri-fac'-tion
petri-fac'-tive
petri-fi-ca'tion
pet'ri-fied
pet'-rify
petro-chem'i-cal
pet-rog'eny
pet'ro-glyph
pet-rog'ly-phy
pet'-ro-graph
pet-rog'ra-pher
petro-graph'ic
272

petro-graph'i-cal
pet-rog'ra-phy
pet'-rol
pet'-rol-age
pet-rol-a'tum
pet'-rol-ene
pet-ro'leum
pet-rol'ic
pet-rol-if'er-ous
pet-rol-ise
petro-log'ic
petro-log'i-cally
pet-rol'-ogist
pet-rol'ogy
pet'-ronel
pet-ro'sal
pet'-rous
pet'-ti-coat
pet'-ti-fog
pet'-ti-fog-ger
pet'-ti-fog-gery
pet'tily
pet'-ti-ness
pet'-tish
pet'-tish-ness
pet'ti-toes
pet'u-lance
pet'u-lancy
pet'u-lant
petu'-nia
pew'-ter
pew'-terer
pfen'-nig
phac'-oid
phac-oid'al
phac'-ol-ite
phac'o-lith
phag'o-cyte

phago-cyt'ic
phago-cyto'sis
phal'-ange
phal-an'-geal
pha-lan'ger
phal-an'ges
phal-an'gid
phal'-an-stery
phal'-anx
phal'a-rope
phal'-lic
phal'-li-cism
phal'-loid
phal-loid'ine
phal'-lus
phan'-ero-gam
phan-er-og'a-mous
phan'o-tron
phan'-tasm
phan-tas'ma
phan-tas-ma-go'ria
phan-tas-ma-gor'ic
phan-tas'-mal
phan'-tom
phar-ma-ceut'ics
phar-ma-ceut'ist
phar'-ma-cist
phar-mac'o-lite
phar-ma-co-log'i-cal
phar-ma-col'-ogist
phar-ma-col'ogy
pharma-co-poe'ia

phar-ma-co-
    poe′ial
phar′-macy
phar-yn′-geal
phar-yn-git′ic
phar-yn-gi′tis
phar-yngo-log′i-
    cal
phar-yn-gol′ogy
phar-yng′o-scope
phar-yn-gos′copy
phar-yn-got′omy
phar′-ynx
pha′si-tron
phel-lan′-drene
phel′-lo-gen
phello-gen-et′ic
phel′-loid
phel-lo-plas′tic
phel-o′nion
phen-ac′etin
phen′a-cite
phen-an′threne
phen-ar′sa-zine
phen′a-zine
phen-et′i-dine
phen′-etole
phen′-gite
pheno-bar′-bi-tal
phe′no-cryst
pheno-crys′tic
phe′-nol
phe′-nol-ate
phe-nol′ic
phe-nol′-ogist
phe-nol′ogy
phenol-phthal′ein
phenom′-ena

phenom′-enal
phenom′-en-al-
    ism
phenom-eno-
    log′i-cal
phenom-en-ol′ogy
phenom′-enon
phe′no-plast
phe′no-type
pheno-typ′ic
phen-ox′ide
phe′-nyl
phenyl-acet-
    al′de-hyde
phen′y-late
phen′-yl-ene
phen-yl-eph′-rine
phenyl-eth′yl-ene
phe-nyl′ic
phenyl-keto-
    nu′ria
phi′ali-form
phil-an′-der
phil-an′-derer
phil′-an-thrope
phil-an-throp′ic
phil-an′thro-pist
phil-an′thropy
phila-tel′ic
phil-at′el-ist
phil-at′ely
phil-har-mon′ic
phil-hel-len′ic
phil-ip′pic
phil′-lip-site
phil-lu′men-ist
phil-lu′mency
philo-den′-dron

phil o-graph
phil-og′yn-ist
phil-og′yny
philo-lo′gian
philo-log′i-cal
phil-ol′-ogist
phil-ol′ogy
phil′o-math
philo-math′ic
phil-om′athy
phil′o-mel
philo-pro-gen′i-
    tive
philos′-opher
philo-soph′ic
philo-soph′i-cal
philo-soph′i-
    cally
philos′-ophise
philos′-ophiser
philos′-ophism
philos′-ophist
philos′-ophy
phleb-it′ic
phleb-i′tis
phlebo-graph′ic
phlebog′ra-phy
phleb′o-lite
phleb′o-lith
phleb-ol′ogy
phleb-ot′omy
phleg-mat′ic
phleg′-mon
phleg′-mon-ous
phlo-ba-phene
phlo-gis′-tic
phlo-gis′-ton
phlog′o-pite

273

PHLOGOSIS

phlog-o'sis
phlog-ot'ic
phlor'i-zin
phlor'i-zin-ise
phloro-glu'ci-nol
pho'-bia
pho'-bic
phobo-tax'is
pho'-cine
pho-co-me'lia
phol-id-o'sis
phon-as-the'nia
pho'-nate
pho-na'tion
phon-au'to-graph
pho-nemat'ic
pho'-neme
pho-ne'mic
pho-ne'mics
pho-nen'do-scope
pho-net'ic
pho-net'i-cally
pho-netic'ian
pho-net'i-cise
pho-net'i-cism
pho-net'i-cist
pho'-netism
pho'-netist
phoni-at'ric
phono-camp'-tic
pho'no-deik
phono-gen'ic
pho'no-gram
pho'no-graph
phono-graph'ic
pho-nog'ra-phy
pho'no-lite
phono-lit'ic

phono-log'i-cal
pho-nol'-ogise
pho-nol'-ogist
pho-nol'ogy
pho-nom'eter
pho-nom'etry
pho'no-phore
pho'no-scope
pho'no-type
phono-typ'ic
pho'no-typy
phor-e'sis
phor'-esy
phor-et'ic
pho'-rone
phos'-gene
phos'-gen-ite
phos'-pha-gene
phos'-pha-tase
phos'-phate
phos-phat'ic
phos'-pha-tide
phos'-pha-tise
phos'-phene
phos'-phide
phos-phin'ic
phos'-phite
phos-pho'nium
phos'-phor
phos'-phor-ate
phos-phor-esc'e
phos-phor-
    esc'ence
phos-phor-
    esc'ent
phos'-phoric

phos'-phor-ise
phos'-phor-ism
phos'-phor-ite
phos'-phor-ous
phos'-phorus
phos-phor'yl-ase
phos'-phuret
phos'-phur-etted
pho'-rics
photo-chem'-is-
    try
photo-chro-
    mat'ic
pho'to-chromy
photo-chron'o-
    graph
photo-elec'-tric
photo-elec'-tron
photo-elec-
    tron'ics
pho'to-en-gra'v-
    ing
pho'to-gen
pho'to-gene
photo-gen'ic
pho'to-glyph
photo-glyph'ic
pho-tog'ly-phy
photo-gram'-
    metry
pho'to-graph
pho-tog'ra-pher
photo-graph'ic
pho-tog'ra-phy
photo-gravu're
photo-kin-e'sis
photo-lith'o-
    graph

274

photo-lith-
　og'raphy
photo-log'ic
pho-tol'o-gy
pho-tol'y-sis
photo-lyt'ic
pho-tom'eter
photo-met'ric
pho-tom'-etry
photo-mi'cro-
　graph
photo-micro-
　graph'ic
photo-microg'-ra-
　pher
photo-microg'-
　ra-phy
pho'-ton
photo-nas'-tic
pho'to-nasty
pho-top'a-thy
photo-pe'riod-ism
pho-toph'il-ic
photo-toph'i-lous
photo-pho'bia
photo-pho'bic
pho'to-phone
photo-phon'ic
pho'-toph'-ony
pho'to-phore
photo-phor-e'sis
pho-top'sy
photo-recep'-tor
photo-sen'-si-
　tive
pho'to-sphere
photo-spher'ic
pho'to-stat

pho'to-stated
photo-syn'-thesis
pho-tot'-onus
pho'to-trope
pho'to-troph
photo-trop'ic
pho-tot'ro-pism
pho'to-type
pho'to-typy
phra's-able
phra'se-monger
phra'seo-gram
phra'seo-graph
phras-eog'ra-phy
phr.aseo-log'ic
phras-eol'-ogist
phras-eol'ogy
phra's-ing
phren-al'gia
phren-as-the'sia
phren-e'sis
phren-et'ic
phreni-cot'-omy
phren-i'tis
phreno-log'i-cal
phren-ol'-ogist
phren-ol'ogy
phren'o-sin
phthal'-ate
phthal'-ein
phthal'i-mide
phthalo-ni'trite
phthi'o-col
phthi-ri'asis
phthi'-sic
phthis'-ical
phthisi-ol'ogy
phthi'-sis

phy-col'ogy
phyco-myce'tous
phyl-ac-ter'ic
phyl-ac'-tery
phy-let'ic
phyl'-lite
phyl-lo-car'-pic
phyl'-loid
phyl-lo-ma'nia
phyl-loph'a-gan
phyl-loph'a-gous
phyllo-tax'is
phyl-loxe'ra
phylo-gen-et'ic
phy-log'eny
phylo-ger-on'tic
phy-lo-nean'ic
phy'-lum
phyma-to'sis
phy-sa-lite
physi-at'rics
phys'i-cal
phys-ic'ian
phys'i-cism
phys'i-cist
phys'-icked
phys'-ick-ing
phys'-ics
phys-ioc'-racy
phys'io-crat
physio-crat'ic
physi-og'eny
physi-og-nom'ic
physi-og'-nom-
　ist
physi-og'-nomy
physi-og'ra-pher
physio-graph'ic

275

physi-og'ra-phy
physi-ol'-ater
physio-log'i-cal
physi-ol'-ogist
physi-ol'ogy
physi-ol'-atry
physi-om'-etry
physio-thera-
peut'-ics
physio-ther'a-
pist
physio-ther'apy
phys-i'que
physo-stig'-mine
phy-sos'to-mous
phyto-gen'-esis
phyto-gen-et'ic
phyto-gen'ic
phy-tog'eny
phy-tog'ra-phy
phy-tol'-ogist
phy-tol'ogy
phy-ton'-omy
phy-toph'a-gous
phy-to'sis
phy-tos'-terol
phy-tot'-omy
phy'-to-tron
pi-ac'u-lar
pi'an-ism
pi'an-ist
pian-ist'e
pian-is'tic
pian'o-forte
pic'a-dor
pic'a-mar
pic-ar-es'que
pic-ar-oon'
276

pica-yu'ne
pic-ca-lil'li
picca-nin'ny
pic'-colo
pic'-colo-ist
pi'-cene
pick'a-back
pick'-axe
pick'-erel
pick'-eter
pick'-et-ing
pick'-ing
pick'-ling
pick'-lock
pick'-pocket
pic'-nic
pic'-nicked
pick'-nicker
pic'-nick-ing
pic'o-line
pico-lin'ic
pic-otee'
pic'o-tite
pic-ram'ic
pic'-rate
pic'-ric
pic'-rite
pic'-to-gram
pic'-to-graph
pic-to-graph'ic
pic-to-graph'i-
cally
pic-tog'ra-phy
pic-to'rial
pic-tor'i-cal
pic'-tur-able
pic'-tural
pic'-ture

pic-tur-es'que
pic'-tur-ing
pid'-dler
pid'-dling
pie'-bald
piec'e-meal
piec'e-work
piec'-ing
pie'-crust
pie'-man
pie'-plant
pier'-age
pierc'-ing
pier'-head
pi-er'i-dine
pi'-etism
pi-etis'tic
pi'-ety
pi-ezom'-eter
piezo-met'ric
pi-ezom'-etry
pig'eon-hole
pig'eon-toed
pig'eon-wing
pig'-gery
pig'-gish
pig'-headed
pig'-ment
pig'-men-tary
pig-men-ta'tion
pig'-nor-ate
pig-nor-a'tion
pig'-nut
pig'-pen
pig'-skin
pig'-stick-ing
pig'-sty
pig'-tail

pig'-weed
pi'ke-let
pi'ke-man
pi'ke-staff
pil-as'ter
pil'-chard
pil'-corn
pil'-crow
pi'-leate
pi'-leated
pi'-leous
pi'le-driver
pil'-fer
pil'-fer-age
pil'-grim
pil'-grim-age
pi-lif'er-ous
pil'-lage
pil'-lager
pil'-lar
pil'-lared
pill'-box
pil'-lor-ied
pil'-lor-ise
pil'-lory
pil'-low
pil'-low-case
pil'low-slip
pil'-lowy
pilo-car'-pine
pi'-lose
pi-los'ity
pi- ot-age
pi- ot-house
pil'u lar
pil'-ul
pim'-e -ate
pim en'to

pi-mi-en'to
pim'-per-nel
pim'-ply
pi-na'ceous
pin'a-coid
pina-coid'al
pin-ac'o-line
pin'a-cone
pin'a-fore
pi'-nane
pi-nas'ter
pin'a-type
pin'-ball
pin'-cers
pinch'-beck
pin'-cushion
pin'-eal
pi'ne-apple
pi'-nene
pi-ne'tum
pin'-feather
pin'-fold
pin'-head
pin'-hole
pin'-ite
pi'-ni-tol
pink'-eye
pink'-ing
pink'-ish
pink'-root
pin'-nace
pin'-nacle
pin'-nate
pin'-ni-form
pin'-ning
pin'-ni-ped
pin'-nu-late
pin'-ochle

pin'-point
pin-ta'do
pin'-tail
pin'-weed
pin'-wheel
pin'-worm
pion-eer'
pion-ee'red
pi'-os-cope
pi-os'ity
pi'-ous
pi'-ously
pi'pe-clay
pi'pe-ful
pi'pe-line
pip-er'a-zine
pip-er'ic
pip-er'i-dine
pip'-er-ine
piper'o-nyl
pi'pe-stem
pi'pe-stone
pip-ett'e
pip-is-trell'e
pip'-kin
pip'-pin
pi'-racy
pi'-rate
pi-rat'i-cal
pir'i-form
pir'-ogue
pir'ou-ette
pir'ou-etted
pir'ou-ett-ing
pis'-cary
pis'-cation
pis-ca-tol'-ogy
pis-ca'tor

pis-ca-to'rial
pis'ca-tory
pis'ci-cul-ture
pis'-ci-form
pis-ci'na
pis'-cine
pis-civ'or-**ous**
pi'si-form
pis'-mire
pis-tach'io
pis'-til
pis'-til-lar
pis'-til-lary
pis'-til-late
pis'-tol
pis'-ton
pitch'-blende
pitch'-fork
pitch'i-ness
pitch'-ing
pitch'-pipe
pitch'-stone
pit'-eous
pit'-eously
pit'-fall
pith-ecan'-
      thro-poid
pith'-ecoid
pith'-ily
pith'i-ness
pit'i-able
pit'i-ful
pit'i-fully
pit'i-less
pit'-man
pit'-tance
pit'-ted

pit'-ting
pitu'-itary
pitu'-itous
pitu'-itrin
pit'y-ing
pity-ri'asis
pit'y-roid
piv'-otal
piv'-oter
pix'i-lation
pix'i-lated
placa-bil'ity
plac'-able
plac'-ard
pla-ca'te
pla-ca'ter
pla-ca't-ing
pla-ca'tion
plac'a-tive
plac'a-tory
pla'ce-able
pla-ce'bo
pla'ce-ment
pla-cen'ta
pla-cen'tary
pla-cen'tate
pla-cen-ta'tion
pla-cen'-ti-form
pla-cen-ti'tis
pla-cid'ity
plac'i-tory
plac'i-tum
plac'o-derm
plac'-oid
pla'giar-ise
pla'giar-is-ing
pla'giar-ism
pla'giar-ist

plagiar-is'tic
pla'gi-ary
pla'gio-clase
plagio-trop'ic
plagi-ot'ro-pism
plain'-ant
plain'-ness
plains'-man
plain'-spoken
plain'-tiff
plain'-tive
plain'-tively
plan-a'rian
plan-a'tion
plan-et-a'rium
plan'-et-ary
plan-etes'i-mal
plan'-et-oid
plan-et-oid'al
plan-et-ol'ogy
plan'-gency
plan'-gent
plan'i-graph
plan-ig'ra-phy
plan-im'eter
plani-met'ric
plan-im'etry
plan'-ish
plan'i-sphere
plank'-ing
plank'-ton
plan'-ner
plan'-ning
plan'o-graph
plan-og'ra-phy
plan-om'eter
plan'-tain
plan'-tar

278

plan-ta'tion
plan'-ti-grade
plant'-ing
plas'-mic
plas'-min
plas-min'-ogen
plas-mo'dium
plas'-mo-lise
plas-mol'y-sis
plas-mo-lyt'ic
plas'-ter
plas'-tered
plas'-terer
plas'-ter-ing
plas'-ter-work
plas'-tic
plas'-ti-cise
plas'-ti-ciser
plas-tic'ity
plas'-tics
plas'-tid
plas'-ti-noid
plas-tom'eter
plas'-tron
pla-teau'
pla'te-ful
plat'-form
plat'-ina
plat'i-nate
plat-in'ic
plat'-in-ise
plat'-in-ite
plat'i-noid
plat'-in-ous
plat'i-num
plat'i-tude
plati-tudi-
na'rian

plati-tu'di-nise
plati-tu'di-nous
pla-ton'ic
pla-toon'
plat'-ter
platy-ceph'a-
lous
platy-kur'-tic
platy-kur-to'sis
plat'y-pus
plat'-yr-rhine
plat-ys'ma
plaud'i-tory
plausi-bil'ity
plaus'-ible
plaus'-ive
play'-able
play'-back
play'-bill
play'-boy
play'-fel-low
play'-ful
play'-fully
play'-ful-ness
play'-goer
play'-ground
play'-house
play'-ing-card
play'-mate
play'-room
play'-script
play'-thing
play'-time
play'-wright
plead'-able
plead'-ing
pleas'ant-ness
pleas'-ing

pleas'ur-able
pleb-e'ian
pleb-is'ci-tary
pleb'i-scite
plec-op'ter-ous
plec-tog'na-
thous
plec'-tron
plec'-trum
pledg'e-able
pledg'-ing
plei-om'er-ous
plei-ot'ro-pism
ple'-narty
ple'-nary
plen-ip'o-tence
plen-ip'o-tent
pleni-po-ten'-
tial
pleni-po-ten'-
tiary
plen'-ish
plen'i-tude
pleni-tu'di-nous
plen'-teous
plen'-ti-ful
ple'-num
ple-och'ro-ism
ple'-on-asm
ple'-on-aste
ple-on-as'tic
pler-o'ma
ple'-sio-saur
pleth'-ora
pleth-or'ic
pleur'-isy
pleur-it'ic
pleur'o-dont

pleuro-dyn'ia
pleuro-gen'ic
pleur-og'en-ous
plex'i-form
plex-im'eter
pli-abil'ity
pli'-able
pli'-ancy
pli'-ant
pli'-cate
pli-ca'tion
plic'a-ture
pli'-ers
plim'-soll
plio-saur'us
pli'o-tron
plod'-ded
plod'-der
plod'-ding
plot'-less
plot'-ter
plot'-ting
plough'-able
plough'-boy
plough'-hand
plough'-ing
plough'-man
plough'-share
pluck'-ily
plug'-board
plug'-ging
plu'-mage
plu'-mate
plum-bagin-
          a'ceous
plum-ba'go
plum'-bate
plum'-beous
280

plum'-bic
plum-bif'er-ous
plumb'-ing
plum'-bism
plum'-bite
plum'-bous
plum'-bum
plum'-mery
plu'-mi-ped
plum'-mer
plum'-met
plu'-mose
plump'-ness
plumu-la'ceous
plu'mu-lar
plu'mu-late
plu'-mule
plu'mu-lose
plun'-der
plun'-der-age
plun'-derer
plun'-der-ous
plung'-ing
plu-per'fect
plu'ral-ise
plu'ral-ism
plu'ral-ist
plu-ral'ity
plu'-rally
plu-rip'ar-ous
pluri-va'lent
plu-toc'-racy
plu'to-crat
pluto-crat'ic
plu-tol'-atry
plu-tol'ogy
plu-ton'ic
plu'-ton-ite

plu-to'nium
plu-ton'omy
plu'-vial
plu-vi-og'ra-phy
plu-vi-om'eter
pluvio-mct'ric
plu'-vi-ous
ply'-ing
ply'-wood
pneu-draul'ic
pneu-mat'ic
pneu-mat'i-cally
pneu-ma-tic'ity
pneu-ma-tol'-
          ogist
pneu-ma-tol'ogy
pneu-ma-tol'y-sis
pneu-ma-to-lyt'ic
pneu-ma-
          tom'eter
pneu-ma-to'sis
pneumo-coc'-cus
pneu-mol'ogy
pneu-mon-ec'-
          tomy
pneu-mo'nia
pneu-mon'ic
pneu-mo-ni'tis
po'-chard
pock'et-book
pock'et-ful
pock'et-knife
pock'-mark
pod-ag'ra
pod-al'gia
pod-al'gic
pod'-ding
pod-esta'

podg'i-ness
po'-dium
pod'-zol-ise
po'-esy
po'et-aster
po'et-ess
po-et'ic
poet'i-cal
poet'i-cally
po-et'ics
po'et-ise
po'-etry
pog'-rom
poign'-ancy
poign'-ant
poi-ki-lit'ic
poi-kil'o-cyte
poin-ci-an'a
poin-set'-tia
point'-edly
point'-less
pois'-ing
pois'on-ous
po'k-ing
pol-ac'ca
polar-im'eter
polari-met'ric
polar-is-a'tion
polar'i-scope
po'lar-ise
po'lar-iser
po'lar-is-ing
po-lar'ity
polar'o-gram
polar'o-graph
polaro-graph'ic
polar-og'ra-phy
po'lar-oid

po'la-touche
po'le-axe
po'le-cat
pol-em'ic
pol-em'i-cal
pol-em'i-cally
pol'-em-ist
pol-en'ta
po'le-star
po'-lia-nite
poli'ce-man
pol'i-cies
poli-clin'ic
pol'-icy
pol'-icy-ho-lder
po'-lio
po-lio-myel-i'tis
pol'-ish
pol'-isher
pol-i'te
pol-i'tely
pol-i'te-ness
pol'i-tic
pol-it'i-cal
pol-it'i-cally
poli-tic'ian
pol-it'i-cise
pol'i-tics
pol'-ity
pol'-lack
pol'-lan
pol'-lard
pol'-len
pol'-len-ise
pol'-len-iser
pol'-li-nate
pol'-li-nat-ing
pol-li-na'tion

pol-li-nif'er-ous
pol-lin'-ium
pol-li-no'sis
pol'-li-wog
poll'-ster
pol-lu'cite
po-llu'tant
po-llu'te
po-llu'ter
pol-lu't-ing
pol-lu'tion
po'lo-ist
pol'-on-aise
po-lo'nium
pol'-ter-geist
pol-troon'
poly-acryl'ic
poly-am'-ide
poly-an'-drous
pol'y-an-dry
poly-an'-thus
pol'y-archy
poly-ar'gyr-ite
poly-ba'sic
poly-ba'site
pol'y-chro-ism
poly-chro-mat'ic
pol'y-chrome
pol'y-chromy
poly-clin'ic
pol'y-crase
poly-cy-the'mia
poly-dac'-tyl
poly-dip'-sia
pol'y-ene
pol'y-esrer
poly-eth'yl-ene
poly-gam'ic

281

pol·yg′a·mist
pol·yg′a·mous
pol·yg′-amy
poly-gen′-esis
poly-gen-et′ic
poly-gen′ic
pol·yg′en-ous
pol·y-glot′-tal
pol′y-gon
pol·yg′-onal
pol′y-graph
poly-graph′ic
pol·yg′ra-phy
pol·yg′yn-ous
pol·yg′yny
poly-he′dral
poly-he′dron
poly-his′-tor
poly-hy′dric
poly-hydrox′y
poly-iso-bu′tyl-
   ene
pol′y-math
pol·ym′-athy
poly′-mer
pol-ym-er′ic
pol-ym-eris-
   a′tion
pol-ym′-erise
pol-ym′-eriser
pol-ym′-erism
pol-ym′-erous
pol′ym-nite
poly-mor′-phic
poly-mor′-phism
poly-mor′-phous
poly-no′mial
poly-nu′cleate

pol′y-onym
poly-on′y-mous
poly-on′ymy
poly-o′pia
poly-pep′-tide
pol-yph′a-gous
pol′y-phase
poly-phon′ic
pol-yph′-ony
pol′y-ploid
pol′y-ploidy
pol′y-pod
pol′y-poid
pol′y-pous
pol′yp-tych
pol′y-pus
poly-sac′-char-
   ose
poly-se′mous
pol′y-semy
poly-sty′rene
poly-syl-lab′ic
poly-syl′-lable
poly-tech′-nic
poly-tech′-ni-cal
poly-the′ism
poly-the′ist
poly-theis′-tic
poly-to′nal-ism
poly-ton-al′ity
poly-troph′ic
poly-u′rethane
poly-va′lent
poly-vi′nyl
poly-zo′a
poly-zo′an
poly-zo′ic

pom′-ace
pom-a′ceous
pom-ad′e
po-man′-der
pom-a′tum
pom′-egran-ate
pom′i-cul-ture
pom-if′er-ous
pom′l-form
pom′-mel
pom′-melled
pomo-log′i-cal
pom-ol′ogy
pom′-pa-dour
pomp′-ano
pom′-pholix
pom′-pom
pom′-pon
pom-pos′ity
pomp′-ous
pon′-cho
pond′-age
pon′-der
pon-der-abil′ity
pon′-der-able
pon′-deral
pon′-der-ance
pon′-der-ancy
pon-der-o′sa
pon-der-os′ity
pon′-der-ous
pon-er-ol′ogy
pon-gee′
pon′-tage
pon′-tiff
pon-tif′i-cal
pon-tif′i-cals
pon-tif′i-cate

pon'-tify
pon'-tine
pon-toon'
poor'-house
poor'-ness
pop'-corn
pop'-eline
pop'-gun
pop'-in-jay
pop'-lar
pop'-lin
poph-te'al
pop'-lit'ic
pop'-over
pop'-per
pop'-pets
pop'-pies
pop'-ping
pop'py-cock
pop'u-lace
pop'u-lar
popu-lar-is-
     a'tion
pop'u-lar-ise
popu-lar'ity
popu-lar'ly
pop'u-late
popu-la'tion
pop'u-list
pop'u-lous
pop'u-lous-ness
por'-beagle
por'-cate
por'-celain
por-cel-la'neous
por'-cel-lan-ite
por'-cine
por'-cu-pine

pori-ci'dal
por-if'er-ous
po'-rism
por-is-mat'ic
por-nog'ra-pher
por-nog'ra-phy
po-rom'-eter
po'-ro-scope
po-ros'copy
po'-rose
po-ro'sis
po-ros'ity
po-rot'ic
po'-rous
por'-phy-rin
por-phyr-ıt'ic
por'-phyry
por'-poise
por-ra'ceous
por'-rect (a.)
por-rect' (v.)
por-rec'-tion
por'-ridge
por'-rin-ger
port-abil'ity
po'rt-able
por-ta'le
po'rta-lе
port-cul'-lis
por-tend'
por'-tent
por-ten'tous
po'rter-age
po'rter-house
po'rt-fire
port-fo'lio

po'rt-hole
po'rt-ico
po'rti-coes
po'rtion-less
po'rt-li-ness
port-man'-teau
porto-lan'
po'rtrait-ure
po'rt-ress
portu-la'ca
portu-la-
     ca'ceous
pos-it'ion
pos-it'ioner
pos'i-tive
pos'i-tively
pos'i-tiv-ism
posi-tiv-is'tic
posi-tri'no
pos'i-tron
posi-tro'-nium
pos-ol'-ogy
pos-sess'
pos-sess'ed
pos-sess'es
pos-ses'sion
pos-sess'-ive
pos-sess'-ive-
     ness
pos-sess'or
pos-sess'-ory
possi-bil'ity
poss'-ible
poss'-ibly
po'st-age
post-ax'ial
po'st-boy
po'st-card

283

post-da´te
post-di-lu´vian
pos-teen´
pos-te´rior
pos-ter´ity
po´st-ern
post-gla´cial
post-grad´u-ate
po´st-haste
pos´thum-ous
pos´thum-ously
post-hyp-not´ic
pos-ti´che
pos´-ti-cous
pos´-til
pos-til´ion
pos´-til-late
post-lim´-in-ary
post-li-min´-ium
post-lim´-iny
po´st-man
po´st-mark
po´st-mas-ter
post-mer-id´ian
post-mil-len´-
             nial
po´st-mis-tress
post-mor´-tem
post-or´bi-tal
po´st-paid
post-po´ne
post-pran´-dial
post-sce´nium
po´st-script
pos´-tu-lant
pos´-tu-late
pos-tu-la´tion
pos´-tu-lator

pos´-tu-lat-ory
pos´-tural
pos´-ture
pos´-tur-ing
po´st-war
pota-bil´ity
po´-table
pot-am´ic
pota-mog´ra-phy
pota-mol´ogy
pot´a-mous
por´-ash
pot-ass´ic
pot-ass´-ium
po-ta´tion
po-ta´to
po-ta´toes
po´ta-tory
pot´-bel-lied
pot´-belly
pot´-boiler
pot´-boy
po´-tency
po´-tent
po´-ten-tate
po-ten´-tial
po-ten-tial´ity
po-ten´-tially
po-ten-tiom´eter
po´-tently
pot´-herb
pot´-hole
pot´-hook
pot´-house
po´-tion
pot´-luck
pot-om´eter
pot´-pie

pot´-sherd
pot´-shot
pot´-stone
pot´-tage
pot´-ted
pot´-ter
pot´-rer-ies
pot´-tery
poutt´-erer
poult´-ice
pounc´-ing
pound´-age
pour´-ing
pout´-ing
pout´-ingly
pov´-erty
pow´-der
pow´-dered
pow´-dery
pow´-ered
pow´er-ful
pow´er-fully
pow´er-house
pow´er-less
pow´-wow
prac-ti-ca-
            bil´ity
prac´-ti-cable
prac´-ti-cal
prac-ti-cal´ity
prac´-ti-cally
prac´-ti-cal-ness
prac´-tice
prac´-tise
prac´-tised
prac´-tiser
prac´-tis-ing
prac-tit´ioner

prae'-cipe
prae'-dial
prae-mu-ni're
prae'-tor
prae-to'rian
prae'-tor-ship
prag-mat'ic
prag-mat'i-cally
prag'-ma-tism
prag'-ma-tist
prais'e-worthy
prais'-ing
pral'-ine
pranc'-ing
pran'-dial
prank'-ish
prank'-ster
praseo-dym'-ium
prat'-in-cole
prat'-tler
pra'yer-ful
preach'-ify
preach'-ing
preach'-ment
pre-am'ble
pre-arra'nge
pre-arra'nge-ment
pre-assu'r-ance
pre-ax'ial
preb'-end
preb'-en-dal
preb'-en-dary
pre-ca'ri-ous
pre-ca'ri-ous-
    ness
pre'-cast
prec'a-tive
preca'a-tory

pre-caut'ion
pre-caut'ion-ary
pre-caut'ious
pre-ce'd-able
pre-ce'de
pre'-cedence
pre'-cedency
pre-cede'n-tial
pre-ce'd-ing
pre-cen'-tor
pre'-cept
pre-cep'-tive
pre-cep'-tor
pre-cep-to'rial
pre-cep'-tory
pre-cep'-tress
pre-ces'sion
pre-ces'sional
pre'-cinct
preci-os'ity
prec'i-pice
pre-cipi-ta-
    bil'ity
pre-cip'i-table
pre-cip'i-tance
pre-cip'i-tancy
pre-cip'i-tant
pre-cip'i-tate
pre-cip'i-tately
pre-cip'i-tate-
    ness
pre-cipi-ta'tion
pre-cip'i-tat-
    ive
pre-cip'i-tator
pre-cip'i-tin
pre-cipi-tin'o-
    gen

pre-cip'i-tous
pre-cip'i-tously
pré'-cis
pré-ci'se
pre-ci'sely
pre-ci'se-ness
pre-cis'ian
pre-cis'ion
pre-ci'sive
pre-clin'i-cal
pre-clu'de
pre-clu'd-ing
pre-clu'sion
pre-clu's-ive
pre-co'cial
pre-co'cious
pre-coc'ity
pre-cog'i-tate
pre-cog-nit'ion
pre-cog'ni-tive
pre-cog-nosc'e
pre-com-po'se
pre-con-ceiv'e
pre-con-ceiv'-ing
pre-con-cep'tion
pre-con-cert'
pre-con-cert'ed
pre-con-is-a'tion
pre'-con-ise
pre-con-sign'
pre-con'-sti-tute
pre-con-struct'
pre-cor'-dial
pre-cor'-dium
pre-cos'-tal
pre-cur'-sive
pre-cur'-sor
pre-cur'-sory

285

pre-da′cious
pre-da′tion
pred′-ator
pred′a-torily
pred′a-tory
pre-de-cease′
pre′-de-cessor
pre′-de-clared
pre-de-si′gn
pre-des′ig-nate
pre-desti-na′rian
pre-des′ti-nate
pre-desti-na′tion
pre-des′tine
pre-de-ter′-mi-
            nate
pre-de-ter-mi-
            na′tion
pre-de-ter′-mine
pre-de-ter′-min-
            ing
predi-ca-bil′ity
pred′i-cable
pre-dic′a-ment
pred′i-cant
pred′i-cate
pred′i-cat-ing
predi-ca′tion
pred′i-cat-ive
pred′i-cat-ory
pre-dict′
pre-dict′-able
pre-dic′-tion
pre-dic′-tive
pre-dic′-tor
pre-diges′t
pre-diges′tion
pre-di-lec′-tion

pre-dis-po′nent
pre-dis-po′se
pre-dis-po′s-ing
pre-dis-posi′tion
pre-dom′i-nance
pre-dom′i-nant
pre-dom′i-nate
pre-domi-na′tion
pre-em′i-nence
pre-em′i-nent
pre-em′i-nently
pre-emp′-tion
pre-emp′-tive
pre-emp′-tor
pre-emp′-tory
pre-en-ga′ge
pre-es-tab′-lish
pre-exam′-ine
pre-exis′-tent
pre-fab′ri-cate
pre-fabri-ca′tion
pre-fab′ri-cator
pref′-ace
pref′-ac-ing
pref′a-torily
pref′a-tory
pre′-fect
pre-fec-to′rial
pre′-fec-ture
pre-fer′
pref-era-bil′ity
pref′-er-able
pref′-er-ably
pref′-er-ence
pref-er-en′-tial
pre-fer′-ment
pre-ferr′ed
pre-fer′-ring

pre-figur-a′tion
pre-fig′ur-at-ive
pre-fig′ure
pre′-fix
pre-for-ma′tion
pre-for′-ma-tive
pre-front′al
pre-ful′gent
preg-na-bil′ity
preg′-nable
preg′-nancy
preg′-nant
pre-hen′-sible
pre-hen′-sile
pre-hen-sil′ity
pre-hen′-sion
pre-hen′-sory
pre-his-tor′ic
pre-his-tor′i-
            cally
prehn′-ite
prehn′i-tene
prehn-it′ic
pre-instruct′
pre-judg′e
pre-judg′-ment
pre-ju′di-cate
pre-judi-ca′tion
prej′u-dice
preju-dic′ial
pre′-ju-dit′ial
prel′-acy
prel′-ate
prel′a-tise
prel′a-tism
prel′a-ture
pre-lect′
pre-lec′-tion

pre-liba'tion
pre-lim'i-nary
prel'-ude
pre-lu'dial
pre-lu'sion
prem'a-ture
prem'a-turely
prema-tu'rity
pre-med'i-cal
pre-med'i-tate
pre-medi-ta'tion
pre-med'i-tat-ive
pre-med'i-tator
prem'ier'
prem'ier-ship
pre-mil-len-
     a'rian
pre-mil-len'ial-
     ism
prem'-ise
prem'-ises
prem'-iss
pre'-mium
pre-mo'lar
pre-mon'-ish
pre-mon-it'ion
pre-mon'i-tory
pre-na'tal
pre'-nomen
pre-no'tion
pren'-tice
pre-ob-tain'
pre-oc'cu-pancy
pre-occu-pa'tion
pre-oc'cu-pied
pre-oc'cupy
pre-op'-tion
pre-o'ral

pre-or-dain'
pre-ord'in-ance
pre-ordi-na'tion
pre-paid'
prep-ara'tion
pre-par'a-tive
pre-par'a-tory
pre-pa're
pre-pa'red
pre-pa'red-ness
pre-pa'rer
pre-pay'
pre-pay'-able
pre-pay'-ment
pre-pen'se
pre-pon'-der-ance
pre-pon'-der-ant
pre-pon'-der-ate
pre-pon'-der-at-
     ing
pre-po'se
prep-osit'ion
prep-osit'ional
pre-pos'i-tive
pre-pos'i-tor
pre-pos-sess'
pre-pos-sess'-ing
pre-pos-ses'sion
pre-pos'ter-ous
pre-pos'ter-
     ously
pre-po'tency
pre-po'tent
pre'-puce
pre-req'ui-site
pre-rog'a-tive
pre-sa'ge
pre-sa'ge-ful

pres-byo-
     phre'nia
pres-by-o'pia
pres'-by-ter
pres-byt'er-ate
pres'-by-te'rial
pres'-by-tery
pre-scind'
pre-scis'sion
pre-scri'be
pre-scri'ber
pre-scri'b-ing
pre'-script
pre-scrip'-tible
pre-scrip'-tion
pre-scrip'-tive
pre-sel-ec'-tive
pres'-ence
pres'-ent (n. a.)
pre-sent' (v.)
pre-sen'table
pres-en-ta'tion
pre-sen'ta-tive
pres-er-va'tion
pre-serv'-ative
pre-ser've
pre-serv'er
pre-si'de
pres'i-dency
pres'i-dent
presi-den'-tial
pre-si'der
pres-id'ial
pre-si'd-ing
pres-id'io
pres-id'ium
pre-sig'-nify
press'-board

287

press'-mark
press'-room
press'-ure
press-ur-is-
      a'tion
press'-ur-ise
press'-work
presti-digi-
      ta'tion
presti-dig'i-
      tator
pres-ti'ge
pres-tig'ious
pre-sto're
pre-su'm-able
pre-su'm-ably
pre-su'me
pre-su'med
pre-su'mer
pre-su'm-ing
pre-sumpt'-tion
pre-sump'-tive
pre-sump'-tuous
pre-sup-po'se
pre-sup-po-
      sit'ion
pre-ten'ce
pre-tend'
pre-tend'ed
pre-tend'er
pre-ten'-sion
pre-ten'-tious
pre-ten'-tious-
      ness
pre-ter-hu'man
pret'-er-ist
pret'-erite
pret-erit'ial

pret-erit'ion
pre-ter'i-tive
pre-ter-mis'sion
pre-ter-mit'
pre-ter-nat'u-ral
pre-ter-sen'-sual
pre'-text
pret'ti-fied
pret'ti-ness
pre-typ'ify
pret'-zel
pre-vail'
pre-vail'-ing
prev'a-lence
prev'a-lent
pre-var'i-cate
pre-vari-ca'tion
pre-var'i-cator
pre-ve'nience
pre-ve'nient
pre-vent'
pre-vent'-able
pre-vent'-ative
pre-vent'er
pre-ven'-tion
pre-ven'-tive
pre'-view
pre'-vious
pre'-viously
pre-vi'se
pre-vis'ion
pre-warn'
pri-ap'ic
pri'a-pism
pri'ce-less
prick'-ling
prick'-li-ness
pri'de-ful

prid'-ian
priest'-craft
priest'-ess
priest'-hood
priest'-li-ness
priest'-ridden
prig'-gery
prig'-gish
pri'-macy
pri'-mage
pri'-mal
pri'-ma-quine
pri'-mar-ily
pri'-mary
pri'-mate
pri-ma'tial
pri-ma-tol'ogy
prima-ve'ra
pri'me-ness
pri-me'val
primi-ge'nial
pri-mip'-ara
pri-mip'-ar-ous
prim'i-tive
prim'i-tiv-ism
prim'-ness
primo-gen'ital
primo-gen'i-tary
primo-gen'i-tive
primo-gen'i-tor
primo-gen'i-ture
pri-mor'-dial
pri-mor'-dium
prim'-rose
prim'-ula
primu-la'ceous
prim'u-line
prin'ce-dom

prin'ce-like
prin'ce-li-ness
prin'-cess
prin-ci-pal'ity
prin'-ci-pally
prin'-ci-pal-ship
prin'-ci-pate
prin-cip'ia
prin'-ciple
print'-able
print'-ery
print'-ing
print'-less
pri'-or-ate
pri'-or-ess
pri-or'ity
pri'-or-ship
pri'-ory
pris-mat'ic
pris'-ma-toid
pris'-moid
pris-moid'al
pris'-oner
pris'-tine
priv'-acy
priva-teer'
priva-teer'-ing
priva-teers'-man
pri'-vately
pri'-vate-ness
pri-va'tion
priv'a-tive
priv'i-lege
priv'i-leged
priv'-ily
priv'-ity

priz'-able
pri'ze-fight
pri'ze-ing
pri'ze-money
prob'-abil-ism
prob-abil'ity
prob'-able
prob'-ably
pro'-bate
pro-ba'tion
pro-ba'tional
pro-ba'tion-ary
pro-ba'tioner
pro'ba-tive
pro'ba-tory
pro'-ber-tite
prob'-ity
prob'-lem
prob-lem-at'ic
prob-lem-at'i-cal
prob-lem-at'i-
    cally
prob-os'ci-date
prob-oscid'-ean
prob-oscid'i-form
pro-bos'cis
pro-bos'cises
pro-ca'cious
pro-cac'ity
pro'-caine
pro'=ca-the'dral
pro-ce'dural
pro-ce'dure
pro-ceed'
pro-ceed'-ing
pro-celeus-mat'ic
pro-cephal'ic

pro'-cess
pro-ces'sion
pro-ces'sional
pro-ces'sion-ary
pro'-cessor
pro-cid'u-ous
pro-claim'
proc-la-ma'tion
pro-clam'a-tory
pro-clit'ic
pro-cliv'ity
pro-cli'vous
pro-con'-sul
pro-con'-su-lar
pro-con'-sul-ate
pro-cras'ti-nate
pro-crasti-
    na'tion
pro-cras'ti-nator
pro'-creant
pro'-create
pro-crea'tion
pro'-creat-ive
pro'-creator
pro-crus'-tean
pro-cryp'-sis
pro-cryp'-tic
proc'-tal
proc-ti'tis
proc-to-log'ical
proc-tol'ogy
proc'-tor
proc-to'rial
proc'-tor-ship
procto-scop'ic
proc-tos'copy
pro-cum'-bent
pro-cu'r-able

289

proc'u-racy
procu-ra'tion
proc'u-rator
proc'u-rat-ory
pro-cu're
pro-cu'red
pro-cu're-ment
pro-cu'rer
proc'u-ress
pro-cu'r-ing
prod'-ding
prod'i-gal
prodi-gal'ity
pro-dig'ious
prod'-igy
prod'-ro-mal
prod'-rome
pro-du'ce (v.)
prod'-uce (n.)
pro-du'cer
pro-du'cible
pro-du'c-ing
prod'-uct (n.)
pro-ducti-bil'ity
pro-duc'tion
pro-duc'tile
pro-duc'tive
pro-duc'tive-ness
pro-ductiv'ity
pro-em'ial
profa-na'tion
pro-fan'a-tory
pro-fa'ne
pro-fa'nely
pro-fa'ner
pro-fa'ning
pro-fan'ity
pro-fec-tit'ious
290

pro'-fert
pro-fess'
pro-fess'ed
pro-fess'edly
pro-fes'sion
pro-fess'ional
pro-fes'sion-al-
           ism
pro-fes'sion-ally
pro-fess'or
prof-esso'rial
prof-esso'riat
pro-fes'sor-ship
prof'-fer
prof'-fered
pro-fic'iency
pro-fic'ient
pro'-file
pro'-filer
pro-fi-lom'-eter
prof'-it-able
prof'-it-ably
profi-teer'
prof'-iter
prof'-it-less
prof'-li-gacy
prof'-li-gate
prof'-lu-ence
prof'-lu-ent
pro-found'
pro-found'ly
pro-ful'gent
pro-fu'se
pro-fu'sely
pro-fu'sion
pro-fu's-ive
pro-gen'i-tor

pro-geni-to'rial
pro-gen'i-ture
pro-ges'ter-one
prog-nath'ic
prog'-na-thous
prog-no'sis
prog-nos'-tic
prog-nos'-ti-cate
prog-nos-ti-
           ca'tion
prog-nos'-ti-
           cator
pro'-gramme
pro'-grammed
pro-gram-mat'ic
pro'-gram-mer
pro'-gram-ming
prog'-ress (n.)
pro-gress' (v.)
pro-gres'sion
pro-gres'sion-ary
pro-gres'sion-ism
pro-gres'sion-ist
pro'-gress-ist
pro-gress'-ive
pro-gress'-ively
pro-gress'-iv-ism
pro-hib'it
pro-hib'-iter
pro-hib-it'ion
pro-hib-it'ion-
                ist
pro-hib'i-tive
pro-hib'i-tory
proj'-ect (n.)
pro-ject' (v.)
pro-jec'ted
pro-jec'-tile

pro-jec'-tion
pro-jec'-tive
pro-jec'-tor
pro-jec'-ture
pro-lam'in
pro-lap'se (v.)
pro'-lapse (n.)
pro'-late
pro-la't-ive
pro-legom'-enon
pro-lep'-sis
pro-lep'-tic
pro-let-a'rian
pro-let-a'rian-
ism
pro-let-a'riat
pro-lif'er-ate
pro-lifer-a'tion
pro-lif'er-at-ive
pro-lif'er-ous
pro-lif'ic
pro-lif'i-cacy
pro-lif'i-cally
pro-lifi-ca'tion
pro-lif-ic'ity
pro-lig'er-ous
pro'-line
pro'-lix
pro-lix'ity
pro-lo-cu'tion
pro-loc'u-tor
pro'-logise
pro'-logue
pro'-long'
pro'-longate
pro-longa'tion
pro-long'ed
pro-lu'sion

pro-lu's-ory
pro'-ma-zine
prom-en-ad'e
prom-en-ad'er
pro-me'thium
prom'i-nence
prom'i-nent
prom'i-nently
prom-is-cu'ity
prom'-ise
prom-isee'
prom'-iser
prom'-is-ing
prom'-isor
prom'-iss-ory
prom'-on-toried
prom'-on-tory
pro-mo'te
pro-mo'ter
pro-mo't-ing
pro-mo'tion
pro-mo'tive
promp'-ti-tude
prompt'-ness
prom'-ul-gate
prom-ul-ga'tion
prom'-ul-gator
pro'-nate
pro-na'tion
pro-na'tor
pro'ne-ness
pro-neph'-ros
prong'-horn
pro-nom'i-nal
pro-no'tum
pro'-noun
pro-nounc'e

pro-nounc'e-able
pro-noun'ce-
ment
pro-nounc'-ing
pro-nuc'-leus
pro'-numeral
pro-nun'-cial
pro-nun-ci-a'tion
proof'-read
proof'-reader
pro-pae-deut'ic
propa-ga-bil'ity
prop'a-gable
propa-gan'da
propa-gan'-dise
propa-gan'-dist
prop'a-gate
propa-ga'tion
prop'a-ga-tive
prop'a-gator
pro'-pane
propa-no'ic
pro'-pa-nol
pro-par'-gyl
pro-pel'
pro-pel'-lant
(n. a.)
pro-pel'-ler
pro-pel'-ling
pro-pen'-dent
pro'-penol
pro-pen'se
pro-pen'-sity
pro-per'-din
prop'-erly
prop'-er-tied
prop'-er-ties
prop'-erty

291

proph'-asis
proph'-ecies
proph'-ecy (n.)
proph'-esied
proph'-esier
proph'-esy (v.)
proph'-et-ess
pro-phet'ic
pro-phet'i-cal
prophy-lac'-tic
prophy-lax'is
pro-pin'-quity
pro-pi-ol'ic
pro'-pi-onate
pro-pi-on'ic
pro'-pi-onyl
pro-pit'iate
pro-pitia'tion
pro-pit'iator
pro-pit'iat-ory
pro-pit'ious
pro-pod'-eon
pro-po'deum
prop'o-lis
pro-po'nent
pro-por'tion
pro-por'tional
pro-por'tion-able
pro-por'tion-ate
pro-por'tion-ately
pro-por'tioned
pro-po'sal
pro-po'se
pro-po'ser
pro-po's-ing
prop-osit'ion
prop-osit'ional
pro-pound'

pro-pound'er
pro-pri'etary
pro-pri'etor
pro-pri'etor-ship
pro-pri'etress
pro-pri'ety
pro-prio-cep'-
tive
pro-prio-cep'-
tor
prop-to'sis
pro-pul'-sion
pro-pul'-sive
por-pul'sory
pro'-pyl
propy-lae'um
pro'-pyl-amine
pro'-pyl-eae
pro-pyl'ic
prop'y-lite
pro-py'lon
pro-ra'table
pro-ra'te
pro-ra'tion
pro'-ro-gate
pro-ro-ga'tion
pro-ro'gue
pro-sa'ic
pro-sa'ic-ally
pro-sce'nium
pro-scri'be
pro-scri'ber
pro'-script
pro-scrip'-tion
pro-scrip'-tive
pro-scrip'-tively
pro-sect'
pro-sec'-tor

pro-sec-to'rial
pros'-ecute
pros-ecu'tion
pros'-ecutor
pros'-ecut-ory
pros'-ecutrix
pros'-elyte
pros'-elyt-ise
pros'-elyt-iser
pros'-elyt-ism
pros-ench'yma
pros-en-chym'a-
tous
pro'-sit
pro-sla'very
proso-di'acal
pros-od'ic
pros-od'i-cal
pros'-odist
pros'-ody
pro-so-pope'ia
pros'o-pyte
pros'-pect (n.)
pros-pect' (v.)
pro-spec'-tive
pro-spec'-tively
pro-spec'-tor
pros-pec'-tus
pros'-per
pros-per'ity
pros'-per-ous
pros'-tate
pros-ta-tec'-
tomy
pros-tat'ic
pros-ta-ti'tis
pros-ter-na'tion
pros-then'ic

pros'-thesis
pros-thet'ic
pros'-thetist
pros-tho-don'-tia
pros-tho-don'-tics
pros'-ti-tute
pros-ti-tu'tion
pros'-trate
pros'-trat-ing
pros-tra'tion
pros'-trator
pro'-style
pro-syl'-lo-gism
pro-tac-tin'-ium
pro'-ta-gon
pro-tag'-on-ist
pro'-ta-mine
pro-tan'-drous
pro-tan'-dry
pro-ta-no'pia
prot'a-sis
pro'-tean
pro'-tease
pro-tect'
pro-tect'-ant
pro-tect'-ing
pro-tect'-ingly
pro-tec'-tion
pro-tec'-tion-ism
pro-tec'-tion-ist
pro-tec'-tive
pro-tec'-tively
pro-tec'-tor
pro-tec'-tor-ate
pro-tec'-tory
pro-tec'-tress
pro'-teid

pro'-tein
pro-tein-a'ceous
pro'-tein-ase
pro-ten'-sion
pro-ten'sity
pro-ten'-sive
pro-teol'-ysis
pro-teo-lyt'-ic
pro'-teose
pro-ter-an'-drous
pro-ter-an'-dry
pro'-test (n.)
pro-test' (v.)
prot'-estant
prot-esta'tion
pro-test'er
pro-test'-ing
pro-tha-la'mion
pro-thal'-lium
proth'-esis
pro-tho'rax
pro-throm'-bin
pro'-tium
proto-ac-tin'-ium
pro'to-cneme
pro'-to-col
pro'-to-gen
pro-to-gen'-esis
pro-to-gen-et'ic
pro-to-gen'ic
pro'-to-gine
pro-tog'yn-ous
pro-tog'yny
proto-mar'-tyr
pro'-ton
proto-ne'ina
proto-no'tary

pro'-to-phyte
pro-to-phyt'ic
pro'-to-plasm
pro-to-plas'-mal
pro-to-plas'-mic
pro'-to-plast
pro-to-plas'-tie
pro-tor'-nis
pro'-to-stele
proto-the'rian
proto-trop'ic
pro'-tot'ropy
pro'-to-typal
pro'to-type
proto-typ'i-cal
pro-tox'-ide
proto-zo'a
proto-zo'al
proto-zo'an
proto-zo'ic
pro-tract'
pro-trac'-ted
pro-tract'-ible
pro-trac'-tile
pro-trac'-tion
pro-trac'-tive
pro-trac'-tor
pro-tru'de
pro-tru's-ile
pro-tru'sion
pro-tru's-ive
pro-tru's-ively
pro-tu'ber-ance
pro-tu'ber-ant
pro-tu'ber-ate
pro'-tyle
proust'-ite
prov'-enance

prov'-ender
pro-ve'ni-ence
prov'-erb
prov-er'bial
prov-er'bial-ise
prov-er'bi-al-ism
prov-er'bi-al-ly
pro-vi'de
pro-vi'ded
prov'i-dence
prov'i-dent
provi-den'-tial
pro-vi'der
pro-vi'd-ing
prov'-ince
pro-vin'-cial
pro-vin'-cial-ism
pro-vin-cial'ity
pro-vin'-cial-ly
pro-vis'ion
pro-vis'ional
pro-vis'ion-ally
pro-vis'ion-ary
pro-vis'ioner
pro-vis'ions
pro-vi'so
pro-vi'sor
pro-vi'sor-ily
pro-vi'sory
pro-vi'sos
provo-ca'tion
pro-voc'a-tive
pro-voc'a-tory
pro-vo'ke
pro-vo'k-ing
prov'-ost
prow'-ess
prox'-ies
294

prox'i-mal
prox'i-mate
prox'i-mately
prox-im'-ity
prox'-imo
prox'y-mite
pru'-dence
pru'-dent
pru-den'-tial
pru'd-ery
pru'd-ish
pru'-in-ose
pru-nel'la
pru-nif'er-ous
pru'n-ing
pru'-ri-ence
pru'-ri-ent
pru-rig'in-ous
pru-ri'go
pru-rit'ic
pru-ri'tus
pruss'i-ate
pry'-ing
pry'-ingly
pryta-ne'um
pryt'-any
psalm'-ist
psalm-od'ic
psalm'-od-ist
psalm'-ody
psal'-ter
psal-te'rium
psal'-tery
psam'-mite
psam-mit'ic
psam'-mo-phile
psam'-mo-phyte
pse-phol'-ogist

pse-phol'ogy
pseud-aes-the'sia
pseud-epig'-
          rapha
pseud-epig'-ra-
          phy
pseudo-aquat'ic
pseud'o-carp
pseud'o-graph
pseud-ol'-ogist
pseud-ol'ogy
pseud'o-morph
pseudo-mor'-
          phic
pseu'do-nym
pseud-on-ym'ity
pseud-on'y-mous
pseudo-ple'gia
pseu'do-pod
pseudo-po'dium
pseud'o-scope
pseudo'-scop'ic
pseud-os'copy
psi-lan'-thropy
psi-lo'sis
psi-lot'ic
psit'-ta-cine
psit-ta-co'sis
psit-ta-cot'ic
pso-ri'asis
psori-at'ic
pso-ro'sis
psy'-cha-gogue
psy-chas-the'nia
psy-chi-at'ric
psy-chi'atrist
psy-chi'atry
psy'-chic

psy'-chi-cal
psy'-chi-cally
psycho-an'-al-ise
psycho-an-al'y-
sis
psycho-an'-al-yst
psycho-ana-lyt'ic
psycho-ana-ly'ti-
cal
psycho-gen'ic
psycho-gen-ic'ity
psy-cho-gon'i-cal
psy-chog'-ony
psy'-cho-gram
psy'-cho-graph
psycho-graph'ic
psy-chog'ra-phy
psycho-log'i-cal
psycho-log'i-
cally
psy-chol'-ogise
psy-chol'-ogism
psy-chol'-ogist
psy-chol'ogy
psy-chom'-achy
psy-chom-man'cy
psy-chom'eter
psycho-met'ric
psy-cho-
metric'ian
psy-chom'-etrist
psy-chom'-etry
psy-cho-neur-
ol'ogy
psycho-neur-o'sis
psycho-neur-ot'ic
psy'cho-path
psycho-path'ic

psy-chop'-athist
psy-cho-path-
ol'ogy
psy-chop'-athy
psy-cho-phys'ics
psy-cho'sis
psycho-som-at'ic
psycho-ther'apy
psy-chot'ic
psy-chrom'eter
psy-chrom'-etry
psy-chro-pho'bia
psyl'-lium
ptar'-mic
ptar'-mi-gan
pteri-dol'ogy
pteri-doph'-olist
ptero-dac'-tyl
pter-o'ic
pter'o-pod
pter-yg'ium
pter'y-goid
ptery-lo'sis
ptil-o'sis
pto'-maine
pto'-sis
pty'a-lin
pty'al-ism
pu'-berty
pu-ber'u-lent
pu-besc'ence
pu-besc'ent
pu'-bic
pubi-ot'omy
pu'-bis
pub'-lic
pub'-li-can
pub-li-ca'tion

pub'-li-cise
pub'-li-cist
pub-lic'ity
pub'-licly
pub'-lish
pub-lish-able
pub'-lisher
puck-ered
puck'-ery
puck'-ish
pud'-dler
pud'-dling
pu'-dency
pu-den da
pu-den'dal
pudg'i-ness
pu'er-ile
puer-il'ity
pu-er'-peral
puer-pe'rium
puff'-ball
puf-fin
puff'i-ness
pug'-garee
pu'-gil-ism
pu'-gil-ist
pu-gil-is'tic
pug-na'cious
pug-na'ciously
pug-nac'ity
puiss'-ance
puiss'-ant
pul'-chri-tude
pul-chri-tu'di-
nous
pul'i-cide
pull'-ing
pul-lo'rum

295

pull'-over
pul'lu-late
pullu-la'tion
pul-mom'eter
pul'-mon-ary
pul'-mon-ate
pul-mon'ic
pulp'i-ness
pulpit-eer'
pulp'-ous
pulp'-wood
pul'sa-tance
pul'-sate
pul'-sa-tile
pul-sa'tion
pul'sa-tive
pul-sa'tor
pul'sa-tory
pul-sim'eter
puls'-ing
pul-som'eter
pul-ta'ceous
pul'-ver-able
pul'-ver-ine
pul'-ver-is-able
pul-ver-is-a'tion
pul'-ver-ise
pul'-ver-iser
pul'-ver-ous
pul-ver'u-lent
pul-vi'nar
pul'-vin-ate
pum'-ice
pu-mic'eous
pum'-mel
pump'-age
pum'-per-nickel
pump'-kin

pun'-cheon
punc'-tate
punc-tated
punc-ta'tion
punc'-ti-form
punc-til'io
punc-til'i-ous
punc'-tual
punc-tu-al'ity
punc'-tu-ally
punc'-tu-ate
punc-tu-a'tion
punc'-tu-ator
punc'-tu-late
punc-tu-la'tion
punc'-tule
punc'-tum
punc'-tur-able
punc'-ture
punc'-tured
punc'-tur-ing
pun'-dit
pun'-gency
pu'ni-ness
pun'-ish
pun'-ish-able
pun'-isher
pun'-ish-ment
pu'ni-tive
pu'ni-tory
pun'-net
pun'-ning
pun'-ster
pu'-pal
pu-pa'rium
pu-pa'tion
pu-pig'er-ous
pu'-pil

pu-pil-lar'ity
pu'-pil-lary
pu'-pil-late
pu-pip'ar-ous
pu-piv'or-ous
pup'-pet
pup-pet-eer'
pup'-petry
pur'-blind
pur'-chas-able
pur'-chase
pur'-chased
pur'-chaser
pur'-chas-ing
pur'-dah
pu're-ness
pur'-fling
pur-ga'tion
pur'-ga-tive
pur-ga-to'rial
pur-ga-to'rian
pur'-ga-tory
purg'-ing
puri-fi-ca'tion
pu'ri-fi-cat-ory
pu'ri-fier
pu'-rify
pu'-rine
pu'-rism
pu'-rist
pu-ris'tic
pu'ri-tan
puri-tan'i-cal
pu'ri-tan-ism
pu'-rity
pur'-lieu
pur'-lin
pur-loin'

pur'-pling
pur'-plish
pur-port' (v.)
pur'-port (n.)
pur'-pose
pur'-pose-ful
pur'-pose-fully
pur'-pose-less
pur'-posely
pur'-pos-ive
pur-pres'-ture
pur-pri'se
pur'-pura
pur'-pu-rate
pur-pu'real
pur-pu'ric
pur'-pu-rin
pur-puro-gal'-lin
purr'-ing
purs'-ing
purs'-lane
pur-su'al
pur-su'-ance
pur-su'-ant
pur-su'-antly
pur-sue'
pur-su'ed
pur-su'er
pur-su'-ing
pur-suit'
pur'-suivant
pur'-ten-ance
pu'ru-lence
pu'ru-lent
pur-vey'
pur-vey'-ance
pur-vey'or
pur'-view

push'-ball
push'-cart
push'-ing
push'-pin
pusil-la-nim'ity
pusil-lan'i-mous
puss'y-foot
pus'-tu-lant
pus'-tu-lar
pus-tu-la'tion
pus'-tule
pus'-tu-lous
pu-ta'men
pu'ta-tive
pu'-teal
put'-log
putre-fa'cient
putre-fac'-tion
putre-fac'-tive
pu'tre-fied
pu'tre-fy-ing
pu-tres'cence
pu-tres'cent
pu-tres'cible
pu-tres'cine
pu'-trid
pu-trid'-ity
put-tee'
puz'zle-ment
puz'-zler
puz'-zling
py-aem'ia
py-aem'ic
pyc-nid'ium
pyc'-nite
pyc-nom'eter
pyc-no'sis

pyc'-no-style
pyc-not'ic
pyel-it'ic
pyel-i'tis
pyelo-graph'ic
py-el-og'ra-phy
py-gid'ium
pyg-me'an
pyk'-nic
py'-lon
pylon-ec'tomy
py-lor'ic
py'-loro-plasty
py-lo'rus
pyo-cy'an-ase
pyo-gen'esis
pyo-gen'ic
py'-oid
py-or-rhe'a
py'-ra-canth
pyr'a-mid
pyr-am'i-dal
pyra-mid'i-cal
pyra-mid'-ion
pyr-am'i-dist
pyr-am'i-don
py'-ran
pyr-ar'-gyr-ite
pyr'a-zine
pyr'a-zole
pyr-az'o-lone
pyr-az'o-lyl
py'-rene
py-re'thrin
py-re'thrum
py-ret'ic
pyr-etol'ogy
py-rex'ia

297

py-rex'ic
pyr-goid'al
pyr-heli-om'eter
py-rid'-azine
py-rid'ic
pyr'i-dine
pyri-dox'-ine
pyr'i-form
pyri-meth'-amine
py-rim'-idine
py'-rite
py-ri'tes
pyr-it'ic
pyri-tif'er-ous
py-rito-he'dral
py-rito-he'dron
pyri-tol'ogy
pyro-clas'-tic
pyro-gal'-lic
pyro-gal'-lol
py'ro-gen
pyro-gen-a'tion
pyro-gen-et'ic
py-rog'en-ous
py-rog-nos'tic
py-rog'ra-pher
pyro-graph'ic
py-rog'ra-phy
py'-ro-grav-ure
py-rol'-ater
py-rol'-atry
pyro-lig'-neous
pyro-lig'nic
py-rol'ogy
pyro-lu'site
py-rol'-ysis
pyro-ma'nia
pyro-ma'niac

298

py-rom'-eter
py-ro-met'ric
py'-rone
py'-rope
pyro-pho'bia
py-roph'-orus
py-roph'-or-ous
pyro-phyl'-lite
py'ro-phyte
py'ro-scope
py-ro'sis
py'-ro-some
pyro-tech'-nic
pyro-tech'-ni-cal
pyro-tech'-nist
pyr-ox'ene
pyr-ox'en-ite
pyr-ox'y-lin
pyr'-rhic
pyr'-rho-tite
pyr'-rhous
pyr-rol'i-dine
pyr'ro-line
pyru-val'-dehyde
pyr-u'vic
pytho-gen'ic
py'-thon
py-thon'ic
pyx'i-date
pyx-id'ium

Q

quack'-ery
quad'-ded
quad-ra-gen-
    a'rian

quadra-ges'i-mal
quad'-rangle
quad-rang'u-lar
quad'-rant
quad-ran'tal
quad'-rat
quad'-rate
quad-rat'ic
quad'-ra-ture
quad-ra'tus
quad-ren'-nial
quad-ren'-nium
quad'-ric
quad-ri-cen-
    ten'-nial
quad'-ri-ceps
quad-ri-cip'i-tal
quad'-ri-cone
quad-ri-cor'-
    nous
quad-rif'er-ous
quad'-ri-fid
quad'-ri-form
quad-ri'ga
quad-ri-gem'-
    inal
quad-ri-gem'-in-
    ate
quad-ri-gem'-in-
    ous
quadri-lat'-eral
quad-ri-ling'ual
quad-ri-lit'-eral
quad-rill'e
quad-ril'lion
quad-ri-loc'u-lar
quad-ri-no'mial
quadri-par'-tite

quad-ri-ple'gia
quadri-ple'gic
quad'-ri-plex
quad-ri-sec'-tion
quad-ri-syl-
     lab'ic
quadri-syl'-lable
quadri-va'lent
quad-riv'-ium
quad-roon'
quad-ru'man-ous
quad-rum'-vir-ate
quad'-ru-ped
quad-ru'pedal
quad-ru'ple
quad-ru'plet
quad'ru-plex
quad-ru'pli-cate
quad-rupli-
     ca'tion
quad-ru'pling
quaes'-tor
quag'-mire
qua'-hog
qua'k-ing
qual'i-fi-able
quali-fi-ca'tion
qual'i-fi-cat-ory
qual'i-fied
qual'i-fier
qual'-ify
qual'i-fy-ing
qual-im'eter
qual'i-tat-ive
qual'i-tat-ively
qual'-ity
qualm'-ish
quan'-dary

quan'-dong
quan'-net
quan'-tic
quanti-fi-ca'tion
quan'-tify
quan'-tile
quan-tim eter
quan'-tise
quan'-ti-tat-ive
quan'-ti-tat-ively
quan'-tity
quan-tiv'a-lence
quan-tom'eter
quan'-tum
quar'-an-tine
quar'-an-tiner
quar'-rel
quar'-relled
quar'-rel-ling
quar'-rel-some
quar'-rier
quar'-tan
quar-ta'tion
quar'-ter
quar'-ter-age
quar'-ter-back
quar'-ter-deck
quar'-tered
quar'-ter-ing
quar'-terly
quar'-ter-mas-ter
quar'-tern
quar-tet'
quar'-tic
quar'-tile
quar'-tos
quartz-it'er-ous
quartz'-ite

quartz-it'ic
quartz'-ose
quass-a'tion
quass'-ative
quater-cen-ten'-
     ary
quat'-ern
quat-ern'-ary
quat-ern'-ate
quat-ern'-ion
quat-er'nity
quat'or-zain
quat'-rain
quat're-foil
qua'ver-ing
queas'-ily
queas'i-ness
queen'-li-ness
quench'-able
quench'-less
quer'-cetin
quer'-cine
quer'-ci-tol
quer'-ci-trin
quer'-ci-tron
quer-civ'or-ous
queri-min'i-ous
quer'u-lous
que'ry-ing
quest'-ing
ques'-tion
ques'-tion-able
ques'-tion-ary
ques'-tioner
ques'-tion-ing
ques'-tion-ingly
ques'-tion=mark
ques-tion-nair'e
299

quet'-zal
queu'-ing
quib'-bler
quib'-bling
quick'-en-ing
quick'-ing
quick'-lime
quick'-ness
quick'-sand
quick'-set
quick-set'-ting
quick-si'ghted
quick'-sil-ver
quick'-step
quick-tem'-pered
quick'-wit-ted
quid'-dany
quid'-dity
quid'-nunc
quiesc'-ence
quiesc'-ent
qui'et-ism
qui'et-ness
qui'et-ude
quilt'-ing
quin'a-crine
quin-al'-dine
quin-cen-ten'ary
quin'cun'cial
quin'-cunx
quin-dec'a-gon
quin-gen-ten'-ary
quin'i-cine
quin'i-dine
quin-i'ne
quin-in'ic
quin'-ise
quin'-ism

quin-iz'arin
quin-oid'-ine
quin'o-line
quin-ol'ogy
quin'-one
quin'o-noid
quin-ox'a-line
quin-qua-
quin-qua-ges'ima
a'rian
quin-qua-gen'-ary
quin-qua-gen-ten'-ary
quin-quan'gu-lar
quin-quen'-niad
quin-quen'-nial
quin-quen-nium
quinque-par'-tite
quin'-tal
quin'-tan
quin'-tant
quin-ter'-nion
quin-tess'-ence
quin-tessen'-tial
quin'-tet'
quin'-tic
quin'-tile
quin-til'lion
quin-troon'
quin-tu'ple
quin-tu'plet
quin-tu'pli-cate
quin-tu'pling
quin'-zaine
quip'-ping
quip'-ster
qui're-wise
quit'-claim
quit'-rent
quit'-tance

quit'-tor
quiv'-ered
quiv'-er-ing
quix-ot'ic
quix-ot'i-cally
quix'-ot-ism
quix'-otry
quiz'-zi-cal
quiz'-zing
quod'-li-bet
quon'-dam
quo'-rum
quot-abil'ity
quo't-able
quo't-able-ness
quo-ta'tion
quo-tid'-ian
quo'-tient
quo't-ing
quo'-tition

R

rab'-bet
rab'-beted
rab'-bin-ate
rab-bin'ic
rab-bin'i-cal
rab'-bit
rab'-bitry
rab'-bler
ra-bid'-ity
rac-coon'
ra'ce-course
ra'ce-horse
ra-ce'me

ra-ce'mic
ra-cem-if'er-ous
ra-cem-is-a'tion
ra'-cem-ose
ra'ce-track
ra'ce-way
rach-it'ic
rach-i'tis
ra'cial-ism
ra'cial-ist
ra'ci-ness
rack-et-eer'
rack'-et-ing
rack'-ets
rack'-ety
ra'dar-scope
radi-al-is-a'tion
ra'di-al-ise
ra'di-ance
ra'di-ancy
ra'di-ant
ra'di-antly
ra'di-ate
radi-a'tion
ra'di-at-ive
ra'di-ator
rad'-ical
rad'-ical-ise
rad'-ical-ism
rad-ical-ity
rad'-ically
rad'-icant
rad'-icate
rad-ica'tion
rad-iciv'-or-ous
rad'-icle
rad-ic'o-lous

rad'-icose
rad-ic'u-lar
rad'-icule
rad-icu-li'tis
rad-ic'u-lose
radio-ac'-tive
radio-ac-tiv'ity
ra'dio-gram
ra'dio-graph
radi-o'gra-pher
radio-graph'ic
radi-og'ra-phy
radio-i'so-tope
radio-la'rian
radio-lo-ca'tion
radio-log'i-cal
radi-ol'-ogist
radi-ol'ogy
radi-om'eter
radio-met'ric
radio-nu'clide
ra'dio-phone
radio-phon'ic
radi-oph'-ony
radio-scler-
          om'eter
ra'dio-scope
radi-os'copy
ra'dio-sonde
radio-tel'-egram
radio-tel'-egraph
radio-tel'-ephone
radio-tel-eph'-
            ony
radio-ther'apy
radio-tho'rium
rad'-ish
rad'-ula

rad'u-lar
rad'u-late
radu-lif'er-ous
rad-u'li-form
raf'-fia
raf'-fin-ate
raf'-fin-ose
raff'-ish
raff'-ishly
raf-flesi-a'ceous
raf'-fling
raf'-ter
rafts'-man
rag'a-muffin
rag'-ged
rag'-ged-ness
rag'-ging
rag'-lan
rag'-let
rag'-man
rag'-picker
rag'-stone
rag'-time
rag'-work
rag'-wort
rail'-head
rail'-ing
rail'-lery
rail'-road
rail'-road-ing
rail'-way
rai'-ment
rain'-band
rain'-bow
rain'-coat
rain'-drop
rain'-fall
rain'-gauge

301

rain'-less
rain'-maker
rain'-proof
rain'-storm
rain'-tight
rain'-water
rais'-ing
ra'ke-hell
ral'-lied
ram'-bler
ram'-bling
ram'-ekin
ramen-ta'ceous
ram'i-cole
ram'i-corn
rami-fi-ca'tion
ram'i-fied
ram'i-form
ram'-ify
ram'i-fy-ing
ram'-jet
ram'-mer
ram'-ming
ram-ol-lesc'ence
ram-pa'ge
ram-pa'geous
ram-pa'ger
ram-pa'g-ing
ramp'-ancy
ram'-pant
ram'-part
ram'-pion
ram'-rod
ram'-shackle
rams'-horn
ram'-sons
ram'u-lose
ra-na'rian

ran-cesc'ent
ranch'-man
ran'-cho
ran'-cid
ran-cid'ity
ran'cor-ous
ran-dan'
ran'-dom
ran'-dom-ise
ra'nge-finder
ran'-ger-ine
ra'ngi-ness
ran'i-form
rank'-ling
rank'-ness
ran'-sack
ran'-som
ran'-somer
rant'-ing
ran-uncu-la'ceous
ra-pa'cious
ra-pa'cious-ness
ra-pac'ity
rap-id'ity
rap'-idly
rap'-ine
rappa-ree'
rap-pee'
rap-pel'
rap-scal'lion
rap'-ta-tory
rap'-tor
rap-to'rial
rap'-ture
rap'-tured
rap'-tur-ise
rap'-tur-ous

ra're-bit
rarofac'-tion
ra're-ness
ras'-cal
ras'-cal-dom
ras-cal'ity
ras'-cally
rash'-ing
rash'-ness
ras-o'rial
rasp-'berry
rasp'-ing
ras'-ter
ras'-trum
rata-fi'a
ratch'-et-ing
ratch'-ing
ratch'-ment
ra'te-able
rate-abil'ity
ra'te-payer
rati-fi-ca'tion
rat'i-fied
rat'-ify
rat'i-fy-ing
ratioc'in-ate
ratiocin-a'tion
ratiom'-eter
ration-al'e
ration-al-is-
      a'tion
rat'ion-al-ise
rat'ion-al-ism
rat'ion-al-ist
ration-al-is'tic
ration-al'ity
rat'ion-ally
rat'-ite

rat'-line
rat'-proof
rat-tan'
rat-teen'
rat'-ten
rat'-ter
rat'-ting
rat'-tler
rat'tle-snake
rat'tle-trap
rat'-tling
rau'-city
rau'-cous
rav'-age
rav'-ager
rav'-ag-ing
rav'-elin
rav'-elled
rav'-el-ling
rav'-ener
rav'-en-ing
rav'-en-ous
ravi'-ne
ravi-o'li
rav'-ish
rav'-isher
rav'-ish-ing
rav'-ish-ment
raw'-boned
raw'-hide
ra'win-sonde
raw'-ness
ray'-less
ray'-on-nant
ra'zor-back
ra'zor-bill
re-act'
re-ac'-tance

re-ac'-tant
re-ac'-tion
re-ac'-tion-ary
re-ac-ti-va'tion
re-ac'-tive
re-ac-tiv'ity
re-ac'-tor
read-abil'ity
read'-able
re-address'
read'i-ness
read'-ing
re-adjust'
re-adjust'-ment
re-admis'sion
re-adopt'
re-adorn'
re-affirm'
re-af-for'-est
re-a'gent
re-al'gar
re-ali'gn
re-ali'gn-ment
re-alis-a'tion
re'-alise
re'-alism
re'-alist
re-alis'tic
re-alis'ti-cally
re-al'ity
re'-altor
re'-alty
ream'-er-ing
re-an'i-mate
re-annex'
re-appar'el
re-appear'
re-appear'-ance

re-appoint'
rear'-dorse
rear'-guard (a.)
re-ar'gue
re-arm'
re-ar'ma-ment
rear'-most
re-arra'nge
re-arra'nge-ment
re-arra'ng-ing
rear'-ward
re-ascend'
reas'on-able
reas'on-able-ness
reas'on-ably
reas'on-ing
re-assem'ble
re-assert'
re-assu'me
re-assu'r-ance
re-assu're
re-assu'r-ing
re-awa'ken
re-ba'te
re-ba'te-ment
re-ba'ter
re-bell'ed
re-bel'-ling
re-bel'lion
re-bel'-lious
re-bel'-liously
re-birth'
re-bi'te
reb'o-ant
rebo-a'tion
re-born'
re-bound'
re-buff'

303

REBUILD

re-build'
re-built'
re-bu'ke
re-bu'k-ing
re-bur'y
re'-bus
re-but'
re-but'-table
re-but'-tal
re-but'-ted
re-but'-ting
re-cal'-ci-trance
re-cal'-ci-trant
re-cal'-ci-trate
re-cal-esc'e
re-cal-esc'ence
re-cal-esc'ent
re-call' (v. n.)
re'-call (n.)
re-cant'
re-can-ta'tion
re'-cap
re-cap-it'u-late
re-cap-itu-
　　　la'tion
re-cap-it'u-lat-
　　　　ory
re-capp'ed
re-cap'-ping
re-cap'-tion
re-cap'-ture
re-cast'
re-ce'de
re-ce'ded
re-ce'd-ence
re-ce'd-ent
re-ce'der
re-ce'd-ing
304

re-ceipt'
re-ceipt'or
re-ceiv'-able
re-ceiv'e
re-ceiv'er
re-ceiv'-er-ship
re-ceiv'-ing
re'-cency
re-cens'e
re-cen'-sion
re'-cent
re'-cently
re-cept'
re-cep'-tacle
re-cep-tac'u-lar
re-cep-tac'u-lum
re-cep-ti-bil'ity
re-cep'-tible
re-cep'-tion
re-cep'-tion-ist
re-cep'-tive
re-cep-tiv'ity
re-cep'-tor
re'-cess
re-cess'er
re-ces'sion
re-ces'sion-al
re-cess'-ive
re-char'ge
re-cid'i-vate
re-cidi-va'tion
re-cid'i-vism
re-cid'i-vist
re-cip'i-ence
re-cip'i-ent
re-cip'ro-cable
re-cip'ro-cal
re-cip'ro-cally

re-cip'ro-cate
re-cipro-cat'ion
re-cip'ro-cat-ive
re-cip'ro-cat-ory
reci-proc'ity
re-cipro-cor'-
　　　　nous
re-cis'ion
re-ci'tal
reci-ta'tion
re-ci'te
re-ci'ter
re-ci't-ing
reck'-less
reck'-lessly
reck'-less-ness
reck'-oner
reck'-on-ing
re-claim'
re-claim'-able
rec-la-ma'tion
re-cli'n-able
rec'-li-nate
rec-li-na'tion
re-cli'ne
re-cli'ner
re-cli'n-ing
re-clo'se
re-clo'the
re-clu'sion
re-clu'sive
rec-og-ni's-able
re-cog'ni-sance
rec'-og-nise
rec=og'-nise
re-cog'ni-see
rec'-og-niser
re-cog'ni-sor

rec-og-nit′ion
re-cog′ni-tive
re-cog′ni-tor
re-coil′
rec-ol-lect′
rec-ol-lec′-tion
re-col′-on-ise
re-com-bi-na′tion
re-com-bi′ne
re-com-men′ce
rec-ommend′
rec-ommend′-able
rec-ommen-
     da′tion
rec-ommend′-
     atory
re-com-mis′sion
re-com-mit′
re-com-mit′-tal
re-com-mit′-ment
re-com-mu′ni-cate
rec′-ompense
rec′-ompenser
rec′-ompens-ing
re-com-po′se
re-com-pound′
re-con′-cen-trate
rec′-oncil-able
rec′-oncile
rec′-oncile-ment
rec-oncili-a-tion
rec-oncil′i-at-
     ory
recon′-dite
re-con-dit′ion
re-con-duct′
re-con-firm′
re-con′nais-sance

rec-onnoit′re
re-con′quer
re-con′quest
re-con′-se-crate
re-con-sid′er
re-con-sider-
     a′tion
re-con′-sti-tute
re-con′-struct
re-con-struc′-
     tion
re-con-ve′ne
re-con′-vert′
re-con-vey′
re-cord′ (v.)
rec′-ord (n.)
re-cord′-able
rec-or-da′tion
re-cord′er
re-cord′-ist
re-count′
re-coup′
re-coup′-ment
re-cours′e
re-cov′er
re-cov′-er-able
re-cov′-ery
rec′-reant
rec′-reate
re-cre-a′te
rec-rea′tion
re-rea′tional
re-cre-a′tive
rec′-reative
rec′-rement
rec-remen′-tal
rec-remen-
     tit′ious

re-crim′i-nate
re-crim′i-nat-ing
re-crimi-na′tion
re-crim′-in-at-
re-crim′-in-at-
     ory
re-crim′-in-at-
     ive
re-cru-desc′e
re-crud-esc′ence
re-crud-esc′ent
re-cruit′
re-cruit′er
re-cruit′-ment
rec′-tal
rec′-tangle
rec-tan′gu-lar
rec′-ti-fi-able
rec-ti-fi-ca′tion
rec′-ti-fied
rec′-ti-fier
rec′-tify
rec′-ti-grade
rec-ti-lin′-eal
rec-ti-lin′-ear
rec-ti-ros′-tral
rec-ti′tis
rec′-ti-tude
rec′-tor
rec′-toral
rec′-tor-ate
rec-to′rial
rec′-tor-ship
rec′-tory
rec′-to-scope
rec′-tum
rec′-tus
rec′u-bant
recu-ba′tion

305

re-cum'-bence
re-cum'-bency
re-cum'-bent
re-cu'per-ate
re-cuper-a'tion
re-cu'per-at-ive
re-cu'per-ator
re-cu'per-at-ory
re-curr'
re-curr'ed
re-cur'-rence
re-cur'-rent
re-cur'-ring
re-cur'-sant
re-cur'-sive
re-cur'-vate
re-cur'-va-ture
re-curvi-ros'-
        tral
re-cur'-vous
rec'u-sancy
rec'u-sant
recu-sa'tion
re-cu'se
re-dact'
re-dac'-tion
re-dac'-tor
red'-bird
red'-breast
red'-bud
red'-cap
red'-coat
red'-den
red-den'-dum
red'-dish
red-dit'ion
red'-di-tive
re-dec'-or-ate
306

re-deem'
re-deem'-able
re-deem'-er
re-demp'-tible
re-demp'-tion
re-demp'-tive
re-demp'-tion-ary
re-demp'-tor
re-demp'-tory
re-deploy'
re-deploy'-ment
re-devel'-op-ment
red'-head
red'-headed
red-hi-bit'ion
red-hib'i-tory
red'-ingote
red-in'te-grate
red-in'te-gration
re-direct'
re-dis'-count
re-dis-cov'er
re-dis-cov'-ery
re-dis-trib'-ute
re-dis-tri-
        bu'tion
re-dis'-trict
redi-vi'vus
red'-ma-nol
red'-ness
red'o-lence
red'o-lent
re-doub'le
re-doub'-ling
re-doubt'
re-doubt'-able
re-dound'
red'-poll

re-draw'
re-dress'
re-dress'er
re-dress'-ible
re-dress'-ive
re-driv'en
red'-sear
red'-shank
rod'-skin
red'-start
re-du'ce
re-du'c-ent
re-du'cer
re-du'c-ible
re-du'c-ing
re-duc'tase
re-duc'tion
re-duc'tive
re-duc'tor
re-dun'-dancy
re-dun'-dant
re-du'pli-cate
re-du'pli-ca'tion
re-du'pli-cat-ive
red'-wing
red'-wood
reed'-ing
re-e-lec'-tion
re-el'i-gible
re-em-bark'
re-en-act'
re-en-fo'rce
re-en-fo'rce-ment
re-en-ga'ge
re-en-list'
re-en'-ter
re-en'-trant
re-es-tab'-lish

re-es-tab'-lish-
    ment
re-exam-in-a'tion
re-exam'-ine
re-ex-port'
re-fash'ion
re-fas'ten
re-fec'-tion
re-fec'-tory
re-fer'
ref'-er-able
ref-eree'
ref'-er-ence
ref-er-en'dum
ref-er-en'-tial
re-ferment'
re-ferr'ed
ref'-errent
re-fer'-ring
re-fill' (v.)
re'-fill (n.)
re-fill'-able
re-fi'ne
re-fi'ned
re-fi'ne-ment
re-fi'ner
re-fi'nery
re-fi'ning
re-fit'
re-fit'-ment
re-fla'tion
re-fla'tion-ary
re-flect'
re-flec'-tance
re-flect'-ible
re-flec'-tion
re-flec'-tive
re-flec-tom'eter

re-flec'-tor
re-flec'-tor-ise
re-flex' (v.)
re'-flex (a.)
re-flex'-ible
re-flex'ion
re-flex'-ive
re-flex-iv'ity
ref'-lu-ent
re'-flux
re-for'-est
re-for-es-ta'tion
re-form'
re-form'-able
ref-or-ma'tion
re-for-ma'tion
re-for'ma-tive
re-for'ma-tory
re-form'er
re-form'-ist
re-fract'
re-frac'-ted
re-frac'-tion
re-frac'-tive
re-frac-tiv'ity
re-frac-tom'eter
re-frac-to-
    met'ric
re-frac-tom'etry
re-frac'-tor
re-frac'-tor-ies
re-frac'-tori-
    ness
re-frac'-tory
ref'ra-gable
re-frain'
re-fran'-gible
re-fresh'

re-fresh'er
re-fresh'-ing
re-fresh'-ment
re-frig'er-ant
re-frig'er-ate
re-friger-a'tion
re-frig'er-ative
re-frig'er-ator
re-frin'-gency
re-frin'-gent
ref'-tone
re-fu'el
ref'-uge
ref'u-gee
re-ful'gence
re-ful'gent
re'-fund (n.)
re-fund' (v.)
re-fur'-bish
re-fur'-nish
re-fu'sal
re-fu'se
ref'-use
re-fu's-ing
re-fu'sion
re-fu't-able
re-fu't-ably
re-fu'tal
refu-ta'tion
re-fu'te
re-fu'ter
re-fu't-ing
re-gain'
re'-gal
re-ga'le
rc-ga'lia
re-ga'ling
re-gal'ity

re'-gally
re-gard'
re-gard'-ant
re-gard'-ful
re-gard'-ing
re-gard'-less
re-gath'er
re'-gel-ate
re-gel-a'tion
re'-gency
re-gen'-er-acy
re-gen'-er-ate
re-gen-er-a'tion
re-gen'-er-at-ive
re-gen'-er-at-or
re-gen'-er-at-ory
re-gen'-esis
re'-gent
regi-ci'dal
reg'i-cide
reg'i-men
reg'i-ment
regi-men'-tal
regi-men'-tals
regi-men'-tary
regi-men-ta'tion
re'-gion
re'-gional
reg'is-ter
reg'is-tered
reg'is-trable
reg'is-trant
reg'is-trar
reg'is-trate
regis-tra'tion
reg'is-try
reg'-let
reg-lett'e

reg'-nal
reg'-nancy
reg'-nant
reg'-num
re-gor'ge
re-gra'te
re-gra't-ing
re-gra'tor
re-gress'
re-gres'sion
re-gress'-ive
re-gress'or
re-gret'
re-gret'-ful
re-gret'-fully
re-gret'-table
re-gret'-tably
re-gret'-ted
re-gret'-ting
reg'-ula
reg'-ular
reg'u-lar-ise
regu-lar-is-
 a'tion
regu-lar'ity
reg'u-larly
reg'u-lat-able
reg'u-late
regu-la'tion
reg'u-lat-ive
reg'u-lator
reg'u-lat-ory
reg'u-line
reg'u-lise
reg'u-lus
re-gur'-gi-tate
re-gur-gi-ta'tion
re-habil'i-tate

re-habili-ta'tion
re-habil'i-tat-
 ive
re-han'dle
re-hang'
re'-hash (n.)
re-hash' (v.)
re-hear'
re-hears'al
re-hears'e
re-hears'er
re-hears'-ing
re-heat'
re-hous'e
re'-ify
re-im-burs'-able
re-im-bur'se
re-im-bur'se-
 ment
re-im-port'
re-im-por-ta'tion
re-incar'-nate
re-incar-na'tion
rein'-deer
re-info'rce
re-info'rce-ment
re-insert'
re-install'
re-instal-la'tion
re-instal'-ment
re-insta'te
re-insta'te-ment
re-insu're
re-in'te-grate
re-inte-gra'tion
re-in-vest'
re-invig'-or-ate
re-is'sue

re-it'er-ate
re-iter-a'tion
re-it'er-at-ive
re-ject' (v.)
re'-ject (n.)
re'-ject'-able
re-ject'er
re-jec'-tion
re-jec'-tive
re-jec'-tor
re-joic'e
re-joic'-ing
re-join'
re-join'-der
re-judg'e
re-ju'-ven-ate
re-ju-ven-a'tion
re-ju'-ven-ator
re-ju-ven-
   esc'ence
re-kin'dle
re-la'bel
re-land'
re-laps'e
re-laps'ed
re-laps'er
re-laps'-ing
re-la'te
re-la'ted
re-la'ter
re-la't-ing
re-la'tion
re-la'tion-ship
rel'a-tive
rel'a-tively
rel'a-tiv-ism
rela-tiv'-ity
re-la'tor

re-lax'
re-lax'-ant
relax-a'tion
re-lax'-edly
re'-lay
re-lay'
re'-layed
re-leas'e
re-leas'ed
re-leas'er
re-leas'-ing
rel'-egable
rel'-egate
rel'-egated
rel-ega'tion
re-lent'
re-lent'-ing
re-lent'-ingly
re-lent'-less
re-lessee''
re-lessor'
rel'-evance
rel'-evancy
rel'-evant
re-liabil'ity
re-li'able
re-li'ably
re-li'ance
re-li'ant
rel'-ict (n.)
re-lict' (v.)
re-li'ed
re-lief'
re-lie've-able
re-lie've
re-lie'ved
re-lie'ver
re-lie've-ing

re-lig'ion
re-lig'i-ose
re-ligi-os'ity
re-lig'ious
re-lig'iously
re-lin'-quish
rel'i-quary
rel'-ish
rel'-ish-able
rel'-ish-ing
re-liv'e
re-load'
re-lo-ca'tion
re-lu'cence
re-lu'cent
re-luc'-tance
re-luc'-tant
re-luc'-tantly
reluc-tiv'ity
re-lu'me
re-lu'mine
re-ly'-ing
re-ma'de
re-main'
re-main'-der
re-main'-ing
re-mains'
re-ma'ke
re-mand'
re-mand'-ment
rem'-an-ence
rem'-an-ent
re-mark'
re-mark'-able
re-mark'-ably
re-mar'-riage
re-mar'ry
re-me'di-able

REMEDIAL

re-me'dial
rem'-edied
rem'-edies
rem'-edi-less
rem'-edy
re-mem'-ber
re-mem'-brance
re-mem'-brancer
rem'i-form
re-mi'grate
re-mi'nd
re-mi'nder
re-mi'nd-ful
remi-nisc'ence
remi-nisc'ent
remi-nisc'ently
remi-nisc'er
remi-nisc'ing
rem'i-ped
re-mi'se
re-miss'
re-missi-bil'ity
re-miss'-ible
re-mis'sion
re-miss'-ive
re-miss'-ness
re-miss'-ory
re-mit'
re-mit'-tal
re-mit'-tance
re-mit'-ted
re-mit-tee'
re-mit'-tent
re-mit'-ter
re-mit'-ting
re-mit'-ti-tur
rem'-nant
re-mod'el

re-mod'-elled
re-mon-et-is-
    a'tion
re-mon'-et-ise
re-mon'-strance
re-mon'-strant
rem'on-strate
remon-stra'tion
re-mon'-stra-tive
remon-stra'tor
re-mon'-tant
rem-on-toir'
rem'-ora
re-mors'e
re-mors'e-ful
re-mors'e-less
re-mo'te
re-mo'tely
re-mo'te-ness
re-mount'
re-mov-abil'ity
re-mov'-able
re-mov'al
re-mov'e
re-mov'ed
re-mov'er
re-mov'-ing
re-mu'ner-able
re-mu'ner-ate
re-muner-a'tion
re-mu'ner-at-ive
re'-nal
re-na'me
re-nasc'ence
re-nasc'ent
ren'-der (v.)
ren'-der-able
ren'-der-ing

rend'-ible
rend'-ing
ren-di'tion
ren'-egade
re-ne'ge
re-ne'ger
re-ne'ging
re-new'
re-new'-able
re-new'al
re-new'ed
re'ni-form
re'-nin
ren'i-tence
ren'i-tent
ren'-net
ren'-nin
re-nom'i-nate
re-nomi-na'tion
re-nounc'e
re-nounc'e-ment
re-nounc'-ing
ren'o-vate
ren'o-vat-ing
reno-va'tion
ren'o-vator
re-nown'
re-nown'ed
rent'-able
ren'-ter
rent'-ing
ren'u-ent
re-nunci-a'tion
re-nun'ci-at-ory
ren-ver'se
re-oc-cu-pa'tion
re-oc'-cupy
re-o'pen

310

re-or-gan-is-
 a'tion
re-or'-gan-ise
re-o'ri-ent
re-ori-en-ta'tion
re-paid'
re-paint'
re-pair'
re-pair'-able
re-pair'er
re-pair'-man
rep'-ar-able
rep-ar-a'tion
re-par'a-tive
re-par'a-tory
rep-ar-tee'
re-par-tit'ion
re-pass'
re-pass'-ant
re-past'
re-pat'ri-ate
re-patri-a'tion
re-pay'
re-pay'-able
re-pay'-ing
re-pay'-ment
re-peal'
re-peal'-able
re-peal'er
re-peat'
re-peat'-able
re-peat'ed
re-peat'-edly
re-peat'er
re-peat'-ing
re-pel'
re-pell'ed
re-pel'-lency

re-pel'-lent
re-pel'-ling
re-pent'
re-pent'-ance
re-pent'-ant
re-peop'le
re-per-cus'sion
re-per-cuss'-ive
rep'-er-toire
rep'-er-tory
rep'-etend
rep-etit'ion
rep-etit'ious
rep-etit'iously
re-pet'i-tive
re-pi'ne
re-pla'ce
re-pla'ce-able
re-pla'ce-ment
re-pla'c-ing
re-plant'
re-plen'-ish
re-plen'-isher
re-plen'-ish-ment
re-ple'te
re-ple'tion
re-ple't-ive
re-plev'in
re-plev'i-sor
re-plev'y
rep'-lica
rep'-li-cate
rep-li-ca'tion
re-pli'ed
re-ply'
re-ply'-ing
re-point'
re-pol'-ish

re-pop'u-late
re-po'rt
re-po'rt-age
re-po'rter
repor-to'rial
re-po'se
re-po'se-ful
re-po's-ing
repo-sit'ion
re-pos'i-tor
re-pos'i-tory
re-pos-sess'
re-pos-ses'sion
rep-rehend'
rep-rehen-si-
 bil'ity
rep-rehen'-sible
rep-rehen'-sion
rep-rehen'-sive
rep-resent'
rep-resent'-able
rep-resen-ta'tion
rep-resen-ta-
 tive
rep-resen'-ter
re-press'
re-press'er
re-press'-ible
re-pres'sion
re-press'-ive
re-press'or
re-prieve
rep'-ri-mand
re-print' (v.)
re'-print (n.)
re-pri'sal
re-pri'se
re-proach'

311

re-proach'-ful
re-proach'-fully
re-proach'-ing
rep'-ro-bacy
rep'-ro-bate
rep'-ro-ba'tion
rep'-ro-bat-ive
rep'-ro-bator
rep'-ro-bat-ory
re-pro-du'ce
re-pro-du'cer
re-pro-du'c-ible
re-pro-du'c-ing
re-pro-duc'tion
re-pro-duc'tive
re-pro-ductiv'ity
re-proof'
re-prov'e
re-prov'-ing
re-prov'-ingly
rep'-tant
rep-ta'tion
rep'-tile
rep-til'ian
rep-ti-lif'er-ous
rep-til'i-form
rep-ti-liv'or-ous
rep'-ti-loid
re-pub'-lic
re-pub'-li-can
re-pub'-li-can-ism
re-pub-li-ca'tion
re-pub'-lish
re-pu'di-ate
re-pudi-a'tion
re-pu'di-ator
re-pug'-nance

re-pug'-nancy
re-pug'-nant
re-pul'se
re-puls'-ing
re-pul'-sion
re-pul'-sive
re-pul'-sory
re-pur'-chase
rep'u-table
rep'u-tably
repu-ta'tion
re-pu'te
re-pu'ted
re-pu't-ing
re-quest'
re-quest'er
re-qui're
re-qui're-ment
re-qui'rer
re-qui'r-ing
req'ui-site
requi-sit'ion
requis'i-tor
re-qui'tal
re-qui'te
re-qui'ted
re-qui't-ing
re-read'
re're-dos
re-sa'le
re-sa'le-able
re-scind'
re-scind'-able
re-scind'-ment
re-sciss'-ible
re-scis'sion
re-sciss'-ory
re'-script

re-scrip'-tion
re-scrip'-tive
res'-cu-able
res'-cue
res'-cued
res'-cuer
res'-cu-ing
re'-search
re-search'er
re-seat'
re-sect'
re-sect'-able
re-sec'-tion
res-eda'ceous
re-seiz'-ure
re-sell'
re-sem'-blance
re-sem'ble
re-sem'-bler
re-sem'-bling
re-sent'
re-sent'-ful
re-sent'-fully
re-sent'-ment
res'-er-pine
res-er-va'tion
re-serv'e
re-serv'ed
re-serv'-edly
re-serv'-ist
res'-er-voir
ro-set'
re-set'-ter
re-set'-ting
re-set'tle
re-set'tle-ment
re-ship'
re-ship'-ment

re-si'de
res'i-dence
res'i-dency
res'i-dent
res'i-den-ter
resi-den'-tial
resi-den'-tiary
re-si'd-ing
re-sid'ual
re-sid'u-ary
res'i-due
res-id'u-ent
re-sid'uum
re-si'gn
res-ig-na'tion
re-si'gned
re-si'gn-edly
re-sil'i-ence
re-sil'i-ency
re-sil'i-ent
re-sil'i-ently
re-sil'-ium
resin-a'ceous
res'in-ate
resin-if'er-ous
resini-fi-ca'tion
res'in-ise
resin-og'raphy
res'in-oid
res'in-ous
resi-pisc'ence
resi-pisc'ent
re-sist'
re-sist'-ance
re-sist'-ant
re-sist'er
re-sisti-bil'ity
re-sist'-ible

res-is-tiv'ity
re-sist'-less
re-sis'tor
re-so'ld
re-sol'-uble
res'-ol-ute
res'-ol-utely
res-ol-u'tion
res-ol-u'tioner
res-ol-u'tive
re-sol'u-tive
re-solv-abil'ity
re-solv'-able
re-solv'e
re-solv'ed
re-solv'-edly
re-solv'-end
re-solv'-ent
re-solv'er
re-solv'-ing
res'-on-ance
res'-onant
res'-onate
res'-onator
re-sorb'-ent
re-sorp'-tion
re-sorp'-tive
re-sort'
re-sound'
re-sound'ed
re-sound'-ing
re-sound'-ingly
re-sourc'e
re-sourc'e-ful
re-sourc'e-fully
re-sourc'e-ful-
     ness

re-spect'
re-spect-abil'ity
re-spect'-able
re-spect'-ably
re-spec'-tant
re-spect'er
re-spect'-ful
re-spect'-fully
re-spect'-ing
re-spect'-ive
re-spect'-ively
res'-pir-able
res-pir-a'tion
res'-pir-ator
res'-pir-at-ory
re-spi're
re-spi'r-ing
res-pir-om'eter
res'-pite
re-splen'-dence
re-splen'-dency
re-splen'-dent
re-spond'
re-spon'-dence
re-spon'-dency
re-spon'-dent
re-spon-den'tia
re-spond'er
re-spons'e
re-spon'-ser
re-sponsi-bil'ity
re-spon'-sible
re-spon'-sibly
re-spon'-sive
re-spon'-sive-ly
re-spon'-sive-
     ness
re-spon'-sor

313

RESPONSORIAL

res-pon-so'rial
re-spon'-sory
re-sta'te
res'-taurant
res-taura-teur'
rest'-ful
res'-ti-form
res'-ti-tute
res-ti-tu'tion
res'-ti-tut-ive
res'-tive
rest'-less
rest'-lessly
rest'-less-ness
re-stock'
res-to-ra'tion
res-to'ra-tive
re-sto're
re-sto'rer
re-sto'r-ing
re-strain'
re-strain'ed
re-straint'
re-strict'
re-stric'-ted
re-stric'-tion
re-stric'-tive
re-sult'
re-sult'-ant
re-su'me
re-su'm-ing
re-sum'mon
re-sump'-tion
re-sump'-tive
re-su'pi-nate
re-supi-na'tion
re-surg'e
re-sur'gence

re-sur'gent
res-ur-rect'
res-ur-rec'-tion
res-ur-rec'-tion-
 ist
res-ur-rec'-tor
re-sus'ci-table
re-sus'ci-tant
re-sus'ci-rate
re-susci-ta'tion
re-sus'ci-tat-ive
re-sus'ci-tator
re'-tail
re'-tailer
re-tain'
re-tain'-able
re-tain'er
re-tain'-ing
re-ta'ke
re-tal'i-ate
re-tali-a'tion
re-tal'i-at-ive
re-tal'i-at-ory
re-tard'
re-tard'-ant
re-tar-da'tion
re-tar'-da-tory
re-tar'ded
re-tell'
re-tene
re-tent'
re-ten'-tion
re-ten'-tive
re-ten-tiv'ity
re-ten'-tor
re'-tiary
ret'i-cence
ret'i-cent

ret'-icle
re-tic'u-lar
re-tic'u-late
re-ticu-la'tion
ret'i-cule
re-tic'u-lin
re-ticu-li'tis
re-ticulo-
  cyto'sis
re-tic'u-lose
re'ti-form
ret'-ina
reti-nac'u-lum
ret'i-nal
re-tin'a-lite
ret'i-nene
reti-ni'tis
retino-choroid-
  i'tis
ret'i-nol
reti-nos'copy
ret'i-nue
re-ti'ral
re-ti're
re-ti'red
re-tiree'
re-ti're-ment
re-ti'r-ing
re-to'ld
re-tor'-sion
re-tort'
re-tort'er
re-tor'tion
re-tor'-tive
re-touch'
re-tra'ce
re-tra'ce-able
re-tra'cing

re-tract'
re-tract-abil'ity
re-tract'-able
re-trac'-ted
re-trac'-tile
re-trac-til'ity
re-trac'-tion
re-trac'-tive
re-trac'-tor
re'-tral
re-tread'
re-treat'
re-tree'
re-trench'
re-trench'-ment
ret'-ri-bute
ret-ri-bu'tion
re-trib'u-tive
re-trib'u-tory
re-trie'v-able
re-trie'val
re-trie've
re-trie'ver
re-trie'v-ing
ret'-ri-ment
ret'-ro-act
retro-ac'tion
retro-ac'tive
retro-ce'de
retro-ce'd-ence
retro-ce'd-ent
retro-ces'sion
retro-cog-nit'ion
ret'ro-curved
ret'ro-date
retro-gra-da'tion
retro-gra'd-atory
ret'ro-grade

ret'ro-gress
retro-gres'sion
retro-gress'-ive
retro-min'-gent
re-trors'e
retro-tror'-sine
ret'ro-spect
retro-spec'-tion
retro-spec'-tive
ret'ro-verse
retro-ver'sion
retro-ver'ted
ret'-ting
re-tund'
re-turn'
re-turn'-able
re-tu'se
re-u'nion
re-uni'te
re-uni't-ing
re-val-or-is-
     a'tion
re-val'-or-ise
re-val'u-ate
re-valu-a'tion
re-val'ue
re-vamp'
re-veal'
re-veal'-able
rev-el-a'tion
rev-el-a'tion-ist
rev'-el-ator
rev'-el-atory
rev'-elled
rev'-el-ler
rev'-el-ling
rev'-elry

rev'-enant
re-ven-di-ca'tion
re-ven'-di-cate
re-venge'
re-venge'e-ful
re-venge'e-ful-
     ness
re-ven'ger
re-veng'-ing
rev'-enue
re-ve'rable
re-ver'-ber-ant
re-ver'-ber-ate
re-ver-ber-a'tion
re-ver'-ber-ator
re-ver'-ber-at-
     ory
re-ve're
rev'-er-ence
rev'-er-end
rev-er-ent
rev-er-en'-tial
rev'-er-ently
rev'-erie
re-ve'ring
re-ver'-sal
re-ver'se
re-ver'ser
re-versi-bil'ity
re-vers'-ible
re-vers'-ing
re-ver'-sion
re-ver'-sion-ary
re-vert'
re-vert'-ant
re-vert'er
re-vert'-ible
re-vert'-ive

REVEST

re-vest'
re-vet'
re-vet'-ment
re-vet'-ted
re-vet'-ting
re-vict'ual
re-vict'ual-ment
re-view'
re-view'-able
re-view'al
re-view'er
re-vig'or-ate
re-vi'le
re-vi'le-ment
re-vi'ler
re-vi'l-ing
re-vin'-di-cate
re-vin-di-ca'tion
re-vi's-able
re-vi'sal
re-vi'se
re-vi'sed
re-vi'ser
re-vis'ion
re-vis'ion-ary
re-vis'ion-ist
re-vis'it
re-visi-ta'tion
re-vi'sor
re-vi's-ory
re-vi'tal-ise
re-vi'val
re-vi'v-al-ism
re-vi'v-al-ist
re-vi've
re-vi'ver
re-vivi-ca'tion
re-viv'ify

re-vi'v-ing
revi-visc'ence
revi-visc'ent
re-vi'vor
revo-ca-bil'ity
rev'o-cable
revo-ca'tion
rev'o-cat-ory
re-vo'ke
re-vo'ker
re-vo'k-ing
re-vo'lt
re-vo'lter
re-vo'lt-ing
re-vo'lt-ingly
rev'-ol-ute
rev-ol-u'tion
rev-ol-u'tion-ary
rev-ol-u'tion-ise
rev-ol-u'tion-ist
re-volv'-able
re-volv'e
re-volv'e-ment
re-volv'er
re-volv'-ing
re-vue'
re-vul'-sion
re-vul'-sive
re-vul'-sor
re-ward'
re-word'
re-wri'te (v.)
re'-write (n.)
rhab'-di-form
rhab'-dium
rhab'-doid
rhab'-do-man-cer
rhab'-do-mancy

rham-na'ceous
rham'-na-zin
rham'-netin
rham'-nose
rham'-nus
rham'-phoid
rhap-sod'ic
rhap-sod'i-cal
rhap'-sodisc
rhap'-sodis-ing
rhap'-sodist
rhap'-sody
rhar'-any
rhe-mat'ic
rhe'-nium
rhe'o-cord
rhe-ol'ogy
rhe-om'eter
rhe-om'-etry
rhe'o-motor
rhe'o-phile
rhe'o-phore
rhe'o-scope
rhe'o-stat
rheo-stat'ic
rhe-otax'is
rhe'o-tome
rhe'o-trope
rhe-ot'ro-pism
rhe'-sus
rhet'-oric
rhe-tor'i-cal
rhet-or-ic'ian
rheu-mat'ic
rheu'-ma-tism
rheu'-ma-toid
rheu-ma-tol'ogy
rhig'-ol-ene

316

rhi´-nal
rhi-nen-ceph´a-lon
rhi´ne-stone
rhi-ni´tis
rhi-noc´eros
rhi´-no-don
rhi-nol´-ogist
rhi-nol´ogy
rhino-plas´-tic
rhi´no-plasty
rhi´no-scope
rhi-nos´copy
rhip´i-date
rhiz-an´-thous
rhi´-zic
rhi-zo´bium
rhizo-car´-pous
rhizo-ceph´a-lous
rhi-zo-gen´ic
rhi´-zoid
rhi-zom´a-tous
rhi´-zome
rhi-zoph´a-gous
rhi-zoph´i-lous
rhi-zoph´-orous
rhi-zot´omy
rho´-dal-ite
rho´-da-mine
rho´-da-nate
rho´-dan-ise
rho´-dic
rho´-di-nol
rho´-dite
rho´-dium
rhodo-chro´site
rho-do-den´-dron
rho´-don-ite

rho-do´ra
rhomb-en-ceph´a-lon
rhomb´-bic
rhombo-he´dral
rhombo-he´dron
rhom´-boid
rhom-boid´al
rhom -bus
rho-pal´ic
rho´-ta-cise
rho´-ta-cism
rhu´-barb
rhum´-ba-tron
rhy´me-less
rhy´m-ster
rhy´m-ing
rhy´o-lite
rhyth´-mal
rhyth´-mic
rhyth´-mi-cal
rhyth´-mi-cally
rhyth´-mise
rhyth-mom´eter
ri´-ancy
ri´-ant
rib´-ald
rib´-aldry
rib´-and
rib´-band
rib´-bing
rib´-bon
rib´-boned
rib´-bon-ite
ribo-fla´vin
ribo-nu´-clease
ribo-nucle´ic
ri´-bo-some

ri´ce-bird
rich´-ness
rici-no-le´ic
rici-no´lein
rick´-ets
rick-ett´-sial
rick´-ety
rick´-shaw
ric´-tus
rid´-dance
rid´-den
rid´-der
rid´-ding
rid´-dling
rid´-dlings
ri´de-able
ri´-dent
ri´der-less
ridg´e-pole
ridg´-ing
rid´i-cule
rid-ic´u-lous
rid-ic´u-lously
ri´fe-ness
rif´-fler
rif´-fling
riff´-raff
ri´fle-man
rig´-ger
rig´-ging
ri´ghteous-ness
ri´ght-ful
ri´ght-fully
ri´ght-ist
ri´ght-ness
ri´ght-whale
rigid´-ity
rig´-ma-role

317

rig'-or-ous
rig'-or-ously
rig'-our
ri'-mate
rim'i-form
rim'-less
rim'-let
rim'-ming
ri'-mose
ri'-mous
rin'-der-pest
ring'-bolt
ring'-bone
ring'-dove
rin'-gent
ring'-ing
ring'-leader
ring'-less
ring'-let
ring'-mas-ter
ring'-side
ring'-ster
ring'-worm
rins'-able
rins'-ing
ri'-oter
ri'ot-ous
ri'ot-ously
ri-pa'rian
ri'pe-ness
ri-pid'o-lite
rip'-pling
rip'-rap
rip'-saw
risi-bil'ity
risk'i-ness
ris-so'le
rit'-ual

rit'u-al-ism
rit'u-al-ist
ritu-al-is'tic
riv'-age
ri'val-ling
riv'-er-ain
riv'-er-bank
riv'-er-ine
riv'-er-side
riv'-eter
riv'-et-ing
riv'u-let
riv'u-lose
road'-bed
road'-house
road'-side
road'-stead
road'-ster
road'-way
rob'-ber
rob'-bery
rob'-bing
rob'-bins
rob'-or-ant
ro'-bur-ite
ro-bust'
ro-bus'-tious
ro-bust'-ness
roc'-am-bole
rock'-bound
rock'-dove
rock'-ery
rocket-eer'
rock'-eter
rock'-etry
rock'-ing
rock'-ling
rock'-rose

ro-co'co
rod'-ding
ro-den'ti-cidal
ro-den'ti-cide
rodo-mon-ta'de
roe'-buck
roent'-gen
roent'-geno-
  graph
roent-gen-og'ra-
  phy
roent-gen-ol'ogy
roent'-gen-
  om'eter
roent'-geno-
  scope
roent-gen-
  os'copy
ro-ga'tion
rog'a-tory
rogu'ish-ness
rois'-ter
rois'-ter-er
rois'-ter-ous
rol'-lick
rol'-lick-ing
rol'-lick-some
roll'-top (a.)
ro-man'ce
ro-man'cer
ro-manc'-ing
ro-man-es'que
ro-man'-tic
ro-man'-ti-cally
ro-man'-ti-cism
ro-man'-ti-cist
ro'-meite
ron'-deau

ron'-del
ron-delet'
ron-dell'e
ron'-dure
ro'neo-graph
roof'-ing
roof'-less
roof'-tree
rook'-ery
room'-age
room'-ful
room'i-ness
room'-mate
root'-less
root'-let
root-stock
ro'pe-dancer
ro'pe-walk
ro'pe-walker
ro'pe-way
ro'pi-ness
ro-rif'er-ous
ror'-qual
ro-sa'ceous
ro-sa'lia
ro-san'-il-ine
ro'-sary
ro'-seate
ro'se-bud
ro'se-bush
ro'se-mary
ro-se'ola
ro-sett'e
ro'se-wood
ros'-in-ate
ro'si-ness
ro-so'lio
ros'-ter

ros'-tral
ros'-trate
ros'-tri-form
ros'-troid
ros'-trum
ros'ula
ros'u-lar
ros'u-late
ro'-tal
ro-tam'eter
ro'-tary
ro-ta't-able
ro'-tate (a.)
ro-ta'te (v.)
ro-ta'tion
ro'ta-tive
ro-ta'tor
ro'ta-tory
ro'-tenone
ro'-ti-fer
ro-tif'er-ous
ro'-ti-form
ro'-to-graph
roto-gravu're
ro'-tor
rot'-ten
rot'-ten-ness
rot'-ten-stone
rot'-ula
ro-tund'
ro-tun'da
ro-tun'-date
ro-tun-di-fo'li-
    ous
ro-tun'-dity
ro-tund'ly
rough'-age
rough'-cast

rough'-dry
rough-hew
rough'-ish
rough'-neck
rough'-ness
rough'-rider
rough'-shod
rou-leau'
rou-lett'e
round'-about
roun'-del
roun-delay
round'-house
round'-ish
round'-ness
rounds'-man
round'-worm
rous'-ant
rous'-ing
rous'-ingly
roust'-about
rou-ti'ne
rou-ti-neer'
rout'-ing
rov'-ing
row'-boat
row'-di-ness
row'dy-ish
row'dy-ism
row'-lock
roy'-al-ism
roy'-al-ist
roy'-ally
roy'-alty
ru-bass'e
rub'-ber
rub'-ber-ise
rub'-bing

319

RUBBISH

rub'-bish
rub'-down
ru-bean'ic
ru-bed'i-nous
ru-befa'cient
ru-befac'-tion
ru-bel'la
ru-bel'-lite
ru-be'ola
ru-besc'ence
ru-besc'ent
ru-bi-a'ceous
ru'-bian
ru'-bi-can
ru'-bi-celle
ru'-bi-cund
ru-bi-cun'-dity
ru-bid'-ium
ru-big'in-ose
ru-big'in-ous
ru'-bric
ru'-bri-cal
ru'-bri-cate
ru-bri-ca'tion
ru'-bri-cator
ru'-bri-cist
ru-bric'ity
ru'-bri-cose
ru'ch-ing
ruck'-sack
ruc-ta'tion
ruc'-tion
rud'-der
rud'-di-ness
ru'de-ness
ru-den'-ture
ru'-di-ment
ru-di-men'-tal
320

ru-di-men'-tary
ru-di-men-ta'tion
rue'-ful
rue'-fully
ru-fesc'ence
ru-fesc'ent
ruf'-fian
ruf' fler
ruf'-fling
ru-fos'ity
ru'-fous
ru'-gate
rug'-ged
ru'-gose
ru-gos'ity
ru'-gu-lose
ru'in-ate
ruin-a'tion
ru'in-ing
ru'in-ous
ru'l-able
ru'l-ing
rum'-bler
rum'-bling
ru'-mi-nant
ru'-mi-nate
ru-mi-na'tion
rum'-mage
rum'-mager
rum'-mag-ing
ru'-mour
rum'-pling
rum'-pus
run'-about
run'a-gate
run'-around
run'-away
run'-cible

run'-ci-nate
run'-date
run'-down (n.)
ru'-nic
run'-let
run'-nel
run'-ner
run'-ning
ru-nol'-ogist
ru-nol'ogy
run'-way
ru-pee'
ru-pesc'ent
ru-pes'tral
ru-pic'o-lous
rup'-tile
rup'-tion
rup'-tur-able
rup'-ture
rup'-tured
rup'-tur-ing
ru'-ral
ru'-ral-ise
ru'-ral-ism
ru'-rally
ru-rig'er-ous
rush'-ing
rush'-light
rus'-tic
rus'-ti-cate
rus-ti-ca'tion
rus'-ti-cator
rus-tic'ity
rust'-ily
rust'i-ness
rus'-tler
rus'-tling
rust'-proof

ruta-ba'ga
ru-ta'ceous
ru-the'ni-ous
ru-the'nium
ruth'-ful
ruth'-less
ruth'-lessly
ruth'-less-ness
ru'-ti-lant
ru'-ti-lated
ru'-tile
ru'-tin
rut'-ted
ry'e-grass

S

sab'bat'i-cal
sab'i-nene
sab'-otage
sab-oteur'
sab'u-lite
sab'u-lose
sabu-los'ity
sab'u-lous
sac'-cate
sac'-char'ic
sac'-char-ide
sac-char-if'er-
    ous
sac'-char-ify
sac-char-im'eter
sac-char-im'etry
sac'-charin
sac'-char-in-ate
sac'-char-ine

sac-char-in'ic
sac-char-in'ity
sac'-char-ise
sac'-char-ite
sac'-char-oid
sac-char-oid'al
sac-char-om'eter
sac-charo-my'ces
sac'-char-ose
sac-cif'er-ous
sac'-ci-form
sac'-cu-lar
sac'-cu-lated
sac-cu-la'tion
sac-er-do'tal
sac-er-do'tal-
    ism

sack'-but
sack'-cloth
sack'-ful
sack'-ing
sac'-ra-ment
sac-ra-men'-tal
sac-ra-men'tary
sac'-ri-fice
sac'-ri-fic'ial
sac'-ri-fic-ing
sac'-ri-lege
sac-ri-le'gious
sac'-ris-tan
sac'-risty
sacro-il'iac
sacro-my'oid
sacro-phar'-ynx
sac'-ro-sanct
sac-ro-sanc'-tity
sacro-sciat'ic
sad'-den

sad'-der
sad'dle-backed
sad'dle-bag
sad'dle-bow
sad'-dler
sad'dlery
sad'dle-tree
sad'-dling
sadis'-tic
sadis'-ti-cally
sad'-ness
sa-far'i
sa'fe-guard
sa'fe-keep-ing
saf'-fian
saf'-flor-ite
saf'-flower
sa-ga'cious
sa-gac'ity
sag'a-more
saga-pe'num
sa'ge-brush
sa-ge'ne
sag'en-ite
sag'-ger
sag'-ging
sag'i-tal
sag'i-tate
sail'-boat
sail'-cloth
sail'-fish
sail'-ing
saint'-hood
saint'-li-ness
sa-laam'
sal-a'cious

321

sal-a'ciously
sal-ac'ity
sal'a-man-der
sala-man'drine
sal-am'ba
sa-lam'i
sal'-ar-ied
sal'-ary
sale-abil'ity
sa'le-able
sal-era'tus
sa'le-room
sa'les-girl
sa'les-man
sa'les-man-ship
sa'les-woman
sali-ca'ceous
sal'i-cet
sali-cc'tum
sal'i-cin
sal-ic'y-late
sali-cyl'ic
salien'-tian
sal-if'er-ous
sali-fi-ca'tion
sal'-ify
sal-ig'enin
sal-im'eter
sa-li'na
sali-na'tion
sal-in-if'er-ous
sal'-ite
sal-in'ity
sali-nom'eter
sal-i'va
sal'i-vant
sal'i-vary
sal'i-vate
322

sali-va'tion
sal'-let
sal'-lied
sal'-low
sal'-ly-ing
sal-ma-gun'dl
sal-mon-el'la
sal-monel-lo'sis
sa-loon'
sal'-pian
sal'-pi-con
sal'-pin-gec'tomy
sal'-pin-gi'tis
sal'-pinx
sal-por'-nis
sal'-sify
sal-so-la'ceous
sal-su'gin-ous
sal'-tant
sal'-tate
sal-ta'tion
sal-ta-to'rial
sal'ta-tory
salt'-cel-lar
salt'-ery
sal'-ti-grade
salt'-ing
sal'-tire
salt'-ness
salt-pe'tre
sal-u'bri-ous
sal-u'brity
salu-tar'ily
sal'u-tary
salu-ta'tion
sal-uta-to'rian
sal-u'ta-tory
sal-u'te

salu-tif'er-ous
sal-u't-ing
sal-va-bil'ity
salv'-able
sal'-vage
sal'-vage-able
sal'-vager
sal'-var-san
sal-va'tion
sal'-ver
sal'-via
salv'-ing
sal-vini-a'ceous
sal vol-at'ile
sam'-ara
sam-ar'i-form
sam-a'rium
sam'-bar
sa'me-ness
sam'i-sen
sam'-ite
sam'-let
sam'o-var
sam'-pan
sam'-phire
sam'-pler
sam'-pling
sam'-son-ite
sam'-urai
san'a-tive
sana-to'rium
san'a-tory
sanc-ti-fi-
    ca'tion
sanc'-ti-fied
sanc'-tify
sanc'-ti-fy-ing
sanc-ti-mo'ni-ous

sanc'-ti-mony
sanc'-tion
sanc'-tion-ary
sanc'-tioner
sanc'-ti-tude
sanc'-tity
sanc'-tu-ary
sanc'-tum
sanc'-tus
san'-dal
san'-dalled
san'-dal-wood
san'-da-rac
sand'-bag
sand'-bank
sand'-bath
sand'-blast
sand'-box
san'-der
san'-der-ling
sand'-glass
sand'-grouse
sand'-hog
sand'-hop-per
sand'i-ness
san'di-ver
san'-dix
sand'-man
san-dor'i-cum
sand'-paper
sand'-piper
sand'-stone
sand'-storm
Sand'-wich
Sand'-wich-man
Sand'-worm
San'-for-ise
Sanga-ree'

sanguif'-er-ous
sangui-fi-ca'tion
san'gui-fier
san'gui-narily
san'gui-nary
sanguin'-eous
sanguin'-ity
sang'ui-suge
sangui-niv'or-ous
sanguin'o-lent
sanguiv'-or-ous
san'-icle
san'i-dine
san'-ify
sani-ta'rian
san'i-tarily
sani-ta'rium
san'i-tary
sani-ta'tion
san'i-tiser
san'-ity
san-ser'if
san-ta-la'ceous
san'-ta-lin
san-ton'-ica
san'-to-nin
sap'a-jou
sa-phe'nous
sap-id'ity
sapien'-tial
sap-in-da'ceous
sap'-less
sap'-ling
sapo-dil'la
sapo-gen'in
sap-on-a'ceous
sap-oni-fi-
    ca'tion

sap-on'-ify
sap'-onin
sap'-on-ite
sapor-if'ic
sapo-ta'ceous
sap'-per
sapph'-ire
sapph'ir-ine
sap'-ping
sap-re'mia
sap-ro-gen'ic
sap-ro-gen-ic'ity
sap-rog'en-ous
sap-ro-pel'ic
sap-roph'a-gan
sap-roph'a-gous
sap'-ro-phile
sap-roph'i-lous
sap'-ro-phyte
sap-ro-phyt'ic
sap'-sucker
sap'-wood
sar'a-band
sar'-casm
sar-cas'-tic
sar-cas'-ti-cally
sar'-cin
sar-ci'tis
sarc'o-carp
sar-co-col'la
sar'-coid
sar-coid-o'sis
sar-co-lem'ma
sar-co-lem'mic
sar-co-log'ic
sar-col'-ogist
sar-col'ogy
sar-co'ma

323

sar-co'ma-toid
sar-coma-to'sis
sar-co'ma-tous
sar-coph'a-gal
sar-coph'agi
sar-coph'a-gus
sar-coph'agy
sar'-co-phile
sar-coph'i-lous
sar'-co-phyte
sar'-co-plasm
sar'co-sine
sar-co'sis
sar'-co-style
sar'-cous
sar-di'ne
sar-don'ic
sar-don'i-cally
sar'-donyx
sar-gass'o
sar'-kin-ite
sar'-ment
sar-men-ta'ceous
sar-men'-tose
sar-men'-tous
sar-men'-tum
sar-ong'
sar'-plar
sar-sa-pa-ril'la
sar'-sen
sar'se-net
sar-to'rial
sar-to'rius
sass'a-fras
sass'o-lite
sa-tan'ic
sa-tan'i-cal

sa-tan'i-cally
sa'tan-ism
sa-teen'
sat'-el-lite
sat'-el-lited
sat'-el-loid
satia-bil'ity
sat i'ety
sat-in-ett'e
sat'-in-ise
sat'-in-spar
sat'-in-wood
sat'-iny
sat'-ire
sat-ir'ic
sat-ir'i-cal
sat'-ir-ise
sat'-ir-is-ing
sat'-ir-ist
sat-is-fac'-tion
sat-is-fac'-
          torily
sat-is-fac'-tory
sat'-is-fied
sat'isfy
sat'-rap
sat'-rapy
sat-su'ma
satu-ra-bil'ity
sat'u-rable
sat'u-rant
sat'u-rate
sat'u-rated
sat'u-rater
sat'u-rat-ing
satu-ra'tion
sat'u-rator
sat-ur-na'lia

sat-ur-na'lian
sat'-ur-nine
sat-ur-nin'ity
sa-tyr'ic
sauc'e-boat
sauc'e-pan
sauc'i-ness
saun'-ter
saun'-ter-ing
sau'-rel
saur'-ian
saur-og'na-thous
saur'-oid
saur-oph'a-gous
saus'-age
saus-su'r-ite
sav'-age
sav'-agely
sav'-age-ness
sav'-agery
sav-an'na
sav'-ant
sav'-eloy
sa'vouri-ness
sa'vour-ous
saw'-buck
saw'-dust
saw'-fish
saw'-fly
saw'-horse
saw'-mill
saw'-pit
saw'-set
saw'-yer
sax'a-tile
sax'-horn
sax-ic'a-vous
sax-ic'o-line

sax-ic'o-lous
saxi-fra-ga'ceous
sax'i-frage
sax'-on-ite
sax'o-phone
sax-oph'on-ist
say'-ing
scab'-bard
scab'-bing
scab'-bler
scab'-bling
scab-er-esc'ent
scab-er'u-lous
scabi-o'sa
sca'bi-ous
scab'-mite
scab'-rid
scab-rid'ity
scab'-rous
scaf'-fold
scaf'-fold-ing
scal-ar'i-form
scal-di'no
sca'li-ness
scal'-lop
scal'-loped
scal'-pel
scal-pel'-li-form
scal-pel'-lum
scal'-per
scal'-pri-form
scal'-prum
scam'-mony
scam'-per
scamp'-ish
scan'-dal
scan-dal-is'-
　　　　ation

scan'-dal-ise
scan'-dal-monger
scan'-dal-ous
scan'-dent
scan'-dia
scan'-dium
scan'-ner
scan'-ning
scan'-sion
scan-so'rial
scan-so'rius
scant'-ily
scant'i-ness
scant'-ling
sca'pe-goat
sca'pe-grace
scaph-an'-der
scaph-id'ium
scapho-ceph'a-
　　　　lous
scaph'-oid
scaph'-opod
sca'pi-form
scap-ig'er-ous
scap'o-lite
scap'-ula
scap'u-lar
scap'u-lated
scara-bae'oid
scar'a-boid
sca'rce-ment
sca're-crow
sca're-monger
scarf'-ing
scari-fi-ca'tion
scar'i-fi-cator
scar'i-fied
scar'i-fier

scar'-ify
sca'ri-ous
scar-la-ti'na
scar'-let
scar'-let-fe'ver
scar'-ring
sca'the-less
scato-log'ic
scato-log'i-cal
scat-ol'o-gy
scat'o-phage
scat-oph'a-gous
scat-os'copy
scat'-ter
scat'-ter-brain
scat'-tered
scat-u'ri-ent
scav'-enge
scav'-en-ger
scav'-eng-ing
scen-ar'io
scen-ar'ist
sce'neo-graph
sce'n-ery
sce'ni-cal
sce'ni-cally
sce'no-graph
sceno-graph'ic
scen-og'ra-phy
scent'-less
scep'-tic
scep'-ti-cal
scep'-ti-cism
sched'-ule
sched'-uled
sched'-ul-ing
scheel'-ite
sche-mat'ic

sche'ma-tism
sche'ma-tist
sche'm-ing
schil'-ling
schin-dy-le'sis
schin-dy-let'ic
schis-mat'ic
schist-a'ceous
schis'to-cyte
schist'ose
schist-os'ity
schis'to-some
schisto-so-
    mi'asis
schiz'o-carp-ous
schizo-gen'-esis
schizo-gen-et'ic
schiz-og'en-ous
schiz-og'on-ous
schiz'-oid
schiz'-oid-ism
schizo-pha'sia
schizo-phre'nia
schizo-phren'ic
schizo-thy'mia
schnap'-per
schol'-ar'ly
schol'-ar-ship
schol-as'-tic
schol-as'-ti-cal
schol-as'-ti-
    cally
schol-as'-ti-cism
scho'li-ast
school'-book
school'-boy
school'-child
school'-girl
326

school'-house
school'-ing
school'-man
school'-mas-ter
school'-mate
school'-mis-tress
school'-room
school'-teacher
school'-work
school'-yard
schor-la'ceous
schrein'-er-ise
sci-aen'oid
sci'a-graph
sci-ag'ra-phy
sci-am'a-chy
scia-ther'ic
sci-at'ic
sci-at'i-ca
sci'-ence
scien'-tial
scien-tif'ic
scien-tif'i-cally
sci'en-tist
sci-li-cet
scillo-ceph'a-
    lous
scim'i-tar
scin-til'la
scin'-til-late
scin'-til-lat'ing
scin-til-la'tion
scin'-til-lator
scin-til-lom'eter
scint'-ling
sci'o-graph
scio-graph'ic
sci'o-lism

sci'o-list
scio-lis'tic
sci-om'achy
sci-oph'i-lous
sci'o-phyte
sci-op'tic
scio-the'ism
scir'-rhoid
scir-rho'sis
scir'-rhous
scir'-rhus
scir'-to-pod
scis-ci-ta'tion
scis'-sel
sciss'-ible
sciss'-ile
scissi-par'ity'
scis'-sors
sciss'-ure
sci'-uroid
scler'a-gogy
sclera-tog'en-ous
scler-ench'yma
scler-i'asis
scler'-ite
scler-it'ic
scler-i'tis
sclero-caul'-ous
scler'o-derm
sclero-der'ma
sclero-der-ma-
    tous
sclero-der'-mia
sclero-der'-mic
scler'o-gen
scler-og'en-ous
scler-o'ma
scler-om'eter

scler-o'sal
scler'o-scope
scler-o'sis
scler-o'tal
scler-ot'ic
sclero-ti'tis
scler-ot'omy
scle'-rous
scob-ic'u-lar
scob'i-form
scob'i-nate
sco'ld-ing
sco'ld-ingly
sco'-lecite
scoli-o'sis
scoli-ot'ic
scolo-pa'ceous
scolo-pen'-dri-form
scolo-pen'-drine
scol'o-phore
scol'y-toid
scom'-ber
scom'-boid
scom'-bri-form
sconc'-ible
scon'-cheon
scoop'-ful
sco'-pate
sco'pi-form
scop-ol'-amine
scop'-tic
scop'-ula
scop'u-late
scop'u-li-form
scop'u-lous
scor-bu'tic
scorch'-ing

sco'-ria
scori-a'ceous
scori-fi-ca'tion
sco'ri-fier
sco'r-ing
scorn'-ful
scorn'-fully
scor'o-dite
scor'-per
scor'-pion
scor'-poid
scor-poid'al
scor'ta-tory
scorzo-ne'ra
scotch'-ing
sco'-ter
scoto-dyn'ia
scot'o-graph
scot-o'ma
scot-om'a-tous
scot-om'eter
scot'-omy
scoto-pho'bia
scot'o-phyte
scot'o-scope
scoun'-drel
scoun-drel-ism
scourg'-ing
scout'-ing
scout'-mas-ter
scowl'-ingly
scrab'-bler
scrab'-bling
scrag'-gi-ness
scram'-bler
scram'-bling
scrap'-book
scrap'-pi-ness

scrap'-ping
scratch'i-ness
scratch'-proof
scrawn'i-ness
scream'-ing
screech'-owl
screen'-ings
screw'-driver
scrib'-bet
scrib'-bler
scrib'-bling
scrim'-mage
scrim'-mager
scrimp'-ily
scrimp'i-ness
scrim'-shaw
scrip'-tion
scrip-to'rium
scrip'-tory
scrip'-tural
scrip'-tur-al-ism
scrip'-tur-al-ist
scrip'-ture
scrip'-tur-ist
scriv'-ener
scrob-ic'u-late
scrob-ic'u-lus
scrof'-ula
scrofu-lo'sis
scrof'u-lous
scro'll-work
scro'ti-form
scro'-tum
scroung'-ing
scrub'-ber
scrub'-bing
scrum'-mage
scrump'-tious

327

scrupu-los'ity
scru'-pu-lous
scru'-pu-lously
scru'-table
scru-ta'tion
scru-ta'tor
scruti-neer'
scru'-ti-nise
scru'-ti-nous
scru'-tiny
scud'-ding
scuf'-fler
scuf'-fling
scul'-lery
scul'-pin
sculpt'-ing
sculp-toon'
sculp'-tor
sculp'-tress
sculp'-tural
sculp'-ture
scum'-ber
scum'-bling
scum'-mer
scum'-mings
scun'-cheon
scup'-per
scurf'i-ness
scur-ried
scur-ril'ity
scur-ri-lous
scur-ry-ing
scurv'-ily
scur'-vi-ness
scu'-tage
scu'-tate
scu'-tel-late
scu-tel-la'tion
328

scu'-ti-form
scu-tig'er-ous
scut'-ter
scut'tle-butt
scut'-tler
scut'-tling
scu'-tum
scypu'-li-form
scy'th-ing
scy-to-dep'-sic
sea'-bear
sea'-board
sea'-borne
sea'-coal
sea'-coast
sea'-cow
sea'-drome
sea'-farer
sea'-far-ing
sea'-food
sea'-fowl
sea'-girt
sea'-going
sea'-kale
sea'-king
seal'-able
seal'-ant
sea'-lark
seal'-ery
seal'-ine
seal'-skin
sea'-man
sea'-man-ship
sea'-mark
sea'-men
seam'i-ness
seam'-less
seam'-stress

sea'-plane
sea'-port
search'-able
search'-ing
search'-light
sear'-ing
sea'-scape
sea'-shore
sea'-sick
sea'-sick-ness
sea'-side
seas'on-able
seas'on-ing
seat'-ing
sea'-wall
sea'-ward
sea'-way
sea'-weed
sea'-wolf
sea-worth'i-ness
sea'-worthy
seb'a-cate
seb-a'ceous
seb-ac'ic
sebor-rhe'a
seca-bil'ity
sec'a-lose
se'-cant
sec'a-teurs
se-ce'de
se-ce'ded
se-ce'der
se-ce'd-ing
se-cern'
se-cern'-ent
se-cern'-ment
se-ces'sion
se-ces'sion-ist

SEGREGATIVE

se-cess'-ive
se-clu'de
se-clu'ded
se-clu'd-edly
se-clu'd-ing
se-clu's-ive
sec'o-dont
sec'-ohm
se-cond'
sec'-ond-arily
sec'-ond-ary
sec'-onder
sec'-ond-hand
sec'-ondly
se'cret-age
sec-retair'e
sec-reta'rial
sec-reta'riat
sec'-retary
se-cre'te
se-cre'ted
se-cre'tin
se-cre'tion
se-cre're'tional
se-cre't-ive
se-cre'to-gogue
se-cre'tor
se-cre'tory
sec'-tant
sec-ta'rial
sec-ta'rian
sec-ta'rian-ise
sec-ta'rian-ism
sec'-tary
sec'-tile
sec-til'ity
sec'-tion

sec'-tional
sec'-tion-al-ise
sec'-tion-al-ism
sec'-tion-ally
sec'-tor
sec'-toral
sec-to'rial
sec'-troid
sec-trom'eter
sec'u-lar
secu-lar-is-
　　　　a'tion
sec'u-lar-ise
sec'u-lar-ism
sec'u-lar-ist
secu-lar'ity
se'-cund
secun'-date
sec'un-dine
se-cu'r-able
se-cu're
se-cu'rely
se-cu'ri-form
sec'u-rite
se-cu'ri-ties
se-cu'r-ity
se-da'te
se-da'tely
se-da'te-ness
sed-a'tion
sed'a-tive
sed'-en-tarily
sed'-en-tary
se-di'le
se-dil'ia
sed'i-ment
sedi-men'-tary
sedi-men-ta'tion

se-dit'ion
se-dit'ion-ary
se-dit'ious
se-du'ce
se-du'ce-ment
se-du'cer
se-du'c-ible
se-du'c-ing
se-duc'tion
se-duc'tive
se-duc'tor
se-du'lity
sed'u-lous
seed'-ing
seed'-less
seed'-ling
seeds'-man
seed'-time
see'-ing
seem'-ing
seem'-ingly
seep'-age
seer'-sucker
see'-saw
seeth'-ing
seg'-ment
seg-men'-tal
seg-men'-tally
seg'-men-tary
seg-men-ta'tion
seg'-ni-tude
seg'-re-ant
seg'-re-gable
seg'-re-gate
seg-re-ga'tion
seg-re-ga'tion-
　　　　ist
seg'-re-gat-ive

329

seis'-mic
seis-mic'ity
seis'-mism
seis'-mo-graph
seis-mog'ra-pher
seis-mo-graph'ic
seis-mog'ra-phy
seis-mo-log'ic
seis-mo-log'i-cal
seis-mol'-ogist
seis-mol'ogy
seis-mom'eter
seis-mo-met'ric
seis-mon-as'ty
seiz'-able
seiz'-ing
seiz'-ure
se'-jant
sel-a'chian
se-lagi-nel'la
sel'-dom
sel-ect'
selec'-tance
selec'-ted
selec-tee'
selec'-tion
selec'-tive
sel-ec-tiv'ity
selec'-tor
sel'-en-ate
sel-en'ic
sel'-en-ide
sel-e'nious
sel-e'ni-scope
sel'-en-ite
sel-e'nium
sel-e'no-dont
sel-e'no-graph

sel-en-og'ra-pher
sel-eno-graph'ic
sel-en-og'ra-phy
sel-e'no-lite
sel-eno-log'i-cal
sel-en-ol'ogy
sel-eno-trop'ic
seis-mo-log'ic
self-assu'r-ance
self-com-mand'
self-con-fi-
        dence
self-con'-fi-dent
self-con'-scious-
        ness
self-con-tain'ed
self-con-tra-
        dic'-tion
self-con-tro'l
self-de-fen'ce
self-de-ni'al
self-de-ter-mi-
        na'tion
self-dis'-ci-pline
self-es-teem'
self-ev'i-dent
self-gov'ern-ment
self-im-po'rt-ance
self-im-po'rt-ant
self-im-po'sed
self'-ish
self'-ishly
self'-ish-ness
self'-less
self-pos-sess'ed
self-pos-ses'sion
self-pres-er-
        va'tion
self-pro-tec'-tion

self-re-gard'
self-re-li'ance
self-re-li'ant
self-re-spect'
self-re-spect'-
        ing
self-sac'-ri-fice
self'-same
self-sat'-is-fied
self-seek'-ing
self-suf-fic'ient
self-su-ppo'rt-
        ing
sell'-ing
sel'-syn
selt'-zer
sel'-vage
sel'-vedge
sem-an'-tic
sem-an'-ti-cist
sem-an'-tics
seman'-tron
sem'a-phore
sema-phor'ic
sem'a-phor-ist
se-masi-ol'ogy
sem-at'ic
sem'-blance
sem'-blant
sem'-bla-tive
semei-ol'ogy
semei-ot'ic
sem'-eme
se'-men
se'-men-cine
sem-es'ter
sem-es'tral
semi-an'nual

semi-ar'id
sem'i-breve
sem'i-circle
semi-cir'cu-lar
sem'i-colon
semi-con'-scious
semi-detach'ed
semi-diam'-eter
sem'i-dine
sem'i-final
semi-lu'nar
semi-month'ly
sem'i-nal
sem'-inar
sem'-in-ar-ist
sem'-in-ary
sem-in-ate'
sem-in-a'tion
sem-in-if'er-ous
sem-in-iv'or-ous
semi-prec'ious
semi-spher'ic
sem'i-tone
semo-li'na
sem-per-vi'rent
sem-pi-ter'-nal
sem-pi-ter'-nity
sen-a'rius
sen'-ary
sen'-ate
sen'a-tor
sena-to'rial
sen'-dal
send'-ing
sen-ec'ti-tude
sen'-ega
sen-esc'ence
sen-esc'ent

sen'-eschal
sen-il'ity
senior'-ity
sen'-night
sen'-nit
sen'-sate
sen-sa'tion
sen-sa'tional
sen-sa'tion-al-
    ism
sen-sa'tion-al-
    ist
sen'se-less
sen-si-bil'ity
sen'-sible
sen'-sibly
sen-sif'er-ous
sen'-sile
sens'-ing
sen-si-tis-a'tion
sen'-si-tise
sen'-si-tive
sen'-si-tive-ness
sen-si-tiv'ity
sen-si-tom'eter
sen-si-tom'-etry
sen-so'rial
sen-so'ri-motor
sen-so'rium
sen'-sory
sen'-sual
sen'-su-al-ise
sen'-su-al-ism
sen'-su-al-ist
sen-su-al-is'tic
sen-su-al'ity
sen'-su-ous

sen'-su-ously
sen'-tence
sen-ten'-tial
sen-ten'-tious
sen'-tience
sen'-tient
sen'-ti-ment
sen-ti-men'-tal
sen-ti-men'-tal-
    ise
sen-ti-men'-tal-
    ism
sen-ti-men'-tal-
    ist
sen-ti-men-
    tal'ity
sen-ti-men'-tally
sen'-ti-nel
sen'-ti-nelled
sen-ti-sec'-tion
sen'-try
sep'-al-ine
sep'-alled
sep'-al-oid
sep'-al-ous
sep-ar-abil'ity
sep'-ar-able
sep'-ar-ate
sep'-ar-ately
sep-ar-a'tion
sep-ar-a'tion-ist
sep'-ar-atist
sep'-ar-at-ive
sep'-ar-ator
sep-ar-a'tum
sep-ic'o-lous
sep'i-ment
se'pio-late

331

SEPSIS

sep'-sis
sep'-tan
sep'-tangle
sep-tan'gu-lar
sep-ta'rian
sep-ta'rium
sep'-tate
sep-ta'tion
sep-tec'-tomy
sep'-tem-fid
sep-tem-par'-tite
sep-tem'-vir
sep-tem'-vir-ate
sep'-ten-ary
sep'-ten-nate
sep-ten'-nial
sep-ten'-tri-onal
sep-tet'
sep'-tic
sep'-ti-cae'mia
sep'-ti-cal
sep-ti-ci'dal
sep-tic'ity
sep-ti-fa-ri'-ous
sep-tif'ra-gal
septi-lat'-eral
sep-til'lion
sep'ti-mal
sep'ti-mole
sep'-tine
septo-na'sal
sep-tua-gen-a'rian
sep-tua-ges'i-mal
sep'-tum
sep'-tuple
sep-tu'-plet
332

sep-tu'pli-cate
sep-ul'-chral
sep-ulchre
sep'-ul-ture
se'-quel
se-que'la
se'-quence
sc'-quent
sequen'-tial
sequen'-tially
seques'-ter
sequescs-tered
seq'ues-trate
seques-tra'tion
seq'ues-trator
se'-quin
se'-quined
ser'-aph
ser-aph'ic
ser'a-phim
ser-en-a'de
ser-en-a'der
ser-en-a'd-ing
ser-en-dip'ity
ser-e'ne
ser-e'nely
ser-en'ity
serf'-dom
se'rial-ise
seri-a'tim
ser-ic'eous
ser'i-cin
ser'i-cite
ser'i-con
ser'i-cul-ture
ser'i-graph
ser-ig'ra-pher
ser-ig'ra-phy

ser'-ine
ser-in-ett'e
ser-in'ga
se'rious-ness
ser'-mon
ser-mon'ic
ser'-mon-ise
ser'-mon-iser
sero-log'ic
sero-log'i-cal
serol'-ogist
serol'-ogy
sero-si'tis
se-ros'ity
ser'o-tine
sero-to'nin
se'-rous
ser'-pent
ser-pen-ta'ria
ser'-pen-tary
ser'-pen-tine
ser-pen'-ti-form
ser-pen-tin'ic
ser'-pet
ser-pett'e
ser-pig'in-ous
ser-pi'go
ser'-po-let
serra-dil'la
ser'-ra-noid
ser'-rate
ser'-rated
ser-ra'tion
ser-rat'u-late
ser'-ra-ture
ser'-ried
ser'-ri-form
ser'-ru-late

ser'-val
ser'-vant
ser'-ver
ser'-very
ser'-vice
serv'ice-able
ser-vi-ent
ser-vi-ett'e
ser'-vile
ser-vil'ity
serv'-ing
ser-vit'ium
ser'-vi-tor
ser'-vi-tude
servo-mech'an-
    ism
servo-mo'tor
ses'a-moid
ses'a-mum
sesqui-al'-tera
sesqui-ba'sic
sesqui-cen-ten'-
    nial
sesqui-ox'-ide
sesqui-ped-a'lian
ses-quip'-li-cate
sess'-ile
ses'-tet
ses-ti'na
se-ta'ceous
set'-back
se-tig'er-ous
set'-tee
set'-ter
set'-ting
set'tle-ment
set'-tler
set'-tling

sev'-en-fold
sev-en-teen'
sev-en-teen'th
sev'-enth
sev'-en-ti-eth
sev'-enty
sev'-er-able
sev'-eral
sev'-er-ally
sev'-er-alty
sev'-er-ance
sev'-ered
sev'-ery
sew'er-age
sew'-ing
sexa-gen-a'rian
sexa-ges'i-mal
sex-an'gu-lar
sex-cen-te'nary
sex-en'-nial
sex-fa'rious
sex'i-fid
sexi-syl-lab'ic
sex-par'-tite
sex'-tain
sex'-tant
sex'-tet
sex-tett'e
sex'-tile
sex-til'lion
sex'-ton
sex'-tuple
sex-tu'plet
sex-tu'pli-cate
sex'-ual
sexu-al'ity
sfer'-ics

shab'-bi-ness
shab'-rack
shack'-ler
shack'-ling
sha'di-ness
sha-di'ne
shad'-ow-graph
shad'owi-ness
shad'-owy
shaft'-ing
shag'-bark
shag'-gi-ness
shag'-ging
sha-green'
sha'ke-down
sha'k-ily
sha'k-ing
shal'-lon
shal-loon'
shal'-lop
shal-lot'
shal'-low
sham'-bling
sha'me-faced
sha'me-ful
sha'me-fully
sha'me-less
sha'me-lessly
sham'-mer
sham'-ming
sham-poo'
sham-poo'ed
sham'-rock
shan'dy-gaff
shang'-hai
shan-tung'
sha'pe-less
sha'pe-li-ness

333

sha're-crop-per
sha're-holder
sha'res-man
shark'-skin
sharp'-ener
sharp'-en-ing
sharp'-ness
sharp'-set
sharp'-shooter
shas'-ter
shat'-ter
shat'-tered
sha've-ling
sha've-tail
sha'v-ing
shear'-ing
shear'-ling
shear'-water
sheath'-ing
shed'-ding
sheep'-fold
sheep'-ish
sheep'-skin
sheep'-walk
sheer'-ness
sheet'-ing
shel'-drake
shel-lac'
shel-lack'ed
shel-lack'-ing
shell'-back
shell'-fish
shell'-proof
shel'-ter
shel'-tered
shel'-ter-ing
shel'-tie
shel'-ver

shelv'-ing
shep'herd-ess
sher'-bet
sher'-iff
shib'-bol-eth
shield'-ing
shift'-ily
shif'ti-ness
shift'-ing
shift'-less
shift'-less-ness
shil-le'lagh
shil'-ling
shim'-mer
shim'-mery
shim'-ming
shin'-bone
ship'-board
ship'-builder
ship'-build-ing
ship'-lap
ship'-load
ship'-mas-ter
ship'-mate
ship'-ment
ship'-owner
ship'-pen
ship'-per
ship'-ping
ship'-pon
ship'-shape
ship'-worm
ship'-wreck
ship'-wright
ship'-yard
shirr'-ing
shirt'-ing
shirt'-sleeve

shirt'-waist
shiv'-ered
shiv'-ery
shock'-ing
shock'-proof
shod'-di-ness
shoe'-black
shoe'-buckle
shoe'-horn
shoe'-ing
shoe'-maker
shoe'-string
shoot'-ing
sho'-phar
shop'-keeper
shop'-lift
shop'-lifter
shop'-per
shop'-ping
shop'-talk
shop'-walker
sho'-ran
sho're-line
sho're-ward
sho'r-ing
short'-age
short'-bread
short'-cake
short-com'ing
short'-en-ing
short'-fall
short'-hand
short'-handed
short'-horn
short'-ness
short'-stop
short'-wave
shot'-gun

shoul'-der-knot
shov'-el-ful
shov'-elled
shov'-eller
shov'-el-ling
shov'-ing
show'-case
show'-down
show'i-ness
show'-ing
show'-man
show'-man-ship
show'-room
shrag'-ger
shrap'-nel
shred'-ded
shred'-ding
shrewd'-ness
shrew'-ish
shriek'-ing
shriev'-alty
shrill'-ness
shrink'-age
shriv'-elled
shriv'-el-ling
shroff'-age
shrub'-bery
shrub'-bi-ness
shrug'-ging
shuck'-ing
shud'-der
shuf'fle-board
shuf'-fling
shun'-ning
shunt'-ing
shut'-down
shut'-ter
shut'-ting

shut'tle-cock
shy'-ness
sny'-ster
siala-gog'ic
sial'a-gogue
si'a-loid
sialo-li-thi'asis
sib'i-lance
sib'i-lant
sib'i-late
sibi-la'tion
sib'i-lus
sib'-ling
sib'y-llic
sib'-yl-line
sic'-cate
sic'ca-tive
sic'-city
sick'-en-ing
sick'-en-ingly
sick'-ish
sick'-li-ness
sick'-ness
sick'-room
si'de-arm
si'de-board
si'de-burns
si'de-light
si'de-long
sid'-eral
sid-er-a'tion
sid'-er-ite
sid-er-og'ra-pher
sid-ero-graph'ic
sid-er-og'ra-phy
sid'-ero-lite
sid'-ero-scope

sid-er-o'sis
sid'-ero-stat
si'de-show
si'des-man
si'de-stroke
si'de-track
si'de-walk
si'de-ways
sieg'-ing
sieg'e-works
sigh'-ing
si'ght-less
si'ght-see-ing
si'ght-seer
sig'il-lary
sig'il-late
sig'-mate
sig-ma'tion
sig'-ma-tism
sig'-moid
sig-moid-ec'tomy
sig-moid-os'tomy
sig'-nal
sig'-nal-ise
sig'-nalled
sig'-nal-ler
sig'-nal-ling
sig'-nally
sig'-nal-man
sig'-nary
sig'-na-tory
sig'-na-ture
si'gn-board
sig'-net
sig-ni-fi'able
sig-nif'i-cance
sig-nif'i-cant
sig-nif'i-cantly

335

sig-nif'i-cate
sig-nifi-ca'tion
sig-nif'i-cat-ive
sig-nif'i-cator
sig-nif'i-cat-ory
sig'-ni-fied
sig'-ni-fy-ing
si'gn-post
sil'-ane
si'lenc-ing
sil-houett'e
sil-houet'-ted
sil'-ica
sil'i-cate
sil-i-cator
sil-ic'eous
sil-ic'ic
sil'i-cide
slli-cif'er-ous
sil-ic'ity
sil'-icle
si'li-cole
sil'i-con
sil'i-cone
sili-co'sis
sili-cot'ic
sil-ic'u-lose
sil'i-qua
sil'i-quous
silk'i-ness
silk'-screen
silk'-weed
silk'-worm
sil'-la-bub
sil'-li-man-ite
sil'-li-ness
sil-ox'en
336

sil-ta'tion
sil-un'-dum
sil-u'rid
sil'-van
sil'-ver
sil'-ver-ing
sil'-ver-ise
sil'-ver-side
sil'-ver-smith
sil'-ver-ware
sil'-ver-work
sil'-very
sil-vi-cul'-tural
sil-vi-cul'-ture
sim'-ial
sim'-ian
sim'i-lar
simi-lar'ity
sim'i-larly
sim'i-lat-ive
sim'-ile
sim'i-lise
sim'i-lor
sim-il'i-tude
sim'-ious
sim'-mer
sim-o'niac
simo-ni'acal
si'mon-ize
sim'-ony
sim'-per
sim'-pered
sim'-perer
sim'-per-ing
sim'-pler
sim'-plest
sim'ple-ton
sim'-plex

sim-plic'ity
sim-pli-fi-
     ca'tion
sim'-pli-fied
sim'-plify
sim'-pli-fy-ing
simu-la'crum
sim'u-lant
sim'u-lar
sim'u-late
sim'u-lat-ing
simu-la'tion
sim'u-lat-ive
sim'u-lator
sim'u-lat-ory
sim'ul-cast
sim-ul-ta'neous
sim-ul-ta'neously
sin'a-pic
sin'a-pine
sin'a-pism
sin'-ar-quism
sin-ce're
sin-ce'rely
sin-cer'ity
sin-cip'i-tal
sin'-ci-put
sin'-ecure
sin'-ecur-ist
sin'-ewy
sin'-ful
sing'-able
sin'ge-ing
sing'-ing
sin'gle-ness
sin'gle-stick
sin'gle-ton
sin'gle-tree

sing'-song
sin'gu-lar
sin'gu-lar-ise
singu-lar'-ity
sin'gu-larly
sin'-is-ter
sin'-is-tral
sin-is-tral'-ity
sin'-is-trorse
sin'-is-trous
sink'-age
sink'-hole
sink'-ing
sin'-less
sin'-ner
sin'-ning
sin'-net
sin-o'pia
sin'-ople
sin'-ter
sin'-ter-ing
sin'u-ate
sinu-a'tion
sinu-os'ity
sin'u-ous
sinu-pal'-li-ate
sinu-si'tis
si'nus-oid
sinus-oid'al
si'phon-age
sip-id'ity
sip'-pet
sip'-ping
sir'-dar
sir-e'nian
sir-i'asis
sir'-loin
sir-oc'co

sis'-kin
sis'-ter
sis'-ter-hood
sis'-terly
sis'-trum
siti-ol'ogy
si-tol'ogy
sito-ma'nia
sito-pho'bia
sito-tro'pism
sit'-ter
sit'-ting
sit'u-ate
sit'u-ated
situ-a'tion
six'-fold
six'-footer
six'-pence
six'-teen
six'-teenth
six'-ti-eth
si'ze-able
si'ze-able-ness
siz'-zling
siz'-zlingly
sjam'-bok
skat'-ole
skel'-etal
skel-et-og'ra-phy
skel-et-ol'ogy
skel'-eton
skel'-eton-ise
sketch'-book
sketch'-ily
sketch'i-ness
skew'-back
skew'-bald
skew'-ered

ski'a-graph
skias'-copy
skid'-ded
skid'-ding
skid'-way
ski'-ing
skil'-ful
skil'-fully
skil'-ful-ness
skil'-let
skim'-mer
skim'-ming
skimp'-ily
skin'-flint
skin'-ner
skin'-ni-ness
skin'-tight
skip'-jack
skip'-per
skip'-pet
skip'-ping
skir'-mish
skir'-misher
skir'-ret
skirt'-ing
skit'-ter
skit'-tish
skul-dug'-gery
skulk'-ing
skull'-cap
sky'-lark
sky'-light
sky'-line
sky'-rocket
sky'-scraper
sky'-ward
slab'-ber
slab'-bing

slack'-ened
slack'-ness
sla'k-ing
slam'-ming
slan'-der
slan'-derer
slan'-der-ous
slang'-ily
slang'-iness
slant'-ing
slant'-wise
slap'-ping
slap'-stick
slash'-ing
slat'-ted
slat'-tern
slat'-ternly
slaugh'-ter
slaugh'-terer
slaugh'-ter-house
slaugh'-ter-man
slaugh'-ter-ous
sla'ver-ing
sla'vish-ness
slay'-ing
sled'-ding
sledg'e-ham-mer
sleek'-er-ing
sleek'-ers
sleep'-ily
sleep'i-ness
sleep'-ing
sleep'-less
sleep'-walker
sleep'-walk-ing
sleet'i-ness
sleev'e-less
sleigh'-ing

slen'-der
slen'-der-ise
slen'-der-ness
slick'-en-side
slick'-ness
sli'ght-ing
sli'mi-ness
slim'-ness
sling'-shot
slink'-ing
slip'-per
slip'-pered
slip'-peri-ness
slip'-pery
slip'-pi-ness
slip'-ping
slip'-shod
slip'-stream
slip'-way
slith'-ery
sloe'-bush
slob'-ber
slob'-ber-ing
sloe'-berry
slog'-ging
slop'-pily
slop'-pi-ness
slop'-ping
sloth'-ful
slot'-ted
slouch'-ily
slouch'-ing
slough'-ing
slov'en-li-ness
slow'-coach
slow'-match
slow'-ness
slub'-ber

slub'-bing
slug'-gard
slug'-gish
sluic'e-way
sluic'-ing
slum'-ber
slum'-berer
slum'-ber-ous
slum'-brous
slum'-ming
slur'-ring
slush'i-ness
slut'-tish
sly'-ness
smack'-ing
small'-ish
small'-ness
small'-pox
small'-sword
smalt'-ine
smar-ag'-dine
smart'-ness
smart'-weed
smat'-ter
smat'-ter-ing
smec'-tite
smed'-dum
smell'i-ness
smell'-ing
smila-ca'ceous
smi'l-ing
smi'l-ingly
smirk'-ing
smith-er-eens'
smit'-ten
smock'-ing
smo'k-able
smo'ke-house

smo'ke-jack	snort'-ing	social-is'tic
smo'ke-less	snow'-ball	so'cial-ite
smo'ke-screen	snow'-bank	social'-ity
smo'ke-stack	snow'-bird	so-ci'etal
smo'k-ing	snow'-blind	so-ci'ety
smooth'-ness	snow' bound	so-cio-log'ic
smudg'-ily	snow'-capped	so-cio-log'i-cal
smudg'-ing	snow'-drift	so-cio-log'i-
smug'-gling	snow'-drop	cally
smut'-ti-ness	snow'-fall	so-ci-ol'-ogist
snag'-ging	snow'-flake	so-ci-ol'ogy
sna'ke-root	snow'-line	so-ci-om'etry
snap'-dragon	snow'-man	so'cio-path
snap'-per	snow'-storm	soci-op'a-thy
snap'-ping	snub'-ber	sock-dol'-ager
snap'-pish	snub'-bing	so'-da-lite
snap'-shot	snuff'-box	so-dal'-ity
snarl'-ing	snug'-gery	so'-da-mide
snarl'-ingly	snug'-gling	sod'-den
snarl'-ish	snug'-ness	sod'-ding
sneak'-ily	soak'-age	so'-dium
sneak'-i-ness	soak'-ing	sod'-om-ite
sneak'-ing	soap'-boiler	sod-om-it'ic
sneer'-ing	soap'-box	sod'-omy
sneez'-ing	soap'i-ness	so'-far
snick'-er-ing	soap'-stone	sof'-fit
sniff'-ing	soap'-suds	sof'ten-ing
snif'-ter	soap'-wort	soft'-ish
snig'-ger	soar'-ing	soft'-ness
snip'-pet	sob'-bing	soft'-wood
snip'-pety	so-bri'ety	sog'-gily
snip'-ping	soc'-age	sog'-gi-ness
sniv'-el-ler	soc'-cer	soil'-age
sniv'-el-ling	socia-bil'ity	so'-journ
snob'-bery	social-is-a'tion	so'-journer
snob'-bish	so'cial-ise	sol'-ace
snoop'-ery	so'cial-ism	sol'-aced
snor'-kel	so'cial-ist	sol'-acer

339

sol'-ac-ing
so-la-na'ceous
so-lan'-der
so'-la-nine
so-lan'o
so'-lar
solar-is-a'tion
so'-lar-ise
so'lar-ism
so-la'rium
so-la'tium
sol'-ecise
sol'-ecism
sol'-ecist
sol-ecis'tic
sol'-emn
sol-em-nis-a'tion
sol'-em-nise
sol-em'-nity
sol'-emnly
so'len-oid
so-len-oid'al
sol-fa-ta'ra
sol-fer-i'no
sol-ic'it
sol-ic'i-tant
sol-ici-ta'tion
sol-ic'i-tor
sol-ic'i-tous
sol-ic'i-tude
sol-ici-tu'di-nous
soli-dar'ic
soli-dar-is'tic
soli-dar'ity
sol-idi-fi-ca'tion
sol-id'i-fied
sol-id'-ify
340

sol'-id-ism
sol-id'-ity
sol'-idly
sol'-id-ness
sol'i-dum
soli-dun'gu-lar
soli-dun'gu-late
sol'i dus
soli-fid'-ian
soli-fid'i-an-ism
sol-il'-oquise
sol-il'-oquist
sol-il'-oquy
sol'i-ped
sol'-ip-sism
sol'i-taire
sol'i-tar-ily
sol'i-tary
sol'i-tude
sol'-lar
sol'-mi-sate
sol-mi-sa'tion
sol'-ograph
so'lo-ist
sol'-stice
sol-stit'ial
sol'u-bil-iser
solu-bil'ity
sol'-uble
so'-lum
sol'-ute
sol-u'tion
sol'u-tiser
sol'u-tive
solv-abil'ity
solv'-able
sol'-vency
sol'-vent

solv'-ing
sol-vol'y-sis
so-mat'ic
so-mat'i-cally
so'-ma-tism
so'-ma-tist
so-ma-to-gen'ic
so-ma-tol'ogy
so-ma-tot'omy
so-mato-typ'ic
som-bre'ro
som'-brous
som'e-body
som'e-day
som'e-how
som'e-one
som'er-sault
som'e-thing
som'e-time
som'e-times
som'e-what
som'e-where
som-nam'-bu-
        lant
som-nam'-bu-
        la'tion
som-nam'-bu-
        lator
som-nam'-bu-
        lism
som-nam'-bu-list
som-nam-bu-lis'-
        tic
som-ni-fa'cient
som-nif'er-ous
som-nif'ic
som-nil'-oquence
som-nil'-oquist

som-nil'-oquous
som-nil'-oquy
som'-nol-ence
som'-nol-ent
som'-nol-ently
som-nol-esc'ent
som'-nol-ism
so'-nance
so'-nancy
so'-nant
so-nan'-tal
so'-nar
son-at'a
song'-bird
song'-ster
song'-stress
soni-fac'-tion
son-if'er-ous
son'-net
son-net-eer'
son'o-buoy
son-om'eter
son-o'rant
son-or-esc'ence
son-or-esc'ent
son-or-if'er-ous
son-or-if'ic
son-or'-ity
son-o'ro-phone
son-o'rous
son-o'rously
soon'-est
sooth'-ing
sooth'-ingly
sooth'-say
sooth'-sayer
soot'i-ness
soph'i-cal

soph'-ism
soph'-ist
soph'-is-ter
soph-is'tic
soph-is'-ti-cate
soph-is'-ti-cated
sophis-ti-ca'tion
soph'-is-try
suph'o-more
sopho-mor'ic
so'-por
sop-or-if'er-ous
sop-or-if'ic
sop'-ping
so-pran'o
sor-be-fa'cient
sor'-bent
sor'-bet
sor'-bic
sor'-bin
sor'-bite
sor'-bi-tol
sor'-bose
sor'-cerer
sor'-cer-ess
sor'-cery
sor'-did
sor'-didly
sor'-dine
sor-do'no
so're-ness
sor'-ghum
so-ri'tes
so-rit'i-cal
sor-o'ral
sor-o'ri-ally
sor-or'i-cide
sor-or'ity

sor-o'sis
sor'-rel
sor'-rily
sor'-ri-ness
sor'-row
sor'-row-ful
sor'-row-fully
sort'-able
sor'-tie
sor'-ti-lege
sor-tit'ion
so'-rus
sos'-trum
so-teri-ol'ogy
sot'-tish
sou-brett'e
sou-chong'
souf'-flé
sough'-ing
soul'-ful
soul'-fully
soul'-less
sound'-ing
sound'-less
sound'-ness
sound'-proof
sour'-ness
south=east'-erly
south=east'-ern
south'ern-most
south'ern-wood
south'-ing
south'-land
south'-ward
south=west'-erly
south=west'-ern
sou-venir'
sov'-er-eign

341

sov'-er-eignty
sov'-prene
spa-ghet'ti
spa-gyr'ic
spal'-peen
span'-drel
span-e'mia
spank'-ing
span'-ner
span'-ning
spar'-able
spa're-ness
spa're-rib
spark'-let
spark'-ling
spark'-lingly
spar'-ling
spar'-ring
spar'-roid
spar'-row
spar'-sity
spar'-teine
spas-mod'ic
spas-mod'i-cally
spas-mol'y-sis
spas-mol-yt'ic
spas'-tic
spas'-ti-cally
spas-tic'ity
spatch'-cock
spa-rha'ceous
spatial'-ity
spatiog'-ra-phy
spat'-ter
spat'-ting
spat'-ula
spat'u-lar
spat'u-late

spat'-ule
spav'-ined
speak'-able
speak'-easy
speak'-ing
spear'-fish
spear'-head
spear'-man
spear'-mint
special-is-a'tion
spec'ial-ise
spec'ial-ism
spec'ial-ist
special'-ity
spec'i-fi-able
specif'i-cally
speci-fi-ca'tion
specif-fic'ity
spec'i-fied
spec'i-fier
spec'i-fy-ing
spec'i-men
specios'-ity
speck'-ling
speck-tion-eer'
spec'-tacle
spec'-tacled
spec-tac'u-lar
spec-tac'u-larly
spec-ta'tor
spec-ta-to'rial
spec'-tral
spec'-tro-gram
spec'-tro-graph
spec-trog'ra-phy
spec-tro-he'lio-
gram

spec-trol'ogy
spec-trom'eter
spec-trom'etry
spec'-tro-phone
spec'-tro-scope
spec-tro-scop'ic
spec-tro-scop'i-
cal
spec-tros'co-pist
spec-tros'copy
spec'-trum
spec'u-lar
spec'u-late
spec'u-lat-ing
specu-la'tion
spec'u-lat-ive
spec'u-lator
spec'u-lum
speech'-ify
speech'-less
speed'-boat
speed'-ily
speed'i-ness
speed'-ing
speed-om'eter
speed'-ster
speed'-way
speed'-well
spel-ae'an
spelae-ol'-ogist
spelae-ol'ogy
spell'-binder
spell'-bound
spell'-ing
spel'-ter
spel-unk'er
spen'-cer
spend'-able

spend'-ing
spend'-thrift
sper-ma-ce'ti
sper-ma-go'nium
sper-mat'ic
sper-ma-tif'er-
ous
sper'-ma-tin
sper-ma-tis-a'tion
sper'-ma-tise
sper'-ma-tism
sper-mat'o-cele
sper-mato-ci'dal
sper-mat'o-cyte
sper-ma-to-gen'-
esis
sper-ma-tog'eny
sper-mat'o-phyte
sper-mato-phyt'ic
sper-ma-tor-rhe'a
sper-ma-to-zo'ic
sper-ma-to-zo'id
sper-ma-to-zo'on
sperm'-ine
sperm'-ism
sper-mol'ogy
spha'-cel-ate
sphag'-num
sphal'-er-ite
sphe'-no-don
sphe'no-gram
sphe'no-graph
sphe-nog'ra-phy
sphe'-noid
sphe-noid'al
spher'i-cal
spheri-cal'ity
spher-ic'ity

spher'-ics
sphe'-roid
sphe-roid'al
sphe-roid'ally
sphe-roid-ic'ity
sphe-rom'eter
spher'u-lar
spher'-ule
spher'u-lite
sphinc'-ter
sphinc'-teral
sphingo-my'elin
sphin'-go-sine
sphra-gis'-tics
sphyg'-mic
sphyg-mo-car'dia-
gram
sphyg-mo-car'dia-
graph
sphyg'-mo-graph
sphyg'-moid
sphyg-mol'ogy
sphyg-mo-man-
om'eter
sphyg-mom'eter
sphyg'-mo-phone
sphyg'-mo-scope
sphyg'-mus
spi'ce-bush
spic'-ula
spic'u-lar
spic'-ule
spic'u-lum
spi'ke-let
spi'ke-nard
spi'ki-ness
spill'-age
spill'-ing

spill'-way
spi'lo-site
spin-a'ceous
spin'-ach
spin'-dler
spin'-dling
spin'-dly
spin'-drift
spi'ne-less
spinif'-er-ous
spi'ni-form
spin'-na-ker
spin'-ner
spin-neret'
spin'-ney
spin'-ning
spinos'-ity
spin'-ster
spin'-ster-hood
spin-thar'i-scope
spin'-ule
spinu-lesc'ent
spin'u-lose
spirac'u-lar
spi'ral-ling
spirif'-er-ous
spiril'-lum
spir'-ited
spir'-it-ism
spir-it-is'tic
spir'-it-less
spir'i-tual
spiri-tu-al'ity
spir'i-tual-ise
spir'i-tual-ism
spir'i-tual-ist
spiri-tual-is'tic
spir'i-tually

343

spiri-tu-ell'e
spiri-tu-os'ity
spir'i-tu-ous
spir'-ket
spir'-ket-ting
spi'ro-chaete
spiro-chae-to'sis
spi'ro-graph
spi'ro-meter
spi-rom'eter
spi-ro-met'ric
spi'ro-phore
spiss'-ated
spiss'i-tude
spitch'-cock
spi'te-ful
spit'-fire
spit'-ting
spit-toon'
splanch'-nic
splanch-ni-cec'-
    tomy
splanch-nol'ogy
splash'-ing
spleen'-ish
spleen'-wort
splen'-dent
splen'-did
splen'-didly
splen-dif'er-ous
splen'-dor-ous
splen'-dour
splen-ec'tomy
splen-et'ic
splen-i'tis
splen'i-tive
spleno-meg'-aly
splen-ot'omy
splint'-age
344

splin'-ter
splin'-tered
split'-ting
spo'-dium
spod'u-mene
spoil'-age
spoil'-ing
spoils'-man
spo'ke-shave
spo'kes-man
spo'li-ate
spo-li-a'tion
spo'-li-at-ive
spon-da'ic
spon'-dee
spon'-dyl
spon-dy-li'tis
spon'-dyl-ous
spong'i-ness
spong'-ing
spon'-sal
spon'-sible
spon'-sion
spon'-son
spon'-sor
spon-so'rial
spon'-sor-ship
spon-ta-ne'ity
spon-ta'neous
spook'-ish
spoon'-bill
spoon'-drift
spoon'-er-ism
spoon'-ful
spor-ad'ic
spor-ad'i-cally
spor-an'-gia
spor-an'-gial

spor-an'-gium
spo-ri-ci'dal
spor'i-desm
spo-rif'er-ous
spo'-ro-cyst
spo-ro-gen' esis
spo-ro-gen'ic
spor-og'en-ous
spo-ro-go'nium
spo'-ro-phyll
spo'-ro-phyte
spo-ro-zo'an
spo-ro-zo'-ite
spor'-ran
spo'rt-ing
spo'rt-ive
spo'rts-caster
spo'rts-man
spo'rts-man-ship
spor'u-late
sporu-la'tion
spor'-ule
spot'-less
spot'-less-ness
spot'-light
spot'-ted
spot'-ter
spot'-ting
sprawl'-ing
spread'-ing
spri'ght-li-ness
spring'-board
spring'-bok
spring'-box
spring'-halt
spring'i-ness
spring'-ing
spring'-tail

spring'-tide
spring'-time
sprink'-ler
sprink'-ling
sprit'-sail
spru'c-ing
spu-mesc'ence
spu-mesc'ent
spu-mif'er-ous
spu'-mous
spu'-ri-ous
spu'-ri-ously
spurn'-ing
spur'-rier
spur'-ring
spur'-tive
sput'-nik
sput'-ter-ing
spu'-tum
spy'-glass
spy'-ing
squab'-bler
squab'-bling
squad'-ron
squal-id'ity
squa-ma'tion
squam-o'sal
squam'u-lose
squan'-der
squan'-dered
squan'-der-ing
squa'r-ing
squash'i-ness
squash'-ing
squat'-ted
squat'-ter
squat'-ting
squat-toc'-racy

squawk'-ing
squeak'-ily
squeak'-ing
squeal'-ing
squeam'-ish
squee'-gee
squeez'-able
squeez'-ing
squint'-ing
squir'-rel
squirt'-ing
stab'-bing
stabil-is-a'tion
sta'bil-is-ator
sta'bil-ise
sta'bil-iser
stab-il'ity
sta'ble-mate
stack'-ing
stack'-yard
stac-tom'eter
stad-im'eter
stadi-om'eter
sta'ge-coach
sta'ge-craft
sta'ge-hand
stag'-gard
stag'-ger
stag'-ger-ing
stag'-gers
stag'-hound
stag'-nancy
stag'-nant
stag'-nate
stag-na't-ing
stag-na'tion
stain'-ing
stain'-less

stair'-case
stair'-way
sta'ke-holder
sta'k-ing
stal-ac'-tic
stal-ac'-ti-form
stal'-ac-tite
stal-ac-tit'ic
stal-ac-tit'i-
          cally
stal'-ag-mite
stal-ag-mit'ic
stal-ag-mit'i-
          cally
stal-ag-mom'eter
sta'le-mate
sta'le-ness
stalk'-ing
stall'-age
stall'-fed
stam'-ina
stam'i-nal
stam'i-nate
stam-in-if'er-ous
stam'-in-ody
stam'-mel
stam'-mer
stam'-merer
stam'-mer-ing
stam-pe'de
stan'-chion
stan'-dard
stan-dard-is-
         a'tion
stan'-dard-ise
stand'-ing
stand'-pipe
stand'-point

stand'-still
stan'-nar-ies
stan'-nic
stan-nif'er-ous
stan'-nite
stan'-nous
stan'-num
staph'y-line
staphy-lo-coc'-
        cus
staphy-lo'ma
staphy-lot'-omy
star'-board
star-cha'mber
starch'i-ness
star'-fish
star'-gazer
star'-less
star'-let
star'-light
star'-like
star'-ling
star'-lit
star'-ri-ness
star'-ring
start'-ling
star-va'tion
star've-ling
starv'-ing
sta'te-craft
sta'te-hood
sta'te-less
sta'te-li-ness
sta'te-ment
sta'te-room
sta'tes-man
sta'tes-man-ship
sta'te-wide
346

stat'i-cally
stat'-ics
sta'tion-ary
sta'tion-ery
stat-is'tic
stat-is'ti-cal
stat-is'ti-cally
stat-is-tic'ian
stat-is'tics
stat'o-scope
stat'u-ary
statu-esq'ue
statu-ett'e
stat'-ure
stat'-ute
stat'u-tory
staur'o-lite
staur'o-scope
staur'o-scop'ic
stay'-ing
stay'-sail
stead'-fast
stead'-ily
stead'i-ness
stead'-ing
stealth'-ily
stealth'i-ness
steam'-boat
steam'-fit-ter
steam'-roller
steam'-ship
steam'-tight
stearop'-tene
steato-pyg'ic
steatop'y-gous
steel'-works
steel'-yard

steen'-bok
steep'le-chase
steep'le-jack
steep'-ness
steer'-age
steer'-age-way
steers'-man
steers'-man-ship
steg-an-og'ra-
        phist
steg-an-og'ra-
        phy
stego-my'ia
steg'o-saur
stego-saur'-us
stel'-lar
stel'-late
stel-lif'er-ous
stel'-li-form
stell'u-lar
stell'u-late
stem'-less
stem-mat'o-pus
stem'-ming
sten'-cil
sten'-cilled
sten'-cil-ling
sten'o-chrome
sten-och'-romy
sten'o-graph
sten-og'ra-pher
steno-graph'ic
steno-graph'i-
        cally
sten-og'ra-phist
sten-og'ra-phy
steno-ha'line
steno-pa'ic

sten-o'sis
sten-ot'ic
sten'o-type
sten'o-typ-ist
sten'o-typy
sten-to'rian
step'-brother
step'-child
step'-daugh-ter
step'-father
step'-lad-der
step'-mother
step'-ney
step'-per
step'-ping
step'-sis-ter
step'-son
ster-a'dian
ster-cor-a'ceous
ster'-cor-ate
ster-cor-a'tion
ster-cor-ic'o-
          lous
ster-culi-a'ceous
ster'eo-graph
ster'eog'ra-pher
stereo-graph'ic
ster-eog'ra-phy
ster-eom'eter
stereo-met'ric
ster-eom'etry
stereo-phon'ic
ster-eoph'-ony
ster-eop'-sis
ster-eop'-ti-con
ster-eop'-tics
ste'reo-scope

stereo-scop'ic
ster-eos'-co-pist
ster-eos'-copy
ster-eot'omy
ster-eot'ro-pism
ster'eo-type
ster'eo-typer
ster'eo-typ'-ing
ster'i-cally
ster'-ile
ster-il-is-a'tion
ster'-il-ise
ster'-il-iser
ster-il'ity
ster'-let
ster'-ling
ster'-ness
stern'-post
stern'-sheets
stern'-son
ster-nu-la't-ive
ster'-num
ster-nu-ta'tion
ster-nu-ta't-ory
stern'-way
ster'-oid
ster-oid'al
ster'-tor
ster'-tor-ous
steth-om'eter
steth'o-scope
stetho-scop'ic
steth-os'copy
stet'-ted
ste've-dore
stew'-ard
stew'-ard-ess
stew'-ard-ship

stew'-pan
stib'-bler
stib'-ine
stib'-ium
stib'o-gram
stich-om'etry
stick'-ful
stick'i-ness
stick'-ing
stick'le-back
stiff'-ener
stiff'-en-ing
stiff'-ness
stig-mas'-terol
stig'-mata
stig-mat'ic
stig-mat'i-cal
stig-ma-tis-
          a'tion
stig'-ma-tise
stig'ma-tism
stig'-ma-tist
stig'-ma-tose
stig-ma-to'sis
stil'-bene
stil-boes'-trol
stil-et'to
still'-born
stil'-li-form
still'-ing
still'-ness
stil'-ton
stim'u-lant
stim'u-late
stimu-la'tion
stim'u-lat-ive
stim'u-lator
stim'-uli

347

STIMULUS

stim'u-lus
stin'gi-ness
sting'-ing
sting'-ray
stink'-ing
stink'-stone
stink'-weed
stint'-ing
sti'-pend
sti-pen'-di-ary
sti'-pes
sti'-pi-form
stipi-tat'ic
stip'-pler
stip'-pling
stip'u-late
stip'u-lat-ing
stipu-la'tion
stip'u-lator
stip'u-lat-ory
stip'-ule
stir'i-ated
stir'-pi-cul-ture
stir'-ring
stir'-rup
stitch'-ing
stitch'-wort
sti'-ver
stoch-as'-tic
stoch-as'-ti-cally
stock-a'de
stock'-broker
stock'-brok-ing
stock'-dove
stock'-fish
stock'-holder
stock-in-ett'e

stock'-ing
stock'-lst
stock'-job-ber
stock'-man
stock'-pile
stock'-pot
stock'-whip
stock'-yard
stodg'i-ness
sto'-ical
stoi-chi-ol'ogy
stoi-chio-met'ric
stoi-chi-om'etry
sto'-icism
sto'ke-hold
sto'ke-hole
sto'k-ing
stol-id'ity
stol'-idly
sto'-lon
sto-lon-if'er-ous
stom'ach-ache
sto'-mata
sto'ma-tal
stoma-ti'tis
stoma-tol'ogy
sto-mat'-omy
sto-mat'o-scope
sto'ne-chat
sto'ne-crop
stone-cur'-lew
sto'ne-less
sto'ne-mason
sto'ne-wall
sto'ne-ware
sto'ne-work
sto'ni-ness
stop'-cock

stop'-gap
stop'-pago
stop'-per
stop'-ping
stop'-watch
sto'-rax
sto're-house
sto're-keeper
sto're-room
sto'ri-ated
stori-ett'e
storm'-cock
storm'-ily
storm'i-ness
storm'-proof
stout'-ness
sto've-pipe
stow'-age
stow'-away
stra-bis'-mal
stra-bis-mom'eter
stra-bis'-mus
stra-bot'omy
strad'-dler
strad'-dling
strag'-gler
strag'-gling
straight'-away
straight'-ener
straight-for'-ward
straight'-way
strain'-ing
strait'-ened
strait'-jacket
strait'-laced
stra-min'-eous

stra-mo'nium
stram'-ony
stra'nge-ness
stran'gu-late
strangu-la'tion
strap'-ping
strat'-agem
stra-te'gic
stra-te'gi-cal
strat'-egist
strat'-egy
strath-spey'
stra-tic'u-late
strati-fi-ca'tion
strat'i-fied
strat'i-form
strat'-ify
strat'i-fy-ing
strati-graph'ic
stra-tig'ra-phy
strat-oc'-racy
strat'-ocrat
strat-on'ic
strat'-ose
strat'o-sphere
strato-spher'ic
straw'-berry
straw'-board
stray'-ing
streak'i-ness
stream'-ing
stream'-led
stream'-line
stream'-lined
streb-lo'sis
strength'-en-ing
strength'-less
stren'u-ous

strep'i-tant
strepi-ta'tion
strep'i-tous
strep'-or-ous
strep-si-ne'ma
strep-sip'-ter-
       ous
strep'-si-tene
strep-to-coc'-cic
strep-to-coc-
       co'sis
strep-to-coc'-cus
strep-to-kin'ane
strep-to-my'cin
strepto-thri'cin
stri-a'ted
stri-a'tion
strict'-ness
stric'-ture
stri'-dency
stri'-dent
stri'-dor
strid'u-late
stridu-la'tion
strid'u-lat-ory
strid'u-lous
strig'il-ate
strig'il-lose
stri'-gose
stri'k-ing
strin'-gency
strin-gen'do
strin'-gent
string'-halt
string'i-ness
string'-ing
string'-piece
strip'-ling

strip'-per
strip'-ping
strobi-la'ceous
strob'-ile
strob-il-if'er-ous
strob-il'i-form
strob'i-line
strob'i-loid
strob'o-scope
strobo-scop'ic
stro'-bo-tron
stro-mat'ic
strong'-box
strong'-hold
strong'-point
stron'-gyle
stron-gyl-o'sis
stron'-tia
stron'-tian-ite
stron'-tium
stro-phan'-thin
stro-phan'-thus
stroph'-ic
stroph'io-late
stroph'i-ole
stroph'u-lus
strop'-ping
struc'-tur-al
struc'-tur-ally
struc'-ture
strug'-gler
strug'-gling
stru-mat'ic
stru-mec'-tomy
stru-mi'tis
strum'-ming
stru'-mose
stru-mo'sis

349

stru'-mous
strum'-pet
stru'-thi-ous
strut'-ted
strut'-ting
strych'-nic
strych'-nine
stub'-bi-ness
stub'-bing
stub'-born
stub'-born-ness
stuc'-coer
stuc'-co-work
stud'-book
stud'-ded
stud'-ding
stud'-ied
stud'-iedly
stu'-dio
stu'-dious
stud'y-ing
stuff'-ily
stuff'i-ness
stuff'-ing
stul-ti-fi-
     ca'tion
stul'-ti-fied
stul'-ti-fy
stul'-ti-fy-ing
stul-til'-oquence
stul-til'-oquent
stum'-bling
stump'-age
stun'-ning
stu-pefa'cient
stu-pefac'-tion
stu-pefac'-tive
stu'-pefied

stu'-petier
stu'-pefy
stu'-pefy-ing
stu-pen'-dous
stu'-pid
stu-pid'-ity
stu'-pidly
stu'-por
stu'-por-ous
sub-aquat'ic
sub'-class
sub-con'-scious
sub-con'-ti-nent
sub-con'-tract
sub-con-trac'-tor
sub-div-i'de
sub-div-is'ion
sub-due'
su-ber'ic
su'-berin
su'-ber-ise
sub'-fusc
sub'-group
sub-head'-ing
sub-hu'-man
sub-ja'cency
sub-ja'cent
sub'-ject (n. a.)
sub-ject' (v)
sub-jec'-tion
sub-jec'-tive
sub-jec'-tiv-ism
sub-jec-tiv'ity
sub'-join
sub-join'-der
sub'-ju-gate
sub-ju-gat'-ing

sub-ju-ga'tion
sub'-ju-gator
sub-junc'-tive
sub'-late
sub-la'tion
sub-leas'e
sub-lessee'
sub-less'or
sub'-let
sub-let'-ting
sub-lieuten'-ant
sub'-jim-able
sub'-li-mate
sub-li-mat'-ing
sub-li-ma'tion
sub-li'me
sub-li'mely
sub-lim'-inal
sub-lim'ity
sub-lin-ea'tion
sub-lu'nary
sub'-mar-ine
sub-max'-il-lary
sub-me'dial
sub-me'dian
sub-me'di-ant
sub-merg'e
sub-merg'ed
sub-merg'-ence
sub-merg'-ible
sub-mers'e
sub-mers'ed
sub-mers'-ible
sub-mers'-ing
sub-mer'-sion
sub-mis'sion
sub-miss'-ive
sub-mit'

sub-mit'-ted
sub-mit'-ting
sub-mon'-tane
sub-mul'-tiple
sub-nor'-mal
sub-nor-mal'ity
sub-or'-di-nate
sub-or'-di-nate-ly
sub-or'-di-na'tion
sub-or'-di-nat-ive
sub-orn'
sub-or-na'tion
sub-or'ner
sub-pan-a'tion
sub-poe'na
sub-poe'naed
sub-poe'na-ing
sub-rep'-tion
sub-rep'-tive
sub'-ro-gate
sub-ro-ga'tion
sub-scri'be
sub-scri'ber
sub-scri'b-ing
sub-scrip'-tion
sub-scrip'-tive
sub-sec'-tion
sub-sec'-tive
sub-sec'u-tive
sub-sen'-sible
sub'-sequence
sub'-sequent
sub-sequen'-tial
sub-serv'e
sub-ser'-vi-ence
sub-ser'-vi-ent
sub-serv'-ing

sub-si'de
sub-si'd-ence
sub-sid'i-ary
sub-si'd-ing
sub-si-dĭs-a'tion
sub'-si-dise
sub'-sidy
sub'sist'
sub-sist'-ence
sub-sist'-ent
sub-sis-ten'-tial
sub'-soil
sub-son'ic
sub'stance
sub-stan'-tial
sub-stan-tial'ity
sub-stan'-tially
sub-stan'-tiate
sub-stan-tia'tion
sub-stan-tive
sub'-station
sub-stit'u-ent
sub'-sti-tut-able
sub'-sti-tute
sub'-sti-tuted
sub'-sti-tut-ing
sub-sti-tu'tion
sub'-sti-tut-ive
sub-strat'o-sphere
sub-stra'tum
sub-struc'-ture
sub-sty'lar
sub-sul'-ti-tory
sub-sul'-tive
sub-su'me
sub-sump'-tion
sub-sump'-tive

sub-tend'
sub-tens'e
sub'-ter-fuge
sub-ter-ra'nean
sub-ter-ra'neous
sub'-tile
sub'-ti-lin
sub-til'ity
sub'-title
sub-tract'
sub-tract'er
sub-trac'-tion
sub-trac'-tive
sub'-tra-hend
sub-treas'ury
sub-trop'i-cal
sub-tru'de
su'bu-late
sub'-urb
sub-ur'ban
sub-ur'ban-ite
sub-ven'-tion
sub-ver'-sion
sub-ver'-sion-ary
sub-vers'-ive
sub-vert'
sub-vert'er
sub-vert'-ible
sub'-way
suc-ceda'neous
suc-ceda'neum
suc-ce'dent
suc-ceed'
suc-cent'or
suc-cess'
suc-cess'-ful
suc-cess'-fully
suc-ces'sion

suc-cess'-ive
suc-cess'or
suc-cid'u-ous
suc-cif'er-ous
suc'-cin
suc-cin-am'ic
suc'-ci-nate
suc-cinct'
suc-cinct'ly
suc-cin'ic
suc'-cin-ite
suc'-cinyl
suc-civ'or-ous
suc'-cose
suc'-co-tash
suc'-cour
suc'-cu-bous
suc'-cu-bus
suc'-cu-lence
suc'-cu-lent
suc-cumb'
suc-cur'-sal
suc-cuss'
suc-cus-a'tion
suc-cus'sion
suc-cuss'-ive
suck'-ler
suck'-ling
su'-crose
suc'-tion
suc-to'rial
suc-to'rian
su-da'men
su'-dary
su-da'tion
suda-to'rium
su'da-tory
sud'-den

sud'-denly
sudor-if'er-ous
sudor-if'ic
sudor-ip'ar-ous
su'-dor-ous
suf'-fer
suf'-fer-able
suf'-fer-ance
suf'-ferer
suf'-fer-ing
suf-fi'ce
suf-fi'ced
suf-fi'cer
suf-fi'ciency
suf-fic'ient
suf-fi'c-ing
suf'-fix
suf-fix'ion
suf-fla'te
suf-fla'tion
suf'-fo-cate
suf'-fo-cat-ing
suf-fo-ca'tion
suf'-fo-cat-ive
suf'-fra-gan
suf'-frage
suf-fra-gett'e
suf-fra-gett'-ism
suf-frag'in-ous
suf'-fra-gist
suf-fru-tesc'ent
suf-fru'ti-cose
suf-fu'mi-gate
suf-fumi-ga'tion
suf-fu's-able
suf-fu'se
suf-fu's-ing
suf-fu'sion

suf-fu's-ive
su'gar-bush
su'gari-ness
su'gar-loaf (n.)
su'gar-plum
suggest-ibil'ity
suggest'-ible
sugges'-tion
sugges'-tive
suggil-a'tion
suici'd-ally
su'-ing
suit-abil'ity
suit'-able
suit'-ably
suit'-case
suit'-ing
sul'-cate
sul-ca'tion
sul'-cus
sulk'-ily
sulk'i-ness
sul'-lage
sul'-len
sul'-lenly
sul'-len-ness
sul'-lied
sul'-pha
sul-pha-cet'a-mide
sul-pha-di'azine
sul-pha-guan'i-dine
sul-pha-nil'a-mide
sul-pha-nil'ic
sul-pha-py'ri-dine

sulph-ar′-sen-ide
sul′-phate
sul-pha-thi′azole
sul-phat′ic
sul-pha′tion
sulph-hy′dryl
sul′-phide
sul-phin′ic
sul′-phi-nyl
sul′-phite
sul-phon′a-mide
sul′-phon-ated
sul′-phon-ator
sul-phon′ic
sul-pho′nium
sul′-phosol
sulph-ox′-ide
sul′-phur
sul′-phu-rate
sul-phu-ra′tion
sul-phu-ra′tor
sul-phu′-reous
sul-phu-ret-ted
sul-phu′ric
sul-phu-ris-
          a′tion
sul′-phur-ise
sul′-phur-ous
sul′-phuryl
sul′-tan
sul-tan′a
sul′-tan-ate
sul-tan′ic
sul′-tri-ness
su′-mac
sum′-mar-ily

sum-mar-isa′tion
sum′-mar-ise
sum′-mary
sum-ma′tion
sum′-mer
sum′-mer-time
sum′-mery
sum′-ming
sum′-mit
sum′-mon
sum′-moned
sum′-moner
sum′-mon-ing
sum′-monsed
sum′-pit
sum′-pi-tan
sump′-ter
sump′-tu-ary
sump--tu-os′ity
sump--tu-ous
sun-ba′the
sun′-beam
sun′-bon-net
sun′-burn
sun′-burned
sun′-burnt
sun′-burst
sun′-dae
sun′-der
sun′-der-ance
sun′-dew
sun′-dial
sun′-down
sun′-downer
sun′-fast
sun′-fish
sun′-flower
sun′-glasses

sun′-less
sun′-light
sun′-lit
sun′-ning
sun′-proof
sun′-rise
sun′-set
sun′-shade
sun′-shine
sun′-spot
sun′-stroke
sun′-struck
sun′-ward
sun′-wise
super-abil′ity
su′per-able
super-abound′
super-abun′-
          dance
super-abun′-dant
super-an′-nu-ate
super-an′-nu-
          ated
super-an-nu-
          a′tion
su-perb′
su-perb′ly
su′per-cargo
super-charg′e
super-charg′er
super-cil′i-ary
super-cil′i-ous
super-col-um′-
          nar
super-con-duc-
          tiv′ity
super-cool′-ing
super-e′go

353

super-el-eva'tion
super-er'o-gate
super-ero-ga'tion
super-erog'a-
  tory
super-foeta'tion
super-fic'ial
super-ficial'-ity
super-fic'ially
super-fic'ies
su'per-fine
super-flu'ity
su-per'flu-ous
su'per-heat
super-heat'ed
super-het'-ero-
  dyne
super-hu'man
super-im-po'se
super-im-po-
  sit'ion
super-in-du'ce
super-in-tend'
super-in-tend'-
  ency
super-in-tend'-
  ent
su-pe'rior
su-peri-or'-ity
super-ja'cent
su-per'la-tive
super-lu'nary
super-lu'nary
su'per-man
su'per-mar-ket
super-nac'u-lar
super-nac'u-lum
super-na'tant
354

super-nat'u-ral
super-natu-ral-
  is'tic
super-nu'mer-ary
su'per-pose
super-po-sit'ion
su'per-power
su'per-scribe
super-scrip'-tion
super-se'de
super-se'deas
super-se'd-ence
super-se'd-ing
super-se'dure
super-sen'-sible
super-sen'-si-
  tive
super-sen'-sory
super-sen'-sual
super-sen'-su-ous
super-ses'sion
su'per-son'ic
su'per-sound
super-stit'ion
super-stit'ious
super-struc'-ture
super-ton'ic
super-tu'ned
super-ve'ne
super-ve'nience
super-ven'-ing
super-ven'-tion
su'per-vise
su'per-vis-ing
super-vis'ion
super-vi'sor
super-vi's-ory
su'-pin-ate

su-pin-a'tion
su'-pin-ator
su'-pine
su-pi'nely
sup'-per
sup'-per-time
sup'-ping
sup-plant'
sup-plan-ta'tion
sup-plant'er
sup'-plement
sup-plemen'-tal
sup-plemen'-
  tarily
sup-plemen'-tary
sup-plemen-
  ta'tion
sup-plemen'-tor
sup'ple-ness
sup'-pletive
sup'-pli-ance
sup'-pli-ant
sup'-pli-cate
sup'-pli-cat-ing
sup-pli-ca'tion
sup'-pli-cat-ory
sup-pli-ca'vit
sup-pli'ed
sup-pli'er
sup-ply'-ing
sup-po'rt
sup-port-abil'ity
sup-po'rt-able
sup-po'rter
sup-po'rt-ing
sup-po'rt-ive
sup-po's-able
sup-po'sal

sup-po′se
sup-po′sed
sup-po′s-edly
sup-po′s-ing
sup-po-sit′ion
sup-po-sit′ion-
    ally
sup-posi-tit′ious
sup-pos′i-tive
sup-pos′i-tory
sup-press′
sup-press′-ible
sup-pres′sion
sup-press′-ive
sup-press′or
sup′-pu-rate
sup′-pu-rat-ing
sup-pu-ra′tion
sup′-pu-rat-ive
supra-lim′-inal
supra-mol-ec′u-
    lar
supra-nat′ional
supra-re′nal
supra-seg-men′-
    tal
su-prem′acy
su-pre′me
su-pre′mely
su′-rah
su′-ral
sur′-amin
sur′-base
sur-ceas′e
sur′-charge
sur′-cingle
sur′-coat
sur′-cu-lose

sur′-cu-lus
sur′-di-mute
su′re-ness
sur′-face
sur′-faced
sur′-face-man
sur′-facer
sur′-fac-ing
sur-fac′-tant
sur′-feit
sur′-gent
sur′-geon
sur′-gery
sur′-gi-cal
su′ri-cate
sur′li-ness
sur′-mas-ter
sur-mi′s-able
sur-mi′se
sur-mi′ser
sur-mi′s-ing
sur-mount′
sur-mount′-able
sur-mount′ed
sur′-name
sur-nom′-inal
sur-pass′
sur-pass′-able
sur-pass′-ing
sur′-plice
sur′-plus
sur′-plus-age
sur-pri′s-able
sur-pri′sal
sur-pri′se
sur-pri′sed
sur-pri′s-edly
sur-pri′s-ing

sur-re′al-ism
sur-re′al-ist
sur-real-is′tic
sur-rebut′
sur-rebut′-tal
sur-rebut′-ter
sur-rejoin′
sur-re-join′-der
sur-ren′-der
sur-rend-eree′
sur-rend′-erer
sur-rend′-eror
sur-rep′-tion
sur-rep-tit′ious
sur′-rey
sur′-ro-gate
sur′-ro-gated
sur′-ro-gat-ing
sur-ro-ga′tion
sur-ro-ga′tum
sur-ro′sion
sur-round′
sur-round′ed
sur-round′-ing
sur′-tar-brand
sur′-tax
sur′-tout
sur-vcil′-lance
sur-veil′-lant
sur-vey′ (v.)
sur′-vey (n.)
sur-vey′al
sur-vey′-ance
sur-vey′-ing
sur-vey′or
sur-vi′val
sur-vi′ve
sur-vi′vor

sur-vi'vor-ship
sus-cep'-tance
sus-cep-ti-
       bil'ity
sus-cep'-tible
sus-cep'-tion
sus-cep'-tive
sus-cep-tiv'ity
sus-cep'-tor
sus-cip'i-ent
sus'-ci-tate
sus-ci-ta'tion
sus'-pect (n.)
sus-pect' (v.)
sus-pend'
sus-pen'ded
sus-pen'der
sus-pend'-ible
sus-pen'se
sus-pen'-sible
sus-pen'-sion
sus-pen'-sive
sus-pen'-sor
sus-pen-so'rium
sus-pen'-sory
sus-pic'ion
sus-pic'ious
sus-pi'ral
sus-pir-a'tion
sus-pi're
sus-pir'i-ous
sus-tain'
sus-tain'ed
sus-tain'er
sus-tain'-ing
sus-tain'-ment
sus'-ten-ance
sus-ten-tac'u-lar

sus-ten-tac'u-lum
sus-ten-ta'tion
sus'-ten-tat-ive
sus'-ten'-tator
sus-ten'-tion
sus-ten'-tive
sus'-ti-nent
su-sur'rant
su-sur-ra'tion
su-sur'-rus
sut'-ler
sut-tee'
su'-tural
su'-ture
su'tur-ing
su'-zer-ain
su'-zer-ainty
swab'-bing
swad'-dling
swag'-ger
swal'low-tail
swal'low-tailed
swal'low-wort
swamp'-land
swan'-like
swan'-nery
swans'-down
swan'-skin
swarm'-ing
swarth'-ily
swarth'i-ness
swash'-buck-ler
swash-buck'-ling
swas'-tika
sway'-backed
sway'-ing
swear'-ing
sweat'-ily

sweat'i-ness
sweat'-shop
sweep'-ing
sweep'-stake
sweet'-bread
sweet'-brier
sweet'-ened
sweet'-ener
sweet'-en-ing
sweet'-heart
sweet'-ish
sweet'-meats
sweet'-ness
swell'-fish
swell'-ing
swel'-ter
swel'-ter-ing
swerv'-ing
swif'-ter
swift'-ness
swim'-mer
swim'-meret
swim'-ming
swim'-mingly
swin'-dler
swin'-dling
swi'ne-herd
swing'e-ing
swin'-ger
swing'-ing
swin'gle-tree
swirl'-ing
switch'-back
switch'-board
switch'-gear
switch'-man
swiv'-elled
swiv'-el-ling

swoon'-ing
sword'-belt
sword'-fish
swords'-man
swords'-man-ship
sword'-stick
syb'-ar-ite
syb-ar-it'ic
syb'-ar-it-ism
syc'a-mine
syc'a-more
sych-no-car'-pous
syc'o-more
sy-co'nium
syc'o-phancy
syc'o-phant
syco-phan'-tic
sy'co-phan-try
sy-co'sis
sy'-en-ite
sy-en-it'ic
syl'-la-bary
syl-lab'ic
syl-lab'i-cate
syl-lab'i-cat-ing
syl-labi-ca'tion
syl-labi-fi-
           ca'tion
syl-lab'i-fied
syl-lab'i-fy
syl-lab'i-fy-ing
syl'-la-bise
syl'-la-bism
syl'-lable
syl'-la-bus
syl-lep'-sis
syl-lep'-tic
syl-lo-gis-a'tion

syl'-lo-gise
syl'-lo-gism
syl-lo-gis'tic
syl-lo-gis'ti-cal
sylph'-like
syl'-van
syl'-van-ite
syl-ves'tral
syl-ves'trene
syl'-vic
syl'-vi-cul-ture
syl'-vine
syl'-vin-ite
syl'-vite
sym'-biont
sym-bio'sis
sym-biot'ic
sym'-bol
sym-bol'-atry
sym-bol'ic
sym-bol'i-cal
sym-bol-is-a'tion
sym'-bol-ise
sym'-bol-ism
sym'-bol-ist
sym-bol-is'tic
sym-bol-og'ra-
              phy
sym'-bol-ogy
sym-met'ral
sym-met'rian
sym-met'ric
sym-met'ri-cal
sym-metris-a'tion
sym'-metrise
sym-metro-
        pho'bia
sym'-metry

sym'-morph
sym-path-ec'-
            tomy
sym-path-et'ic
sym-path-et'i-
            cally
sym'-pa-thin
sym'-path-ise
sym'-path-iser
sym'-path-is-ing
sym'-pathy
sym-pet'-al-ous
sym'-phile
sym'-phil-ous
sym-phon'ic
sym-pho'ni-ous
sym'-phon-ise
sym'-phon-ist
sym'-phony
sym-phyl'-lous
sym-phys'-ial
sym'-phy-sis
sym-phyt'ic
sym-po'dium
sym-po'siac
sym-po'si-arch
sym-po'si-ast
sym-po'sium
symp-tom
symp-to-mat'ic
symp-to-mat'i-
            cally
symp'-toma-tise
symp-toma-
          tol'ogy
symp-to'sis
symp-tot'ic
syna-del'-phite

357

SYNAERESIS

syn-acr'-esis
syn-aes-the'sia
syn'a-gogue
syn-al'gia
syn-al-lag-mat'ic
syna-loeph'a
syn-an'-drous
syn-an'-ther-ous
syn-an'-thous
syn'-apse
syn-ap'-sis
syn-ap'-tic
syn'-archy
syn-ar-thro'dial
syn-ar-thro'sis
syn-cat-egor-emat'ic
syn-chon-dro'sis
syn-chon-drot'-omy
syn-chor-e'sis
synchro-cy'clo-tron
synchro'-mesh
synchron-is-a'tion
synch'ron-ise
synch'ron-iser
synch'ron-is-ing
synch'ron-ism
synchron-is'tic
syn-chron'o-graph
synchron-ol'ogy
synch'ron-ous
syn-chro-scope
syn'chro-tron
syn'-chy-gy
syn-clas'-tic

syn-cli'nal
syn'-cline
syn-cli-no'rium
syn'-co-pate
syn'-co-pated
syn'-co-pat-ing
syn-co-pa'tion
syn'-co-pator
syn'-cope
syn-cop'ic
syn'-cret'ic
syn'-cretism
syn'-cretise
syn'-cri-sis
syn'-cryp'-tic
syn-des-mog'ra-phy
syn-des-mol'ogy
syn-des-mo'sis
syn-des-mot'ic
syn-det'ic
syn'-dic
syn'-di-cal-ism
syn'-di-cate
syn'-di-cat-ing
syn-di-ca'tion
syn'-di-cator
syn'-drome
syn-ec'-doche
syn-ec-doch'i-cal
syn-ec'-dochism
syn-ecol'ogy
syn-ec-pho-ne'sis
syn-er-get'ic
syn-er'gic
syn'-er-gism
syn-er-gis'tic
syn-er-gis'ti-cal

syn'-ergy
syn'-esis
syn'ga-mous
syn-gen-et'ic
syn'-graph
syni-ze'sis
syn'-odal
syn-od'ic
syn-od'i-cal
syn-od'i-cally
syn-oec'ious
syn'-onym
syn-on-ym'ic
syn-onym'i-con
syn-on'y-mist
syn-onym'-ity
syn-on'y-mous
syn-on'ymy
syn-op'-sis
syn-op'-tic
syn-op'-tl-cal
syn-os'-teol-ogy
syn-os-to'sis
syn-o'via
syno-vi'tis
syn-sac'-rum
syn-tac'-tic
syn-tac'-ti-cal
syn'-tax
syn-tech'-nic
syn-tec'-tic
syn-ten-o'sis
syn-tex'is
syn-ther'mal
syn'-thesis
syn'-thesise
syn'-thesiser
syn'-thesis-ing

358

syn'-thesist
syn'-thet'ic
syn-thet'i-cal
syn-thet'i-cally
syn'-thetise
syn'-thol
syn'-thronus
syn-ton'ic
syn'-tonin
syn-ton-is-a'tion
syn'-ton-ise
syn'-tony
syph'-ilis
syph'-il-ise
syph-li-it'ic
syph-il-ol'ogy
syph-il-o'ma
syr'-cis
syr-in'ga
syr-in'ge
syr-in'-geal
syr-in-gi'tis
syr-ingo-mye'lia
syr-ingot'-omy
syr'-inx
syr'-tic
syss-ar-co'sis
sys-tal'-tic
sys'-tem
sys-tem-at'ic
sys-tem-at'i-
    cally
sys-tem-atis-
    a'tion
sys'-tem-atise
sys'-tem-atism
sys'-tem-atist
sys-tem-atol'ogy

sys-tem'ic
sys-tem-is-a'tion
sys'-tem-ise
sys'-tem-oid
sys'-tole
sys-tol'ic
sys'-tyle
syz-yg'ial
syz'-ygy

T

tab'-ard
tab'-aret
tab-as'co
tab'-a-sheer
tab'-bi-net
tab'-bing
tab'-by-ing
tab-efac'-tion
tab'-efy
tab'-er-nacle
tab-er-nac'u-lar
tab-esc'ence
tab-esc'ent
tab-et'ic
tab'-la-ture
tab'-leau
tab'-leaux
ta'ble-cloth
ta'ble-land
ta'ble-spoon
ta'ble-spoon-ful
tab'-let
ta'ble-ware
tab'-loid
tab'-oret

tab'-or-ine
tab'-ouret
tab'-u-lar
tabu-lar-is-
    a'tion
tab'u-lar-ise
tab'u-late
tab'u-lat-ing
tabu-la'tion
tab'u-lator
tac'-a-ma-hac
tach'-ina
tachis'-to-scope
tach'o-graph
tach-om'eter
tacho-met'ric
tach-om'etry
tachy-car'-dia
tachy-gen-et'ic
tachyg'-ra-pher
tachy-graph'ic
tachy-graph-
    om'eter
tachyg'-ra-phy
tach'y-lyte
tachy-lyt'ic
tachyni'-eter
tach-yn_'etry
tach-yp-noe'a
tachys-terol
tachy-tel'ic
tac'i-turn
taci-tur'-nity
tack'i-ness
tack'-ler
tack'-ling
tac'-on-ite
tact'-ful

359

tact'-fully
tac'-ti-cal
tac'-ti-cally
tac-tic'i-ty
tac'-tics
tac'-tile
tac-til'i-ty
tac'-tion
tac'-tism
tact'-less
tac-tom'eter
tac'-tual
tad'-pole
tae-nia
tae-nia-cide
tae-ni'asis
taen'i-form
taen'i-oid
taf'-feta
taff'-rail
tag'a-tose
tag'-ging
tag'il-lite
tag'-lia
tail'-ing
tail'-less
tail'-ored
tail'-or-ess
tail'-or-ing
tail'-piece
tail'-race
tail'-stock
tain'-ture
tal-a'ria
tal-ar'ic
tal'-bo-type
tal'-cite

tal'-cose
tal'-cum
ta'le-bearer
ta'le-bear-ing
tal'-ent
ta'les-man
tal'-ion
tali-on'lc
tal'i-ped
tal'-is-man
tal'-ites
talk'-ative
tal'-lage
tal'-lant
tall'-boy
tal'-lied
tal'-lies
tal'-lith
tal'-low
tal'-ly-man
tal'-oned
tal'-ose
tal-pa-ta'te
tam-an'dua
tam'-anu
tam'-ar-ack
tam'-ar-in
tam'-ar-ind
tam'-ar-isk
tam'-bac
tam'-bour
tam'-bourin
tam-bour-i'ne
ta'me-able
ta'me-ness
tam'-pan
tam'-per

tam'-pin
tamp'-ing
tam'-pon
tam-pon-a'de
tan'a-ger
tan'a-grine
tan'-bark
tan'-dem
tan'-gelo
tan'-gency
tan'-gent
tan-gen'-tial
tan-gen'-tially
tan'-ger-ine
tan-gi-bil'ity
tan'-gible
tan'-gram
tan'-is-try
tan'-ite
tank'-age
tank'-ard
tan'-nate
tan'-ner
tan'-nery
tan'-nic
tan-nif'er-ous
tan'-nin
tan'-ning
tan'-rec
tan'-ta-late
tan-tal'ic
tan-ta-lis-a'tion
tan-ta-lise
tan-ta-liser
tan-ta-li's-ing
tan-ta-lite
tan-ta-lum
tan'-ta-lus

tan'-ta-mount

tan-tiv'y

tan'-tony

tan'-trum

tapa-cu'lo

tapa-de'ra

ta'per-ing

tap'-estsy

tap-e'tum

ta'pe-worm

tapi-o'ca

tap'io-lite

tap'-per

tap'-pet

tap'-ping

tap'-room

tap'-root

tap'-ster

tar-an-tel'la

tar'-an-tism

tar-an'tula

tar-ax'a-cin

tar-ax'a-cum

tar'-boosh

tar'di-grade

tar'di-ness

tar'-get

tar'-iff

tar'-la-tan

tar'-mac

tar'-nish

tar'-nish-able

tar'-pan

tar-paul'in

tar-paul'-ing

tar'-pon

tar'-ra-gon

tar'-ried

tar'-ring

tar'ry-ing

tar'-sal

tar-sal'gia

tar'-sia

tar'-sier

tar'-si-oid

tarso-meta-tar'-
        sal

tarso-meta-tar'-
        sus

tar'-sus

tar'-tan

tar'-tar

tar-ta'reous

tar-tar'-ic

tar-tar-is-a'tion

tar'-tar-ise

tar'-tar-ous

tar'-trate

tar'-trated

tar'-vi-ated

tas-eom'eter

tas-im'eter

tasi-met'ric

tas-im'etry

task'-mas-ter

tas'-man-ite

tass'-elled

tass'-el-ling

ta'ste-ful

ta'ste-less

ta'sti-ness

tat'-ter

tat-ter-dema'lion

tat'-tered

tat'-ting

tat'-tler

tat'tle-tale

tat'-tling

tat-too'

tat-too'er

taunt'-ing

taunt'-ingly

taur'-ian

taur'i-form

taur'-ine

tauro-bol'-ium

tauro-cho'lic

tauro'-coll

taur-om'achy

taut'o-chrone

taut-och'ron-ous

tauto-log'ic

tauto-log'i-cal

taut-ol'-ogise

taut-ol'-ogism

taut-ol'-ogist

taut-ol'ogy

taut-om'er-ism

taut-om'eter

tauto-met'ric

taut'-onym

taut-on'y-mous

tauto-phon'i-cal

taut-oph'-ony

tav'-ern

tav'-erner

taw'-dri-ness

tawn'i-ness

tax-abil'ity

tax'-able

tax-a'tion

tax=ex-empt'

tax'i-cab

taxi-der'-mic

361

TAXIDERMIST

tax'i-der-mist
tax'i-dermy
tax'-ied
tax'-ine
tax'-ing
tax-ol'ogy
taxo-nom'ic
tax-on'omy
tax'-payer
teach'-able
teach'-ing
tea'-cup
team'-mate
team'-ster
team'-work
tea'-pot
tea'-poy
tear'-ful
tear'-ing
tear'-less
tea'-room
teas'-ing
tea'-spoon
tea'-spoon-ful
tea'-time
tech-ne'tium
tech'-ni-cal
tech-ni-cal'-ity
tech-nic'ian
tech'-nics
tech'-ni-phone
tech-ni'que
tech-noc'-racy
tech'-no-crat
tech-nog'ra-phy
tech-no-log'ic
tech-no-log'i-cal
tech-nol'-ogist

tech-nol'ogy
tec-nol'-ogy
tec'-ti-form
tec-tol'ogy
tec-ton'ic
tec-ton'-ics
tec-to'rial
tec'-trices
tec-tric'ial
tec'-trix
tec'-tum
ted'-der
tedi-os'ity
te'di-ous
teeth'-ing
tee-to'tal
tee-to'tal-ler
tee-to'tal-ism
teg'-men
teg-men'-tal
teg-men'-tum
teg'-minal
teg'-ula
teg'u-lar
teg'u-lated
teg'u-men
teg'u-ment
tegu-men'-tary
tein'o-scope
tek-nom'-in-ous
tek-nom'-iny
tek'-tite
tel-aes-the'sia
tel-aes-thet'ic
tel'a-mon
tel-angi-ec-
        ta'sia
tel-angi-o'sis

tel-aut'o-gram
tel-aut'o-graph
tel-auto-graph'ic
tele-bar-om'eter
tel'e-cast
tcle-com-muni-
        ca'tion
tele-con-trol'
tele-gen'ic
tele-gon'ic
tel-eg'ony
tel'e-gram
tele-gram'-mic
tel'e-graph
tel-eg'ra-pher
tele-graph'ic
tel-eg'ra-phist
tel-eg'ra-phy
tele-kine'sis
tele-kin-et'ic
tel-elec'-tric
tel'e-mark
tel'e-meter
tele-met'ric
tel-em'etry
tel'e-motor
tel-en-ceph'a-lon
teleo-log'i-cal
tele-ol'ogy
tel'e-cost
tele-os'-tian
tcle-path'ic
tel-ep'a-thise
tel-ep'a-thist
tel-ep'a-thy
tel'e-phone
tele-phon'ic
tel-eph'on-ist

362

tel-eph'ony
tele-pho'to-graph
tele-pho-tog'ra-
    phy
tele-plas'-tic
tele-prin'-ter
tele-promp'-ter
tel'-eran
tel'ergy
tel'e-scope
tele-scop'ic
tele-scop'i-cally
tel-es'copy
tele-scrip'-ter
tel'e-seme
tel'-esis
tele-spec'-tro-
    scope
tele-ster'eo-
    scope
tel-es'tic
tel'e-stich
tele-ther-
    mom'eter
tel'e-tron
tele-ty'pe-writer
tel'e-typ-ist
tele-view'er
tel'e-vise
tel'e-vision
tel'e-visor
tell'-ing
tell'-tale
tel-lu'ral
tel'-lu-rate
tel'-lu-ret-ted
tel-lu'rian
tel-lu'ric

tel'-lu-ride
tel-lu-rif'er-ous
tel-lu'rion
tel'-lu-rite
tel-lu'rium
tel-lu-rom'eter
tel-lu-ro'nium
tel'-lu-rous
tel'o-phase
tel'-pher
tel'-pher-age
tel'-son
tem'-blor
tem-er-a'rious
tem-er'ity
tem'-er-ous
tem-nos-pon'-dy-
    lous
tem'-per
tem'-pera
tem'-pera-ment
tem-pera-men'-tal
tem'-per-ance
tem'-per-ate
tem'-per-at-ive
tem'-pera-ture
tem'-pered
tem'-perer
tem'-per-ing
tem'-pest
tem-pes'tu-ous
tem'-plar
tem'-plate
tem'-plet
tem'-poral
tem-por-al'ity
tem-por-al'ty
tem'-por-arily

tem'-por-ary
tem-por-is-a'tion
tem'-por-ise
tem'-por-iser
tempt'-able
temp-ta'tion
tempt'-ing
temp'-tress
tem'u-lence
tem'u-lent
ten-abil'ity
ten'-able
ten-a'cious
ten-ac'ity
ten-ac'u-lum
ten'-ancy
ten'-ant
ten'-ant-able
ten'-antry
ten-brif'ic
tend'-ance
tend'-ency
ten-den'-tious
ten'-der
ten'-der-foot
ten'der-hearted
ten'der-iser
ten'-der-ling
ten'-der-ness
ten'-din-ous
ten'-don
ten'-dril
ten'-drilled
ten'-dron
ten-eb'rity
ten'-ebrose
ten'-ebrous
ten'-ement

363

TENEMENTAL

ten-emen'-tal
ten-emen'-tary
ten-en'-dum
ten'-fold
ten'-nan-tite
ten'-nis
ten-on-i'tis
ten'-or-ite
ten-ot'omy
ten'-penny
ten'-pins
ten'-sible
ten'-sile
ten-sil'ity
ten-sim'eter
ten'-sion
ten'-sive
ten'-sor
ten-so'rial
ten'-tacle
ten-tac'u-lar
ten-tac'u-late
ten-tac'u-lite
ten-tac'u-lo-cyst
tent'-age
ten'-ta-tive
ten'-ter
ten'-ter-hook
ten-til'la
ten'u-ate
ten-u'ity
ten'u-ous
ten'-ure
ten-u'rial
tep'-efy
teph'-rite
teph-rit'ic

teph'-ro-ite
tepi-da'rium
tep-id'ity
tera-mor'-phous
ter'-aph
ter'a-phim
tera-to-gen'ic
tera-rog'eny
ter'a-toid
tera-to-log'i-cal
tera-tol'-ogist
tera-tol'ogy
tera-to'ma
tera-to'sis
ter'-bia
ter'-bium
ter'-cel
ter-cen-te'nary
ter-cen-ten'-nial
ter'-cet
ter'-ebene
ter-eb'ic
ter'-ebinth
ter-ebin'-thi-
    nate
ter-ebin'-thine
ter'-ebra
ter'-ebrant
ter'-ebrate
ter-ebra'tion
ter-e'do
ter'-gal
ter'-gant
ter'-gite
ter'-gi-ver-sate
ter-gi-ver-
    sa'tion
ter'-gi-ver-sator

ter'-gum
ter'-ma-gant
ter'-min-able
ter'-minal
ter'-min-ate
ter-min-a'tion
ter'-min-at-ive
ter'-min-ator
ter'-miner
ter'-mini
ter-min'-ism
ter-mino-log'i-
    cal
ter-min-ol'ogy
ter'-minus
ter-mi-ta'rium
ter'-mi-tary
ter'-mite
ter-mit'ic
ter'-nary
ter'-nate
ter'-nion
ter'-pene
ter-pin'-eol
ter-pin'-olene
terp-si-chore'an
ter'-race
ter-rain'
ter-ra-my'cin
ter-ra'nean
ter-ra'neous
ter-ra-pin
ter-ra'queous
ter-ra'rium
ter-raz'zo
ter-re'ne
ter-res'-trial

ter'-ret
ter'-rible
ter'-ribly
ter'-ri-cole
ter-ri-co'lous
ter'-rier
ter-rif'ic
ter-rif'i-cally
ter'-ri-fied
ter'-rify
ter-rig'en-ous
ter'-rine
ter-ri-to'rial
ter'-ri-tory
ter'-ror
ter-ror-is-a'tion
ter'-ror-ise
ter'-ror-ism
ter'-ror-ist
ter'-ry-cloth
ter'-se-ness
ter'-sion
ter'-tial
ter'-tian
ter'-tiary
ter-va'lent
tess'-el-lar
tess'-el-late
tess-el-lated
tess-el-la'tion
tess'-era
test'-able
tes-ta'cean
tes-ta'ceous
tes'-tacy
tes'-tament
tes-ta-men'-tary
tes-ta'mur

tes'-tate
tes-ta'tor
tes-ta'trix
tes'-ter
tes'-ticle
tes-tic'u-lar
tes-tif'i-cate
tes-ti-fi-ca'tion
tes'-tify
tes-ti-mo'nial
tes'-ti-mony
tes'-ti-ness
tes'-tis
tes-tos'-ter-one
tes-tu'di-nal
tes-tu-di-na'rian
tes-tu'di-nous
tet-an'ic
tet'an-ise
tet'a-nus
tet'-any
tet-arto-he'dra
teth'-ered
tetra-ba'sic
tetra-bran'chi-
        ate
tetra-bro'mo
tet'ra-caine
tet'ra-cene
tetra-chlo'ride
tet'ra-chord
tetra-chor'-dal
tetra-chot'o-mous
tet'-ract
tet'-rad
tetra-dac'-tyl
tet-rad'ic

tetra-did'y-mous
tet'-ra-dite
tet-rad'y-mite
tet'ra-gon
tet-rag'-onal
tet-rag'on-ous
tet'ra-gram
tetra-he'dral
tetra-he'drite
tetra-he'dron
tetra-hy'drate
tet'ra-lin
tet-ral'-ogy
tet-ram'er-ous
tet-ram'eter
tetra-mor'-phic
tetra-ni'trate
tetra-ple'gia
tet'ra-ploid
tet'ra-ploidy
tet'ra-pod
tet-rap'ody
tet'ra-rap'-teran
tet'-rap-tote
tet'-rarch
tet-rar'chic
tet'-rarchy
tet'ra-stich
tetras'-ti-chous
tet'-ra-style
tetra-syl-lab'ic
tet'ra-syl-lable
tetra-the'ism
tetra-tom'ic
tet'ra-va'lent
tet'ra-zine
tet'ra-zole
tet'-rode

365

tet'-ronal
tet'-rose
tet-rox'-ide
tet'-ryl
text'-book
tex'-tile
tex-to'rial
tex'-tual
tex'-tu-ary
tex'-tu-ral
tex'-ture
thal-am'ic
thal'a-mus
thal-ass'ic
thal-ass-og'ra-
          phy
thal-ass-om'eter
thal-id'o-mide
thal'-lic
thal-lif'-er-ous
thal'-li-form
thal'-line
thal'-li-ous
thal'-lium
thal-lo-gen
thal'-loid
thal'-lo-phyte
thal'-lose
thal'-lus
thana-pho'bia
than'a-tism
than'a-tist
thana-tog-nom-
          on'ic
thana-tog'ra-phy
than'a-toid
thana-tol--ogy

thana-top'-sis
thana-to'sis
thank'-ful
thank'-ful-ness
thank'-less
thanks'-giv-ing
thar'-an-dite
thatch'-ing
thaum'a-site
thauma-tog'eny
thauma-tol'-atry
thauma-tol'ogy
thaum'a-trope
thaum'a-turge
thaumata-tur'-gic
thauma-tur'-gist
thaum'a-turgy
the-a'ceous
the-an'dric
the-an-throp'ic
the-an'thro-pism
the'-archy
the-at'ri-cal
the-atri-cal'ity
thea-tric'ian
the'ba-ine
the'-ine
the'-ism
the'-ist
the-is'tic
the-mat'ic
the-mat'i-cally
them-sel'ves
the'-nal
the'-nar
then'ce-forth
thence-for'-ward
the-oc'-racy

the-oc'-rasy
the'o-crat
theo-crat'ic
the-od'icy
the-od'o-lite
theo-gon'ic
the-og'ony
theo-lo'gian
theo-log'i-cal
the-ol'-ogise
the-ol'-ogist
the-ol'ogy
the-om'-achy
theo-ma'nia
theo-man'-tic
theo-mor'-phic
theo-mor'-phism
theo-path-et'ic
theo-path'ic
theo-op'a-thy
theo-phan'ic
theo-oph'-any
theo-phyl'-line
theo-op-neus'ic
theo-op-neus'ty
the-or'bo
the'-orem
theor-em-at'ic
the-or-et'ic
theor-et'i-cal
theor-ctic'ian
theor-is-a'tion
the'-or-ise
the'-or-ist
the'-ory
the'o-soph
the-os'-opher

theo-soph'ic
the-os'-ophise
the-os'-oph-ist
the-os'-ophy
ther'a-lite
thera-peut'ic
thera-peut'i-
     cally
ther'a-pist
ther'-apy
there-abouts'
there-af'ter
there'e-fore
there-upon'
there-with'
the'-riac
theri-an-throp'ic
theri-an'thro-
     pism
theri-at'-rics
therio-mor'-phic
therio-mor'-phous
ther'-mal
ther-man'ti-date
ther-ma-tol'ogy
ther'-mic
ther'-mi-cally
ther'-mion
thermi-on'ic
ther-mis'-tor
ther'-mite
ther-mo-chem'-
     is-try
ther'-mo-couple
ther-mo-du'ric
ther-mo-dyn-am'ic
ther-mo-elec'-
     tric

ther-mo-gen'-esis
ther-mo-gen-et'ic
ther'-mo-gram
ther'-mo-graph
ther-mog'ra-pher
ther-mo-graph'ic
ther-mog'ra-phy
ther-mol'y-sis
ther-mo-lyt'ic
ther-mom'eter
ther-mo-met'ric
ther-mo-met'ri-
     cally
ther-mom'-etry
ther-mo-nu'clear
ther'mo-phile
ther-moph'-ily
ther'-mo-pile
thermo-plas'-tic
ther'mo-scope
ther-mo-scop'ic
ther'-mo-stat
ther-mo-stat'ic
thermo-tax'is
thermo-ten'-sile
thermo-ther'apy
ther-mot'ic
ther-mot'ro-pism
ther'mo-type
the'-roid
ther-sit'i-cal
the'-ses
the'-sis
the'-tic
the-ur'gic
the-ur'gist
the'-urgy
thi'a-mide

thi-am'i-nase
thi'a-mine
thi-an'-threne
thi'a-zine
thi'a-zole
thi-az'-oline
thick'-en-ing
thick'-ness
thick'-set
thiev'-ery
thiev'-ing
thiev'-ish
thigh'-bone
thig-mo-trop'ic
thig-mot'ro-pism
thim'ble-ful
thi-mer'o-sal
think'-able
think'-ing
thin'-ner
thin'-ness
thin'-ning
thio-cy'an-ate
thio-cyan'ic
thi-on'ic
thi'o-nine
thio-pen'-tone
thi'o-phene
thio-u'ra-cil
thio-ure'a
thirl'-age
thirst'-ily
thirst'i-ness
thir'-teen
thir'-ti-eth
this'tle-down
thix'o-trope
thixo-trop'ic

367

thix-ot'ropy
tho'-lo-bate
tho'-lus
thora-cen-te'sis
tho-rac'ic
tho-raci-col-
    um'-bar
thor-ac'o-plasty
tho-rac'o-scope
tho-ra-cot'omy
tho'-rax
tho'-ria
tho'-ria-nite
tho'-ri-ate
tho'-rite
tho'-rium
thorn'-back
thorn'-bill
tho'-ron
thor'ough-bred
thor'ough-fare
thor'ough-go'ing
thor'ough-ness
thought'-ful
thought'-fully
thought'-ful-ness
thought'-less
thought'-less-
    ness
thou'-sand
thou'-sand-fold
thou'-sandth
thral'-dom
thra-son'i-cal
thread'-bare
thread'-worm
threat'-en-ing
threat'-ful
368

three'-fold
three'-pence
three'-score
three'-some
thre'-itol
threm-ma-tol'ogy
thren-et'ic
thren'-ode
thren-od'ic
thren'-odist
thren'-ody
thre'-onine
threp-sol'ogy
thrift'-ily
thrift'i-ness
thrift'-less
thrill'-ing
throat'i-ness
throb'-bing
throm-bec'-tomy
throm'-bin
thrombo-angi-
    i'tis
throm'-bo-cyte
throm-bo-cyt'ic
throm-bo-phil'ia
throm-bo-plas'-
    tic
throm-bo-plas'-
    tin
throm'-bose
throm-bo'sis
throm-bot'ic
throm'-bus
throt'-tling
through-out'
thrust'-ful
thrust'-ing

thud'-ding
thug'-gery
thu'-lite
thu'-lium
thum'-bat
thumb'-nail
thumb'-screw
thum'-mim
thun'-der
thun'-der-bird
thun'-der-bolt
thun'-der-cloud
thun'-derer
thun'-der-head
thun'-der-ous
thun'-der-ously
thun'-der-shower
thun'-der-storm
thun'-der-struck
thun'-dery
thu'-rible
thu'-ri-fer
thu-rif'er-ous
thu-ri-fi-ca'tion
thu'-rify
thy'-la-cine
thy-mec'-tomy
thy'-mic
thy'-mine
thy'-mol
thy-mol-phthal'-
    ein
thy'-mus
thy'ra-tron
thy'-roid
thy-roid'al
thy-roid-ec'-tom-
    ise

thy-roid-ec'-tomy
thy-roid-i'tis
thyro-toxi-co'sis
thy-rox'-ine
thyr'-soid
thyr'-sus
thysa-nu'rian
thysa-nu'ri-form
thysa-nu'rous
tib'-ial
tick'-eter
tick'-ing
tick'-ler
tick'-lish
ti'de-rip
ti'des-man
ti'de-water
ti'di-ness
tie'-mann-ite
tif'-fany
tif'-fin
ti'ger-ish
ti'ght-ener
ti'ght-en-ing
ti'ght-rope
tig'-lic
ti'-glon
til'-bury
tili-a'ceous
till'-able
till'-age
tim'-bal
tim'-ber
tim'-bered
tim'-ber-man
tim'-ber-wolf
tim'-ber-work
tim'-brel

tim'-brelled
tim-brol'ogy
ti'me-keeper
ti'me-li-ness
ti'me-piece
ti'me-table
tim-id'ity
tim-oc'racy
timo-crat'ic
tim'-or-ous
tim'-othy
tim'-pani
tim'-pan-ist
tim'-pano,
tinc-to'rial
tinc'-ture
tin'-der
tin'-foil
tin'ge-ing
tink'-ling
tin'-ner
tin-ni'tus
tin'-plate
tin'-sel
tin'-selled
tin'-smith
tin-tin-nab'u-
          late
tin-tin-nabu-
        la'tion
tin-tin-nab'u-
        lous
tint-om'eter
tin'-type
tin'-ware
tip'-per
tip'-pet
tip'-ping

tip'-pler
tip'-pling
tip'-si-ness
tip'-staff
tip'-ster
tip'-toe
ti-ra'de
ti're-less
ti're-some
tir'-ret
tis'-sue
ti'-ta-nate
ti-tan'ic
ti-tan-if'er-ous
ti'-tan-ite
ti-ta'nium
ti-tan'-ous
tit'-ter
ti-thon'ic
ti-thon-ic'ity
ti-thon-om'eter
titian-es'que
tit'-il-late
tit-il-la'tion
tit'-il-lator
tit'i-vate
titi-va'tion
tit'-mouse
ti'-trant
ti-tra'ta-ble
ti'-trate
ti-tra'tion
ti-trim'eter
tit'-ter
tit'u-bate
tit'u-bant
titu-ba'tion
tit'u-lar

369

titu-lar'ity
tit'u-lary
tme'-sis
toad'-stool
toast'-mas-ter
tobac'-co-nist
tobac'-cos
tobog'-gan
tobog'-ganer
toc-cat'a
toc-ol'o-gy
toc-oph'-erol
toc'-sin
tod'-dler
tod'-dling
tof'-fee
togeth'er-ness
tog'-gery
tog'-ging
tog'-gler
toil'-etry
toil'-some
toil'-worn
tol'-booth
tol-bu'ta-mide
tol'-er-able
tol'-er-ably
tol'-er-ance
tol'-er-ant
tol'-er-ate
tol-er-a'tion
tol'i-dine
toll'-booth
toll'-gate
tol'u-ate
tol'u-ene
tol-u'ic
tol-u'idine

tol'-uol
tom'a-hawk
tom-al'-ley
tom-a'to
tom-a'toes
tom'-bac
tom'-boc
tom'-boy
tomb'-stone
tom'-cat
tom-en'-tose
tomen'-tous
tomen'-tum
tom-fool'-ery
tom-og'ra-phy
tom'-pion
to'nal-ite
tonal'-ity
to'ne-less
tonet'-ics
tong'ue-less
ton-ic'ity
to-ni'ght
ton-neau'
tonom'-eter
tono-met'ric
tonom'-etry
ton'-sil
ton'-sile
ton-sil-ec'-tomy
ton-sil-i'tis
ton'-sil-lar
ton-sil-ot'omy
ton-so'rial
ton'-sure
ton'-tine
tool'-holder
tool'-ing

tooth'-ache
tooth'-brush
tooth'-ings
tooth'-less
tooth'-paste
tooth'-pick
tooth'-some
to'paz-ine
topaz'-olite
top'-coat
top-ec'tomy
top-gal'-lant
topi-a'rian
to'pi-ar-ist
to'pi-ary
top'-ical
top'-knot
top'-mast
top'-most
top-og'ra-pher
topo-graph'i-
       cally
top-og'ra-phy
topo-log'i-cal
top-ol'ogy
topo-nym'ic
top-on'ymy
to'po-type
top'-per
top'-ping
top'-pling
top'-sail
top'-side
top'-soil
tor'-ban-ite
tor'-ber-nite
tor'-bite
torch'-bearer

torch'-ing
torch'-light
tor'-chon
torch'-wood
tor-eador'
tor-e'ro
tor-eu'tic
tor'-ment' (v.)
tor'-ment (n.)
tor'-men-til
tor-men'-tor
tor-na'do
tor-na'does
tor-nog'ra-phy
tor-pe'do
tor-pe'does
tor'-pid
tor-pid'-ity
tor'-pi-tude
tor'-por
tor-por-if'ic
tor-re-fac'-tion
tor'-refy
tor'-rent
tor-ren'-tial
to-ren'ti-coles
tor'-rid
tor-sa'de
tor'-sel
tor-si-bil'ity
tor'-sio-graph
tor'-sion
tor'-sional
tor'-sive
tor'-ti-cone
tor'-tile
tor-til'lity
tor'-tious

tor'-toise
tor'-tu-ose
tor-tu-os'ity
tor'-tu-ous
tor'-tu-ously
tor'-ture
tor'-turer
tor'-tur-ingly
tor'-tur-ous
tor'u-loid
tos'-can-ite
toss'-ing
to'-tal-ling
to'tal-is-ator
to'tal-ise
to'tal-iser
totali-ta'rian
totali-ta'rian-
     ism
total'-ity
to'ta-quine
to'tem-ism
toti-pal'-mate
tot'-ter
tou'-can
touch'-able
touch'-down
touch'-ily
touch'i-ness
touch'-ing
touch'-stone
touch'-wood
tough'-ness
tour'-aco
tour-bil'lion
tour'-ism
tour'-ist
tour'-ma-line

tour'-na-ment
tour'-ney
tour'-ni-quet
tour'-nure
tow'-age
tow'-boat
tow'el-ling
tow'er-ing
tow'-head
tow'-line
town'-house
towns'-folk
town'-ship
towns'-man
towns'-people
tow'-path
tow'-rope
tox-ae'mia
tox-ae'mic
tox'i-cant
toxi-ca'tion
tox-ic'ity
toxi-co-log'i-cal
toxi-col'-ogist
toxi-col'ogy
toxi-co-ma'nia
toxi-coph'a-gous
toxi-co'sis
toxi-pho'bia
tox'-oid
tox-oph'a-gous
tox-oph'i-lite
trab'-eated
tra-bec'-ula
tra-bec'u-lar
tra-bec'u-late
tra'ce-able
tra-che'a

tra-che'al
tra-che'idal
tra-chei'tis
trach'el-ate
tra-cheot'-omy
tra-cho'ma
tra-chom'a-tous
trach'-yte
tra-chyt'ic
track'-age
track'-less
track'-man
track'-walker
trac-ta-bil'ity
trac'-table
trac'-tate
trac'-tile
trac-til'ity
trac'-tion
trac'-tive
trac'-tor
tra'de-mark
tra'des-man
tra-dit'ion
tra-dit'ional
tra-dit'ion-al-
    ism
tra-dit'ion-al-ist
tra-dit'ion-ally
tra-dit'ion-ary
trad'i-tive
trad'i-tor
tra-du'ce
tra-du'cer
tra-du'cian
tra-du'cian-ism
tra-du'c-ible
tra-duc'tor

traf'-ficked
traf'-ficker
traf'-fick-ing
trag'a-canth
traga-can'-thin
tra-ge'dian
tra-gedienn'e
tra-gel'a-phus
trag'i-cal
trag'i-cally
trag'i-com'-edy
trag'o-pan
trag'u-line
train'-able
train'-ing
train'-load
train'-man
trait'or-ous
tra-ject'
tra-jec'-tile
tra-jec'-tion
tra-jec'-tory
tra-la-tit'ious
tram'-mel
tram'-melled
tram'-mel-ling
tra-mon'-tane
tram'-pling
tram'-pol-ine
tram-pol-in'-ist
tram'-way
tran'-quil
tran'-quil-lise
tran'-quil-liser
tran-quil'-lity
trans-act'
trans-ac'tion
trans-ac'-tor

trans-am'-in-ase
trans-at-lan'-tic
trans-ca'lent
trans-ceiv'er
tran-scend'
tran-scen'-dency
tran-scen'-dent
tran-scen-den'tal
tran-scen-den'-
    tal-ism
trans'-co-late
trans-con-ti-
    nen'-tal
tran-scri'be
tran-scri'ber
tran'-script
tran-scrip'-tion
tran-scrip'-tive
trans-du'cer
trans-duc'-tor
tran-sect' (v.)
tran'-sect (n.)
tran-sen'na
tran-sept'
tran-sep'-tate
trans'-fer (n. v.)
trans-fer' (v.)
trans-fer-
    abil'ity
trans-fer'-able
trans'-fer-ase
trans-feree'
trans'-fer-ence
trans-fer-en'-
    tial
trans-fer'or
trans-fer'o-type
trans-ferr'ed

trans-fer'-rer
trans-fer'-ring
trans-figur-
    a'tion
trans-fig'-ure
trans-fix'
trans-fix'ion
trans-form' (v.)
trans'-form (n.)
trans-form'-able
trans-form-a'tion
trans-form'a-tive
trans-for'mer
trans-form'-ism
trans-form'-ist
trans-fu's-able
trans-fu'se
trans-fu'sion
trans-fu's-ive
trans-fu'sor
trans-gress'
trans-gress'-ive
trans-gres'sion
trans-gress'or
tran-ship'-ping
trans-hu'mance
tran'-si-ency
tran'-si-ent
tran'-si-ently
tran-sil'i-ence
tran-sil'i-ent
trans-il-lu'mi-
    nate
trans-il-lumi-
    na'tion
tran-sis'-tor
tran'-sit
tran-sit'ion

tran-sit'ional
tran-si'tion-ary
tran'-si-tive
tran'-si-tory
tran'-si-tron
trans-la't-able
trans-la'te
trans-la'tion
trans-la't-ive
trans-la'tor
trans-lit'-er-ate
trans-lit-er-
    a'tion
trans-lit'-er-
    ator
trans-lo'-cate
trans-lo-ca'tion
trans-lu'cence
trans-lu'cency
trans-lu'cent
trans-mi'grant
trans'-migrate
trans-migra'tion
trans'-migrator
trans-mi'grat-ory
trans-miss'-ible
trans-mis'sion
trans-mis-
    som'eter
trans-mit'
trans-mit'-table
trans-mit'-tal
trans-mit'-tance
trans-mit'-ter
trans-mit'-ting
trans-mogri-fi-
    ca'tion
trans-mog'-rify

trans-mon'-tane
trans-mut-
    abil'ity
trans-mu't-able
trans-mu-ta'tion
trans-mu'te
trans-mu'ter
trans-ocean'ic
tran'-som
tran-son'ic
trans-pa-cif'ic
trans-pa'rency
trans-pa'rent
tran-spi'r-able
tran-spi-ra'tion
tran-spi're
trans-plant'
trans-plan-
    ta'tion
tran-splen'-dency
tran-splen'-dent
tran-spon'-der
trans-po'nible
trans-po'rt (v.)
trans'-port (n.)
trans-po'rt-able
trans-por-ta'tion
trans-po'rter
trans-po's-able
trans-po'sal
trans-po'se
trans-po-sit'ion
trans-pos'i-tive
trans-pos'i-tor
tran-sub-stan'-
    tiate
tran-sub-stan-
    tia'tion

TRANSUBSTANTIATOR

tran-sub-stan'-
    tiator
tran-su-da'tion
tran-su'da-tory
tran-su'de
tran-sumpt'
tran-sump'-tion
tran-sump'-tive
trans-uran'ic
trans-ura'nium
trans-vec'-tion
trans-ver'-sal
trans-ver'-sary
trans-ver'se (v.)
trans'-verse (a. n.)
trans-ver'ser
trans-ver'-sion
trans-ver'ter
trans-vert'-ible
tra-pan'
trap'-door
tra-pe'ze
tra-pe'zi-form
tra-pe'zium
tra-pezo-he'dron
trap-ezoid
trap-ezoid'al
trap'-per
trap'-pings
trap'-poid
trau-mat'ic
traum'a-tin
traum'a-tism
tra-vail'
trav'-elled
trav'-el-ler
trav'-el-ling
trav'-elogue

tra-vers'-able
tra-vers'al
trav'-erse (n.)
tra-vers'e (v. n.)
trav'-ers-ing
trav'-er-tine
trav'-esty
treach'-er-ous
treach'-ery
tread'-ing
tread'-mill
treas'on-able
treas'on-ous
treat'-able
treat'-ies
treat'-ise
treat'-ment
treb'u-chet
tree'-ing
tree'-less
tree'-nail
tree'-top
tre'-foil
tre'-hal-ose
trek'-ker
trek'-king
trel'-lis
trel'-lised
trel'-lis-work
trem'a-tode
trem'-bling
trem'-blingly
trem'-el-loid
tremen'-dous
tremen'-dously
trem'o-lant
trem'o-lite
trem'u-lous

tre'-nail
trench'-ancy
trench'-ant
trepa-na'tion
trepan'-ning
tre-phi'ne
trepi-da'tion
trep-id'ity
trepo-nema-
    to'sis
trepo-nem-i'asis
tres'-pass
tri'-able
tria-conta-
    he'dral
tri'-act
tri-ac'-tinal
tri-ac'-tive
tri-ad'ic
tri'-age
tri'-al-ism
tri-al'ity
tri'a-logue
tri'-angle
tri-an'gu-lar
tri-an'gu-late
tri-angu-la'tion
tri-an'gu-loid
tri-ap'-sal
tri-ap'si-dal
tri'-archy
tri-aryl-meth'-
    ane
tri-atom'ic
tri'a-zine
tri'a-zole
tri'bal-ism
tri'bes-man

374

trib'-let
tri-bom'eter
tri'-brach
tri-bromo-
　　　　eth'anol
tri-bromo-eth'yl
tribu-la'tion
tri-bu'r.
trib'u-nate
trib'-une
tribu-nic'ial
trib'u-tary
trib'-ute
tri-cen'-nial
tri-cen'-ten-ary
tri-ceph'a-lous
tri'-ceps
tri-ce'rion
trich-i'asis
trich-i'na
trich'-in-ise
trichi-no'sis
trichi-not'ic
trich-it'ic
tri-chlo'-ride
tri-chloro-meth'-
　　　　ane
trich'o-gen
trich-og'en-ous
trich'-oid
trich-ol'-ogist
trich'-ology
trich'-ome
tri'-chord
trich-or-rhe'a
trich-o'sis
tri-chot'o-mous
tri-chot'omy

tri-chro'ic
tri-chro-mat'ic
tri-chro'ma-tism
tri-chro'mic
trick'-ery
trick'-ily
trick'i-ness
trick'-ling
trick'-ster
tri-clin'ic
tri'-colour
tri-con-son-
　　　　an'tal
tri'-corn
tric'o-tine
tri-crot'ic
tri'-crot-ism
tri-cus'-pid
tri'-cycle
tri-cy'clic
tri'-dent
tri-den'-tate
tri-dimen'-sional
trid'y-mite
tri-en'-nial
tri'-er-archy
tri-fa'rious
tri'-fid
tri-fo'cal
tri-fo'li-ate
tri-fo'lio-late
tri-fo'lium
tri-fo'rium
tri'-form
tri'-fur-cate (a.)
tri-fur'-cate (v.)
tri-fur-ca'tion
trig'a-mist

trig'a-mous
trig'-amy
tri-gem'-inal
trig'-ger
tri'-glot
tri'-glyph
tri-glyph'ic
tri'-gon
trig'-onal
tri-gon'ic
tri-gon-i'tis
trig-on-om'eter
trig-ono-met'ric
trig-on-om'etry
trig'-on-ous
tri'-gram
tri-gram-mat'ic
tri'-graph
tri-he'dral
tri-he'dron
tri-hy'dric
tri'-labe
tri-lam'-inar
tri-lat'-eral
tri-lem'ma
tri-lin'-ear
tri-lin'gual
tri-lit'-eral
tri'-lith
tri-lith'ic
tril'-lium
tri'-lo-bite
tril'-ogy
tri-men'-sual
trim'-er-ous
tri-mes'-tral
trim'-eter
tri-met'ro-gon

375

trim'-mer
trim'-ming
trin-ac'ri-form
tri'-nal
tri'-nary
tri-nitro-tol'u-ene
trin'-ity
tri-no'mial
tri'-ode
tri'-olein
tri'o-let
tri'o-nal
tri'-onym
tri-ox'-ide
tri-par'-tite
tri-par-tit'ion
trip'-edal
tri'-phane
tri-phe'nyl
tri-phib'i-ous
tri'-phone
triph'-thong
triph'-yl-ite
trip'-let
trip'-lex
trip'-li-cate
trip-li-ca'tion
trip-lic'ity
trip'-loid
trip'-loidy
tri'-pod
trip'-odal
tri-pod'ic
trip'-ody
trip'o-lite
tri'-pos
trip'-per

trip'-pingly
trip'-sis
trip'-ter-ous
trip'-tote
trip'-tych
tri-quet'ra
tri-quet'-ral
tri-quet'-ric
tri-quet'-rous
tri'-reme
tri-sect'
tri-sec'-tion
tri-sec'-trix
tri'-seme
tri-se'mic
tri-se'rial
tri-se'ri-ate
tris'-kele
tris-kel'-ion
tris-oc-ta-
    he'dron
tri-so'mic
tri'-spast
tri-ste'arin
tris'-tich
tris'-ti-chous
tri-sul'-cate
tri-sul'-phide
tri-syl-lab'ic
tri-syl'-lable
tri'te-ness
tri-ter'nate
tri-the'ism
tri-thi'on-ate
trit-ic'eous
tri'-ton
tri'-tone
tri-to'rium

trit'u-rate
tritu-ra'tion
trit'u-rator
tri'-umph
tri-um'phal
tri-um'phant
tri-umph-ing
tri-um'-vir
tri-um'-vir-al
tri-um'-vir-ate
tri'-une
tri-va'lence
tri-va'lent
triv'-ial
trivi-al'ity
triv'-ium
tro'-car
tro-cha'ic
tro-chan'-ter
tro'-chee
tro-chil'ic
troch'i-lus
troch'-lea
troch'-lear
tro'-choid
tro-choid'al
tro-chom'eter
troc'-to-lite
trod'-den
trog'-lo-dyte
trog-lo-dyt'ic
tro'-ilite
trol'-ley
trol'-lop
trom-bi-di'asis
trom-bo'ne
trom-bo'n-ist
trom'-mel

tro-mom'eter
troop'-ship
troos'-tite
tro-pae'-olin
troph'-esy
troph-ol'o-gy
tro'-pho-plasm
tro'-phy
trop'-ical
tro'-pism
trop-is'tic
tro-pol'o-gy
trop'o-pause
trop-oph'i-lous
trop'o-phyte
tropo-phyt'ic
trop'o-sphere
trot'-ter
trot'-ting
troub'a-dour
troub'-ler
troub'le-some
troub'-ling
trounc'-ing
troup'-ial
tro'-ver
trow'el-ler
trow'el-ling
tru'-ancy
tru'-ant
truck'-age
truck'-ler
truck'-ling
truck'-man
truc'u-lence
truc'u-lent
trudg'-ing

tru'-ism
tru-is'tic
tru'-meau
trum'-pery
trum'-pet
trum'-peter
trunc'-ate'
trunc'-ated
trunc-a'tion
trunc'a-ture
trun'-cheon
trun'-dler
trun'-dling
trunk'-ful
trun'-ion
truss'-ing
tustee'-ship
trust'-ful
trust'-ily
trus'ti-ness
trust'-ing
trust'-worthi-
          ness
trust'-worthy
truth'-ful
truth'-ful-ness
try'-ing
try'-out (n.)
trypano-ci'dal
tryp'ano-some
tryp'o-graph
trypo-graph'ic
tryp'-sin
tryp-sin'o-gen
tryp'-tic
tryp'-to-phan
try'-sail

tub'-bable
tubec'-tomy
tu'-bercle
tu-ber'cu-late
tu-ber'cu-lin
tu-ber'cu-lose
tu-bercu-lo'sis
tu-ber'cu-lous
tu-ber-if'er-ous
tu'-beri-form
tu-ber-os'ity
tu'-ber-ous
tu-bic'o-lous
tubi-fa'cient
tu'bi-form
tu'bi-pore
tu'bu-lar
tu'bu-late
tubu-la'tion
tu'-bule
tu-bu'-li-form
tues'-ite
tu-fa'ceous
tuf-fa'ceous
tug'-boat
tru-it'ion
tu-it'ional
tu-it'ion-ary
tu-la-rae'mia
tu'-lip
tu'-lip-wood
tum'ble-down
tum'-bler
tum'ble-weed
tum'-bling
tum'-brel
tu-mefa'cient
tu-mefac'-tion

377

tu'-mefied
tu'-mefy
tu-mesc'ence
tu-mesc'ent
tu'-mid
tu-mid'ity
tu'-mor-ous
tu'-mour
tu'-mu-lar
tu'-mu-late
tu'-mu-lose
tu-mu-los'ity
tu'-mult
tu-mul'tu-ary
tu-mul'tu-ous
tu'-mu-lus
tun'-dra
tu'ne-ful
tu'ne-less
tung'-state
tung'-sten
tung-sten'ic
tung-sten-if'er-
ous
tung'-stic
tung'-stite
tu'-nic
tu'-ni-cated
tu'-nicked
tun'-nel
tun'-nelled
tun'-nel-ler
tun'-nel-ling
tun'-nery
tu'-pelo
tu'ra-cin
tu'-ran-ose
tur'-ban

tur'-baned
tur'-bary
tur'-bid
turbi-dim'eter
tur-bi-di-met'ric
tur-bid'ity
tur'-bi-nal
tur'-bi-nate
tur'-bine
tur-bi-nec'-tomy
tur-bin'i-form
tur'-bi-noid
tur'bo-charger
tur'-bot
tur'-bu-lator
tur'-bu-lence
tur'-bu-lent
tur'-dine
tur'-doid
tur'-gency
tur'-gently
tur-gesc'ence
tur-gesc'ent
tur'-gid
tur-gid'ity
tur'-gor
tu'-rion
tur'-key
tur'-keys
tur'-meric
tur'-moil
turn'-buckle
turn'-coat
turn'-cock
turn'-down
turn'-ery
turn'-ing
tur'-nip

turn'-key
turn'-out
turn'-over
turn'-pike
turn'-spit
turn'-stile
turn'-table
tur'-pen-tine
tur'-peth
tur'-pi-tude
tur'-quoise
tur'-ret
tur-ric'u-late
tur'-ri-lite
tur'tle-dove
tus'-kar
tuss'-ock
tu'-tel-age
tu'-telar
tu'-tel-ary
tu'-tenag
tu ti-or-ism
tu'-tor
tu'-tored
tu-to'rial
tu-to'rially
tut'-san
tux-e'do
tweez'-ers
twen'-ti-eth
twid'-dling
twi'-light
twin'ge-ing
twink'-ling
twin'-ning
twit'-ter
twit'-ting
two'-fold

two'-some
ty'-chism
ty'-coon
ty'-ing
tyl'-arus
ty'lo-pod
ty-lop'o-dous
ty-lo'sis
ty'lo-tate
tym'-pan
tym'-pani
tym-pan'ic
tym-pan'i-form
tym'-pan-ist
tym-pa-ni'tes
tym-pan-nit'ic
tym-pan-i'tis
tym'-pa-num
tym'-pany
tyn-dall-im'etry
ty'pe-cast
ty'pe-founder
ty'pe-script
ty'pe-set-ter
ty'pe-write
ty'pe-writer
ty'pe-writ-ing
ty'pe-writ-ten
typh-lit'ic
typh-li'tis
typh-lol'ogy
typh-lo'sis
ty'-phoid
ty-phoid'al
ty-phoid'in
ty-phon'ic
ty-phoon'
ty'-phous

ty'-phus
typ'i-cal
typi-fi-ca'tion
typ'i-fied
typ'i-fier
typ'-ify
ty-pog'ra-pher
ty-po-graph'ic
ty-po-graph'ical
ty-pog'ra-phy
typ'o-lite
typo-log'i-cal
typ-pol'ogy
typ-tol'-ogist
typ-tol'ogy
tyr-an'-ni-cal
tyr-an'-ni-cide
tyr'-an-nise
tyr'-an-nous
tyr'-an-nously
tyr'-anny
ty'-rant
tyr'o-lite
ty'ro-sin-ase
ty'ro-sine
tyro-sin-o'sis
tyro-tox'i-con

U

u'ber-ous
ubiqui-ta'rian
ubiq'ui-tary
ubiq'ui-tous
ud'-der
udom'-eter
udo-met'ric

udom'-etry
udom'o-graph
ug'li-ness
ukul-e'le
ul'-cer
ul'-cer-ate
ul-cer-a'tion
ul-cer-at'ive
ul'-cered
ul'-cer-ous
u'lex-ite
ulig'in-ous
ull'-age
ull'-ing
ul-ma'ceous
ul'-mate
ul'-mic
ul'-min
ul'-mous
ul'-nar
ul-na're
ulot'ri-chan
ulot'ri-chous
ulot'-richy
ul-te'rior
ul'-tima
ul'-ti-macy
ul'-ti-mate
ul-ti-ma'tum
ul'-timo
ul-ti-mo-gen'i-
    ture
ul'-tion
ultra-cen'-tri-
    fuge
ul'tra-ism
ul'tra-ist

379

ultra-mar-i′ne
ultra-mi′cro-
    scope
ultra-mon′-tane
ultra-mon′-tan-
    ism
ultra-mun′-dane
ultra-son′ic
ultra-vi′olet
ultra-vi′rus
ul-tro′neous
u′lu-lant
u′lu-late
ulu-la′tion
um′-bel
um′-bel-late
um-bel-lif′er-ous
um-bel′-li-form
um′-ber
um-bil′i-cal
um-bili-ca′tion
um-bil′i-cus
um′-bonal
um′-bon-ate
um′-bra
um-brac′u-late
um-bracu-lif′er-
    ous
um-brac′u-li-
    form
um-brac′u-lum
um′-brage
um-bra′geous
um′-bral
um′-bra-tile
um-brat′i-lous
um-bra′tion
um′-brel

um-brel′la
um-brett′e
um-brif′er-ous
um′-brine
um′-brose
um′-brous
um′-pir-age
um′-pire
un-abash′ed
un-aba′ted
un-abridg′ed
un-ab′-ro-gated
un-aca-dem′ic
un-ac-cen′ted
un-ac-cept′-able
un-ac-com′-mo-
    dat-ing
un-ac-com′pan-ied
un-ac-count′-able
un-ac-cred′ited
un-ac-cus′-tomed
un-achiev′-able
un-achiev′ed
un-ac-knowl′-
    edged
un-ac-quain′ted
un-ac-qui′red
un-ac-quit′-ted
un-adap′-ted
un-ad-dress′ed
un-adop′-ted
un-ador′ned
un-adul -ter-ated
un-af-fec′-ted
un-af-flic′-ted
un-aid′ed

u′na-list
un-al-lay′ed
un-al-le′vi-ated
un-al-loy′ed
un-al′ter-able
un-al′tered
un-am-big′u-ous
un-am-bit′ious
un-a′miable
un-an-neal′ed
una-nim′ity
unan′i-mous
un-an-nex′ed
un-an-noun′ced
un-an′swer-able
un-ap-peal′-able
un-ap-peas′ed
un-ap-pli′ed
un-ap-prec′ci-
    ated
un-ap-pre′ci-at-
    ive
un-ap-proach′-
    able
un-ap-pro′-pri-
    ated
un-ar′-gued
un-arm′ed
un-ar-raign′ed
un-ar-ra′nged
un-as-cer-tain′-
    able
un-as′-cer-tained
un-asha′med
un-ask′ed
un-as-pi′ring
un-as-sail′-able
un-as-sis′ted

un-as-su'm-ing
un-at-tach'ed
un-at-tain'-able
un-at'ten'ded
un-at-tes'-ted
un-at-trac'-tive
un-auth'or-ised
un-avail'-ing
un-aven'ged
un-avoid'-able
un-avow'ed
un-awa're
un-bal'-lanced
un-bal'-las-ted
un-bar'
un-bear'-able
un-beat'en
un-be-com'-ing
un-be-fit'-ting
un-be-got'-ten
un-be-known'
un-be-lief'
un-be-liev'-able
un-be-liev'er
un-be-liev'-ing
un-bend'
un-bend'-ing
un-ben'-eficed
un-bent'
un-be-queath'ed
un-bi'ased
un-bid'-den
un-bi'nd
un-bla'm-able
un-bleach'ed
un-blem'-ished
un-blink'-ing
un-blush'-ing

un-bo'lt
un-bo'lted
un-born'
un-bos'om
un-bound'
un-boun'ded
un-braid'
un-break'-able
un-bri'dled
un-bro'ken
un-broth'erly
un-buck'le
un-built'
un-bur'-den
un-bus'iness-like
un-but'-ton
un-cal'-cu-lated
un-can'ny
un-can-on'i-cal
un-caught'
un-ceas'-ing
un-cer-emo'ni-ous
un-cer'-tain
un-cer'-tainty
un-chain'
un-chain'ed
un-chal'-lenged
un-cha'nge-able
un-cha'nged
un-char'i-table
un-char'ted
un-cha'ste
un-check'ed
un-chris'-tian
un-church'
un'-cial
un-cif'er-ous
un'-ci-form

un'-ci-nate
un-cir'-cum-cised
un-civ'il
un-civ'-il-ised
un-clad'
un-clasp'ed
un-clean'
un-clench'
un-clo'se
un-cloud'ed
un-coil'
un-com'fort-able
un-com-mit'ted
un-com'-mon
un-com-mu'ni-
                cat-ive
un-com-plain'-
                ing
un-com'-pro-
                mis-ing
un-con-ceal'ed
un-con-ceiv'-able
un-con-cern'
un-con-cern'ed
un-con-cil'ia-
                tory
un-con-dit'ional
un-con-fi'ned
un-con-firm'ed
un-con-form'-
                able
un-con-ge'nial
un-con-nec'-ted
un-con'-quer-
                able
un-con'quered
un-con'-scion-
                able

un-con'-scious
un-con'-scious-
     ness
un-con'-se-crated
un-con-sid'-ered
un-con-sti-
    tu'tional
un-con-strain'ed
un-con-tain'-able
un-con-tro'l-
    lable
un-con-tro'lled
un-con-ven'-
    tional
un-con-ver'ted
un-con-vinc'-ing
un-cor-rect'
un-cor-rupt'
un-cor-rup'-ted
un-coun'ted
un-coup'le
un-cour'teous
un-couth'
un-cov'-enan-ted
un-cov'er
un-cov'ered
un-crown'ed
un-crush'-able
unc'-tion
unc-tu-os'ity
unc'-tu-ous
unc'u-lar
un-cul'-ti-vated
un-cul'-tured
un-cu'red
un-cut'
un'-date
un-da'ted
382

un-daun'ted
un-dec'a-gon
un-de-cay'ed
un-de-ceiv'e
un-de-cen'-nary
un-de-cen'-nial
un-de-ci'ded
un-dec'i-mal
un-de-cla'red
un-ded'i-cated
un-de-fa'ced
un-de-feat'ed
un-de-fen'-ded
un-de-fi'led
un-de-fi'n-able
un-de-fi'ned
un-demo-crat'ic
un-de-mon'-
    strable
un-de-mon'-stra-
    tive
un-de-ni'able
un-de-nom'i-
    national
under-arm'
under-bid'
under-bit'-ten
un'der-body
under-bred'
un'der-brush
under-char'ge
un'der-clay
un'der-cliff
un'der-clothes
un'der-cloth'ing
un'der-coat
un'der-cover
under-croft'

un'der-cur-rent
un'der-cut
under-devel'-
    oped
un'der-dog
under-don'e
under-es'ti-mate
under-feed'
under-foot'
un'der-glaze
under-gon'e
under-grad'-
    uate
un'der-ground
un'der-growth
un'der-hand
under-han'ded
un'der-hold
un'der-hung
un'der-lay
un'der-lease
under-iet'
under-lie'
under-li'ne (v.)
un'der-line (n.)
under-ly'-ing
under-mi'ne
un'der-most
under-neath'
under-nour'ished
under-paid'
un'der-pass
under-pay'
under-pin'
under-play' (v.)
un'der-play (n.)
under-priv'i-
    leged

un'der-proof
under-prop'
under-ra'te (v.)
un'der-rate (n.)
under-sco're
un'der-shirt
un'der-shoot
un'der-shot
un'der-side
under-si'gn
under-si'gned
un'der-sized
un'der-slung
under-stand'
under-stand'-ing
under-sta'te
un'der-state-ment
under-stood'
un'der-study
under-ta'ke
un'der-taker
un'der-tak-ing
un'der-tone
under-took'
un'der-tow
under-valu-a'tion
under-val'ue
un'der-water
un'der-wear
un'der-weight
under-went'
un'der-world
un'der-write
un'der-writer
un'der-written
un-de-serv'ed
un-de-serv'-ing
un-de-si'gned

un-de-si'r-able
un-de-ter'-mined
un-de-ter'red
un-de-vel'-oped
un-dig'en-ous
un-dig'-nified
un-di'nal
un'-dine
un-dis-cern'-ing
un-dis-charg'ed
un-dis'-ci-plined
un-dis-clo'sed
un-dis-cov'-ered
un-dis-gui'sed
un-dis-may'ed
un-dis-pu'ted
un-dis-so'ci-ated
un-dis-trib'u-ted
un-dis-turb'ed
un-di-ver'-si-
        fied
un-div-i'ded
un-di-vulg'ed
un-do'-ing
un-don'e
un-doubt'ed
un-doubt'-edly
un-dream'ed
un-dreamt'
un-dress' (v.)
un'-dress (n.)
un-drink'-able
un-due'
un'-du-lant
un'-du-late
un'-du-lated
un'-du-la'tion
un'-du-lat-ory

un-du'ly
un-dy'-ing
un-earn'ed
un-earth'
un-earth'ly
un-eas'-ily
un-eas'i-ness
un-eas'y
un-eat'-able
un-ec-on-om'ic
un-ed'u-cated
un-em-bar'-
        rassed
un-em-ploy'-able
un-em-ploy'ed
un-em-ploy'-
        ment
un-end'-ing
un-en-du'r-able
un-en-li'ght-ened
un-en'-vi-able
un-e'qual
un-e'qualled
un-equiv'o-cal
un-err'-ing
un-e'ven
un-e'ven-ness
un-event'-ful
un-ex-am'pled
un-ex-cep'-tion-
        able
un-ex-cep'-tional
un-ex-pec'-ted
un-ex-pi'red
un-ex-plain'ed
un-ex-plo'red
un-ex'-pur-gated
un-fa'd-ing

un-fail'-ing
un-fair'
un-faith'-ful
un-fal'ter-ing
un-fam-il'iar
un-fash'-ion-able
un-fas'ten
in-fath'-om-able
un-fath'-omed
un-fa'vour-able
un-fed'
un-feel'-ing
un-feign'ed
un-feign'-edly
un-fet'-ter
un-fet'-tered
un-fil'-ial
un-fin'-ished
un-fit'
un-fit'-ted
un-fit'-ting
un-fix'
un-flag'-ging
un-fledg'ed
un-flinch'-ing
un-fo'ld
un-fore-see'-
　　　　　able
un-fo're-seen
un-for-get'-table
un-for-giv'-able
un-form'ed
un-for'-ti-fied
un-for'-tu-nate
un-foun'ded
un-frequen'-ted
un-friend'ly
un-frock'
384

un-fruit'-ful
un-fun'ded
un-furl'
un-fur'-nished
un-gain'ly
un-gen'-er-ous
un-gen'tle
un-gen'tle-manly
un-gird'
un-god'ly
un-gov'ern-able
un-gra'cious
un-gram-mat'i-
　　　　cal
un-gra'te-ful
un-ground'ed
un-grudg'ing
un-guard'ed
un'guen-tary
unguen'-tous
un'gui-corn
un'gui-nal
unguic'u-lar
unguic'u-late
un'gui-form
un'gui-nous
un'gu-lar
un'gu-late
ungu'li-grade
un-hal'-lowed
un-ham'-pered
un-hand'
un-hand'y
un-hap'-pily
un-hap'-pi-ness
un-hap'py
un-harm'ed
un-har'-ness

un-health'y
un-heard'
un-heed'ed
un-heed'-ing
un-help'-ful
un-her'-alded
un-hes'i-tat-
　　　　ingly
un-hin'ge
un-hitch'
un-ho'ly
un-hon'oured
un-hook'
un-hors'e
un-hur'-ried
un-hurt'
uni-ax'-ial
uni-biva'lent
uni-cam'-eral
uni-cel'lu-lar
u'ni-corn
un-iden'ti-fied
un-idi-o-mat'ic
u'ni-fi-able
uni-fi-ca'tion
u'ni-fied
uni-fi'lar
uni-fo'li-ate
uni-fo'lio-late
u'ni-form
uni-formi-ta'rian
uni-form'-ity
u'ni-formly
u'ni-fy-ing
uni-gen'i-ture
uni-ju'gate
uni-lat'-eral
uni-loc'u-lar

un-im-ag'in-able
un-im-ag'in-ative
un-im-pair'ed
un-im-peach'-able
un-im-po'rt-ance
un-im-po'rt-ant
un-im-po's-ing
un-im-prov'ed
un-in-cor'-por-
    ated
un-in-flam'-mable
un-in-form'ed
un-in-hab'i-ted
un-in-hib'i-ted
un-in-it'iated
un-in'-jured
un-in-struc'-ted
un-in-tel-lec'-
    tual
un-in-tel'-li-gent
un-in-tel'-li-
    gible
un-in-ten'-tional
un-in'-terested
un-in-ter-rup'-
    ted
uni-nu'clear
un-in-vi'ted
un-in-vi't-ing
u'nion-ism
u'nion-ist
uni-par'-tite
u'ni-ped
uni-per'-sonal
uni-pla'nar
uni-po'lar
uni-sex'-ual
u'ni-son

un-iss'ued
u'nit-age
u'ni-tary
u'ni-tise
u'ni-tive
uni-va'lence
uni-va'lent
u'ni-valve
uni-ver'-sal
uni-ver-sal-is-
    a'tion
uni-ver'-sal-ise
uni-ver-sal'ity
u'ni-verse
uni-ver'-sity
uni-ver-sol'-
    ogist
uni-ver-sol'ogy
univ'o-cal
un-just'
un-jus'ti-fiable
un-kempt'
un-ki'nd
un-ki'nd-li-ness
un-ki'nd-ness
un-know'-able
un-know'-ingly
un-known'
un-la'ce
un-la'de
un-latch'
un-law'-ful
un-learn'ed
un-leash'
un-leav'ened
un-less'
un-let'-tered
un-li'censed

un-li'ke
un-li'ke-li-hood
un-li'kely
un-lim'-ber
un-lim'i-ted
un-liq'ui-dated
un-lis'ted
un-load'
un-lock'
un-loos'e
un-lov'ely
un-luck'y
un-ma'de
un-maid'-enly
un-man'
un-man -age-
    able
un-man'ly
un-man'-nerly
un-mar'-ried
un-mask'
un-mask'ed
un-mean'-ing
un-meas'ur-able
un-mel'-lowed
un-mend'-able
un-men'-tion-
    able
un-mer'-chant-
    able
un-mer'-ci-ful
un-mer'i-ted
un-mi'nd-ful
un-mis-ta'k-able
un-mit'i-gable
un-mit'i-gated
un-mix'ed
un-mor'al

un-mort'-gaged
un-moun'-ted
un-mov'ed
un-nat'u-ral
un-necess-ar'ily
un-necess'-ary
un-neigh'-bourly
un-nerv'e
un-no'ticed
un-num'-bered
un-ob-jec'-tion-
    able
un-ob-serv'-ant
un-ob-serv'ed
un-ob-tain'ed
un-ob-tru's-ive
un-oc'-cu-pied
un-of-fic'ial
un-o'pened
un-or'-gan-ised
un-orig'-inal
un-or'-tho-dox
un-os-ten-
    ta'tious
un-pack'
un-pa'ged
un-paid'
un-pal'-at-able
un-par'-al-leled
un-par'-don-able
un-pa'ved
un-per-ceiv'-able
un-per'-for-ated
un-per-turb'ed
un-pin'
un-pla'ced
un-pleas'ant
un-pleas'ant-ness
386

un-pol'-ished
un-pop'u-lar
un-popu-lar'ity
un-prac'-ti-cal
un-pre-ceden'ted
un-pre-dict'-able
un-prej'u-diced
un-pre-med'i-
    tated
un-pre-pa'red
un-pre'-pos-
    sess-ing
un-pre-ten'-tious
un-prin'cipled
un-print'-able
un-pro'-cessed
un-pro-duc'-tive
un-pro-fes'sional
un-prof'-it-able
un-prom'-is-ing
un-pro-noun'ce-
    able
un-pro-pit'ious
un-pros'-per-ous
un-pro-tec'-ted
un-pro-vo'ked
un-pub'-lished
un-pun'-ished
un-qual'i-fied
un-quench'-able
un-ques'-tion-
    able
un-ques'-tioned
un-qui'et
un-quo'te
un-rav'el
un-read'
un-read'-able

un-read'y
un-re'al
un-re-al'ity
un-reas'on-able
un-rec'-og-nis-
    able
un-re-con-struc'-
    ted
un-re-fi'ned
un-re-flec'-tive
un-re-gen'-er-ate
un-re-lent'-ing
un-re-li'able
un-re-mit'-ted
un-re-mit'-ting
un-re-mu'ner-
    ated
un-re-mu'ner-
    at-ive
un-rep-re-sent'-
    ative
un-re-qui't-able
un-re-qui'ted
un-re-serv'ed
un-rest'
un-re-strain'ed
un-re-stric'-ted
un-rid'dle
un-ri'ght-eous
un-ri'pe
un-ri'valled
un-ro'll
un-ruf'fled
un-ru'ly
un-sad'dle
un-sa'fe
un-said'
un-sa'le-able

un-san'i-tary
un-sat-is-fac'-
     tory
un-sat'-is-fied
un-sat'u-rated
un-sa'voury
un-sca'thed
un-schol'-arly
un-scien-tif'ic
un-scram'ble
un-screw'
un-scru'pu-lous
un-search'-able
un-seas'on-able
un-seat'
un-sea'-worthy
un-secu'red
un-seem'ly
un-seen'
un-self'-ish
un-self'-ish-ness
un-ser'-vice-able
un-set'tle
un-set'tled
un-sha'k-able
un-sha'ken
un-sha'ven
un-sheath'e
un-ship'
un-shod'
un-si'ghtly
un-si'gned
un-skil'ful
un-skill'ed
un-snarl'
un-so'ciable
un-so'lder
un-sol-ic'i-ted

un-sol-ic'i-tous
un-soph-is'-ti-
     cated
un-sought'
un-sound'
un-spa'ring
un-speak'-able
un-spec'ial-ised
un-spec'i-fied
un-spec'u-lat-ive
un-spoil'ed
un-spo'rts-man-
     like
un-sta'ble
un-stain'ed
un-stead'-ily
un-stead'y
un-stop'
un-stress'ed
un-strung'
un-stud'-ied
un-sub-stan'-tial
un-sub-stan'-
     tiated
un-suc-cess'-ful
un-suit'-able
un-suit'ed
un-sul'-lied
un-sup-po'rted
un-sur-pass'ed
un-sus-cep'-tible
un-sus-pec'-ted
un-sus-pic'ious
un-sym-met'ri-
     cal
un-sym-pa-thet'ic
un-tain'ted
un-ta'm-able

un-ta'med
un-tang'le
un-tar'-nished
un-taught'
un-ten'-able
un-think'-able
un-think'-ing
un-ti'dy
un-tie'
un-til'
un-ti'mely
un-ti'r-ing
un-ti'tled
un-to'ld
un-touch'-able
un-touch'ed
un-toward'
un-train'ed
un-tram'-melled
un-trans-la't-
     able
un-trav'-elled
un-tra-vers'-able
un-tri'ed
un-trod'-den
un-troub'led
un-true'
un-tru'ly
un-trust'-worthy
un-truth'
un-truth'-ful
un-tu'tored
un-twi'ne
un-twist'
un-u'sed
un-u'sual
un-u'sual-ness
un-ut'-ter-able

un-var'-nished
un-va'ry-ing
un-veil'
un-ven'-ti-lated
un-ver'i-fied
un-vir'-tu-ously
un-vit'ri-fied
un-voic'ed
un-want'ed
un-wa'rily
un-war'-rant-able
un-war'-ranted
un-wa'ry
un-wash'ed
un-wa've-ring
un-wear'ied
un-wel'-come
un-well'
un-who'le-some
un-wield'y
un-will'-ing
un-will'-ing-ness
un-wi'nd
un-wi'se
un-wit'-ting
un-wit'-tingly
un-wo'nted
un-work'-able
un-world'ly
un-wor'thi-ness
un-wor'thy
un-wo'ven
un-wrap'
un-writ'-ten
un-yield'-ing
un-yo'ke
up-braid'
up'-bring-ing
388

up-cast' (v.)
up'-cast (n.)
up'-date
up-end'
up-gra'de
up-heav'al
up-heav'e
up-held'
up'-hill
up-ho'ld
up-ho'lster
up-ho'lsterer
up-ho'lstery
up'-keep
up'-land
up'-lift (n.)
up-lift' (v.)
up'-per
up'-per-cut
up'-per-most
up'-pish
up'-right
up'-right-ness
up-ri's-ing
up'-roar
up-roar'i-ous
up-roar'i-ously
up'-root
up'-set (n.)
up-set' (v. a.)
up'-shot
up'-side
up'-stage
up'-stairs
up-stand'-ing
up'-start
up'-stream
up'-stroke

up'-surge
up'-take
up'-thrust
up'-turn'
up'-wards
u'ra-chus
u'ra-cil
ura-lis-a'tion
u'ral-ite
ura-lit'ic
u'ra-nate
u'ra-nide
u'ra-nifer-ous
u'ra-nin
uran'i-nite
ura-nis'cus
u'ra-nite
ura-nit'ic
ura-no-graph'ic
ura-nog'ra-phy
ura-no-log'i-cal
ura-nol'ogy
ura-nom'-etry
ura-nos'copy
u'ra-nous
u'ra-nyl
ura-to'ma
ur'-ban
ur-ba'ne
ur'-ban-ise
ur-ban'ity
ur'-bi-cul-ture
ur'-ceo-late
ur'-ceous
ur'-chin
uream'-eter
uream'-etry
ure'di-um

ure'do-spore
ureter-i'tis
ureth-ri'tis
ure'yl-ene
ur'-gency
ur'-gently
urg'-ing
uri-bil'in
uri-col'-ysis
uri-col-yt'ic
uri-dro'sis
uri-nae'mia
u'ri-nal
uri-nal'-ysis
u'ri-nant
u'ri-nary
u'ri-nate
uri-na'tion
u'ri-nator
uri-nif'er-ous
uri-nif'ic
uri-nol'ogy
uri-nom'eter
uri-nom'-etry
uri-nos'copy
u'ri-nose
u'ro-dele
uro-gas'-ter
uro-gas'-tric
uro-gen'-ital
urog'-ra-phy
uro-log'ic
urol'-ogist
urol'-ogy
uro-poie'sis
uro-poiet'ic
uro-pyg'ium

uro-sa'cral
uros'-copy
u'ro-some
u'ro-sthene
uro-sthen'ic
uro-sty'lar
u'ro-style
uro-tro'pine
ur'-si-form
ur'-sine
ur'-son
ur-ti-ca'ceous
ur-ti-cal
ur-ti-ca'ria
ur-ti-ca'rious
ur'-ti-cate
ur-ti-ca'tion
u'se-ful
u'se-tul-ness
u'se-less
u'se-less-ness
ush-er-ett'e
u'si-tate
usi-ta't-ive
us-ti-lagin-
a'ceous
us'-tion
us-to'ri-ous
us'-tu-late
us-tu-la'tion
usu-ca'pi-ent
u'su-capt
usu-cap'-tible
usu-cap'-tion
u'su-fruct
usu-fruc'-tu-ary
usu'ri-ous
usurp-a'tion

usur'pa-tory
uten'-sil
u'ter-ine
uter-i'tis
uter-og'ra-phy
util-is-a'tion
u'til-ise
u'til-iser
utili-ta'rian
utili-ta'rian-ism
util'-ity
ut'-most
utric'u-lar
utric'u-late
utricu-lif'er-ous
utric'u-li-form
ut'-ter
ut'-ter-able
ut'-ter-ance
ut'-terly
ut'-ter-most
uvar'o-vite
uvi-ton'ic
u'vu-lar
uvu-li'tis
ux-o'rial
uxori-ci'dal
uxo'ri-cide
uxo'ri-ous

V

va-ca'te
va-ca't-ing
va-ca'tion
va-ca'tion-ist
va-ca'tur

vac'-ci-nal
vac'-ci-nate
vac-ci-na'tion
vac'-ci-nator
vac-ci'ne
vac-cini-a'ceous
vac-cin'-ial
vac'il-late
vac'il-lat-ing
vacil-la'tion
vac'il-lat-ory
vac'u-ist
va-cu'ity
vac'uo-lar
vac'uo-late
vacuo-la'tion
vac'u-ole
vacu-om'eter
vac'u-ous
vac'u-ously
vac'-uum
vag'a-bond
vag'a-bond-age
vag'a-bon-dise
vag'a-bon-dism
va-ga'ri-ous
va-gi'na
vag'in-ate
vagin-ec'tomy
vagin-ic'o-lous
vagin-i'tis
va'gue-ness
vain'-glo'ri-ous
vain'-glory
vain'-ness
val'-ance
val-edic'-tion
val-edic-to'rian
390

val-edic'-tory
val'-en-tine
val'-en-tin-ite
val-e'rian
val-eria-na'ceous
val-eri-an'ic
val-er'ic
val-etudi-na'rian
val-etu'd-in-ary
val-lec'u-late
val'-iancy
val'-iant
val'i-date
vali-da'tion
val-id'ity
val'-ine
va-li'se
val-la'tion
val-lec'-ula
val-lec'u-lar
val'-ley
val'-leys
val-o'nia
val-or-is-a'tion
val'-or-ous
val'-or-ously
val'-our
val'u-able
val'u-ably
val'u-ate
valu-a'tion
val'u-ator
val'ue-less
val'u-ing
val'-val
val'-vate
val'-vu-lar
val'-vu-late

val-vu-li'tis
val-vu-lot'omy
vam'-pire
vam'-pir-ism
van'-a-date
va-nad'ic
va-nad'in-ite
va-na'dium
van'a-dous
van'-dal
van'-dal-ism
van-dy'ke
van'-guard
van-il'la
van-il'-lic
van-il'-lin
van'-ish
van'-ity
van'-ner
van'-ning
van'-quish
van'-quisher
van'-tage
vap-id'ity
vap'-idly
vapog'-ra-phy
vapor-esc'ence
vapor-esc'ent
vapor-if'ic
va'pori-form
vapor-im'eter
va'por-is-able
vapor-is-a'tion
va'por-ise
va'por-iser
vapor-os'ity
va'por-ous
vapu-la'tion

vap'u-la-tory

var-is'-tor

veg-eta'rian-ism

var'a-noid

var'-let

veg'-etate

varia-bil'ity

var'-nish

veg-eta'tion

va'ri-able

var'-nisher

veg-eta'tional

va'ri-ance

vas'-cu-lar

veg'-etat-ive

va'ri-ant

vas'-cu-lar-ise

veg'-etive

va'ri-ate

vas-cu-lar'ity

ve'-hemence

va'ri-ated

vas'-culi-form

ve'-hement

vari-a'tion

vas'-cu-lose

ve'-hemently

var-icel'la

vas'-cu-lum

ve'-hicle

var-icel'-lar

vas-ec'-tomy

ve-hic'u-lar

var-icel'-lous

vas'i-form

veil'-ing

var'-icated

vaso-con-stric'-tor

vein'-ing

var'-ico-cele

vein'-ous

va'ri-coloured

vaso-dila'tion

vein'-stone

var'-icose

vaso-dila'tor

vein'-ule

var-ico'sis

vaso-for'ma-tive

vel-a'men

var-icos'-ity

vaso-mo'tor

ve'-lar

var-icot'-omy

vass'al-age

vel-a'rium

va'ri-egate

vas'-ti-tude

ve'-late

va'ri-egated

vast'-ness

vela-tu'ra

vari-ega'tion

vat'i-cide

veli-ta'tion

var-i'etal

vat-ic'i-nal

vel-le'ity

var-i'ety

vat-ic'i-nate

vel'-li-cate

va'ri-form

vat-ici-na'tion

vel-li-ca'tion

va-ri'ola

vat-ic'i-nator

vel'-li-cat-ive

va'rio-late

vault'-ing

vel'-lum

vario-la'tion

vaunt'-ing

velo-cim'eter

va'ri-ole

vav'a-sor

vel-oc'i-pede

va'rio-lite

vec'-tion

vel-oc'ity

vario-lit'ic

vec'-tor

ve'-lum

va'rio-loid

vec-to'rial

vel-u'ti-nous

vari-o'lous

vec'-tor-scope

vel'-vet

vari-om'eter

veer'-ingly

vel-vet-cen'

vari-o'rum

veg'-etable

vel'-vety

va'ri-ous

veg'-etal

ve'-nal

va'ri-ously

veg'-etant

ve-nal'-ity

var'-is-cite

veg-eta'rian

ve-nat'ic

ve-na'tion
ven'-dace
ven'-dee
ven-det'ta
ven-det'-tist
vend'-ible
ven-dit'ion
ven'-dor
ven-eer'
ven-eer'er
ve-nef'i-cal
ven'-en-ate
ven'-en-ous
ven'-er-able
ven'-er-ate
ven-er-a'tion
ven'-er-ator
ve-ne'real
ve-nereol'-ogy
ven'-ery
ven'-esect
ven-esec'-tion
ven'-geance
ven'ge-ful
ve'-nial
veni-al'ity
ven'i-punc-ture
ven'-ison
ven'-nel
ven'-om-ous
ve-nos'ity
ve'-nous
ve'-nously
ven'-tage
ven'-ter
ven'-ti-duct
ven'-ti-fact
ven'-til
392

ven'-ti-late
ven-ti-la'tion
ven'-ti-lator
ven'-tose
ven-tos'ity
ven'-tral
ven'-tricle
ven'-tri-cose
ven'-tri-cous
ven-tric'u-lar
ven-tri-lo'quial
ven-tril'-oquise
ven-tril'-oquism
ven-tril'-oquist
ven-tril-oquis'-
    tic
ven-tril'-oquy
ven'-ture
ven'-turer
ven'-ture-some
ven'-tur-ing
ven'-tur-ous
ven'-ule
ver-a'cious
ver-a'ciously
ver-ac'ity
ver-an'-dah
ver-at'-ric
ver'a-trine
ve-rat'-royl
ve-ra'trum
ver'-bal
ver-bal-is-a'tion
ver'-bal-ise
ver'-bal-iser
ver'-bal-ism
ver'-bal-ist
ver-bal'ity

ver'-bally
ver-ba'rian
ver-bas'-cum
ver-ba'tim
ver-be'na
ver-ben-a'ceous
ver'-bi-age
ver'-bi-cide
ver-bi-fi-ca'tion
verb'-ify
ver-big'er-ate
ver-biger-a'tion
ver-bo'se
ver-bos'ity
ver'-dancy
ver'-dant
ver'-derer
ver'-det
ver'-dict
ver'-di-gris
ver'-din
ver'-dite
ver'-diter
ver'-di-ture
ver'-doy
ver'-dure
ver'-dur-ous
ver'-dur-ous-
    ness
ver'-ecund
ver'-ger
verg'-ing
ver-id'i-cal
ver-id'i-cally
ver-id'i-cous
ver'i-fi-able
veri-fi-ca'tion
ver'i-fied

ver'-ify
veri-sim'-ilar
veri-si-mil'i-tude
ve'-rism
ve'-rist
ve-ris'-tic
ver'i-table
ver'-ity
ver'-juice
ver'-meil
ver-meol'-ogy
ver'-mian
ver-mi-cel'li
ver-mi-ci'dal
ver'-mi-cide
ver-mic'u-lar
ver-mic'u-late
ver-micu-la'tion
ver'-mi-cule
ver-mic'u-lite
ver-mic'u-lous
ver'-mi-form
ver-mif'u-gal
ver'-mi-fuge
ver'-mi-grade
ver-mil'ion
ver'-min
ver'-mi-nate
ver-mi-na'tion
ver'-min-ous
ver'-min-ously
ver'-miny
ver-miv'or-ous
ver-mouth'
ver-nac'u-lar
ver-nac'u-lar-
     ism
ver'-nal

ver-nal-is-a'tion
ver'-nal-ise
ver-nal'ity
ver'-nally
ver-na'tion
ver'-nicle
ver'-ni-cose
ver'-nier
ver'-onal
ver-on'-ica
ver-ru'ca
ver-ru'ci-form
ver'-ru-cose
ver'-ru-cous
ver'-sant
ver'-sa-tile
ver'-sa-tilely
ver-sa-til'ity
ver'-set
ver'-sicle
ver'-si-colour
ver-sic'u-lar
ver-si-fi'ca'tion
ver'-si-fied
ver'-si-fier
ver'-si-form
ver'sify
ver'-sine
ver'-sion
ver'-sional
ver'-sion-ist
ver'-sus
ver'-tebra
ver'-tebrae
ver'-tebral
ver'-tebrate
ver-tebra'tion
ver'-tex

ver'-ti-cal
ver'-ti-cally
ver'-ti-ces
ver'-ti-cil
ver-ti-cil-las'-ter
ver-tic'il-late
ver-tic'ity
ver-tig'in-ous
ver'-tigo
ver'-vain
ver'-vet
ves'i-cal
ves'i-cant
ves'i-cate
vesi-ca'tion
ves'i-cat-ory
ves'-icle
ves'-icula
ves-ic'u-lar
ves-icu-la'tion
ves-ic'u-lose
ves'-per
ves'-peral
ves'-per tine
ves'-piary
ves'-pine
ves'-poid
ves'-tal
ves'-ti-ary
ves-tib'u-lar
ves'-ti-bule
ves-ti-bu-li'tis
ves'-tige
ves-tig'ial
ves-tig ially
ves'-ti-ture
vest'-ment
ves'-try

ves'-try-man
ves'-tural
ves'-ture
vet'-eran
vet-er-in-a'rian
vet'-er-in-ary
vet'i-ver
ve'-toed
ve'-toer
ve'-toes
ve'-to-ing
vex-a'tion
vex-a'tious
vex'-edly
vex'-il-lary
vi-abil'ity
vi'-able
vi'-aduct
vi-am'eter
vi'-ands
vi-at'ic
vi-at'i-cum
vi-a'tor
vi'-bex
vi-brac'u-lum
vi'-brancy
vi'-brant
vi'-brate
vi-bra-tile
vi-bra-til'ity
vi'-brat-ing
vi-bra'tion
vi-bra'tional
vi'-bra-tive
vi-bra'tor
vi'-bra-tory
vib'-rio
vib-ri-on'ic
394

vib-ri-o'sis
vi-briss'a
vi'bro-gen
vi'-bro-graph
vi'-bro-scope
vi-brom'eter
vi-bur'-num
vic'-ar-age
vi-ca'rial
vi-ca'ri-ate
vi-ca'ri-ous
vi-ca'ri-ously
vice-ge'rent
vic'-en-ary
vi-cen'nial
vice-re'gal
vi'ce-roy
vi'ce-roy-alty
vic'in-age
vicin'-ity
vic'ious-ness
viciss'i-tude
vicissi-tu'd-in-
                ous
vic'-tim
vic-tim-is-a'tion
vic'-tim-ise
vic'-tor
vic-tor-ine
vic-to'ri-ous
vic'-tory
vict'ual-ler
vid'i-mas
vid'u-age
vid'-ual
view'-point
vi-ges'imal
vig'-il-ance

vig'-il-ant
vig-il-an'-tism
vignet'-ter
vig'-or-ous
vig'-our
vi'-king
vila-yet'
vi'le-ness
vili-fi-ca'tion
vil'i-fier
vil'-ify
vil'i-fy-ing
vil'i-pend
vil'-lage
vil'-lager
vil'-lain
vil'-lain-ous
vil'-lainy
vil-la-nell'e
vil-lat'ic
vil'-lein
vil'-li-form
vil'-lose
vil-los'ity
vil'-lus
vim'i-nal
vim-in'eous
vi-na'ceous
vin-aigrett'e
vi-nass'e
vin-ci-bil'ity
vin'-cible
vinc'u-lum
vin-de'mial
vin-de'mi-ate
vin'-di-cable
vin'-di-cate
vin-di-ca'tion

vin'-di-cat-ive
vin'-di-cator
vin'-di-cat-ory
vin-dic'-tive
vin-dic'-tively
vin'-egar
vin'-egary
vini-cul'-tural
vin'i-cul-ture
vi-nif'era
vini-fi-ca'tion
vin-ol'ogy
vin-om'eter
vi-nos'ity
vi'-nous
vin'-tage
vin'-tager
vint'-ner
vi'-nyl
vi-nyl-a'tion
vi'-nyl-ene
vi-nyl'-idene
vi-o'la
vi'-ol-able
vio-la'ceous
vi'-ol-ate
vi-ol-a'tion
vi'-ol-at-ive
vi'-ol-ator
vi'-ol-ence
vi'-ol-ent
vi-olesc'ent
vi'-olet
vi-olin'
vi-olin'-ist
vi-olon-cel'list
vi-olon-cel'lo
vio-lo'ne

vi-os'-terol
vi'-per
vi'-per-ine
vi'-per-ous
vir-a'go
vi-re'mia
vi-resc'ence
vi-resc'ent
vir'-gate
vir'-gin
vir'-ginal
vir-gin'ity
vir-gin'-ium
vir'-gule
vir'-ial
viri-ci'dal
vi'ri-cide
viri-desc'ence
viri-desc'ent
vir-id'-ian
vir'i-dite
vir-id'ity
vir'-ile
vir-il-esc'ence
vir-il-esc'ent
vir'-il-ism
vir-il'ity
vir-o'le
vi-rol'ogy
vi'-rose
vi-ro'sis
vir'-tual
vir-tu-al'ity
vir'-tue
vir-tu-os'ity
vir-tu-o'so
vir'-tu-ous
vir-u-lence

vir'u-lent
vi'-rus
vis'-age
vis'-aged
vis'-cera
vis'-ceral
vis'-cer-ate
vis'-cid
vis-cid'ity
vis'-cin
vis-com'eter
vis-com'-etry
vis'-co-scope
vis'-cose
vis-cos-im'eter
vis-cos'ity
vi'scount-ess
vis'-cous
vis'-cum
visi-bil'ity
vis'-ible
vis'-ile
visio-gen'ic
vis'ion-ary
vis'i-tant
visi-ta'tion
vis'i-tor
visi-to'rial
vis'-ual
visu-al-isa-'tion
vis'u-al-ise
vis'u-al-iser
visu-al'ity
vis'u-ally
vi-ta'ceous
vi'-tal
vi-tal-is-a'tion
vi'-tal-ise

VITALISM

vi'-tal-ism
vi'-tal'ity
vit'-amin
vit'a-min-ise
vi'-ta-scope
vit-el'-lin
vit'i-cide
vit'i-cul-ture
viti-cul'-tur-ist
vit-if'er-ous
viti-li'go
vit'-rain
vit-reos'-ity
vit'-reous
vit-resc'ence
vit-resc'ent
vit-resc'ible
vit'-reum
vit'-ric
vit'-rics
vit-ri-fac'-tion
vit-ri-fac'-ture
vit'-ri-fiable
vit-ri-fi-ca'tion
vit'-ri-form
vit'-rify
vit'-rine
vit'-riol
vit'-ri-ol-ated
vit-ri-ol'ic
vit-ri-ol-ise
vit-ri-os'ity
vit'u-lar
vit'u-line
vit-u'per-ate
vit-uper-a'tion
vit-u'per-at-ive
viv-a'cious

viv-a'ciously
viv-ac'ity
vi-va'rium
viv'ia-nite
viv-id'ity
viv'-idly
viv'-id-ness
vivi-fi-ca'tion
viv'i-fied
viv'-ify
vivi-par'ity
vi-vip'ar-ous
vi-vip'ar-ously
viv'i-sect
vivi-sec'-tion
vivi-sec'-tion-ist
vivi-sec'-tive
vivi-sec'-tor
vivi-sep'-ul-ture
vix'-en-ish
viz'-ard
vo'-cable
vo-cab'u-lary
vo'-cal
vo-cal-is-a'tion
vo'-cal-ise
vo'-cal-iser
vo'-cal-ism
vo-ca'tion
vo-ca'tional
voc'a-tive
voc'a-tively
vo-cif'er-ant
vo-cif'er-ate
vo-cifer-a'tion
vo-cif'er-ous
vo-cif'er-ously
vo-cord'er

voc'u-lar
voc'-ule
voic'e-less
voic'-ing
void'-able
void'-ance
vo'-lant
vo'-lar
vol'-atile
vol-atil-is-a'tion
vol'a-til-ise
vola-til'ity
vol-can'ic
vol'-can-ise
vol-ca'no
vol-ca'noes
vol-ca-nol'ogy
vol'-ery
vol'i-tant
voi'i-tate
voli-ta'tion
vol-it'ion
vol'i-tive
voli-to'rial
vol'-ley
vol'-ley-ball
vol'-plane
vol'-plan-ist
vo'lt-age
vol-ta'ic
vol-tam'eter
vol-ta-met'ric
vol'-tin-ism
vo'lt-meter
volu-bil'ity
vol'-uble
vol'u-crine
vol'-ume

396

volu-men-om'eter
volu-u'meter
volu-met'ric
vol-u'mi-nal
vol-umin-os'ity
vol-u'min-ous
volu-mom'eter
vol'-un-tarily
vol'-un-tar-ism
vol'-un-tary
vol'-un-tary-ism
vol'-un-tary-ist
vol-un-teer'
vol-un-teer'ed
vol-up'tu-ary
vol-up'tu-ous
vol-up'tu-ously
vol-up'tu-ous-
       ness
vol-u'te
vol'u-tin
vol-u'tion
vol'u-toid
vol'-vu-lus
vo'-mer
vo'-mer-ine
vom'-ica
vom'i-ter
vom'i-tive
vom'-ito
vom'i-tory
vomi-tur-it'ion
vom'i-tus
voo'-doo
voo'-doo-ism
vo-ra'cious
vo-rac'ity
vo-ra'go

vo'-rant
vor'-tex
vor'-ti-cal
vor'-ti-cally
vor-ti-cel'la
vor'-ti-ces
vor'-ti-cism
vor'-ti-cist
vor'-ti-cose
vor-tic'ity
vor-tic'u-lar
vor-tig'in-ous
vo'-tar-ess
vo'-tar-ist
vo'-tary
vo'-tive
vouch-sa'fe
vowel'-lise
voy'-age
voy'-ager
vul-can-is-a'tion
vul'-can-ise
vul'-can-iser
vul'-can-ism
vul'-can-ist
vul'-can-ite
vul-can-ol'ogy
vul'-gar
vul-ga'rian
vul-gar-is-
      a'tion
vul'-gar-ise
vul'-gar-ism
vul-gar'ity
vul'-garly
vul-ner-abil'ity
vul'-ner-able
vul'-ner-ary

vul'-pi-cide
vul'-pine
vul-pin'ic
vul'-pi-nite
vul-sel'la
vul'-sin-ite
vul'-ture
vul'-tur-ine
vul'-tur-ous
vul'-var
vul'-vate
vul'-vi-form
vul-vi'tis
vy'-ing

W

wad'-dler
wad'-dling
wad'-set
wad'-set'ter
waft'-age
wag'-gery
wag'-ging
wag'-gish
wag'-gling
wag'-gon
wag'-gon-age
wag'-goner
wag'-gon-load
wagon-ett'e
wag'-tail
wail'-ing
wain'-age
wain'-scot
wain'-scot-ing
wain'-wright

397

waist'-band
waist'-coat
waist'-line
wait'-ing-room
wait'-ress
wa'ke-ful
wa'ke-ful-ness
wa'ken-ing
walk'-able
walk'-away
walk'-ing
walk'-ing-stick
wall'-aby
wall'-aroo
wall'-board
wall'-flower
wall'-ing
wall'-oper
wall'-op-ing
wall'-ow-ing
wall'-paper
wall'-wort
wam'-merah
wam-pee'
wam'-pum
wan'-derer
wan'-der-ing
wan'-der-lust
wan'-deroo
wan'-ness
want'-age
want'-ing
wan'-ton
wan'-tonly
wan'-ton-ness
wap'-en-take
war'-bler
war'-bling

war'-den
war'-den-ship
war'-der-ship
war'-dian
ward'-mote
ward'-robe
ward'-room
ward'-ship
wa're-house
wa're-house-man
wa're-room
war'-fare
war'-faring
war'-head
wa'ri-ness
war'-like
war'-lock
war'-monger
warn'-ing
warp'-age
warp'-ing
war'-ragal
war'-ran-dice
war'-rant
war'-rant-able
war-rantee'
war'-ranter
war'-ran-tor
war'-ranty
war'-ren
war'-ring
war'-rior
war'-ship
war'-time
wash'-able
wash'-basin
wash'-board

wash'-bowl
wash'-cloth
wash'er-woman
wash'-ing
wash'-leather
wash'-room
wash'-stand
wash'-tub
wasp'-ish
wass'-ail
wass'-ailer
wa'st-age
wa'st-rel
watch'-case
watch'-dog
wa'ste-ful
wa'ste-land
wa'ste-paper
wa'st-ing
watch'-ful
watch'-ful-ness
watch'-maker
watch'-man
watch'-word
wat'er-age
wat'er-borne
wat'er-course
wat'er-cress
wat'er-fall
wat'er-fowl
wat'er-front
wat'er-glass
wat'eri-ness
wat'er-line
wat'er-log
wat'er-logged
wat'er-man
wat'er-mark

wat'er-power
wat'er-proof
wat'er-shed
wat'er-side
wat'er-spout
wat'er-tight
wat'er-way
wat'er-wheel
wat'er-works
watt'-age
watt'-ling
watt'-meter
wa've-length
wa've-let
wa've-meter
wa'ver-ing
wa'ver-ingly
wax'-bill
wax'-cloth
wax'i-ness
wax'-ing
wax'-works
way'-bill
way'-farer
way'-far-ing
way'-laid
way'-lay
way'-leave
way'-side
way'-ward
way'-worn
wayz'-goose
weak'-ened
weak'-ish
weak'-ling
weak'-ness
weapon-eer'
wear'-able

wear'i-ful
wear'i-less
wear'i-ness
wear'-ing
wear'i-some
wear'i-somely
weas'-and
weath'-er-beaten
weath'-er-board
weath'-er-cock
weath'-er-ed
weath'-er-ing
weath'-er-man
weath-er-om'eter
weath'-er-proof
weath'-er-vane
weath'-er-wise
weav'-er-bird
weav'-ing
web'-bing
wed'-ded
wed'-ding
wedg'-ing
wedg'e-wise
weed'-lock
week'-day
week'-end
weep'-ing
weev'-iled
weft'-age
weigh'-able
weight'i-ness
weird'-ness
wel'-come
wel'-com-ing
weld'-able
wel'-fare
wel'-kin

wells'-ite
well'-spring
wel'-ter
wel'-ter-weight
wend'-ing
we're-wolf
west'-er-ing
west'-erly
west'-ern
west'-erner
west'-ern-most
west'-ing
west'-most
west'-ward
wet'-ness
wet'-ting
whack'-ing
wha'le-back
wha'le-boat
wha'le-bone
wharf'-age
wharf'-ing
wharf'-in-ger
what-ev'er
what'-not
what-so-ev'er
wheat'-ear
wheed'-ler
wheed'le-some
wheed'-ling
wheel'-bar-row
wheel'-base
wheel'-horse
wheel'-house
wheel'-ing
wheel'-wright
wheez'-ily
wheez'i-ness

399

wheez'-ingly	whip'-poor-will	who'le-saler
when-ev'er	whip'-saw	who'le-some
when-so-ev'er	whip'-stall	whom-so-ev'er
wher'e-abouts	whip'-ster	whoop'-ing
wher'e-fore	whip'-stitch	whop'-per
where-so-ev'er	whirl'i-gig	whop'-ping
where-upon'	whirl'-ing	whor'tle-berry
wher-ev'er	whirl'-pool	who-so-ev'er
where-with'	whirl'-wind	wick'-edly
wher'e-withal	whir'-ring	wick'-ed-ness
wher'ry-man	whis'-ker	wick'-ered
whet'-stone	whis'-kered	wick'-er-work
whet'-ted	whis'-key	wi'den-ing
whet'-ting	whis'-kies	wi'de-spread
which-ev'er	whis'-per	wid'-ower
which-so-ev'er	whis'-pered	wid'-ow-hood
whif'-fle-tree	whis'-per-ing	wield'-able
whif'-fling	whis'-tler	wiel'di-ness
whim'-brel	whis'-tling	wi'fe-hood
whim'-per	whi'te-bait	wi'fe-less
whim'-pered	whi'te-beam	wig'-gery
whim'-perer	whi'te-fish	wig'-ging
whim'-per-ing	whi'te-ness	wig'-gler
whim'-si-cal	whi'ten-ing	wig'-gling
whim-si-cal'ity	whi'te-thorn	wig'-wag
whim'-si-ness	whi'te-throat	wig'-wam
whin'-chat	whi'te-wall	wi'ld-cat
whin'-nied	whi'te-wash	wil'de-beest
whin'-stone	whi'te-wood	wil'-der-ness
whip'-cord	whit'-leather	wi'ld-fire
whip'-jack	whit'-ling	wi'ld-fowl
whip'-lash	whit'-low	wi'ld-ness
whip'-per	whit'-tling	wi'ld-wood
whip'-per-snap-	whiz'-zer	wil'-ful
per	whiz'-zing	wil'-fully
whip'-pet	who-ev'er	wil'-ful-ness
whip'-ping	who'le-hearted	wi'li-ness
whip'ple-tree	who'le-sale	wil'-lem-ite

wil'-let

wil'-ley

will'-ing-ness

wil'-lock

wil'-low

wil'-low-herb

wil'-lowy

win'-cey

win-cey-ett'e

winc'-ing

wind'-age

wind'-bag

wind'-blown

wind'-bound

wind'-break

wind'-breaker

wind'-fall

wind'-flower

wind'i-ness

wi'nd-ing

wi'nd-ing-sheet

wind'-jam-mer

wind'-lass

wind'-less

win'dle-straw

wind'-mill

win'-dow

win'-dow-pane

win'-dow-sill

wind'-pipe

wind'-row

wind'-shield

wind'-storm

wind'-ward

wi'ne-glass

wi'ne-grower

wi'ne-press

wi'ne-skin

wing'-edly

wing'-less

wing'-spread

wink'-ing

win'-ner

win'-ning

win'-now

win'-nower

win-now-ing-fan

win'-some

win'-some-ness

win'-ter

win'-ter-green

win'-ter-time

win'-tri-ness

win'-try

wi're-drawn

wi're-less

wi're-photo

wi're-way

wi're-weed

wi're-work

wi're-worker

wi're-worm

wi'ri-ness

wi'r-ing

wis'-dom

wi'se-acre

wi'se-crack

wis'-erine

wish'-bone

wish'-ful

wis-ta'ria

wist'-ful

wist'-fully

witch'-craft

witch'-ery

witch'-ing

with-draw'

with-draw'al

with-drawn'

with-drew'

with'-ered

with'-er-ing

with'-er-ite

with-er-lock

with'-ers

with-held'

with-ho'ld

with-ho'ld-ing

with-out'

with-stand'

with-stand'-ing

wit'-less

wit'-ness

wit'-ti-cism

wit'-tily

wit'-ti-ness

wit'-tingly

wiz'-ard

wiz'-ardry

wiz'-ened

wob'-bli-ness

wob'-bling

wob'-bu-lator

woe'-be-gone

woe'-ful

woe'-ful-ness

wolf'-hound

wolf'-ish

wolf'-ishly

wolf'-ram

wolf'-ram-ite

wol'laston-ite

wolver-i'ne

wom'an-hood

wom'an-ish
wom'an-kind
wom'an-like
wom'an-li-ness
wom'-bat
wom'en-folk
won'-der
won'-dered
won'-der-ful
won'-der-land
won'-der-ment
won'-drous
won'-drously
wood'-bine
wood'-chuck
wood'-cock
wood'-craft
wood'-cut
wood'-cut-ter
wood'-enly
wood'-en-ware
wood'i-ness
wood'-land
wood'-man
wood'-pecker
wood'-pile
wood'-ruff
wood'-shed
woods'-man
wood'-work
wool'-gath-er-ing
wool'-len
wool'-li-ness
wool'-pack
wool'-sack
word'-age
word'-ily
word'i-ness

word'-ing
word'-less
word'-ster
work-abil'ity
work'-able
work'-a-day
work'-bas-ket
work'-bench
work'-book
work'-box
work'-day
work'-horse
work'-house
work'-ing
work'-ing-man
work'-man
work'-man-like
work'-man-ship
work'-men
work'-out
work'-room
work'-shop
work'-shy
work'-table
work'-week
world'-li-ness
world'-ling
world'-wide
worm'-cast
worm'-hole
worm'-wood
wor'ri-ment
wor'ri-some
wor'ry-ing
wor'sen-ing
wor'-ship-ful
wor'ship-ping
worth'-ily

wor'thi-ness
worth'-less
worth'-while
wrack'-wort
wrap'-page
wrap'-per
wrap'-ping
wrath'-ful
wreath'-ing
wreck'-age
wreck'-fish
wres'-tler
wres'-tling
wretch'-edly
wretch'-ed-ness
wrig'-gler
wrig'-gling
wring'-ing
wrink'-ling
wrist'-band
wrist'-let
wrist'-lock
wrist'-watch
writ'-ten
wrong'-doer
wrong'-do-ing
wrong'-ful
wry'-bill
wry'-neck
wry'-ness
wu'lfen-ite
wurtz'-ite
wy'-vern

X

xalo-stock'-ite
xan'-thate
xan-tha'tion
xan'-thein
xan-thel-as'ma
xan'-thene
xan'-thic
xan'-thine
xan'-thium
xan-tho-car'-
pous
xan-thoch'roi
xan-tho-chro'ic
xan'-tho-chroid
xan-thoch'ro-ism
xan-tho-chro'mia
xan-tho'ma
xan-thom'a-tous
xan-tho-mel'-an-
ous
xan'-tho-phore
xan'-tho-phyll
xan-thop'-sia
xan-thop'-sin
xan-thop'-terin
xan-thor-rhe'a
xan-tho-sid'er-
ite
xan-tho'sis
xan'-thous
xe'-bec
xen-ar'-thral
xe'-nia
xe'-nial
xe'no-cryst

xen-og'amy
xeno-gen'-esis
xeno-gen-et'ic
xen-og'en-ous
xeno-gloss'ia
xen'o-iith
xeno-lith'ic
xeno-ma'nia
xen'o-phobe
xeno-pho'bia
xeno-pho'bic
xen-oph'-oby
xen-oph'ya
xeno-pias'-tic
xen'o-time
xe-ran'-sis
xe-ran'-tic
xe-ra'sia
xe'-ric
xero-der'ma
xero-der-mat'ic
xero-der'-ma-tous
xero-der'-mia
xero-graph'ic
xe-rog'ra-phy
xe'ro-phil
xe-roph'i-lous
xe-roph'-ily
xe-roph-rhal'-mia
xe'ro-phyte
xero-phyt'ic
xe'ro-sere
xe-ro'sis
xero-sto'mia
xe-rot'ic
xiphi-ster'-num
xiph'-oid

xiph-op'-agus
xipho-phyl'-lus
xipho-su'ran
xo'a-non
xy'-lem
xy'-lene
xy'-lenol
xy'-lic
xyl'i-dine
xylo-bai'sa-mum
xy'lo-carp
xylo-car'-pous
xy'lo-chrome
xy'lo-gen
xy-log'en-ous
xy'lo-graph
xy-log'ra-pher
xy-lo-graph'ic
xy-log'ra-phy
xy'-loid
xy-loid'in
xy-loi'ogy
xy-lo'ma
xy-lom'eter
xy-lon'ic
xy'-lo-nite
xy-loph'a-gan
xy'lo-phage
xy-loph'a-gous
xy'lo-phil
xy-loph'i-lous
xy'lo-phon'ic
xylo-phon'ic
xy'lo-phon-ist
xy-lo-pyrog'ra-
phy
xy'-lose
xy'-lo-side

xy-lot′o-mous
xy-lot′omy
xylo-typo-
graph′ic
xylo-typ-og′ra-
phy
xy′-lo-yl
xy′-lu-lose
xy′-lyl
xy′-lyl-ene
xys′-ter
xyx′-tus

Y

yacht′-ing
yachts′-man
yap′-per
yap′-ping
yard′-age
yard′-arm
yard′-mas-ter
yard′-stick
yar′-row
yash′-mak
yat′a-ghan
yau′-pon
yaw′-ing
yaw -meter
yawn′-ing
yawn′-ingly
yean′-ing
year′-ling
year′-long
yearn′-ing
yeast′i-ness
yel′-low
404

yel′-low-bird
yel′-low-fin
yel′-low=ham-mer
yel′-low-ish
yel′-low-jacket
yeo′-man
yeo′-manry
yer′-cum
yes′-ter-day
yield′-able
yield′-ing
yo′-del
yo′-deler
yo′-del-ing
yo-him′-bine
yo′ke-fel-low
yo′-kel
yon′-der
young′-berry
young′-ish
young′-ling
young′-ster
your-self′
your-sel′ves
youth′-ful
youth′-fully
y′per-ite
yp-sil′i-form
yp′-si-loid
yt-ter′-bium
yt-ter′-bous
yt′-tria
yt′-tric
yt-trif′er-ous
yt′-trium
yt-tro-ce′rite
yt-tro-tan′-ta-
                lite

yt-tur′-pic

Z

za-lamb′-do-
           dont
zam′-in-dar
zan-el′la
za′ni-ness
za-oth′ra
zar′a-tite
zar-e′ba
zar′-nec
zar′-nich
zas-tru′ga
zealot′-ical
zeal′ot-ism
ze′-bra
ze′-brass
ze′-brine
ze′-broid
ze′-brule
zed′o-ary
zel-o′so
zelo-typ′ia
zem′-in-dar
zem′-in-dary
zen-an′a
zen′-ith
zen′i-thal
zc′o-lite
zeo-lit′ic
zeo-lit′i-form
zeph-yre′an
zep′-pelin
ze′-roes
ze′-ros

ze-rum'-bet
zest'-ful
zest'-fully
ze-tet'ic
zeug'-lo-dont
zeug-mat'ic
zeux'-ite
zib'-el-ine
zib'-er-line
zig'-gu-rat
zig'-zag
zig'-zag-ging
zinc'-ate
zinci-fi-ca'tion
zinc'-ify
zinc'-ite
zinc'-ode
zinc'o-graph
zin-cog'ra-pher
zin-cog'ra-phy
zinc'-oid
zin-col'y-sis
zinc'o-lyte
zinc'o-site
zinc'o-type
zinc'-ous
zin'-ken-ite
zin'-nia
zip'-per
zirc'-ite
zir'-con
zir'-con-ate
zir-co'nia
zir-con'ic
zir-co'nium
zir'-co-nyl
zith'-er-ist

zo-an-throp'ic
zo-an'-thropy
zo'-diac
zo-di'acal
zo'e-trope
zo-idi-oph'i-lous
zo-il'ean
zo'-il-ism
zo'-il-ist
zo'-is-ite
zo'-ism
zo'-ist
zom'-bie
zo'-nal
zo-nary
zo'-nate
zo-na'tion
zo-nif'er-ous
zo-nu're
zo-ochem'-istry
zo-odyn-am'ics
zo-og'a-mous
zo-og'amy
zo-ogen'ic
zo-og'eny
zo'-ograph
zo-ogeo-graph'ic
zo-ogeog'-ra-phy
zo-ogle'a
zo-og'ra-pher
zo-og'ra-phy
zo'-oid
zo-ol'ater
zo-ol'a-try
zo-'olite
zo-olog'i-cal
zo-ol'ogist
zo-ol'ogy

zo-om'eter
zo-omor'-phic
zo-on'ic
zo-on-if'ic
zo'-on-ite
zo'-onol
zo-ono'sis
zo-on'tomy
zo-opath-ol'ogy
zo-ophil'ia
zo-oph'il-ist
zo-oph'ily
zo-ophys'-ics
zo-oph'orus
zo'-ophyte
zo-oplas'-tic
zo-os'copy
zo-osperm
zo-osper-mat'ic
zo-ospor-
⠀⠀⠀⠀⠀⠀an'gium
zo-ospore
zo-os'terol
zo-otaxy
zo-otechny
zo-othap'-sis
zo-ot'omy
zo-otroph'ic
zor'-gite
zor'-ille
zos'-ter
zum'-boo-ruk
zu'n-yte
zur'-lite
zur'-ron
zyg'a-dite
zygo-branch'i-
⠀⠀⠀⠀⠀⠀ate

405

ZYGODACTYL

zygo-dac′-tyl
zygo-dac′-tyl-ous
zy′go-dont
zygo-don′-tous
zy′go-ite
zy-go′ma
zygo-mat′ic
zygo-mor′-phic
zy′-gon

zy′go-phyte
zy′-gose
zy-go′sis
zy′-gote
zy-got′ic
zy′-mase
zy′-mic
zy-mo-gen′ic
zy-mog′en-ous

zy-mol′-ogy
zy-mom′eter
zymo-plas′-tic
zy-mo′sis
zy-mos′-terol
zy-mos-then′ic
zy-mot′ic
zy′-murgy

SPELLING GUIDE

The following is a list of words which have not been included in the earlier part of the book because they should not normally be divided, or because they may present difficulties of spelling. It includes most foreign words which have retained their original form or pronunciation. These are shown in italics without stress marks.

abaca'
aback'
abaft'
aba'se
  aba'sed
abash'
  abash'ed
aba'sia
ab urbe condita
à bon marché
a capella
à deux
a fortiori
à la mode
a latere
a natura rei
à point
a posteriori
a priori
a tempo
ab initio
aba'te

aba'ted
aba'tor
abe'le
abet'
abi'de
  abi'ded
abla'ze
a'ble
  a'bly
aboard'
abo'de
abort'
  abort'ed
  abor'tion
abound'
  abound'ed
about'
abov'e
abra'de
  abra'ded
  abra'sion
abreast'
abridg'e

abridg'ed
abroad'
absente reo
absit
abu'se
  abu'sed
  abu'ser
abut'
abysm'
abyss'
  abyss'al
aca'cia
acan'thus
acaud'al
accelerando
ace
ace'dia
acer'ic
acesc'ence
  acesc'ent
acet'ic
  acet'ify
ac'etone

aceton'ic
ace'tous
ace'tum
ac'etyl
ache
  ached
ache'ne
  ache'nial
achiev'e
  achiev'ed
ac'id
  acid'ic
  acid'ify
  acid'ity
ack emma
aclin'ic
ac'me
ac'ne
a'corn
a'cre
  a'cred
ac'rid
  acrid'ity
acro'lein
acroph'ony
across'
acryl'ic
act
  act'ed
ac'tual
acu'ity
acu'te
  acu'tely
acy'clic
ad astra
ad hoc
ad infinitum
ad interim
408

ad libitum
  (*ad lib*)
ad modum
ad nauseam
ad rem
ad valorem
ad verbum
ad vivum
ad'age
adagio
adapt'
  adapt'ed
  adapt'er
  adapt'or
add
  add'ed
ad'der
ad'dle
  ad'dled
ad'ept (n.)
adept' (a.)
  adept'ly
adieu
adieux
adiós
adip'ic
ad'it
ad'miral
ado'
ado'be
adopt'
  adopt'ed
  adopt'er
ado're
  ado'red
  ado'rer
adorn'
  adorn'ed

adre'nal
adrift'
adroit'
  adroit'ly
adsum
ad'ult
adult'erer
  adul'tery
advocatus diaboli
adze
aeg'is
ae'on
aer'ial
aer'ie
aer'ify
aero'bic
aerol'ic
aes alienum
afar'
affaire de coeur
affeer'
  affeer'ed
affettuoso
affo'rd
  affo'rded
aficionado
afield'
afi're
afla'me
afloat'
afoot'
afraid'
afresh'
aft
af'ter
again'
again'st
agam'ic

aga'pe

ag'ate

age

  aged

  a'ging

agen'da

a'gene

a'gent

  a'gency

  agen'tial

agent provocateur

aghast'

ag'ile

  ag'ilely

  agil'ity

agitato

aglow'

agnus dei

agog'

agon'ic

ag'ony

ag'ora

agraph'ia

agra rian

agree'

  agreed'

agron'omy

aground'

a'gue

ahead'

ahem'

ahoy'

aid

  aid'ed

aide de camp

aide mémoire

aig'rette

aiguill'e

ail'eron

aim

  aimed

air

  aired

  air'er

  air'ily

  air'y

aisle

ajar'

akim'bo

akin'

alac'rity

ala'lia

a'lar

  a'lary

  a'late

alarm'

  alarm'ed

alar'um

al'chemy

al'der

alert'

  alert'ly

alex'ia

alex'in

al'ga

  al'gal

al'gin

a'lias

al'ibi

a'lien

ali'ght

  ali'ghted

ali'gn

  ali'gned

ali'ke

ali've

al'kali

alla breve

allegretto

allegro

allemande

allonge

ally (v.)

al'ly (n.)

alma mater

almi'ghty

al'mond

al'most

alms

al'nage

  al'nager

al'oe

aloft'

alog'ical

alo'ne

along'

aloof'

aloud'

alp

alph'a

alread'y

al'so

al'tar

al'ter

  al'tered

alter ego

although'

altissimo

al'to

altogeth'er

alto relievo

al'um

alu'mina

alumni

409

alumnus
al'ways
am'ah
amain'
amass'
  amass'ed
ama'ze
  ama'zed
am'ble
  am'bled
amen'
amend'
  amend'ed
  amends'
amende
amende honorable
ament'
amen'tia
amerc'e
a'miable
  amiabil'ity
am'ice
amicus curiae
amid'
  amid'st
amid'ic
amigo
amiss'
amoeb'a
amok'
among'
  among'st
amor'al
  amor'ally
amoretto
amoroso
amount'
amour

amour propre
am'phora
  am'phorae
am'ple
am'plify
am'uck
amu'se
  amu'sed
am'yl
am'ylum
anaem'ia
  anaem'ic
anal'ogy
a'nal
an'chor
  an'chored
  an'choret
a'ncient
  a'nciently
andante
andantino
anem'one
anent'
aneur'in
anew'
ang ary
a'ngel
an'gelus
an'ger
  an'gered
  an'grily
a'ngry
an'gle
  an'gled
  an'gler
  an'gling
ango'ra
Angst

an'guish
  an'guished
an'il
ani'on
  anion'ic
ank'er
ank'le
an'na
Anno Domini
an'nual
annus mirabilis
an'ode
ano'dal
anod'ic
anoint'
  anoint'ed
  anoint'er
anom'aly
anon'
anoth'er
an'swer
  an'swered
an'ta
ante
ante meridiem
      (AM)
an'tiar
anu'rous
a'nus
anxi'ety
anx'ious
  anx'iously
aor'ta
  aor'tal
  aor'tic
apa'ce
apache
apart'

ape
  aped
  a'per
  a'pery
  a'pian
  a'ping
  a'pish
  a'pishly
apep'sy
aperçu
a'pex
  a'pexes
apha'sia
  apha'sic
aphe'lion
  aphe'lian
aphet'ic
aph'id
  aph'is
apho'nia
  aphon'ic
apho'tic
aphra'sia
apie'ce
aplomb'
aplus'tre
apoc'ope
ap'ophthegm
apoph'yge
apos'tle
ap'ple
appoggiatto
appoggiatura
apport
a'pron
apse
apt
  apt'ly

aqua'rium
aquat'ic
arc
arch
  arched
  arch'er
  arch'es
archa'ngel
a'rea
  a'real
are'na
are'ola
arête
ar'ia
ar'id
  arid'ity
arietta
ariette
ar'il
arioso
ari'se
  aris'en
aro'se
arm
  armed
ar'my
  ar'mies
aro'ma
around'
arous'e
  arous'al
  arous'ed
arpeggio
arrière pensée
arriviste
arrondissement
art
  ar'ty

ar'ticle
  ar'ticled
ascor'bic
ase'ity
asex'ual
ash
  ash'en
  ash'es
  ash'y
asha'me
  asha'med
asho're
asi'de
ask
  asked
  ask'er
askanc'e
askew'
aslant'
asleep'
asp
ass
  ass'es
assai
as'suetude
astat'ic
astern'
as'thma
astrad'dle
astir'
astray'
astri'de
asty'lar
asun'der
asy'lum
atax'ia
  atax'ic
  atax'y

411

atelier
athwart'
at'oll
at'om
  atom'ic
ato'ne
  ato'nal
  aton'ic
atro'cious
  atro'ciously
atroph'ic
aubade
au contraire
au courant
au fait
au fond
au gratin
au naturel
au pair
au revoir
au secours
auberge
aub'urn
aud'it
auf wiedersehen
aug'er
aught
aug'ite
aug'ur
  augur'ed
  aug'ury
august'
auk
aul'ic
aunt
aur'a
  aur'al
aure'ity

aur'ic
auric'ula
auth'or
autobahn
autoc'racy
auto da fé
autog'eny
autop'sy
autostrada
aut'umn
avail'
  avail'ed
avant garde
avast'
aveng'e
  aveng'ed
  aveng'er
aver'
  averr'ed
avers'e
avert'
  avert'ed
a'vian
av'id
  av'idly
avoid'
  avoid'ed
  avoid'er
avouch'
  avouch'ed
  avouch'er
  avouch'es
avow'
  avow'al
  avow'ed
  avow'ry
avuls'e
await'

await'ed
awa'ke
  awa'ken
awo'ke
award'
  award'ed
  award'er
awa're
awash'
away'
awe
  awed
aw'ful
  aw'fully
aweigh'
awhi'le
awl
awry'
axe
ax'il
ax'iom
ax'is
  ax'ial
ax'le
  ax'led
ax'on
ay'ah
aza'lea
azo'ic
azon'ic
azo'te
  azot'ic
a'zure
bab'ble
  bab'bled
babe
ba'bel
ba'by

ba'bies
back
  backed
  back'er
ba'con
badge
badg'er
bad'ly
baf'fle
  baf'fled
bag
  bagged
  bag'gy
bail
  bailed
  bailee'
  bail'er
  bail'or
bail'ey
bait
  bait'ed
  bait'er
baize
bake
  baked
  ba'ker
bald
  bald'ly
bale
  baled
  ba'ler
  ba'ling
baleen'
balk
  balked
  balk'er
ball
  balled
balm

balm'y
bal'sa
  bal'sam
ban
  banned
ba'nal
band
  band'ed
bandeau
ban'dy
  band'ied
  band'ies
bane
bang
  banged
  bang'er
ban'gle
  ban'gled
ban'jo
bank
  banked
  bank'er
banns
bar
  barred
barb
  barbed
bard
bare
  bared
  ba'rely
barge
  barged
ba'rium
  ba'ric
bark
  barked
  bark'er
barm

barm'y
barn
bar'ney
bar'on
barouch'e
bar'que
bar'yon
base
  ba'sal
  based
  ba'sic
  ba'sing
  ba'sis
  ba'sely
bash
  bashed
  bash'er
  bash'es
bas'il
ba'sin
bask
  basked
bass
  ba'ss
basso profundo
basso-relievo
bast
baste
  ba'sted
  ba'sting
batch
  batched
  batch'es
bate
  ba'ted
  ba'ting
bath
bathe
  ba'thed

413

ba'ther
ba'thing
ba'thos
bat'on
bat'tle
bat'tled
baub'le
bawd
bawd'ry
bawd'y
bawl
bawled
bawl'er
bay
bayed
ba'you
beach
beached
beach'es
bead
bead'ed
bead'y
bead'le
beag'le
beak
beaked
beak'er
beam
beamed
beam'er
bean
bear
bea'rer
bo're
bo'rne
beard
beard'ed
béarnaise

beast
beast'ly
beat
beat'en
beat'er
beau
beaux
beau geste
beau idéal
beau monde
beaut'y
beaut'ify
beav'er
beck
beck'on
beck'oned
beck'oner
beck'et
beech
beech'en
beech'es
beef
beef'y
beev'es
beer
beer'y
beet
beet'le
beg
begged
beige
bel
bel canto
belch
belched
belch'er
bell
belled

belle
belles lettres
bel'ly
bell'ied
bell'ies
belt
belt'ed
bench
benched
bench'er
bench'es
bend
bend'ed
bend'er
bent
benedicite
benet'
ben'zoin
berceuse
ber'et
ber'ry
berth
berthed
ber'yl
bes'om
best
best'ed
bes'tial
bet
be'ta
bête noire
bev'el
bev'y
bey
bez'el
bi'as
bi'ased
bi'assed

bibelot
bi'ble
bice
bick'er
  bick'ered
bi'cycle
bid
bide
  bi'ded
  bi'ding
bidet
bier
big'amy
bight
big'ot
  big'oted
  big'otry
bijou
bijouterie
bikin'i
bile
  bil'ious
  bil'iously
bilge
bilk
  bilked
  bilk'er
bill
  billed
  bill'er
billet
billet-doux
bil'liards
bil'lion
  bil'lionth
bin
bind
  bi'nder

bound
bound'en
bing
bin'go
birch
  birched
bird
birth
bis
bish'op
bisque
bis'tre
  bis'tred
bit
  bite
  bi'ter
  bi'ting
bitt
bizarr'e
blab
  blabbed
black
  blacked
  black'en
  black'ly
black'guard
  black'guardly
blade
  bla'ded
blame
  blamed
blanch
  blanched
blancmange
bland
  bland'ly
blank
  blanked

blank'ly
blanquette
blare
  blared
  bla'ring
blasé
blast
  blast'ed
  blast'er
bla'tant
  bla'tancy
  bla'tantly
blaze
  blazed
bla'zer
bla'zon
bleach
  bleached
  bleach'er
  bleach'es
bleak
  bleak'ly
blear
  blear'y
bleat
  bleat'ed
bleb
  bleb'by
bleed
  bled
  bleed'er
blench
  blenched
blend
  blend'ed
  blend'er
bless
  blessed

blight
  bli'ghted
  bli'ghter
blind
  bli'nded
  bli'nder
  bli'ndly
blink
  blinked
  blink'er
bliss
blithe
  bli'thely
blitz
bloat
  bloat'ed
bloat'er
bloc
block
  blocked
blood
  blood'ed
  blood'ily
blond
  blonde
bloom
  bloomed
  bloom'er
bloss'om
  bloss'omed
blot
blotch
  blotched
  blotch'y
blouse
  bloused
blow
  blew

blow'er
blown
blow'y
blowz'y
bludg'eon
blue
bluff
  bluffed
  bluff'er
  bluff'ly
blunt
  blunt'ed
  blunt'ly
blur
  blurred
  blur'ry
blurb
blurt
  blurt'ed
blush
  blushed
  blush'er
  blush'es
bo'a
boar
board
  board'ed
  board'er
boast
  boast'ed
  boast'er
boat
  boat'er
boat'swain
    (bo'sun)
bob
  bobbed
bob'ble

bode
  bo'ded
  bo'ding
bod'y
  bod'ied
  bod'ies
  bod'ily
bog
  bogged
  bog'gy
bog'gle
  bog'gled
bo'gy
boil
  boiled
  boil'er
bold
  bo'ldly
bole
bo'll
  bo'lled
bo'lster
  bo'lstered
bolt
  bo'lted
  bo'lter
bomb
  bombed
  bomb'er
bon mot
bon vivant
bon voyage
bona fide
bona fides
bone
  boned
  bo'ning
  bo'ny

bond
bond'ed
bond'er
bonne
bonne chance
bon'ny
bo nus
boob'y
boob'ies
book
booked
boom
boomed
boon
boor
boost
boost'ed
boost'er
boot
boot'ed
bootee'
booth
booth'es
boot'y
bore
bored
bo'rer
bo'real
bor'ic
born
bor'ough
bosk
bosk'y
bos'om
bos'omed
boss
bossed
boss'es

boss'y
botch
botched
botch'er
botch'y
both
both'er
both'ered
both'y
bot'tle
bot'tled
bou'clé
bough
bouillabaisse
bouilli
bouillon
boul'der
bouleversement
boult
boult'er
bounce
bounced
bounc'er
bound
bound'ed
bound'er
boun'ty
boun'ties
bour'geon
bourn
bourée
bourse
bout
boutique
bow
bowed
bow'er
bow'el

bow'elled
bow'er
bow'ery
bow'ie
bowl
bowled
bo'wler
box
boxed
box'er
box'es
boy
brace
braced
bra'cer
bra'ces
bra'cing
bra'chial
brack'en
brack'et
brad
brag
bragged
braggadocio
braid
braid'ed
brail
braille
brain
brain'y
braise
braised
brake
braked
bra'king
bram'ble
bram'bled
bram'bly

417

bran
branch
  branched
  branch'er
  branch'es
brand
  brand'ed
  brand'er
bran'dy
  brand'ied
brash
  brash'y
brass
  brass'ily
  brass'y
brat
brave
  braved
  bra'vely
  bra'ving
brav'o
bravura
brawl
  brawled
  brawl'er
brawn
  brawn'y
brax'y
bray
  brayed
  bray'er
braze
  bra'zen
  bra'zenly
bra'zier
breach
  breached
  breach'es

bread
breadth
break
  break'er
  broke
  bro'ken
bream
breast
  breast'ed
breath
breathe
  breathed
  breath'er
brecc'ia
breech
  breeched
  breech'es
breed
  bred
  breed'er
breeze
  breez'ily
  breez'y
breg'ma
breve
brev'et
brevier'
brew
  brewed
  brew'er
bri'ar
bribe
  bribed
  bri'ber
bric'=a=brac
brick
  bricked
bride

bri'dal
bridge
  bridged
bri'dle
  bri'dled
  bri'dling
brief
  brief'ly
bri'er
brig
bright
  bri'ghten
  bri'ghtly
brill
brim
  brimmed
brin'dle
  brin'dled
brine
  bri'ny
bring
  bring'er
  brought
brink
brioche
brisk
  brisk'ly
bristle
  bris'tled
  bris'tly
brit'tle
broach
  broached
  broach'es
broad
  broad'en
  broad'ly
brock

brock'et
brogue
broid'er
broil
  broiled
  broil'er
bro'ker
bron'co
bronze
  bronzed
brooch
brood
  brood'ed
  brood'er
  brood'y
brook
  brooked
broom
broth
broth'el
broth'er
  broth'erly
brougham
brow
brown
  browned
browse
  browsed
  brows'er
bruise
  bruised
  bruis'er
bruit
  bruit'ed
brunt
brush
  brushed
  brush'er

brush'es
brusque
brus'quely
brus'querie
brute
bru'tal
bub'ble
  bub'bled
buck
  bucked
  buck'er
  buck'et
  buck'le
  buck'led
  buck'ler
bud'dle
  budge
  budged
  budg'et
  budg'eter
buff
  buff'er
buffet
bug
  bugged
  bugg'er
bu'gle
  bu'gler
  bu'gling
buhl
build
  build'er
  built
bulb
  bulbed
bulge
  bulged
  bul'gy

bulk
  bulk'y
bull
  bu'llion
bu'lly
  bu'llies
bum'ble
bump
  bumped
  bump'y
bunch
  bunched
  bunch'es
  bunch'y
bun'dle
  bun'dled
bung
  bunged
bung'le
  bung'led
  bung'ler
  bung'ling
bun'ion
bunk
  bunked
  bunk'er
bunt
buoy
  buoyed
bur'ble
  bur'bled
bur'gh
bur'gle
  bur'gled
  burg'ling
bur'ly
burn
  burned

419

burn'er	cab'in	calk'er
burnt	ca'ble	call
burr	ca'bled	called
bu'rro	ca'bling	call'er
bur'sa	ca'bre	cal'la
burst	cache	calm
bur'y	*cachet*	calmed
bur'ial	cack'le	calm'ly
bur'ied	cack'led	ca'lyx
bus	cack'ler	ca'lices
bus'es	cac'ti	cam'bric
bus'by	cad	cam'el
bush	cad'dy	cam'elry
bushed	ca'dence	cam'eo
bu'shy	ca'dency	*cameraderie*
bu'shel	*cadenza*	cam'ion
bus'iness	cadge	camp
buss	cadged	camped
bust	cadg'er	camp'er
bust'ed	cad're	can
bus'tle	*cafard*	canned
bus'tled	caf'é	*canaille*
bus'y	cage	*canapé*
bus'ied	caged	*canard*
bus'ily	ca'ging	can'dle
bu'tcher	cairn	can'dy
bu'tchered	cake	cand'ied
butt	caked	cand'ies
bux'om	ca'king	cane
buy	calced	caned
bought	calf	ca'ning
buy'er	calve	cank'er
buzz	calved	cank'ered
buzzed	cal'id	can'na
buzz'er	ca'liph	can'ny
byre	ca'lix	can'nily
caballero	calk	canoe'
ca'ber	calked	canoed'

can'on
can'onry
cant
cant'ed
cantabile
canto
canzone
canzonetta
cap
capped
ca'pable
ca'pably
cape
ca'per
ca'pered
ca'perer
ca'pon
caraf'e
car'at
card
card'ed
card'er
care
cared
ca'ring
car'et
car'go
ca'ries
carillon
cark
car'ob
car'ol
car'olled
carp
carped
carp'er
car'ry

cart
cart'ed
cart'er
carte blanche
carve
carved
carv'en
carv'er
case
cased
ca'sing
ca'seate
ca'seic
ca'sein
ca'seous
cash
cashed
cash'ew
cask
casque
cas'sia
cast
cast'er
caste
cas'tle
cas'tled
cas'tling
castrato
casus belli
cat
cat'ty
catch
catch'er
catch'y
caught
ca'ter
ca'tered
ca'terer

ca'teran
cat'tle
cauc'us
caud'le
caul
caul'is
caulk
caulked
caulk'er
cause
caus'al
caused
caus'er
cause célèbre
cave
caved
ca'ving
caveat
cav'il
cav'illed
cav'iller
ca'vy
cease
ceased
ce'city
ce'dar
cede
ce'ded
ce'der
ce'ding
ceil
cell
celled
cel'lo
'cel'list
cens'er
cent
centime

cen'to

cen'tre
  cen'tred
  cen'tring

cere

ce'real

cerge

ce'ric

ceris'e

certiorari

chafe
  chafed
  cha'fing

cha'fer

chaff
  chaffed

chagrin'
  chagrin'ed

chain
  chained

chair
  chaired

chaise

chaise longue

chal'et

chalk
  chalk'y

chamade

cha'mber
  cha'mbered

cham'ois

champ
  champed

champignon

champlevé

chance
  chanced
  chanc'ing

chanc'y

chanc're

change
  changed
  cha'nger

chanson

chant
  chant'ed
  chant'er

cha'os
  chaot'ic

chap
  chapped

chapeau

chap'el

chap'eron
  chap'eronage

char
  charred

charad'e

chard

charge
  charged
  chargé
    d'affaires

char'ger

char'lotte

cha'ry
  cha'rily

charm
  charmed
  charm'er

charmeus'e

chart
  chart'ed

chase
  chased
  cha'ser

chasm

chassepot

chasseur

chass'is

chaste

cha'sten
  cha'stened
  cha'stener

chat
  chat'ted
  chat'tily
  chat'ty

château

chaun'try

cheap
  cheap'en
  cheap'ly

cheat
  cheat'ed
  cheat'er

check
  checked
  check'er

cheek
  cheek'y

cheep
  cheeped
  cheep'er

cheer
  cheered
  cheer'er
  cheer'y

cheese
  chees'y

chef

chef d'oeuvre

chem'ic

chenill'e

cheque
cheq'uer
  cheq'uered
cheroot'
cher'ry
cher'ub
chess
chest
  chest'y
chew
  chewed
chiaroscu'ro
chic
chica'ne
chick
  chick'en
chic'le
chide
  chid
  chi'ded
chief
  chief'ly
chignon
child
chill
  chilled
  chill'y
chil'li
chime
  chimed
  chi'mer
  chi'ming
chin
  chinned
chi'na
chine
chink
chintz

chip
  chipped
chirp
  chirped
  chirp'er
  chirp'y
chis'el
chit
chives
chiv'y
chlam'ys
chlo'ral
chlo'ric
chock
choice
  choic'ely
choir
choke
  choked
  cho'ker
  cho'ky
chol'er
chol'ic
choose
  choos'er
  chose
  cho'sen
chop
  chopped
  chop'py
chop suey
chor'tle
  chor'tled
cho'rus
cho'ral
chor'ic
chrism
chris'om

chris'ten
  chris'tened
chro'ma
chrome
  chro'mic
chron'ic
chthon'ic
chub
chub'by
chuck
  chucked
  chuck'er
chuck'le
  chuck'led
chuff
  chuffed
chuff'y
chug
  chugged
chuk'ka
chum
  chum'my
chump
chunk
  chunk'y
church
  churched
  church'es
  church'ly
churl
churn
  churned
  churn'er
chute
chyle
chyme
  chy'mify
chyp're

CICERONE

cicerone
ci'der
ci-devant
cigar'
cinque-centist
cinque-cento
ci'pher
circa
circiter
cir'cle
  cir'cled
cite
  ci'table
  ci'ted
  ci'ter
  ci'ting
cit'y
  cit'ify
civ'et
civ'ic
civ'il
clach'an
clad
clag'gy
claim
  claimed
  claim'er
clam
clam'my
clamp
  clamped
clan
clang
  clanged
  clang'er
  clang'our
clank
  clanked

clap
  clapped
claque
  claq'ueur
clar'et
clar'ify
cla'ry
clash
  clashed
clasp
  clasped
  clasp'er
class
  classed
  class'ify
class'ic
class'is
clause
  claus'al
cla'vis
claw
  clawed
clay
clean
  cleaned
  clean'er
  clean'ly
cleanse
  cleansed
  cleans'er
clear
  cleared
  clear'ly
cleat
cleave
  cleav'er
cleft
clove

clef
clench
  clenched
cler'gy
  cler'ic
clerk
  clerk'ly
clev'er
clev'is
clew
cliché
click'
  clicked
  click'er
cli'ent
cliff
  cliffed
  cliff'y
climb
  climbed
  cli'mber
clinch
  clinched
  clinch'er
  clinch'es
cling
  clung
clin'ic
clink
  clinked
  clink'er
clip
  clipped
clique
  cliq'uey
cloak
  cloaked
cloche

clock
  clocked
  clock'er
clod
clog
  clogged
clogs
clon'ic
close
  closed
  clo'sely
  clo'ser
clos'et
clot
cloth
clothe
  clothed
  clothes
cloud
  cloud'ed
  cloud'y
clout
  clout'ed
clove
clo'ven
clown
  clowned
cloy
  cloyed
club
  clubbed
cluck
  clucked
clue
clump
  clumped
clum'sy
  clum'sily

clutch
  clutched
coach
  coached
  coach'er
  coach'es
coal
  coaled
coarse
  coars'ely
  coars'en
coast
  coast'al
  coast'ed
  coast'er
coat
  coatee'
coax
  coaxed
  coax'er
cob
cob'ble
  cob'bled
  cob'bly
coc'ci
cock
  cocked
  cock'ily
  cock'y
cock'er
cock'le
  cock'led
cocoon'
cocotte
cod
co'da
code
  co'ded

co'der
co'ding
codg'er
co'dify
cog
  cogged
cog gle
  cog'gly
cogn ac
cognoscente
coif
coign
coil
  coiled
coin
  coined
  coin'er
coir
coke
col
cold
  co'lded
  co'ldly
col'ic
  col'icky
col'lier
  col'liery
col'onel
  col'onelcy
coloratura
col'our
  col'oured
colt
col'umn
  col'umned
col'za
co'ma
comb

425

COMBED

combed
cu'mber
combe
come
    came
    com'er
    com'ing
com'ely
com'et
com'fort
    com'forted
    com'forter
com'ic
com'ma
comme il faut
com'pany
    com'panies
com'pass
    com'passed
    com'passes
com'po
compôte
con
    conned
conch
conch'a
concierge
cone
    con'ic
confrère
cong'a
congé
cong'er
con'quer
    con'quered
    con'querer
    con'quest
contre danse

contretemps
conversazione
coo
    cooed
cook
    cooked
    cook'er
cool
    cooled
    cool'er
    cool'ly
    cool'ie
coom
coombe
coon
coop
    cooped
    coop'er
cope
    coped
    co'ping
cop'ra
copse
cop'y
    cop'ier
coquet'
    coquett'e
    coquet'ry
cor'al
coranto
cord
    cord'ed
cordillera
core
    cored
    co'rer
    co'ring
cor'gi

cork
    corked
    cork'er
    cork'y
corn
    corned
    corn'y
corps
corpse
corpus delicti
corsage
cost
    cost'ly
co'sy
    co'sily
cot
coterie
couch
    couched
cough
    coughed
    cough'er
could
couloir
count
    count'ed
    count'er
    coun'try
    coun'ty
    coun'ties
coup
coup d'état
coupé
coup'le
    coup'led
courante
course
    coursed

426

cours'er
court
court'ed
court'ly
cous'in
cous'inly
cous'inry
cou'teau
couture
couturier
couva'de
cove
cov'en
cov'er
cov'ered
cov'et
cov'eted
cov'ey
cow
cowed
cow'er
cowl
cowled
cow'rie
cox
cox'a
cox'al
cox'swain
coy
coy'ly
coy'ote
coy'pu
coz'en
coz'ened
coz'ener
crab
crack
cracked

crack'er
crack'le
crack'led
cra'dle
cra'dled
cra'dling
craft
craft'y
crag
cragged
crag'gy
cram
crammed
cramp
cramped
cran
crane
craned
cra'ning
cra'nium
cra'nial
crank
crank'ily
crank'y
cran'ny
crape
crash
crashed
crash'es
cra'sis
crass
crass'ly
crate
cra'ted
cra'ter
crave
craved
cra'ver

cra'ven
craw
craw,
crawled
crawl'er
craw'ly
cray on
craze
crazed
cra'zy
creak
creaked
creak'y
cream
creamed
cream'y
crease
creased
crèche
cred'it
cred'ited
Credo
creed
creed'al
creek
creel
creep
creep'er
creep'y
crept
crème de menthe
cren'el
crêpe
crêpe-de-chine
crep'on
crescendo
cress
crest

crest'ed

crет'in

crew

  crewed

crew'el

crib

  cribbed

crib'ble

crick

  cricked

crick'et

crime

crimp

  crimped

crimp'er

cringe

  cringed

  cring'er

cring'le

crink'le

  crink'led

  crink'ly

crip'ple

  crip'pled

cri'sis

  cri'ses

crisp

  crisp'ly

crit'ic

critique

croak

  croaked

  croak'er

croche

cro'chet

  cro'cheter

crock

  crock'et

croft

croft'er

croissant

crone

cro'ny

crook

  crooked

croon

  crooned

  croon'er

crop

  cropped

cro'quet

croquette

cro'sier

cross

  crossed

crosse

cross'ly

crotch

crotch'et

crot'tle

crouch

  crouched

croup'

  croup'y

croute

crouton

crow

  crowed

crowd

  crowd'ed

crown

  crowned

croze

crude

  cru'dely

cru'el

  cru'elly

  cru'elty

cru'et

cruise

  cruised

  cruis'er

crumb

  crumb'y

crum'ble

  crumb'led

crum'ple

  crum'pled

crunch

  crunched

  crunch'y

cruse

crush

  crushed

crust

  crust'ed

  crust'y

crutch

  crutched

  crutch'es

crux

cry

  cried

  cri'er

  cries

crypt

cub

  cubbed

cub'by

cube

  cubed

cud

cud'dle

  cud'dled

cud'dy

cudg'el

cue

cued
cuff
  cuffed
cuisine
cul de sac
cull
  culled
culott'e
cult
cum'in
cu'neal
cup
  cupped
cup'board
cu'rate
cur
curb
  curbed
curd
  curd'le
    curd'led
cure
  cured
  cu'rer
curé
cu'ria
cu'rie
cu'rio
curl
  curled
  curl'er
  curl'y
cur'ry
curse
  cursed
  curst
curt
  curt'ly

curt'sy
curve
  curved
cu'shion
  cu'shioned
cusp
cuss
  cuss'ed
cute
  cu'tely
cu'ticle
cut'tle
cut'ty
cy'cle
cy'ma
cyme
cyn'ic
cyst
dab
  dabbed
dab'ble
  dab'bled
da capo
d'accord
dace
da'cite
da'do
daft
  daft'ly
da'go
da'hlia
dain'ty
dair'y
da'is
dais'y
dale
dal'ly
dam

dammed
dame d'honneur
damn
  damned
damp
  damp'ly
  damp'en
  dam'per
dance
  danced
  danc'er
dan'dle
  dan'dled
dan'dy
  dand'ies
da'nger
dang'le
  dang'led
  dang'ler
  dang'ling
dank
danse macabre
danseur
danseuse
dap'ple
  dap'pled
dare
  dared
dark
  dark'en
  dark'ly
darn
  darned
  darn'er
dart
  dart'ed
  dart'er
dash

dashed
dash'er
da'ta
da'tary
date
da'tal
da'ted
da'tive
daub
daubed
daub'er
daunt
daunt'ed
dauphin
dav'it
daw'dle
daw'dled
dawn
dawned
day
dail'y
daze
dazed
daz'zle
daz'zled
de bonne grace
de facto
de fide
de jure
de luxe
de nouveau
de novo
de profundis
de rigueur
de trop
dead
dead'en
dead'ly

deaf
dcaf'en
deal
deal'er
dealt
dean
dear
dear'ly
dearth
death
death'ly
deb'it
deb'ited
deb'ris
debt
debt'or
début
decil'lion
deck
decked
deck'le
deck'led
décolletage
décolleté
décor
decrescendo
deed
deem
deemed
deep
deep'en
deep'ly
deer
deft
deft'ly
defy'
dégagé
de-i'ce

de-i'ced
de-i'cer
deign
deigned
del credere
dele
delenda
dell
del'ta
delve
delved
delv'er
démarche
démenti
démodé
demoiselle
dem'y
den
dene
deng'ue
den'im
dénouement
dense
dens'ely
dent
dent'ed
deny'
deo volente (DV)
dep'ot
depth
dernier cri
dernier ressort
déshabille
desk
des'uetude
détente
deuce

deus ex machina
dev'il
   dev'illed
devoir
dew
   dew'y
dhôbi
dhôti
dhow
diablerie
di'al
diamanté
di'ary
dias'pora
dib'ble
dice
   diced
   di'cer
dic'ta
did'dle
   did'dled
die
   died
dies non
dies'el
di'et
   di'eted
   di'eter
dig
   dug
dig'it
dilettan'te
dill
dim
   dim'ly
   dimmed
   dim'ple
   dim'pled

din'ar
dine
   dined
   di'ner
   dinett'e
   di'ning
ding'hy
   ding'hies
ding'le
ding'o
din'gy
   din'gily
din'ic
dint
dip
   dipped
dire
   di'rely
dirge
dirk
dirn'dl
dirt
   dirt'ied
   dirt'ily
   dirt'y
disc
diseur
diseuse
dishev'el
   dishev'elled
distingué
distrait
ditch
   ditched
   ditch'er
   ditch'es
dith'er
dit'to

dit'ty
   dit'ties
dive
   dived
   di'ver
   di'ving
divertissement
div'ot
dix'ie
diz'zy
do
   done
   do'er
dock
   docked
   dock'er
dock'et
dodge
   dodged
   dodg'er
   dodg'y
do'do
doe
doff
   doffed
   doff'er
dog
   dogged
do'ge
dog'ma
doil'y
dolce
dole
doll
   doll'y
   dolled
dolt
dome

domed

don
  donned

dona nobis

dood'le
  dood'led

dook
  dooked

doom
  doomed

door

dope
  doped
  do'per
  do'pey

dor'ic

do'ry

dose
  dosed

dot
  dot'ty

dote
  do'ted
  do'ter

douane

doub'le
  doub'led
  doub'ly

double entendre

doubt
  doubt'ed
  doubt'er

douceur

douche
  douched

dough
  dough'y

dought'y

douse
  doused
  dous'er

dove

dow'dy
  dow'dily

dow'er
  dow'ry

dow'el

down
  downed
  down'y

dowse
  dows'er

dox'y

doy'en

doze
  dozed
  do'zer
  do'zy

doz'en

drab
  drab'ly

drach'ma

draff

draft
  draft'ed

drag
  dragged
  drag'gle
  drag'gled
  drag'on

drail

drain
  drained
  drain'er

drake

dram

dram'a

dramatis
            personae

drape
  draped
  dra'per

draught
  draught'ily
  draught'y

draw
  draw'ee
  draw'er
  drawn
  drew

drawl
  drawled
  drawl'er

dray

dread
  dread'ed

dream
  dream'er
  dreamt
  dream'y

drear
  drear'y

dredge
  dredged
  dredg'er

dregs

drench
  drenched
  drench'es

dress
  dressed
  dress'er

drib'ble
  drib'bled

drift
  drift'ed
  drift'er
drill
  drilled
drink
  drank
  drink'er
  drunk
drip
  dripped
drive
  driv'en
  dri'ver
  drove
driv'el
driz'zle
  driz'zled
  driz'zly
drogue
droit
droll
  dro'lly
drone
  droned
  dro'ner
droop
  drooped
  droop'y
drop
  dropped
drop'sy
dross
  dross'y
drought
dro'ver
drown
  drowned

drowse
  drowsed
  drows'y
drub
  drubbed
drudge
  drudged
drug
  drugged
dru'id
  druid'ic
drum
  drummed
drunk
  drunk'en
drupe
druse
  drused
  dru'sy
drux'y
dry
  dried
  dries
  dry'er
  dry'ly
  dry'ad
du'al
dub
  dubbed
duc'at
duch'y
duck
  ducked
duct
dud
dudg'eon
due
  du'ly

du'el
duet'
duf'fle
duke
  du'kery
dull
  dulled
  dull'y
dulse
dumb
  dumb'ly
dum'my
  dum'mies
dump
  dumped
  dum'py
dun
  dunned
dunce
dune
dung
duo
dupe
  duped
  du'per
du'ple
dusk
  dusk'y
dust
  dust'ed
  dust'er
  dust'y
du'ty
dwarf
  dwarfed
dwell
  dwell'er
  dwelt

dwin'dle
   dwin'dled
dy'ad
dye
   dyed
   dy'er
dyke
each
eag'er
   eag'erly
eag'le
eag're
ear
   eared
earl
   earl'y
earn
   earned
   earn'er
earth
   earth'en
   earth'ly
   earth'y
ease
   eased
   eas'y
eas'el
east
eat
   eat'en
   eat'er
eaves
eau de Cologne
eau de vie
ebb
   ebbed
eb'on
ech'elon

echid'na
ech'o
   ech'oes
   echo'ic
éclair
éclat
eclip'se
   eclip'sed
ed'dy
edge
   edged
   edg'y
e'dict
ed'it
   ed'ited
   edit'ion
edu'ce
   edu'ced
   educt'
eel
eer'ie
eft
e'gence
e'gency
egest'
   eges'ta
egg
   egged
e'go
e'gress
   egres'sion
e'gret
eid'er
eight
   eighth
   eighth'ly
   eight'y
eisteddfod

elth'er
eject'
   ejec'ta
eke
   eked
   e'king
élan
e'land
elap'se
   elaps'ed
ela'te
   ela'ted
   ela'tion
el'der
elect'
elev'en
   elev'enth
elf
   elf'in
   elves
elic'it
   elic'ited
eli'de
elis'ion
élite
elix'ier
elk
ell
ellag'ic
ell'ops
elm
éloge
e'longate
   e'longated
   elonga'tion
elo'pe
   elo'ped
   elo'per

else
elu'de
  elu'ded
  elu'sion
elu'te
  elu'ter
  elu'tion
embarras de
    richesse
embonpoint
emend'
  emend'ed
emerg'e
  emerg'ed
emet'ic
émigré
emi'r
emit'
  emis'sion
emo'te
  emo'tion
  emo'tive
emp'ty
e'mu
en arrière
en avant
en bloc
en effet
en famille
en fête
en masse
en passant
en rapport
en route
en tout
en tout cas
e'nate
  ena'tion

enceinte
encore
end
  end'ed
enfant terrible
enig'ma
ennui
enough'
ensemble
entente
entente cordiale
entourage
entr'acte
entre nous
entrechat
entrecôte
entrée
entrements
entrepreneur
en'vy
e'pact
épée
eper'gne
eph'od
ep'ic
epis'tle
e'poch
  ep'ochal
equ'able
e'qual
  equal'ity
  e'qualled
equa'te
  equa'ted
  equa'tion
equa'tor
eq'uerry
eq'uine

equip'
  equipp'ed
equ'us
  equ'oid
eq'uity
e'ra
era'se
  era'sed
  era'ser
erect'
  erect'ly
erg
ergo
er'ica
ero'de
  ero'ded
  ero'sion
erot'ic
err
  erred
eruct'
erupt'
esprit de corps
espy'
estaminet
estancia
etch
  etched
  etch'er
e'ther
e'thos
eth'yl
étude
eva'de
  eva'ded
  eva'sion
e'ven
  e'venly

435

event'
ev'er
evert'
 ever'sion
ev'ery
evict'
e'vil
 e'villy
evinc'e
 evinc'ed
evoe
evo'ke
 evo'ked
evolv'e
 evolv'ed
ewe
ew'er
Ewigkeit
ex cathedra
ex curia
ex dono
ex gratia
ex libris
ex officio
ex parte
exact'
 exact'ly
exalt'
 exalt'ed
exa'men
exam'ple
exempt'
excrt'
 exert'ed
exeunt
exhaust'
exhib'it
exhort'
436

ex'ile
 ex'iled
exist'
 exist'ed
ex'it
 ex'ited
exot'ic
exposé
ex'udo
 exu'ded
exult'
 exult'ed
ey'as
eye
 eyed
ey'rie
fa'ble
 fa'bled
face
 faced
fa'cial
fac'et
 fac'eted
fac'ile
fact
fad
 fad'dy
fade
 fa'ded
fag
 fagged
fai'ence
fail
 failed
faint
 faint'ed
 faint'ly
fair

fair'ly
fair'y
fait accompli
faith
fake
 faked
fa'ker
fa'king
fakir'
fall
 fall'en
 fell
false
 fals'ely
falt'er
fame
 famed
fa'mous
 fa'mously
fan
 fanned
fan'cy
fane
fang
 fanged
fan'ion
fan'on
far
 far'ad
farce
fare
 fared
fa'ring
farm
 farmed
 farm'er
fa'ro
farouche

fas'ces
fas'cia
fash'ion
  fash'ioned
fast
fas'ting
fas'ten
  fas'tened
  fas'tener
fat
  fat'ty
fate
  fa'tal
  fa'tally
  fa'ted
fath'er
  fath'erly
fath'om
  fath'omed
faubourg
fault
  fault'y
faun
faun'a
faute de mieux
fauteuil
fauv'ism
faux pas
fa'vour
  fa'voured
  fa'vourer
fawn
  fawned
  fawn'er
feal'ty
feast
  feast'ed
  feast'er

feat
  feat'ly
feath'er
fee
feeb'le
  feeb'ly
feed
  fed
  feed'er
feign
  feigned
feint
  feint'ed
feel
  feel'er
  felt
fell
  felled
  fell'er
fel'on
felt
  felt'ed
  felt'er
femme fatale
fe'mur
fen
fence
  fenced
  fenc'er
fend
  fend'ed
fen'ny
fer de lance
fe'ral
fern
  fern'y
fer'ry
fetch

fetched
fête
fet'tle
feu
  feu'ar
  feued
feu de joie
feud
feuilleton
few
fey
fez
  fezzed
  fez'zes
fiancé
fiancée
fias'co
fiat
fib
  fibbed
fi'bre
  fi'bred
fich'u
fick'le
fid'dle
  fid'dled
fidg'et
  fidg'eted
  fidg'ety
fie
fief
field
  field'ed
  field'er
fiend
fierce
  fierc'ely
fieri facias

437

fies'ta

fife
  fi'fer
fifth
  fif'thly
fif'ty
fig
fight
  fought
filch
  filched
  filch'er
file
  filed
  fi'ler
fill
  filled
  fill'er
fil'let
fil'lip
fil'ly
film
  filmed
  fil'my
filth
  filth'y
fin
  finned
  fin'ny
fin de siecle
final'e
finan'ce
  finan'cial
  finan'cier
finch
  finch'es
find
  fi'nder

found
fine
  fined
  fi'ning
fi'nely
fi'nery
fing'er
  fing'ered
finis
fioritura
fir
  fir'ry
fire
  fired
  fi'ery
firm
  firm'ly
first
  first'ly
fish
  fished
  fish'er
  fish'es
  fish'y
fis'sion
fist
  fis'tic
fit
  fit'ly
fix
  fixed
  fix'er
fizz
  fizz'y
fiz'zle
  fiz'zled
fjord
flab'by

flag
  flagged
fla'grant
fla'grancy
flagrante delicto
flail
  flailed
flair
flake
  flaked
  fla'ky
flame
  flamed
  fla'ming
fla'men
flaneur
flange
  flanged
flank
  flanked
  flank'er
flap
  flapped
flare
  flared
flash
  flashed
  flash'es
  flash'y
flask
flat
flatt'er
  flatt'erer
  flatt'ery
  flat'ly
fla'tus
flaunt
  flaunt'ed

FLEW

flaunt'er
flav'in
fla'vour
  fla'voured
flaw
  flawed
flax
  flax'en
flay
  flayed
flea
fleam
fleck
  flecked
fledge
  fledged
flee
  fled
fleece
  fleeceɑ
  fleec'y
fleer
fleet
  fleet'ly
flesh
  fleshed
  flesh'ly
  flesh'y
flesh'er
fletch'er
fleur de lis
flex
  flexed
  flex'ion
  flex'or
flick
  flicked
  flick'er

flick'er
  flick'ered
flight
  fli'ghty
flim'sy
flinch
  flinched
fling
  fling'er
  flung
flint
  flint'y
flip
  flipped
flirt
  flirt'ed
  flirt'er
flit
flitch
float
  float'ed
  float'er
flock
  flocked
floe
flog
  flogged
flood
  flood'ed
floor
  floored
flop
  flopped
  flop'py
flo'ra
  flor'al
  flor'et
flor'id

flor'in
floss
  floss'y
flounce
  flounced
flour
  floured
  flour'y
flour'ish
  flour'ished
flout
  flout'ed
  flout'er
flow
  flowed
flow'er
  flow'ered
  flow'eret
  flow'ery
flue
fluff
  fluffed
  fluff'y
flu'id
fluke
flume
flur'ry
flush
  flushed
flute
  flu'ted
  flu'ter
  flu'ty
flux
flux'ion
  flux'ional
fly
  flew

439

fli'er
flown
fly'er
foal
  foaled
foam
  foamed
  foam'y
fob
  fobbed
foe
fog
  fogged
  fog'gily
  fog'gy
foib'le
foie gras
foil
  foiled
  foil'er
foist
  foist'ed
  foist'er
fold
  fo'lded
  fo'lder
folk
fol'ly
fond
  fond'ly
fon'dle
  fon'dled
fondue
font
  font'al
food
fool

fooled
foot
  feet
  foot'ed
  foot'le
  foot'led
fop
for'ay
  for'ayer
force
  forced
  force majeure
ford
  fo'rded
fore
  fo'recastle
      (fo'c'sle)
forego'
for'eign
  for'eigner
forge
  forged
  forg'er
fork
  forked
form
  formed
fort
  forte
  forth
fortissimo
for'ty
forzando
foth'er
foul
  fouled
  foul'ly

found
  found'ed
  found'er
foun'dry
fount
four
  fourth
  fourth'ly
fowl
  fowl'er
fox
  foxed
  fox'es
  fox'y
foy'er
frac'as
fra'grance
fra'grant
fra'grantly
frail
  frail'ty
fraise
frame
  framed
  fra'mer
franc
frank
  franked
  frank'ly
frappé
Frau
Fraülein
fraud
fraught
fray
  frayed
fraz'il

440

fraz'zle
  fraz'zled
freak
freck'le
  freck'led
  freck'ly
free
  freed
  freel'y
freeze
  freez'er
  froze
  fro'zen
freight
  freight'ed
  freight'er
fre'nal
fren'zy
fres'co
fresh
  fresh'en
  fresh'er
  fresh'ly
fret
frett
fri'ar
fricassée
friend
  friend'ly
frieze
fright
  fri'ghten
frig'id
frill
  frilled
  frill'y
fringe
  fringed

frisk
  frisk'y
friv'ol
frizz
  frizz'y
friz'zle
  friz'zled
frock
frog
  frogged
frol'ic
frond
front
  front'al
  front'ed
frost
  frost'ed
  frost'y
froth
  frothed
  froth'y
frown
  frowned
  frown'er
frowst
  frow'sty
  frow'zy
fruit
  fruit'y
frump
  frump'y
fry
  fried
  fri'er
  fry'er
fu'chisa
fud'dle
  fud'dled

fudge
fu'el
fug
  fug'gy
fugato
fugue
ful'gency
  fulgen'ic
ful'gent
ful'gid
full
  fu'lly
fum'ble
  fum'bled
fume
  fumed
fun
  fun'ny
fund
  fund'ed
fung'us
  fung'al
  fung'i
  fung'oid
  fung'ous
funk
  funk'y
fur
  furred
  fur'ry
furioso
furl
  furled
fur'ther
  fur'thest
fu'ry
furze
fuse

fused
fu'sion
fuss
  fussed
  fuss'er
  fuss'y
fus'ty
fuzz
  fuzz'y
gab
  gab'ble
  gab'bied
ga'ble
  ga'bled
  ga'bling
ga'by
gad
  gadd'ed
gadg'et
  gadg'etry
gaff
  gaffed
gaffe
gag
  gagged
gage
  gaged
  ga'ger
  ga'ging
gag'gle
gain
  gained
  gain'er
gait
  gait'ed
gait'er
gal'a

gale
gall
  galled
galop'
gam'ble
  gam'bled
game
  ga'mely
  ga'ming
gamin
gamine
gam'ma
gam'ut
gang
  ganged
  gang'er
  gan'glia
  gan'gling
  gan'glion
  gan'grene
gaol
  gaol'er
gap
  gapped
gape
  gaped
  ga'per
  ga'ping
garb
  garbed
gar'ble
  gar'bled
garçon
gar'gle
  gar'gled
ga'rish
  ga'rishly
gas

ga'seous
gas'es
gassed
gash
  gashed
gasp
  gasped
gate
  ga'ted
gâteau
gâteaux
gath'er
gauche
  gauch'ely
gaucho
gaud
  gaud'y
gaudeam'us
gauge
  gauged
  gaug'er
gaunt
  gaunt'ly
gauze
  gauz'y
gav'el
ga'vial
gaw'ky
gay
  gail'y
gaze
  gazed
  ga'zer
gean
gcar
  geared
geck'o
geish'a

geld
  geld'ed
gel'id
gem
  gemmed
gendarme
gendarmerie
gene
ge'nie
genre
gen'tle
  gen'tly
ge'on
georgett'e
germ
gesso
gey'ser
ghar'ry
ghast'ly
ghet'to
ghost
  gho'stly
ghoul
gi'ant
gibe
  gibed
  gi'ber
  gi'bing
gid'dy
gift
  gift'ed
gig
gig'gle
  gig'gled
gild
  gild'ed
  gild'er

gill
gilt
gimp
gin
ging'ham
gird
  gird'ed
  girt
gir'dle
  gir'dled
girl
girth
gist
give
  gave
  giv'en
  giv'er
gla'brate
gla'brous
glacé
glad
  glad'ly
glade
glair
glance
  glanced
gland
glare
  glared
glass
  glass'es
  glass'y
glaze
  glazed
  gla'zer
gleam
  gleamed

glean
  gleaned
  glean'er
glebe
glee
glen
glib
  glib'ly
glide
  gli'ded
  gli'der
glimpse
  glimpsed
glint
  glint'ed
glissando
glis'ten
  glis'tened
gloat
  gloat'ed
  gloat'er
globe
gloom
  gloomed
  gloom'y
glo'ry
  glo'ried
gloss
  glossed
  gloss'y
glove
  gloved
  glov'er
glow
  glowed
  glow'er
  glow'ered

glue
　glued
　glu'ey
glum
　glum'ly
glume
glut
glycer'ic
glyc'erol
glyc'eryl
glyph
　glyph'ic
gnarl
　gnarled
gnash
　gnashed
gnat
gnath'ic
gnaw
　gnawed
　gnaw'er
gneiss
　gneiss'ic
gnome
gnu
goad
　goad'ed
goal
goat
goatee'
gob'ble
　gob'bled
go'by
　go'bies
god
　god'ly
gog'gle
　gog'gled

goit're
gold
　go'lden
golf
　golfed
　golf'er
gon'ad
gong
　gonged
good
　good'ly
goose
　geese
gore
　gored
gorge
　gorged
　gorg'er
gorse
go'ry
　go'rily
gouge
　gouged
gourd
gout
　gout'y
gow'an
gown
　gowned
grab
　grabbed
grace
　graced
gra'cious
gra'ciously
grack'le
grade
　gra'ded

gra'der
graft
　graft'ed
　graft'er
grain
　grained
　grain'er
gramme
grand
　grand'ly
grandioso
grange
grant
　grant'ed
　grantee'
　grant'or
grape
　gra'pery
graph
　graph'ic
grap'ple
　grap'pled
grasp
　grasped
　grasp'er
grass
　grassed
　grass'y
grate
　gra'ted
　gra'ter
gratin
grave
　gra'vely
grav'el
　gra'ven
gray
graze

444

grazed
gra'zer
grease
  greased
  greas'er
  greas'y
great
grebe
greed
  greed'y
green
greet
  greet'ed
grey
grid
grid'dle
grief
  grieve
  grieved
grill
  grilled
grille
grilse
grim
  grim'ly
grime
  grimed
  gri'my
grin
  grinned
grind
  gri'nder
  ground
grip
  gripped
gripe
  griped

gri'ping
gris'ly
gris'tle
  gris'tled
  gris'tly
grit
  grit'ty
griz'zle
  griz'zled
groan
  groaned
groat
gro'cer
  gro'cery
grog
  grog'gy
groin
groom
  groomed
groove
  grooved
grope
  groped
gross
  gro'ssly
grot'to
grouch
  grouch'y
ground
  ground'ed
group
  grouped
grouse
  groused
  grous'er
grout
  grout'er

grove
grov'el
  grov'elled
grow
  grew
  grow'er
  grown
growl
  growled
  growl'er
grub
  grubbed
  grub'by
grudge
  grudged
gru'el
gruff
  gruff'ly
grum'ble
  grum'bled
grum'py
grunt
  grunt'ed
  grunt'er
gryph'on
guan'o
guar'anty
guard
  guard'ed
guav'a
gudg'eon
guenon'
guess
  guessed
  guess'er
guest
guild

445

guile
guillo'che
guilt
  guilt'y
guinea
guipu're
guise
guitar'
gulf
gull
gul'ly
gulp
  gulped
gum
  gummed
  gum'my
gum'bo
gun
  gunned
gun'ny
gun'wale
gup'py
gur'gle
  gur'gled
gush
  gushed
  gush'er
gust
  gus'ty
gus'to
gut
guy
  guyed
guide
  gui'ded
guid'on
guz'zle
  guz'zled

446

gybe
  gy'bing
gyp'sy
  gyp'sies
habeas corpus
hab'it
hacienda
hack
  hacked
hack'le
hadji
haft
hag
  hagged
hag'gle
  hag'gled
hail
  hailed
hair
  hair'y
hake
hale
half
  halved
  halves
ham
ha'mose
hand
  hand'ed
han'dle
  han'dled
han'dy
hang
  hanged
  hang'er
  hung
hang'ar
hank

hank'er
  hank'ered
hap
  hap'ly
hap'py
hard
  hard'y
hard'en
hard'ly
hare
ha'rem
hark
harm
  harmed
harp
  harped
harp'er
har'py
har'ry
har'ried
harsh
harsh'ly
hart
hash
hasp
haste
ha'stily
ha'sting
ha'sty
ha'sten
ha'stened
hat
hatch
  hatched
  hatch'es
hatch'et
hate
  ha'ted

ha'ter
ha'ting
ha'tred
haught'y
haul
  hauled
haul'ier
haunch
  haunch'es
  haunched
haunt
  haunt'ed
  haunt'er
Hausfrau
haut'boy
hauteur
have
  had
  hav'ing
ha'ven
hav'oc
haw
hawk
haw'ker
hawse
hay
haze
  ha'zy
ha'zel
head
  head'ed
  head'er
  head'y
heal
  healed
  heal'er
health
  health'y

heap
  heaped
hear
  heard
  hear'er
hearse
heart
  heart'ed
  heart'y
  heart'en
hearth
heat
  heat'ed
  heat'er
heath
  heath'er
heave
  heaved
  heav'er
  hove
  heav'en
  heav'enly
  heav'y
  heav'ily
heck'le
  heck'led
hedge
  hedged
  hedg'er
heed
  heed'ed
heel
  heeled
  heeler
hef'ty
heif'er
height

height'en
hein'ous
heir
hell
hel'lion
hello'
  hallo'
  hullo'
helm
hel'ot
help
  helped
  help'er
helve
hem
  hemmed
hemp
  hemp'en
hence
hen'na
hen'ry
herb
  herb'al
herd
  herd'ed
  herd'er
here
he'reby
herein'
hereof'
hereto'
he'ro
  he'roes
her'on
Herr
Herren
hew
  hewed

hewn
hew'er
hide
hid
hie
hied
hig'gle
hig'gled
high
high'ly
hike
hiked
hi'ker
hill
hill'y
hilt
hilt'ed
hind
hi'nder
hinge
hinged
hint
hint'ed
hip
hipped
hire
hired
hi'rer
hiss
hissed
hit
hitch
hitched
hith'er
hive
hoar
hoar'y
hoard

hoard'ed
hoard'er
hoarse
hoars'ely
hoax
hoaxed
hoax'er
hob
hob'ble
hob'bled
hob'by
ho'bo
hock
hock'ey
hod
hoe
hoed
ho'er
hog
hogged
hoi polloi
hoist
hoist'ed
hoist'er
ho'kum
hold
held
ho'lder
hole
holed
ho'ley
holly
holy
home
ho'mely
ho'mer
ho'ming
homo sapiens

hone
honed
ho'ning
hon'est
hon'estly
hon'esty
hon'ey
hon'eyed
honk
honked
hon'our
hon'oured
hood
hood'ed
hoof
hoofed
hooved
hooves
hook
hooked
hook'er
hoop
hooped
hoot
hoot'ed
hoot'er
hop
hopped
hope
hoped
ho'ping
horde
horn
horned
horn'y
hors de combat
hors d'oeuvre
horse

hors'y
hose
  hosed
  ho'sing
host
hot
  hot'ly
hound
  hound'ed
hour
  hour'ly
  hour'i
house
  housed
hov'el
hov'er
  hov'ered
how
howl
  howled
  howl'er
hub
  hubbed
hud'dle
  hud'dled
hue
  hued
buff
  huff'y
huge
  hu'gely
hu'la
hulk
hull
  hulled
hum
  hummed
hum'ble

hum'bled
hum'bly
hu'mour
hu'moured
hump
  humped
hunch
  hunched
hun'ger
  hun'gered
  hun'gry
  hun'grily
hunt
  hunt'ed
  hunt'er
hur'dle
  hur'dled
hurl
  hurled
hur'ry
hurt
hur'tle
  hur'tled
hush
  hushed
husk
  husked
  husk'er
hus'ky
huss'y
hus'tle
  hus'tled
hut
hutch
hymn
  hymned
iamb
i'bex

i'bis
ice
  iced
  i'cily
  i'cing
  i'cy
i'chor
icicle
i'con
  icon'ic
id
id est (i.e.)
ide'a
  ide'ate
  ide'ated
  idea'tion
ideal'
  ide'ally
idée fixe
idem
i'dle
  i'dled
  i'dler
  i'dling
  i'dly
i'dol
id'yll
ig'loo
ignis fatuus
iguan'a
i'lex
ilk
ill
ima'go
imp
impasto
imprimatur
imprimis

in absentia
in camera
in extremis
in loco parentis
in memoriam
in re
in situ
in toto
in vacuo
inch
  inched
in'fra
ingénue
in'gle
ink
  ink'y
in'ly
inn
insofar'
inter alia
inter se
in'terest
  in'terested
inter'nal
in'to
i'on
io'ta
ipso facto
ire
i'ris
irk
  irked
i'ron
  i'roned
i'rony
  iron'ic
i'singlass
i'sland
450

i'slander
isle
i'slet
is'sue
  is'sued
is'tle
itch
  itch'ed
  itch'y
i'tem
i'vory
i'vy
  i'vied
jab
  jabbed
jab'ot
ja'cent
jack
  jacked
jack'al
jack'et
jade
  ja'ded
jag
  jagged
jail
  jailed
jail'or
jalousie
jam
  jammed
jam'my
jamb
jan'gle
  jan'gling
  jan'gled
  jan'gly
jar

jarred
jardinière
jaspé
jaunt
  jaunt'ed
  jaunt'y
jaw
jay
jazz
  jazzed
jeep
jeer
  jeered
jel'ly
jem'my
  jem'mied
jen'ny
jerk
  jerked
  jerk'y
jess
  jessed
jest
  jest'ed
  jest'er
jet
  jet'ted
  jet'ty
jeunesse dorée
jew'el
jew'ellery
jib
  jibbed
jibe
  jibed
jif'fy
jig
  jigged

jig'gle
  jig'gled
jilt
  jilt'ed
jin'gle
  jin'gled
  jin'gling
  jin'gly
jin'go
job
jock'ey
jog
  jogged
jog'gle
  jog'gled
joie de vivre
join
  joined
  join'er
joint
  joint'ed
  joint'ly
joist
  joist'ed
joke
  joked
  jo'ker
jol'ly
jolt
  jo'lted
jos'tle
  jos'tled
jot
jour'nal
jour'ney
  jour'neyed
joust
  joust'ed

joust'er
jowl
joy
judge
  judged
ju'do
jug'gle
  jug'gled
juice
  juic'y
jum'ble
  jum'bled
jum'bo
jump
  jumped
  jump'er
  jump'y
jun'gle
  jun'gly
junk
  junk'er
  junk'et
junta
junto
ju'ry
  ju'ries
  ju'ror
jus
just
  just'ly
jut
  jutt'ed
jute
kaffiyeh
kail
kak'a
kale
kame

Kamerad
kamikaze
ka'pok
kap'pa
kar'ma
kar'ri
karst
kaur'i
kav'a
kay'ak
keck'le
kedge
keel
  keeled
keen
  keen'er
  keen'ly
keep
  keep'er
  kept
keg
kelp
kelt
ken
kepi
kerb
kerf
kern
ketch
ketch'up
ket'tle
key
  keyed
khak'i
khediv'e
kib'ble
kick
  kicked

KICKER

kick'er

kid
kid'dle
kill
  killed
  kill'er
kiln
ki'lo
kilt
  kilt'ed
kil'ter
kin
kind
  ki'ndly
kin'dle
  kin'dled
  kin'dler
king
  king'ly
kink
  kinked
  kink'y
ki'osk
kip
kirk
kir'tle
kish
kiss
  kissed
kit
  kitt'ed
kitch'en
kite
kith
kit'ty
ki'wi
klink'er
knack

knack'er
knag
knag'gy
knap
kna've
knead
  knead'ed
  knead'er
knee
kneel
knelt
knell
knife
  knifed
  knives
knight
  knight'ed
  knight'ly
knit
  knit'tle
knob
  knob'bly
knock
  knocked
  knock'er
knoll
knot
  knot'ty
knout
know
  knew
  known
knuck'le
  knuck'led
knurl
  knur'ly
kohl
kok'ra

kopje
kowtow
kraal
kris
krona
  kronen
krone
  kroner
ku'dos
ku'kri
la'bel
  la'belled
la'bia
  la'bial
  la'biate
  la'bium
la'bile
la'bour
  la'boured
  la'bourer
la'brum
lace
  laced
  la'cing
  la'cy
lach'es
lack
  lacked
  lack'ey
lad
lade
  la'ded
  la'den
  la'ding
la'dle
  la'dled
  la'dler
  la'dling

la'dy
 la'dies
lag
 lagged
lag'an
la'ger
lair
laird
laissez-faire
lake
la'ma
lamb
la'mé
lame
 lamed
 la'mely
la'mia
lamp
la'nate
lance
 lanced
 lanc'er
land
 land'ed
lane
lan'guage
lan'guid
 lan'guidly
lan'guish
 lan'guished
lan'guor
lank
 lank'y
la'nose
lap
 lapped
lapse
 lapsed

larch
lard
large
 larg'ely
 larghetto
 largo
lark
lar'va
lash
 lash'ed
 lash'er
lass
lasso
 lasso'er
last
 last'ed
 last'ly
latch
 latched
 latch'et
late
 la'tely
 la'tish
la'tent
 la'tence
 la'tency
la'tex
lath
lathe
lath'er
 lath'ered
laud
 laud'ed
laugh
 laughed
 laugh'er
launch
 launch'ed

launcher
launch'es
laur'el
lav'a
lave
 laved
 la'ver
 la'ving
law
lax
lax'ly
lay (v.)
 laid
 lain
 lay'er
lay (a.)
 la'ic
 la'ical
 la'icise
laze
 lazed
 la'zily
 la'zy
lea
lead
 led
 lead'er
 lead'en
lea.
 leaf'y
 leaves
league
 leagued
 leag'uer
leak
 leaked
 leak'y
lean

453

leaned
leant
leap
  leaped
  leap'er
  leapt
learn
  learned
  learn'er
  learnt
lease
  leased
  leas'er
  lessee'
  less'or
leash
  leashed
  leash'es
least
leath'er
  leath'ern
  leath'ery
leave
  left
  leav'en
  leav'ened
Lebensraum
lech'er
ledge
ledg'er
lee
leech
  leech'es
leek
leer
  leered
lees
leet
454

leg
  leg'gy
le'gal
  le'gally
  legal'ity
  le'gist
lega'te
legato
leg'end
legerdemain
leg'ible
  leg'ibly
le'gion
leis'ure
  leis'ured
  leis'urely
lem'on
le'mur
lend
  lend'er
  lent
length
  length'en
  length'y
le'nient
  le'nience
  le'niently
lens
  lens'es
lentamente
lentando
lento
leop'ard
lep'er
lese majesty
le'sion
less
  less'en

less'er
less'on
let
le'thal
  lethal'ity
lettre de cachet
lev'ée
lev'el
le'ver
  le'vered
lev'y
  lev'ied
lewd
  lewd'ly
liais'on
lia'na
li'bel
  li'belled
libid'o
libret'to
  libret'ti
  libret'tist
lic'it
  lic'itly
lick
  licked
  lick'er
lid
lido
lie
  li'ar
  lied
lief
lieg'e
lien
life
  lives
lift

lift'ed
lift'er
light
  li'ghted
  li'ghten
  li'ghter
  li'ghtly
  lit
like
  liked
  li'king
like
  li'kened
  li'kely
lilt
lil'y
limb
  limbed
lim'bo
lime
  limed
  li'ming
lim'it
limn
  limned
limp
  limped
  limp'ly
line
  lined
  li'ner
  li'ning
ling
lin'ger
  lin'gered
  lin'gerer
lin'gerie
lin'go

lingua franca
lin'gua
lin'gual
lin'gually
lin'guist
link
  linked
links
lint
  lint'er
li'on
lip
  lipped
liq'uate
  liqua'tion
liq'uefy
  liq'uefied
liqueur'
liq'uid
liq'uor
lira
lire
lisle
lisp
  lisped
  lisp'er
list
  list'ed
litch'i
lithe
lith'ic
lit're
lit'tle
live (to)
  lived
live
  li'vely
  li'ven

liv'er
liver-wurst
liv'id
llam'a
loach
load
  load'ed
  load'er
loaf (n.)
  loaves
loaf (v.)
  loafed
  loaf'er
loam
  loam'y
loan
  loaned
loathe
  loathed
lob
  lobbed
lob'by
lobe
  lobed
loch
lock
  locked
  lock'er
lock'et
locum tenens
lode
lodge
  lodged
  lodg'er
loft
  loft'ed
  loft'y
log

logged
loggia
log'ic
  logic'ian
loin
loll
  lolled
  loll'er
lone
  lo'nely
long
  longed
  lon'ger
longeron
loof'ah
look
  looked
loom
  loomed
loon
  loon'y
loop
  looped
loose
  loosed
  loos'er
  loos'ely
loot
  loot'ed
  loot'er
lop
  lopped
lope
  loped
  lo'ping
lord
  lord'ed
  lord'ly

lore
lorgn'ette
lor'ry
lo'ry
lose
  lo'sable
  lost
  lo'ser
  lo'sing
loss
lot
loth
loud
  loud'ly
lounge
  lounged
  loun'ger
louse
  lice
  lous'y
lout
louvre
love
  lov'able
  loved
  lov'er
  lov'ely
low
  low'ly
  low'er
  low'ered
loy'al
  loy'ally
luck
  luck'y
lu'cre
luff
  luffed

lug
  lugged
lull
  lulled
lump
  lumped
  lump'er
  lump'y
lunch
  lunched
  lunch'es
lung
lunge
  lunged
  lun'ger
  lun'ging
lurch
  lurched
  lurch'er
lure
  lured
  lu'ring
lurk
  lurked
  lurk'er
lus'cious
lush
  lush'ly
lust
  lust'ed
  lust'er
lus'tre
lus'ty
lute
lux
lux'ury
lycée
lye

lymph
lynch
  lynched
lynx
  lynx'es
lyre
lyr'ic
mace
macédoine
mache'te
mack'le
  mack'led
mac'le
  mac'led
macra'mé
mad
  mad'ly
mad'am
madame
mademoiselle
madge
mad'ia
mad'id
madon'na
maestoso
maestro
maf'ia
mag'ic
ma'gi
mag'ma
magnificat
magnum opus
mahjongg'
maid
  maid'en
maid'an
maig're
mail

mailed
maim
  maimed
main
  main'ly
main'or
maisonett'e
maître d'hôtel
maize
ma'jor
make
  made
  ma'ker
makimo'no
mal de mer
male
mala fide
mal'aise
ma'lar
ma'lic
malt
mañana
mane
  maned
manège
ma'nes
ma'nge
ma'ngy
man'gel-wur'zel
man'ger
man'gle
  man'gled
  man'gler
  man'gling
man'go
  man'goes
ma'nia
ma'niac

manly
man'na
mann'ed
man'or
manqué
manse
man'suetude
manteau
man'tle
man'y
man'yplies
map
  mapped
ma'ple
maquis
mar
  marred
mar'ble
  mar'bled
marc
march
  marched
  march'er
  march'es
mare
mar'id
mark
  marked
  mark'er
marl
  marled
marquise
marron glacé
mar'ry
marsh
  marsh'es
  marsh'y
mas'cle

mash

  mashed

  mash'er

  mash'es

mash'ie

mask

  masked

ma'son

  ma'sonry

mas'que

mass

  massed

masse

mass'if

mat

  mat'ted

match

  matched

  match'es

maté

mate

  ma'ted

  ma'ting

matelot

mater familias

materia medica

matinée

ma'trix

matt

maul

  mauled

maund

maun'dy

mauvaise honte

mauve

mavour'neen

maw

max'im

may

may'or

ma'ze

me judice

mea culpa

mead

meag're

  meag'rely

meal

  meal'y

mean

  meant

  mean'ly

meas'les

meas'ly

meas'ure

  meas'ured

  meas'urer

meat

  meaty

med'al

med'dle

  med'dled

meed

meek

  meek'ly

meet

  met

  meet'ly

mélange

meld

melée

mel'ic

mell

mel'on

melt

  melt'ed

mem'o

memoirs

ménage

mend

  mend'ed

  mend'er

men'hir

men'u

mer'cy

mere

  me'rely

merge

  merged

  mer'ging

mering'ue

mer'it

mer'ry

me'sa

mésalliance

mesdames

mesh

  meshed

  mesh'es

me'sne

mess

messieurs

met'al

metall'urgy

mete

  me'ted

me'ter

  me'tered

meth'od

meth'yl

métier

me'tre

metri'tis

met'tle

  met'tled

...ew	mil'lionth	mir'th
mewed	*milord*	mir'za
...ews	mil'reis	mise
...eze'rium	milt	*mise en scène*
...ez'zo	mime	mi'ser
...iaow'	mimed	mi'serly
...ias'ma	mi'mer	*misère*
mias'mal	mi'ming	*miserere*
...i'ca	mim'ic	miser'icord
...id	mi'na	miss
...id'dle	mince	missed
...id'dy	minced	miss'es
...idge	minc'er	miss'al
...id'get	mind	miss'el
...idinette	mi'nder	mis'sion
...idst	mine	mis'sioner
...ien	mi'nable	mist
...ight	mined	mis'ty
migh'ty	mi'ner	mite
	mi'ning	
...i'graine	minestro'ne	*mitrailleuse*
...ihrab'	min'gle	mi'tre
...il	min'gled	mi'tred
...ila'dy	min'gling	mix
...ilch	min'gy	mixed
...ild	min'im	mix'er
mi'ldly	min'ion	mix'es
...ile	mink	miz'zen
mi'ler	mi'nor	miz'zle
...ilk	mint	mne'me
milked	mint'ed	mne'mic
milk'er	mint'er	mnemon'ic
milk'y	mi'nus	moan
...ill	minx	moaned
milled	*mirabile dictu*	moan'er
mill'er	*mirabilia*	moat
millefiori	mire	moat'ed
mil'lion	mi'ry	mob

459

mobbed

mock

 mocked

 mock'er

mode

mod'el

moderato

mo'dus

modus operandi

modus vivendi

moil

 moiled

moir'a

moir

moist

 mois'ten

 moist'ly

mole

molest'

 molest'ed

 molest'er

mo'lten

 mo'lter

molto

mon'ad

mon'ey

 mon'eyed

mon'ger

mon'goose

mon'grel

monk

monk'ey

monseigneur

monsieur

monsignor

monsignore

month

 month'ly

mon'tre

mood

 mood'**y**

moon

moor

 moored

moose

moot

mop

 mopped

mope

 moped

mo'per

mo'ping

mo'pish

mo'ra

morain'e

mor'al

morass'

mo'ray

more

morel'

morgue

mo'ron

mor'phia

morse

mort

mosque

moss

most

 mo'stly

mot juste

mote

moth

moth'er

 moth'erly

moto perpetuo

mo'tor

mottle

 mottled

mot'to

mouchoir

mould

 mould'ed

 mould'er

 mould'y

moulin

moult

mound

mount

 mount'ed

mourn

 mourned

 mourn'er

mouse

 mice

 mous'er

 mous'y

mousse

mouss'eline

moustach'e

 moustach'ed

mouth

 mouth'ed

move

 moved

 mov'er

mow

 mow'ed

 mow'er

 mown

mozet'ta

much

muck

mud

 mud'dy

mud'dle
mudir'
muezz'in
muff
  muff'ed
muff'in
muf'fle
  muf'fled
muf'ti
mug
muggy
mulch
  mulch'ed
mulct
mule
  mu'lish
mull
  mulled
  mull'er
mul'lion
  mul'lioned
multum in parvo
mum
mum'ble
  mum'bled
mum'my
mump
  mumped
  mum'pish
mumps
munch
  munched
  munch'er
  munch'es
  mung'o
murk
  murk'y
mur'ra

mur'rain
mus'cle
  mus'cled
muse
  mused
  mu'ser
  mu'sing
mush
  mush'y
musk
  musk'y
muss'el
must
  mus'ty
mutatis mutandis
mute
  mu'ted
  mu'tely
mu'tual
mutuus consensus
muzz'le
  muzz'led
muzzy
mynheer'
myrrh
myth
  myth'ic
nab
  nabb'ed
na'bob
na'cre
  na'creous
na'crite
na'dir
nag
  nagged
nai'ad
nail

nailed
nai've
  nai'vely
  nai'vety
na'ked
  na'kedly
na'ker
name
  named
  na'mely
na'nism
  na'noid
nan'ny
nap
na'palm
nape
na'pery
nap'py
nard
na'res
  na'rial
  na'rine
na'sal
  na'sally
na'scency
  na'scent
nas'ty
na'sute
na'tal
  na'tant
natale solum
na'tion
  nat'ional
  nat'ionally
na'tive
na'trium
na'tron
nat'ty

461

na'ture
  na'tured
naught
naugh'ty
naus'ea
naut'ic
na'vy
  na'vies
na'val
na've
na'vel
na'vew
nav'vy
nawab'
naze
na'zir
ne plus ultra
ne temere
ne'ance
  nean'ic
neap
near
  nearby'
  near'ly
neat
  neat'ly
neb
neck
necro'sis
  necrot'ic
née
need
  need'ed
  need'y
need'le
neglect'
négligé
  négligée

ne'gro
  ne'gress
  ne'groid
  negroid'al
ne'gus
neigh
  neighed
  neith'er
ne'on
neph'ew
ne'reid
nerve
  nerv'y
ne'science
  ne'scient
nest
nes'tle
  nes'tled
net
  nett'ed
neth'er
nett
net'tle
  net'tled
neur'al
neur'on
nev'er
new
  new'ly
new'el
news
  new'sy
newt
next
nex'us
nib
  nibb'ed
nib'ble

nib'bled
nice
  ni'cely
  ni'cety
niche
nick
  nicked
  nick'er
nick'cl
nic'ol
nid
  nide
nidge
niece
nig'gle
  nig'gled
nigh
night
  ni'ghtly
ni'hil
nihil ad rem
nihil obstat
nil
nil desperandum
nim'ble
nimi'ety
n'importe
nine
  ninth
  ni'nthly
ni'nety
nin'ny
ninon'
nip
  nipped
  nip'py
nip'ple
ni'si

nisi prius
nit'id
ni'tre
nob'ble
  nob'bled
no'ble
  no'bly
noblesse oblige
nock
nod
nod'dle
nod'dy
node
  no'dal
nog
no'how
noise
  nois'y
noisett'e
nolens volens
nolo contendere
nom de guerre
nom de plume
nom'ic
non assumpsit
non compos
   -mentis
non est
non licet
non liquet
non obstante
non placet
non possumus
non prosequitur
non sequitur
nonce
none
non'such

nood'le
  nood'les
nook
noon
noose
norm
north
  north'ern
nose
  nosed
  no'sing
nota bene
notch
  notched
  notch'es
note
  no'ted
  no'ting
noth'ing
nought
noun
  noun'al
nour'ish
  nour'ished
nous
nouveau riche
no'va
nov'el
  nov'elty
novel'la
nowed
now'el
now'y
now'yed
nox'a
  nox'al
nox'ious
  nox'iously

noyan
noz'zle
  noz'zled
nude
nudge
  nudg'ed
  nudg'er
null
nulle secundus
numb
  numb'ed
  numb'ly
nun
nunc dimitis
nurse
  nursed
nut
  nut'ty
nux vomica
nuz'zle
  nuz'zled
nymph
  nym'pha
  nym'phal
oak
  oak'en
  oak'um
oar
  oar'ed
oa'sis
  oa'ses
oast
oat
  oat'en
oath
obe'ah
obe'se
obey'

obey'ed
ob'it
obiter
obiter dictum
objet d'art
obli'ge
  obli'ged
  obli'ger
obli'que
  obli'quely
o'boe
o'cean
  ocean'ic
oc'elot
o'chre
  ochra'ceous
odd
  odd'ly
ode
  od'ic
  o'dist
o'dium
o'dour
oede'ma
oer'sted
off'al
of'ten
o'gee
og'ham
o'give
  ogi'val
o'gle
  o'gled
  o'gling
o'gre
  o'gress
ohm
  ohm'ic

oil
oiled
oil'er
oil'y
okap'i
old
  o'lden
olea'ceous
o'leate
olefi'ant
o'lefine
o'lein
ole'ic
o'lent
o'leo
ol'id
o'lio
ol'la
oma'sum
om'bre
o'mega
om'elet
  omelett'e
o'men
o'mer
omi'cron
omit'
on dit
once
oneir'ic
on'ion
only
on'to
o'nus
on'yx
oog'amy
oog'eny
  oogenet'ic

ooid'al
o'olite
oolit'ic
ool'ogy
ool'ong
oom'eter
oothe'ca
ooze
  oozed
  ooz'ily
  ooz'y
o'pal
opa'que
  opa'quely
o'pen
  o'pened
  o'pener
  o'penly
ophit'ic
opi'ne
  opi'ned
opin'ion
  opin'ioned
o'pium
oposs'um
opt
  opt'ed
op'time
o'pus
opus probandi
opus'cle
  opus'cule
o'ral
  o'rally
o'rant
ora'rian
ora'rion
ora'rium

ora'te
  ora'ted
  ora'tion
orb
  orbed
orc
ore
ore rotundo
o'read
orfe
or'gy
o'riel
o'rient
o'riole
o'rotund
or'yx
o'sier
ossia
ostinato
os'tier
oth'er
o'tic
o'tiose
  otios'ity
oti'tis
ot'tar
ottava rima
ot'ter
oubliett'e
ought
oui'ja
ounce
our
ous'el
oust
  oust'ed
  oust'er
out

out'er
outré
ouz'el
ouz'o
o'va
o'val
o'vate
o'void
ova'tion
o'vary
  ova'rian
ov'en
o'ver
  o'verly
o'vert
  o'vertly
o'vine
o'vist
ovo'lo
o'vule
o'vum
owe
  owed
owl
  owl'et
own
  owned
  own'er
ox
  ox'en
oy'er
oyez'
o'zone
pac'a
pace
  pa'cer
  pa'cing
pac'ify

pack
  packed
  pack'er
  pack'et
pact
pad
  pad'dle
  pad'dled
  pad'dy
padre
padrone
pae'an
  pae'on
pae'ony
pa'gan
pag'eant
  pag'eantry
page
  paged
  pa'ger
  pa'ging
pail
paillette
paillon
pain
  pained
paint
  paint'ed
  paint'er
pair
  paired
paie
  paled
  pa'lish
palea'ceous
pa'ling
pall
  palled

465

palm
  palm**'y**
palm**'er**
palp
pals**'tave**
pals**'y**
  pals**'ied**
palt**'er**
palt**'ry**
pan
  panned
panach**'e**
pan**'da**
pane
  paned
pan**'el**
pang
pan**'ic**
  pan**'icky**
pan**'sy**
  pan**'sies**
pant
  pant**'ed**
pants
papa**'in**
papaw**'**
papa**'ya**
pa**'per**
  pa**'pery**
papier-mâché
par
par avion
par excellence
par exemple
para**'**
parch
  parched
pare

pared
pa**'rer**
pa**'ring**
pa**'rent**
parfait
par**'iah**
pari passu
park
  parked
par**'ka**
parr
par**'ry**
pars**'e**
  pars**'ed**
par**'sley**
part
  part**'ed**
  part**'ly**
parti
parti pris
partim
par**'ty**
pas de deux
pass
  passed
  pass**'er**
passé
pass**'im**
pas**'sion**
past
pa**'ste**
  pa**'sted**
  pa**'ster**
  pa**'sting**
pa**'stry**
  pa**'stries**
pa**'sty (a.)**
pas**'ty (n.)**

pat
patch
  patched
  patch**'er**
  patch**'es**
  patch**'y**
patchouli
pate
pâté de foie   *gras*
pat**'en**
pa**'tent**
  pa**'tency**
  patentee**'**
  pa**'tently**
  pa**'tentor**
pa**'ter**
pater familias
pater noster
path
pa**'thos**
pa**'tience**
pa**'tient**
pat**'io**
patisserie
pat**'ois**
pa**'triot**
pa**'tron**
patte
pat**'ty**
pauc**'ity**
paunch
  paunch**'y**
paup**'er**
pause
  paus**'al**
pavan**'e**
pave

paved
pa'ving
pavé
pav'id
paw
pawed
pawl
pawn
pawned
pawnee'
pawn'er
pax
pax vobiscum
pay
paid
payee'
pay'er
pea
peace
peach
peak
peaked
peak'y
peal
pealed
pean
pear
pearl
pear'ler
pear'ly
peas'ant
peas'antry
peat
peat'y
peb'ble
peb'bled
pecan'
peccavi

peck
pecked
peck'er
pecu'liar
peculiar'ity
pecu'liarly
ped'al
ped'dle
ped'dled
peel
peeled
peel'er
peep
peeped
peep'er
peer
peered
peg
pegged
peg'gy
peignoir
pelt
pelt'ry
pen
penned
pent
pe'nal
pe'nally
penates
penchant
pend
pen'na
pen'ny
penseroso
pe'on
peop'le
peop'led
peop'ling

per annum
per capita
per cent
per contra
per curiam
per diem
per mensem
per se
per stirpes
perch
perched
perch'er
perch'es
perdendo
perdu
pe'ri
per'il
per'illed
pe'riod
period'ic
perk
perk'y
perpetuum mobile
per'ry
perse
persona grata
persona non grata
pert
pert'ly
pesante
peseta
peso
pest
pest'er
pes'tle
pet
pet'al
pe'ter

467

pe'tered

petit

petite

petitio principii

pet'ty

pew

peyote

phaet'on

phase

pha'sic

pheas'ant

pheas'antry

phen'yl

phe'on

phi'al

phi'alled

phil'tre

phlegm

phlo'em

phon

phon'ic

phot

pho'to

phrase

phra'sal

phrased

phra'try

phren'ic

phthal'ic

phthal'in

phys'ic

pia mater

pi'al

pianissimo

pia'no

piano'la

piassav'a

piastre

468

piaz'za

pi'broch

pi'ca

pice

pic'eous

pick

picked

pick'er

pick'et

pick'le

pick'led

pic'ot

picque

picqued

picq'uet

pic'ul

pid'dle

pid'dled

pidg'in

pie

piece

pieced

piec'er

pièce de

résistance

pied

pied à terre

piend

pier

pierce

pierced

pierc'er

pif'fle

pig

pig'eon

pign'on

pike

pilaff'

pillau'

pilch

pile

piled

pi'ling

pill

pil'lion

pi'lot

pimp

pim'ple

pim'pled

pim'ply

pin

pinned

pince-nez

pinch

pinched

pinch'er

pinch'es

pine

pined

pi'nery

ping

pinged

pin'guid

pin'guefy

pinguid'ity

pin'guin

pin'ion

pin'ioned

pink

pin'na

pino'le

pint

pin'tle

pin'to

pip

pipped

pipe
  piped
  pi'per
  pi'ping
pip'it
piq'uancy
  piq'uant
pique
  piqued
piquet'
pirag'ua
piran'ha
pis aller
pit
pitch
  pitched
  pitch'er
pith
  pith'y
pith'os
piton
pit'y
piu mosso
piv'ot
pix'ie
  pix'y
pizzicato
place
  placed
  pla'cer
  pla'cing
placet
plac'id
  plac'idly
plack'et
plafond
pla'gal
pla'gium

plague
  plagued
  pla'guily
  pla'guy
plaice
plaid
plain
  plain'ly
plaint
plait
  plait'ed
plan
  planned
pla'nar
  planar'ity
planchet'
  planchett'e
plane
  planed
  pla'ner
plan'et
plank
plant
  plant'ed
  plant'er
plaque
plash
  plashed
plasm
  plas'ma
plat
plate
  pla'ted
  pla'ter
  pla'ting
plat'en
plaud'it
play

played
play'er
plaz'a
plea
plead
  plead'ed
  plead'er
pled
pleach
pleas'ance
  pleas'ant
  pleas'antly
  pleas'antries
  pleas'antry
plea'se
pleas'ure
pleat
  pleat'ed
pledge
  pledged
  pledgee'
  pledg'er
  pledg'et
pleno jure
plen'ty
pleur'a
  pleur'al
plex'or
plex'us
pli'ca
plight
  pli'ghted
  pli'ghter
plinth
plod
plop
  plopped
plot

plough
ploughed
plough'er
plov'er
ploy
pluck
plucked
pluck'y
plug
plugged
plum
plumb
plumbed
plumb'er
plume
plumed
plump
plumped
plump'er
plunge
plunged
plun'ger
plunk
plunked
plu'ral
plus
plush
plush'y
ply
plies
plied
pli'er
pneuma
poach
poached
poach'er
pochett'e
pock

pock'et
poco
pod
podg'y
po'em
po'et
poilu
poind
poind'ed
poind'er
poind'ing
point
point'ed
point'er
point-device
point'el
poise
poised
pois'on
pois'oned
pois'oner
poke
poked
po'ker
po'king
po'ky
po'lar
po'lder
pole
poled
po'ling
poli'ce
poll'cing
politesse
politique
po'lka
poll
po'lled

po'ller
poll'ee
po'lo
polo'ny
pol'yp
pomp
pond
pon'iard
po'ny
po'nies
pood
pood'le
pool
pooled
poop
poor
poor'ly
pop
popped
pop'py
porch
po'rches
pore
pored
po'ring
pork
po'rker
po'rky
port
po'rtal
portamento
portemonnaie
po'rter
portière
po'rtion
po'rtioned
po'rtioner
po'rtly

470

po'rtrait
portray'
  portray'al
    portray'ed
posaun'e
pose
  posed
  po'ser
  po'sing
poseur'
pos'it
poss'e
poss'et
post
  po'stal
  po'sted
  po'ster
post meridiem
post obitum
poste restante
po'sy
pot
pot pourri
potage
poth'er
pouch
  pouched
pouffe'e
poult
  poult'ry
pounce
  pounced
pound
  pound'ed
  pound'er
pour
  poured
  pour'er

pout
  pout'ed
  pout'er
pow'er
  pow'ered
pox
prair'ie
praise
  praised
pram
prance
  pranced
  pranc'er
prank
prate
  pra'ted
  pra'ting
prat'tle
  prat'tled
prawn
pray
  prayed
  pray'er
preach
  preached
  preach'er
prec'edent
prec'ious
preen
  preened
première
pre science
  pre'scient
press
  pressed
  press'er
prestissimo
presto

prett'y
  prett'ify
  prett'ily
prey
  preyed
price
  priced
  pri'cing
prick
  pricked
  prick'er
  prick'ly
pride
  pri'ded
  pri'ding
prie-dieu
priest
  priest'ly
prig
prim
prima donna
prima facie
prime
  primed
  pri'mely
  pri'mer
  pri'ming
primo
pri'mus
prince
  prin'cely
prink
  prinked
print
  print'ed
  print'er
pri'or
prise

prised
pri'sing
pris'm
pris'on
priv'et
priv'y
prize
  prized
pro bono publico
pro forma
pro patria
pro tempore
probatum est
probe
  probed
  pro'bing
prod
pro'em
prof'it
prog'eny
prompt
  prompt'ed
  prompt'er
  prompt'ly
prone
prong
  pronged
pronunciamento
proof
  proofed
  proof'er
prop
  propped
prop'er
proph'et
prose
  pro'sily
  pro'sy

protégé
protègèe
proud
  proud'ly
prove
  prov'able
  proved
  prov'en
  prov'ing
provost marshal
prow
prowl
  prowled
  prowl'er
proximo
prox'y
prude
prune
  pruned
  pru'ner
psy'che
pter'in
pry
  pried
  pries
psalm
puce
puck
  puck'er
pu'dding
pud'dle
  pud'dly
pudg'y
puff
  puffed
  puff'er
  puff'y
pug

puke
  puked
  pu'king
pule
  pu'ling
pull
  pulled
  pull'et
  pull'ey
pulp
  pulped
  pulp'er
  pulp'y
pu'lpit
pulse
  pulsed
pu'ma
pump
  pumped
  pump'er
pun
  punned
punch
  punched
  punch'er
punk'ah
punt
  punt'er
pu'ny
pup
  pupped
  pup'py
pu'pa
pure
  pu'rely
pur'fle
purge
  purged

purg'er
pur'im
purl
  purled
  pur'ler
pur'ple
  pur'ply
pun
  punned
purr
  purred
purse
  pursed
  purs'y
purs'er
pur'vey (v.)
pus
push
  pushed
  pu'sher
puss
put
pu'trefy
putt
  putt'ed
  putt'er
  putt'ing
putt'y
puz'zle
  puz'zled
pyg'my
pyjam'as
pyre
pyx
quack
  quacked
quadrill'e
quaff

quaffed
quag
quag'ga
quail
  quailed
quaint
  quaint'ly
quake
  quaked
qualm
quant
quar'ry
  quar'ried
quart
quart'o
quartz
quash
  quashed
quasi
quas'sia
qua'ver
  qua'vered
  qua'very
quay
quean
queas'y
queen
  queened
  queen'ly
queer
  queer'ly
quell
  quelled
quench
  quenched
  quench'er
quern
que'ry

que'ried
quest
queue
  queued
qui vive
quib'ble
  quib'bled
quick
  quick'en
  quick'ly
quid
quid pro quo
quiesc'e
qui'et
  qui'eten
  qui'etly
quie'tus
quiff
quill
  quill'er
quilt
qui'nary
  qui'nate
quince
quin'ol
quin'sy
quip
  quipp'ed
quire
quirk
quirt
quit
quitch
quite
quiv'er
quiz
  quizzed
quo jure

quo vadis
quo warranto
quoad
quod erat
demonstrandum
(*QED*)
quod erat
faciendum (*QEF*)
quod vide (*q.v.*)
quoin
quoit
quo'ta
quote
  quo'ted
rab'bi
rab'ble
rab'id
ra'bies
race
  raced
  ra'cer
  ra'cing
ra'cial
  ra'cially
ra'cism
  ra'cist
ra'cy
rack
  racked
rack'et
raconteur'
ra'dar
rad'dle
  rad'dled
ra'dio
ra'dium
ra'dius
  ra'dial

ra'dian
ra'dii
ra'dix
ra'dome
raf'fle
  raf'fled
raft
rag
rage
  raged
  ra'ging
ragoût
raid
  raid'ed
  raid'er
rail
  railed
rain
  rained
  rain'y
raise
  raised
  rais'in
raison d'être
rake
  raked
  ra'ker
  ra'king
  ra'kish
rallentando
ral'ly
ram
  rammed
ram'ble
  ram'bled
ramp
  ramped
ranch

ranch'er
ranc'our
range
  ranged
  ra'nger
  ra'nging
  ra'ngy
rank
  ranked
  rank'er
rank'le
  rank'led
  rank'ly
rant
  rant'ed
  rant'er
rap
  rapped
rape
  raped
  ra'per
  ra'ping
rap'id
ra'pier
rapport
rapprochement
rapt
  rapt'ly
rara avis
rare
  ra'rely
  ra'rity
ra'refy
  ra'refied
rash
  rash'ly
rasp
  rasped

rat

ratch

  ratch'et

rate

  ra'ted

  ra'ting

ra'ther

ra'tio

rat'ion

  rat'ioned

rat'ional

rat'tle

  rat'tled

rave

  raved

  ra'ving

rav'el

ra'ven

raw

  raw'ly

ray

ray'on

raze

  razed

ra'zor

reach

  reached

  reach'es

read

  read'er

read'y

  read'ily

real

  real'ly

realm

ream

reap

  reaped

reap'er

rear

  rear'ed

reas'on

  reas'oned

  reas'oner

reb'el (n. & a.)

rebel' (v.)

réchauffé

récherché

rec'ipe

recitative

recitativo

reck

reck'on

  reck'oned

reclu'se

recto

red

redan'

redd

reductio ad

      absurdum

reed

  reed'ed

  reed'y

reef

  reefed

  reef'er

reek

  reeked

reel

  reeled

reeve

reft

regat'ta

régime

regius

reign

  reigned

rein

  reined

rel'ic

rely'

rencontre

rend

rendezvous

rent

  rent'al

  rent'ed

rente

rentier

req'uiem

requiescat in

           pace

rese'da

res'in

rest

  rest'ed

résumé

retch

  retched

retour

retroussé

reveille

rev'el

revers'

rhe'a

rheum

  rheum'y

rhex'is

rhomb

rhyme

  rhymed

  rhy'mer

rhyth'm

rib

  ribbed

rice

ricercare

rich

  rich'es

  rich'ly

rick

  ricked

ric'ochet

  ric'ocheted

rid

rid'dle

  rid'dled

ride

  ri'der

  ri'ding

  rode

ridge

  ridged

  ridg'y

rifacimento

rife

rif'fle

  rif'fled

ri'fle

  ri'fled

  ri'fling

rift

rig

  rigged

right

  ri'ghtly

ri'ghteous

  ri'ghteously

rig'id

  rig'idly

ri'gor

rigor mortis

rile

  ri'led

  ri'ling

rill

rim

  rimmed

rime

rind

ring

  rang

  ringed

  ring'er

rink

rinse

  rinsed

  rins'er

ri'ot

rip

  ripped

ripe

  ri'pen

ripo'ste

rip'ple

  rip'pled

rise

  ris'en

  ri'ser

  ri'sing

ri'sible

risk

  risk'y

risoluto

risorgimento

risotto

risqué

rite

ri'val

ri'valled

ri'valry

rive

  riv'en

riv'er

riv'et

roach

road

roam

  roamed

  roam'er

roan

roar

  roar'er

roast

  roast'ed

  roast'er

rob

  robbed

robe

  ro'bed

  ro'bing

rob'in

ro'bot

rock

  rocked

  rock'er

  rock'y

rock'et

rod

ro'dent

ro'deo

roe

rogue

  ro'guery

  ro'guish

role

roll

rolled
ro'ller
romp
romped
romp'er
ronde
rondo
rone
rood
roof
roofed
rook
room
roomed
room'y
roost
roost'er
root
root'ed
rope
roped
ro'ping
ro'pery
rose
ro'sery
ro'sy
ro'sily
ros'in
rot
ro'ta
rote
rôtisserie
roub'le
roué
rouge
roug'ing
rough
rough'en

rough'ly
roulade
round
round'ed
round'er
round'ly
rouse
roused
rous'er
rout
rout'ed
route
roux
rove
roved
ro'ver
row
rowed
row'er
row'ing
row'an
row'dy
rowd'ily
row'el
row'elled
roy'al
rub
rubbed
rubato
rub'ble
ru'ble
ru'by
ru'befy
ru'bies
ruche
ruched
ruck
rucked

rud'dy
rude
ru'dely
rue
rued
ruff
ruffed
ruf'fle
ruf'fled
rug
ru'in
ru'ined
rule
ruled
ru'ler
rum
rum'my
rum'ba
rum'ble
rum'bled
rump
rum'ple
rum'pled
run
rune
runk'le
runk'led
runt
runt'y
ruse
rush
rushed
rush'er
rush'es
rush'y
rusk
russ'et
rust

rust'y

rus'tle
  rus'tled

rut
  rut'ty

ruth

rye

sa'ble

sab'ot

sa'bre

sac

sach'et

sack
  sacked

sacra'rium

sa'cred

sa'cring

sa'crist

sa'crum
  sa'cral

sad

sad'ly

sad'dle
  sad'dled

sa'dism
  sa'dist

safe
  sa'fely
  sa'fety

sag
  sagged

sag'a

sage
  sa'gely

sa'go

sail
  sailed
  sail'or

saint
  saint'ed
  saint'ly

sake

sa'ke

sa'ker

sak'i

sal'ad

sale

sal'ep

sa'lience
  sa'lient

sa'line

sal'ly
  sal'lied

sal'mi

salm'on

sal'on

salt
  salt'ed
  salt'er
  salt'y

saltando

saltato

salve
  salved
  salv'or

sal'vo

sam'ba

sam'ple
  sam'pled

sanctus

sand
  sand'ed
  sand'y

sane
  sa'nely

sang'froid

san'guine

sans souci

sap
  sapped
  sap'py

sap'id

sa'pience
  sa'pient

sa'por

sard

sar'i

sash
  sashed
  sash'es

satch'el

sate
  sa'ted
  sa'ting

sa'tiate
  sa'tiable
  sa'tiated

satia'tion

sat'in

sa'tive

sat'yr

sauce
  sauc'y
  sauc'er

Sauerbraten

Sauerkraut

sauna

sauté

sautereau'

sauterell'e

sauve-qui-peut

sauvegarde

save
  sa'vable

saved
sa'ver
sa'ving
sa'viour
savoir-faire
savoir-vivre
sa'vory
sa'vour
sa'voury
saw
  sawed
  saw'er
  sawn
say
  said
scab
  scabbed
  scab'by
sca'bies
scad
scagl'ia
scagl'iola
sca'la
sca'lar
sca'lary
scaid
  scald'ed
  scald'er
scale
  sca'lable
  scaled
  sca'ling
sca'lene
sca'ler
scal'lion
sca'ly
scalp
  scalped

scamble
scamp
  scamped
scan
  scanned
scant
  scant'ily
  scant'y
scan'tle
scape
sca'pha
scar
  scarred
scar'ab
scarce
  sca'rcely
  sca'rcity
scare
  scared
  sca'ring
scarf
  scarves
scarp
  scarped
sca'thing
scaup'er
sce'na
scene
sce'nic
scent
  scent'ed
scep'tre
  scep'tral
  scep'tred
sche'ma
scheme
  schemed
  sche'mer

scherzando
scherzo
schism
schist
schnapps
Schnitzel
schol'ar
scho'lia
school
  schooled
schoon'er
schottische
sci'on
scis'sion
scle'ral
scoff
  scoffed
  scoff'er
scold
  sco'lded
sconce
scone
scoop
  scooped
  scoop'er
scoot'er
scope
scorch
  scorched
  scorch'er
  scorch'es
score
  scored
  sco'rer
scorn
  scorned
  scorn'er
scotch

479

scotched
scour
scoured
scour'er
scourge
scourged
scourg'er
scout
scout'ed
scowl
scowled
scrab'ble
scrab'bled
scrag
scragg'ed
scrag'gy
scrag'gly
scram'ble
scram'bled
scrap
scrapped
scrap'py
scrape
scraped
scra'per
scra'ping
scratch
scratch'es
scratched
scratch'er
scratch'y
scrawl
scrawled
scraw'ny
scream
screamed
scream'er
scree
480

screech
screeched
screech'er
screech'y
screed
screen
screened
screen'er
screw
screwed
scrib'ble
scrib'bled
scribe
scri'bal
scri'ber
scri'bing
scrim
scrimp
scrimped
scrimp'y
scrip
script
scroll
scrolled
scrounge
scrounged
scroung'er
scrub
scrubbed
scrub'by
scruff
scruff'y
scrum
scru'ple
scru'pled
scud
scuff
scuffed

scuf'fle
scuf'fled
scull
sculled
scull'er
scul'lion
sculpsit
sculpserunt
scum
scum'my
scurf
scur'fy
scur'ry
scur'vy
scut
scutch
scutch'er
scutch'eon
scut'tle
scut'tled
scythe
scythed
sea
seal
sealed
seam
seamed
seam'y
se'ance
sear
seared
search
searched
search'er
seas'on
seas'onal
seas'oned
seat

seat'ed

seat'er

se'bum

sec

secco

se'cret

  se'cretly

sect

secundo

secundum

sedan'

sederunt

sedge

see

  saw

  seen

  seer

seed

seed'ed

seed'y

seek

  seek'er

  sought

seem

  seemed

  seem'ly

seep

  seeped

seethe

  seethed

segno

segue

seigneur

  seigneural

seise

  seised

  seis'in

seize

seized

seiz'er

seiz'or

sell

  sell'er

  sold

sem'ble

semper idem

semper vivum

semplice

sempre

sen

send

  send'er

senhor

senhora

senhorita

se'nile

se'nior

sen'na

señor

señora

señorita

sense

  sensed

sent

sep'al

se'pia

se'poy

sept

sequa'cious

  sequac'ity

seraglio

sera'i

serang'

se're

serf

serge

ser'geant

  ser'geancy

se'rial

  se'rially

se'ries

ser'if

ser'in

se'rio-comic

serioso

se'rious

  se'riously

se'rum

serve

ses'ame

ses'sion

  ses'sional

set

sett

set'tle

  set'tled

sev'en

sev'er

seve're

  seve'rely

  sever'ity

sew

  sewed

  sewn

sew'age

  sew'er

sex

  sexed

  sex'y

sforzando

shab'by

shack

shack'le

  shack'led

shad
shade
  sha'ded
  sha'ding
  sha'dy
shad'ow
shaft
  shaft'ed
shag
  shag'gy
shake
  sha'ken
  sha'ker
  sha'ky
shak'o
shale
  sha'ly
shall
sham
sham'ble
  sham'bled
  sham'bles
shame
  shamed
  sha'ming
shank
  shank'ed
shan'ty
shape
  shaped
  sha'pely
  sha'per
  sha'ping
shard
share
  sha'red
  sha'rer
  sha'ring

shark
sharp
  sharp'en
  sharp'er
  sharp'ly
shave
  sha'ved
  sha'ven
  sha'ver
shawl
sheaf
  sheav'es
shear
  sheared
  shear'er
  shorn
sheath
  sheathed
sheave
shed
sheen
sheep
sheer
  sheer'ly
sheet
  sheet'ed
sheikh
shek'el
shelf
  shelv'es
shell
  shelled
shelve
  shelved
  shelv'er
shep'herd
sher'ry
shield

shield'ed
shiel'ing
shift
  shift'ed
  shift'er
  shift'y
shin
  shinned
shine
  shone
shin'gle
  shin'gled
  shin'gles
  shin'ty
ship
  shipped
shirk
  shirked
  shirk'er
shirr
  shirred
shirt
shiv'er
shoal
shock
  shocked
  shock'er
shod
shod'dy
shoe
shoot
  shoot'er
  shot
shop
  shopped
shore
  shored
short

short'en
short'ly
should
shoul'der
shoul'dered
shout
shout'ed
shove
shoved
shov'el
show
showed
shown
show'y
show'er
show'ery
shred
shrew
shrewd
shrewd'ly
shriek
shrieked
shrike
shrill
shrill'y
shrimp
shrine
shrink
shrank
shrunk
shrunk'en
shrive
shriv'en
shri'ving
shriv'el
shroud
shroud'ed
shrub

shrub'by
shrug
shrugged
shuf'fle
shuf'fled
shun
shunned
shunt
shunt'ed
shunt'er
shut
shut'tle
shut'tled
shy
shied
shies
shy'ly
sib'yl
sic
sick
sick'en
sick'ly
sick'le
side
si'ded
si'ding
side'real
si'dle
si'dled
si'dling
siege
sien'na
sier'ra
sies'ta
sieve
sieved
sift
sift'ed

sift'er
sigh
sighed
sight
si'ghted
si'ghter
si'ghtly
sig'il
sig'ma
sign
signed
si'gner
signor
signora
signore
signorina
si'lage
si'lence
si'lenced
si'lencer
si'lent
si'lently
si'lex
silic'ify
silk
silk'en
silk'y
sill
sil'ly
si'lo
silt
silt'y
simpatico
sim'ple
sim'ply
sin
since
sine

483

sine die
sine qua non
  sin'ew
  sin'ewed
  sin'ewy
sinfonia
sing
  sang
  sing'er
  song
  sung
singe
  singed
sin'gle
  sin'gled
  sin'gling
  sin'gly
sin'glet
Singspiel
sink
  sank
  sink'er
  sunk
si'nus
  si'nuses
sip
  sipped
si'phon
  si'phonal
  si'phoned
  siphon'ic
sire
  sired
  si'ring
si'ren
si'sal
sit
  sat

site
  si'ted
six
  sixth
  six'ty
size
  sized
  si'zer
  si'zing
  siz'zle
  siz'zled
skate
  ska'ted
  ska'ter
  ska'ting
skein
skep
sker'ry
sketch
  sketched
  sketch'er
  sketch'es
  sketch'y
skew
  skew'er
ski
  ski'er
skid
skiff
skill
  skilled
skimp
  skimped
  skimp'y
skin
  skinned
  skin'ny
skip

skipped
skirt
  skirt'ed
skit
  skit'tle
skoal
sku'a
skulk
  skulked
  skulk'er
skull
skunk
sky
slab
  slabbed
slack
  slacked
  slack'en
  slack'er
  slack'ly
slag
slake
  slaked
slam
  slammed
slang
  slanged
slant
  slant'ed
slap
  slapped
slash
  slashed
  slash'er
  slash'es
slat
slate
  sla'ted

sla'ter
sla'ting
sla'ty
slave
slaved
sla'very
sla'ving
sla'vish
sla'ver
sla'vered
slay
slay'er
sleave
sleaved
sleaz'y
sledge
sleek
sleek'ly
sleep
sleep'er
sleep'y
slept
sleet
sleet'y
sleeve
sleeved
sleigh
sleight
sleuth
slew
slewed
slice
sliced
sli'cer
sli'cing
slick
slick'ly
slide

slid
sli'der
sli'ding
slight
sli'ghted
sli'ghtly
slim
slimmed
slime
sli'my
sling
slung
slink
slink'y
slunk
slip
slipped
slip'py
slipe
slit
slith'er
sliv'er
sloe
slog
slogged
slo'gan
sloop
slop
slopped
slop'py
slope
sloped
slo'ping
slot
sloth
slouch
slouched
slouch'er

slough
sloughed
slov'en
slov'enly
slow
slowed
slow'ly
slub
slubbed
sludge
sludg'er
sludg'y
slug
slugged
sluice
sluiced
slum
slump
slumped
slur
slurred
slur'ry
slush
slush'y
slut
sly
sli'ly
sly'ly
smack
smacked
small
smart
smart'ed
smart'en
smart'ly
smash
smashed
smell

smelled

smell'y

smelt

smelt

smelt'ed

smelt'er

smi'lax

smile

smiled

smi'ler

smirch

smirched

smite

smote

smith

smith'y

smock

smocked

smog

smoke

smoked

smo'ker

smo'ky

smolt

smooth

smoothed

smooth'er

smooth'ly

smoth'er

smoth'ered

smould'er

smould'ered

smudge

smudged

smudg'y

smug

smug'ly

smug'gle

smug'gled

smut

smut'ty

snack

snaf'fle

snaf'fled

snag

snagged

snag'gy

snail

snake

sna'kily

sna'kish

sna'ky

snap

snapped

snap'py

snare

snared

sna'ring

snarl

snarl'ed

snatch

snatched

snatch'er

snatch'es

sneak

sneaked

sneak'y

sneer

sneered

sneer'er

sneeze

sneezed

sneez'er

sneez'y

snick

snicked

snick'er

sniff

sniffed

sniff'er

sniff'le

snip

snipped

snipe

sniped

sni'per

sni'ping

sniv'el

snob

snood

snook'er

snoop

snooped

snoop'er

snooze

snoozed

snore

snored

sno'rer

sno'ring

snort

snort'ed

snort'er

snout

snow

snowed

snow'y

snub

snubbed

snuff

snuffed

snuff'er

snuf'fle

snuf'fled

snuff'ly

snug

   snug'ly

soak

   soaked

soap

   soaped

   soap'y

soar

   soared

sob

   sobbed

sobe'it

so'ber

   so'berly

so'briquet

so'cial

   so'ciable

   so'cially

sock

sock'et

sod

so'da

so'fa

soft

   soft'ly

soft'en

   soft'ened

   soft'ener

sog'gy

soi-disant

soigné

soil

   soiled

soirée

sol'der

   so'ldered

sol'dier

so'ldierly

so'ldiery

sole (a. v.)

   so'lely

   so'ling

sol'fa

sol'id

so'lo

solve

   solv'ed

   solv'er

som'bre

   som'brely

some

son

sonatina

son'ic

soon

soot

   soot'y

sooth

soothe

   sooth'ed

   sooth'er

sop

   sopp'ed

   sop'py

sore

   so'rely

sor'ry

sort

   sort'er

sostenuto

sotto voce

soubrette

soufflé

sound

   sound'er

sound'ly

soupçon

sour

   soured

   sour'ly

souse

   soused

soutan'e

souterrain

south

   south'erly

   south'ern

   south'erner

sow

   sowed

   sow'er

   sow'ing

   sown

soy'a

space

   spaced

   spa'cer

   spa'cing

   spa'cious

spade

   spa'ded

   spa'ding

spa'dix

   spadic'eous

   spa'dices

span

   spanned

span'gle

   span'gled

span'iel

spank

   spanked

   spank'er

spar
  sparred
spare
  spared
  spa'rely
  spa'ring
spark
  sparked
spar'kle
  spar'kled
  spar'kler
sparse
  spars'ely
spasm
spate
spathe
  spathed
  spath'ic
spa'tial
  spa'tially
spav'in
spawn
  spawned
speak
  speak'er
  spoke
  spo'ken
spear
  speared
spec'ial
  special'ity
  spec'ially
spe'cie
spe'cies
spec'ify
  specif'ic
spe'cious
speck

speck'le
  speck'led
spec'tre
speech
  speech'es
speed
  sped
  speed'er
  speed'y
spell
  spelled
  spell'er
  spelt
spend
  spend'er
  spent
sperm
spew
sphere
  sphe'ral
  spher'ic
sphinx
spi'ca
spiccato
spice
  spiced
  spi'cily
  spi'cing
  spi'cy
spi'der
  spi'dery
spig'ot
spike
  spiked
  spi'king
  spi'ky
spill
  spilled

spill'er
  spilt
spilo'ma
spin
  spun
spin'dle
spine
  spi'nal
  spi'nate
  spi'nous
  spi'ny
spinel'
  spin'et
spinesc'ence
  spinesc'ent
spi'node
spi'racle
spirae'a
spi'ral
  spi'ralled
  spi'rally
spi'rant
spire
  spired
spir'it
  spiritoso
spit
  spat
spite
  spi'ted
  spi'ting
spit'tle
splash
  splashed
  splash'er
  splash'es
  splash'y
splay

splayed	sprawled	spies
spleen	sprawl'er	spied
splen'ic	spray	squab
sple'nium	sprayed	squab'ble
sple'nial	spray'er	squab'bled
splice	spread	squad
spliced	spread'er	squal'id
spli'cer	spree	squal'or
spli'cing	sprig	squall
splint	sprigged	squall'y
splint'ed	spri'ghtly	squa'mous
split	spring	square
splotch	spring'y	squared
splotch'y	sprung	squa'rely
splurge	sprink'le	squash
spoil	sprink'led	squashed
spoiled	sprint	squash'es
spoil'er	sprint'ed	squash'y
spoilt	sprit	squat
sponge	sprite	squaw
spong'er	sprock'et	squawk
spong'y	sprout	squawked
spook	sprout'ed	squawk'er
spook'y	spruce	squeak
spool	spruced	squeaked
spoon	sprue	squeak'er
spoor	spry	squeak'y
spore	spry'ly	squeal
sport	spume	squealed
spot	spu'my	squeal'er
spot'ty	spur	squeeze
spouse	spurred	squeezed
spous'al	spurge	squeez'er
spout	spurn	squelch
spout'ed	spurned	squelched
spout'er	spurt	squib
sprat	spurt'ed	squid
sprawl	spy	squig'gle

489

squig'gly
squill
squint
  squint'ed
squire
  squired
  squi'ring
squirm
  squirmed
  squirm'er
  squirm'y
squirt
  squirt'ed
stab
  stabbed
sta'bile
sta'ble
  sta'bled
  sta'bling
staccato
stac'te
sta'dium
  sta'dia
staff
  staffed
stag
stage
  staged
  sta'ger
  sta'ging
staid
  staid'ly
stain
  stained
stair
stake
  staked
stalk

stalked
stalk'er
stall
  stalled
stal'lion
stal'wart
sta'men
  sta'mened
  stamin'eal
stamp
  stamped
  stamp'er
stance
stand
  stood
stan'za
stapes
sta'ple
  sta'pled
  sta'pler
  sta'pling
star
  starred
  star'ry
starch
  starched
  starch'es
  starch'y
stare
  stared
  sta'ring
stark
  stark'ly
start
  start'ed
  start'er
  star'tle
  star'tled

starve
  starved
sta'sis
state
  sta'tely
stat'ic
  stat'ics
stat'ice
sta'tion
  sta'tioned
sta'tioner
sta'tist
stat'ue
sta'tus
status quo
staunch
  staunched
  staunch'ly
stave
  staved
stay
  stayed
  stay'er
stead
  stead'y
steak
steal
  steal'er
  stole
  sto'len
stealth
  stealth'y
steam
  steamed
  steam'er
  steam'y
steap'sin
ste'arate

ste'arin
 stear'ic
ste'atite
 steatit'ic
steato'ma
steato'sis
steel
 steeled
 steel'y
steep (a.)
 steep'en
 steep'ly
steep (v.)
 steeped
steep'le
 steep'led
steer
 steered
 steer'er
stem
 stemmed
stench
step
 stepped
steppe
stere
ster'ic
stern
 stern'ly
stern'al
ster'ol
stet
stew
 stewed
sthen'ic
stich
 stich'ic
stick

stick'er
stick'y
stuck
stick'ler
stiff
 stiff'en
 stiff'ly
sti'fle
 sti'fled
 sti'fling
stig'ma
stile
still
 stilled
 still'y
stilt
 stilt'ed
sting
 sting'er
 stung
 sting'y
 stin'gily
stink
 stank
 stink'er
stint
 stint'ed
stip'ple
 stip'pled
stir
 stirred
stirp
 stirpes
stitch
 stitched
 stitch'er
stith'y
stoccado

stock
 stocked
 stock'y
stodge
 stodg'y
sto'ic
stoke
 stoked
 sto'ker
stol'id
sto'ma
stom'ach
 stom'ached
 stom'acher
 stomacn'ic
stone
 sto'nily
 stoned
 sto'ning
 sto'ny
stook
stool
stoop
 stooped
stop
 stopped
store
 sto'rage
 stored
 sto'ring
stork
storm
 stormed
 storm'y
sto'ry
 sto'ried
stoup
stout

stoutly
stove
  stoved
stow
  stowed
strad'dle
  strad'dled
strag'gle
  strag'gled
  strag'gly
straight
  straight'en
strain
  strained
  strain'er
strait
  strait'en
  strait'ly
strand
  strand'ed
strange
  stra'ngely
  stra'nger
stran'gle
  stran'gled
  stran'gler
  stran'gling
strap
  strapped
stra'tum
  stra'ta
straw
stray
  strayed
streak
  streaked
  streak'y
stream

  streamed
  stream'er
street
strength
  streng'then
stress
  stressed
stretch
  stretched
  stretch'er
  stretch'es
strewn
strick'en
strict
  strict'ly
stride
  stri'der
  stri'ding
strode
strife
strig'il
strike
  stri'ker
  struck
string
  stringed
  string'er
  string'y
  strung
stringendo
strip
  stripped
stripe
  striped
strive
  stri'ving
  striv'en

strove
stroke
  stroked
  stro'king
stroll
  strolled
  stro'ller
strong
  strong'ly
strop
  stropped
stro'phe
strudel
strug'gle
  strug'gled
strum
  strummed
strut
stub
  stubbed
  stub'by
  stub'ble
  stub'bly
stuc'co
stud
stu'dent
  stud'y
stuff
  stuffed
  stuff'y
stump
  stumped
  stump'y
stunt'ed
sturd'y
sty'mie
  sty'mied
suave

suav'ely
sub judice
sub rosa
sub specie
sub voce
subt'le
  subt'lety
  subt'ly
suck
  sucked
  suck'er
suck'le
  suck'led
sue
  sued
suede
su'et
su'gar
  su'gared
  su'gary
suggest'
su'icide
sui generis
suit
  suit'ed
suite
suit'or
suivez
sulk
  sulked
  sulk'y
sul'ly
sul'try
sum
  summed
sump
sun
  sunned

sun'ny
sun'dry
  sun'dries
sup
  supped
sup'ple
sup'ply
supply'
surd
sure
  su'rely
  su'rety
surf
surge
  surged
  surg'ing
sur'ly
  sur'lily
svelte
swab
  swabbed
swad'dle
  swad'dled
swag
swain
swall'ow
  swall'owed
swamp
  swamped
  swamp'y
swan
swarm
  swarmed
swarth'y
swathe
  swathed
  swa'thing
sway

swayed
swear
  swear'er
  swore
  sworn
sweat
  sweat'ed
  sweat'y
sweat'er
sweep
  sweep'er
  swept
sweet
  sweet'en
  sweet'ly
swell
  swelled
  swo'llen
swerve
  swerved
swift
  swift'ly
swig
  swigged
swill
  swilled
  swill'er
swim
  swam
swin'dle
  swin'dled
swine
  swi'nish
swing
  swing'er
  swung
swinge
swipe

swiped

swi'ping

swirl

swirled

swish

swished

switch

switched

switch'es

swiv'el

swoon

swooned

swoop

swooped

sword

sylph

sylph'id

syng'amy

syn'od

syr'up

tab

tabbed

tab'by

ta'bes

ta'ble

ta'bled

ta'bling

table d'hôte

taboo'

ta'bor

ta'bour

tac'it

tac'itly

tack

tacked

tack'er

tack'le

tack'led

tack'ler

tack'y

tact

tag

tagged

tail

tailed

tail'er

tail'or

taint

taint'ed

take

ta'ken

ta'ker

ta'king

took

talc

tale

talk

talked

talk'er

tall

tal'ly

tal'on

tame

ta'mable

tamed

ta'mely

ta'mer

ta'ming

tamp

tamped

tan

tanned

tang

tan'gle

tan'gled

tang'ling

tang'o

tang'oed

tank

tank'er

tann'oid

tan'sy

tap

tapped

tape

taped

ta'ping

ta'per

ta'pered

ta'pir

tar

tarred

tarr'y

tar'dy

tar'dily

tare

targe

tarn

tar'ry

tart

tart'ly

task

task'er

tass'el

taste

ta'sted

ta'ster

ta'sting

ta'sty

tat'tle

tat'tled

taunt

taunt'ed

taut

taut'en
taut'ly
taw'dry
taw'ny
t ax
  taxed
  tax'er
  tax'or
tax'i
tax'is
tazza
Te Deum
tea
teach
  taught
  teach'er
teak
teal
team
  teamed
tear
  tear'er
  tore
  torn
tease
  teased
  teas'er
teas'el
teat
ted
te'dium
tee
  teed
teem
  teemed
teet'er
tell
  tell'er

told
tole'do
tem'ple
tempo
tempore
tempt
  tempt'ed
  tempt'er
ten
  tenth
tench
tend
  tend'ed
  tend'er
ten'et
ten'on
ten'or
tense
  tensed
  tens'ely
tent
  tent'ed
  tent'er
te'pee
tep'id
terce
term
  termed
  term'or
tern
terne
ter'ra-cot'ta
terra firma
terse
  ters'ely
tertio
tertium quid
tertius

test
  test'ed
  test'er
test'y
  test'ily
tetch'y
  tetch'ily
tête-à-tête
teth'er
text
thane
thank
  thanked
  thank'er
thatch
  thatched
  thatch'er
thaw
  thawed
the'atre
theft
theme
thence
thereby'
therein'
thereof'
thereon'
thereto'
therm
thesaur'us
the'ta
thick
  thick'en
  thick'ly
thick'et
thief
  thieves
thieve

thigh
thim'ble
thin
  thinned
  thin'ly
thing
think
  think'er
  thought
third
  third'ly
thirst
  thirst'ed
thir'ty
this'tle
  this'tly
thith'er
thole
thong
  thonged
thorn
  thorned
  thorn'y
thor'ough
  thor'oughly
though
thrall
thrash
  thrashed
thread
  thread'ed
  thread'er
  thread'y
threat
  threat'en
thresh
  threshed
  thresh'er

thresh'ing
thresh'old
thrice
thrift
  thrifty
thrill
  thrilled
  thrill'er
thrips
thrive
  thrived
  thri'ving
  throve
throat
  throat'ed
  throat'ily
  throat'y
throb
  throbbed
throes
throne
  throned
throng
  thronged
thros'tle
throt'tle
  throt'tled
through
throw
  threw
  throw'er
  thrown
thrum
  thrummed
thrush
thrust
  thrust'er
thud

thug
thule
thumb
  thumbed
thump
  thumped
  thump'er
thus
thwart
  thwart'ed
  thwart'er
thyme
  thy'my
tiar'a
tib'ia
tick
  ticked
  tick'er
  tick'et
tick'le
  tick'led
  tick'ly
tide
  ti'dal
  ti'dings
ti'dy
  ti'died
  ti'dily
tie
  tied
  tier
  ty'ing
tier'
  tier'ed
tierce
tiff
ti'ger
  ti'gress

tight
  d'ghten
  ti'ghtly
tile
  tiled
  ti'ler
  ti'ling
till
  tilled
  till'er
tilt
  tilt'ed
  tilt'er
tilth
timbre
time
  timed
  ti'mely
  ti'meous
  ti'meously
  ti'mer
  ti'ming
tim'id
  tim'idly
tin
  tinned
  tin'ny
tine
  tined
tinge
  tinged
tin'gle
  tin'gled
  tin'gling
  tin'gly
tink'er
tink'le
  tink'led

tink'ly
tint
  tint'ed
  tint'er
ti'ny
tip
  tipped
tip'ple
  tip'pled
tip'sy
  tip'sily
tire
  tired
ti'redly
ti'ring
ti'tan
tithe
  ti'thable
  tithed
ti'ther
ti'thing
tit'ian
ti'tle
  ti'tled
  ti'tling
toad
toad'y
  toad'ies
toast
  toast'ed
  toast'er
tobac'co
toccata
today'
tod'dle
  tod'dled
tod'dy
to'ga

togeth'er
tog'gle
  tog'gled
toil
  toiled
  toil'er
toile
toil'et
toilette
to'ken
toll
  tolled
tomb
tome
tomor'row
ton
  ton'nage
tone
  to'nal
  toned
  ton'ic
  to'ning
tong'a
tongs
tongue
  tongued
  tong'uing
tool
  tooled
  tool'er
tooth
  teeth
  toothed
top
  topped
to'paz
tope
  to'per

497

topee'	*tout de même*	train'er
top'ic	*tout de suite*	trait
top'ple	*tout ensemble*	trait'or
top'pled	*tout le monde*	trait'ress
toque	tow	tram
torch	towed	trammed
torque	tow'er	tramp
torqued	toward'	tramped
torse	tow'el	tramp'er
tor'so	tow'elled	tram'ple
tort	tow'er	tram'pled
toss	tow'ered	trance
tossed	town	tranced
toss'er	tox'ic	*transeunt*
tot	tox'in	trap
to'tal	toy	trapped
to'talled	toyed	trash
to'tally	trace	trash'ily
to'tem	traced	trash'y
totem'ic	tra'cer	traum'a
touch	tra'cery	trav'el
touched	tra'cing	trawl
touch'y	track	trawled
touché	tracked	trawl'er
tough	track'er	tray
tough'en	tract	treac'le
tough'ly	trade	treac'ly
toupée	traded	tread
toup'et	tra'der	tread'er
tour	tra'ding	trod
toured	trag'edy	tread'le
tour'er	trag'ic	treas'on
tour de force	trail	treas'ure
tous'le	trailed	treas'urer
tous'led	trail'er	treas'ury
tout	train	treat
tout'ed	trained	treat'ed
tout à fait	trainee'	treat'er

treat'y

treb'le

  treb'ly

tree

trek

  trekked

trem'ble

  trem'bled

  trem'bly

tremolo

trem'or

trench

  trenched

  trench'er

  trench'es

trend

trepan'

tress

  tressed

  tress'es

tres'tle

trews

tri'ad

tri'al

tribe

  tri'bal

  tri'bally

trib'ble

trice

trick

  tricked

  trick'y

trick'le

  trick'led

tri'fle

  tri'fled

  tri'fler

  tri'fling

trig

trill

  trilled

tril'lion

  tril'lionth

trim

  trimmed

  trim'ly

trink'et

tri'o

trip

  tripped

tripe

trip'le

  trip'ly

triptique

trite

  tri'tely

triv'et

troik'a

troll

  trolled

troop

  trooped

  troop'er

trope

tro'phy

  tro'phies

trop'ic

troppo

trot

troub'le

  troub'led

trough

trounce

  trounced

troupe

  troup'er

trous'ers

trouss'eau

trout

trove

trow'el

truce

truck

  truck'er

truck'le

  truck'led

trudge

  trudged

true

  tru'ly

truf'fle

trug

trump

  trumped

trun'dle

  trun'dled

trunk

  trunc'al

  trunked

truss

  trussed

  truss'es

trust

  trust'ed

  trustee'

  trust'y

truth

try

  tries

  tried

tri'er

try'er

tryst

  try'sted

tset'se-fly

tub
  tubbed
  tub'by
tu'ba
tube
  tubed
  tu'bing
tu'ber
  tu'berose
tuck
  tucked
  tuck'er
tu'fa
tuff
tuft
  tuft'ed
  tuft'er
  tuft'y
tug
  tugged
tulle
tum'ble
  tum'bled
tun
tu'na
tune
  tuned
  tu'ner
  tu'ning
tun'ny
tup
tureen'
turf
  turfed
  turf'y
turn

turned
turn'er
tur'tle
tusk
  tusked
  tusk'er
tus'sle
  tus'sled
twad'dle
twain
twang
  twanged
tweak
  tweaked
tweed
  tweed'y
twelve
  twelf'th
twen'ty
twice
twid'dle
  twid'dled
  twid'dly
twig
  twig'gy
twill
  twilled
twin
twine
  twined
twinge
  twinged
twin'kle
  twink'led
twirl
  twirled
twist

twist'ed
twist'er
twist'y
twit
twitch
  twitched
  twitcher
two
type
  ty'pal
  typed
  ty'per
  ty'pist
tyre
ubiq'uity
ug'ly
  ug'lify
uka'se
ul'na
um'bles
u'mlaut
unc'ate
unc'le
undo'
ung'ual
ung'uent
ung'ula
u'nify
u'nion
uniq'ue
  uniq'uely
u'nit
uni'te
  uni'ted
  u'nity
un'to
upon'

utaem'ia
uraem'ic
u'rate
ura'nium
  uran'ic
ure'a
  ure'al
ure'ter
ure'thra
urge
  urged
u'rine
  u'ric
u'rial
urn
use
  u'sable
  u'sage
  u'sance
  used
  u'sing
ush'er
  ush'ered
usquebaugh
u'sual
  u'sually
usurp'
  usurp'ed
  usurp'er
u'sury
  u'surer
u'terus
uto'pian
uve'a
u'vula
va'cant
  va'cancy
va'gary

va'grant
  va'grancy
va'gue
  va'guely
vain
  vain'ly
vale
va'lence
  va'lent
val'et
val'id
val'ue
  val'ued
  val'uer
valve
vamp
van
vane
  vaned
vap'id
va'pour
vaquero
vare
va'ry
  va'ried
vase
vass'al
vast
  vast'ly
vat
vaud'eville
vault
  vault'ed
  vault'er
vaunt
  vaunt'ed
veal
veer

veered
veil
  veiled
vein
  veined
veld (t)
velour
vend
  vend'or
ven'om
vent
venue
verb
verboten
verbum sapienti
verge
  verged
vers libre
verse
  versed
ver'so
verve
ver'y
vess'el
vest
  vest'ed
  vestee'
vet
vetch
ve'to
vex
  vexed
via
via media
vi'al
vibrato
vic'ar
vice

vic'ious
vic'iously
vice versa
vic'inal
vict'ual
  vict'ualled
vicu'na
view
  viewed
  view'er
vig'il
vign'ette
vigoroso
vile
  vi'lely
vil'la
vine
  vi'nery
  vin'eyard
vi'ol
vir'id
vi'sa
vis-à-vis
vi'scount
vis'ion
  vis'ional
vis'it
vi'sor
vis'ta
vite
vit'iate
  vit'iated
  vitia'tion
  vit'iator
viva voce
vivace
viv'id
vix'en
502

vizier'
vod'ka
voe
vo'gue
voice
  voiced
void
voile
vol-au-vent
vole
volt
volte-face
vom'it
vote
  vo'ted
  vo'ter
  vo'ting
vouch
  vouched
  vouch'er
vow
  vowed
  vow'el
wad
  wad'dle
  wad'dled
wade
  wa'ded
  wa'der
  wa'ding
wa'fer
waf'fle
waft
  waft'ed
wag
  wagged
wage
  waged

wa'ging
wa'ger
  wa'gered
wag'gle
  wag'gled
wagon-lit
waif
wail
  wailed
wain
waist
  waist'ed
wait
  wait'ed
  wait'er
waive
  waived
wake
  wa'ken
  wa'kened
  wa'king
  woke
wale
walk
  walked
  walk'er
wall
  walled
  wall'et
  wall'ow
wal'nut
wal'rus
waltz
  waltzed
  waltz'es
wan
  wan'ly
wand

wane
  waned
  wa'ning
wan'gle
  wan'gled
  wan'gling
want
  want'ed
war
  warred
war'ble
  war'bled
ward
  ward'ed
  ward'er
ware
warm
  warmed
  warm'er
  warm'ly
warn
  warned
warp
  warped
wart
wa'ry
  wa'rily
wash
  washed
  wash'er
wasp
waste
  wa'sted
  wa'ster
watch
  watched
  watch'er
wat'er

wat'ered
wat'ery
watt
wat'tle
  wat'tled
wave
  waved
  wa'ving
  wa'vy
wa'ver
  wa'vered
  wa'verer
wax
  waxed
  wax'er
  wax'y
way
weak
  weak'er
  weak'ly
weal
wealth
  wealth'y
wean
  weaned
weap'on
wear
  wear'er
  wore
  worn
wear'y
  wear'ied
  wear'ily
weas'el
weath'er
weave
  weav'er
  wove

wo'ven
web
  webbed
wed
wedge
  wedged
weed
  weed'ed
  weed'er
  weed'y
week
  week'ly
weep
  wept
weev'er
weev'il
weft
weigh
  weighed
  weigh'er
weight
  weight'y
weir
weird
  weird'ly
weld
  weld'ed
  weld'er
welt
  welt'ed
wench
wend
  wend'ed
went
were
west
  west'er
weth'er

whack

whale

  wha'ler

  wha'ling

wharf

  wharves

what

wheat

  wheat'en

wheed'le

  wheed'led

wheel

  wheeled

wheeze

  wheezed

  wheez'y

whelk

whelp

  whelped

when

whence

where

  whereas'

  whereby'

  wherein'

  whereof'

  whereon'

wher'ry

  wher'ries

whet

wheth'er

whey

which

whiff

while

whim

  whim'sy

whin

whine

  whined

  whi'ner

  whi'ning

whin'ny

whip

  whipped

whirr

  whirred

whirl

  whirled

whisk

  whisked

whis'ky

whist

whis'tle

  whis'tled

whit

white

  whi'ten

whith'er

whi'ting

whit'tle

  whit'tled

whizz

  whizzed

who

whom

whose

whole

  who'lly

whoop

  whooped

whore

whorl

  whorled

why

wick

wick'ed

wick'er

wick'et

wide

  wi'den

  wi'dened

widg'eon

wid'ow

wield

  wield'ed

  wield'er

wife

  wives

  wi'fely

wig

  wigged

wig'gle

  wig'gled

  wig'gly

wild

  wi'ldly

wile

will

  willed

wilt

  wilt'ed

wim'ple

win

  won

wince

  winced

winch

wind

  wind'ed

  wind'y

wind (v)

  wi'nder

  wi'nding